MCSA 70-741
Cert Guide

Michael S. Schulz

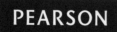

800 East 96th Street
Indianapolis, Indiana 46240 USA

MCSA 70-741 Cert Guide

ISBN-13: 978-0-7897-5704-3
ISBN-10: 0-7897-5704-4

Library of Congress Control Number: 2017936408

Printed in the United States of America

First Printing: June 2017

Trademarks

Warning and Disclaimer

Special Sales

For information about buying this title in bulk quantities, or for special sales opportunities (which may include electronic versions; custom cover designs; and content particular to your business, training goals, marketing focus, or branding interests), please contact our corporate sales department at corpsales@pearsoned.com or (800) 382-3419.

For government sales inquiries, please contact governmentsales@pearsoned.com.

For questions about sales outside the U.S., please contact intlcs@pearson.com.

Cover image ©Sata Production/ShutterStock

Editor-in-Chief
Mark Taub

Product Line Manager
Brett Bartow

Acquisitions Editor
Michelle Newcomb

Development Editor
Christopher Cleveland

Managing Editor
Sandra Schroeder

Senior Project Editor
Tonya Simpson

Copy Editor
Krista Hansing Editorial Services, Inc.

Indexer
Ken Johnson

Proofreader
Chuck Hutchinson

Technical Editor
Chris Crayton

Publishing Coordinator
Vanessa Evans

Cover Designer
Chuti Prasertsith

Compositor
Studio Galou

Contents at a Glance

Table of Contents

About the Author

Michael S. Schulz has been working with Microsoft Server products and technologies since 1999. He holds the Microsoft Certified Trainer (MCT) certification and several other Microsoft certifications, such as MCSA and MSCE. During two decades as an IT trainer, he has instructed thousands of IT students about networking, Windows Server, Exchange Server, SQL Server, and PowerShell. He has worked as an item writer for Microsoft in Seattle. *MCSA 70-741 Cert Guide* is his third book. Together with Thomas Lee (MVP and author) Michael has written the courseware "50604A: First Look Windows Server 2012," which published in 2012 worldwide through the Microsoft Courseware library, and the courseware "Windows Server 2016 Workshop," which was self-published through Amazon. Since 2015 Michael has been CEO of his own IT consulting and training company, ConsuIT GmbH in Switzerland. He also works as an IT engineer, trainer, and Azure technical consultant for the European cloud service provider ALSO AG (www.also.com) and NORDCLOUD from Finland (www.nordcloud.com). Michael's home country is Germany. Together with his wife and his two sons he lives near Zurich, Switzerland. His hobbies include technology, science, books, traveling, skiing, swimming, and cycling.

Dedication

This book is dedicated to my two boys, Samuel (16) and Robin (13), and my wife, Isabel. They often had to renounce their father and husband because writing a technical book like this takes a lot of time, nerves, and endurance.

Acknowledgments

I thank Chris Cleveland and Chris Crayton, who helped me to improve this Cert Guide. Thanks also to Michelle Newcomb and the production team: Tonya Simpson, Krista Hansing, Ken Johnson, Louisa Adair, and Chuck Hutchinson.

About the Technical Reviewer

Chris Crayton (MCSE) is an author, technical consultant, and trainer. He has worked as a computer technology and networking instructor, information security director, network administrator, network engineer, and PC specialist. Chris has authored several print and on-line books on PC repair, CompTIA A+, CompTIA Security+, and Microsoft Windows. He has also served as technical editor and content contributor on numerous technical titles for several leading publishing companies. He holds numerous industry certifications, has been recognized with many professional teaching awards, and has served as a state-level SkillsUSA competition judge.

We Want to Hear from You!

As the reader of this book, *you* are our most important critic and commentator. We value your opinion and want to know what we're doing right, what we could do better, what areas you'd like to see us publish in, and any other words of wisdom you're willing to pass our way.

We welcome your comments. You can email or write to let us know what you did or didn't like about this book—as well as what we can do to make our books better.

Please note that we cannot help you with technical problems related to the topic of this book.

When you write, please be sure to include this book's title and author as well as your name and email address. We will carefully review your comments and share them with the author and editors who worked on the book.

Email: feedback@pearsonitcertification.com

Mail: Pearson IT Certification
            ATTN: Reader Feedback
            800 East 96th Street
            Indianapolis, IN 46240 USA

Reader Services

Register your copy of *MCSA 70-741 Cert Guide* at www.pearsonitcertification.com for convenient access to downloads, updates, and corrections as they become available. To start the registration process, go to www.pearsonitcertification.com/register and log in or create an account*. Enter the product ISBN 9780789757043 and click Submit. When the process is complete, you will find any available bonus content under Registered Products.

*Be sure to check the box that you would like to hear from us to receive exclusive discounts on future editions of this product.

Introduction

Congratulations! If you are reading this, you have in your possession a powerful tool that can help you accomplish some important goals:

- Improve your awareness and knowledge of Windows Server 2016 networking

- Increase your skill level in implementing Windows Server 2016 networking features

- Prepare for the MCSA: Networking with Windows Server 2016 70-741 Microsoft certification exam

As you prepare for the MCSA: Windows Server 2016 certification, this book will help you gain the knowledge to get started and prepared. We wrote this book with you in mind, and together we will explore the critical ingredients for configuring Windows Server 2016 networks. We focus on both the objectives for the 70-741 Microsoft exam and integration with real-world best practices and examples as we take you on a journey through the world of network security.

The 70-741 Networking with Windows Server 2016 exam is required for the MCSA: Windows Server 2016 Solutions Associate certification. This book covers all the topics listed in Microsoft's exam blueprint. Each chapter includes key topics and preparation tasks to assist you in mastering this information. Reviewing tables and practicing test questions will help you practice your knowledge on all subject areas.

About the 70-741 Networking with Windows Server 2016 Exam

The 70-741 Networking with Windows Server 2016 exam is the second of three required exams to achieve the MCSA: Windows Server 2016 Solutions Associate certification and is aligned with the job role of a Microsoft Network Administrator. You can find more about the MCSA: Windows Server 2016 Microsoft certification and all necessary Microsoft exams at https://www.microsoft.com/en-us/learning/mcsa-windows-server-2016-certification.aspx.

The 70-741 Networking with Windows Server 2016 exam is a computer-based test with 40 to 60 questions that you must answer within 120 minutes. Microsoft manages all exam information, so candidates should continually monitor the Microsoft site for the 70-741 exam at https://www.microsoft.com/en-us/learning/exam-70-741.aspx. You can take the exam at Pearson VUE testing centers and register at www.vue.com/cisco.

You can read the Microsoft exam policies and FAQs at https://www.microsoft.com/en-us/learning/certification-exam-policies.aspx.

This exam measures your ability to accomplish the technical tasks listed next. The percentages indicate the relative weight of each major topic area on the exam.

Exam Topic	Weight
Implement Domain Name System (DNS)	15%–20%
Implement DHCP	15%–20%
Implement IP Address Management (IPAM)	15%–20%
Implement network connectivity and remote access solutions	25%–30%
Implement core and distributed network solutions	10%–15%
Implement an advanced network infrastructure	10%–15%

You also should visit the Microsoft Certification exams site to find out about the exam formats and the available question types: https://www.microsoft.com/en-us/learning/certification-exams.aspx

70-741 Exam Topics

Table I-1 lists the topics of the 70-741 exam and indicates the chapter in the book that covers them.

Table I-1   70-741 Exam Topics

Exam Topic	Chapter
1.0 Install and configure DNS servers	Chapters 1–5
1.1 Install and configure DNS servers	Chapter 1
1.1.1 Determine DNS installation requirements	Chapter 1
1.1.2 Determine supported DNS deployment scenarios on Nano Server	Chapter 1
1.1.3 Install DNS, configure forwarders	Chapter 1
1.1.4 Configure Root Hints	Chapter 1
1.1.5 Configure delegation	Chapter 1
1.1.6 Implement DNS policies	Chapter 1
1.1.7 Configure and implement DNS global settings using Windows PowerShell	Chapter 1
1.1.8 Configure Domain Name System Security Extensions (DNSSEC)	Chapter 1
1.1.9 Configure DNS Socket Pool	Chapter 1
1.1.10 Configure cache locking	Chapter 1
1.1.11 Enable Response Rate Limiting	Chapter 1
1.1.12 Configure DNS-based Authentication of Named Entities (DANE)	Chapter 1

Exam Topic	Chapter
6.1.7 Enable and configure Virtual Machine Multi-Queue (VMMQ)	Chapter 14
6.1.8 Enable and configure Single-Root I/O Virtualization (SR-IOV) on a supported network adapter	Chapter 14
6.2 Determine scenarios and requirements for implementing software-defined networking (SDN)	**Chapter 14**
6.2.1 Determine deployment scenarios and network requirements for deploying SDN	Chapter 14
6.2.2 Determine requirements and scenarios for implementing Hyper-V Network Virtualization (HNV) using Network Virtualization Generic Route Encapsulation (NVGRE) encapsulation or Virtual Extensible LAN (VXLAN) encapsulation	Chapter 14
6.2.3 Determine scenarios for implementation of Software Load Balancer (SLB) for North-South and East-West load balancing	Chapter 14
6.2.4 Determine implementation scenarios for various types of Windows Server Gateways, including L3, GRE, and S2S, and their use	Chapter 14
6.2.5 Determine requirements and scenarios for distributed firewall policies and network security groups	Chapter 14

About the *MCSA 70-741 Cert Guide*

This book maps to the topic areas of the Microsoft 70-741 exam and uses features to help you understand the topics and prepare for the exam.

Objectives and Methods

This book uses several key methodologies to help you discover the exam topics on which you need more review, to help you fully understand and remember those details, and to help you prove to yourself that you have retained your knowledge of those topics. This book does not try to help you pass the exams only by memorization; it seeks to enable you to truly learn and understand the topics. This book is designed to help you pass the Microsoft 70-741 exam by using the following methods:

- Helping you discover which exam topics you have not mastered
- Providing explanations and information to fill in your knowledge gaps
- Supplying exercises that enhance your ability to recall and deduce the answers to test questions
- Providing practice exercises on the topics and the testing process via test questions on the companion website

Book Features

To help you customize your study time using this book, the core chapters have several features that enable you to make the best use of your time:

- **"Do I Know This Already?" Quiz:** Each chapter begins with a quiz that helps you determine how much time you need to spend studying that chapter.

- **Foundation Topics:** These are the core sections of each chapter. They explain the concepts for the topics in that chapter.

- **Exam Preparation Tasks:** After the "Foundation Topics" section of each chapter, the "Exam Preparation Tasks" section lists a series of study activities. Each chapter includes the activities that make the most sense for studying the topics in that chapter:

  - **Review All the Key Topics:** The Key Topic icon appears next to the most important items in the "Foundation Topics" section of the chapter. The "Review All the Key Topics" activity lists the key topics from the chapter, along with their page numbers. Although the contents of the entire chapter could be on the exam, you should definitely know the information listed in each key topic.

  - **Complete the Tables and Lists from Memory:** To help you memorize some lists of facts, many of the more important lists and tables from the chapter are included in a document on the companion website. This document lists only partial information, allowing you to complete the table or list.

  - **Define Key Terms:** Although the exam will not likely ask a question such as "Define this term," the 70-741 exam does require that you learn and know networking terminology. This section lists the most important terms from the chapter and asks you to write a short definition and then compare it to the glossary at the end of the book.

  - **End-of-Chapter Review Questions:** Confirm that you understand the content that you just covered by answering these questions.

- **Web-based practice exam:** The companion website includes the Pearson Test Prep practice test software, which you can use to take practice exam questions. Use it to prepare with a sample exam and to pinpoint topics where you need more study.

How This Book Is Organized

This book contains 14 core chapters. Chapter 15 includes some preparation tips and suggestions for how to approach the exam. Each core chapter covers a subset of the topics on the 70-741 exam. The core chapters are organized into parts that map directly to the 70-741 exam topic areas and cover the concepts and technologies that you will encounter on the exam.

Companion Website

Register this book to get access to the Pearson IT Certification test engine and other study materials, plus additional bonus content. Check this site regularly for new and updated postings written by the author that provide further insight into the more troublesome topics on the exam. Be sure to check the box that you would like to hear from us to receive updates and exclusive discounts on future editions of this product or related products.

To access the companion website, follow these steps:

1. Go to www.pearsonITcertification.com/register and log in or create a new account.

2. Enter the ISBN, 9780789757043.

3. Answer the challenge question as proof of purchase.

4. Click the **Access Bonus Content** link in the Registered Products section of your account page to go to the page where your downloadable content is available.

Note that many of our companion content files are very large, especially image and video files.

If you cannot locate the files for this title by following the steps, visit www.pearsonITcertification.com/contact and select the Site Problems/Comments option. Our customer service representatives will assist you.

Pearson Test Prep Practice Test Software

As noted previously, this book comes with the Pearson Test Prep practice test software and two full exams. These practice tests are available to you either online or as an offline Windows application. To access the practice exams that were developed with this book, see the instructions in the card inserted in the sleeve at the back of the book. The card includes a unique access code that enables you to activate your exams in the Pearson Test Prep software.

Accessing the Pearson Test Prep Software Online

The online version of this software works on any device that has a browser and connectivity to the Internet, including desktop machines, tablets, and smartphones. To start using your practice exams online, simply follow these steps:

1. Go to http://www.PearsonTestPrep.com.

2. Select Pearson IT Certification as your product group.

3. Enter your email/password for your account. If you don't have an account on PearsonITCertification.com or CiscoPress.com, you need to establish one by going to PearsonITCertification.com/join.

4. In the My Products tab, click the **Activate New Product** button.

5. Enter the access code printed on the insert card at the back of your book to activate your product.

6. The product then is listed in your My Products page. Click the Exams button to launch the exam settings screen and start your exam.

Accessing the Pearson Test Prep Software Offline

If you want to study offline, you can download and install the Windows version of the Pearson Test Prep software. The book's companion website has a download link for this software, or you can enter this link in your browser:

http://www.pearsonitcertification.com/content/downloads/pcpt/engine.zip

To access the book's companion website and the software, follow these steps:

1. Register your book by going to PearsonITCertification.com/register and entering the ISBN: 9780789757043.

2. Respond to the challenge questions.

3. Go to your account page and select the **Registered Products** tab.

4. Click the **Access Bonus Content** link under the product listing.

5. Click the **Install Pearson Test Prep Desktop Version** link under the Practice Exams section of the page to download the software.

6. When the software finishes downloading, unzip all the files on your computer.

7. Double-click the application file to start the installation, and follow the on-screen instructions to complete registration.

8. When installation is complete, launch the application and click the **Activate Exam** button on the My Products tab.

9. Click the **Activate a Product** button in the Activate Product Wizard.

10. Enter the unique access code found on the card in the sleeve at the back of your book and click the **Activate** button.

11. Click **Next**, and then click **Finish** to download the exam data to your application.

12. You can now start using the practice exams by selecting the product and clicking the **Open Exam** button to open the exam settings screen.

Note that the offline and online versions sync, so saved exams and grade results recorded on one version are available to you on the other as well.

Customizing Your Exams

From the exam settings screen, you can choose to take exams in one of three modes:

- Study Mode
- Practice Exam Mode
- Flash Card Mode

Study Mode enables you to fully customize your exams and review answers as you are taking the exam. This is typically the mode you use first to assess your knowl-edge and identify information gaps. Practice Exam Mode locks certain customization options and presents a realistic exam experience. Use this mode when you are preparing to test your exam readiness. Flash Card Mode strips out the answers and presents you with only the question stem. This mode is great for late-stage prepa-ration when you really want to challenge yourself to provide answers without the benefit of seeing multiple-choice options. This mode does not provide the detailed score reports that the other two modes do, so do not use it if you are trying to identify knowledge gaps.

In addition to selecting your desired mode, you can select the source of your questions. You can choose to take exams that cover all the chapters, or you can narrow your selection to a single chapter or the chapters that make up specific parts in the book. All chapters are selected by default. If you want to narrow your focus to individual chapters, simply deselect all the chapters and then select only the ones you want to focus on in the Objectives area.

You can also select desired exam banks. Each exam bank has a full exam of questions that cover topics in every chapter. The two exams printed in the book are available, along with two additional exams of unique questions. You can have the test engine serve up exams from all four banks or from just one bank by selecting the desired banks in the exam bank area.

You can make several other customizations to your exam on the exam settings screen, such as the time of the exam, the number of questions served up, whether to randomize questions and answers, whether to show the number of correct answers for multiple-answer questions, and whether to serve up only specific types of questions. You can also create custom test banks by selecting only questions that you have marked or questions on which you have added notes.

Updating Your Exams

If you are using the online version of the Pearson Test Prep software, you always have access to the latest version of the software and the exam data. If you are using the Windows desktop version, every time you launch the software, it checks for updates to your exam data and automatically downloads any changes since the last time you used the software. This requires that you connect to the Internet at the time you launch the software.

If the exam data is not fully downloaded when you activate your exam and you find that figures or exhibits are missing, you might need to manually update your exams.

To update a particular exam that you have already activated and downloaded, simply select the Tools tab and click the Update Products button. This is an issue only with the desktop Windows application.

If you want to check for updates to the Pearson Test Prep exam engine software, Windows desktop version, simply select the Tools tab and click the Update Application button. This ensures that you are running the latest version of the software engine.

This chapter covers the following subjects:

- **Installing and configuring DNS servers:** DNS service has existed for many years and, in that time, DNS base functionality has continued to improve. Windows Server 2016, the latest version in a long hierarchy of Microsoft operating systems, also includes some new DNS improvements. This section traces previous DNS settings and explores new possibilities with Windows Server 2016 DNS. It delivers a comprehensive, detailed view on DNS scenarios and settings. It also covers all the knowledge needed to pass the exam questions on that topic and solve DNS problems in real-world environments. Specifically, this section covers installation requirements, deployment scenarios on Nano Server, DNS server installation, forwarders, root hints, delegation, policies, global settings, DNSSEC, socket pool, cache locking, Response Rate Limiting, DANE, logging, delegated administration, and recursion settings.

- **Creating and configuring DNS zones and records:** Name resolution data, or the resource records in the DNS zones, is the most important data type on a DNS server. This section covers all the settings and configurations for DNS zones and DNS resource records: zone types, primary zones, secondary zones, AD-integrated zones, stub zones, GlobalNames zone, analysis of zone-level statistics, DNS resource records (RR), zone scavenging, record options, round robin, secure dynamic update, unknown record support, audit events, analytical events, zone scopes, record configuration in zone scopes, and configuration of DNS Policies for zones.

## CHAPTER 1

Installing and Configuring DNS Servers

This chapter covers the different aspects of the installation and configuration of Windows Server 2016 DNS servers. It reviews some DNS server features of earlier Windows Server versions as well because these foundation subjects are also required for the exam.

Windows Server 2016 DNS server can also now be deployed on Nano Server, and this chapter discusses that topic. Nano Server does not support the domain controller role. For that reason, a Windows Server 2016 DNS server on a Nano Server cannot host AD-integrated zones; it can host only file-based DNS zones, such as primary or secondary zones with zone files.

DNS Policies are another important new Windows Server 2016 feature. DNS Policies enable you to create rules to determine how DNS servers respond to client queries based on several different factors (for example, location, time of day, and transport protocol). This supports new traffic management scenarios, such as redirecting users to specific servers based on location, implementing split-brain DNS in a new way, and blocking malicious domains or ensuring that clients can resolve only specific names.

With PowerShell Version 5.0, Windows Server 2016 DNS server and name resolution gain new possibilities. This chapter also covers the most important new PowerShell cmdlets for this issue.

"Do I Know This Already?" Quiz

The "Do I Know This Already?" quiz enables you to assess whether you should read this entire chapter or simply jump to the "Exam Preparation Tasks" section for review. If you are in doubt, read the entire chapter. Table 1-1 outlines the major headings in this chapter and the corresponding "Do I Know This Already?" quiz questions. You can find the answers in Appendix A, "Answers to the 'Do I Know This Already?' Quizzes and End-of-Chapter Review Questions."

Table 1-1 "Do I Know This Already?" Foundation Topics Section-to-Question Mapping

Foundation Topics Section	Questions Covered in This Section
DNS Fundamentals Windows Server 2016 DNS Installation	1, 2
Windows Server 2016 DNS Installation	3, 4
Configure and Implement DNS Global Settings Using PowerShell	5, 6
Configure Forwarders	7
Configure DNS Delegation	8
Configure DNS Socket Pool	9
Configure Cache Locking	10
Configure DNS Logging	11
Configure DNS Delegated Administration	12

CAUTION The goal of self-assessment is to gauge your mastery of the topics in this chapter. If you do not know the answer to a question or are only partially sure of the answer, you should mark that question as wrong for purposes of the self-assessment. Giving yourself credit for an answer you correctly guess skews your self-assessment results and might provide you with a false sense of security.

1. Which types of DNS resource records cannot be created automatically? (You do not want to use scripts.)

    a. SRV

    b. TXT

    c. A

    d. MX

2. Which global DNS setting can be used as a DNS load-balancing configuration setting?

    a. Enable DNSSEC

    b. Enable Round Robin

    c. Enable Cache Against Pollution

    d. Enable BIND Secondaries

3. Which DNS zone type uses RPC network traffic for replication of DNS data?

    a. Primary zone type

    b. Secondary zone type

    c. AD-integrated zone type

    d. Stub zone type

4. You have two domains named pearson.com and a child domain named usa.pearson.com. The test.com zone (ADintegrated) resides on DNS1 and DNS2 (both in pearson.com). You must replicate the DNS data from test.com through AD replication only to DNS3 (usa.pearson.com). Which AD partition should you use?

    a. DomainDNSZones

    b. ForestDNSZones

    c. Custom application directory partition

    d. Configuration partition

5. You want to back up only your Active Directory–integrated zone (pearson.com) on your Windows Server 2016 DNS server named DNS1. Which command you can use for that?

    a. **dnscmd DNS1 /ZoneExport "pearson.com" "pearson.com.bak"**

    b. **Export-DnsServerZone -Name "pearson.com" -FileName "pearson.com"**

    c. **Wbadmin.exe Start SystemStateBackup -backuptarget: E:**

    d. **Export-Csv -path pearson.com.csv**

6. You use an ISATAP router to allow network connections between your IPv4 network and your IPv6 network through an ISATAP tunnel. Which DNS server configuration do you need on your DNS server in the IPv4 network?

    a. Configure SRV Record

    b. Configure DNSSEC

    c. Configure GlobalQueryBlockList

    d. Configure Round Robin

7. You add a DNS server with the IP address of 172.16.0.20 to the server-based forwarders list on your DNS server named DNS1, which is the authoritative DNS server for pearson.com. A conditional forwarder for the zone pearsonucertify.com still exists with the same IP address for the authoritative DNS server for pearsonucertify.com. To which DNS server will DNS1 forward DNS requests?

   a. DNS server in the forwarder list

   b. DNS server in the conditional fowarder list

8. You have two domain controllers with an AD-integrated DNS server, named DNS1 and DNS2, in the forest root domain pearson.com. You also have one domain controller with an AD-integrated DNS server named DNS3 in the child domain usa.pearson.com. Now you set up an additional domain controller DNS4 at usa.pearson.com. You use the Active Directory Installation Wizard to promote DNS4 to a domain controller. On the DNS Options page, you notice the yellow note on the top of that page: "A delegation for this DNS server cannot be created because the authoritative parent zone cannot be found." You need a solution with the least administrative effort. What is your next configuration step?

   a. Cancel the Active Directory Installation Wizard and set up the domain controller with PowerShell.

   b. Ignore the note and go forward with the Active Directory Installation Wizard.

   c. Restart DNS3 and repeat all steps in the Active Directory Installation Wizard.

   d. Ensure that DNS4 has a network connection to DNS1 or DNS2 and repeat all steps in the Active Directory Installation Wizard.

9. You verify the DNS server settings. You control the socket pool size value with the PowerShell commands **$dns = get-dnsserver** and **$dns.ServerSetting.SocketPoolSize**. You notice a socket pool size value of 7500. You want to reconfigure that to the default settings. Which socket pool size should you choose?

   a. 3500

   b. 2500

   c. 3000

   d. 2000

10. You want to overwrite DNS server cache entries before the Cache TTL expires and you want to provide enhanced security against poisoning attacks. Which commands do you use? (Choose two.)

   a. **Dnscmd /config /CacheLockingPercent 90**

   b. **Dnscmd /config /CacheLockingPercent 50**

   c. **Restart-Service DNS**

   d. **Dnscmd /clearcache**

11. You want to get information about DNS request types and DNS query packet content. What kind of DNS logging do you need to enable to get that information?

   a. DNS server log

   b. Debug logging

   c. Analytic event logging

   d. DNS monitoring

12. You are responsible for the administration of your Windows Server 2016 DNS server, which is installed on a domain controller as an AD-integrated DNS server. Paul, a new employee, also needs full administrative rights for the DNS server. Which security group must he become a member of?

   a. DomainAdmins

   b. DNSAdmins

   c. Administrators

   d. DNSUpdateProxy

Foundation Topics

DNS Fundamentals

To use a Windows Server 2016 DNS server, you must first install it. Installing the DNS Server service on a GUI-based Windows Server 2016 server is simple, and only slightly more complex on a Windows Server 2016 Server Core. The most modern option is to integrate a DNS server into a Nano Server image. You can use the **New-NanoServer Image** PowerShell command for this. The process of installing a Windows Server 2016 Nano Server with a DNS role is explained in the section "Installing a DNS Server on a Nano Server" later in this chapter.

To manage your Windows Server 2016 DNS Server service, it is essential to understand the main DNS server components available and their purpose. For that reason, this chapter first covers the most important DNS components. For the exam, it is important to know which DNS feature is based on which OS server version. Table 1-2 provides an overview of the important DNS features.

Table 1-2 Comparison of Important DNS Features

Feature	Windows Server 2012	Windows Server 2012 R2	Windows Server 2016
Authoritative server	✓	✓	✓
Recursive resolver	✓	✓	✓
AD integration	✓	✓	✓
IPv6 support (except root hints)	✓	✓	✓
PowerShell 5.0			✓
EDN50	✓	✓	✓
DNSSEC	✓	✓	✓
Enhanced key management for signed zones		✓	✓
Analytical and audit logging		✓	✓
DNS Server Policies			✓
Selective recursion control			✓
Response Rate Limiting (RRL)			✓
DNS-Based Authentication Named Entities (DANE)			✓
Management of unknown record types			✓
Support for internationalized domain names/ support for IDNs that contain characters that cannot be represented in ASCII			✓
IPv6 root hints			✓
Nano Server support			✓

Not every IT professional has to deal with DNS server and its settings on a daily basis. At this point, we cover some basic name resolution topics to ensure that you are familiar with basic Windows Server DNS terminology and configurations.

DNS Queries

A DNS query is a name resolution query that is sent to a DNS server. The DNS server provides either an authoritative or a nonauthoritative response to the client query.

> **TIP** It is important to know that DNS servers also can act as DNS resolvers and send DNS queries to other DNS servers.

Difference Between Authoritative and Nonauthoritative Responses

The following list explains the main differences between an authoritative and a nonauthoritative response from a DNS server. It describes the distinction between a DNS server that is the official nameserver and one that is not.

- **Authoritative:** An authoritative response is one in which the server returns an answer that it knows is correct because the request is directed to the authoritative server that manages the domain. A DNS server is authoritative when it hosts a primary or secondary copy of a DNS zone. A DNS server hosting an AD-integrated zone is also authoritative.

- **Nonauthoritative:** A nonauthoritative response is one in which the DNS server that contains the requested domain in its cache answers a query by using forwarders or root hints. Because the answer provided might not be accurate, it is called a nonauthoritative response.

If the Windows Server 2016 DNS server is authoritative for the query's namespace, the DNS server checks the relevant zone and returns either the requested IP address or the authoritative answer, such as "Name does not exist." If the local DNS server is nonauthoritative for the query's namespace, the DNS server responds in one of three ways:

- It checks its cache and returns a cached response.

- It forwards the unresolvable query to a specific server, called a forwarder.

- It uses well-known addresses of multiple root servers to find an authoritative DNS server to resolve the query.

This process uses root hints. With the command **dnscmd** */clearcache*, you can clear the DNS server hostname cache.

Recursive Queries

The requester (client) asks the DNS server to obtain a fully resolved IP address of the requested resource before it returns the answer to the requestor. The DNS server might have to perform several queries to other DNS servers before it finds the answer.

A recursive query has two possible results: 1) The DNS server returns the IP address of the host requested. 2) The DNS server cannot resolve an IP address. For security reasons, sometimes recursive queries must be disabled on a DNS server so that the DNS server does not attempt to forward its DNS requests to another server. This is useful when you do not want a particular DNS server to communicate outside its local network.

You can disable recursion on a Windows Server 2016 server in the DNS management console through global DNS server settings using the **dnscmd.exe** utility or the PowerShell cmdlet **Set-DnsServerRecursion**:

```
dnscmd <servername> /config /NoRecursion 1
Set-DnsServerRecursion -Enable 0
```

Iterative Queries

Iterative queries access domain name information that resides across the DNS system. You can use iterative queries to quickly and efficiently resolve names across many servers.

When a DNS server receives a request that it cannot answer using its local database or cached lookups, it forwards the request to another DNS server by using an iterative query. When this other DNS server receives the iterative query, it might answer either with the IP address for the domain name (if known) or with a referral to the DNS servers that are responsible for the domain being queried.

The DNS server continues this process either until it locates a DNS server that is authoritative for the queried name or until an error or timeout condition is met.

Forwarding

A Windows Server 2016 DNS server that forwards queries for external names to DNS servers outside or inside its network is called a *forwarder*. You also can create and use *conditional forwarders* to quickly forward queries to specific domain names.

When you designate a network DNS server as a forwarder, other DNS servers in the network forward the queries that they cannot resolve locally to that server. By using a forwarder, you can manage name resolution for names outside your network, such as names on the Internet. This improves the efficiency of name resolution for your network's computers. In addition, you can forward to DNS servers inside your network.

The forwarder managing name resolution for names outside your network must be capable of communicating with the DNS server that is located on the Internet. This means that either you configure it to forward requests to another DNS server or you configure it to use root hints to communicate.

With the following PowerShell command, you add the IPv4 address of another DNS server to the list of forwarders on a local DNS server (in Windows Server 2016 DNS server, you also can add IPv6 addresses of DNS servers as forwarders):

`Add-DnsServerForwarder` -IPAddress 192.168.1.201 -PassThru

With the PowerShell command **Get-DnsServerForwarder | FL ***, you can list all forwarder settings on a local Windows Server 2016 DNS server.

TIP Use a central DNS server as the forwarder for the complete Internet name resolution. This improves security because you can isolate the forwarding DNS server in a DMZ, to ensure that no server within the network is communicating directly to the Internet about name resolution. Then you have a central point of control over the name resolution traffic to and from the Internet.

Round Robin

A round robin approach is often used to load-balance requests among multiple web servers.

Consider this example: A company has one domain name and three identical copies of the same website residing on three servers with three different IP addresses. When one user accesses the home page, it is sent to the first IP address. The second user who accesses the home page is sent to the next IP address, and the third user is sent to the third IP address. In each case, after the IP address is given out, it goes to the end of the list. The fourth user then is sent to the first IP address, and so forth.

Figure 1-1 displays the default setting on a Windows Server 2016 DNS server for round robin, which is enabled by default.

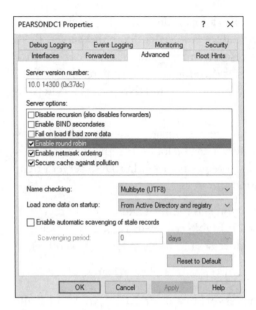

Figure 1-1 DNS Server Round Robin Setting

Conditional Forwarding

A *conditional forwarder* is a DNS server on a network that forwards DNS queries to other DNS servers. For example, you can configure a DNS server to forward all queries that it receives for names that end with corp.pearson.com to the IP address of a specific DNS server or to the IP addresses of multiple DNS servers. Figure 1-2 shows where to create a new conditional forwarder in the DNS server management tool.

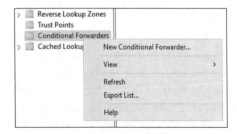

Figure 1-2 Creating a New Conditional Forwarder

Since Windows Server 2012 R2, you can store the conditional forwarder in Active Directory, to replicate it to all DNS servers in the domain. You save time doing so because all DNS servers in the domain then automatically have the same conditional forwarder configured; you do not have to configure it manually or through scripting. Conditional forwarder replication is not possible with DNS servers that are pre-Windows Server 2003 domain controllers.

With the following PowerShell command, you can add an AD-integrated conditional forwarder with forest replication scope (DNS servers that are also domain controllers in the complete forest):

```
Add-DnsServerConditionalForwarderZone -Name "pearson.com"
-ReplicationScope "Forest" -MasterServers 172.23.90.124 -PassThru
```

If you have a connected S2S VPN tunnel to Microsoft Azure, you also can forward from your on-premises (internal) DNS servers to DNS servers hosted on virtual networks in Azure.

> **TIP**   Conditional forwarding is the fastest and best solution if you have to forward to multiple namespaces and other DNS servers. You need to know the IP address of the responsible DNS server for the relevant namespace.

DNS Server Caching

Windows Server 2016 DNS caching increases the performance of the organization's DNS system by decreasing the time it takes to provide DNS lookups.

As an example, consider what you are doing when you want to telephone a known friend. You quickly search for his name in your contact list and press the Call button. You not have to call for directory assistance because you have his telephone number stored in your contact list. Now replace the term *contact list* with *cache* and replace the term *directory assistance* with *DNS server*, and you know the main advantages of DNS server caching.

When a Windows Server 2016 DNS server successfully resolves a hostname, it adds the name to its cache.

> **TIP**   With the PowerShell cmdlet **Get-DnsServerCache**, you can retrieve DNS server cache settings. With the PowerShell cmdlet **Show-DnsServerCache**, you can display the content (records) in the DNS server cache.

Over time, this builds a cache of domain names and their associated IP addresses for most of the domains that the organization uses or accesses. The default time to keep a name in the cache is 1 hour.

> **TIP**   With the PowerShell cmdlet **Get-DnsServerResourceRecord**, you can display the Time To Live value of a DNS resource record.

The zone owner can change the default time by modifying the start of authority (SOA) record for the appropriate DNS zone.

A caching-only server is the ideal type of DNS server to use as a forwarder. It does not host any DNS zone data; it only answers lookup requests for DNS clients.

In Windows Server 2016, you can access the content of the DNS server cache by selecting Advanced view in the DNS Manager console. In this view, cached content displays as a node in DNS Manager. You also can delete single entries (or the entire cache) from the DNS server cache. Alternatively, you can use the Windows Power-Shell cmdlet **Get-DNSServerCache** to view the cache content.

The DNS client cache is stored on the local computer by the DNS client service. To view client-side caching, at a command prompt, run the **ipconfig /displaydns** command. This displays the local DNS client cache. If you need to clear the local cache, you can use the Windows PowerShell **Get-DNSClientCache** and **Clear-DNSClientCache** cmdlets or use the **ipconfig /flushdns** command.

Cache Locking

To prevent DNS client caches from being overwritten, use the DNS Cache Locking feature. With this feature enabled, the cached records cannot be overwritten for the duration of the Time To Live (TTL) value. Cache locking provides improved security against cache poisoning attacks, which occur when an attacker's DNS server provides false name resolution. This false data is kept in the cache for as long as the attacker's DNS server has set the TTL value for that record and therefore falsifies, or poisons, the cache.

> **TIP**   With the PowerShell cmdlet **Set-DnsServerCache** and the parameter **LockingPercent**, you can configure DNS cache locking.

Resource Record Types

Table 1-3 shows the different kinds of resource records and how they are configured. CNAME, MX, and TXT resource records cannot be created automatically.

Table 1-3   Windows Server 2016 DNS Resource Record Types

Resource Record Type	Automatic Creation	Manual Creation
SOA	Yes	No
NS	Yes	No
A	Yes	Yes
PTR	Yes	Yes
CNAME	No	Yes
MX	No	Yes
SRV	Yes	Yes
TXT	No	Yes

TIP   If new DNS servers reside on the namespace of the master DNS server, A and NS resource records of the new DNS servers are registered on the primary zone and then automatically are transferred to the stub zone DNS server. The IP addresses of the new DNS servers can then be used to forward DNS requests to the new DNS servers.

File-Based Zone Types

File-based zone types are stored without using the Active Directory database. Instead, they save their zone data in a text file. For security reasons, using AD-integrated zones is better than using file-based zones. Table 1-4 shows the different types of file-based DNS zones.

Table 1-4   Comparison of DNS Server File-Based Zone Types

Primary Zone (File Based)	Secondary Zone (File Based)	Stub Zone (File Based)
Can be hosted on a standalone server without running a DC	Can be hosted on a standalone server without running a DC	Can be hosted on a standalone server without running a DC
Read/write copy of DNS database	Read-only copy of DNS database	Read-only copy of DNS database (has only SOA, A, and NS resource records of DNS servers)
DNS data saved in zone file	DNS data saved in zone file	DNS data saved in zone file
Active Directory independent	Active Directory independent	Active Directory independent

Primary Zone (File Based)	Secondary Zone (File Based)	Stub Zone (File Based)
AXFR and IXFR replication	AXFR and IXFR replication	AXFR and IXFR replication
	Unsecured DNS data replication from primary zone to secondary zone	Unsecured DNS data replication from primary zone to stub zone
Zone file security: NTFS permissions, no records-based permission	Zone file security: NTFS permissions, no records-based permission	Zone file security: NTFS permissions, no records-based permission
No secure dynamic update	No secure dynamic update	No secure dynamic update

Active Directory–Integrated Zone Types

AD-integrated zones can run only on domain controllers. Primary, secondary, and stub zone DNS data can be saved in Active Directory. All domain controllers that host the DNS zone in the AD DS database are considered primary zone servers for the zone, and they can accept changes to the DNS zone and then replicate those changes to all other domain controllers. With AD DS replication, each change is sent securely via encrypted replication traffic. If a domain controller with an Active Directory–integrated DNS zone fails, as long as other domain controllers exist within the Active Directory–integrated zone, DNS functionality for that zone and the domain will continue to operate correctly. The benefits of an Active Directory–integrated zone follow:

- **Multimaster updates:** As in standard primary zones, which can be modified by only a single primary server, Active Directory–integrated zones can be written to by any writeable domain controller to which the zone is replicated. This offers redundancy functionality. Clients can update their DNS records without having to connect to a potentially geographically distant primary server.

- **DNS zone data replication using AD DS replication:** Only changed attributes are replicated. An Active Directory–integrated zone can thus avoid replicating the entire zone file as in traditional DNS zone transfer models.

- **Secure dynamic updates:** An Active Directory–integrated zone can enforce secure dynamic updates.

- **Detailed security:** An Active Directory–integrated zone supports the delegated administration of zones, domains, and resource records by modifying the access control list (ACL) on the zone.

Dynamic Update

A dynamic update is an update to DNS in real time. Dynamic updates are important for DNS clients that change locations because they can dynamically register and update their resource records without manual intervention. Before a DNS client can automatically update its resource records on the DNS server, you must use the PowerShell cmdlet **Set-DnsClientServerAddress** to configure which DNS server the DNS client should use.

> **TIP**   When an administrator executes the PowerShell cmdlet **Register-DNSClient** or runs **ipconfig /registerdns** at a command prompt, the dynamic update process runs.
>
> The new PowerShell Windows Server 2016 cmdlet **Get-NetIPConfiguration** gives you IP configuration information for all the nonvirtual connected interfaces on a DNS client. You also can verify whether the DNS client knows the correct DNS server to use to perform dynamic updates.
>
> Example:
>
> PS C:\Windows> **Get-NetIPConfiguration**
>
> | | |
> |---|---|
> | InterfaceAlias | : Wi-Fi |
> | InterfaceIndex | : 7 |
> | InterfaceDescription | : Intel Centrino Advanced-N 6205 |
> | NetProfile.Name | : SchulzM |
> | IPv4Address | : 192.168.1.121 |
> | IPv6DefaultGateway | : |
> | IPv4DefaultGatewa | : 192.168.1.1 |
> | DNSServer | : 192.168.1.1 |

You also can configure the DHCP server to register the records on the client's behalf. By default, a client registers its A resource record and the DHCP server registers the PTR record. By default, Windows operating systems attempt to register their records with their DNS server they have configured as the first DNS server on their network interface. You can modify this behavior in the client IP configuration or through Group Policy.

Delegating DNS Administration

Delegation involves applying permissions to specific IT professionals so they can do their work. You always have to keep in mind the concept of least privileges.

The Domain Admins security group has full permissions to manage all of the DNS server in its home domain. Figure 1-3 shows the example DNS server properties.

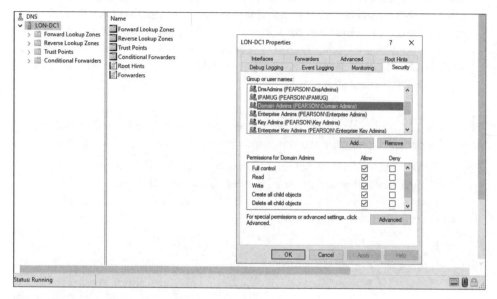

Figure 1-3 Example DNS Server Properties

The Enterprise Admins security group has full permissions to manage all aspects of all DNS servers in any domain in the complete forest.

The DNS Admins security group can be used if you need to delegate the administration of a DNS server to a different user or group. Add the user or group to the DNS Admins security group for a given domain in the forest. Members of the DNS Admins group get the following permissions:

- View and modify all DNS data
- Perform DNS settings and configurations

DNS Logging

By default, DNS maintains a DNS server log, which you can view in the Event Viewer. This event log is located in the Applications and Services Logs folder in the Event Viewer.

The DNS server log records common events such as these:

- DNS service starting and stopping
- Background loading and zone signing events
- Changes to DNS configuration settings
- Various warnings and error events

Debug logging must be explicitly enabled and can be used for the following logging options:

- Direction and contents of packets
- Transport protocol
- Request type
- Filtering based on IP address
- Name and location of the log file, which is located in the %windir%\ System32\DNS directory
- Log file maximum size limit

Debug logging is resource intensive. It can affect overall server performance and consumes disk space. Therefore, you should enable it only temporarily when you require more detailed information about server performance. To enable debug logging on the DNS server, do the following:

Step 1.   Open the DNS console.

Step 2.   Right-click the applicable DNS server, and then click **Properties**.

Step 3.   In the Properties dialog box, click the Debug Logging tab.

Step 4.   Select **Log Packets for Debugging**, and then select the events for which you want the DNS server to record debug logging (see Figure 1-4).

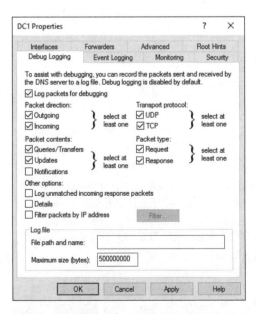

Figure 1-4   Debug Logging Properties

> **TIP**   Logging can generate a large number of files and, if left on too long, can fill a drive. Recommended practice is to turn on logging only while you are actively troubleshooting; at all other times, logging should be turned off.

Aging and Scavenging

In some cases, DNS resource records are not deleted automatically when they are no longer required. If a computer registers its own A resource record and is improperly disconnected from the network, the A record will not be deleted in the zone. These kinds of records are referred to as *stale records*. Windows Server 2016 can search for those stale records and, based on the aging of the record, scavenge (remove) them from the DNS database.

The aging and scavenging features are disabled by default on a Windows Server 2016 DNS server. Figure 1-5 shows the Zone Aging/Scavenging properties.

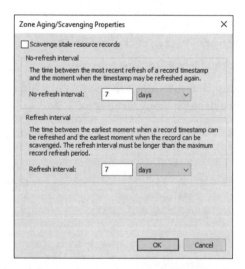

Figure 1-5   Zone Aging/Scavenging Properties

You must enable automatic scavenging and determine the interval at which it will take place in the Advanced properties of the DNS server. Each individual zone then is configured to indicate whether the stale records should be scavenged and the aging settings that determine when records become stale. The aging settings are found in the General tab for the zone's properties.

> **TIP**   Static records that are manually entered have a time stamp value of 0. They are not removed through the aging and scavenging process, so you must remove them manually from the zone.

DNS Backup

If your Windows Server 2016 DNS zone is an Active Directory–integrated zone, your DNS zone data is stored in the AD database (ntds.dit file). If the DNS zone is a primary zone and is not stored in the AD DS, the file is stored as a DNS file in the %SystemRoot%\System32\Dns folder. You can back up a primary zone simply by copying the individual zone file (zonename.dns), which is located in the %windir%\System32\DNS directory. Active Directory–integrated zones are stored in the AD DS and are backed up as part of a system state or a full server backup. Additionally, you can back up just the Active Directory–integrated zone by using the **dnscmd** command-line tool or PowerShell. To back up an AD-integrated zone with Power-Shell, perform the following command:

```
Export-DnsServerZone -Name pearson.com -Filename pearson
```

If you want to back up an AD-integrated zone with **dnscmd**, perform the following command:

```
Dnscmd /ZoneExport pearson.com pearson.com.bak
```

TIP   If DNSSEC is configured, the security information is not exported with these commands.

Netmask Ordering

With netmask ordering enabled (default setting), IP addresses of hosts that are on the same subnet as the requesting client have a higher priority in the DNS response to the client computer. Netmask ordering is also termed LocalNetPriority and is similar to round robin in function; however, its main job is to reorder and give preference to clients' queries using the addresses assigned to DNS server multiple network interface cards. Assume that a client generates a DNS query and sends it to a DNS server. If its IP address is in the same subnet as the client, the server reorders its IP addresses and moves it to the top of the list, to greatly improve its response to client queries. The netmask ordering feature is enabled (default setting) on the DNS server advanced properties (refer to Figure 1-1, earlier in this chapter).

Socket Pool

The DNS socket pool feature enables a DNS server to use source port randomization when it issues DNS queries. DNS socket pool is enabled by default in Windows Server 2016. The following list explains some of the DNS socket pool features and settings:

- **Random port numbers from the socket pool:** When the DNS service starts, the server chooses a source port from a pool of sockets that are available for issuing queries. Instead of using a predicable source port, the DNS server uses a random port number that it selects from the DNS socket pool.

- **Improved security through the DNS socket pool feature:** The DNS socket pool makes cache-tampering attacks more difficult because a malicious user must correctly guess both the source port of a DNS query and a random transaction ID to successfully run the attack.

- **DNS socket pool default value:** The default DNS socket pool size is 2,500.

- **DNS socket pool size value:** When you configure the DNS socket pool, you can choose a size value from 0 to 10,000. The larger the value, the greater the protection you have against DNS spoofing attacks.

- **DNS socket pool exclusion list:** DNS spoofing is another form of the DNS cache poisoning attack, in which a malicious user uploads incorrect IP addressing information into your DNS system. If the DNS server is running Windows Server 2008 R2 or newer, you can also configure a DNS socket pool exclusion list. The socket pool exclusion list enables you to specify port ranges that will never be used as a source port for DNS queries.

Nano Server

Starting with Windows Server 2016, a new server installation option is to use Nano Server.

Nano Server can be administered only remotely and is OS optimized for private clouds and datacenters. It is similar to Server Core but is much smaller, has no local logon capability, and supports only 64-bit applications, tools, and agents. Nano Server takes up far less disk space, sets up significantly faster, and requires far fewer updates and restarts than Windows Server. When it does restart, it restarts faster.

Nano Server is available for Windows Server 2016 Standard and Datacenter editions. It is ideal as a "compute" host for Hyper-V VMs whether in a cluster or not, as a storage host for SOFS (Scale-Out File Server), and as a DNS server.

You can use Windows Server 2016 Nano Server as a DNS server through the Nano Server package **Microsoft-NanoServer-DNS-Package**. With the **New-NanoServerImage** PowerShell cmdlet, you can prepare a Nano Server Image with a DNS server. You find out more about this topic later in this chapter in the section "Installing a DNS Server on a Nano Server."

Windows Server 2016 DNS Installation

The DNS server role is part of Windows Server 2016. You can install it on a Windows Server 2016 GUI or Server Core, as well as on Windows Server 2016 Nano Server, Standard or Datacenter version. You can install it with the Server Manager or PowerShell. First, however, you must determine whether your DNS Server service depends on Active Directory. On a domain with Active Directory, DNS is required.

Basically, you can install the DNS server role on a Windows Server 2016 server using the following PowerShell command:

```
Install-WindowsFeature -name DNS -IncludeAllSubFeatures
-IncludeManagementTools
```

Using DNS with Active Directory

You can install DNS after installing the first domain controller either in two steps or in one step together with the Active Directory installation. If you install DNS server as part of the Active Directory installation process, an Active Directory–integrated zone is automatically configured. With an Active Directory–integrated zone, you have the following advantages:

- Automatic encrypted replication of DNS data between domain controllers (RPC traffic)

- Every DNS record in the DNS zone becomes an Active Directory object and is protected with Active Directory permissions

- Secure dynamic update feature

AD-integrated DNS data usually is stored in the DomainDNSZones partition of Active Directory. You can change the replication scope to the ForestDNSZones partition to replicate the DNS data to all forest domain controllers instead of only to domain controllers in the domain. Suppose you want to replicate AD-integrated DNS data only to exclusive domain controllers independently from their domain membership; you then can create a new DNS application directory partition and replicate DNS data only to enlisted AD-integrated DNS servers (which are also domain controllers). You can create a DNS application directory partition with the PowerShell cmdlet **Add-DnsDirectoryPartition** and you can enlist and register a DNS server in a DNS application directory partition with the PowerShell cmdlet **Register-DnsServerDirectoryPartition**.

Using DNS Without Active Directory

You also can install a DNS server as a primary or secondary DNS server. Both DNS server types save DNS data in a zone file, not in the Active Directory database. This provides less zone security than with Active Directory as a repository for DNS data. If you have no domain controller on your server and you need a DNS server there, you cannot configure an Active Directory–integrated DNS server on that machine.

Example for primary/secondary: Suppose you have a branch office without domain controllers and you want to transfer DNS zone data from the zone pearson. local to a branch office DNS server. You can configure a secondary DNS server in that branch office and then use the Active Directory–integrated DNS server in the main office as the primary DNS server for the secondary DNS server in the branch. You can transfer the zone through zone transfer settings. The zone transfer network traffic is not encrypted, by default.

DNS Server Installation Options

Installing a DNS server can be accomplished in many different ways. If you are familiar with the graphical DNS manager utility, you might prefer to install the DNS server on a GUI-based server through Server Manager. You also can install a special kind of DNS server with a read-only AD-integrated DNS zone on a read-only domain controller (RODC) in a branch office, to keep the DNS query traffic locally inside the branch. To save resources, you might choose a Windows Server 2016 Nano Server for your DNS server installation. To save infrastructure costs, you might opt for an Azure virtual machine as a DNS server. The following are the most common options for installing a DNS server:

- DNS server on a Windows Server 2016 GUI-based server

- DNS server on a Windows Server 2016 Core

- DNS server on a Windows Server 2016 Nano Server

- DNS server on a read-only domain controller (RODC)

- DNS server on an Azure virtual machine

Tools for DNS Server Installation

You can use different tools to install a Windows Server 2016 DNS server. The following describe some of the common DNS server installation tools:

- Windows Server 2016 Server Manager

- Active Directory Installation Wizard

- Windows PowerShell

- DISM

Installing DNS with Server Manager

AD DS can be installed in Windows Server 2016 by using the Add Roles Wizard in Server Manager, followed by the Active Directory Domain Services Configuration Wizard. The Active Directory Domain Services Installation Wizard (dcpromo.exe) is deprecated beginning in Windows Server 2012, but dcpromo.exe can still be used as a command-line utility.

Installing a DNS server as part of Active Directory installation (forest root domain controller) with Server Manager involves these steps:

Step 1.   Log in to the Windows Server 2016 server locally as an administrator. In Server Manager, under Manage, select **Add Roles and Features** (see Figure 1-6).

Figure 1-6   Add Roles and Features in Server Manager

Step 2.   In the Before You Begin window (see Figure 1-7), click **Next**.

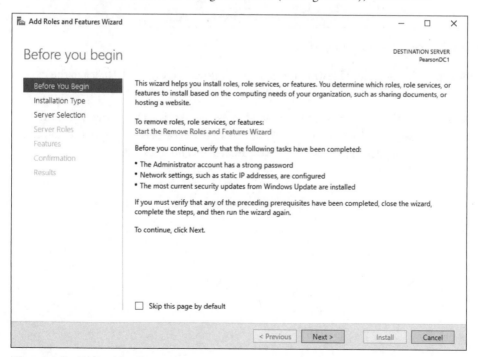

Figure 1-7   Before You Begin Page

Step 3.   In the Select Installation Type window (see Figure 1-8), leave the default selection and click **Next**.

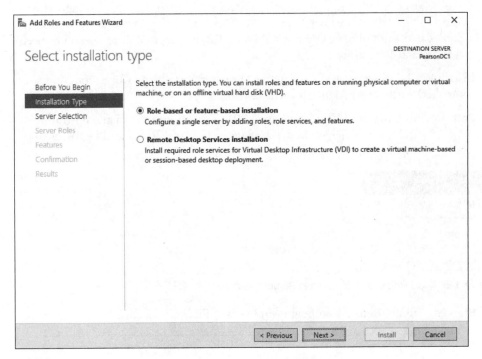

Figure 1-8   Select Installation Type Page

Step 4.   In the Select Destination Server window (see Figure 1-9), leave the default selection and click **Next**.

Step 5.   In the Select Server Roles window, select **Active Directory Domain Services** (see Figure 1-10) and click **Next**. You are prompted to add the dependent features. Click **Add Features** and click **Next**.

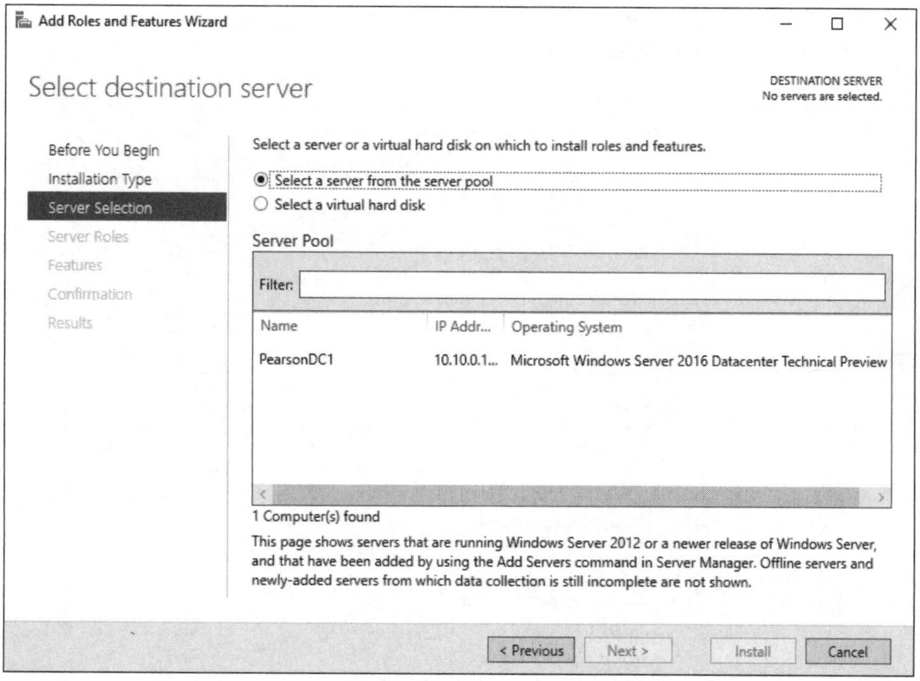

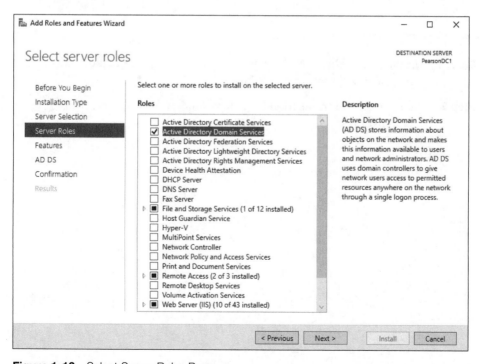

Figure 1-9   Select Destination Server Page

Figure 1-10   Select Server Roles Page

Step 6.   In the Select Features window (see Figure 1-11), keep the default selection and click **Next**.

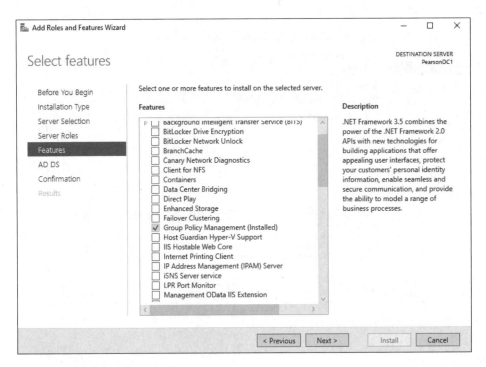

Figure 1-11   Select Features Page

Step 7.   In the Active Directory Domain Services window (see Figure 1-12), read the description and click **Next**.

Step 8.   In the Confirm Installation Selections window (see Figure 1-13), click **Install**.

Figure 1-12   Active Directory Domain Services Page

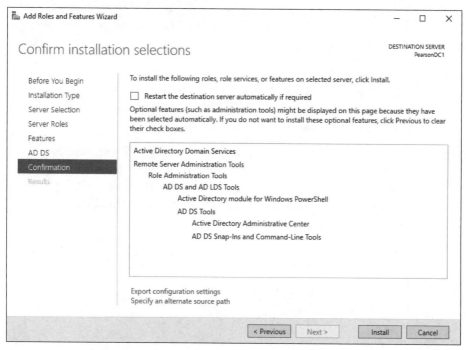

Figure 1-13   Confirm Installation Selections Page

Step 9.   When installation finishes, click the link **Promote This Server to a Domain Controller** (see Figure 1-14).

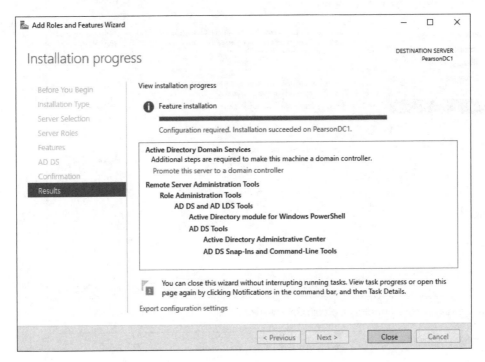

Figure 1-14   Installation Progress Page

Step 10.   In the Active Directory Domain Services Configuration Wizard, select **Add a New Forest** (see Figure 1-15). At Root Domain Name, type **pearson.local** as the name for the domain and enter your correct credentials; then click **Next**.

Step 11.   In the Domain Controller Options window, select **Windows Server 2016** as both Forest and Domain Functional Level options. Under Specify Domain Controller Capabilities, leave the default setting as Domain Name System (DNS) Server and type in a DSRM password (see Figure 1-16).

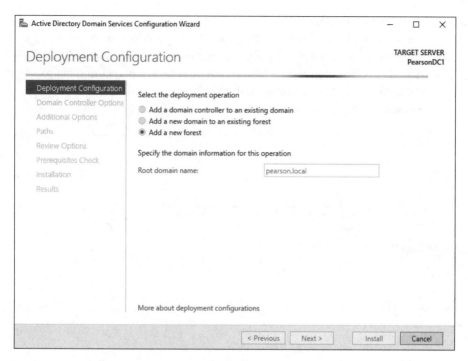

Figure 1-15 Deployment Configuration Page

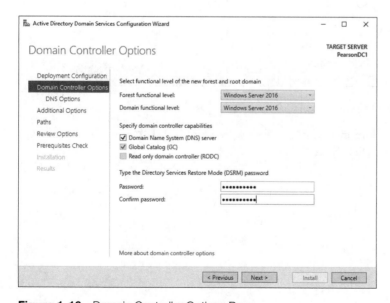

Figure 1-16 Domain Controller Options Page

Step 12. In the DNS Options window, shown in Figure 1-17, leave the default and click **Next**. (You do not have to worry about the yellow warning message because in this example you create a new forest root domain; therefore, you do not want to create a DNS delegation from a parent domain to a child domain. A parent zone cannot be found because, at that moment, no such parent zone exists.)

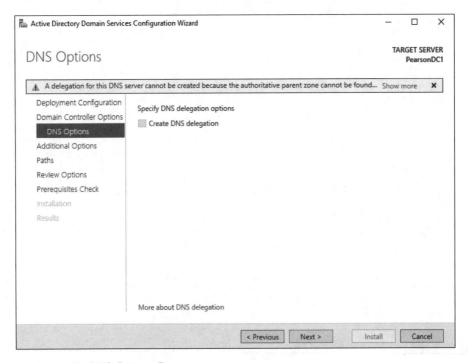

Figure 1-17   DNS Options Page

Step 13. In the Additional Options window (see Figure 1-18), leave the default settings and click **Next**.

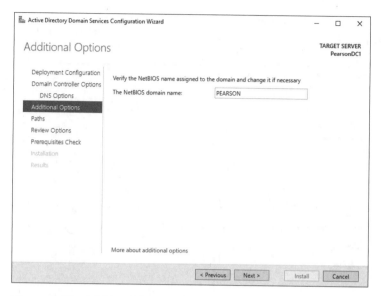

Figure 1-18 Additional Options Page

Step 14. In the Paths window, shown in Figure 1-19, leave the default settings and click **Next**.

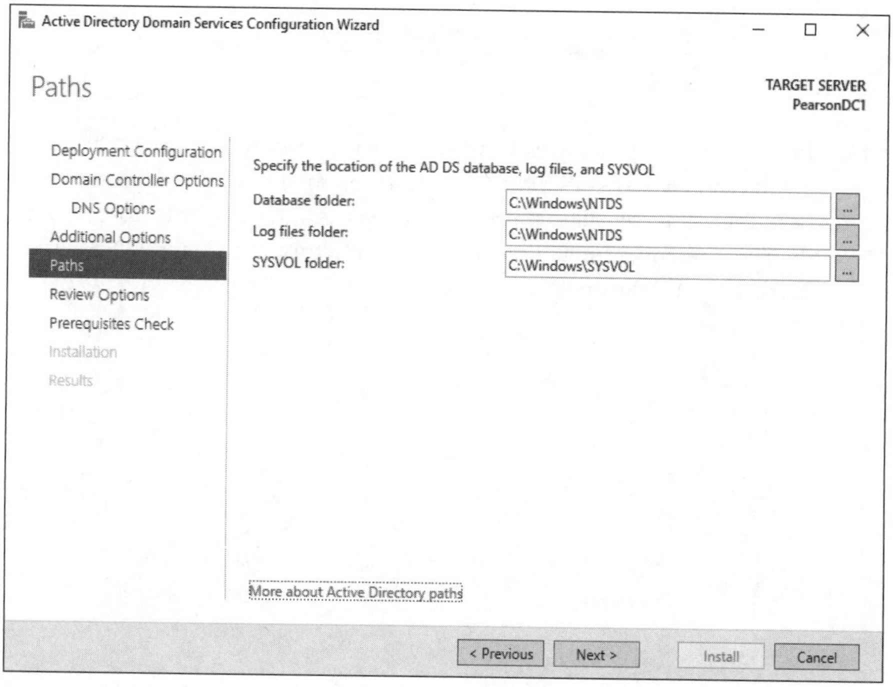

Figure 1-19 Paths Page

Step 15. In the Review Options window (see Figure 1-20), leave the default and
click **Next**.

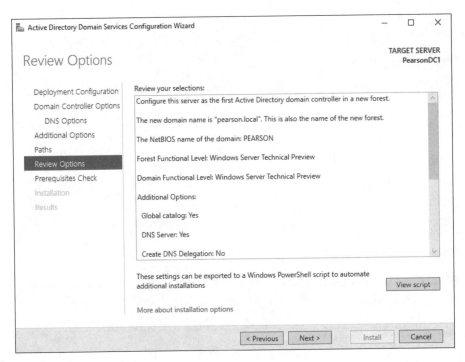

Figure 1-20   Review Options Page

Step 16. In the Prerequisites Check window, shown in Figure 1-21, read the
results and click **Install**. Ignore the warning messages; prerequisites have
been met. The installation process then starts and installs the forest root
domain controller, including an Active Directory–integrated DNS server
hosting the DNS zone pearson.local.

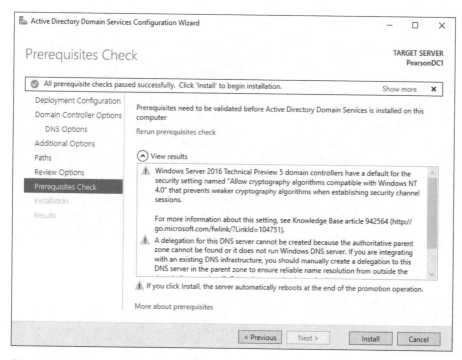

Figure 1-21   Prerequisites Check Page

The server automatically performs a restart and you see the message in Figure 1-22. Be sure to wait for the restart.

Figure 1-22   Signout Message After Active Directory Domain Services Installation

Installing DNS with PowerShell

To install a DNS server as part of Active Directory installation (forest root domain controller) with PowerShell, perform the following steps:

Step 1. Log in to the Windows Server 2016 server locally as an administrator. Open PowerShell and install the Active Directory role with the following command:

```
Install-WindowsFeature -name AD-Domain-Services
  -IncludeManagementTools
```

Step 2. With the following PowerShell commands, you can install the forest root domain controller, including the DNS server. (At press time, in the Windows Server 2016 evaluation version, the domain mode and forest mode are called WinThreshold in the script. In the full version of Windows Server 2016, this is the Windows Server 2016 level.)

```
Import-Module ADDSDeployment
Install-ADDSForest '
-CreateDnsDelegation:$false '
-DatabasePath "C:\Windows\NTDS" '
-DomainMode "WinThreshold" '
-DomainName "pearson.local" '
-DomainNetbiosName "PEARSON" '
-ForestMode "WinThreshold" '
-InstallDns:$true '
-LogPath "C:\Windows\NTDS" '
-NoRebootOnCompletion:$false '
-SysvolPath "C:\Windows\SYSVOL" '
-Force:$true
```

Installing a DNS Server on RODC

If you install a read-only domain controller (RODC), a DNS server is installed automatically on your RODC.

On the Additional Domain Controller Options page in the Active Directory Domain Services Configuration Wizard, the DNS Server option is selected by default. A DNS server installed on a read-only domain controller is a special type of DNS server. This DNS server gets a read-only Active Directory–integrated zone.

Consider the following example PowerShell Script for installing an RODC with a DNS server:

```
Import-Module ADDSDeployment
Install-ADDSDomainController '
```

```
-AllowPasswordReplicationAccountName @("PEARSON\Allowed RODC Password
  Replication Group", "PEARSON\Zuerich RODC Admins", "PEARSON\Zuerich
  RODC Users and Computers") '
-Credential (Get-Credential) '
-CriticalReplicationOnly:$false '
-DatabasePath "C:\Windows\NTDS" '
-DelegatedAdministratorAccountName "PEARSON\Zuerich RODC Admins" '
-DenyPasswordReplicationAccountName @("BUILTIN\Administrators",
"BUILTIN\Server Operators",
  "BUILTIN\Backup Operators", "BUILTIN\Account Operators", "PEARSON
    \Denied RODC Password
  Replication Group") '
-DomainName "corp.pearson.local" '
-InstallDNS:$true '
-LogPath "C:\Windows\NTDS" '
-ReadOnlyReplica:$true '
-SiteName "Default-First-Site-Name" '
-SYSVOLPath "C:\Windows\SYSVOL"
-Force:$true
```

Table 1-5 explains the parameters and values of the **Install-ADDSDomainController** PowerShell cmdlet.

Table 1-5   Install-ADDSDomainController PowerShell Cmdlet Options

Parameter	Example Value	Description
AllowPassword Replication AccountName	@("PEARSON\Allowed RODC Password Replication Group", "PEARSON\ Zuerich RODC Admins", "PEARSON\Zuerich RODC Users and Computers")	Specifies the names of user accounts, group accounts, and computer accounts whose passwords can be replicated to this RODC. Use an empty string ("") if you want to keep the value empty. By default, only the Allowed RODC Password Replication Group is allowed.
LogPath	$true	Specifies the fully qualified, non-UNC path to a directory on a fixed disk of the local computer that will contain the domain log files (for example, C:\Windows\Logs). The default is %SYSTEMROOT%\NTDS.
ReadOnlyReplica	$true	Specifies whether to install the domain controller as an RODC for an existing domain.

Parameter	Example Value	Description
DatabasePath	C:\Windows\NTDS	Specifies the path to a directory on a fixed disk of the local computer that will contain the domain database (for example, C:\Windows\NTDS).
Delegated Administrator AccountName	"PEARSON\Zuerich RODC Admins"	Specifies the name of the user or group that will be the delegated administrator of this domain controller.
DenyPassword Replication AccountName	@("BUILTIN\ Administrators", "BUILTIN\ Server Operators", "BUILTIN\Backup Operators", "BUILTIN\ Account Operators", "PEARSON \Denied RODC Password Replication Group")	Specifies the names of user accounts, group accounts, and computer accounts whose passwords are not to be replicated to this RODC. Use an empty string ("") if you do not want to deny the replication of credentials of any users or computers. By default, Administrators, Server Operators, Backup Operators, Account Operators, and the Denied RODC Password Replication Group are denied. By default, the Denied RODC Password Replication Group includes Cert Publishers, Domain Admins, Enterprise Admins, Enterprise Domain Controllers, Enterprise Read-Only Domain Controllers, Group Policy Creator Owners, the krbtgt account, and Schema Admins.
DomainName	"corp.pearson.local"	Specifies the FQDN for the domain where the domain controller will be installed or added.
InstallDNS	$true	Specifies whether the DNS Server service should be installed and configured on the domain controller. For domain controller installation, if this parameter is left unspecified and the current domain already hosts and stores the DNS names for the domain, then the default for this parameter is *$true* and the DNS server will be installed. Otherwise, if DNS domain names are hosted outside Active Directory, the default is *$false* and no DNS server will be installed.

Parameter	Example Value	Description
LogPath	"C:\Windows\NTDS"	Specifies the fully qualified, non-UNC path to a directory on a fixed disk of the local computer that will contain the domain log files (for example, C:\Windows\Logs).
ReadOnlyReplica	$true	Specifies whether to install the domain controller as an RODC for an existing domain.
SiteName	"Default-First-Site-Name"	Defines the name of an existing site where you can place the new domain controller. The default value depends on the type of installation. For a new forest, the default is Default-First-Site-Name. For all other installations, the default is the site that is associated with the subnet that includes the IP address of this server. If no such site exists, the default is the site of the replication source domain controller.
SYSVOLPath	"C:\Windows\SYSVOL"	Defines the fully qualified, non-UNC path to a directory on a fixed disk of the local computer that will contain the Sysvol data (for example, C:\Windows\SYSVOL).
Force	$true	Suppresses any warnings that might normally appear during the installation and addition of the domain controller, to allow the cmdlet to complete its operation. This parameter can be useful to include when scripting installation.

Installing a DNS Server on Azure

In Microsoft Azure, you can deploy Azure virtual machines and other Azure resources through the Azure Resource Manager. This enables you to provision the DNS server role as part of an Azure VM using a declarative template. In a single template, you can deploy multiple services along with their dependencies. You use the same template to repeatedly deploy your application during every stage of the application lifecycle. For example, you can use Azure ARM templates to deploy an Active Directory forest root domain controller, including a DNS server role (see Figure 1-23).

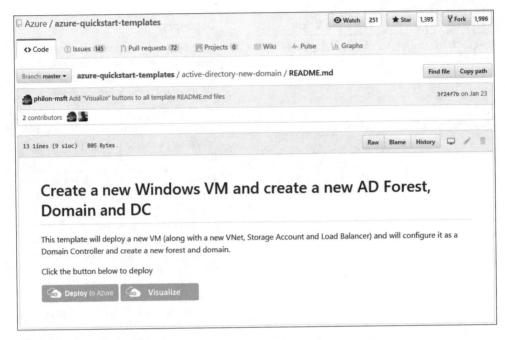

Figure 1-23 Using Azure ARM Templates for DNS Servers

With Microsoft Azure, you can boost your server deployment, especially if you want to build test environments to work through different kinds of DNS scenarios. With Azure Resource Manager (ARM) templates, you can quickly deploy Azure virtual machines. To do so, you need an Azure subscription.

For testing purposes, you can get a one-month free trial Azure subscription at https://azure.microsoft.com/en-us/offers/ms-azr-0044p/.

After you have created the free trial subscription, you can use a ready-made ARM template in the GitHub repository to build a new Azure VM that includes Azure VNet, Azure Storage Account, Azure Load Balancer, and the complete AD configuration. The Azure VM then automatically is usable as the first domain controller and Active Directory–integrated DNS server for a new AD forest.

The URL to the Active-Directory-New-Domain ARM template shown in Figure 1-23 is https://github.com/Azure/azure-quickstart-templates/tree/master/active-directory-new-domain.

On the GitHub page, you must select the README.md file. Then click the **Deploy to Azure** button to automatically connect to the Azure Portal. Fill out the ARM template form. Table 1-6 describes example values for the fields.

Table 1-6   ARM Template Fields

Field	Example Value	Description
Subscription	Pay-As-You-Go	The name of your Azure Subscription.
Resource Group	Create new: *<YourInitials>RG*	Location for creating a new Azure resource group. A resource group is a collection of Azure resources that share the same lifecycle, permissions, and policies.
Location	Nearest location to you	Location where the Azure resources (AzureVM, VNet, and so on) will be created.
Admin Username	AdminX	The name of the Administrator account of the new VM and domain.
Admin Password	Pa$$w0rdPa$$w0rd	The password for the Administrator account of the new VM and domain.
Domain Name	pearsonucertify.com	The FQDN of the Active Directory domain to be created.
Dns Prefix	pearsonucertify	The DNS prefix for the public IP address that the load balancer uses.
Windowsserver	2016-Datacenter	The version of Windows Server to use.
_artifacts Location	Default path	The location of resources, such as templates and DSC modules, that the template depends on.
_artifacts Location Sas Token	empty	Auto-generated token to access _artifactsLocation.

Figure 1-24 shows example parameters for the ARM template, which you can use to build a forest root domain controller in Azure.

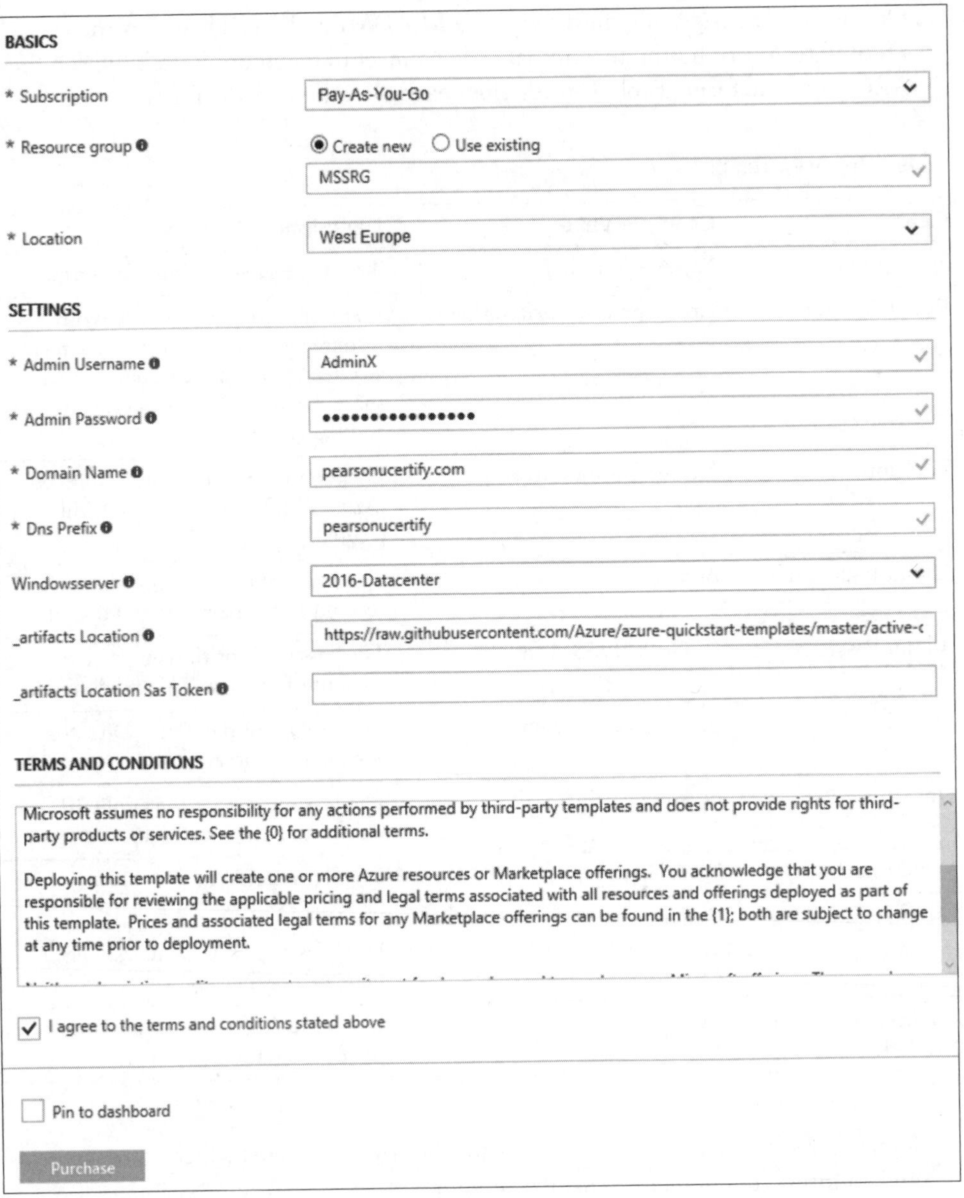

BASICS

| * Subscription | Pay-As-You-Go |

* Resource group ❶   ◉ Create new   ○ Use existing

| | MSSRG |

| * Location | West Europe |

SETTINGS

* Admin Username ❶	AdminX
* Admin Password ❶	••••••••••••••••
* Domain Name ❶	pearsonucertify.com
* Dns Prefix ❶	pearsonucertify
Windowsserver ❶	2016-Datacenter
_artifacts Location ❶	https://raw.githubusercontent.com/Azure/azure-quickstart-templates/master/active-c
_artifacts Location Sas Token ❶	

TERMS AND CONDITIONS

Microsoft assumes no responsibility for any actions performed by third-party templates and does not provide rights for third-party products or services. See the {0} for additional terms.

Deploying this template will create one or more Azure resources or Marketplace offerings. You acknowledge that you are responsible for reviewing the applicable pricing and legal terms associated with all resources and offerings deployed as part of this template. Prices and associated legal terms for any Marketplace offerings can be found in the {1}; both are subject to change at any time prior to deployment.

☑ I agree to the terms and conditions stated above

☐ Pin to dashboard

Purchase

Figure 1-24   ARM Parameters Example

After you have filled out the ARM template parameters, click **OK**. In Custom Deployment under Resource Group, select **Create New** and type the following resource group name: **ADTestDomain**. Select the nearest location to your location under Resource Group Location and then select **Review Legal Terms** under Legal Terms; after that, click **Purchase** to accept the legal terms. Finally, click

Create. You have to wait about 15–20 minutes for the ARM template deployment. The AzureVM named ADVM starts automatically. Be sure to wait until the message shown in Figure 1-25 appears, confirming that the deployment is ready.

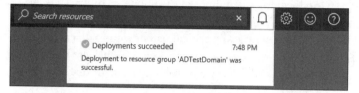

Figure 1-25   Successful Deployment in the Azure Portal

At this point, you simply have to connect through RDP to the Azure virtual machine named ADVM, accept the certificate, and log in with the credentials. Now you have a Windows Server 2016 Datacenter domain controller with DNS server for the test. local domain, for testing purposes.

> **TIP**   If you quickly want to remove all resources that are part of the Azure resource group ADTestDomain, you only have to remove the Resource group in the Azure Portal.

If you want to deploy a testing environment with two domain controllers, you can use the following ARM template:

> https://azure.microsoft.com/en-us/documentation/templates/
> active-directory-new-domain-ha-2-dc/

Installing a DNS Server on a Nano Server

Windows Server 2016 offers a new installation option: Nano Server. The Nano Server operating system can be administered only remotely, with the exception of some settings configurable in the Nano Server Recovery Console. It is optimized for private clouds and datacenters. The Nano Server installation option is much smaller and faster, and it supports only 64-bit applications, tools, and agents. This option is available for Standard and Datacenter editions of Windows Server 2016.

Deploying a Windows Server 2016 Nano Server requires the following prerequisites, which might show up in some 70-741 exam questions:

- Windows Server 2016 ISO image file

- Windows Server 2016 Hyper-V Host

- PowerShell scripts:

    - Convert-WindowsImage.ps1

    - NanoServerImageGeneratorer.psm1

Nano Server Zero Footprint Model

Nano Server adheres to the *zero footprint model*, which is designed to deliver faster speed and lower resource consumption. This means no 32-bit support, no GUI, no MSI installation option, no local logon, and no RDP support. Compared with the full server installation option, a Windows Server 2016 Nano Server boasts a 93 percent smaller VHD size, 92 percent fewer critical patches, and 80 percent fewer reboots. Nano Server employs the zero footprint model so that the base OS is always the same upon deployment. All binaries for roles or features that are to be installed will live outside the server.

Nano Server can be installed into a Hyper-V or Azure VM. It also can be installed as a Bare Metal host. Figure 1-26 shows the three different Windows Server 2016 deployment options.

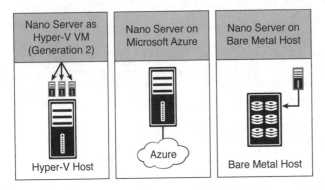

Figure 1-26   Nano Server Deployment Options

Nano Server Deployment Scenarios

A Windows Server 2016 Nano Server can be used for more purposes than just a DNS server. Nano Server is ideal for the following scenarios:

- Host for Hyper-V VMs, clustered/unclustered

- Storage host for SOFS (Scale-Out File Servers)

- Web server running IIS

- Host for applications running in a container or VM guest OS

Nano Server Recovery Console

On a Windows Server 2016 Nano Server, you can use the Nano Recovery Console (also named the Emergency Management Console) to configure some base network settings locally (all other configuration must be done remotely!):

Computer Name	Gateway Address
Domain/workgroup	Primary/secondary DNS
Logon/logoff	MAC address
Shutdown/restart	Network driver name
Enable/disable NIC	Network driver date
IPv4/IPv6 address	Network driver provider
Firewall rules	

Figure 1-27 shows the Network Adapter Settings of the Windows Server 2016 Nano Server Recovery Console.

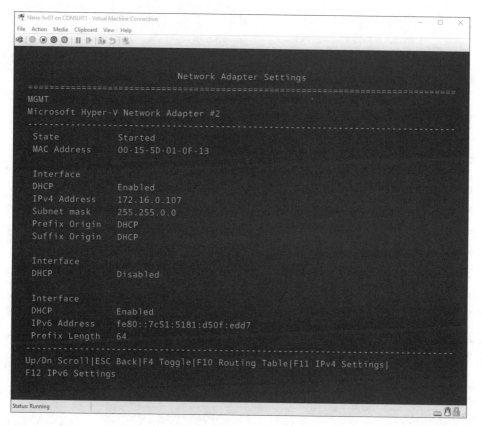

Figure 1-27   Nano Recovery Console NIC Settings

The 70-741 exam might include questions on Nano Server and the Nano Server Recovery Console. Be sure that you know about the following DNS server deployment options for Windows Server 2016 Nano Server:

1. Install a DNS server as part of the Nano Server image building process.

2. Create a Nano Server image and install the DNS Server Package *Microsoft-NanoServer-DNS-Package* after the Nano Server Generation 2 Hyper-V virtual machine is created.

DNS Servers Supported on Nano Server

The deployment of a DNS server onto a Windows Server 2016 Nano Server is available only with file-based DNS; *AD-integrated DNS server is not supported*. Think about that for the 70-741 exam. Running a DNS server on a Windows Server 2016 Nano Server image, you can run your DNS servers with a reduced footprint, quick bootup, and minimized patching.

TIP AD-integrated DNS is not supported on a Nano Server.

Adding Roles on Nano Server

To add functionality or roles to a Windows Server 2016 Nano Server, you need packages. The following tables show the roles and features that are available with Windows Server 2016 Nano Server, along with the Windows PowerShell options that install the packages for them. Some packages are installed directly with their own Windows PowerShell switches (such as **-Compute**); others you install by passing package names to the **-Packages** parameter, which you can combine in a comma-separated list.

You can dynamically list available packages using the **Get-NanoServerPackage** cmdlet.

Table 1-7 through Table 1-10 show the available Nano Server package options. These options are essential to learn for exam preparation.

Table 1-7 Available Roles and Features for Nano Server (1)

Role or Feature	Option
DNS server role	**-Packages Microsoft-NanoServer-DNS-Package**
Hyper-V role (including NetQoS)	**-Compute**
Failover clustering	**-Clustering**

TIP   Failover clustering on Windows Server 2016 Nano Server works the same as it does on Windows Server in Server Core mode, but keep in mind the following:

- Clusters must be managed remotely with Cluster Manager or PowerShell.
- Nano Server cluster nodes must be joined to the same domain.
- Domain accounts must have Administrator privileges on Nano Servers.
- All commands must be run in an elevated command prompt.

Table 1-8   Available Roles and Features for Nano Server (2)

Role or Feature	Option
Basic drivers for a variety of network adapters and storage controllers. This is the same set of drivers included in a Server Core installation of Windows Server 2016.	**-OEMDrivers**
File Server role and other storage components.	**-Storage**

TIP   File Services is not automatically enabled when you use the **-Storage** parameter to install File Services. Enable this feature from a remote computer with Server Manager.

Table 1-9   Available Roles and Features for Nano Server (3)

Role or Feature	Option
Windows Defender Antimalware, including a default signature file	**-Defender**
Reverse forwarders for application compatibility (for example, common application frameworks such as Ruby and Node.js)	Included by default

TIP   **What is the Reverse Forwarders package?** Some APIs are moved from higher-level Windows DLLs into new DLLs. If an app depends on these DLLs, it will fail to load on Nano Server. The Reverse Forwarders package, included by default, enables a subset of Desktop Win32 binaries to run on Nano Server without recompilation. Adding this optional package lets you load your app on Nano Server. Reverse Forwarders automatically routes the app to the correct DLLs on Nano Server.

Table 1-10   Available Roles and Features for Nano Server (4)

Role or Feature	Option
Desired State Configuration (DSC)	**-Packages Microsoft-NanoServer-DSC-Package**
Internet Information Server (IIS)	**-Packages Microsoft-NanoServer-IIS-Package**
Host support for Windows Containers	**-Containers**
System Center Virtual Machine Manager agent	**-Packages Microsoft-NanoServer-SCVMM-Package** **-Packages Microsoft-NanoServer-SCVMM-Compute-Package**
Network Performance Diagnostics Service (NPDS) (Note: This requires the Windows Defender Antimalware package, which you should install before installing NPDS.)	**-Packages Microsoft-NanoServer-NPDS-Package**
Data Center Bridging (including DCBQoS	**-Packages Microsoft-NanoServer-DCB-Package**
Deployment on a virtual machine	**Microsoft-NanoServer-Guest-Package**
Deployment on a physical machine	**Microsoft-NanoServer-Host-Package**
Secure Startup	**-Packages Microsoft-NanoServer-SecureStartup-Package**
Shielded VM	**-Packages Microsoft-NanoServer-ShieldedVM-Package**

TIP   What about language packs? When you install packages, a language pack is also installed based on the configured locale of the administrator account. For example, if your locale is set to German (de_de) but you are configuring a Swedish image (sv_se), you will receive an error stating that the sv_se package is not present. The solution is to use the **-Language** parameter (for example, **-Language sv_se**). You can find the available language packs and their locale abbreviations in the installation media in subfolders named for the locale of the image.

TIP   What about different Nano Server editions? You have the option to specify the Nano Server edition to build either the Standard or Datacenter edition. Use the **-Edition** parameter to specify the Standard or Datacenter editions.

Adding Nano Server to a Domain

In some DNS Nano Server scenarios, you want to have the DNS server part of a domain. In these cases, you must join the Nano Server to a domain. Again, you can use the **New-NanoServerImage** PowerShell cmdlet for this. In the following example, the PowerShell cmdlet harvests a domain blob for the *pearson.com* domain from the local computer (which also has to be part of the same domain). Then it performs offline provisioning of the image using the blob.

```
New-NanoServerImage -Edition Standard -DeploymentType Host
-MediaPath <PathtoMedia> -BasePath.\Base -TargetPath .\
  NanoDNS.vhdx -Computername
  NanoDNS -DomainName pearson
```

When this command completes, you find a computer account named Nano_DNS in your Active Directory.

You can harvest a blob with this command:

```
Djoin /Provision /domain pearson /Machine Nano_DNS
  /SaveFile NanoDNS.djoin
```

Figure 1-28 shows how to add a DNS Nano Server to a domain.

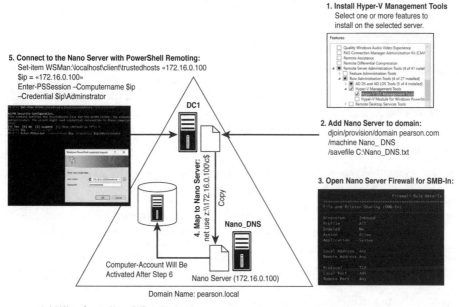

Figure 1-28 Adding a DNS Nano Server to a Domain

Installing a DNS Server Package on Nano Server

You can install a DNS server on a Nano Server through the Nano Server package **Microsoft-NanoServer-DNS-Package** during creation of the Nano Server VHD. Use the following PowerShell command:

```
New-NanoServerImage -BasePath C:\nanotemp -TargetPath C:\Nano\
  NanoDNS.vhd -OEMDrivers
  -Packages Microsoft-NanoServer-DNS-Package -Computer Name NanoDNS
  -DomainName pearson.com
  -Language en-us
```

Setting Static IP Addresses on Nano Server

To use static IP addresses, first you must determine the name or index of the interface you want to modify by using the **Get-NetAdapter** PowerShell cmdlet. Alternatively, you can use the **Nano Server Recovery Console**. You can use the **Ipv6Address**, **Ipv6Dns**, **Ipv4Address**, **Ipv4SubnetMask**, **Ipv4Gateway**, and **Ipv4Dns** parameters to specify the configuration, as in this example:

```
New-NanoServerImage -DeploymentType Host -Edition Standard -MediaPath
  \\Path\To\Media\en_us
  -basePath .\Base -targetPath .\NanoVM.vhd
  -InterfaceNameorIndex Ethernet -IPv4Address 192.168.1.200
  -IPv4SubnetMask 255.255.255.0 -IPv4Gateway 192.168.1.1
  -IPv4Dns 192.168.1.100
```

Adding Drivers on Nano Server

Nano Server includes a basic drivers set. You can install it with the parameter **OEMDrivers**. Keep in mind that the drivers for your network adapter might not be included. In that case, you can add drivers to the Nano Server image by following these steps:

Step 1.   Install Windows Server 2016 on the physical computer where you will run a Nano Server.

Step 2.   Open the Device Manager and identify devices in the following categories: network adapters, storage controllers, and disk drives.

Step 3.   For each device, right-click the device name and click **Properties**. In the dialog box that opens, click the **Driver** tab and then click **Driver Details**.

Step 4.   Note the filename and path for the driver file.

Step 5. Search for the driver file and search for all instances with the following command: **dir** *<filename>* */s /b*.

Step 6. In the elevated prompt, navigate to the directory of the Nano Server VHD and run the following commands:

```
Dism \dism /Mount-Image /ImageFile:.\NanoServer.vhd /Index:1
   /MountDir:.\mountdir
Dism \dism /Add-Driver /image:.\mountdir /driver: C:\Windows\
   System32\ DriverStore\FileRepository\<driverfile>
Dism \dism /Unmount-Image /MountDir:.\MountDir /Commit
```

Step 7. Repeat these steps for each driver file you need on Nano Server.

Injecting Additional Drivers for Nano Server Deployment

Gradually, you will recognize the importance of the **New-NanoServer Image** PowerShell cmdlet for the Windows Server 2016 Nano Server deployment process. Recommended practice is to memorize all the parameters of that cmdlet for the exam. You also can use the **New-Nano ServerImage** PowerShell cmdlet to search the directory for available drivers and inject them into the Nano Server image. You can do this with the following command:

```
New-NanoServerImage -Deploymenttype Host -Edition Standard
-MediaPath \\Path\To\Media\en_us -basePath .\Base -TargetPath
  .\NanoVM.vhdx -DriversPath .\Extra\Drivers
```

Connecting with WinRM to Nano Server

To connect to a Windows Server 2016 Nano Server using WinRM (from another computer that is not on the same subnet), open port 5985 for inbound TCP traffic on the Nano Server image. You can open that port with the **EnableRemote-ManagementPort** parameter:

```
New-NanoServerImage -Deployment type Host -Edition Standard
-MediaPath \\Path\To\Media\en_us -basePath .\Base
-TargetPath .\NanoVM.vhdx -EnableRemoteManagementPort
```

Deploying Nano DNS Server During Image Creation

The following list outlines how to deploy a Nano DNS server during image creation:

Step 1. Mount the Windows Server 2016 ISO. Note the drive in which it is mounted.

Step 2. Copy NanoServerImageGenerator.psm1 and ConvertWindowsImage. ps1 from the \NanoServer folder in the Windows Server 2016 ISO to a folder on your local hard drive.

Step 3. Import the NanoServerImageGenerator script with the following PowerShell command:

```
Import-Module NanoServerImageGenerator.psm1 -Verbose
```

Step 4. Create a VHDX with the following PowerShell commands:

```
Import-Module .\NanoServerImageGenerator.psm1 -verbose
New-NanoServerImage -MediaPath <path to root of media>
-BasePath .\Base -TargetPath .\NanoVM\NanoVM.vhdx -ComputerName
  Nano -Compute -GuestDrivers -packages Microsoft-NanoServer-DNS-
  Package
```

The **New-NanoServerImage** cmdlet does the following:

- Creates the Nano Server image
- Creates the image with the name NanoVM.vhdx
- Sets the computer name as Nano
- Adds the Compute and GuestDrivers packages
- Adds the DNS role package Microsoft-NanoServer-DNS-Package

Step 5. Create a new Generation 2 VM named Nano in Hyper-V Manager and use the VHD. Be sure to also create a virtual switch for your networking. Ensure that DHCP is running so that the Nano Server can be assigned a dynamic IP address.

Step 6. Log on to the Recovery Console. By default with the DNS image, the firewall exceptions for DNS are added. If you want the ping utility to work, you must enable appropriate firewall exceptions.

Deploying Nano Server and Adding the DNS Package Afterward

Follow these steps to deploy Nano Server and then add the DNS package afterward:

Step 1. Mount the Windows Server 2016 ISO. Note the drive in which it is mounted.

Step 2. Copy NanoServerImageGenerator.psm1 and Convert-WindowsImage. ps1 from the \NanoServer folder in the Windows Server 2016 ISO to a folder on your local hard drive.

Step 3. Import the NanoServerImageGenerator script with the following PowerShell command:

```
Import-Module NanoServerImageGenerator.psm1 -Verbose
```

Step 4. Create a VHDX with the following PowerShell commands:

```
Import-Module .\NanoServerImageGenerator.psm1 -verbose
New-NanoServerImage -MediaPath <path to root of media>
-BasePath .\Base -TargetPath .\NanoVM\NanoVM.vhdx
-ComputerName Nano -Compute -GuestDrivers
```

The **New-NanoServerImage** cmdlet does the following:

- Creates the Nano Server image

- Creates the image with the name NanoVM.vhdx

- Sets the computer name to be Nano

- Adds the Compute and GuestDrivers packages

- Note that the DNS role package *Microsoft-NanoServer-DNS-Package* is not installed here during image creation

Step 5. Create a new Generation 2 VM named Nano in Hyper-V Manager and use the NanoVM.vhdx for the VM. Be sure to also create a virtual switch for your networking. Ensure that DHCP is running so that Nano Server can be assigned a dynamic IP address.

Step 6. Use PowerShell Direct to connect to the Nano Server VM:

```
Enter-PSSession -VMName Nano -Credential administrator
```

Step 7. Enter the credentials of the Admin account on the VM.

Step 8. After you have connected to the Nano Server VM through PowerShell Direct, install the Nano Server Package provider with the following command:

```
Install-PackageProvider NanoServerPackage
```

Step 9. To find all available packages, use the following command:

```
Find-NanoServerPackage -Name *
```

Step 10. Install the DNS role type with the following command:

```
Install-NanoServerPackage Microsoft-NanoServer-DNS-Package
```

Step 11. When the package finishes installation, enable the DNS server using the following commands:

```
Enable-WindowsOptionalFeature -Online -FeatureName
  DNS-Server-Full-Role; Import-Module DNSServer
```

Step 12. To view all available DNS server cmdlets, use the following command:

```
Get-Command -Module DNSServer
```

> **TIP** You also can deploy Nano Server in Microsoft Azure. To do so, you must use the **-ForAzure** parameter for the **New-NanoServerImage** PowerShell cmdlet.

Deploying DNS Nano Server to Bare Metal Host

Follow these steps to deploy Nano Server to a Bare Metal host:

Step 1. Mount the Windows Server 2016 ISO. Note the drive in which it is mounted.

Step 2. Copy NanoServerImageGenerator.psm1 and ConvertWindowsImage. ps1 from the \NanoServer folder in the Windows Server 2016 ISO to a folder on your local hard drive.

Step 3. Import the NanoServerImageGenerator script with the following PowerShell command:

```
Import-Module NanoServerImageGenerator.psm1 -Verbose
```

Step 4. Create a VHDX with the following PowerShell commands:

```
Import-Module .\NanoServerImageGenerator.psm1 -verbose
New-NanoServerImage -MediaPath <path to root of media>
-BasePath .\Base -TargetPath .\NanoVM\NanoVM.vhdx
-ComputerName Nano -Compute -GuestDrivers -packages Microsoft-
  NanoServer-DNS-Package
```

The **New-NanoServerImage** cmdlet does the following:

- Creates the Nano Server image

- Creates the image with the name NanoVM.vhdx

- Sets the computer name to be Nano

- Adds the Compute and GuestDrivers packages

- Adds the DNS role package **Microsoft-NanoServer-DNS-Package**

Step 5. Copy the VHDX file to a USB flash drive and insert the drive into the target server.

Step 6. Boot the target server through bootable media (DVD, USB) and press Shift+F10 to get a command prompt.

Step 7. Run diskpart.exe, and then run the following commands:

```
Select disk 0
Clean
Convert gpt
```

```
Create partition EFI size=300
Format quick fs=fat32
Assign letter=s
Create partition primary
Format quick fs=ntfs
Assign letter=c
Exit
```

This prepares the C:\ drive on the target server to get it ready for Nano Server.

Step 8. Copy the Nano Server image from the USB flash drive to the C:\ drive:

```
Copy D:\Nano c:\
```

Step 9. Run diskpart.exe again and run the following commands:

```
select vdisk file=c:\NanoVM.vhdx
attach vdisk
list volume
select volume 4
assign letter=v
exit
```

Step 10. Run the following command:

```
Bdcboot V:\windows /s s: /f uefi
```

Step 11. Remove the USB flash drive and reboot the server. The system boots to the Nano Server OS.

Configuring Nano Server as a DNS Client

Mostly, you want to have Nano Server part of a domain as a DNS client. To do so, you must define the preferred DNS server on the Nano Server. At a GUI-based or core server, this can be done locally through Server Manager or PowerShell.

On Nano Server, you can do this locally through the Nano Server Recovery Console. It is possible to use the Nano Server ImageGenerator.psm1 PowerShell module and **New-Nano ServerImage** PowerShell cmdlet to create a Nano Server image. In addition, as an integral part of the **New-NanoServerImage** cmdlet, you can deliver some important parameters, such as **Computername**, **Ipv4Address**, **Ipv4SubnetMask**, **Ipv4Gateway**, and **DomainName**, during image creation.

For your practical Nano Server setup, and especially for 70-741 exam preparation, keep this point in mind: Before you can add a computer to the domain, you must ensure that this computer knows about the DNS server for its domain.

Why is this important to know? Unfortunately, the **New-Nano ServerImage** PowerShell cmdlet has no parameter such as **DNSServerIpv4Address** or **PreferredDNS server** to define the DNS server IPv4 address at the Nano Server. You can configure the DNS IPv4 address only on Nano Server with PowerShell Desired State Configuration (DSC) or locally through the Nano Server Recovery Console.

Configure and Implement DNS Global Settings Using Windows PowerShell

You can configure and implement many PowerShell cmdlets with Windows Server 2016 DNS global settings. This section highlights five of the most important PowerShell cmdlets relevant to the 70-741 exam:

```
Set-DnsServerGlobalQueryBlockList
Set-DnsServerResponseRateLimiting
Set-DnsServerZoneTransferPolicy
Set-DnsServerRecursionScope
Export-DnsServerZone
```

Set-DnsServerGlobalQueryBlockList

Scenario: You want to allow DNS clients to resolve the IP number of an ISATAP router through a Windows Server 2016 DNS server.

Possible solution: With the PowerShell cmdlet **Set-DnsServerGlobal Query-BlockList**, you can define which records are allowed or denied in a DNS zone. By default, DNS servers use the *globalqueryblocklist* to block the resolution of an ISATAP DNS record. To allow name resolution for this kind of record, you must remove the ISATAP entry from the *globalqueryblocklist* of the DNS Server service for each DNS server.

You still can disable or enable the DNS-globalqueryblocklist without using Power-Shell commands, through the following command:

```
dnscmd <servername> /config /enableglobalqueryblocklist
```

Set-DnsServerResponseRateLimiting

Scenario: You want to prevent DNS amplification attacks on your Windows Server 2016 DNS server. A DNS amplification attack is a kind of a DDoS attack that relies on the use of publicly accessible open DNS servers to overwhelm a victim system with DNS response traffic.

Possible solution: The new Windows Server 2016 PowerShell cmdlet **Set-DnsServerResponseRateLimiting** enables you to prevent DNS amplification attacks. In this type of attack, the attacker sends small queries that can result in very large responses. One of the most famous DNS amplification attacks was the Spamhaus DDos attack, in which multiple DNS servers were forced to send a gigantic amount of traffic to Spamhaus servers. Windows Server 2016 offers a new option to enable Response Rate Limiting to prevent the misuse of DNS servers for running amplification attacks.

A DNS server cannot identify the legality of a single UDP query, but you can take preventive actions. A Windows Server 2016 DNS server can flag potentially malicious queries. Enabling RRL, the DNS server identifies the malicious query and then takes two kinds of preventive actions:

- Do not respond
- Respond with truncation

Enabling RRL

By default, RRL is not enabled on a Windows Server 2016 DNS server. If you use the **Set-DnsServerRRL -Mode Enable** command, you enable the Response Rate Limiting feature on the Windows Server 2016 DNS server.

If a DNS client is genuine, the TCP protocol reverts back, to ensure legitimacy of that client via its three-way-handshake. If the client is not genuine, the DNS server does not respond.

Enabling RRL LogOnly-mode

Suppose you want to log the potential actions as if RRL were enabled and then you want to continue with normal responses. You can use the **Set-DnsServerRRL -Mode LogOnly** command to enable RRL LogOnly-mode.

Configuring RRL Exception Lists

Suppose you have some health monitoring systems, known subnets/domains, or newly released applications that are expected to produce a spike of DNS queries. You do not want to see negative impacts on their name resolution about having enabled RRL. In this case, you can add them to an RRL exception list:

```
Add-DnsServerResponseRateLimitingExceptionlist -Name "SafeApplication"
  -ServerInterface "EQ,10.1.0.10"
Add-DnsServerResponseRateLimitingExceptionlist -Name "SafeDomain"
  -Fqdn "EQ,*.pearson.com"
```

> **TIP**   In document ISC-TN-2012-1-Draft1 (http://ss.vix.su/~vixie/isc-tn-2012-1.txt),
> you can read about DNS Response Rate Limiting in technical detail.

Set-DnsServerZoneTransferPolicy

Scenario: You want to allow zone transfer to a specific subnet.

Possible solution: With the PowerShell cmdlet **Set-DnsServerZoneTransfer-Policy**, you can control whether your DNS server allows zone transfers. You can create policies for zone transfer at either the server level or the zone level. Server-level policies apply on every zone transfer query that occurs on the DNS server. Zone-level policies apply only on the queries on a zone hosted on the DNS server. Zone-level policies are most commonly used to implement block or safe lists.

The following command creates a client subnet named *AllowedNet* using the **Add-DnsServerClientSubnet** PowerShell cmdlet:

```
Add-DnsServerClientSubnet -Name "AllowedNet" -Ipv4Subnet 10.0.0.0/16
   -PassThru
```

The following command creates a DNS zone transfer policy that disallows all customers that do not belong to the *AllowedNet* to transfer the zone. This is a server-level policy and, therefore, applies to all zones on the server:

```
Add-DnsServerZoneTransferPolicy -Name "EUPolicy" -Action IGNORE
   -ClientSubnet "ne,AllowedNet" -PassThru
```

Set-DnsServerRecursionScope

Scenario: You want to allow recursion for internal clients and disallow recursion for all other clients.

Possible solution: With the new Windows Server 2016 PowerShell cmdlet **Set-DnsServerRecursionScope**, you can control whether to allow or deny recursion by using DNS recursion scope policies. A recursion scope contains a list of forwarders and defines whether recursion is enabled. A Windows Server 2016 DNS server can have multiple DNS recursion scopes. With the PowerShell cmdlet **Add-DnsServerRecursionScope**, you can add a recursion scope.

Suppose you want to disable recursion for external DNS clients and enable recursion for internal clients. The legacy recursion settings and forwarder list are referred to as the default recursion scope. You cannot add or remove the default recursion scope identified by the name . (dot).

The following two commands disable the default recursion setting while creating a new recursion scope for internal clients where recursion is enabled:

```
Set-DnsServerRecursionScope -Name . -EnableRecursion $false
Add-DnsServerRecursionScope -Name "InternalCli" -EnableRecursion
  $True
```

 Export-DnsServerZone

Scenario: You want to back up zone content to a file.

Possible solution: With the new Windows Server 2016 PowerShell cmdlet **Export-DnsServerZone**, you can export (back up) zone content into a file containing resource records for an AD-integrated zone for troubleshooting or backup purposes. The file will be placed in the DNS directory at C:\windows\system32\dns.

The following command exports the zone eu.pearson.com to a file called pearsonexported.com:

```
Export-DnsServerZone -Name "eu.pearson.com" -FileName
  "pearsonexported.com"
```

Configure Forwarders

A forwarder is a DNS server that forwards DNS queries to other DNS servers. When a DNS server receives a query, it attempts to resolve it by using the zones that it hosts and by checking its own cache. If it cannot resolve the query, the DNS server tries to forward the query to the DNS server(s) that the DNS administrator has configured.

Types of Forwarders

You can restrict access to Windows Server 2016 DNS server zone information by specifying which internal or external DNS servers you allow to forward DNS requests. To do so, you can configure DNS forwarding. This involves configuring your company DNS servers within the domain as one of the following:

- **Forwarding-only:** DNS server that only caches responses and passes requests to forwarders. This kind of DNS server is also known as a *caching-only DNS server*.

- **Forwarder:** DNS server that receives requests from clients or other DNS servers and forwards the requests to another DNS server.

- **Conditional forwarder:** DNS server that forwards requests based on the DNS domain. This kind of forwarder is useful if your organization has multiple internal domains. Usually this is the most effective and fastest DNS server forwarding option.

- **Disable recursion:** If you want to prevent a DNS server from forwarding to other DNS servers, you have to disable recursion. This is done in the Advanced tab of the DNS server properties at Disable Recursion (Also Disables Forwarders); see Figure 1-29.

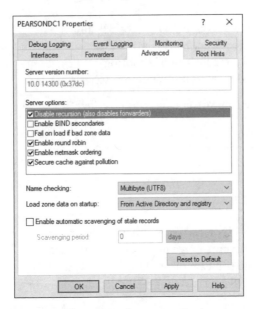

Figure 1-29 Disable Recursion Setting

Configuring DNS Forwarder with PowerShell

You can configure forwarding to a DNS server with the IPv6 address 2001:4888:7010:f100:438f:e6a1:fcaf:698c through the following PowerShell command:

```
Add-DnsServerForwarder -IPAddress 2001:4888:7010:f100:438f:e6a1:fcaf:
698c -PassThru
```

You can configure forwarding to a DNS server with the IPv4 address 172.16.0.20 through the following PowerShell command:

```
Add-DnsServerForwarder -IPAddress 172.16.0.20 -PassThru
```

You can create a conditional forwarder zone called pearson.com and a responsible master DNS server of 172.16.0.20 for pearson.com with the following PowerShell command:

```
Add-DnsServerConditionalForwarderZone -Name "pearson.com"
  -MasterServers 172.16.0.20
```

Suppose you want to store the conditional forwarder in Active Directory, and all DNS servers (which are DCs) in your forest have to get that conditional forwarder automatically replicated through Active Directory replication. You can use the following PowerShell command:

```
Add-DnsServerConditionalForwarderZone -Name "pearson.com"
  -ReplicationScope "Forest" -MasterServers 172.16.0.20
```

Suppose you want to change the replication scope of the previously created conditional forwarder from *forest* to *domain* so that only DNS servers (which are also DCs) from the domain can get the Conditional Forwarder Zone replicated. You can do this using the following PowerShell command:

```
Set-DnsServerConditionalForwarderZone -Name "pearson.com"
  -ReplicationScope "Domain" -PassThru
```

With the **Remove-DnsServerForwarder** PowerShell cmdlet, you can remove an IP address from the forwarders list on a DNS server. With **Get-DnsServerForwarder**, you can list the forwarder settings on a local Windows Server 2016 DNS server.

Configuring Forwarder with DNS Manager Console

In the DNS server properties on the Forwarders tab, you can add the IP address (IPv4 and IPv6) of DNS servers to forward requests (see Figure 1-30).

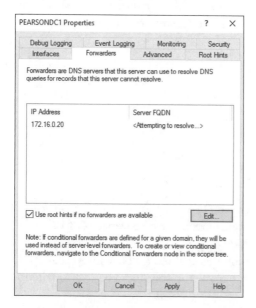

Figure 1-30   DNS Server Forwarders Window

In the DNS Manager console on Conditional Forwarders, you can add conditional forwarders (add the DNS domain and the IPv4 or IPv6 address of the master server of this domain), as Figure 1-31 shows.

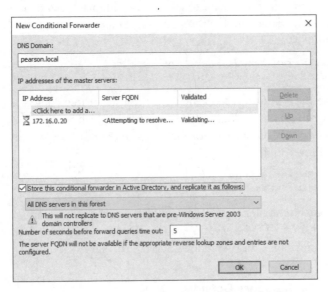

Figure 1-31   New Conditional Forwarder Configuration

As Figure 1-32 shows, you can use the option Store This Conditional Forwarder in Active Directory, and Replicate It As Follows: to save the forwarder as an AD object and replicate it to all DNS servers (which are also DCs) into the forest or domain.

Figure 1-32   Store This Conditional Forwarder in Active Directory, and Replicate It As Follows Option

Selective Recursion Control Using DNS Server Policies

Windows Server 2016 has a new feature named *DNS Policy*. You can use *recursion policies* to implement DNS selective recursion control. Previous versions of Windows Server supported only enabling or disabling recursion for the whole DNS server for all zones. This means that recursion was enabled for both internal and external clients, which made the DNS server an open resolver and basically invited attackers.

Suppose you do not want the DNS server for pearson.local to perform recursive name resolution for external clients, but you want to allow recursion for internal clients. You then configure the default recursion scope and disable recursion with the following PowerShell command:

```
Set-DnsServerRecursionScope -Name . -EnableRecursion $False
```

For the internal clients, you create a new recursion scope, which enables recursion for them:

```
Add-DnsServerRecursionScope -Name "IntClients" -EnableRecursion $True
```

After that, you create the DNS server recursion policies to choose a recursion scope for a set of queries that match specific criteria. The internal recursion scope with recursion enabled is associated with the private network interface:

```
Add-DnsServerQueryResolutionPolicy -Name "SplitBrainRecursionPolicy"
  -Action ALLOW
-ApplyOnRecursion -RecursionScope "IntClients" -ServerInterfaceIP
  "EQ,10.0.0.39"
```

You do not have to restart the DNS Server service to activate the DNS Policies. All new policies are applied automatically.

Configuring Root Hints

The earlier section "DNS Fundamentals" explained root hints. This is not a new feature, but it is important to understand for the 70-741 exam. The only enhancement worth mentioning for the root hints feature in Window Server 2016 is that now also IPv6 root hints is supported.

What is the root hints feature? It is simply a list of DNS servers that are used to resolve queries that the local DNS server cannot resolve on its own. The root hints feature uses iterative queries. If the local DNS server can't resolve a query using its cache or DNS database, it sends a query to one of the root DNS servers of the root hints list on the Internet.

The corresponding DNS root server responds with a referral, which contains the addresses of the DNS servers that are authoritative for the top-level domain (such as .com or .net) in the original query. Using root hints for DNS servers is similar to forwarding. The difference between DNS forwarders and forwarding through the root hints list is that forwarders are used for manual configuration, and root hints work with the DNS server list that is configured by default.

Figure 1-33 shows the Root Hints tab.

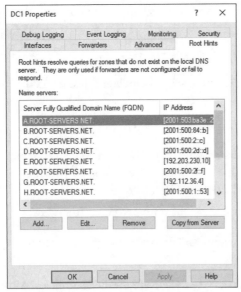

Figure 1-33 DNS Server Root Hints Configuration Window

You also can add and remove DNS servers with the root hints list. However, understand that properly configured forwarders and conditional forwarders often provide quicker responses than root hints. This is also important to remember for the 70-741 exam.

Another difference between root hints and forwarders is that forwarders use recursive queries. When the local DNS server cannot resolve a query, it sends a recursive query to one of the forwarders in its list. This request type informs the forwarder that the local DNS server will accept either a positive or a negative response, but it will *not* accept a referral as through root hints.

Root servers in the root hints list are installed automatically when you install the DNS role. They are copied from the cache.dns file that is included in the DNS role setup files.

If you want to disable all iterative queries, clear the **Use Root Hints If No Forwarders Are Available** check box on the Forwarders tab. If you configure the server to use only a forwarder and you disable root hints, it attempts to send a recursive query to its forwarding server; if the forwarding server does not answer this query, the first server responds that the host could not be found.

Recursion on a DNS server and *recursive queries* are not the same thing. With recursion, a DNS server uses its root hints to try to resolve a DNS query. With a recursive query, a query is made to a DNS server in which the requester asks the server to assume the responsibility for providing a complete answer to the query.

With the PowerShell cmdlet **Get-DnsServerRootHint**, you can get the root hints for the local DNS server. With the PowerShell cmdlet **Import-DnsServer RootHint**, you can copy root hints from a DNS server. You also can search for specific root DNS servers, as in this PowerShell example:

```
Get-DnsServerRootHint | {$_.NameServer.RecordData.NameServer -eq
  "H.Root-Servers.net."}
```

TIP DNS server in Windows Server 2016 supports the native IPv6 root hints. This helps to perform Internet name resolution also using the IPv6 root servers.

TIP Windows Server 2016 Nano Server with DNS server also supports root hints.

Configure DNS Delegation

DNS delegation is not a new feature of Windows Server 2016, but it is still present. In DNS delegation, the authoritative DNS server for a domain receives a request for a subdomain's records and responds with NS records for other DNS servers.

Creating DNS Delegation Automatically

During the Active Directory installation process of a first domain controller with DNS server in a child domain, you can see on the DNS Options page of the Active Directory Domain Services Configuration Wizard that the option Create DNS Delegation is automatically selected. A DNS delegation on the forest root DNS server in the root domain is created automatically. This is useful because you do not have to create a DNS delegation manually on the forest root DNS server.

Ignoring DNS Delegation Option

In any other Active Directory installation process scenario (forest root domain controller, additional domain controller in forest root domain, and so on), you see a yellow information warning in the DNS Options page of the Active Directory Domain Services Configuration Wizard (refer to Figure 1-17). If you have no child domain, you simply click **Next** and ignore that message; it is not relevant if you have no child domains. You do not have to create a DNS delegation if you do not have any child domains.

In the DNS Manager console, you can manually configure a DNS delegation to a DNS server in a child domain (see Figure 1-34).

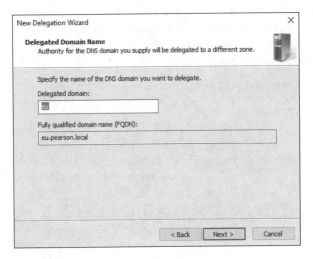

Figure 1-34   New Delegation Wizard

Configuring DNS Delegation with PowerShell

Windows Server 2016 enables you to create a DNS delegation with PowerShell. Using the following PowerShell command, you manually can create a DNS delegation for the child domain EU in the zone pearson.com with the specified name server and IP address:

```
Add-DnsServerZoneDelegation -Name "pearson.com"
-ChildZoneName "EU" -NameServer "DNSEU1.EU.pearson.com"
-IPAddress 172.16.0.20 -PassThru -Verbose
```

Configure DNS Socket Pool

The DNS socket pool feature enables a DNS server to use source port randomization when issuing DNS queries. The DNS service chooses a source port from a pool of sockets that are available for issuing queries.

Instead of using a known source port, the DNS server uses a randomized port number from the socket pool.

A DNS socket pool makes attacks against the cache more difficult because a malicious user must correctly guess both the source port of a DNS query and a random transaction ID to successfully run the attack.

The DNS socket pool is enabled by default in Windows Server 2016.

Using the following PowerShell commands, you can verify the configured socket pool size value:

```
$dns = get-dnsserver
$dns.ServerSetting.SocketPoolSize
```

The default size of the DNS socket pool is 2,500.

When you configure the DNS socket pool, you can choose a size value from 0 through 10,000. The larger the value, the greater the protection you have against DNS spoofing attacks. If the DNS server is running Windows Server 2016, you can also configure a *DNS socket pool exclusion list*.

Use the following command to exclude port ranges used by the socket pool:

```
dnscmd /config /SocketPoolExcludePortRanges <excludedportranges>
```

Keep in mind that every additional socket uses around 2.5 KB of memory.

You can configure the DNS socket pool size by using the **dnscmd** command, as follows:

Step 1.   Open an elevated command prompt.

Step 2.   Run the following command:

```
dnscmd /Config /SocketPoolSize <value>
```

Step 3.   Restart the DNS Server service to apply the changes.

Configure Cache Locking

Cache locking is a Windows Server 2016 DNS server security feature that is enabled by default. You can use this feature to control when the DNS cache information can be overwritten. By default, the cache locking percent value is 100. This means that cached entries will not be overwritten for the entire duration of the TTL. You can verify the cache locking value with the following PowerShell commands:

```
$dnscache = get-dnsservercache
$dnscache.LockingPercent
```

The period of time the DNS server keeps information in its DNS server cache is determined by the TTL value for a resource record. Information in the cache can be overwritten before the TTL expires, if updated information about that resource record is received.

If a malicious user successfully has overwritten records in the cache, that user might be able to redirect your network traffic to a malicious site. When you use cache locking, the DNS server prohibits cached records from being overwritten for the duration of the TTL value.

You configure cache locking as a percentage value. For example, if the cache locking value is set to 50, the DNS server will not overwrite a cached entry for half the duration of the TTL.

You can configure the cache locking value through PowerShell with the following command:

```
Set-DnsServerCache -LockingPercent 50
```

You can configure the cache locking value through the **dnscmd** tool without PowerShell using the following command (after that, you have to restart the DNS Server service to apply changes):

```
dnscmd /config /CacheLockingPercent 50
```

Configure DNS Logging

A Windows Server 2016 DNS server has many options to log what has happened on the DNS server. These include the DNS server log, debug logging, analytical logging, event logging, and monitoring (which works like a testing tool that is part of the DNS server to simulate successful or unsuccessful DNS queries).

With Windows Server 2016, you can enable DNS server debug logging through PowerShell commands.

Use this command to enable DNS server diagnostics of outgoing TCP responses for updates:

```
Set-DnsServerDiagnostics -SendPackets $True -TcpPackets $True -Answers
  $True -Updates $True
```

Use this command to enable all DNS server debug logging options except LogFilePath:

```
Set-DNSServerDiagnostics -All $True
```

Monitoring Tab

On the Monitoring tab (see Figure 1-35) on the DNS server properties, you can run a test that allows the DNS server to determine whether it can resolve simple local queries or perform a recursive query to ensure that the server can communicate with upstream servers. You can schedule this test as well. Possible causes for test failures can include a failed DNS Server service and an upstream server that is not available.

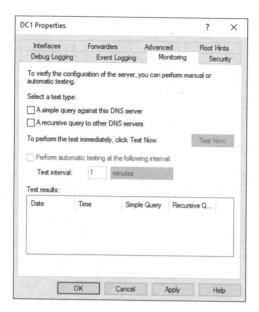

Figure 1-35   DNS Server Monitoring Tab

Auditing and Analytic Event Logging

DNS analytical logs are a new Windows Server 2016 feature and are not enabled by default. One advantage of these logs is that they typically affect DNS server performance only at very high DNS query rates.

For example, a DNS server running on current hardware and getting 100,000 queries per second (QPS) can experience a 5 percent performance degradation when analytic logs are enabled.

Microsoft predicts no noticeable performance impact for query rates of 50,000 QPS and lower.

An audit event gets logged every time a change takes place on a DNS server, zone, or resource record setting. This includes operational events such as zone transfers, dynamic updates, and DNSSEC.

DNS server analytic events enable you to track activity on the DNS server. An analytic event gets logged every time the server sends or receives DNS information.

You can view Windows Server 2016 DNS analytic and debug logs in the Event Viewer (see Figure 1-36).

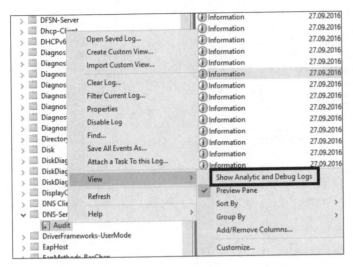

Figure 1-36 Event Viewer Show Analytic and Debug Logs Settings

Configure DNS Delegated Administration

In smaller organizations with fewer DNS servers and IT administrative employees, the person who administers the DNS servers is usually the same person who has domain administration permissions. The larger and more complex an environment is, the more difficult it is to manage and secure. You can add accounts of responsible persons to manage your DNS servers to the built-in local or Active Directory security group DNSAdmins. On an AD-integrated zone, you can configure permissions on every resource and record. Additionally, with the new Windows Server 2016 privileged account management feature, you can use extended capabilities such as just-in-time access or the new just-enough administration feature. You can then control which administrators can use which DNS server PowerShell cmdlets.

DNSAdmins Security Group

To enable a user to manage all DNS server settings of a local Windows Server 2016 DNS server, you have to add the user to the DNSAdmins security group (see Figure 1-37). If the DNS server is installed on a domain controller, you must use the domain local security group (pictured in Figure 1-37). If the DNS server is installed on a member server, you must use the local security group on that member server.

Figure 1-37   DNSAdmins Domain Security Group

Privileged Account Management

With the new Windows Server 2016 security feature PAM (privileged account management), you can reduce opportunities for malicious users to gain access and obtain privileged account access. PAM adds protection to privileged accounts (and is also usable for least-privileged DNS admin accounts).

With PAM, you can assign users to privileged roles that they can activate as needed for *just-in-time access*. As soon as the elevation session expires, the privileged account can no longer access the protected resource. These roles are defined manually and established in a bastion environment.

The PAM components are listed here:

- MIM Service
- MIM Portal
- MIM Service Database
- PAM Monitoring Service
- PowerShell cmdlets
- PAM REST API
- PAM sample portal

PAM needs a minimum of two parallel forests connected through a one-way trust. Forest 1 is a general-purpose corporate forest (CORP) with one or more domains. Forest 2 is a dedicated forest (PRIV) that includes the accommodate privileged groups and accounts that are shadowed from one or more corporate domains.

Suppose John has to get privileged access to manage DNS zones only for one day. Without elevated privileged access, John cannot manage DNS zones. With PAM configured, John has to request privileged access. He can do that with the following PowerShell commands:

```
Import-Module MIMPAM
$r = Get-PAMRoleForRequest | ? {$_.DisplayName -eq "DNSZoneAdmins"}
New-PAMRequest -role $r
Klist purge
```

Exam Preparation Tasks

Review All the Key Topics

Review the most important topics in the chapter, noted with the Key Topics icon in the outer margin of the page. Table 1-11 lists these key topics and the page numbers where each is found.

Table 1-11 Key Topics for Chapter 1

Key Topic Element	Description	Page Number
Step list	Installing a DNS server as part of Active Directory installation with Server Manager	25
Step list	Installing DNS with PowerShell	36
Configuration example	PowerShell Script for installing an RODC with a DNS server	36
List	Prerequisites for deploying a Windows Server 2016 Nano Server	43
Section	Nano Server Recovery Console	45
Section	DNS Servers Supported on Nano Server	46
Table 1-7 through Table 1-10	Adding Roles on Nano Server	46–48

Key Topic Element	Description	Page Number
Section	Adding Nano Server to a Domain	49
Example	Command to harvest a blob	49
Section	Installing a DNS Server Package on Nano Server	50
Section	Setting Static IP Addresses on Nano Server	50
Section	Adding Drivers on Nano Server	50
Section	Connecting with WinRM to Nano Server	51
Step list	Outlines how to deploy a Nano DNS server during image creation	51
Step list	Outlines how to deploy Nano Server and then add the DNS package afterward	52
Step list	Outlines how to deploy Nano Server to a Bare Metal host	54
Section	Demonstrates the **Set-DnsServerGlobalQueryBlockList** PowerShell cmdlet	56
Section	Demonstrates the **Set-DnsServerResponseRateLimiting** PowerShell cmdlet	56
Section	Enabling RRL	57
Section	Enabling RRL LogOnly-mode	57
Section	Configuring RRL Exception Lists	57
Section	Demonstrates the **Set-DnsServerZoneTransferPolicy** PowerShell cmdlet	58
Section	Demonstrates the **Set-DnsServerRecursionScope** PowerShell cmdlet	58
Section	Demonstrates the **Export-DnsServerZone** PowerShell cmdlet	59
Section	Configuring DNS Forwarder with PowerShell	60
Section	Selective Recursion Control Using DNS Server Policies	62
Figure 1-33	DNS Server Root Hints Configuration Window	64
Section	Configuring DNS Delegation with PowerShell	66
Section	Configure DNS Socket Pool	66
Section	Configure Cache Locking	67
Section	Auditing and Analytic Event Logging	69
Section	Privileged Identity Management	71

Complete the Tables and Lists from Memory

Print a copy of Appendix B, "Memory Tables" (on the book's website), or at least the section for this chapter, and complete the tables and lists from memory. Appendix C, "Memory Tables Answer Key," also on the website, includes completed tables and lists to check your work.

Definition of Key Terms

Define the following key terms from this chapter and check your answers in the glossary.

DNSSEC, Nano Server, DANE, DNS server policies, TLSA, Nano Server Recovery Console, reserve forwarders, New-NanoServerImage, IPv6 root hints, cache locking, Response Rate Limiting, DNS socket pool, forwarders, recursion scope, zone transfer policy

End-of-Chapter Review Questions

1. You have installed a Windows Server 2016 DNS server. Now you want to configure the following global DNS settings with PowerShell:

   - Hinder DNS attacks
   - Resolve IP address of the ISATAP router
   - Deny zone transfer to a specific domain or subnet

   Which PowerShell cmdlets can you use to implement the desired global DNS settings? (Choose three.)

   a. **Set-DnsServerGlobalQueryBlockList**

   b. **Set-DnsServerRecursionScope**

   c. **Set-DnsServerResponseRateLimiting**

   d. **Set-DnsServerCache**

   e. **Set-DnsServerZoneTransferPolicy**

   f. **Set-DnsServerGlobalNameZone**

2. You have a new application named App1 that will produce many unwanted DNS queries. You want to optimize your protection against DDoS attacks, and you want to ensure that App1 can run all required DNS queries without problems. Which settings should you configure on your Windows Server 2016 DNS servers? (Choose two.)

   a. **Set-DnsServerDnsSecZoneSetting**

   b. **Set-DnsServerRRL**

   c. **Set-DnsServerEDns**

   d. **Add-DnsServerResponseRateLimitExceptionList**

   e. **Add-DnsServerSigningKey**

3. You are responsible for your DNS server monitoring solution. You have a Windows Server 2016 DNS server. You want to enable DNS server analytic logging. Which tool/command can you use?

   a. **Set-DnsServerDiagnostics**

   b. **tracelog.exe**

   c. **Set-DnsServerSetting**

   d. **wusa.exe**

4. You have a Windows Server 2016 DHCP server named DHCP1 and one Windows Server 2012 R2 NAP server named NAP1. You have the following Windows Server 2016 Nano Servers:

   - N01

   - N02

   - N03

   - N04

   All Nano Servers must get their IP addresses through DHCP reservations from DHCP1. You look into the DHCP log file on DHCP1 and see that the message "A new IP address was leased to a client." is present for N01, N02, and N03, but not for N04. You must troubleshoot this problem. Which configuration step should you take?

   a. Press F4 on Nano Server Recovery Console

   b. Reconfigure NAP server on NAP1

   c. Remove and re-create DHCP reservation

   d. Disable a firewall rule on N04

5. You are responsible for a Windows Server 2016 DNS server named DNS1 that is authoritative for the zone pearson.com. You have configured conditional forwarding to other DNS servers. None of these forwardings is working correctly. Which setting could be the cause of this problem?

   a. Store This Conditional Forwarder in Active Directory

   b. Disable Recursion

   c. Use Root Hints If No Forwarders Are Available

   d. Enable Netmask Ordering

6. You want to maximize performance for your new DNS server. Which command should you use to start the deployment?

   a. **Install-WindowsFeature**

   b. **New-NanoServerImage**

   c. **Add-WindowsFeature**

   d. **New-Container**

7. You have a forest root domain named pearson.com. You have to create a new child domain named eu.pearson.com. You want to implement a DNS delegation from your forest root DNS servers to the eu.pearson.com DNS servers. Which configuration possibility should you use?

   a. **Add-DnsServerForwarder**

   b. **Install-ADDSForest**

   c. Create DNS delegation automatically

   d. **Install-ADDSDomainController**

8. You must configure some settings on a Windows Server 2016 Nano Server locally. Which of the following configurations can you not configure within the Nano Server Recovery Console?

   a. Computer name

   b. Gateway address

   c. DNS server

   d. IPv6 address

This chapter covers the following subjects:

- **Zone types:** On a Windows Server 2016 DNS server, you can use primary and secondary zones, forward and reverse lookup zones, and AD-integrated or file-based DNS zones. In this section, you learn about the different kinds of zones and how you can manage them through DNS Manager and PowerShell.

- **Primary zones:** In this section, you learn about the different types of primary zones on a Windows Server 2016 DNS server. You discover the benefits of using Active Directory as a repository for zone data and see how to manage primary zones through PowerShell commands.

- **Secondary zones:** Here you sort through the advantages and disadvantages of using secondary zones. You learn about the importance of zone transfer settings and possibilities and see how to configure these settings through DNS Manager and PowerShell. You also explore the use of DNS server zone transfer policies, a new feature of Windows Server 2016.

- **Stub zones:** This section defines Windows Server 2016 stub zones, describes their use, and shows how to configure them with DNS Manager and PowerShell.

- **GlobalNames zone:** This section defines GlobalNames zones, gives scenarios in which stub zones can be useful, and shows how to manage GlobalNames zones with PowerShell.

- **DNSSEC:** Here you get an overview of DNSSEC and both its possibilities and improvements in Windows Server 2016. You also learn how to configure DNSSEC through the DNSSEC Zone Signing Wizard and PowerShell.

- **Analyze zone-level statistics:** In this section, you learn about the new enhanced zone-level statistics feature of Windows Server 2016 DNS server and see how to enable or disable it.

- **Zone scavenging:** This section discusses the zone scavenging feature of Windows Server 2016 DNS server and shows how to use new PowerShell commands for aging and scavenging.

- **Record options:** You learn in this section about the most common resource record types and the Windows Server 2016 support for unknown record types. You also get basic information on TLSA records and how you can manage resource records with PowerShell.

- **DNS audit and analytical events:** This section discusses the purpose of DNS audit events and analytical events and shows how you can manage them with command-line tools.

## CHAPTER 2

Creating and Configuring DNS Zones and Records

This chapter covers the different DNS zones and zone data on Windows Server 2016 DNS server. We review some DNS server features of earlier Windows Server versions and also describe the enhancements and new features of Windows Server 2016 DNS server.

Topics include zone types, differences, and usage scenarios. We explain the new DNS zone transfer policy feature of Windows Server 2016 and show an example configuration of a primary/secondary DNS server scenario that uses DNS policies. Related to this, we also look at the new PowerShell commands that Windows Server 2016 DNS server offers for managing the DNS server.

In addition, this chapter delivers an overview of the possibilities of DNSSEC and describes the features of the DNSSEC Zone Signing Wizard. It covers DNSSEC improvements in Windows Server 2016, including DNSSEC, dynamic update, and automatic management of signing, keys, and trust anchors. Chapter 4, "Understanding and Configuring DNSSEC," gives more detailed information on DNSSEC.

This chapter also includes material on zone scavenging, GlobalNames zones, stub zones, resource record options and types, DNS audit events, and analytical event tracing.

"Do I Know This Already?" Quiz

The "Do I Know This Already?" quiz enables you to assess whether you should read this entire chapter or simply jump to the "Exam Preparation Tasks" section for review. If you are in doubt, read the entire chapter. Table 2-1 outlines the major headings in this chapter and the corresponding "Do I Know This Already?" quiz questions. You can find the answers in Appendix A, "Answers to the 'Do I Know This Already?' Quizzes and End-of-Chapter Review Questions."

Table 2-1   "Do I Know This Already?" Foundation Topics Section-to-Question Mapping

Foundation Topics Section	Questions Covered in This Section
Zone Type Overview	1, 2
Primary Zones	3
Secondary Zones	4
Stub Zones	5
GlobalNames Zones	6
DNSSEC	7
Analyze Zone-level Statistics	8
Zone Scavenging	9
Record Options	10
DNS Audit and Analytical Events	11

CAUTION   The goal of self-assessment is to gauge your mastery of the topics in this chapter. If you do not know the answer to a question or are only partially sure of the answer, you should mark that question as wrong for purposes of self-assessment. Giving yourself credit for an answer you correctly guess skews your self-assessment results and might provide you with a false sense of security.

1. Which of the following is part of a Windows Server 2016 stub zone? (Choose two.)

    a. The IP of one or more master servers that you can use to update the zone

    b. Resource records not contained in a DNS server's zone

    c. A cache of domain names and their associated IP addresses for the most common domains that the organization uses or accesses

    d. Requests for all Internet names forwarded to a DNS server at an ISP

    e. The delegated zone's SOA record, NS record, and A record

2. You have less DNS zone security after you have used the **ConvertTo-DnsServerPrimaryZone** PowerShell cmdlet to convert an AD-integrated zone to a file-based DNS zone. Which statement about file-based DNS zones is not correct?

    a. A file-based DNS zone can use the secure dynamic update feature.

    b. A file-based DNS zone cannot use DNSSEC.

    c. Records in a file-based DNS zone have fewer security settings.

    d. File-based DNS zones data can be protected with NTFS.

3. You are managing a Windows Server 2008 R2 domain named pearson.com (productive domain). All domain controllers are Windows Server 2008 R2 with a DNS server role and AD-integrated DNS zones. You want to perform a step-by-step migration from this existing domain to a newly created empty forest root domain (future domain) with the same domain name. You have installed the Windows Server 2016 forest root domain controller of the future domain (including DNS server role with the AD-integrated zone pearson. com). You want to migrate all DNS zone data from the zone pearson.com (productive domain) to the forest root DNS server (future domain) so that this DNS server is authoritative for that zone and DNS data is saved in the Active Directory of the future domain. This has to be done with the least administrative effort. Which configuration steps are the best option?

    a. Create a forest trust between the productive and future domain. Replicate DNS data through Active Directory.

    b. Create a stub zone on the DNS server of the future domain. Convert the stub zone to primary. (Store the zone in Active Directory.)

    c. Activate a zone transfer on the DNS server of the productive domain for pearson.com. Configure the DNS server in the future domain as the secondary DNS server.

    d. Convert the zone type of pearson.com from AD-integrated to primary without Active Directory. Copy the zone file to the %systemroot% \system32\dns folder of the DNS server of the future domain. Create a new primary zone on that DNS server and select **Use This Existing File**. Change the zone type to primary. (Store the zone in Active Directory.)

4. You are responsible for managing your DNS environment. You have a UNIX BIND DNS server named BIND1 that is the master authoritative server for the zone pearson.com with TSIG protection enabled. You want to use a Windows Server 2016 DNS server named SEC1 as the secondary DNS server for this zone. You want to use an additional layer of security for zone transfer between BIND1 and SEC1. Which technology enables you to accomplish this?

    a. TSIG

    b. IPsec

    c. HMAC-MD5

    d. GSS-TSIG

5. You have a forest environment with the following domains: pearson.com, eu.pearson.com, usa.pearson.com, pearsonucertify.com, eu.pearsonucertify.com, and usa.pearsonucertify.com. Every domain has two domain controllers with AD-integrated DNS servers. Each DNS server is authoritative for the name resolution in its own domain. You plan to implement additional DNS servers in usa.pearsonucertify.com. DNS servers in usa.pearson.com must automatically know about the new DNS servers in usa.pearsonucertify.com. Which of the following is the best solution to accomplish this?

   a. Conditional forwarding on DNS servers in usa.pearson.com

   b. File-based stub zone on DNS servers in usa.pearson.com

   c. AD-integrated stub zone on DNS servers in usa.pearson.com

   d. Secondary zone usa.pearsonucertify.com on DNS servers in usa.pearson.com

6. Which command can you use to enable GlobalNames zones? (Choose two.)

   a. Set-DnsServerGlobalNameZone

   b. Dnscmd

   c. Set-DnsServer

   d. Set-DnsServerPrimaryZone

7. You want to sign DNS resource records with NSEC3 and RSA/SHA-2. Which Windows server version can use both standards?

   a. Windows Server 2008

   b. Windows Server 2012

   c. Windows Server 2012 R2

   d. Windows Server 2016

8. You want to get information about DNSKEY record behaviors on your Windows Server 2016 DNS server and your zone pearson.com. You use the following PowerShell command: **$stat = Get-DnsServerStatistics -ZoneName pearson.com**. Now you must use the correct command to get that information you need. Which command do you use?

   a. $stat.ZoneQueryStatistics

   b. $stat.ZoneUpdateStatistics

   c. $stat.ZoneTransferStatistics

   d. $stat.RRLStatistics

9. You have some static A resource records on the DNSSEC-signed zone pearson.com on your Windows Server 2016 DNS server. You have enabled automatic scavenging with default settings. You notice that existing static A records are not removed through the automatic scavenge process; you must manually remove them. In the future, you want static A records to be removed through automatic scavenging. Which of the following is the best solution to accomplish this?

    a. **Dnscmd** *<ServerName>* /*StartScavenging*

    b. Add new static A records through the DNS manager

    c. **Add-DNSServerResourceRecordA**

    d. Unsign zone pearson.com

10. You want to prevent man-in-the-middle attacks, in which an attacker corrupts the DNS cache to point to a different website and provides a certificate issued from a different CA. Which kind of record can you use for this?

    a. TSIG

    b. RRSIG

    c. TLSA

    d. DNSKEY

11. You have enabled analytical event auditing on your Windows Server 2016 DNS server. You have very high DNS query rates, so your DNS server performance has decreased unacceptably. You want to disable analytical event audit tracing, to see whether this feature is the cause of the unacceptable burden. Which command should you use?

    a. **Set-DnsServer Diagnostics -EnableLoggingForServerStartStop Event $true**

    b. **Set-DnsServerDiagnostics -DebugLogging 0x10000**

    c. **Stop-PefTraceSession**

    d. **tracelog -stop Dns**

Foundation Topics

Zone Type Overview

DNS zone content can be stored in a zone file or in the Active Directory database. When the zone is not stored in Active Directory, only one copy of the zone (the primary zone) is a writeable copy; all other copies are read-only (secondary zone). The most commonly used zone types in Windows Server 2016 DNS are forward lookup and reverse lookup zones. Forward lookup zones resolve names to IP addresses and reverse lookup zones resolve IP addresses to hostnames.

Primary Zones

Principally, two kinds of DNS zones exist:

- File-based zones

- Active Directory–integrated DNS zones

A *primary zone* without Active Directory integration stores the zone data in a file. By default, the primary zone file is named zone_name.dns and is located on the server in the %windir%\System32\Dns folder. Figure 2-1 shows that Primary Zone is selected as the actual zone type for pearson.com zone. Figure 2-2 displays the primary zone file for the pearson.com zone.

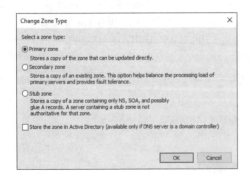

Figure 2-1   Primary Zone Configuration

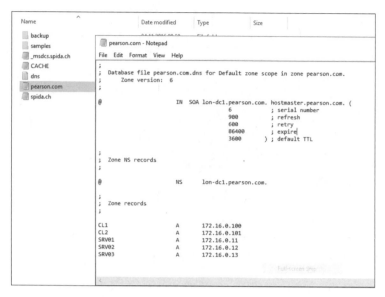

Figure 2-2 Primary Zone File for the pearson.com Zone

When the zone is not stored in AD DS, the primary zone server is the only DNS server that has a writeable copy of the database.

Secondary Zones

Zone information at a *secondary zone* DNS server must be obtained from another DNS server (master) that hosts the primary (file-based or AD-integrated) zone. This secondary zone DNS server must have network access to the *master DNS server* to receive updated zone information. The basic interval time for the secondary zone DNS server to look for changes in the primary zone on the master DNS server is 15 minutes. This can be changed through the SOA record on the master DNS server.

Figure 2-3 shows the secondary zone configuration. (Notice that the Store the Zone in Active Directory setting is not possible. In this example, LON-DC1 is configured as the domain controller. You cannot store a secondary zone in Active Directory.)

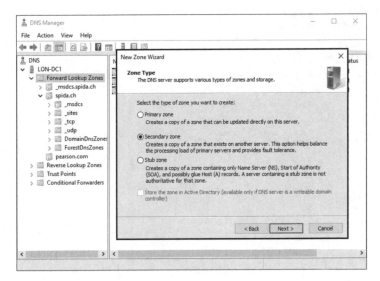

Figure 2-3 Secondary Zone Configuration

Figure 2-4 shows the master DNS servers configuration for a secondary zone. The master DNS server is the primary DNS server, where the zone must be transferred from.

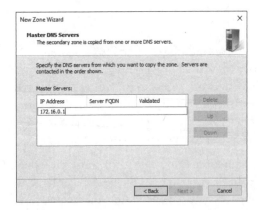

Figure 2-4 Master DNS Servers Configuration for a Secondary Zone

Stub Zones

A stub zone DNS server has a replicated copy of a primary zone (therefore, a stub zone always is a secondary zone because it always needs a master DNS server with a primary zone). A stub zone contains only the resource records that are necessary to identify that zone's authoritative DNS servers. Only the SOA resource record, the A resource records of the DNS servers, and the corresponding NS resource records are present on a stub zone. Other records, such as client resource records and mail server resource records (MX), are not transferred to a stub zone DNS server. A stub zone can store its DNS data in a zone file or in the Active Directory database.

Figure 2-5 shows the stub zone configuration for a new stub zone on a Windows Server 2016 DNS server.

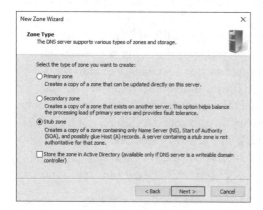

Figure 2-5   Stub Zone Configuration for a New Stub Zone

Use stub zones to accomplish the following goals:

- **Keep delegated zone information current:** By regularly updating a stub zone for one of its child zones, the DNS server hosting both the parent zone and the stub zone maintains a current list of authoritative DNS servers for the child zone. *Advantage:* Automatically keeps the list of DNS servers up to date.

- **Improve name resolution:** Stub zones enable a DNS server to perform recursion using the stub zone's list of name servers without needing to query the Internet or the internal root server for the DNS namespace. *Advantage:* Increased name resolution and forwarding performance.

- **Simplify DNS administration:** By using stub zones, you can distribute a list of the authoritative DNS servers for a zone without using secondary zones. However, stub zones do not serve the same purpose as secondary zones and are not an alternative when considering redundancy and load sharing.

TIP   If new DNS servers reside on the namespace of the master DNS server, the A and NS resource records of these new DNS servers are registered on the primary zone and then automatically transferred to the stub zone DNS server. After that process, the stub zone DNS server can use these automatically transferred IP addresses of that new DNS server to forward DNS requests to that (now) known new DNS server.

File-Based Zone Types

The file-based zone types (primary zone, secondary zone, and stub zone) have some commonalities. They are all hosted on a standalone server without using Active Directory, and zone data is stored in a local zone file. Only a primary zone hosts a read/write copy of the DNS database. The secondary and stub zones are always read-only copies and must get their DNS data transferred from a master DNS (primary). The DNS zone data between a primary zone DNS server and a secondary or stub zone DNS server can be transferred through AXFR or IXFR zone transfer. With AXFR, a full zone transfer occurs when you copy the entire zone from one DNS server to another. Normally, this happens when a secondary or stub zone is newly configured and the DNS data initially must be transferred the first time. When changes occur on the primary zone DNS server (new resource records), only these changes are replicated to the secondary or stub zone DNS server. This is known as incremental zone transfer (IXFR). The section "Secondary Zones," later in this chapter, gives more detailed information about the zone transfer functionality. Table 2-2 provides an overview about DNS server file-based zone types and functionalities.

Table 2-2   Comparison of DNS Server File-Based Zone Types

Primary Zone (File Based)	Secondary Zone (File Based)	Stub Zone (File Based)
Can be hosted on a standalone server without running a DC	Can be hosted on a standalone server without running a DC	Can be hosted on a standalone server without running a DC
Read/write copy of DNS database	Read-only copy of DNS database	**Read-only copy of DNS database (has only SOA, A, and NS resource records of DNS servers)**
DNS data saved in zone file	DNS data saved in zone file	DNS data saved in zone file
Active Directory independent	Active Directory independent	Active Directory independent
AXFR and IXFR replication	AXFR and IXFR replication	AXFR and IXFR replication
Unsecured DNS data replication from primary zone to secondary zone	Unsecured DNS data replication from primary zone to secondary zone	Unsecured DNS data replication from primary zone to stub zone
Zone file security: NTFS permissions; no records-based permission	Zone file security: NTFS permissions; no records-based permission	Zone file security: NTFS permissions; no records-based permission
No secure dynamic update	No secure dynamic update	No secure dynamic update

Active Directory–Integrated Zone Types

Active Directory replication provides an advantage over standard DNS replication with zone transfer. With standard DNS replication, only the primary zone DNS server for a zone can modify the zone. With Active Directory replication, all domain controllers for the domain can modify the zone and then replicate the changes to other domain controllers.

This replication process is known as *multimaster replication* because multiple domain controllers, or masters, can update the zone. Active Directory–integrated zones replicate by using multimaster replication. This means that any standard domain controller that also holds the DNS role can update the DNS zone information, which then replicates to all DNS servers that host the DNS zone.

The DNS server file-based zone types are the primary zone (AD integrated), secondary zone (AD integrated), and stub zone (AD integrated). They have all of the following characteristics:

- Only if DNS server is also a DC

- Read/write copy of DNS database

- DNS data saved in Active Directory

- AD replication (multimaster) of DNS data (domain, forest, partition independent)

- AD replication encrypted network traffic through RPC

- Secure dynamic update

- Every record saved as an AD object secured with AD permissions

Active Directory–Integrated Zones

A DNS server can store zone data in the Active Directory database, provided that the DNS server is an AD DS domain controller. When the DNS server stores zone data in this way, it creates an Active Directory–integrated zone. By default, the Active Directory database (ntds.dit) consists of five partitions:

- Schema partition

- Configuration partition

- Domain partition

- DomainDNSZones partition

- ForestDNSZones partition

When you create a new Active Directory–integrated zone on a Windows Server 2016 DNS server, the zone data is saved in the DomainDNSZones partition. All other DNS servers that are also domain controllers of the same domain get zone data automatically through Active Directory replication.

Figure 2-6 shows the Change Zone Type setting of an Active Directory–integrated DNS zone named pearson.com.

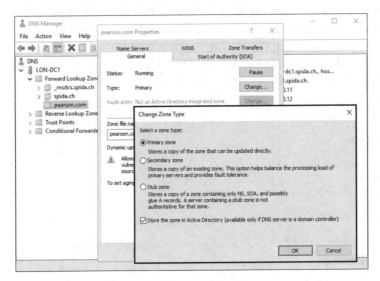

Figure 2-6   Change Zone Type Setting of an Active Directory–Integrated DNS Zone

If you select the setting Store the Zone in Active Directory (Available Only If DNS Server Is a Domain Controller), the DNS data is stored in an Active Directory database. This is possible only if the DNS server is installed on a domain controller.

Advantages of an Active Directory–integrated zone include the following:

- Multimaster updates
- Replication of DNS zone data by using AD DS replication
- Secure dynamic updates
- Detailed security

The zone replication scope can be changed on the Properties page of a zone. You can choose from four possible settings, as Table 2-3 shows.

Table 2-3 Available Active Directory Zone Replication Scopes

Zone Replication Scope	Description
To all DNS servers running on domain controllers in this forest	Replicates DNS zone data to all DNS servers running on DCs in the forest. DNS zone data is stored in the ForestDNSZones partition in AD.
To all DNS servers running on domain controllers in this domain	Replicates DNS zone data to all DNS servers running on DCs in the domain. This option is the default setting for Active Directory–integrated DNS zone replication. DNS zone data is stored in the DomainDNSZones partition in AD.
To all domain controllers in this domain (for Windows 2000 compatibility)	Replicates zone data to all domain controllers in the Active Directory domain.
To all domain controllers in the scope of this directory partition	Replicates DNS zone data according to the replication scope of the specified application directory partition. For a zone to be stored in the specified application directory partition, the DNS server that is hosting the zone must be enlisted in the specified application directory partition. You can create an application directory partition named MyDNSData with the PowerShell command **Add-DnsServer DirectoryPartition -Name "DNSData"**.

_msdcs Zone

The _msdcs subdomain of the forest's root domain automatically is created with the setup of the forest root domain controller with DNS server. The _msdcs zone is an Active Directory–integrated zone and its replication scope is set to all DNS servers in the forest. This means that all content in this zone will be replicated to all DNS servers, and all DNS servers in the forest are authoritative for that zone. Normally, some CNAME records are registered in this zone. For each domain controller in the forest, there must be a CNAME record with the GUID number of the domain controller. The DCs automatically register their records in that zone. AD uses these records to increase AD replication performance. All writeable domain controllers must register a record in this zone for proper AD replication.

Figure 2-7 shows an _msdcs zone.

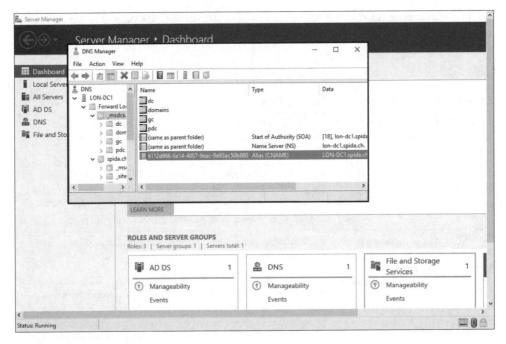

Figure 2-7   _msdcs Zone

> **TIP**   If you ever need the GUID number of a domain controller, you can get it from the ALIAS record in the _msdcs zone.

Primary Zones

When the DNS server is the host and the primary source for information about a DNS zone, the zone is a primary zone. In addition, the DNS server stores the master copy of the zone data either in a local file or in AD DS. When the DNS server stores the zone data in a file, the primary zone file is named zone_name.dns by default and is located on the server in the %windir%\System32\ Dns folder. When the zone is not stored in AD DS, the primary zone server is the only DNS server that has a writeable copy of the database. A primary zone in Windows Server 2016 works like a primary zone in earlier versions. It can be configured as a forward lookup zone or a reverse lookup zone.

Forward Lookup Zones

A primary zone as a forward lookup zone resolves hostnames to IP addresses and hosts these common resource records: A, CNAME, SRV, MX, SOA, TXT, and NS records. This zone type must exist for a DNS zone and is named authoritative.

Client computers send hostnames or FQDNs of the DNS server's domain to the DNS server. The DNS server uses the FQDN to look up a corresponding IP address or to find any resource record type that the client prescribes, such as a domain controller's SRV records. The DNS server returns the IP address or addresses to the client in the DNS response.

Reverse Lookup Zones

The reverse lookup zone resolves an IP address to a domain name and hosts start of authority (SOA), name server (NS), and pointer (PTR) resource records. A reverse zone does the opposite: It returns the hostname if given a particular IP address.

Reverse zones are not configured automatically, but you should configure them to reduce warning and error messages. Many standard Internet protocols rely on reverse zone lookup data to validate forward zone information. For example, if the forward lookup indicates that the zone training.pearson.com resolves to 192.168.2.32, you can use a reverse lookup to confirm that 192.168.2.32 is associated with the zone training.pearson.com. Or try to use the **nslookup** utility after you have installed a new forest root domain controller with an AD-integrated DNS server. You will get the "Default server: Unknown" message because **nslookup** wants to verify the PTR record in the reverse lookup zone of your DNS server. To solve this, you have to manually create the reverse lookup zone.

Having a reverse zone is important if you have applications that rely on looking up hosts by their IP addresses. Many applications log this information in security or event logs. If you see suspicious activity from a particular IP address, you can resolve the host by using the reverse lookup zone information.

Managing Primary Zones with PowerShell

To list all zones on the local DNS server, you use the **Get-DNSServerZone** PowerShell cmdlet (see Figure 2-8).

```
PS C:\> Get-DnsServerZone

ZoneName                    ZoneType    IsAutoCreated   IsDsIntegrated  IsReverseLookupZone  IsSigned
--------                    --------    -------------   --------------  -------------------  --------
0.in-addr.arpa              Primary     True            False           True                 False
127.in-addr.arpa            Primary     True            False           True                 False
255.in-addr.arpa            Primary     True            False           True                 False
pearson.com                 Primary     False           True            False                False
Pearsontest.com             Primary     False           True            False                False
pearsonUCertify.com         Primary     False           True            False                False
TrustAnchors                Primary     False           True            False                False
```

Figure 2-8   Get-DNSServerZone PowerShell Cmdlet and Example Output

To list all available information about a forward lookup zone, use the **Get-DNSServerZone -Name pearson.com | FL *** PowerShell cmdlet (see Figure 2-9).

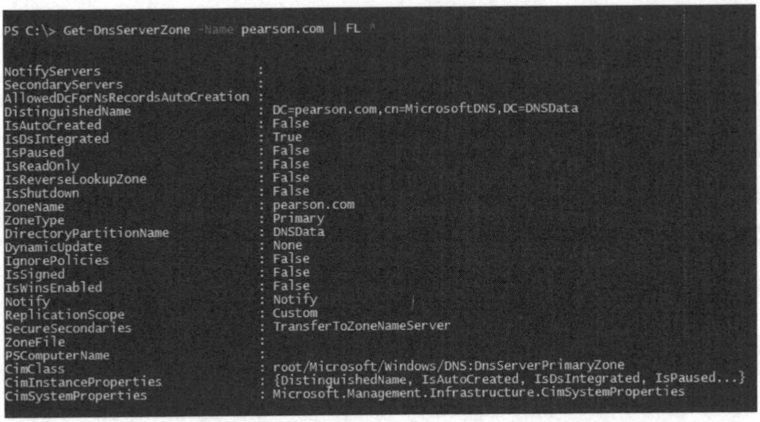

```
PS C:\> Get-DnsServerZone -Name pearson.com | FL *

NotifyServers                         :
SecondaryServers                      :
AllowedDcForNsRecordsAutoCreation     :
DistinguishedName                     : DC=pearson.com,cn=MicrosoftDNS,DC=DNSData
IsAutoCreated                         : False
IsDsIntegrated                        : True
IsPaused                              : False
IsReadOnly                            : False
IsReverseLookupZone                   : False
IsShutdown                            : False
ZoneName                              : pearson.com
ZoneType                              : Primary
DirectoryPartitionName                : DNSData
DynamicUpdate                         : None
IgnorePolicies                        : False
IsSigned                              : False
IsWinsEnabled                         : False
Notify                                : Notify
ReplicationScope                      : Custom
SecureSecondaries                     : TransferToZoneNameServer
ZoneFile                              :
PSComputerName                        :
CimClass                              : root/Microsoft/Windows/DNS:DnsServerPrimaryZone
CimInstanceProperties                 : {DistinguishedName, IsAutoCreated, IsDsIntegrated, IsPaused...}
CimSystemProperties                   : Microsoft.Management.Infrastructure.CimSystemProperties
```

Figure 2-9   Get-DNSServerZone PowerShell Cmdlet and Example Output About the Forward Lookup Zone pearson.com

The pearson.com zone is stored in a DNS application directory partition named DNSData (AD-integrated zone). It is a primary zone with dynamic update disabled. For security reasons, enabling secure dynamic update on that zone is recommended so that only known domain DNS clients can use that zone.

To list all available information about a reverse lookup zone, use the **Get-DNSServerZone -Name 1.168.192.in-addr.arpa | FL *** PowerShell cmdlet (see Figure 2-10).

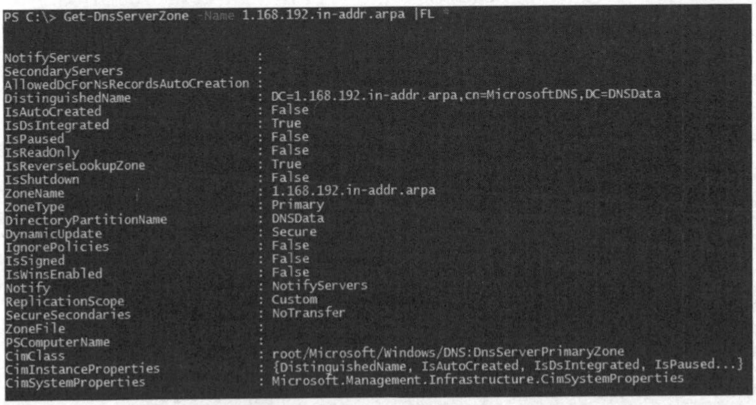

```
PS C:\> Get-DnsServerZone -Name 1.168.192.in-addr.arpa |FL *

NotifyServers                         :
SecondaryServers                      :
AllowedDcForNsRecordsAutoCreation     :
DistinguishedName                     : DC=1.168.192.in-addr.arpa,cn=MicrosoftDNS,DC=DNSData
IsAutoCreated                         : False
IsDsIntegrated                        : True
IsPaused                              : False
IsReadOnly                            : False
IsReverseLookupZone                   : True
IsShutdown                            : False
ZoneName                              : 1.168.192.in-addr.arpa
ZoneType                              : Primary
DirectoryPartitionName                : DNSData
DynamicUpdate                         : Secure
IgnorePolicies                        : False
IsSigned                              : False
IsWinsEnabled                         : False
Notify                                : NotifyServers
ReplicationScope                      : Custom
SecureSecondaries                     : NoTransfer
ZoneFile                              :
PSComputerName                        :
CimClass                              : root/Microsoft/Windows/DNS:DnsServerPrimaryZone
CimInstanceProperties                 : {DistinguishedName, IsAutoCreated, IsDsIntegrated, IsPaused...}
CimSystemProperties                   : Microsoft.Management.Infrastructure.CimSystemProperties
```

Figure 2-10   Get-DNSServerZone PowerShell Cmdlet and Example Output for the Reverse Lookup Zone 1.168.192.in-addr.arpa

The zone 1.168.192.in-addr.arpa is stored in a DNS application directory partition named DNSData (AD-integrated zone). It is a primary zone with secure dynamic update enabled.

To allow zone transfer only to secure servers, apply the Zone Transfer setting for the pearson.com zone, as Figure 2-11 demonstrates.

Figure 2-11   Zone Transfer Setting for the pearson.com Zone

On the DNS server, the setting Only to the Following Servers is selected, which means that only the listed DNS servers are allowed to transfer the DNS zone data from this DNS server.

Figure 2-12 shows the **Get-DNSServerZone -Name pearson.com | FL *** Power-Shell command and example output for the pearson.com forward lookup zone. The value for the **SecureSecondaries** attribute is **TransferToSecureServers**. Through this attribute, you also can verify the secondary DNS servers 192.168.1.120 and 192.1681.121, which are allowed to transfer the zone pearson.com.

```
PS C:\> Get-DnsServerZone -Name pearson.com | FL *

NotifyServers                    :
SecondaryServers                 : {192.168.1.120, 192.168.1.121}
AllowedDcForNsRecordsAutoCreation :
DistinguishedName                : DC=pearson.com,cn=MicrosoftDNS,DC=DNSData
IsAutoCreated                    : False
IsDsIntegrated                   : True
IsPaused                         : False
IsReadOnly                       : False
IsReverseLookupZone              : False
IsShutdown                       : False
ZoneName                         : pearson.com
ZoneType                         : Primary
DirectoryPartitionName           : DNSData
DynamicUpdate                    : None
IgnorePolicies                   : False
IsSigned                         : False
IsWinsEnabled                    : False
Notify                           : Notify
ReplicationScope                 : Custom
SecureSecondaries                : TransferToSecureServers
ZoneFile                         :
PSComputerName                   :
CimClass                         : root/Microsoft/Windows/DNS:DnsServerPrimaryZone
CimInstanceProperties            : {DistinguishedName, IsAutoCreated, IsDsIntegrated, IsPaused...}
CimSystemProperties              : Microsoft.Management.Infrastructure.CimSystemProperties
```

Figure 2-12   Get-DNSServerZone PowerShell Cmdlet and Example Output

Primary DNS Server as a Single Point of Failure

If a file-based primary zone DNS server goes down, you have no other file-based primary zone DNS server to automatically replace the functionality of the down server. Secondary zone servers are read-only, so although they still can resolve names for DNS clients, they cannot store additional records or accept changes. For this reason, a file-based primary zone DNS server is a single point of failure.

Fault Tolerance with AD-Integrated DNS Servers

Make a DNS zone fault tolerant by integrating it into Active Directory. Doing this makes the DNS zone an AD-integrated zone. A DNS server can store zone data only in the AD database, if the DNS server is a DC. After that, DNS records are stored as AD objects. All DCs that host the DNS zone in the AD database are primary zone servers for the zone (multiple masters) with read/write possibility. They can accept changes to the DNS zone and replicate those changes to other DCs (depending on the zone replication setting).

Encrypted DNS Data Replication Traffic

With AD replication, each change is sent securely via encrypted replication traffic (RPC network protocol). If a DC with an AD-integrated DNS zone fails, as long as there are other DCs with the AD-integrated zone, DNS functionality for that zone and the domain will continue to operate properly.

Figure 2-13 shows the AD replication of DNS zone data between two Windows Server 2016 domain controllers with an AD-integrated DNS zone.

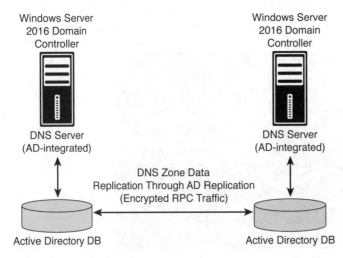

Figure 2-13   AD Replication of DNS Zone Data Between Two Windows Server 2016 Domain Controllers with an AD-Integrated DNS Zone

Benefits of AD-Integrated Zones

The main benefits of AD-integrated DNS zones are as follows:

- **Multimaster updates:** AD-integrated zones can be written to by any write-able DC to which the zone is replicated. This builds redundancy into the DNS infrastructure. Clients can update their DNS records without having to connect to a potentially geographically distant primary server.

- **Replication of DNS zone data by using AD DS replication:** AD replication uses attribute-level replication, in which only changed attributes are replicated. An AD-integrated zone can thus avoid replicating the entire zone file as in traditional DNS zone transfer models.

- **Secure dynamic updates:** An Active Directory–integrated zone can enforce secure dynamic updates.

- **Detailed security:** An AD-integrated zone enables you to delegate the administration of zones, domains, and resource records by modifying the access control list (ACL) on the zone.

Managing AD-Integrated Zones with PowerShell

To create an AD-integrated forward lookup zone called west.pearson.com with forest-wide replication scope, you enter the following:

```
Add-DnsServerPrimaryZone -Name "west.pearson.com" -ReplicationScope
  "Forest" -PassThru
```

To create an AD-integrated class C reverse lookup zone 0.1.10.in-addr.arpa with forest-wide replication scope, you enter the following::

```
Add-DnsServerPrimaryZone -NetworkID "10.1.0.0/24" -ReplicationScope
  "Forest"
```

To convert a zone named west.pearson.com from an AD-integrated zone to a file-backed primary zone on the current server, you enter the following:

```
ConvertTo-DnsServerPrimaryZone -Name "west.pearson.com" -PassThru
  -Verbose -ZoneFile "west.pearson.com " -Force
```

TIP When you convert an AD-integrated DNS zone to a file-based DNS zone, you lose great security possibilities for the zone, such as secure dynamic update, automated AD replication of DNS zone data, and zone records as AD objects with AD permissions. If you convert an AD-integrated DNS zone to a file-based zone, you also remove the DNS data from all other domain controllers in your domain or forest.

To convert a zone named west.pearson.com to an AD-integrated primary zone, you enter the following (the zone then is replicated to all DNS servers in the domain):

```
ConvertTo-DnsServerPrimaryZone "west.pearson.com" -PassThru -Verbose
  -Replication Scope Domain -Force
```

To change the dynamic update setting to **NonsecureAndSecure** for the zone named pearson.com, enter the following:

```
Set-DnsServerPrimaryZone -Name "pearson.com" -DynamicUpdate
  "NonsecureAndSecure" -PassThru
```

To change the replication scope of the zone named pearson.com to **Legacy**, you would enter the following:

```
Set-DnsServerPrimaryZone -Name "pearson.com" -ReplicationScope
  "Legacy" -PassThru
```

Secondary Zones

When the DNS server is the host but is the secondary source for zone information, the zone is a secondary zone. The zone information at this server must be obtained from another DNS server that also hosts the zone (master DNS server).

This DNS server must have network access to the master DNS server to receive updated zone information. Because a secondary zone is a copy of a primary zone that another server hosts, the secondary zone cannot be stored in the AD DS.

The secondary zone on a DNS server is a read-only copy of the original DNS zone from the master DNS server. Secondary zones can be useful if you are replicating data from non-Windows DNS zones.

Zone Transfer Process

Zone transfers occur in a traditional DNS zone without Active Directory if you have primary and secondary DNS servers. The zone transfer network traffic between a primary and a secondary DNS server is unencrypted network traffic, by default. Zone replication occurs in an AD-integrated zone, and such network traffic is encrypted by default.

Figure 2-14 shows the difference between zone transfer and zone replication.

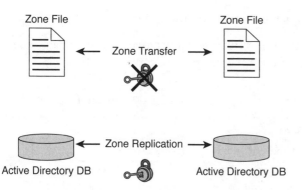

Figure 2-14 Zone Transfer vs. Zone Replication

Zone transfers are used to transfer zone records from a master server to a secondary server. A master server can be any other DNS server that loads the zone, such as the primary server for the zone or another secondary server. When the master server receives the request for the zone, it can reply with either a partial or a full transfer of the zone to the secondary server.

With the following PowerShell command, you can start a zone transfer on the local DNS server for the secondary zone named pearson.com:

```
Start-DnsServerZoneTransfer -Name "pearson.com"
```

Modifying Zone Transfer Settings Using the DNS Manager

To modify the zone transfer setting using the DNS Manager, perform the following steps:

Step 1.   Open the DNS Manager.

Step 2.   Right-click a DNS zone and then click **Properties**.

Step 3.   On the Zone Transfers tab, do one of the following:

■ To disable transfers, clear **Allow Zone Transfers**.

■ To allow transfers, select **Allow Zone Transfers**.

Step 4.   To allow zone transfer to any server, click **To Any Server**.

To allow zone transfers only to the DNS servers that are listed on the Name Servers tab, click **Only to Servers Listed on the Name Servers** tab.

To allow zone transfers only to specific DNS servers, click **Only to the Following Servers**, and then add the IP address of one or more DNS servers.

Modifying Zone Transfer Settings Using the Command Line

You can configure DNS zone transfer settings with the dnscmd.exe command-line utility. Table 2-4 shows the parameters and descriptions for this utility.

Table 2-4   Parameter and Descriptions for Zone Transfer Settings with **dnscmd**

Parameter	Description
dnscmd	The command-line tool for managing DNS servers.
<ServerName>	Required. Specifies the DNS hostname of the DNS server. You can also type the IP address of the DNS server. To specify the DNS server on the local computer, you can also type a period (.).
<ZoneName>	Required. Specifies the fully qualified domain name (FQDN) of the zone.
/NoXfr	Disables zone transfers for the zone.
/NonSecure	Permits zone transfers to any DNS server.
/SecureNs	Permits zone transfers only to DNS servers that are listed in the zone using name server (NS) resource records.
/SecureList	Permits zone transfers only to DNS servers that are specified by *SecondaryIPAddress*.
</SecondaryIPAddress>	Required if **/SecureList** is specified. A list of one or more IP addresses for DNS servers that are permitted to obtain zone transfers.

Figure 2-15 shows the parameters of the **dnscmd /zoneresetsecondaries** command.

Figure 2-15   dnscmd /zoneresetsecondaries Command Parameters

Figure 2-16 shows that the master (primary) DNS server can be an AD-integrated DNS server or a non-AD-integrated file-based DNS server.

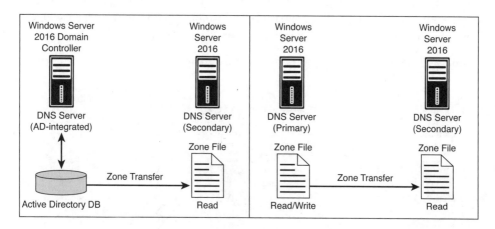

Figure 2-16 Two Possibilities of Zone Transfer

Types of Zone Transfers

The three types of zone transfer are as follows:

- **Full zone transfer:** A full zone transfer occurs when you copy the entire zone from one DNS server to another. A full zone transfer is known as an all-zone transfer (AXFR).

- **Incremental zone transfer:** An incremental zone transfer occurs when an update to the DNS server takes place and only the resource records that were changed are replicated to the other server. This is known as an incremental zone transfer (IXFR).

- **Fast zone transfer:** Windows DNS servers perform fast transfers, which use compression and send multiple resource records in each transmission. Not all DNS server implementations support incremental and fast zone transfers. When integrating a Windows Server 2016 DNS server with a BIND DNS server, you must ensure that the features you need are supported by the BIND version that is installed.

Using DNS Policies in a Primary/Secondary Deployment

Imagine that you are responsible for a company named pearson.com. You provide web and domain hosting solutions for your customers. One of your customers (customer.com) has two datacenters, one in the United States and the other in Europe.

Your customer wants the DNS clients from Europe to be redirected to the Europe datacenter and the DNS clients from the United States to be redirected to the USA datacenter. You have a primary DNS server (10.0.0.1) and two secondary DNS servers (10.0.0.2 and 10.0.0.3). The primary zone customer.com is on the primary DNS server, with read-only copies on Secondary1 and Secondary2.

Figure 2-17 shows the geolocation-based DNS scenario.

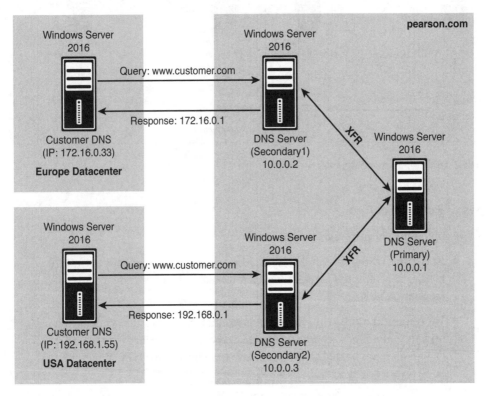

Figure 2-17   Geolocation-based DNS Scenario

The primary server must be configured with zones, zone scopes, client subnets, and DNS server policies. This is the step-by-step description for the solution using new Windows Server 2016 DNS server policies and PowerShell cmdlets:

Step 1.   To create the secondary zones with PowerShell, enter the following:

```
Add-DnsServerSecondaryZone -Name "customer.com" -ZoneFile
   "customer.com.dns"
-MasterServers 10.0.0.1 -ComputerName SecondaryServer1
Add-DnsServerSecondaryZone -Name "customer.com" -ZoneFile
   "customer.com.dns"
-MasterServers 10.0.0.1 -ComputerName SecondaryServer2
```

Step 2.   To allow zone transfer to the specified secondary servers, enter the following:

```
Set-DnsServerPrimaryZone -Name "customer.com -Notify
  -SecondaryServers "10.0.0.2,10.0.0.3"
-SecureSecondaries TransferToSecureServers -ComputerName
  PrimaryServer
```

The **Notify** parameter of the **Set-DnsServerPrimaryZone** can have the following values:

- **NoNotify:** The zone does not send change notifications to secondary servers.

- **Notify:** The zone sends change notifications to all secondary servers.

- **NotifyServers:** The zone sends change notifications to some secondary servers. If you choose this option, specify the list of secondary servers in the **NotifyServers** parameter.

Step 3.   To copy the client subnets, enter the following:

```
Add-DnsServerClientSubnet -ComputerName SecondaryServer1
Get-DnsServerClientSubnet -ComputerName PrimaryServer
Add-DnsServerClientSubnet -ComputerName SecondaryServer2
```

Step 4.   To create the zone scopes on the secondary server, enter the following:

```
Get-DnsServerZoneScope -ZoneName "customer.com" -ComputerName
  PrimaryServer
Add-DnsServerZoneScope -ZoneName "customer.com" -ComputerName
SecondaryServer1 -ErrorAction Ignore
Get-DnsServerZoneScope -ZoneName "customer.com" -ComputerName
  PrimaryServer
Add-DnsServerZoneScope -ZoneName "customer.com" -ComputerName
  SecondaryServer2 -ErrorAction Ignore
```

Step 5.   To configure the DNS server policies, enter the following:

```
$policy = Get-DnsServerQueryResolutionPolicy -ZoneName
  "customer.com" -ComputerName PrimaryServer
$policy | Add-DnsServerQueryResolutionPolicy -ZoneName
  "customer.com" -ComputerName SecondaryServer1
$policy | Add-DnsServerQueryResolutionPolicy -ZoneName
  "customer.com" -ComputerName SecondaryServer2
```

Stub Zones

Use stub zones when you want to redirect a DNS request to a DNS server that can answer it. A DNS server with a stub zone is aware of the authoritative DNS servers for a foreign zone. A conditional forwarder is not an efficient way to keep a DNS server that is hosting a parent zone aware of the authoritative DNS servers for a child zone. This is because whenever the authoritative DNS servers for the child zone change, you must configure the conditional forwarder setting *manually* on the DNS server that hosts the parent zone. With a stub zone, these changes are done automatically through the zone transfer process from the master DNS server to the stub zone DNS server. Use a stub zone in the following scenarios:

- Domain name (child domain/zone)

- Forest-to-forest scenarios, in which DNS servers from one forest have to know about authoritative DNS servers from the other forest

- Delegation below a delegation

A stub zone is a replicated copy (like a secondary zone) of a zone that contains only resource records necessary to identify that zone's authoritative DNS servers. A stub zone resolves names between separate DNS namespaces, which might be necessary when a corporate merger requires that the DNS servers for two separate DNS namespaces resolve names for clients in both namespaces.

A stub zone consists of the following:

- The delegated zone's SOA resource record, NS, and A resource record

- The IP of one or more master servers that you can use to update the stub zone

The master servers for a stub zone are one or more DNS servers that are authoritative for the child zone, usually the DNS server that is hosting the primary zone for the delegated domain name.

Stub Zone Name Resolution Process

When a DNS resolver performs a recursive query operation on a DNS server that is hosting a stub zone, the DNS server uses the resource records in the stub zone to resolve the query (often it forwards the request to the DNS server in the stub zone). During the stub zone's creation, the SOA record is created. SOA record updates occur during transfers to the stub zone from the original, primary zone. If the query was an iterative query, the DNS server returns a referral containing the servers that the stub zone specifies.

Communication Between DNS Servers That Host Parent and Child Zones

A DNS server that delegates a domain to a child zone on a different DNS server is made aware of new authoritative DNS servers for the child zone only when resource records for them are added to the parent zone that the DNS server hosts. This is a manual process that requires administrators for the different DNS servers to communicate often. Stub zones enable a DNS server that is hosting a stub zone for one of its delegated domains to obtain updates on the authoritative DNS servers for the child zone when the stub zone is updated. The update is performed from the DNS server that is hosting the stub zone; the administrator for the DNS server that is hosting the child zone does not need to be contacted.

Managing Stub Zones with PowerShell

To add europe.pearson.com as a file-backed stub zone, enter the following:

```
Add-DnsServerStubZone -Name "europe.pearson.com" -MasterServers
   "172.16.1.12" -PassThru -ZoneFile "europe_pearson.dns"
```

To change the master servers for a stub zone named europe.pearson.com, enter the following:

```
Set-DnsServerStubZone -Name "europe.pearson.com" -MasterServers
   172.16.1.15,172.16.1.20
```

GlobalNames Zones

The DNS server service in Windows Server 2016 provides the GlobalNames zone, which you can use to contain single-label names that are unique across an entire forest. The main advantage of using a GlobalNames zone is that you no longer need NetBIOS-based WINS to provide support for single-label names.

GlobalNames zones provide single-label name resolution for large enterprise networks that do not deploy WINS and that have multiple DNS domain environments.

You must create GlobalNames zones manually, and they do not support dynamic record registration.

Creating a GlobalNames Zone

To create a GlobalNames zone, perform the following steps:

Step 1.   Use the **dnscmd** command-line utility to enable GlobalNames zones support.

Step 2.   Create a new forward lookup zone named GlobalNames (not case sensitive). Do not allow dynamic updates for this zone.

Step 3.   Manually create CNAME records that point to records that already exist in the other zones that are hosted on your DNS servers.

Managing a GlobalNames Zone with PowerShell

You can also use the Windows PowerShell cmdlets **Get-DnsServerGlobalName-Zone** and **Set-DnsServerGlobalName Zone** to configure GlobalNames zones.

To configuring a GlobalNames zone with PowerShell, perform the following steps:

Step 1.   Create an AD-integrated forward lookup zone named pearson.com:

```
Add-DnsServerPrimaryZone -Name pearson.com -ReplicationScope
    Forest
```

Step 2.   Run the following command to enable support for GlobalName zones:

```
Set-DnsServerGlobalNameZone -AlwaysQueryServer $true
```

Step 3.   Create an AD-integrated forward lookup zone named GlobalNames:

```
Add-DnsServerPrimaryZone -Name GlobalNames -ReplicationScope
    Forest
```

Step 4.   Open the DNS Manager console and add a new host record to the pearson.com domain named SRV1 with the IP address 172.16.0.15.

Step 5.   In the GlobalNames zone, create a new alias named SRV1 by using the FQDN of SRV1.pearson.com.

Step 6.   Close the DNS Manager console and close the Windows PowerShell window.

DNSSEC

DNSSEC enables a DNS zone and all records in the zone to be signed cryptographically so that client computers can validate the DNS response. DNS is often subject to various attacks, such as spoofing and cache tampering. DNSSEC helps protect against these threats and provides a more secure DNS infrastructure. On Windows servers, DNSSEC enables your DNS server to do the following:

- Securely sign DNS zones

- Host DNSSEC-signed zones

- Process related records

- Perform both validation and authentication

The DNSSEC improvements in Windows Server 2016 are as follows:

- **DNSSEC enabled by default:** When you install the DNS server service on a Windows Server 2016 server, DNSSEC is enabled by default. If you want to disable it, you can do so by right-clicking the DNS server, selecting Properties, and then clicking the Advanced tab. There you can find the Enable DNSSEC Validation for Remote Responses setting.

- **DNSSEC and secure dynamic update:** In Windows Server 2012 R2, when you enabled DNSSEC for a zone and this zone was an AD-integrated zone with secure dynamic update enabled, you manually had to update all SRV records and other RRs. With Windows Server 2016, you can do this automatically.

- **Automatic management of signing, keys, and trust anchors:** Previously, in Windows Server 2012 R2, you needed to manually configure and manage signings, keys, and trust anchors. With online signing, automated key management, and automated trust anchor distribution, this is no longer required: Windows Server 2016 DNS servers now can do that automatically.

- **Updated DNSSEC standards support:** Windows Server 2016 DNSSEC supports validation of records with updated DNSSEC standards such as NSEC3 and RSA/SHA-2. Older versions did not support signing records with NSEC3 and RSA/SHA-2.

DNSSEC Zone Signing Wizard

Since Windows Server 2012, the DNSSEC Zone Signing Wizard is included in the graphical DNS management tool, to simplify the configuration and signing process and to enable online signing. The wizard enables you to choose zone signing parameters. Since Windows Server 2012, you can enable DNSSEC in the DNS Manager tool. Chapter 4 covers the DNSSEC Zone Signing Wizard and explores its possibilities and settings in more detail.

Analyzing Zone-Level Statistics

Name resolution sometimes requires troubleshooting. Issues can occur when the DNS server, its zones, and its resource records are not configured properly. Identifying such issues can sometimes be difficult because configuration problems are not always obvious. A number of tools are available to configure, manage, and troubleshoot DNS server and name resolution issues. PowerShell has extended functionality in Windows Server 2016 with enhanced zone-level statistics. This is accessible through the **Get-DnsServer Statistics** PowerShell cmdlet.

Windows Server 2012 R2 DNS Server Statistics

Windows Server 2012 R2 introduced a new Windows PowerShell DNS module with numerous cmdlets, including the **Get-DNSServerStatistics** cmdlet:

```
$statistics = Get-DnsServerStatistics -ZoneName pearson.com
$statistics.ZoneQueryStatistics
$statistics.ZoneTransferStatistics
$statistics.ZoneUpdateStatistics
```

Windows Server 2016 Enhanced Zone-Level Statistics

In Windows Server 2016, the **Get-DnsServerStatistics** cmdlet has been extended to enhanced zone-level statistics. Table 2-5 displays details about the **Zone TransferStatistics** cmdlet, which returns information about full and incremental zone transfers.

Table 2-5   ZoneTransferStatistics Cmdlet Parameters

Parameter	Functionality
RequestReceived	Received when the DNS server is a primary server for a zone.
RequestSent	Sent when the DNS server is a secondary server for a zone.
ResponseReceived	Received when the DNS server is a secondary server for a zone.
SuccessReceived	Indicates success. Received when the DNS server is a secondary server for a zone.
SuccessSent	Indicates success. Received when the DNS server is a primary server for a zone.

Table 2-6 displays details about the **ZoneUpdate Statistics** cmdlet.

Table 2-6   ZoneUpdateStatistics Cmdlet Parameters

Parameter	Functionality
DynamicUpdateReceived	Dynamic update requests that are received by the DNS server
DynamicUpdateRejected	Dynamic updates that are rejected by the DNS server

Zone Scavenging

DNS dynamic updates automatically add resource records to the zone, but in some cases, those records are not deleted automatically when they are no longer required.

For example, if a computer registers its own A record and is improperly disconnected from the network, the A record might not be deleted. These records, known as stale records, take up space in the DNS database and can result in an incorrect query response being returned. Windows Server operating systems can search for those stale records and, based on the aging of the record, scavenge them from the DNS database.

An exception to the exception arises if you use the new Windows Server 2016 PowerShell cmdlets, such as **Add-DnsServerResourceRecordPtr** or **Add-DNSServerResourceRecordA**. These cmdlets have a parameter named **AgeRecord**. Using this parameter, the DNS server can use a time stamp for the record that this cmdlets adds.

Enabling and Disabling Scavenging

Aging and scavenging is disabled by default. You can enable aging and scavenging in the Advanced Properties of the DNS server (see Figure 2-18), or you can enable it for selected zones in the zone's Properties (see Figure 2-19) window.

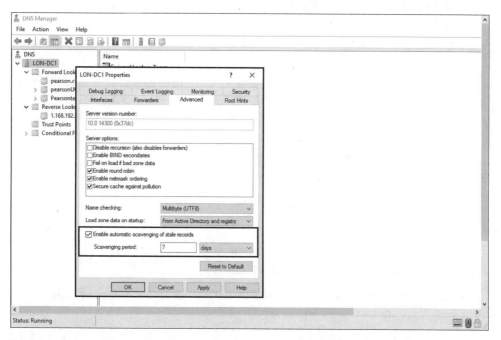

Figure 2-18   DNS Server Enable Automatic Scavenging of Stale Records Setting

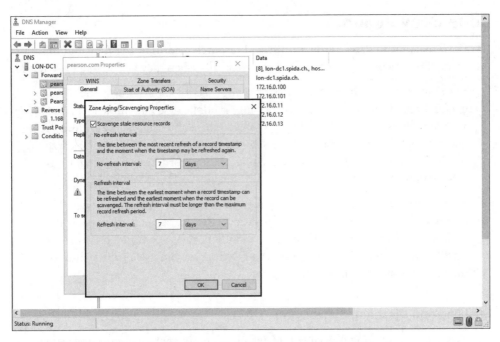

Figure 2-19   Zone Properties Scavenge Stale Resource Records Setting

Aging is determined by using two parameters, the refresh interval and the no-refresh interval. The refresh interval is the date and time that the record is eligible to be refreshed by the client; the default is 7 days. The no-refresh interval is the period of time that the record is not eligible to be refreshed; by default, this is also 7 days.

In the normal course of events, a client host record cannot be refreshed in the database for 7 days after it is first registered or refreshed. However, it then must be refreshed within the next 7 days after the no-refresh interval, or the record becomes eligible for scavenging out of the database. A client attempts to refresh its DNS record at startup and then every 24 hours while the system is running.

Starting the Scavenging Process

To start the scavenging process immediately, perform the following steps:

Step 1.   Open the DNS Manager.

Step 2.   In the console tree, right-click the applicable DNS server and then click **Scavenge Stale Resource Records**.

Step 3.   When you are asked to confirm that you want to scavenge all stale resource records on the server, click **OK**.

You also can start the scavenging process immediately with the following command:

```
Dnscmd <ServerName> /StartScavenging
```

TIP DNS records that are added dynamically are time stamped. Static records that you enter manually have a time stamp value of 0; therefore, they are not affected by aging and will not be scavenged out of the database. Instead, you must remove them manually.

An exception to the exception arises if you use the new Windows Server 2016 Power-Shell cmdlets, such as **Add-DnsServerResourceRecordPtr** or **Add-DNSServer-ResourceRecordA**. These cmdlets have a parameter named **AgeRecord**. Using this parameter, the DNS server can use a time stamp for the record that this cmdlets adds.

Scavenging Configuration with PowerShell

To get the scavenging settings for the local DNS servers, use the following Power-Shell cmdlet:

```
Get-DnsServerScavenging
```

Figure 2-20 shows the **Get-DnsServerScavenging** PowerShell cmdlet and output.

Figure 2-20   Get-DnsServerScavenging PowerShell Cmdlet and Output

To enable aging for the domain named europe.pearson.com and specify a scavenging server, enter the following:

```
Set-DnsServerZoneAging europe.pearson.com -Aging $True
  -ScavengeServers 172.16.1.12 -PassThru -Verbose
```

To change the refresh interval to 1 day for scavenging on a local DNS server, enter the following:

```
Set-DnsServerScavenging -RefreshInterval 1.00:00:00 -Verbose -PassThru
```

Record Options

Resource records specify a resource type and the IP address to locate the resource. The most common resource record is an A record. This is a simple record that resolves a hostname to an IP address. The host can be a workstation, a server, or another network device, such as a router.

Most Common Resource Records

Table 2-7 describes the most common resource records.

Table 2-7   Most Common DNS Resource Records

DNS Resource Record	Description
SOA	Identifies the primary DNS server for a DNS zone, in addition to other specifics, such as Time to Live (TTL) and refresh
A	Acts as the main record that resolves a hostname to an IPv4 address
CNAME	Acts as an alias record type that maps one name to another (for example, www.pearson.com is a CNAME of the A record pearson.com)
MX	Specifies an email server for a particular domain
SRV	Identifies a service that is available in the domain
NS	Identifies a DNS server for a domain
AAAA	Acts as the main record that resolves a hostname to an IPv6 address
PTR	Used to look up and map an IP address to a domain name

TLSA Records and Unknown Record Types

In Windows Server 2016, you also can add Transport Layer Security Authentication (TLSA) records to provide information to DNS clients that state what CA they should expect a certificate from for your domain name. This prevents man-in-the-middle attacks, in which someone corrupts the DNS cache to point to a different website and provides a certificate issued from a different CA. Windows Server 2016 also supports unknown record types that the Windows DNS server does not explicitly support. TLSA records are an example of such unknown record types.

The following PowerShell cmdlets are updated to support unknown record types:

```
Add-DnsServerResourceRecord
Get-DnsServerResourceRecord
Remove-DnsServerResourceRecord
Set-DnsServerResourceRecord
```

Managing Resource Records with PowerShell

To get information about an A record in the zone pearson.com, use the **Get-DnsServerResourceRecord** PowerShell cmdlet (see Figure 2-21).

```
PS C:\> Get-DnsServerResourceRecord -ComputerName lon-dc1 -ZoneName pearson.com -Name cl1 |FL

DistinguishedName     : DC=cl1,DC=pearson.com,cn=MicrosoftDNS,DC=DNSData
HostName              : cl1
RecordClass           : IN
RecordData            : DnsServerResourceRecordA
RecordType            : A
Timestamp             :
TimeToLive            : 01:00:00
Type                  : 1
PSComputerName        :
CimClass              : root/Microsoft/Windows/DNS:DnsServerResourceRecord
CimInstanceProperties : {DistinguishedName, HostName, RecordClass, RecordData...}
CimSystemProperties   : Microsoft.Management.Infrastructure.CimSystemProperties
```

Figure 2-21   Get-DnsServerResourceRecord PowerShell Cmdlet and Output

To add hostname SVR1 to the pearson.com zone for the IP address 172.16.0.1, you enter the following:

```
Add-DNSServerResourceRecordA -Name "SVR1" -ZoneName "pearson.com"
  -IPv4Address "172.16.0.1"
```

To add an MX record named MXX for the zone west.pearson.com with a preference of 10 (Mail exchanger is MX1), you enter the following:

```
Add-DnsServerResourceRecordMX -Preference 10  -Name "MXX" -TimeToLive
  01:00:00 -MailExchange "west.pearson.com " -ZoneName "pearson.com"
```

To add a PTR record in the zone pearson.com, you enter the following:

```
Add-DnsServerResourceRecordPtr -Name "17" -ZoneName "0.168.192.
  in-addr.arpa" -AllowUpdateAny
  -TimeToLive 01:00:00 -AgeRecord -PtrDomainName "host17.pearson.com"
```

The record maps IP address 192.168.0.17 to the name host17.pearson.com. The command includes the **AllowUpdateAny** and **AgeRecord** parameters and provides a TTL value. Because the command includes the **AgeRecord** parameter, a DNS server can scavenge this record.

To add a CNAME resource record with the alias *testserver* to the pearson.com domain for a system named *srv1* in the zone named lab.pearson.com, you enter the following:

```
Add-DnsServerResourceRecordCName -Name "testserver" -HostNameAlias
  "srv1.lab. pearson.com" -ZoneName "pearson.com"
```

To change the TTL value of the record Host01 in the zone pearson.com to 2 hours, you enter the following:

```
$NewObj = $OldObj = Get-DnsServerResourceRecord -Name "Host01"
  -ZoneName "pearson.com" -RRType "A" (Assigns a resource record named
  Host01 in the zone named pearson.com to the variables $NewObj and
  $OldObj)
$NewObj.TimeToLive = [System.TimeSpan]::FromHours(2) (Sets the TTL
  time span for $NewObj to 2 hours)
```

```
Set-DnsServerResourceRecord -NewInputObject $NewObj -OldInputObject
    $OldObj -ZoneName "pearson.com" -PassThru (Changes the properties
    of $OldObj to the settings specified for $NewObj in the previous
    command)
```

DNS Audit and Analytical Events

Microsoft introduced enhanced DNS logging and diagnostics in Windows Server 2012 R2. This is continued in Windows Server 2016.

Although DNS server performance can be affected when additional logging is enabled, the enhanced DNS logging and diagnostics features are designed to have very low impact on performance.

Enabling or Disabling Analytical DNS Logging

DNS audit logs are enabled by default and do not significantly affect DNS server performance. DNS analytical logs are not enabled by default and typically affect DNS server performance only at very high DNS query rates.

However, it is good practice to monitor DNS server performance when additional logging is enabled. An analytic event gets logged every time the server sends or receives DNS information.

To enable DNS server analytical and audit logging, perform the following steps:

Step 1.   Download and install the Windows Driver Kit (WDK) to get the **tracelog.exe** command-line utility. **tracelog.exe** is included when you install the WDK, Visual Studio, and the Windows SDK for desktop apps.

Step 2.   Type the following command to enable DNS server analytical and audit logging: **tracelog.exe -start Dns -guid #{EB79061A-A566-4698-9119-3ED2807060E7} -level 5 -matchanykw 0xFFFFFFFF -f C:\analytic_audit.etl**.

Step 3.   While the trace is active, all analytical and audit events are recorded in the C:\analytic_audit.etl file that was specified on the command line. You can stop tracing by issuing a stop command: **tracelog -stop Dns.**

Step 4.   After stopping the trace, you can view the .etl file in the Event Viewer by clicking **Action** and then clicking **Open Saved Log**.

Exam Preparation Tasks

Review All the Key Topics

Review the most important topics in the chapter, noted with the Key Topics icon in the outer margin of the page. Table 2-8 lists these key topics and the page numbers on which each is found.

Table 2-8 Key Topics for Chapter 2

Key Topic Element	Description	Page Number
Section	Primary Zones	92
Section	Forward Lookup Zones	92
Section	Reverse Lookup Zones	93
Section	Managing Primary Zones with PowerShell	93
Section	Primary DNS Server as a Single Point of Failure	96
Section	Fault Tolerance with AD-Integrated DNS Servers	96
Section	Encrypted DNS Data Replication Traffic	96
Section	Managing AD-Integrated Zones with PowerShell	97
Tip	Converting AD-integrated DNS zone to file-based	97
Section	Zone Transfer Process	98
Text	Starting zone transfer with PowerShell	99
Bullet	Fast zone transfer	101
Section	Using DNS Policies in a Primary/Secondary Deployment	101
List	When to use stub zones	104
Section	Managing Stub Zones with PowerShell	105
Section	Managing a GlobalNames Zone with PowerShell	106
Section	Windows Server 2012 R2 DNS Server Statistics	108
Table 2-5 and Table 2-6	Enhanced zone-level statistics	108
Section	Enabling and Disabling Scavenging	109
Step List	Immediately starting the scavenging process	110
Tip	AgeRecord parameter	111

Key Topic Element	Description	Page Number
Section	Scavenging Configuration with PowerShell	111
Text	Updated PowerShell cmdlets	112
Section	Managing Resource Records with PowerShell	112
Step List	Enabling or Disabling Analytical DNS Logging	114

Complete the Tables and Lists from Memory

Print a copy of Appendix B, "Memory Tables" (on the book's website), or at least the section for this chapter, and complete the tables and lists from memory. Appendix C, "Memory Tables Answer Key," also on the website, includes completed tables and lists to check your work.

Definition of Key Terms

Define the following key terms from this chapter and check your answers in the glossary:

Primary zone, AD-integrated zone, secondary zone, stub zone, AXFR, IXFR, ForestDNSZones, DomainDNSZones, Application Directory partition, DNSSEC, KSK, ZSK, trust anchor, msdcs zone, GlobalNames zone, zone transfer, DNS server transfer policies, zone-level statistics, scavenging, TLSA record, unknown record support, DNS analytical logging

End-of-Chapter Review Questions

1. You have installed a Windows Server 2012 R2 DNS server named DNS1. You want to use DNSSEC and DANE. You have to implement all necessary DNS configuration. You realize that not all kinds of resource records can be created on your DNS server. What change do you have to conduct?

    a. Change the DNS zone to AD integrated with forest replication scope

    b. Upgrade the DNS server to Windows Server 2016

    c. Add another Windows Server 2016 DNS server as the secondary of DNS1

    d. Enable BIND secondaries and use a BIND server as the secondary DNS for DNS1

2. You have a Windows Server 2016 DNS server named DNS1 that is authoritative for the AD-integrated zone eu.pearson.com and is the domain controller for the domain eu.pearson.com. You have implemented DNS2 as the secondary DNS server for that zone. DNS2 is a Windows Server 2012 R2 DNS server and the second domain controller for eu.pearson.com. You want to start the DNS data replication between DNS1 and DNS2 immediately. What step does this quickly?

   a. On DNS2, convert eu.pearson.com zone to an AD-integrated zone

   b. **Start-DnsServerZoneTransfer -Name "eu.pearson.com"** on DNS1

   c. **Repadmin /replicate DNS2 DNS1 DC=eu,DC=pearson,DC=com**

   d. Add DNS2 to the notify list of secondary DNS servers on DNS1

3. You want to change the TTL value of record SRV1 in the zone pearson.com to 4 hours. Which PowerShell command is not a working solution to accomplish this task?

   a. **Get-DnsServerResourceRecord**

   b. [System.TimeSpan]::*FromHours(4)*

   c. **Set-DnsServerResourceRecord**

   d. **Add-DnsServerResourceRecord**

4. You want to enable the analytical DNS logging feature to get more detailed information about incomplete or incorrectly configured DNS records on your Windows Server 2016 DNS server. Which settings or tools can you use to enable analytical DNS logging and analyze recorded analytical DNS logging data?

   a. tracelog.exe

   b. Debug logging

   c. **Test-DnsServer**

   d. **nslookup**

This chapter covers the following subjects:

- **DHCP options, DHCP name protection:** DHCP options on a DHCP server deliver the information DHCP clients must use. If you want to implement the new Windows Server 2016 DNS Policy feature, it is important to know how clients get their correct DNS server IP address with preconfigured DNS Policies.

- **Managing DNS client and server settings with PowerShell:** Windows Server 2016 delivers many new PowerShell cmdlets to manage DNS client and DNS server settings. The exam requires knowledge about the most important.

- **Network troubleshooting with PowerShell:** DNS Policies are an important new Windows Server 2016 feature. Name resolution is only one little piece of the networking components cosmos. DNS Policies are dependent on the underlying network configurations, such as IPv4 or IPv6 TCP/IP settings. Therefore, you must be familiar with the most important network troubleshooting PowerShell cmdlets to get the toolbox for solving such network problems and to be prepared for questions in the 70-741 Microsoft exam.

- **Understanding routing:** To prepare for questions on DNS Policy, it is also important to know the most common commands for troubleshooting routing problems. If you do not get the correct gateway to reach the DNS server configured with DNS Policies, this can have a negative impact on your DNS Policy–based name resolution solution.

- **Split DNS:** You should be familiar with Split DNS. This chapter covers various Split DNS scenarios and purposes. You also see how NRPT settings and Split DNS relate, which influences your DNS Policy planning and configuration.

- **DNS Policies:** DNS Policies are useful for DNS traffic management, application high availability, split-brain configuration, filtering, and forensics. You explore DNS Policy usage scenarios and learn about the purposes of DNS Policies, and you see how to implement DNS Policies with different requirements. This chapter also covers the elements of a DNS Policy and the different types of DNS Policies. Through many practical exercises, you learn when to use DNS Policies and how to configure them with new PowerShell cmdlets. You deepen your knowledge with exercises on configuring DNS Policies based on location (domain and/or subnet) and time of the day. You also use zone- and server-level DNS transfer policies to control which secondary DNS servers get transferred with zone data. You see how to block or allow queries based on different criteria, and you learn how to configure DNS query resolution policies overall.

## CHAPTER 3

Configuring and Managing DNS Policies

This chapter takes a look at the purpose of the new Windows Server 2016 DNS Policy feature and its capabilities. First you get coverage of DHCP options, DHCP name protection, PowerShell cmdlets for managing DNS client and server settings, and fundamental considerations about network troubleshooting and routing. Then you explore the practical use of Split DNS and other important DNS features to get you ready for the 70-741 Microsoft exam and prepare you for dealing with DNS Policies.

DNS Policies are the main topic of this chapter. You investigate the possibilities of the new Windows Server 2016 DNS feature and explore its usage scenarios. This chapter also covers DNS Policy types, elements, and parameters, along with multiple query resolution DNS Policies, DNS Policies based on location, and DNS Policies used for split-brain configuration. In addition, you learn how selective recursion control through DNS recursion policies works and how to configure it.

In practical exercises, you learn how to block DNS queries based on domain names using DNS query resolution policies and how to configure server- and zone-level zone transfer policies with DNS transfer policies. You see how to block or allow queries based on criteria such as domain names, subnet, or time of the day. You also explore how to configure a DNS Policy scenario based on the time of the day by using a Microsoft Azure application server.

DNS Policies on a Windows Server 2016 DNS can be configured only through PowerShell cmdlets, not through the graphical DNS manager interface. Therefore, this chapter introduces many new PowerShell cmdlets that are relevant to the 70-741 Microsoft exam.

"Do I Know This Already?" Quiz

The "Do I Know This Already?" quiz enables you to assess whether you should read this entire chapter or simply jump to the "Exam Preparation Tasks" section for review. If you are in doubt, read the entire chapter. Table 3-1 outlines the major headings in this chapter and the corresponding "Do I Know This Already?" quiz questions. You can find the answers in Appendix A, "Answers to the 'Do I Know This Already?' Quizzes and End-of-Chapter Review Questions."

Table 3-1   "Do I Know This Already?" Foundation Topics Section-to-Question Mapping

Foundation Topics Section	Questions Covered in This Section
DHCP Options	1
DHCP Name Protection	2
Manage DNS Client Settings with PowerShell	3
Manage DNS Server Settings with PowerShell	4
Network Troubleshooting with PowerShell	5
Understanding Routing	6
Split DNS	7
DNS Policies	8

CAUTION   The goal of self-assessment is to gauge your mastery of the topics in this chapter. If you do not know the answer to a question or are only partially sure of the answer, you should mark that question as wrong for purposes of the self-assessment. Giving yourself credit for an answer you correctly guess skews your self-assessment results and might provide you with a false sense of security.

1. You have configured your Windows Server 2016 DHCP server with a scope of 10.0.0.0/16 and the two scope options Option 003: 10.0.0.10 and Option 006: 10.0.0.20. Some of your DHCP clients get a DNS server of 10.0.0.100 and a default gateway of 10.0.0.200 from that DHCP server. What is a possible cause?

    a. DHCP failover

    b. DHCP Policy

    c. DNS Policy

    d. DNSSEC

2. You use a DHCP server to automatically register client resource records on a DNS server. Which feature should you enable on your DHCP server to protect your environment from name squatting attacks?

    a. DHCP server policies

    b. DNS Policies

    c. Name Protection

    d. DNSSEC

3. Which PowerShell cmdlet can you use to configure the DNS server's IP address on a DNS client?

    a. **Set-DnsClientServerAddress**

    b. **Set-NetIPInterface**

    c. **Set-NetIPAddress**

    d. **Set-DnsClient**

4. You want to synchronize DNS zone data and root hint data for a zone to the persistent storage of a Windows Server 2016 Nano Server DNS server. Which PowerShell command can you use for that?

    a. **Start-DnsServerZoneTransfer**

    b. **Sync-DnsServerZone**

    c. **Add-DnsServerZoneTransferPolicy**

    d. **Set-DnsServerZoneTransferPolicy**

5. You are responsible for the DNS zone named pearson.com. Some clients of the subnet named Paris cannot reach resources on your partner company pearsonucertify.com through hostnames. However, they can reach the resources through IP addresses without problems. Clients from other internal networks have no problems accessing such resources. Which network components should you verify? (Choose four.)

    a. DHCP Policy

    b. DNS server options

    c. DNS server zone transfer policy settings

    d. DNS server zone scope settings

    e. DNS server client subnet settings

    f. DNS server recursion policy settings

6. You have established a P2S connection to your Azure VNet. You want to verify the gateway IP address through which the P2S network traffic flows. Which command can you use?

    a. **Get-AzureVNetGateway**

    b. **Get-NetRoute**

    c. **Get-NetIPInterface**

    d. **Get-VpnConnection**

7. You have configured your Windows 10 laptops as DirectAccess clients. Your employee starts his laptop at the airport and will remain there while waiting for a flight. He will use the airport's WLAN connection to connect through a Windows Server 2016 Direct Access Server (Azure VM) to Azure VNet resources. Which source delivers the DNS server resolving internal hostnames?

   a. Airport DHCP server

   b. Company DHCP server

   c. TCP/IP settings of network interface

   d. Name Resolution Policy Table

8. You want to configure selective recursion control on your Windows Server 2016 DNS server in your DMZ to configure different recursion settings for internal and external clients. Which of the following PowerShell commands can you use? (Choose three.)

   a. **Add-DnsServerResourceRecord**

   b. **Set-DnsServerRecursionScope**

   c. **Add-DnsServerRecursionScope**

   d. **Add-DnsServerQueryResolutionPolicy**

   e. **Add-DnsServerClientSubnet**

Foundation Topics

DHCP Options

Clients can obtain their IP address settings from a DHCP server and can also obtain the information about which Domain Name System (DNS) server(s) they must use. DHCP servers can provide information about network resources such as DNS servers and the default gateway. DHCP options are values for common configuration data that apply to the server, scopes, reservations, and class options. You can apply DHCP options at the server, scope, class, and reservation levels on a DHCP server. An option code identifies the DHCP options, and most option codes come from the RFC documentation found on the Internet Engineering Task Force (IETF) website.

Table 3-2 lists the common option codes for Windows-based DHCP client requests.

Table 3-2 DHCP Option Codes

Option Code	Name
1	Subnet mask
3	Router
6	DNS server
15	DNS domain name
31	Perform router discovery
33	Static route
43	Vendor-specific information
47	NetBIOS scope ID
51	Lease time
58	Renewal (T1) time value
59	Rebinding (T2) time value
60	Pre-Boot Execution (PXE) client
66	Boot server hostname
67	Bootfile name
249	Classless static routes

The priority for option settings follows:

reservation > scope policy > server policy > scope level > server level

DHCP Name Protection

During dynamic IP address allocation, the DHCP server automatically creates DNS resource records for DHCP clients in the DNS database.

You should protect the names DHCP registers on DNS servers on behalf of other computers or systems, from being overwritten by non-Windows operating systems that use the same names. You also should protect the names from being overwritten by systems that use static addresses that conflict with DHCP-assigned addresses when they use unsecure DNS and do not have DHCP configured for conflict detections.

As an example, a UNIX-based system named Computer1 could potentially over-write the DNS address that DHCP assigned and registered on behalf of a Windows-based system that is also named Computer1. DHCP name protection addresses this issue.

The term *name squatting* describes the conflict that occurs when one client registers a name with DNS that another client is already using. This problem makes the original machine inaccessible. It typically occurs with systems that have the same names as Windows operating systems.

DHCP name protection addresses this by using a resource record known as a Dynamic Host Configuration Protocol Identifier (DHCID) to track which machines originally requested which names. The DHCP server provides the DHCID record, which is stored in DNS. When the DHCP server receives a request from a machine with an existing name for an IP address, the DHCP server can refer to the DHCID in DNS to verify that the machine requesting the name is the original machine that used the name. If it is not the same machine, the DNS resource record is not updated.

You can implement name protection for both IPv4 and IPv6. In addition, you can configure DHCP name protection at both the server level and the scope level. To enable DHCP name protection for an IPv4 or IPv6 node, you perform the tasks outlined in the following lists.

To enable name protection at the IPv4 or IPv6 node level, follow these steps:

Step 1.   Open the DHCP Microsoft Management Console (MMC) snap-in.

Step 2.   In the console tree, double-click the DHCP server you want to configure, right-click **IPv4** or **IPv6**, and then click **Properties**.

Step 3.   Click **DNS**, click **Advanced**, and then check **Enable Name Protection** (see Figure 3-1).

To enable name protection at the scope level, follow these steps:

Step 1.   Open the DHCP console.

Step 2.   In the console tree, double-click the DHCP server you want to configure, double-click **IPv4** or **IPv6**, right-click the scope you want, and then click **Properties**.

Step 3.   Click **DNS**, click **Configure**, and then check **Enable Name Protection**.

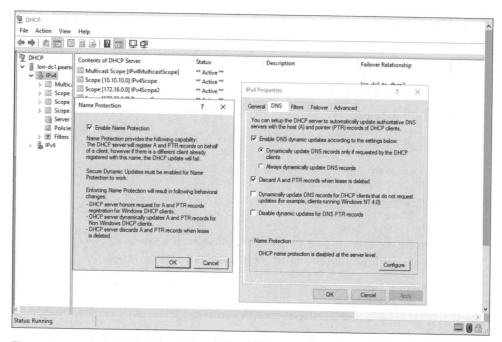

Figure 3-1   Enabling Name Protection at the IPv4 or IPv6 Node Level

Manage DNS Client Settings with PowerShell

Windows Server 2016 includes some new PowerShell cmdlets to configure the local network interface and its TCP/IP configuration (see Table 3-3). It is important to know these before implementing the new Windows Server 2016 DNS server policies feature because you also need to configure the DNS client settings correctly.

Table 3-3   PowerShell Cmdlets to Configure Local Network Interface Settings

Cmdlet	Description
Get-NetIPConfiguration	Delivers the IP network configuration
New-NetIPAddress	Creates a new IP address and binds it to a NIC
Remove-NetIPAddress	Removes an IP address
Set-NetIPAddress	Modifies the configuration of an IP address
Set-NetIPInterface	Enables or disables DHCP on a NIC
New-NetRoute	Creates routing table entries
Set-DnsClientServerAddress	Configures DNS server(s) used for a NIC

The following code is an example of how to configure the interface named Ethernet with the following parameters:

- **Static IP address:** 172.16.0.100

- **Subnet mask:** 255.255.255.0

- **Default gateway:** 172.16.0.1

- **DNS servers:** 172.16.0.200, 172.16.0.201

```
New-NetIPAddress -InterfaceAlias "Ethernet" -IPAddress 172.16.0.200
  -PrefixLength 24 -DefaultGateway 172.16.0.1
Set-DNSClientServerAddress -InterfaceAlias "Ethernet"
  -ServerAddresses 172.16.0.200, 172.16.0.201
```

The following code shows how to configure the interface named Ethernet so that a client can obtain its IP address dynamically through a DHCP server:

```
Set-NetIPInterface -InterfaceAlias "Ethernet" -Dhcp Enabled
  Restart-NetAdapter -Name "Ethernet"
```

Manage DNS Server Settings with PowerShell

Table 3-4 lists all available Windows Server 2016 DNS PowerShell cmdlets. You should know all of them for the exam.

Visit https://technet.microsoft.com/en-us/library/jj649850.aspx and work through the examples for every PowerShell cmdlet. Windows Server 2016 introduces some new ones, including all cmdlets about DNS Policies (**Add-DnsServerQueryResolutionPolicy**, **Add-DnsServerZoneTransfer Policy**, **Disable-DnsServerPolicy**, **Enable-DnsServerPolicy**, **Get-DnsServerQueryResolutionPolicy**, **Get-DnsServerZoneTransferPolicy**, **Remove-DnsServerQueryResolutionPolicy**, and so on). You should also take a look at the ones related to the Response Rate Limiting (RRL) feature. At the very minimum, work through all documentation and examples for highlighted DNS server PowerShell cmdlets in the table.

Table 3-4 Windows Server 2016 DNS Server PowerShell Cmdlets

Cmdlet	Description
Add-DnsServerClientSubnet	Adds a client subnet to a DNS server
Add-DnsServerConditionalForwarderZone	Adds a conditional forwarder to a DNS server
Add-DnsServerDirectoryPartition	Creates a DNS application directory partition
Add-DnsServerForwarder	Adds server-level forwarders to a DNS server

Cmdlet	Description
Add-DnsServerPrimaryZone	Adds a primary zone to a DNS server
Add-DnsServerQueryResolutionPolicy	Adds a policy for query resolution to a DNS server
Add-DnsServerRecursionScope	Adds a recursion scope on a DNS server
Add-DnsServerResourceRecord	Adds a resource record of a specified type to a specified DNS zone
Add-DnsServerResourceRecordA	Adds a type A resource record to a DNS zone
Add-DnsServerResourceRecordAAAA	Adds a type AAAA resource record to a DNS server
Add-DnsServerResourceRecordCName	Adds a type CNAME resource record to a DNS zone
Add-DnsServerResourceRecordDnsKey	Adds a type DNSKEY resource record to a DNS zone
Add-DnsServerResourceRecordDS	Adds a type DS resource record to a DNS zone
Add-DnsServerResourceRecordMX	Adds an MX resource record to a DNS zone
Add-DnsServerResourceRecordPtr	Adds a type PTR resource record to a DNS zone
Add-DnsServerResponseRateLimiting-Exceptionlist	Adds an RRL exception list on the DNS server
Add-DnsServerRootHint	Adds root hints on a DNS server
Add-DnsServerSecondaryZone	Adds a DNS server secondary zone
Add-DnsServerSigningKey	Adds a KSK or ZSK to a signed zone
Add-DnsServerStubZone	Adds a DNS stub zone
Add-DnsServerTrustAnchor	Adds a trust anchor to a DNS server
Add-DnsServerZoneDelegation	Adds a new delegated DNS zone to an existing zone
Add-DnsServerZoneScope	Adds a zone scope to an existing zone
Add-DnsServerZoneTransferPolicy	Adds a zone transfer policy to a DNS server
Clear-DnsServerCache	Clears resource records from a cache on the DNS server
Clear-DnsServerStatistics	Clears all DNS server statistics or statistics for zones
ConvertTo-DnsServerPrimaryZone	Converts a zone to a DNS primary zone
ConvertTo-DnsServerSecondaryZone	Converts a primary zone or stub zone to a secondary zone

Cmdlet	Description
Disable-DnsServerPolicy	Disables DNS server policies
Disable-DnsServerSigningKeyRollover	Disables key rollover on an input key
Enable-DnsServerPolicy	Enables DNS server policies
Enable-DnsServerSigningKeyRollover	Enables rollover on the input key
Export-DnsServerDNSSECPublicKey	Exports DS and DNSKEY information for a DNSSEC-signed zone
Export-DnsServerZone	Exports the contents of a zone to a file
Get-DnsServer	Retrieves a DNS server configuration
Get-DnsServerCache	Retrieves DNS server cache settings
Get-DnsServerClientSubnet	Gets client subnets for a DNS server
Get-DnsServerDiagnostics	Retrieves DNS event logging details
Get-DnsServerDirectoryPartition	Gets a DNS application directory partition
Get-DnsServerDNSSECZoneSetting	Gets DNSSEC settings for a zone
Get-DnsServerDsSetting	Retrieves DNS server Active Directory settings
Get-DnsServerEDns	Gets EDNS configuration settings on a DNS server
Get-DnsServerForwarder	Gets forwarder configuration settings on a DNS server
Get-DnsServerGlobalNameZone	Retrieves DNS server GlobalName zone configuration details
Get-DnsServerGlobalQueryBlockList	Gets a global query block list
Get-DnsServerQueryResolutionPolicy	Gets policies for query resolution from a DNS server
Get-DnsServerRecursion	Retrieves DNS server recursion settings
Get-DnsServerRecursionScope	Gets the DNS server recursion scopes
Get-DnsServerResourceRecord	Gets resource records from a specified DNS zone
Get-DnsServerResponseRateLimiting	Displays the RRL settings on a DNS server
Get-DnsServerResponseRateLimiting-Exceptionlist	Enumerates the RRL exception lists on a DNS server
Get-DnsServerRootHint	Gets root hints on a DNS server
Get-DnsServerScavenging	Gets DNS aging and scavenging settings
Get-DnsServerSetting	Retrieves DNS server settings

Cmdlet	Description
Get-DnsServerSigningKey	Gets zone signing keys
Get-DnsServerStatistics	Retrieves DNS server statistics or statistics for zones
Get-DnsServerTrustAnchor	Gets trust anchors on a DNS server
Get-DnsServerTrustPoint	Gets trust points on a DNS server
Get-DnsServerZone	Gets details of DNS zones on a DNS server
Get-DnsServerZoneAging	Gets DNS aging settings for a zone
Get-DnsServerZoneDelegation	Gets the zone delegations of a DNS server zone
Get-DnsServerZoneScope	Gets the scopes of a zone on a DNS server
Get-DnsServerZoneTransferPolicy	Gets the zone transfer policies on a DNS server
Import-DnsServerResourceRecordDS	Imports DS resource record information from a file
Import-DnsServerRootHint	Copies root hints from a DNS server
Import-DnsServerTrustAnchor	Imports a trust anchor for a DNS server
Invoke-DnsServerSigningKeyRollover	Initiates rollover of signing keys for the zone
Invoke-DnsServerZoneSign	Signs a DNS server zone
Invoke-DnsServerZoneUnsign	Unsigns a DNS server zone
Register-DnsServerDirectoryPartition	Registers a DNS server in a DNS application directory partition
Remove-DnsServerClientSubnet	Removes a client subnet from a DNS server
Remove-DnsServerDirectoryPartition	Removes a DNS application directory partition
Remove-DnsServerForwarder	Removes server-level forwarders from a DNS server
Remove-DnsServerQueryResolutionPolicy	Removes a policy for query resolution from a DNS server
Remove-DnsServerRecursionScope	Removes a recursion scope from a DNS server
Remove-DnsServerResourceRecord	Removes specified DNS server resource records from a zone
Remove-DnsServerResponseRateLimiting-Exceptionlist	Removes an RRL exception list from a DNS server
Remove-DnsServerRootHint	Removes root hints from a DNS server
Remove-DnsServerSigningKey	Removes signing keys

Cmdlet	Description
Remove-DnsServerTrustAnchor	Removes a trust anchor from a DNS server
Remove-DnsServerZone	Removes a zone from a DNS server
Remove-DnsServerZoneDelegation	Removes a name server or delegation from a DNS zone
Remove-DnsServerZoneScope	Removes a zone scope from an existing zone
Remove-DnsServerZoneTransferPolicy	Removes a zone transfer policy from a DNS server
Reset-DnsServerZoneKeyMasterRole	Transfers the role of Key Master for a DNS zone
Restore-DnsServerPrimaryZone	Restores primary DNS zone contents from Active Directory or from a file
Restore-DnsServerSecondaryZone	Restores secondary zone information from its source
Resume-DnsServerZone	Resumes name resolution on a suspended zone
Set-DnsServer	Overwrites a DNS server configuration
Set-DnsServerCache	Modifies cache settings for a DNS server
Set-DnsServerClientSubnet	Updates the IP addresses in a client subnet
Set-DnsServerConditionalForwarder-Zone	Changes settings for a DNS conditional forwarder
Set-DnsServerDiagnostics	Sets debugging and logging parameters
Set-DnsServerDNSSECZoneSetting	Changes settings for DNSSEC for a zone
Set-DnsServerDsSetting	Modifies DNS Active Directory settings
Set-DnsServerEDns	Changes EDNS settings on a DNS server
Set-DnsServerForwarder	Changes forwarder settings on a DNS server
Set-DnsServerGlobalNameZone	Changes configuration settings for a GlobalNames zone
Set-DnsServerGlobalQueryBlockList	Changes settings of a global query block list
Set-DnsServerPrimaryZone	Changes settings for a DNS primary zone
Set-DnsServerQueryResolutionPolicy	Updates settings of a query resolution policy on a DNS server
Set-DnsServerRecursion	Modifies recursion settings for a DNS server
Set-DnsServerRecursionScope	Modifies a recursion scope on a DNS server
Set-DnsServerResourceRecord	Changes a resource record in a DNS zone

Cmdlet	Description
Set-DnsServerResourceRecordAging	Begins aging resource records in a specified DNS zone
Set-DnsServerResponseRateLimiting	Enables Response Rate Limiting (RRL) on a DNS server
Set-DnsServerResponseRateLimiting-Exceptionlist	Updates the settings of an RRL exception list
Set-DnsServerRootHint	Replaces a list of root hints
Set-DnsServerScavenging	Changes DNS server scavenging settings
Set-DnsServerSecondaryZone	Changes settings for a DNS secondary zone
Set-DnsServerSetting	Modifies DNS server settings
Set-DnsServerSigningKey	Changes settings of a signing key
Set-DnsServerStubZone	Changes settings for a DNS server stub zone
Set-DnsServerZoneAging	Configures DNS aging settings for a zone
Set-DnsServerZoneDelegation	Changes delegation settings for a child zone
Set-DnsServerZoneTransferPolicy	Updates a zone transfer policy on a DNS server
Show-DnsServerCache	Shows the records in a DNS server cache
Show-DnsServerKeyStorageProvider	Returns a list of key storage providers
Start-DnsServerScavenging	Notifies a DNS server to attempt a search for stale resource records
Start-DnsServerZoneTransfer	Starts a zone transfer for a secondary DNS zone from master servers
Step-DnsServerSigningKeyRollover	Rolls over a KSK that is waiting for a parent DS update
Suspend-DnsServerZone	Suspends a zone on a DNS server
Sync-DnsServerZone	Checks the DNS server memory for changes and writes them to persistent storage
Test-DnsServer	Tests that a specified computer is a functioning DNS server
Test-DnsServerDNSSECZoneSetting	Validates DNSSEC settings for a zone
Unregister-DnsServerDirectoryPartition	Deregisters a DNS server from a DNS application directory partition
Update-DnsServerTrustPoint	Updates all trust points in a DNS trust anchor zone

Network Troubleshooting with PowerShell

Name resolution sometimes requires troubleshooting. Issues can occur when the DNS server, its zones, and its resource records are not configured properly. When resource records are causing issues, identifying the issue sometimes is difficult because configuration problems are not always obvious. Several tools are available to configure, manage, and troubleshoot DNS server and name resolution issues. The exam includes questions about name resolution issues, so you must know the most common tools to troubleshoot such problems:

- **Nslookup:** Use this tool to query DNS information. Nslookup is flexible and can provide valuable information about DNS server status. You also can use it to look up resource records and validate their configuration. Additionally, you can test zone transfers, security options, and MX record resolution.

- **DNSCmd:** Use this command-line tool to manage the DNS server role. DNSCmd is useful in scripting batch files to help automate routine DNS management tasks or to perform simple unattended setup and configuration of new DNS servers on your network.

- **DNSlint:** Use this tool to diagnose common DNS issues. DNSlint quickly diagnoses configuration issues in DNS and generates a report in HTML format regarding the status of the domain that you are testing. With DNSlint, you can generate reports across more DNS servers simultaneously.

When you troubleshoot name resolution problems, mostly it is because someone cannot reach a remote host, a server, or another device. You must verify the DNS resolver cache on the client experiencing the problem. You can do that with **ipconfig /flushdns** or **Clear-DNSClientCache**. Try to ping the remote host with its IP address instead of the hostname. This helps identify whether the issue is related to name resolution. If the ping works with the IP address but fails with the hostname, the problem is related to name resolution. Suppose you cannot reach a host named pearson-dc1.pearson.com. Try **nslookup.exe -d pearson-dc1.pearson.com > C:\filename.txt** and examine the content of the textfile to identify the failed stage in name resolution.

Table 3-5 lists some of the Windows PowerShell cmdlets you can use to troubleshoot network problems.

Table 3-5 PowerShell Cmdlets for Network Troubleshooting

Cmdlet	Description
Get-NetAdapter	Obtains a list of network adapters in a computer.
Get-NetIPv4Protocol	Gets information about the IPv4 protocol configuration. Note that **Get-NetIPv6Protocol** gets information about the IPv6 protocol configuration.
Restart-NetAdapter	Disables and re-enables a network adapter.
Get-NetIPInterface	Obtains a list of interfaces and their configuration.
Get-NetIPAddress	Obtains a list of IP addresses that are configured for interfaces.
Get-NetRoute	Obtains the list of routes in the local routing table.
Get-NetConnectionProfile	Obtains the type of network (public, private, domain) to which a network adapter is connected.
Get-DnsClient	Retrieves configuration details specific to the different network interfaces on a specified computer.
Get-DnsClientCache	Obtains the list of resolved DNS names stored in the DNS client cache.
Get-DnsClientGlobalSetting	Retrieves global DNS client settings such as the suffix search list.
Get-DNSClientServerAddress	Obtains the list of DNS servers used for each interface.
Register-DnsClient	Registers all the IP addresses on the computer on the configured DNS server.
Set-DnsClient	Sets the interface-specific DNS client configurations on the computer.
Set-DnsClientGlobalSetting	Configures the global DNS client settings, such as the suffix search list.
Set-DnsClientServerAddress	Configures the computer's network adapter with the IP addresses of the DNS server.
Set-NetIPAddress	Sets information about the IP address configuration.
Set-NetIPv4Protocol	Sets information about the IPv4 protocol configuration. Note that **Set-NetIPv6Protocol** returns information about the IPv6 protocol configuration.
Set-NetIPInterface	Modifies the IP interface properties.
Test-Connection	Runs connectivity tests similar to those used by ping.

Cmdlet	Description
Test-NetConnection	Displays the following:
	Results of a DNS lookup
	Listing of IP interfaces
	Option to test a TCP connection
	IPsec rules
	Confirmation of connection establishment
Resolve-Dnsname	Performs a DNS name query resolution for the specified name.

Understanding Routing

If you plan your DNS server environment to include the new DNS server policies, you should understand how routers and routing tables correlate with that. Routers send traffic to destination networks based on a set of data called *routing tables*. Routing tables contain the following:

- All routes of which the router is aware

- Information on which connections lead to different IP address ranges

- Priorities for connections to be used

- Rules for handling both typical and special cases of network traffic

Data stored in routing tables typically is dynamic. This means the data is updated through routing protocols such as Routing Information Protocol (RIP), Open Shortest Path First (OSPF), and Border Gateway Protocol (BGP).

Routing tables contain the following information:

- Network destination
- Network mask
- Gateway
- Interface
- Metric

For example, the entry in Table 3-6 in a routing table points any network traffic destined for the 10.10.0.0/16 network to the gateway at the IPv4 address of 172.16.0.1 with a hop of 1.

Table 3-6   Example of a Routing Table Entry

Network Destination	Netmask	Gateway	Hop
10.0.0.0	255.0.0.0	172.16.0.1	1

Routing with Windows Server 2016

As in older versions of Windows server, you can use a Windows Server 2016 server as a router between a local network and the DMZ or between the DMZ and the public Internet. Windows Server 2016 can be configured to act as a router by installing the Remote Access role with the Routing role service. In most real-world network environments, this is not the preferred solution; most companies use third-party routing solutions.

You can view and manipulate a routing table on a Windows Server 2016 server in the following ways.

You can view the routing table by typing the following PowerShell command:

```
Get-NetRoute -AddressFamily IPv4
```

To create a new routing table entry in the routing table, you can use the following PowerShell command:

```
New-NetRoute -InterfaceIndex 10 -DestinationPrefix 10.10.0.0/16
   -NextHop 192.168.1.1
```

You can change route settings with the **Set-NetRoute** cmdlet. For example, you can change hop values for existing routing entries.

TIP   You cannot modify the **DestinationPrefix** or **NextHop** properties of an existing route by using **Set-NetRoute**.

You still can use the older **route** command for routing table modifications.

To view the routing table, type the following at the command line:

```
route print
```

This command delivers output similar to the PowerShell cmdlet **Get-NetRoute**.

To modify the routing table, you also can use the **route** command with either the **Add**, **Delete**, or **Change** commands. The following command adds a new routing entry to the routing table:

```
route add 10.0.0.0 netmask 255.255.0.0 192.168.1.1 metric 5
```

In addition, you can use the Routing and Remote Access console to add a static route entry to the routing table of a Windows Server 2016 router:

Step 1.   Open the Routing and Remote Access console.

Step 2.   Expand the local server and then expand IPv4.

Step 3.   Right-click **Static Routes** and then select **Show IP Routing Table**.

Step 4.   To add a new route, perform the following steps from within the Routing and Remote Access console:

- Under IPv4, right-click **Static Routes**, and then click **New Static Route** (see Figure 3-2).

- Configure the static route with the appropriate interface, destination, network mask, and gateway.

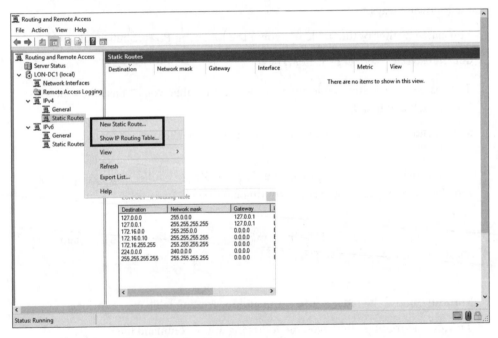

Figure 3-2   Adding a New Static Route

Split DNS

Split DNS enables a hostname to resolve to one IP address on the internal network and another on the external network. In a Split DNS network configuration scenario, some important DNS data, such as SRV resource records of internal domain controllers, should be inaccessible from outside the firewall for unknown clients. At the same time, DNS records of servers and services hosting Internet-level resources such as web, mail, or proxy servers must remain accessible for some Internet clients.

Split DNS, also known as split-brain DNS, uses the same domain name for Internet and internal domain member resources. Normally, the DNS server role is assigned to separate DNS servers for that. In a Split DNS configuration, one or more DNS servers are used for internal name resolution and one or more DNS servers are for Internet name resolution. In such a configuration, internal DNS clients typically are configured with the IP address of internal DNS servers. If an internal DNS client resolves names from resources in the DMZ, this is solved through forwarding. All records at the Internet-facing DNS servers in the DMZ are created manually.

When a query comes from the Internet through the external firewall to the DMZ DNS server requesting a resolution on any domain-level resource (SRV records), the Internet-facing DNS server rejects the query.

Normally, you configure firewall rules on the DMZ inside the firewall to reject all DNS (UDP port 53) queries from the DMZ network to the internal network.

NRPT and Split DNS

Since Windows Server 2012, DirectAccess can connect clients automatically to the corporate network with an Internet connection.

When you use DirectAccess for portable clients, you should realize that when the client cannot locate the URL of the Network Location Server (NLS), the Direct-Access client assumes that it is not connected to the intranet and that it is located on the Internet.

The Name Resolution Policy Table (NRPT) is used for DirectAccess name resolution on a DirectAccess client. When a DirectAccess client cannot communicate with an NLS server in the company's local network, it uses the DNS server listed in the NRPT for name resolution instead of using the DNS server on the TCP/IP settings on the network interface. You also have to know about the behavior of DirectAccess clients. Think about a DNS server in your DMZ. Suppose that you have configured DNS Policies there and you are wondering why these DNS Policies are not working for that DirectAccess client. The answer is that if that DMZ DNS server is not listed in the NRPT, the client will not contact that DNS server for name resolution. To ensure that DNS Policies on the DMZ DNS server will also work for a DirectAccess client that cannot communicate with the NLS server, you must add this DNS server to the NRPT. You do this using the DirectAccess server configuration tool, which transforms the performed NRPT settings into DirectAccess client Group Policy settings. The DirectAccess client must update its Group Policy settings to get the actual NRPT settings from an internal domain controller.

You also have to be careful when you have Split DNS configured because you need to add the FQDN of any Internet-level web server kept in the DMZ to the NRPT as a firewall exception rule.

- **NRPT instead of TCP/IP settings on network interface:** When the client cannot communicate with the NLS server, it uses the Name Resolution Policy Table (NRPT) for name resolution instead of using the TCP/IP settings on its network interface. The NRPT determines which DNS server should be used to resolve the names of resources they are accessing. If the DirectAccess client is internal, the client uses the TCP/IP DNS server settings of its network interface.

- **NRPT and Split DNS:** When you use DirectAccess for portable clients, be aware that when the client is deployed outside the internal network, it uses the NRPT for continued access to internal resources. This sends DNS name queries for internal resources to the Active Directory–integrated DNS servers. With Split DNS and DirectAccess clients, you need to add the FQDN of any Internet-level web servers kept in the perimeter network to the NRPT as a firewall exception rule.

DNS Policies

DNS Policies enable administrators to create rules that define how DNS servers respond to client queries based on different parameters (such as location, time of day, and transport protocol). This enables new traffic management scenarios, such as redirecting users to specific servers based on location, implementing split-brain DNS in a new way, blocking malicious domains, and ensuring that clients can resolve only specific names. The following list describes scenarios in which DNS Policies can be useful.

- **Traffic management:** Directs DNS clients to the closest datacenter or other datacenters based on the time of day

- **Application high availability:** Redirects DNS clients to the best endpoint for the application

- **Split-brain DNS:** Gives DNS clients a response based on whether they are internal or external

- **Filtering:** Blocks a list of malicious IP addresses or FQDNs

- **Forensics:** Redirects DNS clients to a sink hole instead of the destination computer they are trying to reach

DNS Policy Elements

To create DNS Policies, you must identify groups of records in a zone, groups of clients on a network, or other elements.

You can define policies that you apply based on the *client subnet* that generates the requests. For example, you might have a split-brain DNS scenario in which the name resolution request for www.pearson.com can be answered with an internal IP address for internal clients and a different IP address for external clients.

You also can use unique instances of a group of settings that control DNS server recursion, known as *a recursion scope*. The recursion scope holds a list of forwarders and specifies whether recursion is used. A DNS server can have multiple recursion scopes. You can use DNS server recursion policies to choose a recursion scope for a given set of queries. If the DNS server is not authoritative for certain queries, DNS server recursion policies let you control how to resolve those queries. In this case, you can specify which forwarders to use and whether to use recursion.

DNS zones can have multiple *zone scopes*, and each zone scope can contain its own set of DNS resource records. The same resource record can be present across multiple scopes, with different IP addresses depending on the scope. Additionally, zone transfers can be done at the zone scope level. This allows resource records from a zone scope in a primary zone to be transferred to the same zone scope in a secondary zone.

The following points summarize these DNS Policy elements:

- **Client subnet:** This is the IPv4 or IPv6 subnet from which queries are submitted to the DNS server.

- **Recursion scope:** This specifies the list of forwarders and whether recursion is enabled.

- **Zone scope:** A DNS zone can have multiple zone scopes, which each scope containing their own set of DNS records. The same record can be present in multiple scopes, with different IP addresses.

Types of DNS Policies and Differences

DNS Policies are divided by level and type. You can use *query resolution policies* to define how queries are handled and use *zone transfer policies* to define how zone transfers take place. Each policy type can be applied at the server level or the zone level. Recursion policies control how the DNS server performs recursion for a query. Recursion policies apply only when query processing reaches the recursion path. You can choose a value of *DENY* or *IGNORE* for recursion in a set of queries. Alternatively, you can choose a set of forwarders for a set of queries. You can use *recursion policies* to implement a split-brain DNS configuration. In this configuration, the DNS server performs recursion for a set of clients for a query but not for other clients for that query. Table 3-7 summarizes each type of DNS Policy.

Table 3-7   Types of DNS Policies

Query Resolution Policies	Recursion Policies	Zone Transfer Policies
Defines how incoming resolution queries are handled	Controls how the server performs recursion for a query	Controls whether a zone transfer is allowed

DNS Policy Parameters

DNS Policies provide a strong mechanism for controlling the DNS responses based on the criteria parameters in Table 3-8.

Table 3-8   DNS Policy Parameters

Criteria Parameter	Description
Client subnet	Name of a predefined client subnet. Used to verify the subnet from which the query was sent.
Transport protocol	Transport protocol used in the query. Possible entries are UDP and TCP.
Internet protocol	Network protocol used in the query. Possible entries are IPv4 and IPv6.
Server interface IP address	IP address of the network interface of the DNS server that received the DNS request.
FQDN	FQDN of a record in the query. A wildcard may be used.
Query type	Type of record being queried (A, SRV, TXT, and so on).
Time of day	Time of day the query is received.

These criteria can be combined with logical operators (AND/OR) to define policy expressions. When these expressions match, the policies are expected to perform one of the actions outlined in Table 3-9.

Table 3-9   DNS Policies Action Table

Action	Description
Ignore	The DNS server silently drops the query.
Deny	The DNS server replies to that query with a failure response.
Allow	The DNS server responds back with a traffic-managed response.

TIP   Server-level and zone transfer DNS Policies can have only the values *Deny* or *Ignore* as an action.

TIP   Recursion policies can be created only at the server level.

TIP   DNS zone transfer also transfers records added to a zone scope in a primary zone to the same zone scope in a secondary zone.

TIP   Don't mix up the terms! DNS Policies are a new feature of Windows Server 2016 that has nothing to do with Active Directory or local Group Policies.

Multiple Query Resolution DNS Policies

Because you can create multiple query resolution policies at the same level (with different processing order), the DNS server processes incoming queries in the following way:

1. The incoming query looks for all server-level policies and matches them one by one in order of their processing order until it finds a match.

2. If a server-level policy is matched, it is applied.

3. If a server-level policy is not matched and the DNS server is authoritative for the query, the zone-level policies are viewed.

4. If a matching zone-level policy is found, it is applied.

5. If the DNS server is not authoritative for the query, the recursion policies are relevant.

6. If a matching recursion policy is matched, it is applied.

Using DNS Policies Based on Location

Consider the following example for DNS Policies based on location: You have a zone named pearson.com and two subnets named LondonNet (192.168.1.0/24) and ParisNet (192.168.2.0/24). When clients try to reach www.pearson.com, you want clients performing queries from LondonNet to get the IP address 192.168.1.10 and clients performing queries from ParisNet to get the IP address 192.168.2.10. Clients from the LondonNet subnet should get a different IP address (in this case, another web server for www.pearson.com) than clients from the ParisNet subnet.

You can use the new Windows Server 2016 DNS server policy feature to implement such a scenario (based on location), to redirect users to specific servers:

Step 1.   Install the DNS Server with PowerShell:

```
Add-WindowsFeature -Name DNS -IncludeManagementTools
```

Step 2.   Create a zone for testing with PowerShell:

```
Add-DnsServerPrimaryZone -Name pearson.com -ZoneFile
   pearson.com.dns
```

Step 3.   Configure two client subnets with PowerShell:

```
Add-DnsServerClientSubnet -Name LondonNet -Ipv4Subnet
   192.168.1.0/24
```

```
Add-DnsServerClientSubnet -Name ParisNet -Ipv4Subnet
   192.168.2.0/24
```

Step 4.   List the client subnets:

```
Get-DnsServerClientSubnet
```

Step 5.   Divide the zone pearson.com into two zone scopes so that queries from different client subnets can be answered using different DNS resource records:

```
Add-DnsServerZoneScope -ZoneName pearson.com -Name
   LondonZoneScope
Add-DnsServerZoneScope -ZoneName pearson.com -Name ParisZoneScope
```

Step 6.   Display the Zone Scopes with the following PowerShell command:

```
Get-DnsServerZoneScope -ZoneName pearson.com
```

Step 7.   Add records to the zone scopes with the following PowerShell command:

```
Add-DnsServerResourceRecord -ZoneName pearson.com -A -name
   www -Ipv4Address 192.168.1.10
-ZoneScope LondonZoneScope
Add-DnsServerResourceRecord -ZoneName pearson.com -A -name
   www -Ipv4Address 192.168.2.10
-ZoneScope ParisZoneScope
```

Step 8.   To make it possible for everyone to access the servers, add the records to the default zone scope:

```
Add-DnsServerResourceRecord -ZoneName pearson.com -A -name
   www -Ipv4Address 192.168.1.10
Add-DnsServer ResourceRecord -ZoneName pearson.com -A -name
   www -Ipv4Address 192.168.2.10
```

Step 9.   List the records in each scope:

```
Get-DnsServerResourceRecord -ZoneName pearson.com -ZoneScope
  ParisZoneScope

Get-DnsServer ResourceRecord -ZoneName pearson.com -ZoneScope
  LondonZone Scope
```

Step 10.   Create DNS server policies:

```
Add-DnsServerQueryResolutionPolicy -Name LondonPolicy
  -Action ALLOW -ClientSubnet 'eq, LondonNet' -ZoneScope
  'LondonZoneScope,1' -ZoneName pearson.com

Add-DnsServerQuery ResolutionPolicy -Name ParisPolicy -Action
  ALLOW -ClientSubnet 'eq, ParisNet' -ZoneScope
  'ParisZoneScope,1' -ZoneName pearson.com
```

DNS Policies become effective immediately; you do not have to restart the service or reboot. After that, configuration queries from Paris should resolve to 192.168.2.10 and queries from London should resolve to 192.168.1.10.

Step 11.   To see the policies configured for zone pearson.com, use this command::

```
Get-DnsServerQueryResolutionPolicy pearson.com
```

Using DNS Policies for Split-Brain

A known DNS deployment is deemed split-brain (or split-horizon) when two versions of the same single zone exist, one for internal name resolution and the other for external name resolution (see Figure 3-3). Distributing one zone through different DNS servers is done for security. External users can resolve names only for external resources (servers inside the DMZ network) and are not allowed to access DNS records from internal resources. Internal users can resolve internal resources (mail servers, SharePoint servers, and so on).

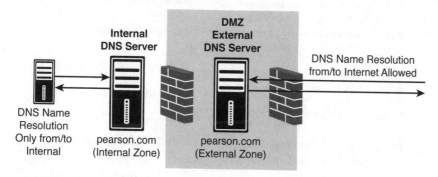

Figure 3-3   DNS Split-Brain Scenario

Using the new Windows Server 2016 DNS Policy feature, it is possible to configure the same scenario without using two DNS servers (see Figure 3-4).

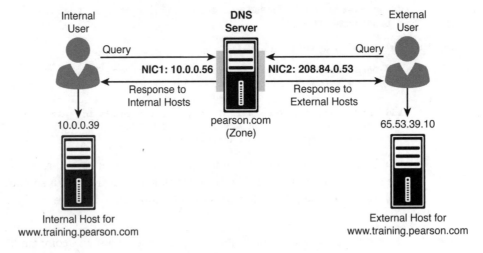

Figure 3-4   DNS Split-Brain with Windows Server 2016 DNS Policies

If the DNS server responsible for the pearson.com zone listens on two network interfaces (one with a public IP address of 208.84.0.53 for external queries and another with a private IP address of 10.0.0.56 for internal queries), the administrator can follow these steps to achieve split-brain DNS deployment through DNS Policies:

Step 1.   Create the scopes of the zone with PowerShell:

```
Add-DnsServerZoneScope -ZoneName "pearson.com" -Name "internal"
```

Step 2.   Add records to the zone scopes with PowerShell:

```
Add-DnsServerResourceRecord -ZoneName "pearson.com" -A -Name
   www.training -IPv4address "65.53.39.10"
Add-DnsServerResourceRecord -ZoneName "pearson.com" -A -Name
   www.training -IPv4address "10.0.0.39 -ZoneScope "internal"
```

No **-ZoneScope** parameter is used for the first resource record because it is added to the default zone scope.

Step 3.   Create the DNS Policies with PowerShell:

```
Add-DnsServerQueryResolutionPolicy -Name "SplitBrainZonePolicy"
-Action ALLOW -ServerInterface "eq, 10.0.0.56"
```

For mapping the default zone scope, no policy is required. When a request comes from an internal user, the DNS Policy **SplitBrainZonePolicy** allows the internal interface to receive the IP address 10.0.0.56 from the internal host. DNS queries received on the public network interface card of the DNS server get a response with the public IP address in the default zone scope (see Figure 3-5).

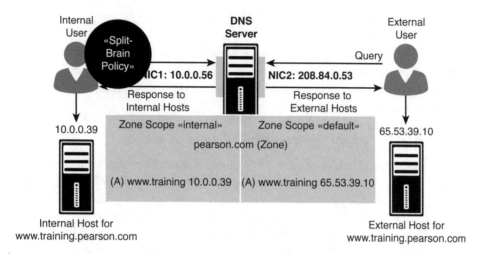

Figure 3-5   Configuring Split-Brain DNS Policies

Selective Recursion Control with DNS Policies

In Figure 3-5, the same DNS server was used for both external and internal clients; it simply responded with different answers. Some deployments require the same DNS server to perform recursive name resolution for the internal clients, apart from acting as the authoritative name server for pearson.com.

For this, recursion should be enabled on the DNS server. But when the DNS server is also listening to external queries, the recursion is enabled for external clients as well and the DNS server becomes an open resolver. This makes the server vulnerable.

No reason exists for why the pearson.com DNS server should do recursive name resolution for external clients. The solution is to do selective recursion control through DNS recursion policies. Recursion should be allowed for internal clients and blocked for external clients.

To implement a scenario with selective recursion control through DNS Policies, you can perform the following steps:

Step 1.   Create recursion scopes with PowerShell:

```
Set-DnsServerRecursionScope -Name -EnableRecursion $false
Add-DnsServerRecursionScope -Name "InternalClients"
  -EnableRecusion $true
```

Step 2.   Create recursion policies with PowerShell:

```
Add-DnsServerQueryResolutionPolicy -Name "SBRecursionPolicy"
  -Action ALLOW
-ApplyOnRecursion -RecursionScope "InternalClients"
  -ServerInterfaceIP "EQ, 10.0.0.39"
```

In Step 1, the default recursion setting was disabled; then a new recursion scope for internal clients was created and recursion was enabled for them. With Step 2, the DNS server recursion policy named **SBRecursionPolicy** was created for a set of queries matching certain criteria.

How Selective Recursion Control with DNS Policies Works

If the DNS server receives a query for which it is not authoritative (for example, www.nasa.org), the request is evaluated against the DNS server policies. If no query zone resolution policy exists for the request, the zone-level policies are not evaluated—instead, recursion policies are evaluated. The queries received on the private interface matching the **SBRecursionPolicy** criteria point to a recursion scope where recursion is enabled. Then the DNS server performs recursion (forwarding) to get the answer for www.nasa.org. If a query comes from the Internet to the external interface, default recursion settings are applied, preventing the server from acting as an open resolver for external clients.

Practice: Block Queries for a Domain with DNS Policies

You can block queries that come from a specific subnet. The following example creates a subnet for 172.16.0.0/16 and then creates a policy to ignore all queries from that subnet:

```
Add-DnsServerClientSubnet -Name "BlockedSubnet" -IPv4Subnet
  172.16.0.0/16
Add-DnsServerQueryResolutionPolicy -Name "Blackhole Policy" -Action
  IGNORE -ClientSubnet "EQ, BlockedSubnet"
```

Practice: Create a Server-Level Zone Transfer Policy

Allow zone transfer for any server on a specific subnet:

```
Add-DnsServerClientSubnet -Name "AllowedNet" -IPv4Subnet 172.16.0.0/16
Add-DnsServerZoneTransferPolicy -Name "SwissPolicy"
-Action IGNORE -ClientSubnet "ne, AllowedNet"
```

Practice: Create a Zone-Level Zone Transfer Policy

Ignore any zone transfer requests for pearson.com that come from a specific server interface (10.0.0.50):

```
Add-DnsServerZoneTransferPolicy -Name "IntTransfer" -Action IGNORE
    -ServerInterfaceIP "ne,10.0.0.50" -PassThru -ZoneName "pearson.com"
```

Practice: Block Queries from a Domain

Block any query with the domain baddomain.com:

```
Add-DnsServerQueryResolutionPolicy -Name "BLPol" -Action IGNORE -FQDN
    "EQ, *.baddomain.com" -PassThru
```

Practice: Allow Queries Only from a Domain

Allow only devices and computers in the domain pearson.com and child domains to query the DNS server:

```
Add-DnsServerQueryResolutionPolicy -Name "AllowListPolicyDomain"
    -Action IGNORE -FQDN "NE, *.pearson.com" -PassThru
```

Responses Based on Time of Day

You can use DNS Policies based on the time of the day to distribute traffic across different geographic instances. Suppose that you want to direct your network traffic in one time zone to alternate application servers that are in another time zone. For that, you can load-balance traffic across application instances during peak time periods when your primary servers are overloaded.

The example in Figure 3-6 uses the fictional company Pearson Gift Services, which provides online gifting solutions across the globe through the website pearsongiftservices.com.

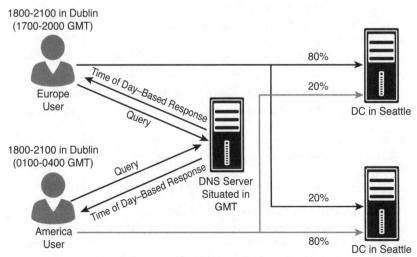

Figure 3-6 DNS Policies for Responses Based on Time of Day

The website is in two datacenters: Dublin and Seattle. After performing site analysis, IT pros discover that, between 6 p.m. and 9 p.m. local time, the web servers experience increased traffic. Pearson Gift Services wants to redirect 20 percent of the Dublin traffic to Seattle application servers and 20 percent of the Seattle traffic to Dublin application servers, but only between 6 p.m. and 9 p.m. for both locations. When the DNS server is configured with time-of-day DNS Policies, then between 6 p.m. and 9 p.m. at each location, the DNS server should do the following:

- Answer the first four queries with the IP address of the web server in the local datacenter

- Answer the fifth query with the IP address of the web server in the remote datacenter

For that, you should configure the following:

- Create the DNS client subnets

- Create the zone scopes for Seattle and Dublin

- Add the web server records to the zone scopes

- Create the DNS Policies, including processing order

These are the configuration steps for the scenario:

Step 1. Create the DNS client subnets with PowerShell:

```
Add-DnsServerClientSubnet -Name "AmericaSubnet" -IPv4Subnet
  "192.0.0.0/24, 182.0.0.0/24"
Add-DnsServerClientSubnet -Name "EuropeSubnet" -IPv4Subnet
  "141.1.0.0/24, 151.1.0.0/24"
```

Step 2. Create the zone scopes with PowerShell:

```
Add-DnsServerZoneScope -ZoneName "pearsongiftservices.com" -Name
  "SeattleScope"
Add-DnsServerZoneScope -ZoneName "pearsongiftservices.com" -Name
"DublinScope"
```

Step 3. Add records to the zone scopes with PowerShell:

```
Add-DnsServerResourceRecord -ZoneName "pearsongiftservices.com"
  -A
-Name "www" -IPv4Address "192.0.0.1" -ZoneScope "SeattleScope
Add-DnsServerResourceRecord -ZoneName "pearsongiftservices.com"
  -A
-Name "www" -IPv4Address "141.1.0.3" -ZoneScope "DublinScope"
```

Step 4. Create the DNS Policies with PowerShell:

```
Add-DnsServerQueryResolutionPolicy -Name "USA6To9Policy" -Action
  ALLOW -ClientSubnet "eq,
AmericaSubnet" -ZoneScope "SeattleScope,4; DublinScope,1"
  -TimeOfDay "EQ,01:00-04:00"
```

```
-ZoneName "pearsongift services.com" -ProcessingOrder 1
```
Add-DnsServerQueryResolutionPolicy -Name "EU6To9Policy" -Action
  ALLOW -ClientSubnet "eq, EuropeSubnet"
```
-ZoneScope "SeattleZScope,1; DublinScope,4" -TimeOfDay
  "EQ,17:00-20:00" -ZoneName "pearsongift services.com"
-ProcessingOrder 2
```
Add-DnsServerQueryResolutionPolicy -Name "USAPolicy"
```
-Action ALLOW -ClientSubnet "eq, America Subnet" -ZoneScope
  "SeattleScope,1" -ZoneName "pearson giftservices.com"
-ProcessingOrder 3
```
Add-DnsServerQueryResolutionPolicy -Name "EUPolicy"
```
-Action ALLOW -ClientSubnet "eq, EuropeSubnet" -ZoneScope
  "DublinScope,1" -ZoneName "pearsongiftservices.com"
-ProcessingOrder 4
```
Add-DnsServerQueryResolutionPolicy -Name "RestOfWorldPolicy"
  -Action ALLOW --ZoneScope
```
"DublinScope, 1; SeattleScope,1" -ZoneName
  "pearsongiftservices.com" -ProcessingOrder 5
```

Time-of-Day Responses with Azure App Server

You can use DNS Policies based on the time of the day to distribute application traffic across different geographical instances. You can direct traffic in one time zone to alternative application servers in another time zone. The alternative application servers also can be on an Azure virtual machine.

The example in Figure 3-7 again uses the fictional company Pearson Gift Services, which provides online gifting solutions across the globe through the website pearsongiftservices.com.

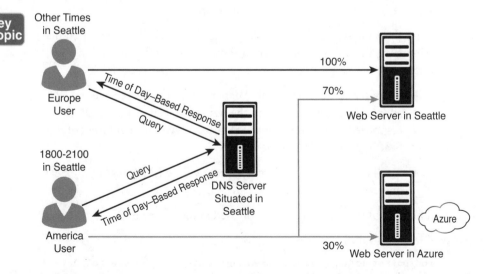

Figure 3-7 DNS Policies for Responses Based on Time of Day with Azure App Server

The website and the DNS server are hosted on a single on-premises datacenter in Seattle with a public IP address of 192.68.30.2. During a site analysis, IT professionals discover that, every evening between 6 p.m. and 9 p.m. local time, traffic increases to the Seattle web server. To ensure that pearsongiftservices.com customers get a responsive experience between 6 p.m. and 9 p.m., they rented an Azure virtual machine with an additional web server. The public IP address for this web server is 192.68.31.44. This web server is automatically turned on at 6 p.m. and off at 9 p.m. through Azure automation.

The DNS server should be configured with zone scopes and DNS Policies so that, between 6 p.m. and 9 p.m. every day, 30 percent of the queries are sent to the instance of the web server that is running in Azure.

These are the configuration steps for this scenario:

Step 1.   Create the scopes of the zone with PowerShell:

```
Add-DnsServerZoneScope -ZoneName "pearsongiftservices.com" -Name
   "AzureZoneScope"
```

Step 2.   Add records to the zone scopes with PowerShell:

```
Add-DnsServerResourceRecord -ZoneName "pearsongiftservices.com"
   -A
-Name "www" -IPv4address "192.68.31.44"
-ZoneScope "SeattleZoneScope"-TimeToLive 600
Add-DnsServerResourceRecord -ZoneName "pearsongiftservices.com"
   -A
-Name "www" -IPv4address "192.68.30.2"
```

No **-ZoneScope** parameter is used for the second resource record because it is added to the default zone scope.

After the zone scopes are created, you can create DNS Policies that distribute the incoming queries across these scopes so that the following occurs:

- From 6 p.m. to 9 p.m. daily, 30 percent of clients receive the IP address of the web server in the Azure datacenter in the DNS response, while 70 percent of clients receive the IP address of the Seattle on-premise web server.

- At all other times, all the clients receive the IP address of the Seattle on-premise web server.

The time of the day should be expressed in local time of the DNS server.

Step 3.   Create the DNS Policies with PowerShell:

```
Add-DnsServerQueryResolutionPolicy -Name "Pearson6to9Policy"
-Action ALLOW -ZoneScope
```

```
"pearsongiftservices.com,7; AzureZoneScope,3" -TimeOfDay
"EQ,18:00-21:00" -ZoneName
"pearsongiftservices.com" -ProcessingOrder 1
```

Explanation: **-ZoneScope "pearsongiftservices.com,7; AzureZoneScope,3" -TimeOfDay "EQ,18:00-21:00"** configures the DNS server with a ZoneScope and weight combination that instructs the DNS server to send the IP address of the Seattle web server 70 percent of the time and send the IP address of the Azure web server 30 percent of the time.

Exam Preparation Tasks

Review All the Key Topics

Review the most important topics in the chapter, noted with the Key Topics icon in the outer margin of the page. Table 3-10 lists these key topics and the page numbers where each is found.

Table 3-10 Key Topics for Chapter 3

Key Topic Element	Description	Page Number
List	DNS Policies usage scenarios	138
Table 3-7	Types of DNS Policies	140
Table 3-8	DNS Policy Parameters	140
Tips	DNS Policies tips	141
Section	Multiple Query Resolution DNS Policies	141
Step List	Using DNS Policies based on location	142
Section	Using DNS Policies for Split-Brain	143
Step List	Using DNS Policies for split-brain	144
Step List	Selective recursion control with DNS Policies	145
Practice	Block Queries for a Domain with DNS Policies	146
Practice	Create a Server-Level Zone Transfer Policy	146
Practice	Create a Zone-Level Zone Transfer Policy	147
Practice	Block Queries from a Domain	147
Practice	Allow Queries Only from a Domain	147
Figure 3-6	DNS Policies for Responses Based on Time of Day	147

Key Topic Element	Description	Page Number
Step List	DNS Policies for responses based on time of day	148
Figure 3-7	DNS Policies for Responses Based on Time of Day with Azure App Server	149
Step List	DNS Policies for time-of-day responses with Azure App Server	150

Complete the Tables and Lists from Memory

Print a copy of Appendix B, "Memory Tables" (on the book's website), or at least the section for this chapter, and complete the tables and lists from memory. Appendix C, "Memory Tables Answer Key," also on the website, includes completed tables and lists to check your work.

Definition of Key Terms

Define the following key terms from this chapter and check your answers in the Glossary:

NRPT, DNS Policies, DHCP options, DHCP name protection, Split DNS, recursion policies, transfer policies, query resolution policies, server-level zone transfer policy

End-of-Chapter Review Questions

1. You are the administrator of the Pearson Corporation. You are responsible for your name resolution environment.

Site	Subnet	Subnet Name	Important Server IP Number	Subnet: Member of Zone Scope?	Server: Member of Zone Scope?	Zone Scope	DNS Server Policy
DE	172.16.1.0/24	DESubnet1	172.16.1.5	No	Yes	DEScope	DEPolicy
DE	172.16.2.0/24	DESubnet2	172.16.2.8	Yes	Yes	DEScope	DEPolicy
CH	172.16.3.0/24	CHSubnet1	172.16.3.12	Yes	Yes	CHScope	CHPolicy
CH	172.16.4.0/24	CHSubnet2	172.16.4.23	Yes	Yes	CHScope	CHPolicy
NY	172.16.5.0/24	NYSubnet1	172.16.5.56	Yes	Yes	NYScope	NYPolicy
NY	172.16.6.0/24	NYSubnet2	172.16.6.60	No	Yes	NYScope	NYPolicy
LA	172.16.7.0/24	LASubnet1	172.16.7.22	Yes	Yes	LAScope	LAPolicy
LA	172.16.8.0/24	LASubnet2	172.16.8.12	No	Yes	LAScope	LAPolicy

Subnets 172.16.3.0/24 and 172.16.6.0/24 are identified as being infected with malware. You want to block name resolution through DNS server policy. Which PowerShell cmdlet should you use to accomplish this?

- **a.** **Add-DnsServerQuery ResolutionPolicy -Name MalwarePolicy -Action DENY -ClientSubnet 'EQ, CHSubnet1' -Disable $false**

- **b.** **Add-DnsServerQuery ResolutionPolicy -Name MalwarePolicy -Action DENY -ClientSubnet 'EQ, NYSubnet2' -Disable $false**

- **c.** **Add-DnsServerQuery ResolutionPolicy -Name MalwarePolicy -Action IGNORE -ClientSubnet 'EQ, CHSubnet1' -Disable $false**

- **d.** **Set-DnsServerQuery ResolutionPolicy -Name NYPolicy -Action IGNORE -ClientSubnet 'EQ, NYSubnet2' -Disable $true**

2. You want to allow DNS queries only from clients from the subnet AllowedNET (172.16.0.0/16). You create a DNS server query resolution policy with the following command: **Add-DnsServer QueryResolutionPolicy -Name "AllowSubnetPolicy"-Action IGNORE -ClientSubnet "NE, AllowedNET" -PassThru**. However, clients from all subnets still successfully can send queries to your DNS server. What additional PowerShell cmdlet should you use to solve that problem?

- **a.** **Add-DnsServerClientSubnet**

- **b.** **Remove-DnsServerClientSubnet**

- **c.** **Add-DnsServerResourceRecord**

- **d.** **Add-DnsServerZoneScope**

3. You have a DNS server named DNS1 (10.0.0.10) with an AD-integrated DNS zone for pearson.com, and you have configured three secondary DNS servers named DNS2 (10.0.0.49), DNS3 (10.0.0.50), and DNS4 (10.0.0.51) as secondary DNS servers. You want to restrict zone transfer from DNS1 only to DNS3 through DNS server zone transfer policies. Which command can you use?

- **a.** **Add-DnsServerZoneTransferPolicy -Name "IntTransfer" -Action IGNORE -ServerInterfaceIP "ne,10.0.0.10" -PassThru -ZoneName "pearson.com"**

- **b.** **Add-DnsServerZoneTransferPolicy -Name "IntTransfer" -Action IGNORE -ServerInterfaceIP "ne,10.0.0.50" -PassThru -ZoneName "pearson.com"**

- **c.** **Add-DnsServerZoneTransferPolicy -Name "IntTransfer" -Action ALLOW -ServerInterfaceIP "ne,10.0.0.49" -PassThru -ZoneName "pearson.com"**

- **d.** **Add-DnsServerZoneTransferPolicy -Name "IntTransfer" -Action ALLOW -ServerInterfaceIP "ne,10.0.0.51" -PassThru -ZoneName "pearson.com"**

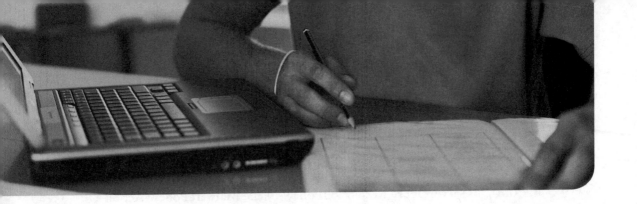

This chapter covers the following subjects:

- **DNSSEC planning:** This section gives a short overview of the most important topics involved in planning the deployment of DNSSEC.

- **Enabling DNSSEC:** You learn about the different possibilities for enabling DNSSEC on Windows Server 2016.

- **DNSSEC functionality:** DNSSEC protects clients that are making DNS queries from accepting false DNS responses. You learn about the core functionality of DNSSEC.

- **DNSSEC Zone Signing Wizard:** The DNSSEC Zone Signing Wizard simplifies DNSSEC configuration. The wizard enables you to choose the zone signing parameters step by step.

- **Trust anchors:** A trust anchor for DNSSEC is represented by a public key. The TrustAnchors zone on a Windows Server 2016 DNS server stores preconfigured public keys that are associated with a specific zone.

- **KSK rollover process:** This section explains the rollover update process behind the scenes and covers that subject to promote a better DNSSEC understanding.

- **DNSSEC clients:** This section covers configuration of DNSSEC clients through the Name Resolution Policy Table and compares the behavior of both security-aware and non-security-aware DNSSEC clients.

- **DNSSEC and delegation:** Delegations establish a chain of authentication for child zones. This section looks at DNSSEC delegation scenarios.

- **Chain of trust:** This section covers the chain of trust and explains the dependencies among the different kinds of keys and trust anchors.

- **Redesigning DNSSEC zone:** Information includes details on the reconfiguration of signed DNSSEC zones in the case of re-signing.

- **DS records configuration:** This section explains the use and advantages of DS records and shows you how to add and configure DS records.

- **DNSSEC resource records:** In this section, you learn about the most important DNSSEC-relevant resource record types and their purposes.

## CHAPTER 4

Understanding and Configuring DNSSEC

This chapter covers the use, installation, and configuration of Windows Server 2016 DNSSEC. It explains DNSSEC functionality issues and all the relevant subjects you need to get a better understanding of DNSSEC and its components for real-world configuration and for the exam.

You learn how to enable DNSSEC with the DNSSEC Wizard and how to configure it with PowerShell commands. You learn about trust anchors, DNSSEC resource record types and their use, and the configuration of DNSSEC clients through the Name Resolution Policy Table.

Windows Server 2016 DNSSEC offers some DNSSEC enhancements to isolate the key management process from primary DNS servers that are not the key masters of the zone. The process of signing key generation, storage, rollover, retirement, and deletion now can be done only from the key master; other primary servers can continue the zone signing by accessing these keys. In addition, a new feature is support for AD-integrated DNS scenarios, including using the DNS dynamic update feature together with DNSSEC signed zones.

In this chapter, you learn about the updated DNSSEC standards, automated trust anchor distribution through Active Directory, and automated trust anchor rollover support per RFC 5011 and the easier extraction of the root trust anchor with Windows Server 2016.

"Do I Know This Already?" Quiz

The "Do I Know This Already?" quiz enables you to assess whether you should read this entire chapter or simply jump to the "Exam Preparation Tasks" section for review. If you are in doubt, read the entire chapter. Table 4-1 outlines the major headings in this chapter and the corresponding "Do I Know This Already?" quiz questions. You can find the answers in Appendix A, "Answers to the 'Do I Know This Already?' Quizzes and End-of-Chapter Review Questions."

Table 4-1 "Do I Know This Already?" Foundation Topics Section-to-Question Mapping

Foundation Topics Section	Questions Covered in This Section
Enabling DNSSEC	1
DNSSEC Zone Signing Wizard	2
Trust Anchors	3, 4
ZSK/KSK Rollover Process	5, 6
DNSSEC Clients	7
DNSSEC and Delegation	8
Chain of Trust	9
DNSSEC Record Types	10

CAUTION The goal of self-assessment is to gauge your mastery of the topics in this chapter. If you do not know the answer to a question or are only partially sure of the answer, you should mark that question as wrong for purposes of the self-assessment. Giving yourself credit for an answer you correctly guess skews your self-assessment results and might provide you with a false sense of security.

1. You want to enable DNSSEC verification for your Windows Server 2016 DNS server. Which setting or command can you use?

    a. Advanced tab of DNS server properties

    b. **(Get-DnsServer).DNSSetting.EnableDnsSec**

    c. **Get-DnsServerDnsSecZoneSetting**

    d. **DnsCmd.exe** *<servername>* **/Config /enableDNSSEC 2**

2. You are responsible for the domain pearson.com. You don't use hardware solutions to safeguard cryptographic keys. You have three domain controllers with the DNS server role installed: DC1, DC2, and DC3 (RODC). The DNSSEC key master DC1 for the file-based zone pearson.com goes offline. You try to transfer the DNSSEC key master role from DC1 to DC2. You get the following message: "The DNS server DC1.pearson.com is the Key Master, Status: Inactive." DC1 cannot be recovered. You want to seize the key master role to DC2. You not want to redistribute trust anchors. From which location can DC2 get private key data for the zone?

    a. Certificate

    b. Active Directory on DC2

    c. Active Directory on DC3

    d. HSM

3. You want to add a DS record to your Windows Server 2016 DNS server. Which of the following configuration options is not a valid solution?

    a. DNSSEC Zone Signing Wizard

    b. DS resource record set

    c. DNS Manager

    d. PowerShell

4. You unsign the zone pearson.com on a Windows Server 2016 DNS server. After doing so, you notice that validation requests fail and DNS resolution for the zone fails. Which component do you need to remove to solve the problem?

    a. RRSIG records

    b. Trust anchor

    c. NRPT settings

    d. RRset

5. You plan to roll over a DNSSEC KSK that is waiting for a parent DS update. You manually have updated the DS record in the parent zone. Now you want to force the rollover. Which PowerShell cmdlet can you use?

    a. Invoke-DnsServerSigningKeyRollover

    b. Step-DnsServerSigningKeyRollover

    c. Enable-DnsServerSigningKeyRollover

    d. Grant-HgsKeyProtectorAccess

6. You want to plan your ZSK/KSK rollover process. Select the preferred rollover method for each kind of key. (Choose two.)

    a. ZSK: Prepublishing

    b. ZSK: Double signing

    c. KSK: Prepublishing

    d. KSK: Double signing

7. You have configured both Enable DNSSEC in This Rule and Require DNS Clients to Check That Name and Address Data Has Been Validated by the DNS Server in the Default Domain Policy of your domain pearson.com. Your DNSSEC-configured DNS is named DNS1. In the Default Domain Policy, you add a rule for sec.pearson.com with *DNSSEC (Validation)* = *"Yes"* and *DNSSEC (IPsec)* = *"No"*. You want to ensure that the value for DNSSECValidationRequired is True on client1 (Windows 10). Which PowerShell command can you use? (Choose two.)

    a. **Gpupdate /force**

    b. **Resolve-dnsname dc1.sec.pearson.com -server dns1 -DNSSECok**

    c. **Get-dnsclientnrptpolicy**

    d. **Resolve-dnsname -name sec.pearson.com -type dnskey -server dns1 -DNSSECok**

8. Your environment consists of one parent domain named pearson.com and two child domains named usa.pearson.com and eu.pearson.com. You must plan the DNSSEC chain of trust, including delegations. Which statement is correct?

    a. One DS trust anchor is installed for the child zone.

    b. One DS trust anchor is installed for the parent zone.

    c. One trust anchor is installed for every zone that a caching DNS server can validate.

    d. Two trust anchors are installed for the parent zone.

9. You have one domain named pearson.com and a child domain named eu.pearson.com. You want to start with your DNSSEC chain of trust configuration. On your root Windows Server 2016 DNS server, you see in Trust Points and the root folder that no DS record exists. Which configuration can you use to install a root trust anchor using the RSA/SHA256 algorithm as the starting point of your chain of trust? (Choose two.)

    a. **Import-DnsServerTrustAnchor**

    b. **Dnscmd /retrieveroottrustanchors**

    c. **Add-DnsServerTrustAnchor -Root**

    d. **Add-DnsServerTrustAnchor -KeyProtocol DNSSEC -CryptoAlgorithm RsaSha256**

10. You want to produce a statement if you try to find a record that does not appear on your Windows Server 2016 DNS server. You also want to use hashing security for existing hosts. Which kinds of resource records do you need? (Choose two.)

    a. DNSKEY

    b. RRSIG

    c. NSEC

    d. NSEC3

    e. NSEC3PARAM

Foundation Topics

DNSSEC Planning

Domain Name System Security Extensions (DNSSEC) enables a DNS zone and all records in the zone to be signed cryptographically. Clients then can validate the DNS response. DNS is often subject to attacks such as spoofing and cache tampering. DNSSEC helps protect against these threats and provides a more secure DNS infrastructure. DNSSEC protects clients that are making DNS queries from accepting false DNS responses. When a DNS server with a DNSSEC-protected zone gets a query, the server returns the digital signatures along with the requested records. A resolver or another server can obtain the public key of the public/private key pair from a trust anchor and then validate that the responses are authentic and have not been tampered with. To do this, the resolver or server must be configured with a *trust anchor* for either the signed zone or a parent of the signed zone. A trust anchor is an entity represented by a public key. The TrustAnchors zone stores preconfigured public keys that are associated with a specific zone.

You also need the Name Resolution Policy Table (NRPT) to control the DNS client behavior for sending DNS queries and processing the responses from those queries. Group Policy is the preferred method of configuring the NRPT.

To deploy DNSSEC for a zone on a Windows Server 2016 DNS server, you can use the DNSSEC Configuration Wizard of PowerShell.

DNSSEC Requirements

A DNSSEC deployment does not require all DNS servers to be Windows Server 2012 or a later operating system to host a signed zone. But it is recommended to have all DNS servers hosting the signed zone upgraded to a minimum of Windows Server 2012 or Windows Server 2012 R2 before validation is enabled on resolvers; only one authoritative DNS server running Windows Server 2012 or Windows Server 2012 R2 is required. For a DNS deployment, you must choose the zone to protect with DNSSEC, choose a DNSSEC key master (the server where you will initiate the DNSSEC parameter values), sign the zone, and then verify the zone signing. If the zone is an AD-integrated zone, you must verify the replication of the signed zone. You also must configure the DNS clients and which DNS clients will require DNSSEC validation to be performed for DNS queries in this zone. You must deploy the trust anchors to all nonauthoritative DNS servers that will perform validation for the zone. And you must deploy the NRPT to DNSSEC clients. In addition, you should review the impact of zone signing with DNSSEC on your DNS servers and infrastructure. Table 4-2 lists some of the most important DNSSEC requirements.

Table 4-2   DNSSEC Requirements

Category	Requirement	Details
Operating system	Windows Server 2012 or later.	DNS servers must be running Windows Server 2012 or a later operating system to sign a zone with DNSSEC or validate DNSSEC signatures.
		Mixed-mode environment is supported, which means that a server running Windows Server 2008 R2 can host a static offline-signed zone, but DNSSEC settings on a zone signed with Windows Server 2008 R2 cannot be modified by DNS servers running Window Server 2012 or later.
		A zone signed on Windows Server 2012 or later is loaded as an unsigned zone on a secondary or AD-integrated DNS server running Windows Server 2008 R2.
Server roles	DNS server role.	The DNS server role must be installed and running.
		To host an AD-integrated DNS zone, the DNS server must also be a domain controller.
		Additional roles and role services are optional.
Features	Features are required to perform administrative tasks.	The Group Policy Management utility is required to configure the NRPT.
		DNS Server Tools are required to sign or unsign a zone using DNS Manager, Windows PowerShell, or **dnscmd.exe**.

Category	Requirement	Details
Network	Same as for the DNS protocol.	DNS servers can be on the same network or on different networks.
		Static IP addresses are configured on all network adapters.
EDNS0	DNS servers must support EDNS0.	EDNS0 must be enabled on all DNS servers that will host or validate DNSSEC-signed zones.
		EDNS0 enables large (greater than 512-byte) UDP packet support in DNS, which is required to send DNSSEC-enabled DNS responses.
		Network infrastructure must be capable of passing large UDP-formatted network packets.
DNS servers	At least one primary, authoritative DNS server is required.	One or more primary, authoritative DNS servers are required to sign or unsign a zone with DNSSEC.
		At least one primary, authoritative DNS server is required to be the key master.
		Additional DNS servers are optional and can be primary, secondary, or resolving DNS servers.
DNS zones	At least one primary DNS zone is required.	Forward and reverse lookup zones can be signed with DNSSEC.
		Zones can be Active Directory–integrated or file backed.
		When a zone is signed on a DNS server running Windows Server 2012 or a later operating system, the zone automatically is signed on all other primary DNS servers running Windows Server 2012 or later.
		A secondary DNS server depends on the primary DNS server to sign the zone and transfers a signed version of the zone from the primary server that supports DNSSEC validation.
Domain membership	Not required.	DNS servers can be workgroup or domain members. Workgroup computers cannot host AD-integrated DNS zones.

Identifying Goals

The first consideration with DNSSEC-staged deployments is to determine your goals. Possible goals follow:

- **Security improvements:** DNSSEC signing can protect against DNS spoofing attacks.

- **Compliance with corporate policies:** Your company might have security policies that require DNSSEC.

- **Government mandates:** Your government might require you to use DNSSEC.

- **Proof of concept:** Deploy DNSSEC in a test environment to learn about the technology.

DNSSEC Staging

DNSSEC deployment does not require that all DNS servers run at least Windows Server 2012 or later to host a signed zone. Only DNS servers running Windows Server 2012 or a later operating system will host a signed copy of a zone that was signed using Windows Server 2012 or Windows Server 2012 R2. Servers running earlier versions of Windows will host an unsigned version of the zone. In a mixed-mode Active Directory environment, with some DNS servers running Windows Server 2012 or a later operating system and some DNS servers running Windows Server 2008 R2 or a previous operating system, the Active Directory schema must be upgraded before signing a DNS zone. Schema update occurs automatically if you promote a computer running Windows Server 2012 or Windows Server 2012 R2 to be a domain controller.

You can use the following DNSSEC deployment steps to stage DNSSEC:

Step 1. **Choose a zone.** Start by signing a single zone or only a few zones. The zones should be small enough to monitor easily, but of sufficient size to enable thorough testing.

Step 2. **Choose a key master.** Select a primary, authoritative DNS server to be the key master for your zone. This is the server where you will initiate zone signing, and it should be online at all times.

Step 3. **Choose methods and settings.** Decide whether you want to use DNS Manager or Windows PowerShell to sign the zone, and document the DNSSEC parameter values that you use.

Step 4. **Sign the zone.** Use the methods and settings that you have chosen to initiate zone signing on the key master and to monitor progress.

Step 5. **Verify zone signing.** Verify that zone signing was successful on the key master. If the zone is Active Directory–integrated, verify that replication of the signed zone was successful. If secondary servers are configured, verify that zone transfers were successful. Also verify that the zone functions as expected. Signing a zone with DNSSEC does not affect your capability to add, delete, or update resource records.

Step 6. **Choose DNS clients.** Select which DNS clients will require DNSSEC validation performed for DNS queries in this zone. The choice of DNS clients also affects which DNS servers will require trust anchors. DNS clients that require validation must use DNS servers that have valid trust anchors for the zone.

Step 7. **Deploy trust anchors.** Deploy trust anchors to all nonauthoritative DNS servers that will perform validation of DNS queries for the zone. If applicable, this includes deploying DS records to DNS registrars that manage parent DNS zones.

Step 8. **Configure and deploy name resolution policy.** If desired, deploy name resolution policy in your environment. Configure the NRPT to require validation of DNS queries for the signed zone, and deploy this policy only to DNS clients that use DNS servers that are capable of DNSSEC validation. If some authoritative DNS servers in your environment are not capable of hosting a signed version of the zone, ensure that these DNS servers are not queried when DNSSEC validation is required.

Step 9. **Verify name resolution policy.** Verify that NRPT settings are applied to DNS clients and that all DNS queries were successful.

Step 10. **Monitor and manage.** Review the impact that zone signing has on your DNS server and support infrastructure. Initiate the key rollover process or wait for automated key rollover to occur and verify that the zone was successfully re-signed. Redistribute trust anchors as needed after key rollover.

Enabling DNSSEC

Windows Server 2016 DNS Security Extensions (DNSSEC) is an advanced security feature that provides a way to protect DNS responses to DNS client queries so that malicious users cannot tamper with them. DNSSEC does not encrypt DNS data. Instead, it enables cryptographic signing of both a DNS zone and all the records in that zone so that DNSSEC-enabled clients can validate the DNS response. DNS is often subject to various attacks, such as spoofing and cache tampering. DNSSEC helps protect against these threats and provides a more secure DNS infrastructure. In Windows Server 2016, you easily can enable and configure DNSSEC through the DNSSEC Zone Signing Wizard. Figure 4-1 displays the first page of the wizard.

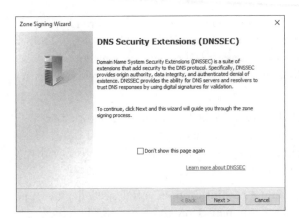

Figure 4-1   Windows Server 2016 DNSSEC Zone Signing Wizard

TIP   Previous Windows Server versions used the Advanced tab of DNS server properties to accomplish DNSSEC validation. In Windows Server 2016, this setting is no
longer present. Instead, you can verify DNSSEC status with the following Power-
Shell command:

```
(Get-DnsServer).DNSSetting.EnableDNSSEC
```

In this example, DNSSEC validation is disabled (Dword: 0). If you want to enable
DNSSEC validation with dnscmd.exe, you must configure the value to *1*.

You also can modify and check the status of this setting with the **dnscmd.exe** utility
using the following command:

```
Dnscmd /info /enableDNSSEC

Query result:
Dword: 0(00000000)
Command completed successfully.
Dnscmd /config /enableDNSSEC 1

Query result:
Dword: 1(00000001)
Command completed successfully.
```

DNSSEC Functionality

A known attack involves intercepting DNSSEC and tampering with DNS query responses. If malicious users alter DNS responses or use spoofed responses to point clients to their own servers, they can get unwanted access to sensitive information of your organization. Any service that relies on DNS for the initial connection is vulnerable. DNSSEC protects clients that are making DNS queries from accepting false DNS responses. When a DNS server that hosts a digitally signed zone receives a query, it returns the digital signatures and requested records. A resolver or another server can obtain the public key of the public/private key pair from a trust anchor (in DNS, the trust anchor is the DNSKEY or DS resource record) and validates that the responses are authentic and have not been tampered with. To do this, you must configure the resolver or server with a trust anchor for the signed zone or for a parent of the signed zone.

DNSSEC and RODCs

In Windows Server 2008, Windows Server 2008 R2, Windows Server 2012, Windows Server 2012 R2, and also Windows Server 2016, read-only domain controllers (RODCs) host AD-integrated copies of all DNS zones, but a zone on an RODC always is read-only. A DNS server on an RODC cannot make any updates to the zone that it hosts. Updates can occur only through AD replication from other DNS servers.

When an AD-integrated zone is signed with DNSSEC, the private keys are also replicated to all DNS servers running DCs, with one exception: Private keys are not replicated to an RODC because RODCs are intended to operate in an insecure environment.

If an RODC identifies a DNSSEC-signed zone in Active Directory, it does not load the zone as an AD-integrated zone. Instead, it creates a secondary copy of the zone. Then the RODC uses the closest domain controller as the primary DNS server. The problem is, you manually have to allow a zone transfer on that primary DNS server for the DNSSEC-signed zone so that the RODC can transfer the zone data. If the zone transfer is not enabled, an error occurs. Figure 4-2 illustrates that behavior.

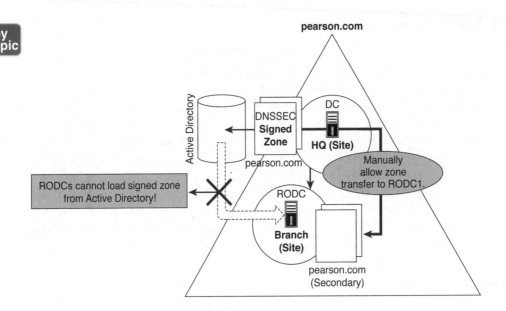

Figure 4-2   RODC and DNSSEC

DNSSEC Zone Signing Wizard

Since Windows Server 2012, the DNSSEC Zone Signing Wizard helps to simplify the DNSSEC configuration and signing process and to enable online signing. Figure 4-3 shows where you can start to configure signing a zone with the DNSSEC Zone Signing Wizard.

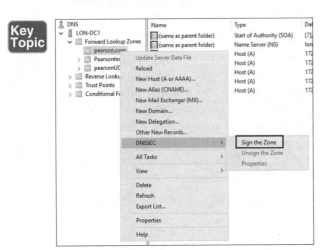

Figure 4-3   Windows Server 2016 DNSSEC Sign the Zone Setting

The wizard enables you to choose the zone-signing parameters, as you saw in Chapter 2, "Creating and Configuring DNS Zones and Records." If you choose to configure the zone-signing settings instead of using parameters from an existing zone or using default values, you can use the wizard to configure settings such as these:

- Key signing key (KSK) options

- Zone signing key (ZSK) options

- Trust anchor distribution options

- Signing and polling parameters

The following figures explain the detailed settings of the DNSSEC Zone Signing Wizard.

Figure 4-4 shows the Signing Options page of the DNSSEC Zone Signing Wizard. You can choose among the following signing options:

- Customize Zone Signing Parameters

- Sign the Zone with Parameters of an Existing Zone

- Use Default Settings to Sign the Zone

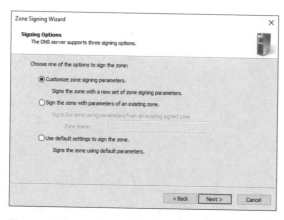

Figure 4-4   Signing Options Page of the DNSSEC Zone Signing Wizard on a Windows Server 2016 DNS Server

If you select Use Default Settings to Sign the Zone, you get the default settings shown in Figures 4-5 through 4-9.

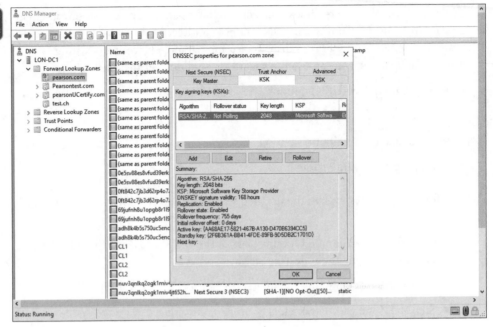

Figure 4-5 KSK Default Settings

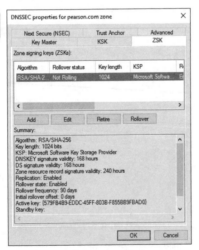

Figure 4-6 ZSK Default Settings

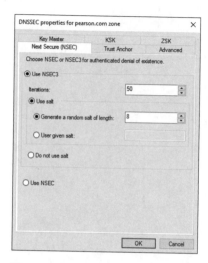

Figure 4-7 Next Secure (NSEC) Default Settings

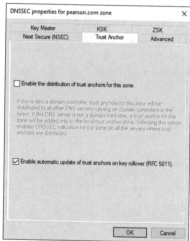

Figure 4-8 Trust Anchor Default Settings

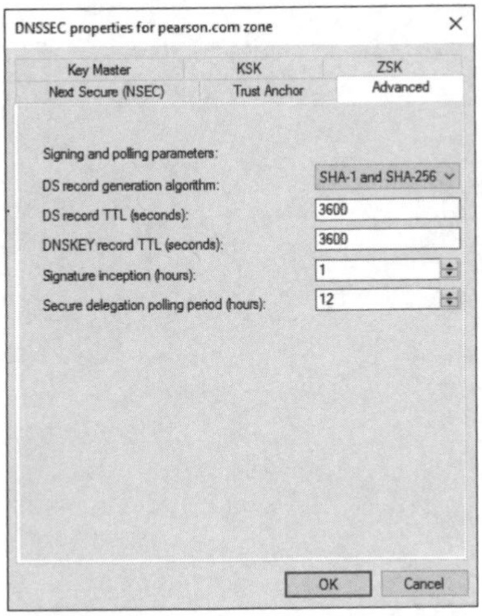

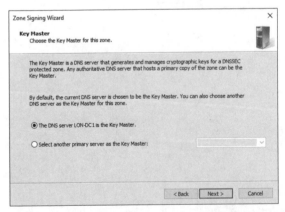

Figure 4-9   Advanced Default Settings

Key Master

The key master is the server that generates/maintains keys for a signed DNS zone. Each signed zone has one key master, and a single server can be the key master for multiple zones. After a zone has been signed, the key master role can be moved to another DNS server. This new server must meet the following requirements:

- It is running Windows Server 2012 or later.

- It is authoritative for the zone in question.

- It hosts a primary (writeable) copy of the zone.

Figure 4-10 shows the Key Master page of the DNSSEC Zone Signing Wizard. You can choose your DNS server or another DNS server as the key master.

Figure 4-10   Key Master Page of the DNSSEC Zone Signing Wizard on a Windows Server 2016 DNS Server

Transferring the Key Master

You can transfer the DNSSEC key master role to another DNS server. The new key master does not have to be a DC; however, this adds security for the private key data. If a non-DC becomes the new DNSSEC key master, you should ensure that only the DNS server role is installed on the server, to minimize attack possibilities. These are the two different key master transferring scenarios:

- Online key master transfer
- Offline key master transfer

If the zone's key master is online, it can be transferred to another DNS server through the Use the Following DNS Server as the Key Master setting in the Key Master tab of the DNSSEC properties in DNS Manager. There you can select the appropriate server from the drop-down list or simply type the desired server's name into the field.

If the key master goes offline and cannot be recovered, it is still possible to move the role to another server. This is known as *seizing* the role. When you want to seize the key master role, the new server must have access to the zone's existing private key data. This is the case if the keys are stored in AD (only for AD-integrated zones) or another shared location, such as a certificate or hardware security module (HSM). If the zone's private key data is not available, the role can still be seized, but new keys must be generated and the zone must be re-signed with them. Any distributed trust anchors for the zone must then be redistributed.

Suppose that you have two DCs named DC1 and DC2 with a DNS server and an AD-integrated DNSSEC-signed zone pearson.com installed. DC1 goes offline. On DC2, in the DNS Manager console in the DNSSEC properties, the following message displays after a delay:

```
Unable to load DNSSEC settings for zone DNSSEC-pearson.com from Key
   Master DC1.pearson.com. Do you want to load DNSSEC settings from DNS
   server DC1?
```

You know that DC1 is not online, but you select Yes. The Key Master tab appears and you see the following message:

```
The DNS server DC1.pearson.com is the Key Master, Status: Inactive.
```

Select the Use the Following DNS Server as the Key Master setting and select dc2.pearson.com as the new Key Master. After that, the following message appears:

```
The following is the summary of changes made on the zone
   DNSSEC-pearson.com: The Key Master setting has been changed to
   dc2.pearson.com. Click Yes to proceed or No to abort the operation.
```

If DC2 cannot locate the zone's private key data, a dialog box appears indicating that new keys must be generated, the zone must be re-signed, and trust anchors must be redistributed. Click Yes to seize the role anyway. If you proceed, new keys will be automatically generated. You must manually re-sign the zone to generate new keys. When the role has been seized, you get the following message:

```
The Key master for the zone DNSSEC-pearson.com has been updated
   successfully.
```

If DC1 (old Key Master) comes back online, it automatically discovers that it is no longer the key master and operates normally. No additional configuration is necessary.

You also can seize the key master role with the PowerShell command **Reset-DnsServerZoneKey MasterRole**. The following command transfers the key master role for the zone pearson.com to the server dc2.pearson.com:

```
Reset-DnsServerZoneKeyMasterRole -ZoneName "pearson.com"
  -KeyMasterServer "dc2.pearson.com"
```

Key Signing Key

The KSK validates a DNSKEY record. The KSK signs the ZSK (stored in a DNSKEY record). The KSK creates an RRSIG for the DNSKEY. As with the public ZSK, the DNS server publishes the public KSK in another DNSKEY record. Both the public KSK and the public ZSK are signed by the private KSK. Resolvers can use the public KSK to validate the public ZSK. Why use separate ZSKs and KSKs? Swapping out an old or compromised KSK is difficult, whereas changing the ZSK is much easier. A smaller ZSK minimizes the amount of data that the server has to send with each response.

Figure 4-11 shows the Key Signing Key (KSK) Description page of the DNSSEC Zone Signing Wizard. Be sure to read the descriptive text in this figure.

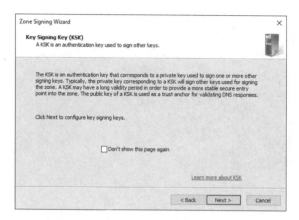

Figure 4-11 Key Signing Key (KSK) Description Page of the DNSSEC Zone Signing Wizard on a Windows Server 2016 DNS Server

Figure 4-12 shows the Key Signing Key (KSK) Configuration page of the DNSSEC Zone Signing Wizard. Here you configure parameters for the KSK or add KSKs. You can specify a maximum of three KSKs.

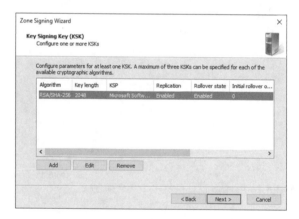

Figure 4-12 Key Signing Key (KSK) Configuration Page of the DNSSEC Zone Signing Wizard on a Windows Server 2016 DNS Server

Figure 4-13 shows the KSK settings of the default KSK in Figure 4-12.

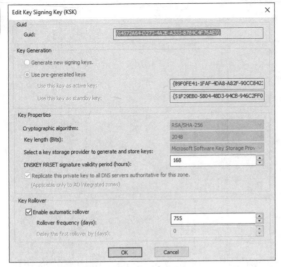

Figure 4-13   Key Signing Key (KSK) Settings Page of the DNSSEC Zone Signing Wizard on a Windows Server 2016 DNS Server

The following KSK settings are available:

- Guid

- Key Generation

- Key Properties

- Cryptographic Algorithm

- Key Length (Bits)

- Key Storage Provider

- DNSKEY RRset Signature Validity Period (Hours)

- Key Rollover

TIP   In the Edit Key Signing Key (KSK) window, you must replicate the private key to all DNS servers that are authoritative for the zone (applicable only to AD-integrated zones) for the default KSK key. Only if you add another KSK can you disable the Replicate This Private Key to All DNS Servers Authoritative for This Zone setting so that the key will not be replicated through Active Directory to other DNS servers. If you have a primary zone without Active Directory, there is no default KSK on this page; then you can add a new KSK, but you cannot activate the Replicate This Private Key to All DNS Servers Authoritative for This Zone Setting for that KSK because the zone is not an AD-integrated zone.

TIP   When a zone on a Windows Server 2016 DNS server is signed, you cannot change the zone type and replication scope of that zone. First, you must unsign the zone. Also keep in mind that a zone that is signed on a Windows Server 2018 R2 cannot be unsigned on a Windows Server 2016 with the PowerShell cmdlet **Invoke-DnsServerZoneUnsign**.

Figure 4-14 shows the ZSK Description page of the DNSSEC Zone Signing Wizard. Be sure to read the descriptive text in this figure.

Figure 4-14   Zone Signing Key (ZSK) Description Page of the DNSSEC Zone Signing Wizard on a Windows Server 2016 DNS Server

Figure 4-15 shows the Zone Signing Key (ZSK) Configuration page of the DNSSEC Zone Signing Wizard.

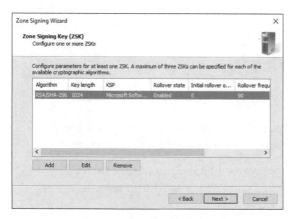

Figure 4-15   Zone Signing Key (ZSK) Configuration Page of the DNSSEC Zone Signing Wizard on a Windows Server 2016 DNS Server

Figure 4-16 shows the ZSK settings of the default ZSK key of the DNSSEC Zone Signing Wizard.

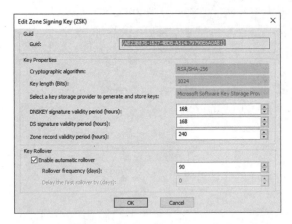

Figure 4-16   Edit Zone Signing Key (ZSK) Page of the DNSSEC Zone Signing Wizard on a Windows Server 2016 DNS Server

The following ZSK settings are available:

- Guid
- Key Properties
- Cryptographic Algorithm
- Key Length (Bits)
- Key Storage Provider
- DNSKEY Signature Validity Period (Hours)
- DS Signature Validity Period (Hours)
- Zone Record Validity Period (Hours)

Understanding ZSK

Each zone in DNSSEC has a ZSK pair: The private portion of the key digitally signs each RRset in the zone, and the public portion verifies the signature.

To enable DNSSEC, a zone operator creates digital signatures for each RRset using the private ZSK and stores them in their name server as RRSIG records.

This is like saying, "These are my DNS records; they come from my server and they should look like this."

However, these RRSIG records are useless unless DNS resolvers find a way to verify the signatures. The zone operator makes the public ZSK available by adding it to a DNSKEY record. When a DNSSEC resolver requests a particular record type, the DNS server also returns the corresponding RRSIG. The resolver then pulls the DNSKEY record containing the public ZSK from the DNS server.

Together, the RRset, RRSIG, and public ZSK can validate the response. If you trust the ZSK in the DNSKEY record, you can trust all records in that zone. You can view the properties of an RRSIG record named CL1 using the following PowerShell cmdlet:

```
Get-DnsServerResourceRecord -name CL1 -zonename pearson.com -RRType
    RRSIG | FL *
```

RRSIG records have a TTL and a signature expiration date/time. Figure 4-17 shows example RRSIG settings.

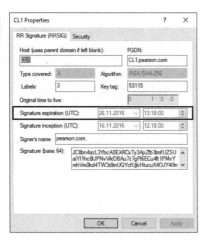

Figure 4-17   RRSIG Record Settings

Figure 4-18 shows the Next Secure (NSEC) page of the DNSSEC Zone Signing Wizard. Here you can choose between NSEC and NSEC3 resource records to provide authenticated denial of existence.

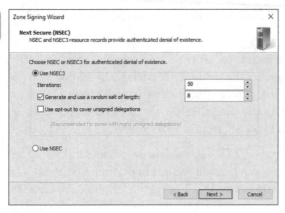

Figure 4-18 Next Secure (NSEC) Page of the DNSSEC Zone Signing Wizard on a Windows Server 2016 DNS Server

NSEC3 is a hashed version of NSEC records that prevents attacks by enumerating the zone. DNSSEC-aware servers can choose to send an NSEC3 record instead of an NSEC record when they cannot find a record. The NSEC3 record is signed, but instead of including the name directly, the NSEC3 record includes a cryptographically hashed value of the name. Therefore, NSEC3 is more secure, but it generates greater cryptographic overhead for recursive validators and has a slightly more complicated DNS configuration.

Figure 4-19 shows the Trust Anchors (TAs) page of the DNSSEC Zone Signing Wizard.

Figure 4-19 Trust Anchors Page of the DNSSEC Zone Signing Wizard on a Windows Server 2016 DNS Server

In the Zone Signing Wizard on the Trust Anchors page, you can configure the distribution of trust anchors and rollover keys. You can choose between the following two settings:

- **Enable the Distribution of Trust Anchors for This Zone:** With this setting, you enable trust anchor distribution in Active Directory. If this setting is enabled and the DNS server is also a domain controller, trust anchors are distributed to all DNS servers running on domain controllers in the Active Directory forest. If the DNS server is not a domain controller, a trust anchor for the zone is added only to the local trust anchor store, located by default in %windir%\system32\dns\TrustAnchors.dns.

- **Enable Automatic Update of Trust Anchors on Key Rollover (RFC 5011):** You must redistribute trust anchors each time a zone is re-signed unless re-signing occurs as part of an automatic key rollover and trust anchors are distributed automatically on key rollover (RFC 5011). Trust anchors can also be distributed automatically in Active Directory to all AD-integrated DNS servers within the replication scope for the zone. Support for RFC 5011 is enabled on the authoritative DNS server on a zone-by-zone basis. However, trust anchor updates are supported only for automated key rollover.

TIP   If you manually re-sign or unsign a zone, or if you manually roll over zone signing keys, trust anchors on validating DNS servers are not automatically updated.

TIP   Trust anchors that have been enabled for RFC 5011 automatic updates have information that is stored in the file %windir%\system32\dns\RFC5011.csv on the DNS server where the trust anchor is installed.

To enable automatic update of trust anchors on key rollover using Windows PowerShell, you can use the following command:

```
Get-DnsServerSigningKey -ZoneName secure.pearson.com |
  Enable-DnsServerSigningKey Rollover -Force
```

Figure 4-20 shows the Signing and Polling Parameters page of the DNSSEC Zone Signing Wizard. Here you can configure the following parameters:

- DS Record Generation Algorithm
- DS Record TTL (Seconds)
- DNSKEY Record TTL (Seconds)
- Secure Delegation Polling Period (Hours)

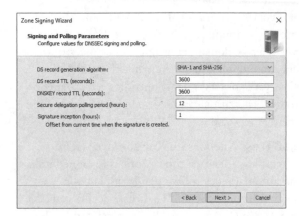

Figure 4-20   Signing and Polling Parameters Page of the DNSSEC Zone Signing Wizard on a Windows Server 2016 DNS Server

By default, the parent zone queries every 12 hours (**SecureDelegationPolling-Period**) for DNSKEY from the child zone. When it receives the DNSKEY RRset, the parent zone creates a DS of the new DNSKEY.

DNSSEC Monitoring

Windows Server 2016 DNS server audit events permit you to track changes on the DNS server. An audit event gets logged every time changes occur to server, zone, or resource record settings. This includes operational events such as DNSSEC zone signing and unsigning. You can also use the Event Viewer to view DNSSEC events. In addition, you can use some third-party tools to monitor DNSSEC issues such as DNSViz or the DNSSECAnalyzer.

Event Viewer

You can view DNSSEC events in the DNS Server log part of the Event Viewer. Figure 4-21 shows an example of a DNSSEC event.

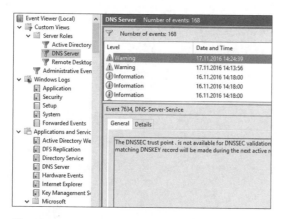

Figure 4-21   DNSSEC Events in Event Viewer

In the exam, DNSSEC events can produce messages such as "The DNS server has successfully assumed Key Master responsibilities for zone pearson.com. The Key Master role was transferred to this server from…". Another example is the warning event about the DNSSEC trust point shown in Figure 4-21. You must run DNSSEC testing as much as possible and view the relevant events in the DNS server log in the Event Viewer. This example should point out that you have no other way to test DNSSEC for yourself and to experiment with DNSSEC events.

DNSSEC Outages

If you need to get an overview of major DNSSEC outages and validation failures from the past, you can get a list of such DNSSEC failures through the following site:

https://ianix.com/pub/DNSSEC-outages.html

DNSSEC Status Verification

If you want to verify the DNSSEC status of a DNS zone, you can do that with the DNSViz tool: http://dnsviz.net/. For example, if you want to verify the authentication chain of trust for a given name, you can graphically display that through DNSViz (see Figure 4-22).

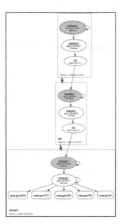

Figure 4-22   Authentication Chain of nasa.gov in DNSViz

You also can use the VERISIGN DNSSEC Analyzer (http://DNSSEC-debugger.verisignlabs.com/) to verify DNSSEC configurations and locate DNSSEC problems. Figure 4-23 shows example output for pearson.com in the DNSSEC Analyzer.

Figure 4-23   VERISIGN DNSSEC Analyzer Example for pearson.com

Trust Anchors

A trust anchor is an authoritative entity that is represented by a public key. The TrustAnchors zone on a Windows Server 2016 DNS server stores preconfigured public keys that are associated with a specific zone. In DNS, the trust anchor is the DNSKEY or DS resource record.

TIP A DS record is smaller in size than a DNSKEY record because it contains only a hash of the public key. To add a DS record, you must manually add or import it. DNSKEY records can be added automatically through the DNSSEC Zone Signing Wizard.

DS records must be added to each parent zone in a chain of authentication. For example, DS records for finance.corp.pearson.com must be added to corp.pearson.com to complete a chain of authentication from finance.corp.pearson.com to pearson.com.

Figure 4-24 shows where to add trust anchor records in the DNS Manager console.

Figure 4-24   Adding DNSKEY/DS Records

When you select the Enable the Distribution of Trust Anchors for This Zone setting on the Trust Anchor page of the DNSSEC Zone Signing Wizard (refer to Figure 4-19), the following two DNSKEY records will be created under Trust Points if you enable DNSSEC for the zone pearson.com. These DNSKey records are the trust anchors. In Figures 4-26 and 4-27, on the properties of the records, you can see that the FQDN of each record is pearson.com.trustanchors; this shows that these records are the trust anchors (more on that in the upcoming sections).

Figure 4-25 shows the trust points configuration in the DNS Manager.

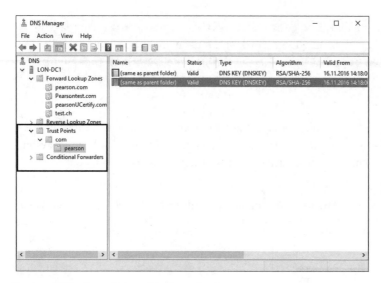

Figure 4-25   Trust Points Configuration for pearson.com

Figures 4-26 and 4-27 show the two trust anchor DNSKEY records for the pearson.com zone.

Figure 4-26   First Trust Anchor DNSKEY Record for pearson.com

Figure 4-27   Second Trust Anchor DNSKEY Record for pearson.com

A DNS server running Windows Server 2016, Windows Server 2012, or Windows Server 2012 R2 displays configured trust anchors in the DNS Manager console tree in the Trust Points container. A trust anchor is a public cryptographic key for a signed zone. Trust anchors must be configured on every nonauthoritative DNS server that attempts to validate DNS data.

Client computers use trust anchor records such as DNSKEY or DS records to build trust chains.

You must configure a trust anchor from the zone on every domain Windows Server 2016 DNS server to validate responses from that signed zone.

If the DNS server is a DC, then AD-integrated zones can distribute the trust. A validating DNS server must be configured with one or more trust anchors to perform validation. TAs are stored in the forest directory partition in AD DS and can be replicated to all DCs in the forest.

On standalone Windows Server 2016 DNS servers, trust anchors are stored in the file TrustAnchors.dns.

You can use the PowerShell cmdlet **Get-DnsServerTrustAnchor** to display trust anchors on a Windows Server 2016 DNS server, or you can use Dnscmd.exe to view trust anchors. For example, you can list the trust anchors for pearson.com with the following PowerShell command:

```
Get-DnsServerTrustAnchor -Name "pearson.com"
```

With the following PowerShell command, you can obtain a DNSKEY resource record from the DNS server DNS1 for pearson.com and then add the trust anchor to the current DNS server for this zone:

```
Get-DnsServer ResourceRecord -ZoneName "sec.contoso.com" -RRType
  "DNSKEY"
-ComputerName DNS1 | %{ $_.RecordData | Add-DnsServerTrustAnchor
  -PassThru -Verbose
-Name "pearson.com"}
```

DS Resource Record Set

A DS record is a hash of a public key. DS records are smaller than DNSKEY records. To add a DS record, you manually add or import it. The DS resource record set (DSSET) is automatically added as a file to the key master when a zone is signed.

You can use this file with the **Import-DnsServerResourceRecordDS** PowerShell cmdlet to import DS records to the parent zone. With the following example, you can use the **Import-DnsServer ResourceRecordDS** cmdlet to import DS records to a parent zone:

```
Import-DnsServerResourceRecordDS -ZoneName pearson.com -DSSetFile "c:\
  windows\system32\dns\dsset-corp.pearson.com"
Get-DnsServerResourceRecord -ZoneName pearson.com -RRType DS
```

In the preceding example, the DS records for the child zone corp.pearson.com are imported into the parent zone, pearson.com, by using the DSSET file that is located in the C:\windows\system32\dns folder. The DSSET file is located in this directory because the local DNS server is the key master for the child zone. If the key master DNS server for a child zone is not the same computer as the primary authoritative DNS server for the parent zone where you are adding the DS record, you must obtain the DSSET file for the child zone and make it available to the primary authoritative server for the parent zone. Alternatively, you can manually add DS records.

Updating and Removing Trust Anchors

Trust anchors must be updated if the public key for a zone changes, such as when a zone is re-signed.

If trust anchors are distributed after a zone is signed and the zone becomes unsigned later, trust anchors for the zone must be removed. If trust anchors are not removed when a zone is unsigned, DNS servers will continue to attempt validation of DNS responses for the zone; however, this validation will fail and, therefore, DNS resolution for the zone will also fail.

Trust Anchor Types

Two types of Windows Server 2016 DNSSEC trust anchor records exist:

- DNSKEY (public key from a DNSKEY resource record)
- DS (hash of a public key)

Windows Server 2008 R2 supported only DNSKEY trust anchors.

Windows Server 2012 and 2012 R2 and Windows Server 2016 support DNSKEY and DS trust anchors.

Trust Anchor Status

When a zone has been signed with DNSSEC, the success or failure of a DNS query also depends on the trust anchor status. Trust anchors are installed on DNS servers. A trust anchor has these status options:

- Available and valid
- Available and invalid
- Missing

A security-aware DNS server automatically attempts to validate a DNS response if the server has a trust anchor installed for the specified zone. You cannot install a trust anchor on a DNS server that does not support DNSSEC.

You can verify the trust anchor status with the following PowerShell command for the zone pearson.com:

```
Get-DnsServerTrustAnchor -Name pearson.com
```

Trust Anchor Status Verification

To view the status of a trust anchor on a Windows Server 2016 DNS server, you can use the DNS Manager or PowerShell. Trust anchors are displayed in the DNS Manager console tree under Trust Points. The PowerShell cmdlets **Get-DnsServerTrustAnchor** and **Get-DnsServerTrustPoint** provide status information. The PowerShell cmdlets **Get-DnsServerTrust Anchor** and **Get-DnsServerTrustPoint** display all configured trust anchors on the DNS server if a name is not specified. Table 4-3 outlines the possible trust anchor states.

Table 4-3 Windows Server 2016 Trust Anchor States

Status	Description
Valid or Active	Trusted for DNSSEC validation
Add Pending	Not yet trusted for DNSSEC validation, but becomes valid after an additional hold-down period
Missing	Trusted for DNSSEC validation, but was not found during the last active refresh cycle
Revoked	Revoked by an administrator and no longer valid for DNSSEC validation
DS Pending	Waiting for a matching DNSKEY, which then becomes a valid trust anchor
DS Invalid	Matched with a DNSKEY that cannot be a valid trust anchor

Root Zone Trust Anchor

The most obvious trust anchor to add is the one for the root zone. IANA publishes the root zone trust anchor online, along with signatures and certificates to determine its authenticity. If you are not sure whether your TLD (that your domain zone is a child zone of) is signed, you can find that information on this ICANN page on the TLD (generic top-level domain) DNSSEC Report:

http://stats.research.icann.org/dns/tld_report/

At https://data.iana.org/root-anchors/root-anchors.xml, you can retrieve the root trust anchor.

Your Windows Server 2016 DNS server must know this URL to deploy a root trust anchor from the IANA using that URL. It is specified in the **RootTrustAnchors-URL** property of the DNS server. You can view the RootTrust AnchorsURL by using **Get-DnsServerSetting**:

```
Get-DnsServerSetting -All | Select RootTrustAnchorsURL


RootTrustAnchorsURL
-------------------
https://data.iana.org/root-anchors/root-anchors.xml
```

With that information (see Figure 4-28), you can create the DS record on your Windows Server 2016 DNS server.

```
<?xml version="1.0" encoding="UTF-8"?>
<TrustAnchor source="http://data.iana.org/root-anchors/root-anchors.xml" id="AD42165F-3B1A-4778-8F42-D34A1D41FD93">
    <Zone>.</Zone>
    <KeyDigest id="Kjqmt7v" validFrom="2010-07-15T00:00:00+00:00">
        <KeyTag>19036</KeyTag>
        <Algorithm>8</Algorithm>
        <DigestType>2</DigestType>
        <Digest>49AAC11D7B6F6446702E54A1607371607A1A41855200FD2CE1CDDE32F24E8FB5</Digest>
    </KeyDigest>
</TrustAnchor>
```

Figure 4-28   Root-anchors.xml

You can add the trust anchors for the DNS root zone with **dnscmd.exe**. It retrieves the DS records for the root zone, adds them, and enables DNSSEC validation all in one command:

Dnscmd.exe /RetrieveRootTrustAnchors

```
Are you sure you want to Retrieve and add root trust anchors
    (activating DNSSEC validation)? (y/n) y
```

```
The root trust anchors were successfully retrieved and added as DS
    trust anchors. They will become effective when the server is able
    to convert them to DNSKEY trust anchors during an active refresh.
```

```
Command completed successfully.
```

You also can add the trust anchors for the DNS root zone with PowerShell using the following command:

Add-DnsServerTrustAnchor -Root

DNSSEC Priming

In DNSSEC priming, a validating DNS server that uses a DS trust anchor must query the authoritative DNS server to obtain the full DNSKEY resource record set. This forces the validating server to acquire up-to-date information.

Trust Anchor Distribution with Active Directory

You can distribute trust anchors through Active Directory. You can use the DNS Manager console or PowerShell for that. To enable automatic distribution of trust anchors through Active Directory for a zone that is already signed for DNSSEC, you perform the configuration steps outlined in the following sections.

Trust Anchor Distribution in Active Directory Using DNS Manager

By default, trust anchors are updated automatically upon key rollover. Normally, you want this to happen. If not, you need to manually update trust anchors upon key rollover. The option to enable the distribution of trust anchors for the zone is the best choice when the DNS server is running on a domain controller because the DNS server then replicates the trust anchors for the zone to all domain controllers running DNS servers in the AD forest. Following are the steps to configure this:

Step 1. Open the DNS Manager and right-click the zone where you want to enable trust anchor distribution. Point to **DNSSEC** and click **Properties**.

Step 2. Click the **Trust Anchor** tab.

Step 3. Select the **Enable the Distribution of Trust Anchors for This Zone** check box and the **Enable Automatic Update of Trust Anchors on Key Rollover (RFC 5011)** check box, and click **OK**.

Trust Anchor Distribution in Active Directory Using PowerShell

If the DNS server is not Active Directory–integrated, trust points are stored on the DNS server as a text file. By default, the list of trust points is stored in the file %windir%\system32\dns\TrustAnchors.dns. If the DNS server is also a domain controller, trust points are stored in Active Directory. You can distribute trust anchors in Active Directory by using PowerShell with the following commands. Membership in the Administrators group, or equivalent, is the minimum requirement for these steps.

Step 1. Open an elevated Windows PowerShell prompt on a primary, authoritative DNS server.

Step 2. Use the following PowerShell commands to enable distribution of trust anchors in Active Directory:

```
Set-DnsServerDNSSECZoneSetting zuerich.pearson.com
  -DistributeTrustAnchor DnsKey
Get-DnsServerDNSSECZoneSetting zuerich.pearson.com | fl -Property
  Zone, Name,DistributeTrustAnchor
```

ZSK/KSK Rollover Process

You have secured your zone with DNSSEC. The longer a key is used, the longer intruders have to break it. From time to time, key algorithms need updating, to lower the risk that someone will steal your private keys. All these problems have the same solution: Replace your keys with updated newer keys. This is called key rollover. You can roll over KSKs and ZSKs.

Changing a KSK or ZSK certainly risks breaking the chain of trust, so the goal of key rollover is to still have a valid chain of trust. If a DNS server can verify any one of those signatures through the chain of trust, the zone stays secure. Extra signatures do not harm DNS or DNSSEC, but your timing must be very good so that resolvers do not try to use a key that is not valid or one that has been removed or rolled from cache.

Two standard rollover methods are used: double signature and prepublishing. With the *double signature* method, you simultaneously sign the zone with both the old and new keys. Recursive clients get both signatures. Both signatures are held in the zone until all caches have had enough time to expire the old public key from the zone. When the time passes, the old key is removed. This is a risk-reducing method, but it doubles the size of your zone. With the *prepublishing* method, you make the new DNSKEY record available before signing. You then propagate the key to all client caches, remove the old signatures, and create new ones with the new key. This method does not double the size of your zone; it replaces signatures as they expire. However, it is more complicated. Best practice is to use prepublishing for ZSK rollovers and double signing for KSK.

Windows Server 2016 has some new PowerShell cmdlets to help you perform a ZSK/KSK rollover process. One is **Step-DnsServerSigningKeyRollover**, which you can use to roll over a KSK that is waiting for an update from a parent delegation signer (DS). If a server that hosts a securely delegated zone cannot check whether the DS record in a parent is updated, use this cmdlet to force a rollover. *Important:* You must manually update the DS record in the parent before you run this cmdlet.

The root's KSK pair was first generated in the year 2010. The KSK rollover will take place in eight steps, a process that is expected to take about 2 years.

ISPs and network operators that have enabled DNSSEC validation must update their systems with the new public part of the KSK, known as the root's trust anchor.

Developers of software that supports DNSSEC validation should ensure that their product supports RFC 5011. If so, the KSK will be updated automatically at the appropriate time.

For software that does not conform to RFC 5011, or for software that is not configured to use it, the new trust anchor file can be manually updated. This file is available at http://data.iana.org/root-anchors/.

DNSSEC Clients

A DNSSEC security-aware DNS client is a client that understands DNSSEC. A non-security-aware DNS client is a DNS client that does not understand DNSSEC. Table 4-4 summarizes DNS client security-aware status.

Table 4-4   DNSSEC DNS Client DNSSEC Security-aware Status

Operating System	Security-aware
Windows XP, Windows Server 2003, and previous OS	No
Windows Vista and Windows Server 2008	No
Windows 7, 8, 8.1, and 10; Windows Server 2008 R2; Windows Server 2012; Windows Server 2012 R2; and Windows Server 2016	Yes

When a zone has been signed with DNSSEC, the success or failure of a DNS query depends on the following settings:

1. Name Resolution Policy

2. Trust anchor status

3. Security-aware status

Name Resolution Policy

The Name Resolution Policy Table (NRPT) contains rules that control the DNS client behavior for sending DNS queries and processing the responses from those queries.

Settings from the NRPT can be applied only to *security-aware* DNS clients. *Non-security-aware* clients ignore such settings. GPOs can be configured to either require DNSSEC validation or not require DNSSEC validation for a given namespace (see Figure 4-29).

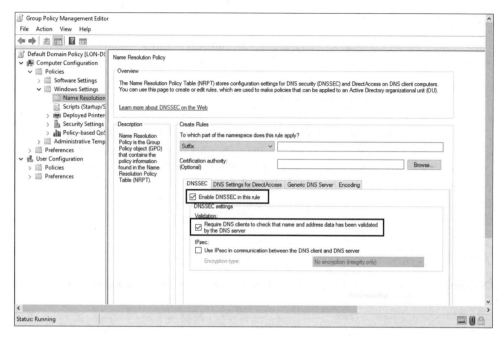

Figure 4-29   NRPT DNSSEC Settings

For example, a DNSSEC rule prompts the client computer to check for validation of the response for a particular DNS domain suffix. As a best practice, you should use GPOs as the preferred method for delivering NRPT settings. If no NRPT is present, the client computer accepts responses without validating them.

In Windows 8, Windows Server 2012, Windows 8.1, and Windows Server 2012 R2, the DNS client service continues to be nonvalidating and security-aware, the same as computers running Windows 7 and Windows Server 2008 R2. When the DNS client issues a query, it can indicate to the DNS server that it understands DNSSEC. However, the client is nonvalidating. When issuing queries, the DNS client relies on the local DNS server to indicate that validation was successful. If the server fails to perform validation or reports that validation was unsuccessful, the DNS client service can be configured to return no results.

With the following PowerShell command, you can retrieve the effective DNS client NRPT:

```
Get-DnsClientNrptPolicy -Effective
```

Security-aware Status

A security-aware (DNSSEC-enabled) client can still be protected by DNSSEC because a DNS server with an installed trust anchor automatically attempts to validate all responses in that namespace and discards invalid (spoofed) responses. A non-security-aware client ignores Name Resolution Policy requirements for DNSSEC validation. Therefore, if a trust anchor is not installed on a DNS server that is used by the client, and NRPT policy requires that validation be performed, only a security-aware DNS client will fail DNS resolution. The behavior of a non-security-aware client is the same as the behavior of a security-aware client that does not have any NRPT rules applied. Table 4-5 summarizes how DNSSEC validation works for security-aware and non-security-aware DNS clients under different conditions.

Table 4-5 DNSSEC Validation

DNSSEC Validation	TA Status	Non-security-aware	Security-aware
No	TA: none	Success	Success
No	TA: valid	Success	Success
No	TA: invalid	Failure	Failure
Yes	TA: none	Success	Failure
Yes	TA: valid	Success	Success +RRSIG
Yes	TA: invalid	Failure	Failure

DNSSEC and Delegation

A delegation is a referral of authority from one DNS server to a different DNS server for a specific namespace. Delegations are commonly used to assign authority for child zones. For example, the Internet root DNS servers delegate DNS authority for .com to generic top-level domain (gTLD) servers. See the following example for nslookup.exe:

```
nslookup -q=NS microsoft.com. a.root-servers.net

com     nameserver = m.gtld-servers.net
com     nameserver = l.gtld-servers.net
com     nameserver = k.gtld-servers.net
com     nameserver = j.gtld-servers.net
```

```
com    nameserver = i.gtld-servers.net
com    nameserver = h.gtld-servers.net
com    nameserver = g.gtld-servers.net
com    nameserver = f.gtld-servers.net
com    nameserver = e.gtld-servers.net
com    nameserver = d.gtld-servers.net
com    nameserver = c.gtld-servers.net
com    nameserver = b.gtld-servers.net
com    nameserver = a.gtld-servers.net
```

The gTLD servers delegate authority for microsoft.com to msft.net authoritative DNS servers. See the following example:

nslookup -q=NS microsoft.com. a.gtld-servers.net

```
microsoft.com    nameserver = ns3.msft.net
microsoft.com    nameserver = ns1.msft.net
microsoft.com    nameserver = ns5.msft.net
microsoft.com    nameserver = ns2.msft.net
microsoft.com    nameserver = ns4.msft.net
```

Delegations are important because they establish a chain of authentication for child zones. If all zones in the chain are signed with DNSSEC, resolving DNS servers can have only a single delegation signer (DS) trust anchor installed, as long as the appropriate DS records are available in the parent zone.

With delegations, installing a trust anchor is not always necessary for every zone that a caching DNS server can validate. Under certain conditions, you can build a chain of authentication (a chain of trust) in which it is sufficient for the DNS server to have only a DS trust anchor installed for the parent zone.

Chain of Trust

During secure name resolution, a resolver builds a chain of trust: It starts from a trusted key and follows the path to the queried resource records while verifying signatures of resource records and secure links represented by DS-DNSKEY records.

Figure 4-30 shows the steps that a DNSSEC client (with only the root zone key as the secure entry point) follows to trust a resource record of the pearson.com zone.

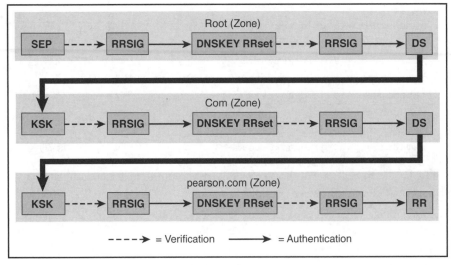

Figure 4-30   DNSSEC Chain of Trust

At each step, you see the same scheme: A DS resource record allows trust for a KSK, a KSK allows trust for all the zone keys (the DNSKEY RRset), and ZSKs allow trust for other resource records of the zone.

TIP   Storing a KSK or ZSK for a zone as a certificate is also possible. With the following command, you can create a ZSK or KSK certificate with the corresponding signing key in the certificate: **dnscmd** */OfflineSign /GenKey /Alg /Flags /Length /Zone /SSCert /FriendlyName*. In the Microsoft Script Center, you can find the DNSSEC Zone Sign/Rollover Sample Script to aid in signing or rolling over a zone using DNSSEC. By default, the script uses the RSA/SHA-1 signing algorithm and 1024-bit key lengths. Supported rollover methods include prepublished ZSK, double signature ZSK, and double signature KSK. For example, with the **Generate-Key** function in this script, you can create a ZSK or KSK for the pearsontest.com zone using the following commands: **Generate-Key** *zsk pearsontest.com* or **Generate-Key** *ksk pearsontest.com*. Afterward, you have two new certificates in the local computer certificate store under MS-DNSSEC/Certificates (see Figure 4-31).

Figure 4-31 DNSSEC KSK and ZSK Certificates with Signing Keys

An attacker that owns a compromised key for a given zone can forge any resource record for this zone and generate signatures for these RRs. Then the attacker can send these RRs with their associated signatures to the target cache server or a resolver to provide false information. Moreover, with this key, the attacker can generate an entire false zone and its delegations. It can also create a false or forged child zone (and so on) because it owns a secure entry point in the DNS tree.

However, if the chain of trust is broken, a child zone must have its own trust anchor installed. For example, DNS responses for the signed zone A.B.C.com can be validated using a trust anchor for the signed zone C.com, as long as B.C.com is also signed. If B.C.com is not signed, then C.com becomes an island of trust and requires its own trust anchor.

After a zone is DNSSEC-signed, and if the parent of the zone is also DNSSEC-signed, the signed delegation records must be added to the parent zone and then the parent zone must be re-signed.

This process must be performed every time a new child zone is signed for the first time or when a child zone is re-signed with a new key signing key.

If you own a signed zone but do not own the children of the zone, and if the children zones are in the process of being DNSSEC-signed one at a time, you must re-sign your zone after adding the delegation records each time a new child zone is signed. However, you optimize the process of signing multiple zones if you own the parent as well as the children zones that are to be signed.

DNSSEC Record Types

With DNSSEC you get new resource record types that contain the encryption information and hashes used to perform DNSSEC validation. The six most important DNSSEC record types are TA, DNSKEY, DS, RRSIG, NSEC, and NSEC3.

Table 4-6 describes the base functionality of DNSSEC resource records.

Table 4-6   DNSSEC Resource Records

Resource Record	Purpose
TA	Acts as the DNSSEC trust authority record. This record is part of a deployment proposal for DNSSEC without a signed DNS root. It uses the same format as the DS record.
DNSKEY	Publishes the public key for the zone. It checks the authority of a response against the private key held by the DNS server. These keys require periodic replacement through key rollovers. Windows Server 2016 supports automated key rollovers. Every zone has multiple DNSKEYs that are then broken down to the ZSK and KSK.
DS (Delegation Signer)	Acts as a delegation record that contains the hash of the public key of a child zone. This record is signed by the parent zone's private key. If a child zone of a signed parent also is signed, the DS records from the child must be manually added to the parent to create a chain of trust.
RRSIG (Record Signature)	Holds a signature for a set of DNS records. It is used to check the authority of a response. The signature of an RRSIG record can expire.
NSEC (Next Secure)	Authenticates that the host does not exist when the DNS response has no data to provide to the client.
NSEC3	Is a hashed version of the NSEC record that prevents alphabet attacks by enumerating the zone.

RRset

A resource record set (RRset) is simply a collection of records of the same domain name, record class, and record type. Resolvers return entire RRsets when answering queries. If you make a DNS query for www.pearson.com, you get a single A record in answer. This is the most simple complete RRset. If you ask for the host www.google.ch, however, you get six records. Those six records are a single RRset. Suppose that you get an error message such as "Not enough valid signatures over SOA RRset found." A possible cause of the problem is that either the SOA RRset didn't come with RRSIG records or none of the RRSIG that did come with it were valid and cryptographically sound. An SOA RRset can be one SOA record or a group of SOA records. Why is it important to know about RRsets? DNSSEC does not sign single DNS records; instead, it signs complete RRsets.

DNSKEY Record

The DNSKEY records contain a zone's public key. This is an example DNSKEY resource record, followed by some explanation of its components:

```
Resolve-DnsName -Name pearson.com -Type DNSKEY | FL *
```

```
QueryType        : DNSKEY
Flags            : 257
Protocol         : DNSSEC
Algorithm        : 8
Key              : {3, 1, 0, 1...}
Name             : pearson.com
Type             : DNSKEY
CharacterSet     : Unicode
Section          : Answer
DataLength       : 270
TTL              : 3600
```

Flags: DNSKEY records use only two flags: 256 = record is a ZSK, 257 = record is a KSK.

Algorithm: 5 = RSASHA (old), 8 = RSASHA256 (recommended)

DS Record

The DS (Delegation Signer) record is based on a zone's KSK and contains a hash of the zone's active KSK, along with information about the algorithm used and the associated key tag. An example for a DS resource record follows, along with an explanation of its components:

Example DS resource record:

pearson.com 86400 IN DS 12086 5 2 GD216607…

pearson.com = domain

86400 = TTL (Time to Live value)

IN DS = this labels this as an Internet DS record

12086 = Key Tag (A tag is unique for any zone, but isn't unique between zones)

5 = algorithm (5=RSASHA1, 8=RSA/SHA-256, 10=RSA/SHA-512)

2 = Digest type (algorithm used to compute this hash; 1=SHA1, 2=SHA256)

GD216607… = Hash of the Public Key

RRSIG Record

The RRSIG (Resource Record Signature) record gives the digital signature of an RRset. If a DNSSEC-secured zone has an RRset for www.pearson.com, that RRset includes an RRSIG record. An example for an RRSIG resource record follows, along with an explanation of its components:

```
Resolve-DnsName -Name pearson.com -Type RRSIG

QueryType         : RRSIG
Key               : 53115
TypeCovered       : NS
Algorithm         : 8
LabelCount        : 2
OriginalTtl       : 3600
Expiration        : 26.11.2016 13:18:00
Signed            : 16.11.2016 12:18:00
KeyTag            : 53115
Signer            : pearson.com
Signature         : {123, 110, 37, 254...}
Name              : pearson.com
Type              : RRSIG
CharacterSet      : Unicode
Section           : Answer
DataLength        : 168
TTL               : 3600
```

TypeCovered: Type of DNS resource (in this case, an NS record) the signature applies to. It can be A, SOA, NS, MX, or any other sort of DNS record.

Algorithm: Type of algorithm (5=RSASHA1, 8=RSA/SHA-256).

LabelCount: Number of labels (for example, www.pearson.com has three labels and pearson.com has two labels).

OriginalTTL: Time to Live, in seconds. Validating a DNSSEC signature requires the original TTL.

Expiration: Date the signature expires.

Signed: Date the signature becomes valid.

Signature: Digital signature (the signature is generated by signing the zone data with the ZSK).

NSEC/NSEC3 Records

The "next secure" records offer proof that a record does not exist. You want to generate a statement if you try to find a record that does not appear in DNS. A disadvantage of NSEC records is that an attacker can use them to enumerate the entries in a zone. NSEC3 is better because NSEC3 records hash the names of existing hosts. Consider this example for an NSEC recourse record, followed by an explanation of its components:

```
usa.pearson.com. 900 IN NSEC www.pearson.com. A TXT AAAA RRSIG NSEC
    DNSKEY
```

> **usa.pearson.com.** = Name of valid host in the zone
>
> **900** = TTL for this record
>
> **IN NSEC** = Identification as an Internet NSEC record
>
> **www.pearson.com.** = Name of the next valid host in the zone
>
> **A TXT AAA RRSIG NSEC DNSKEY** = The host with which usa.pearson.com has these records associated

An example for a NSEC3 recourse record follows, along with an explanation of its components:

```
ZUAQT15EZT56UT1ZUET.pearson.com. 3600 IN NSEC3 1 0 10 03F92714
    bzewf26zgf2gd72gd A RRSIG
```

> **ZUAQT15EZT56UT1ZUET** = Hash of a valid hostname
>
> **3600** = TTL for this record
>
> **IN NSEC3** = Identification of an Internet NSEC3 record
>
> **1** = Algorithm used to generate the hash
>
> **0** = NSEC3 flags
>
> **10** = Number of times the hostname is passed through the hashing algorithm
>
> **03F92714** = Hexadecimal salt used for that calculation
>
> **bzewf26zgf2gd72gd** = Hashed hostname for the next host in the zone
>
> **A RRSIG** = List of valid resource records associated with this host

A zone using NSEC3 also has a NSEC3PARAM record, which is necessary for the proper functioning of NSEC3. Figure 4-32 shows an example of the NSEC3PARAM resource record.

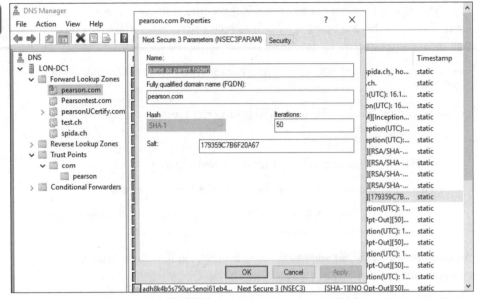

Figure 4-32   NSEC3PARAM Resource Record

Exam Preparation Tasks

Review All the Key Topics

Review the most important topics in the chapter, noted with the Key Topics icon in the outer margin of the page. Table 4-7 lists these key topics and the page numbers where each is found.

Table 4-7   Key Topics for Chapter 4

Key Topic Element	Description	Page Number
Tip	Verifying DNSSEC status only with PowerShell	164
Figure 4-2	RODC and DNSSEC	166
Figure 4-3	Windows Server 2016 DNSSEC Sign the Zone Setting	166
List	Configuration settings of DNSSEC Zone Signing Wizard	167
Figure 4-5	KSK Default Settings	168
Figure 4-6	ZSK Default Settings	168
Figure 4-8	Trust Anchor Default Settings	169

Key Topic Element	Description	Page Number
Figure 4-13	Key Signing Key (KSK) Settings Page of the DNSSEC Zone Signing Wizard on a Windows Server 2016 DNS Server	174
Tip	KSK Active Directory replication	174
Section	Understanding ZSK	176
Text	Verifying RRSIG properties with PowerShell	177
Figure 4-17	RSIG Record Settings	177
Figure 4-18	Next Secure (NSEC) Page of the DNSSEC Zone Signing Wizard on a Windows Server 2016 DNS server	178
List	Zone Signing Wizard settings to configure the distribution of trust anchors and rollover keys	179
Tip	Manually re-sign or unsign a zone	179
Tip	Where to find trust anchors that have been enabled for RFC 5011 automatic updates	179
Text	Enabling automatic update of trust anchors on key rollover using PowerShell	179
Tip	Important differences between DNSKEY and DS records	183
Figure 4-26	First Trust Anchor DNSKEY Record	184
Figure 4-27	Second Trust Anchor DNSKEY Record	185
Text	Displaying trust anchors	185
Section	Updating and Removing Trust Anchors	186
Table 4-3	Windows Server 2016 Trust Anchor States	188
Text	Deploying a root trust anchor	188
Section	DNSSEC Priming	189
Section	Trust Anchor Distribution with Active Directory	189
Table 4-4	DNSSEC DNS Client DNSSEC Security-aware Status	192
Text	Applying NRPT settings	192
Table 4-5	DNSSEC Validation	194
Section	Chain of Trust	195
Figure 4-30	DNSSec Chain of Trust	196
Table 4-6	DNSSEC Resource Records	198
Section	NSEC/NSEC3 Records	200
Figure 4-32	NSEC3PARAM Resource Record	202

Complete the Tables and Lists from Memory

Print a copy of Appendix B, "Memory Tables" (on the book's website), or at least the section for this chapter, and complete the tables and lists from memory. Appendix C, "Memory Tables Answer Key," also on the website, includes completed tables and lists to check your work.

Define Key Terms

Define the following key terms from this chapter and check your answers in the glossary.

DNSSEC, trust anchors, root zone trust anchor, trust anchor state, DNSSEC priming, chain of trust, DNSKEY, DS record, trust point, KSK rollover process, NRPT

End-of-Chapter Review Questions

1. Your Active Directory environment consists of one forest with two trees and six domains (see Figure 4-33). Every domain has two domain controllers named DC1 and DC2 with an installed DNS server role. You have created an AD-integrated zone named devtestenv.com on dc1.pearson.com. The zone is signed with DNSSEC. DNS data of this zone is stored in a custom DNS application directory partition. Only the DC1 domain controllers from all domains are enlisted in the scope of that partition. You must ensure that all domain controllers from all domains can get the DNS data replicated from devtestenv.com and that the zone is signed. What is your first step?

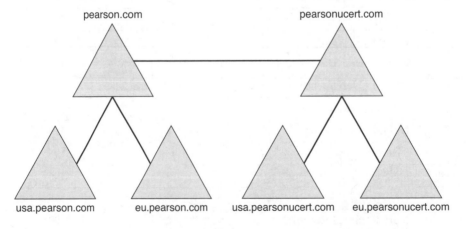

Figure 4-33   Active Directory Environment, End-of-Chapter Review Question 1

a. Change the replication scope of zone devtestenv.com.

b. Unsign the zone devtestenv.com. Change the replication scope to all domain controllers running DNS servers in this forest. Re-sign the zone.

c. Change zone devtestenv.com to Primary. Apply zone type AD integrated with forest replication scope.

d. Create a new zone named devtestenv2.com. In the DNSSEC Zone Signing Wizard, select Sign the Zone with Parameters of an Existing Zone.

2. You have a domain named pearson.com and two domain controllers with the DNS server role installed (DC1 and DC2). The zone pearson.com is a signed AD-integrated zone. You have installed a new Azure virtual machine DC3 as an additional domain controller. Your company site is connected through an Azure S2S tunnel to Azure. You successfully have tested AD replication for all domain controllers. You want to transfer the key master role from DC1 to DC3 and you want to get confirmation messages. Which tools or commands can you use?

a. On DC3, select Use the Following DNS Server as the Key Master on DC3 and then choose DC3 as the new key master.

b. On DC1, select Use the Following DNS Server as the Key Master on DC3 and then choose DC3 as the new key master.

c. On DC3, use **Reset-DnsServerZoneKeyMasterRole -SeizeRole**.

d. On DC3, use **Reset-DnsServerZoneKeyMasterRole -Force**.

3. You want to stage a Windows Server 2016 DNSSEC deployment with Windows 10 clients. You have only writeable domain controllers and Windows Servers. You know about the 10 DNSSEC deployment steps. Which of the following two deployment steps are wrong?

a. Choose a zone

b. Choose a key master

c. Choose methods and settings

d. Sign the zone

e. Verify zone signing

f. Add DLV records

g. Choose DNS clients

h. Deploy trust anchors

i. Configure BIND

j. Configure and deploy name resolution policy

k. Verify name resolution policy

l. Monitor and manage

4. Your environment consists of one domain named pearson.com and two sites named HQ and Branch (a physically unsecure location). A firewall secures the network traffic between both sites. The HQ site consists of two domain controllers, named DC1 and DC2, with the DNS server role installed. The zone pearson.com is a signed AD-integrated zone. You install a new Windows Server 2016 RODC at the Branch site. After you do so, you find that the DNS server on that RODC does not have the pearson.com zone. Which configuration should you perform so that the DNS server on the RODC can work as a DNS server for DNS clients at the Branch site?

   a. Make sure your firewall isn't blocking UDP DNS replies that are larger than 512 bytes.

   b. Allow zone transfer with Set-DnsServerPrimaryZone.

   c. Install an additional writeable domain controller at the Branch site.

   d. Install an additional RODC at the Branch site.

5. You have the following DNS servers:

   ■ **DNS1:** Windows Server 2008 R2; Signed Zone: pearson1.com

   ■ **DNS2:** Windows Server 2012; Signed Zone: pearson2.com

   ■ **DNS3:** Windows Server 2012 R2; Signed Zone: pearson3.com

   ■ **DNS4:** Windows Server 2016; Signed Zone: pearson4.com

   All zones were signed locally by a DNS server. You want to use the PowerShell cmdlet **Invoke-DnsServerZoneUnsign** to unsign all the zones. Which zone can you not unsign in this way?

   a. pearson1.com

   b. pearson2.com

   c. pearson3.com

   d. pearson4.com

This chapter covers the following subjects:

- **DANE overview:** DANE offers two functionalities: 1) enabling you to specify which Certificate Authority (CA) is allowed to issue digital certificates and 2) authenticating TLS client and server entities without a Certificate Authority. This section covers the base DNS functionality and its usage, criteria, statements, and operation modes. It also explains common DANE bottlenecks.

- **DANE security:** This section explains the security aspects of DANE. It compares DANE with public CAs, shows an example of a nonvalidated web server certificate, and illustrates how the client becomes informed about that issue.

- **TLSA records:** This section details using TLSA records for DANE validation. It explains the important fields of TLSA records, including Certificate Usage, Selector, and Matching Type.

- **Configuring DANE:** This section demonstrates how to use PowerShell commands to create a TLSA record with relevant parameters and how to verify the successful TLSA record deployment through PowerShell, DNS Manager, and the Event Viewer.

- **Common DANE failures:** This section explains some of the most common DANE failures, including update failures, unsupported certificate types, and firewall considerations.

## CHAPTER 5

Understanding and Configuring DANE

This chapter covers some of the most important aspects of Windows Server 2016 DANE and TLSA records. It gives an overview of DANE functionality and usage; explains the common DANE criteria, statements, operation modes, and bottlenecks; and shows the interoperability between DNSSEC and DANE.

With Windows Server 2016, unknown records are supported on Windows Server 2016 DNS servers. Through that new enhancement, Windows Server 2016 also supports DANE and TLSA records to validate certificates, CA certificates, trust anchors, and self-signed certificates.

The focus of this chapter is to deliver knowledge about DANE and TLSA records and how to use them to protect against man-in-the-middle attacks and to form TLSA certificate associations with TLSA records to validate self-signed certificates and X.509 certificates from certification authorities.

This chapter explains the different fields of TLSA records (such as Certificate Usage, Selector, and Matching Type) and delves into their usage and administrative implementation. You learn how to use TLSA records for certificate and record validation, and you get practical guidance on how to implement TLSA records.

You also learn how to use the **Add-DnsServerResourceRecord** PowerShell cmdlet to add TLSA records to a Windows Server 2016 DNS server and how to verify existing TLSA records through PowerShell, DNS Manager, and other tools.

The key topic selection, memory tables, key term definitions, and exam preparation questions in this chapter give you powerful tools to increase your knowledge about DANE and TLSA records for the Microsoft 70-741 exam and your work.

"Do I Know This Already?" Quiz

The "Do I Know This Already?" quiz enables you to assess whether you should read this entire chapter or simply jump to the "Exam Preparation Tasks" section for review. If you are in doubt, read the entire chapter. Table 5-1 outlines the major headings in this chapter and the corresponding "Do I Know This Already?" quiz questions. You can find the answers in Appendix A, "Answers to the 'Do I Know This Already?' Quizzes and End-of-Chapter Review Questions."

Table 5-1   "Do I Know This Already?" Foundation Topics Section-to-Question Mapping

Foundation Topics Section	Questions Covered in This Section
DANE Overview	1, 2
DANE Security	3
TLSA Records	4, 5, 6
Configuring DANE	7
Common DANE Failures	8

CAUTION   The goal of self-assessment is to gauge your mastery of the topics in this chapter. If you do not know the answer to a question or are only partially sure of the answer, you should mark that question as wrong for purposes of the self-assessment. Giving yourself credit for an answer you correctly guess skews your self-assessment results and might provide you with a false sense of security.

1.   What are two core functionalities of DANE? (Choose two.)

    a.   Enables you to specify which CA is allowed to issue certificates for a resource

    b.   Authenticates TLS client and server entities without a Certificate Authority

    c.   Improves DNS response performance from Windows Server 2016 DNS servers

    d.   Simplifies certificate validation in a mixed IPv4/IPv6 environment

2. Which of the following is not a DANE operation mode?

   a. CA Constraints

   b. Service Certificate Constraints

   c. Trust anchor assertion

   d. Self-Signed Certificate Constraint

   e. Domain-issued certificate

3. You have three web servers deployed on your DMZ. You also use Exchange Server 2016. All your servers are Windows Server 2016 servers. They are reachable from the Internet and are secured through SSL certificates delivered from a public CA. You want to prevent your environment against man-in-the-middle attacks. Which kinds of records should you use if you want to add certificate validation to your solution? (Choose two.)

   a. RRSIG

   b. DNSKEY

   c. TLSA

   d. DS records

4. You want to test DANE and TLSA records in your testing environment. You want to use only certificates that do not have to be signed by a valid CA. Which value should you use for the **CertificateUsage** parameter when you create your TLSA records with the PowerShell cmdlet **Add-DnsServerRecourseRecord**?

   a. **ServiceCertificateConstraint**

   b. **DomainIssuedCertificates**

   c. **CAConstraint**

   d. **TrustAnchor Assertion**

5. You are the administrator of pearson.com. You want to specify to your DNS clients the CA from which they should expect certificates for usa.pearson.com. You want to prevent man-in-the-middle attacks. The client has to trust only the referenced SHA-256 certificate in the TLSA record. Which TLSA record is correct?

   a. _443._tcp.usa.nutex.com. IN TLSA 0 1 1 ea0fccb0f5a7f7a4c67...

   b. _443._tcp.usa.nutex.com. IN TLSA 1 1 1 ea0fccb0f5a7f7a4c67...

   c. _443._tcp.usa.nutex.com. IN TLSA 2 1 2 ea0fccb0f5a7f7a4c67...

   d. _443._tcp.usa.nutex.com. IN TLSA 3 1 1 ea0fccb0f5a7f7a4c67...

6. You are the administrator of pearson.com. You have configured DNSSEC on your Windows Server 2016 DNS servers. You want your SMTP mail servers to validate each other's TLS certificate. For that, you add some records to your DNS zone, as in the following PowerShell command:

```
Add-DnsServerResourceRecord
   -TLSA
   -Name _25._tcp
   -ZoneName pearson.com
   -CertificateUsage DomainIssuedCertificate
   -Selector SubjectPublicKeyInfo
   -MatchingType Sha256Hash
   -CertificateAssociationPath 831B8309F329E52731A
```

Which new Windows Server feature allows you to add such records?

   a. DANE

   b. DNS policies

   c. Response Rate Limiting

   d. Unknown record support

   e. IPv6 root hints

7. You must create a TLSA record for a server authentication certificate signed from your internal enterprise root ca. The certificate is for your web server named SRV01.pearson.com. You want to add the TLSA record correctly on your Windows Server 2016 DNS server and verify it. Determine the necessary steps for this process and put them in the correct order.

   a. Fill in the Usage, Selector, and Matching Type fields. _____

   b. Use the thumbprint of your certificate as the **CertificateAssociation-Data** parameter value on your **Add-DnsServerResourceRecord** command. _____

   c. Paste the X.509 binary data of the certificate into the TLSA record generator. _____

   d. Fill in the port number with 443. _____

   e. Export the X.509 binary certificate data to the .CER file. _____

   f. Fill in the transport protocol with TCP. _____

   g. Fill in the domain name with srv01.pearson.com. _____

   h. Fill in the domain name with pearson.com. _____

   i. Open the TLSA record generator. _____

    j. Select Generate. ____

    k. Use the key value from the generated TLSA record as the **Certificate-AssociationData** parameter value on your **Add-DnsServerResourceRecord** command. ____

    l. Add the TLSA record with **Add-DnsServerResourceRecord**. ____

8. You want to update your DNSSEC implementation. Which of the following is the proper procedure if you plan to deploy a new planned certificate chain related to DANE and TLSA records?

    a. Leave the existing TLSA records and publish TLSA records that match the planned certificate chain. After deploying the planned certificate chain, remove the old TLSA records.

    b. Remove the current TLSA records. Publish the TLSA records that match the planned certificate chain.

    c. Publish the TLSA records that match the planned certificate chain and overwrite the current TLSA records with the settings of the new TLSA records.

    d. Publish the TLSA records that match the planned certificate chain. Edit the existing TLSA records.

Foundation Topics

DANE Overview

Windows Server 2016 supports the DNS-based Authentication of Named Entities (DANE) protocol. DANE uses Transport Layer Security Authentication (TLSA) records to state which Certificate Authority (CA) clients should expect to get a certificate from.

NOTE If you need a refresher or a better understanding of TLSA records, you should read the next section, "TLSA Records," before you read this section.

Through the support of unknown resource records in Windows Server 2016, you now can use TLSA records on those servers. DANE support is specified in the Internet Engineering Task Force (IETF) Request For Comments (RFC) 6394 and 6698.

DANE has two core functionalities:

- DANE allows a domain owner to specify which CA is allowed to issue certificates for a resource.

- DANE provides a way to authenticate TLS client and server entities without a CA. Figure 5-1 shows an example.

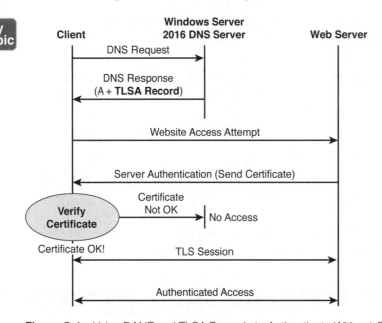

Figure 5-1   Using DANE and TLSA Records to Authenticate Without CA

Using DANE, a Windows Server 2016 administrator can specify which CA is allowed to issue certificates for a particular resource and to securely specify exactly which TLS/SSL certificate an application or service should use to connect to a site. This prevents man-in-the middle attacks in which someone corrupts the DNS cache to point to a different website and provides a certificate issued from a different CA.

For example, suppose that your organization hosts a secure website using HTTPS at www.pearson.com by using a certificate from a well-known authority named CA1. Someone might still be able to get a certificate for www.pearson.com from a different, relatively unknown Certificate Authority named CA2. At that point, an entity hosting the fake www.pearson.com website might be able to corrupt the DNS cache of a client or server to point www.pearson.com to its fake site. The end user then would be presented a certificate from CA2 and might acknowledge it and connect to the fake site. With DANE, the client makes a request to the DNS server for pearson.com asking for the TLSA record and discovers that CA1 issued the certificate for www.pearson.com. If another CA offers the client a certificate, the connection is terminated.

DANE Criteria

DANE allow certificates to be bound to DNS names using DNSSEC. A client then has to evaluate the server certificate to decide whether the certificate is sufficient to establish the server's identity. This decision is usually based on two criteria:

- The certificate contains the desired domain name.

- The certificate is issued under a trusted Certificate Authority (CA).

With DNSSEC, clients can obtain authenticated data directly from the DNS server. Using DNSSEC and DANE means that DNS server administrators have more security functions, but they also are likely to inherit many of the security troubles that CA administrators experience today. DNS server administrators thus need to strengthen their security posture accordingly.

DANE Statements

DNSSEC allows clients to securely ask the DNS server of a domain about which certificates to accept for that domain. DANE allows domain administrators to make statements about how clients should judge TLS certificates for their domains, but what kinds of statements should DANE allow them to make? Three major types of statements exist:

- **CA Constraints:** The client should accept certificates issued under only a specific CA.

- **Service Certificate Constraints:** The client should accept only a specific certificate.

- **Trust Anchor Assertion:** The client should use a domain-provided trust anchor to validate certificates for that domain.

CA Constraints and Service Certificate Constraints statements limit the scope. The Trust Anchor Assertion statement provides the client with a new trust anchor with limited scope. DANE can work perfectly with existing TLS certificates issued by CAs.

DANE Operation Modes

DANE defines four different operation modes (Certificate Usage field of a TLSA record):

- **0: CA specification:** Defines the CA that will provide TLS certificates for the domain. The domain will then accept TLS certificates from only that specific CA. If the browser or other application using DANE validation sees a TLS certificate from another CA, the app should reject that TLS certificate as bogus.

- **1: Specific TLS certificate:** Specifies the exact TLS certificate that can be used for the domain. This certificate must be issued by a valid CA.

- **2: Trust anchor assertion:** Specifies the trust anchor to be used for validating the TLS certificates for the domain. For example, if a company operated its own CA that was not in the list of CAs typically installed in client applications, this usage of DANE could supply the certificate (or fingerprint) for that CA.

- **3: Domain-issued certificate:** Specifies the exact TLS certificate that should be used for the domain. However, in contrast to Usage 1, the TLS certificate does *not* need to be signed by a valid CA. This allows for the use of self-signed certificates.

DANE Bottlenecks

DANE improves security because it approves the CA that is allowed to issue certificates for a particular resource. However, it also brings some caveats. For example, you might have to work with a different certificate, network traffic for DNS responses increases, and your routers must forward DANE-specific network traffic. The following list explains some of the most important bottlenecks with DANE:

- **Different certificates through IPv4 and IPv6:** The difference between IPv4 and IPv6 certificates is problematic for DANE TLSA with domain-issued certificates because one domain name normally has one associated TLSA record. In such a case, one TLSA record cannot match two different certificates.

- **Too-large TLSA packages:** A TLSA response can contain multiple TLSA records, either for certificate rollover or for different assertions. With DNSSEC enabled and multiple RRs, a TLSA response is more likely to be problematically large. This is a common problem of DNS responses and is not limited to TLSA. Recommendations include limiting the number of TLSA records for one domain name, using hash matching instead of exact matching, and limiting the number of RRs to avoid future possible IP fragmentation.

  Adding DNSSEC to the TLS connection process can also add significant latency to the TLS connection process. In addition to completing the TLS handshake and certificate validation, the client has to wait for several DNS round-trips and then validate the chain of DNSSEC signatures. These combined delays can add up to multiple seconds of latency in connection establishment.

- **DNS APIs:** Although some DNS libraries have robust DNSSEC support, many of the major DNS application programming interfaces (APIs) that applications use do not provide any information about the DNSSEC status of the results returned. Application developers might have to refactor their DNS support and also query for new record types. If more sites come to rely on DANE, this process could also draw increasing attention to the various types of intermediaries that cause DNSSEC breakage (for example, home gateways that set DNS flags improperly).

■ **DNS forwards blocking DNSSEC:** Some routers or forwarders might not be up to date with recent standards such as DNSSEC. Most recursive resolvers from ISPs can properly process DNSSEC queries; however, home routers and older routers, for example, might not be able to forward that information to the end users because they are not DNSSEC-aware.

DANE Security

DNSSEC delivers the security for DANE and ensures that a TLSA record has not been altered.

Using DNSSEC, clients can obtain authenticated data directly from DNS servers. DNSSEC should allow clients to securely ask the domain administrator about which certificates they should accept as credentials for that domain.

DNSSEC forms certificates (binding an identity to a key) by combining a DNSKEY or DS record with an associated RRSIG record. These records then form a signing chain extending from the client's trust anchors to the record of interest. Although DNSSEC does not enforce it, DNSKEYs are often marked with a SEP flag indicating whether the key is a zone signing key (ZSK) or a key signing key (KSK). ZSKs protect records in the zone (including DS record) and KSKs protect ZSK DNSKEY records. This allows KSKs to be stored offline.

The TLSA record type allows keys from the DNSSEC PKI hierarchy to authenticate keys wrapped in certificates for a particular hostname, protocol, and port.

All of these certificates constrain the keys they identify to names that are within the zone signing the certificate. The domain's DNSKEY must be configured as the trust anchor.

DNSKEYs are limited in what they can sign. Public CAs are not typically constrained by what names they can sign, so a compromise of even one CA allows the attacker to generate a certificate for any name in the DNS. Because a TLSA certificate association is constrained to its associated name, protocol, and port, the certificate is similarly constrained, even if its public CAs signing the certificate are not.

If the certificate from a web server cannot be validated through DANE and TLSA records, the client gets an error message (see Figure 5-2).

Figure 5-2   TLSA Validation Error

TLSA Records

Without DANE, the certificate validation happens as shown in Figure 5-3.

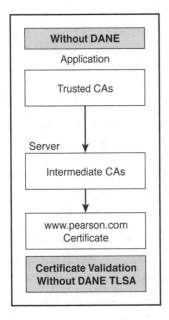

Figure 5-3   Certificate Validation Process Without DANE

The TLSA resource record is used to associate a TLS server certificate or public key with the domain name where the record is found, thus forming a TLSA certificate association. TLSA resource records are not class dependent and have no TTL.

TLSA records can be used to validate self-signed certificates and X.509 certificates from certification authorities (Symantec, Comodo, StartSSL, CACert, and so on). A TLSA record contains the hash of an X.509 certificate (or the full certificate) and

stores it on the DNS server. The owner of the domain is the owner of the certificate. TLSA records consist of the following fields:

- **Certificate Usage field:** Specifies the provided association that will be used to match the certificate presented in the TLS handshake:

  - **0 (PKIX-TA):** Certificate Usage 0 specifies either a CA certificate or the public key of such certificate that *must* be found in any of the certification paths for the end entity certificate given by the server in TLS. This certificate usage is also named CA constraint because it limits which CA can be used to issue certificates for a given service on a host. The presented certificate *must* pass certification validation and a CA certificate that matches the TLSA record *must* be included as part of a valid certification path. Figure 5-4 shows the DANE-based Certificate Usage 0.

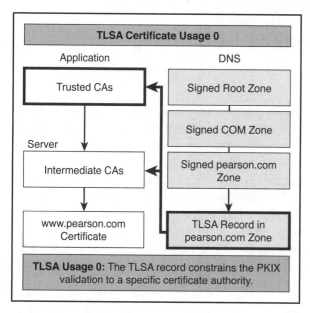

Figure 5-4 TLSA Usage 0

  - **1 (PKIX-EE):** Certificate Usage 1 specifies either an end entity certificate or the public key of such certificate that *must* be matched with the end entity certificate given by a server in TLS. This certificate usage is also named service certificate constraint because it limits which end entity certificate a given service can use on a host. The target certificate *must* pass certification path validation and *must* match the TLSA record. Figure 5-5 shows the DANE-based Certificate Usage 1.

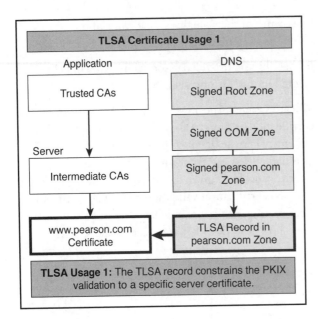

Figure 5-5   TLSA Usage 1

- **2 (DANE-TA):** Certificate Usage 2 specifies either a certificate or the public key of such a certificate that *must* be used as the trust anchor when validating the end entity certificate given by the server in TLS. This certificate usage is also named trust anchor assertion and allows a domain name administrator to specify a new trust anchor. For example, this becomes relevant if the domain issues its own certificates under its own CA that is not expected to be in the end user's collection of trust anchors. The target certificate *must* pass certification path validation, with any certificate matching the TLSA record considered to be a trust anchor for this certification path validation. Figure 5-6 shows the DANE-based Certificate Usage 2.

- **3 (DANE-EE):** Certificate Usage 3 specifies either a certificate or the public key of such a certificate that *must* match the end entity certificate given by the server in TLS. This certificate usage is also named domain-issued certificate because it allows for a domain name administrator to issue certificates for a domain without involving a third-party CA. The target certificate must match the TLSA record. Certificate pass validation is not required for Certificate Usage 3. Figure 5-7 shows the DANE-based Certificate Usage 3.

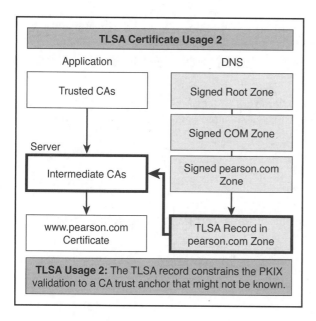

Figure 5-6   TLSA Usage 2

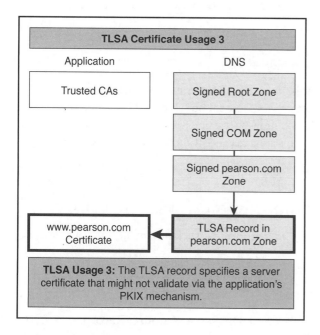

Figure 5-7   TLSA Usage 3

The certificate usage types CA Constraint and Service Certificate Constraint can coexist with and strengthen public CA systems. The Trust Anchor Assertion and Domain-Issued Certificate usage types can operate without public CAs.

- **Selector field:** Specifies which part of the TLS certificate presented by the server will be matched against the associated data. The selector field can have the following values:
  - **0:** Full certificate
  - **1:** SubjectPublicKeyInfo

- **Matching Type field:** Specifies how the certificate association is presented.
  - **0:** Exact match
  - **1:** SHA-256 hash
  - **2:** SHA-512 hash

Consider the following TLSA record examples.

The following is an example of a hashed (SHA-256) association of a PKIX CA certificate:

    _443._tcp.www.pearson.com. IN TLSA (0 0 1
    d2abde240d7cd3ee6b4b28c54df034b9...)

_443._tcp.www.pearson.com defines the protocol used (in this case, 443 for https) and the protocol name of the transport protocol on which a TLS-based service is assumed to exist (in this case, tcp). Transport names can be tcp, udp, and sctp. www.pearson.com is the base domain name, the FQDN of the TLS server.

The following is an example of a hashed (SHA-512) subject public key association of a PKIX and entity certificate:

    _443._tcp.www.pearson.com. IN TLSA (1 1 2 92003ba34942dc74152e2f2c...)

The following is an example of a full certificate association of a PKIX and entity certificate:

    _443._tcp.www.pearson.com. IN TLSA (3 0 0
    30820307308201efa00302010202...)

You can use the PowerShell cmdlet **Add-DnsServerResourceRecord** to verify the necessary TLSA record fields. Simply type **Add-DnsServerResourceRecord -TLSA**. PowerShell asks you for the zone name parameters. Type the name of an existing zone. You then are asked about the **CertificateUsage** parameter. Leave this and all coming parameters empty and press Enter; you get an error message such as the following:

```
Add-DnsServerResourceRecord: Cannot validate argument on parameter
  'CertificateUsage'. The argument "" does not belong to the set
  "CAConstraint,ServiceCertificateConstraint,TrustAnchor Assertion,Do
  mainIssuedCertificate" specified by the ValidateSet attribute.
  Supply an argument that is in the set and then try the command
  again.
```

This error message tells you the possible values for the **CertificateUsage** parameter. In PowerShell parameters, you must use strings instead of numbers for the **CertificateUsage** field of a TLSA record described earlier. For PowerShell parameters, you can choose from the following values:

- **CAConstraint** (0)
- **ServiceCertificateConstraint** (1)
- **TrustAnchorAssertion** (2)
- **DomainIssuedCertificate** (3)

For the **MatchingType** parameter of the PowerShell cmdlet, you can use the following values:

- **ExactMatch** (0)
- **Sha256Hash** (1)
- **Sha512Hash** (2)

For the **Selector** parameter of the PowerShell cmdlet, you can use the following values:

- **FullCertificate** (0)
- **SubjectPublicKeyInfo** (1)

Figure 5-8 demonstrates how to use the PowerShell cmdlet **Add-DnsServerResourceRecord** to add a TLSA record for a server authentication certificate for the pearson.com zone.

```
PS C:\> Add-DnsServerResourceRecord -TLSA

cmdlet Add-DnsServerResourceRecord at command pipeline position 1
Supply values for the following parameters:
ZoneName: pearson.com
CertificateUsage: DomainIssuedCertificate
MatchingType: Sha256Hash
Selector: FullCertificate
CertificateAssociationData: _
```

Figure 5-8 Add-**DnsServerResourceRecord** – TLSA

You can create TLSA records with a trusted CA signed certificate and also with a self-signed certificate. In all cases, a TLSA check is valid through only the first TLS certificate that is correctly signed by a trusted CA with its correct common name. This is the main advantage of DANE: Self-signed certificates can be used even with incorrect names, as long as the certificate itself is the correct one published in DNS.

Configuring DANE

To configure DANE, you must configure TLSA records.

DANE Example Configuration

Suppose you have a domain pearson.com and you have deployed an internal enterprise root CA. You have a web server with an intranet web page, which is accessible through https://intranet.pearson.com and you want to protect TLS access to that website through the use of a TLSA record. An A-record named intranet with the IP address of the intranet web server 172.16.0.10 exists on your Windows Server 2016 DNS server. Your zone pearson.com is signed with DNSSEC.

You have to generate a TLSA record.

For that you can use the TLSA record generator tool (https://www.huque.com/bin/gen_tlsa). In this generator you will be asked about the Base64-encoded X.509 certificate data (which is NOT the **CertificateAssociationData** parameter of the PowerShell cmdlet **Add-DnsServerResourceRecord**).

You can get that kind of data, if you export your existing server authentication certificate in Base64-encoded X.509 format to a .CER file and copy the content into the **Enter/paste PEM format X.509 certificate here** field of the TLSA record generator page as shown in Figure 5-9.

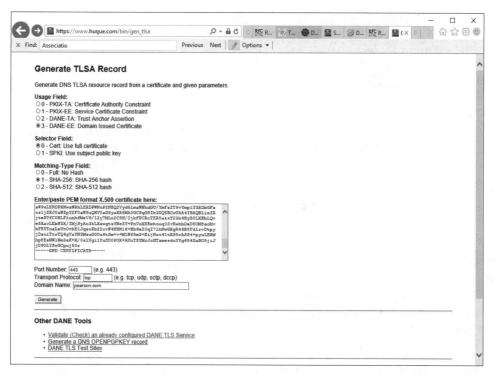

Figure 5-9 TLSA Generator Page with Completed Fields and Imported Base64-encoded X.509 Certificate Data

The TLSA record generator can create a correct TLSA record for verifying the domain-issued web server certificate (issued from the enterprise root CA of pearson. com) if you select the correct fields in the generator. You must select **3 - DANE-EE: Domain Issued Certificate** for the Usage Field, select **0 - Cert: Use full certificate** for the Selector Field, and select **1 - SHA-256: SHA-256 hash** for the Matching-Type Field. You also must fill in the Port Number field with port **443** for https, the transport protocol field with **TCP**, and the Domain Name field with the zone name **pearson.com**. Then click the **Generate** button at the bottom of the page.

The TLSA record generator has created a TLSA record like the following:

```
_443._tcp.pearson.com. IN TLSA 3 0 1 919371d9a16343919371d9a16343…
```

```
Serial: 16000000041b5760da7d63b7f6000000000004
Issuer : DC=com, DC=pearson, CN=pearson-LON-DC1-CA
Subject: CN=pearson.com
Certificate Inception: 2016-11-22 10:30:16+00:00 UTC
Certificate Expiration: 2018-11-22 10:30:16+00:00 UTC
```

```
TLSA Parameters:
Usage: 3 - DANE-EE: Domain Issued Certificate
Selector: 0 - Cert: Full Certificate
Matching Type: 1 - SHA-256: SHA-256 Hash
Service Parameters:
Port: 443, Transport: tcp, Domain name: pearson.com.
```

To effectively add the TLSA record to your DNS server, you must use the Power-
Shell cmdlet **Add-DnsServerResourceRecord** because Windows Server 2016 also
supports unknown record types. With the following PowerShell command, you can
add the TLSA record:

```
Add-DnsServerResourceRecord -TLSA -CertificateAssociationData
   "919371d9a16343…"

-CertificateUsage DomainIssuedCertificate -MatchingType Sha256Hash
   -Selector FullCertificate

-ZoneName pearson.com -name _443._tcp.intranet.pearson.com.
```

Table 5-2 displays the mandatory parameters for the
Add-DnsServerResourceRecord PowerShell cmdlet when you use
the **-TLSA** parameter to add a TLSA record.

Table 5-2   Add-DnsServerRecourseRecord TLSA Record Parameters

Parameter	Values	Description
ZoneName	Example: pearson.com	The name of the zone where you want to add the TLSA record.
CertificateUsage	*CAConstraint*	Specifies either a CA certificate or the public key of such certificate that *must* be found in any of the certification paths for the end entity certificate given by the server in TLS.
	ServiceCertificateConstraint	Specifies either an end entity certificate or the public key of such certificate that *must* be matched with the end entity certificate given by a server in TLS.
	TrustAnchorAssertion	Specifies either a certificate or the public key of such a certificate that *must* be used as the trust anchor when validating the end entity certificate given by the server in TLS.
	DomainIssuedCertificate	Specifies either a certificate or the public key of such a certificate that *must* match the end entity certificate given by the server in TLS. It is also usable for self-signed certificates.

Parameter	Values	Description
MatchingType	*ExactMatch*	Specifies that the same algorithm used to build the hash is the one used in the certificate.
	Sha256Hash	Specifies that the Sha256 algorithm will be used to build the hash.
	Sha512Hash	Specifies that the Sha512 algorithm will be used to build the hash.
Selector	*FullCertificate*	Must be used when you have to add a TLSA record for a certificate signed from a CA.
	SubjectPublicKeyInfo	Must be used when you have to add a TLSA record for a certificate based on a self-signed certificate.
Certificate Association Data	Example: 919371d9a163...	The certificate association data to be matched. You can generate this through the TLSA record generator.
name	Examples: *_443._tcp.srv01.pearson.com* *_25._tcp.exchange.pearson.com*	The name, port, and protocol of the certificate.

After adding the TLSA record, you can view the record as an unknown record with a record type number value of *52* (official TLSA record type number applied through IANA) and a time stamp value of *static* (TLSA records have no TTL) in the Windows Server 2016 DNS Manager console (see Figure 5-10).

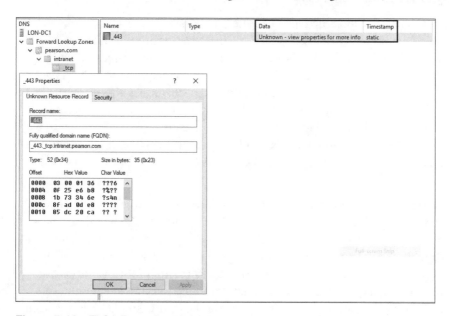

Figure 5-10 TLSA Record in DNS Manager

You also can view the created TLSA record through PowerShell with the PowerShell cmdlet **Get-DnsServerResourceRecord** (see Figure 5-11).

```
PS C:\> Get-DnsServerResourceRecord -ZoneName pearson.com -name _443._tcp.intranet |FL

DistinguishedName  : DC=_443._tcp.intranet,DC=pearson.com,cn=MicrosoftDNS,DC=DNSData
HostName           : _443._tcp.intranet
RecordClass        : IN
RecordData         : DnsServerResourceRecordTLSA
RecordType         : TLSA
Timestamp          :
TimeToLive         : 01:00:00
Type               : 52
PSComputerName     :
CimClass           : root/Microsoft/Windows/DNS:DnsServerResourceRecord
CimInstanceProperties : {DistinguishedName, HostName, RecordClass, RecordData...}
CimSystemProperties  : Microsoft.Management.Infrastructure.CimSystemProperties
```

Figure 5-11   TLSA Record Details with PowerShell

In the Event Viewer, you can verify whether the TLSA record (record type 52) was created successfully (see Figure 5-12).

DNS Client Eve	ⓘ Information	22.11.2016 13:09:39	DNS-Server
DNS-Server	ⓘ Information	22.11.2016 13:05:18	DNS-Server
Audit	ⓘ Information	22.11.2016 12:09:37	DNS-Server
DriverFramewo	ⓘ Information	22.11.2016 12:09:37	DNS-Server

Event 515, DNS-Server

General | Details

A resource record of type 52, name _443._tcp.intranet.pearson.com., TTL 3600 and RDATA 0x030001360F25E6B81B73346E8FAD0DE885DC20CAAEE2A86A97FC53920F85322E0DC837 was created in scope Default of zone pearson.com. [virtualization instance: .].

Figure 5-12   TLSA Record Creation Event in Event Viewer

Common DANE Failures

When a web browser looks up named entities, it queries the site's DNS zone for the IP address of its server, then queries the servers for the certificate, and then uses the servers' CA list to verify the certificate. Using DANE, a browser queries the DNS server for the IP address *and* the TLSA record, then connects to the web server, and determines whether the returned certificate matches what it has already learned and verified from the DNS. Any man-in-the-middle attack is thus thwarted before it even starts. This is the advantage of DANE, but some disadvantages come into play as well: DANE involves more planning and administrative effort on the administrator's side. The following list explains some aspects of DANE that can be possible bottlenecks:

- **DNSSEC DS records and DANE TLSA records published as a fashion statement:** Administrators who expect to "fire and forget" should not publish DNSSEC-signed zones or DANE TLSA records. Alternatively, they can pay others to host their zones and DANE TLS services. Operating poorly maintained DNSSEC zones or TLSA records creates problems not only for the domain in question, but also for all the domains trying to communicate with such a domain. Everyone is better off if DNSSEC and DANE are taken seriously.

- **Failure to update TLSA records before updating the matching server certificate chain:** Multiple domains have left stale TLSA records in effect while updating the server certificate chain. Before deploying the planned certificate chain, make sure that TLSA records that match the planned certificate chain are published in addition to the records that match the current chain. After deploying the planned certificate chain, you can remove the TLSA records that match the previous chain removed.

   When your TLSA records are CNAMEs to a location where your organization's issuing authority maintains suitable TLSA records for you, you can deploy new certificates from that authority without updating the server's TLSA records. The burden of key rollover falls on that authority before it issues any certificates via a new certificate or key.

- **Unsupported certificate usage for SMTP:** For SMTP, the TLSA record certificate usage *must* be either DANE-TA(2) or DANE-EE(3). PKIX-TA(0) and PKIX-EE(1) are not supported.

- **Firewall filtering of TLSA queries:** If your domain is DNSSEC validated, make sure that your firewalls allow TLSA queries to reach your name servers over every address type. (Some firewalls block TLSA lookups only for IPv4.)

Exam Preparation Tasks

Review All the Key Topics

Review the most important topics in the chapter, noted with the Key Topics icon in the outer margin of the page. Table 5-3 lists these key topics and the page numbers where each is found.

Table 5-3 Key Topics for Chapter 5

Key Topic Element	Description	Page Number
List	DANE core functionality	214
Figure 5-1	Using DANE and TLSA Records to Authenticate Without CA	214
Section	DANE Operation Modes	215
List	DANE bottlenecks	216
Section	DANE Security	217
Text and list	TLSA record usage and fields	218

Key Topic Element	Description	Page Number
Example	Adding TLSA records with PowerShell	223
Section	Configuring DANE	224
Table 5-2	**Add-DnsServerRecourseRecord** TLSA Record Parameters	226
List	Common DANE failures	228

Complete the Tables and Lists from Memory

Print a copy of Appendix B, "Memory Tables" (on the book's website), or at least the section for this chapter, and complete the tables and lists from memory. Appendix C, "Memory Tables Answer Key," also on the website, includes completed tables and lists to check your work.

Definition of Key Terms

Define the following key terms from this chapter and check your answers in the glossary.

DANE, DANE criteria, DANE statements, DANE operation modes, TLSA, CAConstraint, ServiceCertificateConstraint, TrustAnchorAssertion, DomainIssuedCertificate, SEP flag

End-of-Chapter Review Questions

1. You want to add a TLSA record with the **Add-DnsServerResourceRecord** PowerShell cmdlet. You are asked for a value for the **CertificateAssociation-Data** parameter. Which value can you use for that parameter?

    a. Public key of the certificate

    b. Thumbprint of the certificate

    c. PEM format X.509 certificate data

    d. Serial number of the certificate

2. You have created a TLSA record and added this record to your pearson.com zone on your Windows Server 2016 DNS server, as in Figure 5-13.

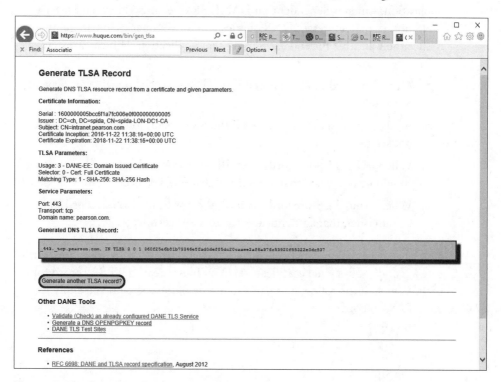

Figure 5-13 Exhibit for Question 2

You now must secure the TLSA record. You also have to ensure that clients can reach your intranet web server through https://intranet.pearson.com with secure DANE validation. Which implementation should you use?

   a. Request a new server certificate and bind it to your website

   b. Sign the pearson.com zone

   c. Remove Everyone from the ACL of the TLSA record

   d. Activate the two NRPT GPO settings: Enable DNSSEC in This Rule and Require DNS Clients to Check That Name and Address Data Has Been Validated by the DNS Server

3. You have added some SRV records to your zone pearson.com. You use DANE to protect these SRV records. Developers are running tests with a new LOB application, which is dependent on DANE SRV records. They have used a DNS library that addresses DNS queries and TLSA queries in parallel to reduce the wait time for end users using that application. Which two statements are correct?

   a. An SRV record can be ignored if the TLSA record on which it depends is not secure.

   b. A TLSA record can be ignored if the SRV record on which it depends is not secure.

   c. When using TLSA records with SRV records, at least one TLSA record should be published that authenticates the server's certificate.

   d. When using TLSA records with SRV records, no TLSA record should be published that authenticates the server's certificate.

4. You have a web server certificate #0, a CA certificate #1, a trust anchor certificate #2, and a self-signed certificate #3. You must create a TLSA record for each. Which of the following certificate usage options should you apply for each TLSA record?

   a. PKIX-TA

   b. PKIX-EE

   c. DANE-TA

   d. DANE-EE

Certificate	Certificate Usage Option
Certificate 0	
Certificate 1	
Certificate 2	
Certificate 3	

This chapter covers the following subjects:

- **DHCP fundamentals:** The DHCP server role is a core networking feature supported on Windows Server 2016. This chapter covers the benefits of DHCP, the differences between stateless and stateful configuration types, DHCP address allocation, the lease generation and renewal process, the DHCP database and backups, and issues related to DHCP moving and migration.

- **DHCP server installation:** A Windows Server 2016 DHCP server can be installed through the DHCP Manager or with PowerShell commands and scripts. This chapter shows you how to authorize a DHCP server in Active Directory and configure important DHCP server settings, with the focus on PowerShell commands.

- **DHCP scopes:** This chapter covers the different types of DHCP scopes, including IPv4 and IPv6 scopes, multicast scopes, and superscopes. It explains the differences, illustrates the configurations, and discusses the scope properties in detail. You learn how to use PowerShell to manage Windows Server 2016 DHCP scopes.

- **DHCP options:** Through DHCP options, you can deliver additional IP configurations to DHCP clients such as DNS servers, routers, and SNTP servers. You learn about the different scope options for IPv4 and IPv6 on a Windows Server 2016 DHCP server and how to configure them using PowerShell and the DHCP Manager.

- **DHCP relay agent:** If DHCP network traffic has to flow through routers, you should understand the purpose of a DHCP relay agent. This chapter explains the main purpose of DHCP relay agents and illustrates their use.

- **DHCP security options:** Here you learn about DHCP security options, including the importance of limited network access for rogue DHCP servers, DHCP auditing possibilities, and DHCP Name Protection and how to configure it.

- **DHCP high availability:** Windows Server 2016 DHCP servers support different high-availability configuration possibilities, such as failover clustering, split scopes, and DHCP failover configuration. The focus is the DHCP failover feature.

- **DHCP Policies:** Windows Server 2016 DHCP servers support DHCP Policies, which enable you to deliver specific IP addresses and optional information to clients based on criteria such as MAC addresses and FQDNs. In this chapter, you get an overview of the important DHCP Policy settings, conditions, and PowerShell cmdlets for managing DHCP Policies.

## CHAPTER 6

Installing and Configuring Windows Server 2016 DHCP Server

This chapter covers DHCP fundamentals that an administrator needs to know, including stateless and stateful configuration, address allocation, lease generation and renewal, backups, and moving and migration issues. It explains the necessary steps for installing a Windows Server 2016 DHCP server, including post-installation tasks and authorization with the DHCP Manager and PowerShell.

You learn about IPv4 and IPv6 DHCP scope management, multicast and superscopes, Windows Server 2016 DHCP scope overall configuration settings, DHCP options, DHCP relay agents, and important DHCP security options. DHCP auditing and DHCP Name Protection are also integral parts of this chapter.

In addition, this chapter discusses DHCP high-availability considerations; points out the differences in failover clustering, split scope, and DHCP failover hot standby or load sharing mode; and shows when to use which technology.

DHCP Policies can be used to fine-tune IP address delivery and DHCP options based on client criteria conditions, to build individual DHCP server solutions with less administrative effort and resources. This chapter helps you understand how to create and configure DHCP Policies for foreign DHCP clients using a guest DNS suffix.

Key topic selections, memory tables, key term definitions, and exam preparation questions give you some powerful tools to increase your knowledge about Windows Server 2016 DHCP server configuration for both the Microsoft exam 70-741 and your daily work.

"Do I Know This Already?" Quiz

The "Do I Know This Already?" quiz enables you to assess whether you should read this entire chapter or simply jump to the "Exam Preparation Tasks" section for review. If you are in doubt, read the entire chapter. Table 6-1 outlines the major headings in this chapter and the corresponding "Do I Know This Already?" quiz questions. You can find the answers in Appendix A, "Answers to the 'Do I Know This Already?' Quizzes and End-of-Chapter Review Questions."

Table 6-1 "Do I Know This Already?" Foundation Topics Section-to-Question Mapping

Foundation Topics Section	Questions Covered in This Section
DHCP Fundamentals	1
DHCP Server Installation	2
DHCP Scopes	3
DHCP Options	4
DHCP Relay Agent	5
DHCP Security Options	6
DHCP High Availability	7, 8
DHCP Policies	9

CAUTION   The goal of self-assessment is to gauge your mastery of the topics in this chapter. If you do not know the answer to a question or are only partially sure of the answer, you should mark that question as wrong for purposes of the self-assessment. Giving yourself credit for an answer you correctly guess skews your self-assessment results and might provide you with a false sense of security.

1. You want to migrate the DHCP configuration (including scope configuration) of an existing Windows Server 2012 R2 DHCP server to a new Windows Server 2016 DHCP server. Which PowerShell command should you use?

    a. **Export-DhcpServer**

    b. **Import-DhcpServer**

    c. **Backup-DhcpServer**

    d. **Restore-DhcpServer**

2. You manage a domain named pearson.com. You have a Windows Server 2016 DHCP server named DHCP1 and you want to implement DHCP failover with hot standby mode. You want to choose DHCP2, which is a Windows Server 2016 Nano Server, as a partner server. Which changes must you make so that you can use DHCP2 as a DHCP failover replication partner for DHCP1? (Choose two.)

    a. Authorize DHCP server DHCP2 in ADDS

    b. Add DHCP server DHCP2 to the domain pearson.com

    c. Replace DHCP2 with a Windows Server 2016 Datacenter server

    d. Install the DHCP server role on DHCP2 and authorize DHCP2

3. In the DHCP Manager on your Windows Server 2016 DHCP server, you select New Scope to create an IPv4 multicast scope starting with 224. You cannot create the scope. What is the best solution for this problem?

   a. Use the PowerShell cmdlet **Add-DhcpServerv4Scope**

   b. Create another scope and use **Set-DhcpServerv4Scope**

   c. Use the PowerShell cmdlet **Add-DhcpServerv4MulticastScope**

   d. Use the PowerShell cmdlet **Add-DhcpServerv4Superscope**

4. You have set up a Windows Server 2016 WDS server that includes the DHCP server role on the server wds.pearson.com. You have configured your DHCP scope with the PowerShell cmdlet **Add-DhcpServerv4OptionDefinition** using the necessary DHCP scope options for clients. Which scope option do you also need to configure that requires using a different command?

   a. Option 59

   b. Option 60

   c. Option 66

   d. Option 67

5. Your company consists of one domain with two sites named Paris and Chicago. Subnet1 (10.10.0.0/16) resides in Paris; Subnet2 (192.168.2.0/24) resides in Chicago. You have installed a Windows Server 2016 DHCP server named DHCP1 in Subnet1. Clients from Subnet2 have problems getting IP addresses from DHCP1. A router between Paris and Chicago does not support the RFC 1541 standard. It is not possible to install a DHCP server in Subnet2. What is the best solution to resolve this issue?

   a. Install a second DHCP server in Subnet1

   b. Install and configure a DHCP relay agent in Paris

   c. Install and configure a DHCP relay agent in Chicago

   d. Install a DHCP relay agent in Paris and a DHCP relay agent in Chicago

6. You have enabled server logging on your Windows Server 2016 DHCP server. You also have configured that server to dynamically update DNS requests on behalf of the DHCP clients with default settings. You want to view the log information about failed DNS dynamic update events. How do you accomplish this?

   a. View failed DNS dynamic update events on the DNS server

   b. View events with an event ID of 31 on the DHCP server

   c. View failed DNS dynamic update events on the DHCP client

   d. View events with an event ID of 30 on the DHCP server

7. You want to split your DHCP scope with a ratio of 70:30 between two DHCP servers. You want to use a solution without changing the default settings. Which split-scope solution is the best option for this scenario?

   a. Use two DHCP servers configured for DHCP failover with load sharing mode

   b. Use two DHCP servers with manually configured DHCP IPv4 scopes

   c. Use two DHCP servers configured for DHCP failover with hot standby mode

   d. Use two DHCP servers and replicate the DHCP scope through a PowerShell script

8. You think about a high-availability solution for your DHCP service. You have two virtual DHCP servers with Windows Server 2016 Datacenter running on a Windows Server 2016 Hyper-V host. The servers are in the same domain, but in different subnets. You want to implement the solution with the least amount of administrative effort and automatic failover functionality for DHCP scopes. Which solution is the best option?

   a. Failover cluster with two nodes

   b. DHCP failover with hot standby mode

   c. DHCP failover with load sharing mode

   d. Hyper-V Replica feature

9. You want to register domain clients of a partner company domain named also.ch on a guest DNS suffix zone in your DNS server named guests.pearson.com when they try to obtain IP address configuration from your DHCP server. Which kind of policy must you create for that?

   a. Group Policy with Name Resolution Policy Table settings

   b. DHCP Policy based on FQDN and operator Is Not Single Label

   c. DHCP Policy based on FQDN and operator Is Single Label

   d. DHCP Policy based on MAC address condition

   e. DNS Policy with zone scope configuration

   f. DNS Policy with recursion policy settings

Foundation Topics

DHCP Fundamentals

The DHCP server role simplifies the client device configuration by distributing network configuration information to network devices and network-enabled services.

The DHCP protocol simplifies the configuration of IP clients in a network environment. Manually configuring the network interface settings (IP address, subnet mask, gateway address, DNS server) of thousands of desktop computers, laptops, servers, printers, scanners, handhelds, and other network devices is not efficient and probably prone to error.

The solution is a DHCP server that manages the IP address information centrally and delivers it automatically to DHCP clients running the DHCP client service. All Windows-based clients are configured to automatically get an IP address after initial installation.

With the PowerShell cmdlet **get-service DHCP | FL ***, you can verify the existence, running state, and properties of the DHCP client service (see Figure 6-1).

```
C:\
PS> get-service DHCP

Status   Name               DisplayName
------   ----               -----------
Running  DHCP               DHCP Client


PS> get-service DHCP | FL *

Name               : DHCP
RequiredServices   : {NSI, Afd, Tdx}
CanPauseAndContinue : False
CanShutdown        : True
CanStop            : True
DisplayName        : DHCP Client
DependentServices  : {NcaSvc, iphlpsvc, WinHttpAutoProxySvc, NcdAutoSetup...}
MachineName        : .
ServiceName        : DHCP
ServicesDependedOn : {NSI, Afd, Tdx}
ServiceHandle      :
Status             : Running
ServiceType        : Win32ShareProcess
StartType          : Automatic
Site               :
Container          :
```

Figure 6-1 Getting DHCP Client Service Information Through PowerShell

This DHCP Server service ensures that all DHCP client devices have appropriate IP address configuration information, which helps to eliminate human error during configuration. When an IP address configuration changes, you can update the DHCP clients centrally using the DHCP Server service; you do not have to change the information directly on each device locally. The DHCP Server service runs only on computers that have the DHCP server role configured.

DHCP is also a key service for mobile users who often change networks. By using DHCP servers, administrators can configure a complex network configuration information offering to nontechnical users.

DHCP clients can use the assigned IP address for a certain period (a *lease*). You can set the lease time to optimize your overall IP address scheme. Clients normally renew their lease automatically after 50 percent of the lease period has passed. As long as IP addresses are available, DHCP continues to provide the renewals.

A Windows Server 2016 DHCP server also supports DHCP version 6 (v6) stateful and stateless configurations for clients in an IPv6 environment:

- **Stateful configuration:** The DHCPv6 server assigns IPv6 addresses and additional DHCP data.

- **Stateless configuration:** The router assigns IPv6 addresses, but the DHCPv6 server assigns additional DHCP data.

DHCP Address Allocation Process

DHCP allocates IP addresses on a dynamic basis, otherwise known as a *lease*. Although you can set the lease duration from a few minutes to unlimited, you typically want to set the duration for only a few hours or days. Here are some important facts about DHCP address allocation:

- The default lease time is 8 days for wired clients and 3 days for wireless clients.

- The DHCP server offers the next available IP address from the pool.

- The IP address can be reversed, based on the MAC address of the client's NIC.

- DHCP initiation traffic is the broadcast network traffic.

- DHCP servers are limited to communication within their IP subnet.

- A non-DHCP client has a manual locally configured IP address.

DHCP Lease Generation

DHCP uses a four-step lease-generation process to assign an IP address to clients. Understanding how each step of this process works helps you troubleshoot problems when clients cannot obtain an IP address. The following list outlines the DHCP lease generation process.

1. The client broadcasts a DHCPDISCOVER packet to every computer in the subnet. The DHCP server or the devices/routers that run a DHCP relay agent respond. In the latter case, the DHCP relay agent forwards the message to the DHCP server for which it is configured to relay requests.

2. A DHCP server responds with a DHCPOFFER packet, which contains a potential IP for the client.

3. The client receives the DHCPOFFER packet. It might receive packets from multiple servers. If it does, it usually selects the server that made the fastest response to its DHCPDISCOVER, which normally is the closest DHCP server. The client broadcasts a DHCPREQUEST that contains a server identifier informing the DHCP servers receiving the broadcast that the client has chosen to accept that server's DHCPOFFER.

4. The DHCP servers receive the DHCPREQUEST. DHCP servers that the client has not accepted use this message as notification that the client has declined that server's offer. The chosen DHCP server stores the IP address client information in the DHCP database (dhcp.mdb) and responds with a DHCPACK message. If the DHCP server cannot provide the IP that was offered in the initial DHCPOFFER, the DHCP server sends a DHCPNAK message.

DHCP Lease Renewal Process

The default DHCP lease renewal process works as follows:

1. The DHCP client sends a DHCPREQUEST packet.

2. The DHCP server sends a DHCPACK packet.

3. If the client fails to renew its lease after 50 percent of the lease duration has expired, the DHCP lease renewal process begins again after 87.5 percent of the lease duration has expired.

4. If the client fails to renew its lease after 87.5 percent of the lease has expired, the DHCP lease generation process starts over again, with a DHCP client broadcasting a DHCPDISCOVER.

When the DHCP lease reaches 50 percent of the lease time, the client automatically attempts to renew the lease. This process occurs in the background. A device might have the same DHCP-assigned IP address for a long time if the computer is not restarted because the device renegotiates the lease periodically.

Every time a client device restarts within the lease period, it contacts the configured default gateway. If the gateway does not respond, the client considers itself to be on a new subnet and enters the discovery phase.

Of course, client devices might be moved while they are turned off (for example, a laptop might be plugged into a new subnet), so client devices also attempt renewal during the startup process or when they detect a network change. If renewal is successful, the lease period is reset.

DHCP Database

The DHCP database of a Windows Server 2016 DHCP server is a dynamic database containing data that relates to scopes, address leases, and reservations. It contains the data file that stores both the DHCP configuration information and the lease data for clients that have leased an IP address from the DHCP server.

By default, the DHCP database files are stored in the %systemroot%\System32\Dhcp folder. Table 6-2 describes the DHCP database files.

Table 6-2   DHCP Database Files

File	Description
Dhcp.mdb	This is the DHCP server database file.
Temp.edb	Tmp.edb is a temporary file that the DHCP database uses as a swap file during database index maintenance operations. Following a system failure, tmp.edb sometimes remains in the Systemroot\System32\Dhcp directory.
J50.log and J50res#####.jrs	J50.log and J50res#####.jrs are logs of all database transactions. The DHCP database uses these logs to recover data when necessary.
J50.chk	J50.chk is a checkpoint file used in truncating the transaction log for the DHCP server.

DHCP Backup

The DHCP database is automatically backed up every 60 minutes. You can manually back up the database anytime in the DHCP management console by right-clicking the DHCP server and selecting Backup or by using the PowerShell cmdlet **Backup-DhcpServer**. If you want to export the DHCP configuration, including scope configuration (without DHCP data), you can use the PowerShell cmdlet **Export-DhcpServer**.

The following items are backed up:

- All scopes
- Reservations
- Leases
- All options, including server options, scope options, reservation options, and class options
- All registry keys and other configuration settings that are set in DHCP server properties.

You can initiate the database restoration process from the DHCP console by right-clicking the DHCP server and then clicking Restore or by using the PowerShell cmdlet **Restore-DhcpServer**. During the restoration, process the DHCP Server service is automatically restarted.

Moving a DHCP Database

You might have to move the DHCP server role to another server (for example, as part of the migration process from Windows Server 2012 R2 to Windows Server 2016). If so, you also need to move the DHCP database to the same target server. This ensures that client leases are retained and reduces the likelihood of client configuration issues.

The steps for moving a DHCP database follow:

Step 1.   Back up the DHCP database on the old server.

Step 2.   Stop the old DHCP Server service.

Step 3.   Copy the DHCP database to the new server and, if necessary, install the DHCP server role.

Step 4.   Restore the database.

Step 5.   Start the DHCP Server service.

DHCP Server Migration

When you decommission an outdated or old server (for example, Windows Server 2003), you must migrate the services from the old server to a new server. Migrating the DHCP server is not difficult, but you must use command-line utilities to export the DHCP data from the old server to a file and then import the data from that file to the new DHCP server. You can use **netsh** or Windows PowerShell commands to accomplish this. The following list outlines how to migrate a DHCP server.

Step 1.   Install the DHCP server role on the computer that will be the new DHCP server.

Step 2.   Stop the DHCP service on the current DHCP server.

Step 3.   Export the DHCP data from the current server.

Step 4.   Copy the DHCP data to the new server (or make it available on the network).

Step 5.   Import the DHCP data to the new server.

Use Windows PowerShell to export DHCP data with the **Export-DhcpServer** cmdlet. The following command exports DHCP data from the DHCP server D1 to a file named d1.xml:

```
Export-DhcpServer
-ComputerName D1
-Leases
-File C:\d1.xml
```

DHCP Data Import

Use Windows PowerShell to import DHCP data with the **Import-DhcpServer** cmdlet. The following command imports DHCP data from the DHCP data file D1.xml to the new DHCP server D2:

```
Import-DhcpServer
-ComputerName D2
-Leases
-File C:\export\d1.xml
-BackupPath C:\dhcp\
```

Exporting and Importing DHCP Data with netsh

You also can still use **netsh** commands by opening an elevated command prompt and pressing Enter at the end of each line:

You export DHCP data with **netsh** in this way:

```
Netsh
DHCP
Server D1
Export C:\D1.txt all
```

You import DHCP data with **netsh** as follows:

```
Netsh
DHCP
Server D2
Import C:\D1.txt all
```

DHCP Server Installation

As a first step to implementing a DHCP solution, you need to know how to install and authorize a DHCP server. You can install the DHCP server role by using the following:

- The Add Roles and Features Wizard in Server Manager
- Windows PowerShell (**Add-WindowsFeature** *DHCP*)

The DHCP server role can be installed only on Windows Server operating systems. You can install the DHCP server on a DC, but any server running Windows Server can host the DHCP server (except a Windows Server 2016 Nano Server). For example, a branch office file and print server might also act as the local DHCP server. Local administrative rights are required to perform the installation, and the server must have a static IP address.

TIP A DHCP server cannot be installed on a Windows Server 2016 Nano Server: no Nano Server package is available for a DHCP server.

TIP You should *not* install a DHCP server on an application server, Exchange, or SQL Server.

The following list outlines the main steps of a DHCP server installation process:

Step 1.   Install the DHCP server role with Server Manager or PowerShell (**Add-WindowsFeature DHCP -includeManagementTools**).

Step 2.   Perform DHCP server post-installation tasks (creating DHCP security groups, restarting DHCP service, authorizing DHCP server in ADDS).

Step 3.   Configure the DHCP server settings.

Figure 6-2 shows how to install the DHCP server role with PowerShell.

Figure 6-2 Installing the DHCP Server Role with PowerShell

Figure 6-3 shows a successful DHCP server role installation and verification with PowerShell.

Figure 6-3 DHCP Server Role Installation and Verification with PowerShell

Figures 6-4 and 6-5 show the DHCP server post-installation configuration tasks in the Server Manager.

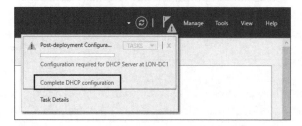

Figure 6-4   DHCP Server Post-installation Tasks (Initial Step)

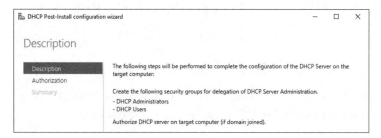

Figure 6-5   DHCP Server Post-Install Configuration Wizard (Description)

Figure 6-6 shows the DHCP Post-Install Configuration Wizard Authorization page. On the Authorization page, you choose the credentials to be used to authorize the DHCP server in ADDS (the user must be a member of the Enterprise Admins security group).

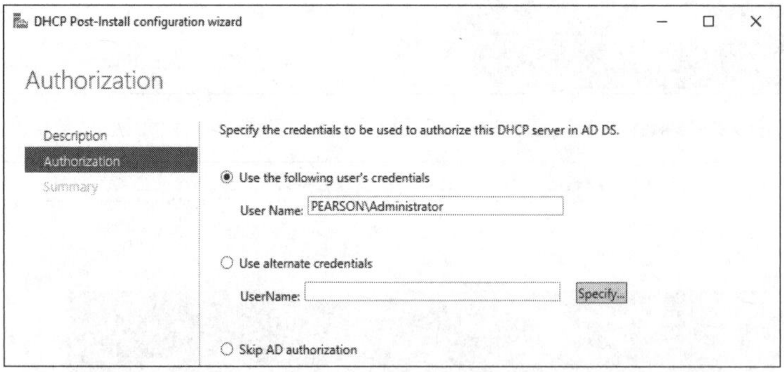

Figure 6-6   DHCP Server Post-Install Configuration Wizard (Authorization)

Figure 6-7 shows the Summary page of the DHCP Post-Install Configuration Wizard.

Figure 6-7   DHCP Server Post-Install Configuration Wizard (Summary)

Alternatively, you can authorize a DHCP server through PowerShell (see Figure 6-8).

Figure 6-8   Authorize and Verify Successful DHCP Server Authorization with PowerShell

You also can authorize a DHCP server through the DHCP Manager (see Figures 6-9 and 6-10).

Figure 6-9   DHCP Manager: Manage Authorized Servers

Figure 6-10   Authorize DHCP Server Through the DHCP Manager

You can verify which DHCP servers are authorized in ADDS through the DHCP Manager and the Manage Authorized Servers window (see Figure 6-11).

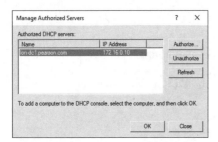

Figure 6-11   Verifying Authorized DHCP Servers in the DHCP Manager

You also can verify that your DHCP server is successfully authorized in ADDS through the DHCP Manager. When you see the green check marks by IPv4 and IPv6, as in Figure 6-12, you know that the DHCP server is authorized.

Figure 6-12   DHCP Manager Green Check Marks by IPv4 and IPv6

Performing DHCP Post-Installation Tasks with PowerShell Commands

You can perform the DHCP post-installation tasks using the following commands:

Step 1.   Create the security groups: **Netsh** *DHCP Add SecurityGroups*

Step 2.   Restart the service: **Restart-Service** *DHCPServer*

Step 3.   Authorize the DHCP server in ADDS: **Add-DHCPServerinDC**
<hostname or IP address>

If you want to manage a remote DHCP server, you must install the Remote Server Administration Tools (RSAT) component. The following PowerShell command installs the DHCP Manager utility on your system:

```
Add-WindowsFeature RSAT-DHCP
```

To get all authorized DHCP servers in Active Directory, you can use the following PowerShell cmdlet:

```
Get-DhcpServerinDC
```

To get the list of all DHCP scopes on DHCP server DHCP1, use the following PowerShell cmdlet:

```
Get-DhcpServerv4Scope -computername DHCP1
```

To create a new DHCP IPv4 scope with a range of IP addresses from 172.16.0.1 to 172.16.0.100 on a DHCP server named *DHCP1* use the following PowerShell command:

```
Add-DhcpSrverv4Scope -StartRange 172.16.0.1 -EndRange 172.16.0.100
  -Name TestScope
-SubnetMask 255.255.255.0 -State Active -Computername DHCP1
```

Use the following PowerShell command to configure the DHCP server parameters of DNS server, domain, and router address for the created IPv4 scope:

```
Set-DhcpServerv4OptionValue -computername DHCP1 -DnsServer
  172.16.0.200 -DnsDomain pearson.com -Router 172.16.0.99
```

To exclude the range of 172.16.0.80 to 172.16.0.100 from the IP addresses given for the created scope, use the following PowerShell command:

```
Add-DhcpServerv4ExclusionRange -computername DHCP1 -ScopeID 172.16.0.0
  -StartRange 172.16.0.80 -EndRange 172.16.0.100
```

To create a reservation for a client named CL1 with the IP address 172.16.0.80, use the following PowerShell command:

```
Get-DhcpServerv4Lease -computername CL1 -IPAddress 172.16.0.80 |
  Add-DhcpServerv4Reservation -computername CL1
```

To perform a mass reservation of IP addresses for computers listed in a CSV file, first create a text file, as in the following example:

```
ScopeID,IPAddress,Name,ClientID,Description
172.16.0.81, Client1, b1-ac-5a-f1-9e-6f,Reservation Client1
172.16.0.82, Client2, f1-bc-7a-f1-9a-1a,Reservation Client2
172.16.0.83, Client3, D1-a9-5b-e1-2a-6f,Reservation Client3
```

Save this file as C:\reservations.csv and run the following PowerShell command to create the DHCP reservations:

```
Import-Csv -Path C:\reservations.csv | Add-DhcpServerv4Reservation
  -computername DHCP1
```

To deactivate an IPv4 scope, use the following PowerShell command:

```
Set-DhcpServerv4Scope -computername DHCP1 -ScopeID 172.16.0.0 -State
  InActive
```

To get DHCP server statistics, use the following PowerShell command:

```
Get-DhcpServerv4Statistics -computername DHCP1
```

Figure 6-13 shows the output of that PowerShell command.

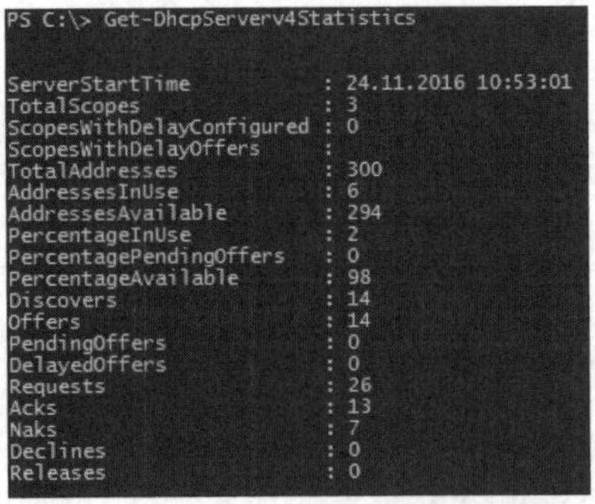

Figure 6-13   Get-DhcpServerv4Statistics Example Output

You can also use a PowerShell script that installs the DHCP server role, authorizes the DHCP server in ADDS, adds a DHCP server IPv4 scope, sets DHCP options for that scope, and changes the lease duration time, as in the following example:

```
$DNSDomain="pearson.com"
$DNSServerIP="172.16.1.10"
$DHCPServerIP="172.16.1.10"
$StartRange="172.16.1.150"
$EndRange="172.16.1.200"
$Subnet="255.255.255.0"
$Router="172.16.1.1"

Install-WindowsFeature -Name 'DHCP' -IncludeManagementTools
cmd.exe /c "netsh dhcp add securitygroups"
Restart-service dhcpserver
Add-DhcpServerInDC -DnsName $Env:COMPUTERNAME
Set-ItemProperty -Path registry::HKEY_LOCAL_MACHINE\SOFTWARE\
  Microsoft\ ServerManager\Roles\12 -Name ConfigurationState -Value 2
Add-DhcpServerV4Scope -Name "DHCP Scope" -StartRange $StartRange
  -EndRange $EndRange -SubnetMask $Subnet
Set-DhcpServerV4OptionValue -DnsDomain $DNSDomain -DnsServer
  $DNSServerIP -Router $Router
Set-DhcpServerv4Scope -ScopeId $DHCPServerIP -LeaseDuration
  1.00:00:00
```

DHCP Authorization

Because the DHCP protocol is based on broadcasts, an unknown DHCP server can provide invalid information to clients. You can avoid this by authorizing the server. Administrators use a process called *DHCP authorization* to register the DHCP server in the AD domain before it can support DHCP clients.

Active Directory Requirements

You must authorize a Windows Server 2016 DHCP server in AD DS before it can begin leasing IP addresses. It is possible to have a single DHCP server providing IP addresses for subnets that contain multiple Active Directory domains.

TIP You must use an Enterprise Administrator account to authorize the DHCP server.

Standalone DHCP Server Considerations

A standalone DHCP server is a Windows Server 2016 DHCP server without domain membership. If the standalone DHCP server detects an authorized DHCP server in the domain, it does not lease IP addresses and automatically shuts down.

Unauthorized DHCP Servers

Many routers and firewalls can act as DHCP servers, but often these servers do not recognize DHCP-authorized servers and might lease IP addresses to clients. When you detect unauthorized DHCP servers, you should disable the DHCP service or functionality on them.

DHCP Scopes

You need to configure your Windows Server 2016 DHCP server with the range of IP addresses and DHCP options to be distributed to the clients. These ranges of IP addresses are called *scopes*. After the initial configuration of the DHCP server, you must create a scope. A DHCP scope is a range of IP addresses that a DHCP server manages. A DHCP scope typically is confined to the IP addresses in a given subnet, although a DHCP server can host scopes for multiple different subnets.

A DHCP scope for the network 192.168.5.0/24 (subnet mask of 255.255.255.0) can support a range from 192.168.5.1 through 192.168.5.254. When a computer or device on the 192.168.5.0/24 subnet requests an IP address, the scope that defined the range in this example allocates an address between 192.168.5.1 and 192.168.5.254.

Table 6-3 describes the four types of DHCP scopes.

Table 6-3 DHCP Scopes

Scope Type	Description	Example
IPv4 scope	IPv4 range of IP addresses	10.10.0.0/16
IPv4 multicast scope	IPv4 range of IP addresses starting with 224	224.0.0.0/8
IPv4 superscope	Aggregation of two or more IPv4 scopes	10.10.0.0/16 and 172.16.0.0/
IPv6 scope	IPv6 range of IP addresses	2001::..../64

Superscopes

A superscope is a collection of individual scopes that are grouped for administrative purposes. You use a superscope to allow clients to receive an IP address from multiple logical subnets even when the clients are located on the same physical subnet. You can create a superscope only if you have two or more IP scopes already created.

To understand the benefit of a superscope, you must think about what you need to do when a scope runs out of addresses and you cannot add more addresses from the subnet. The solution is to add a new subnet to the DHCP server. This scope will lease addresses to clients in the same physical network, but the clients will be in a separate network logically. This process is known as *multinetting*. After you add a new subnet, you must configure routers to recognize the new subnet so that you ensure local communications in the physical network. In addition, suppose that you need to move clients gradually into a new IP numbering scheme. Having both numbering schemes coexist for the original lease's duration means that you can transparently move clients into the new subnet. When you have renewed all client leases in the new subnet, you can retire the old subnet and remove the superscope.

You can create, configure, and remove DHCP superscopes with PowerShell. Figure 6-14 shows the available DHCP server superscope PowerShell cmdlets.

```
PS C:\> get-command *superscope*

CommandType     Name                                    Version    Source
-----------     ----                                    -------    ------
Function        Add-DhcpServerv4Superscope              2.0.0.0    DhcpServer
Function        Get-DhcpServerv4Superscope              2.0.0.0    DhcpServer
Function        Get-DhcpServerv4SuperscopeStatistics    2.0.0.0    DhcpServer
Function        Remove-DhcpServerv4Superscope           2.0.0.0    DhcpServer
Function        Rename-DhcpServerv4Superscope           2.0.0.0    DhcpServer
```

Figure 6-14   DHCP Server Superscope PowerShell Cmdlets

Multicast Scopes

A multicast scope is a collection of multicast addresses from the class D IP address range of 224.0.0.0 to 239.255.255.255 (224.0.0.0/3). These addresses are used when applications need to communicate with numerous clients efficiently and simultaneously. Multiple hosts then listen to traffic for the same IP address.

A multicast scope is commonly known as a Multicast Address Dynamic Client Allocation Protocol (MADCAP) scope. Applications that request addresses from these scopes need to support the MADCAP API. Windows Deployment Service (WDS) is an example of an application that supports multicast transmissions. Multicast scopes allow applications to reserve a multicast IP address for data and content delivery.

You can create, configure, and remove DHCP multicast scopes with PowerShell. Figure 6-15 shows the available DHCP server multicast scope PowerShell cmdlets.

```
PS C:\> get-command *multicast*

CommandType     Name                                          Version    Source
-----------     ----                                          -------    ------
Function        Add-DhcpServerv4MulticastExclusionRange       2.0.0.0    DhcpServer
Function        Add-DhcpServerv4MulticastScope                2.0.0.0    DhcpServer
Function        Get-DhcpServerv4MulticastExclusionRange       2.0.0.0    DhcpServer
Function        Get-DhcpServerv4MulticastLease                2.0.0.0    DhcpServer
Function        Get-DhcpServerv4MulticastScope                2.0.0.0    DhcpServer
Function        Get-DhcpServerv4MulticastScopeStatistics      2.0.0.0    DhcpServer
Function        Remove-DhcpServerv4MulticastExclusionRange    2.0.0.0    DhcpServer
Function        Remove-DhcpServerv4MulticastLease             2.0.0.0    DhcpServer
Function        Remove-DhcpServerv4MulticastScope             2.0.0.0    DhcpServer
Function        Set-DhcpServerv4MulticastScope                2.0.0.0    DhcpServer
```

Figure 6-15   DHCP Server Multicast Scope PowerShell Cmdlets

You can create IPv4 scopes, IPv4 superscopes, and IPv4 multicast scopes in the DHCP Manager (see Figure 6-16).

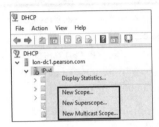

Figure 6-16   Create IPv4 Scopes in the DHCP Manager

You can create only IPv6 scopes in the DHCP Manager because it does not have the capability to create IPv6 superscopes or IPv6 multicast scopes (see Figure 6-17).

Figure 6-17   IPv6 Superscopes and Multicast Scopes Are Not Possible in the DHCP Manager

When you use the New Scope Wizard to create a scope and you try to create a multicast scope starting with 224 in that wizard, you get an error message (see Figure 6-18). The solution is to use the New Multicast Scope Wizard to create IPv4 multicast scopes.

When you try to create an IPv6 scope starting with Fe80::, which is a link-local address, this is not possible and you get the error message in Figure 6-19.

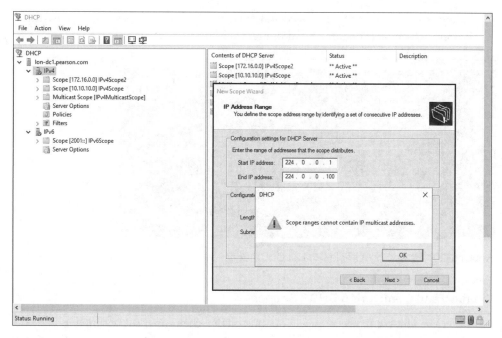

Figure 6-18   IPv4 Scope Ranges Cannot Contain IP Multicast Addresses

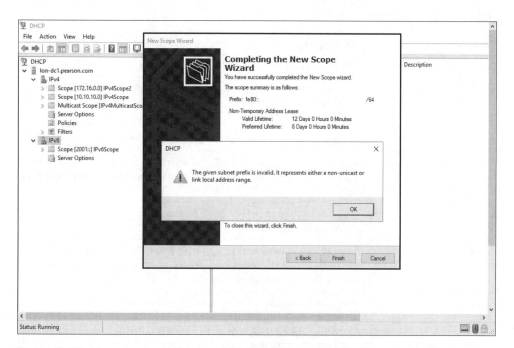

Figure 6-19   Nonunicast and Link-Local Address Ranges Are Not Allowed in IPv6 Scopes in the DHCP Manager

When you want to verify the successful creation of all scope types, you can use the PowerShell cmdlets demonstrated in Figure 6-20.

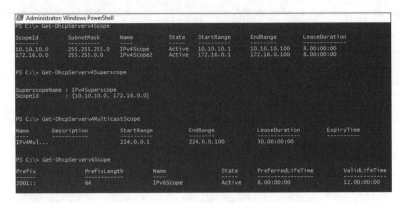

Figure 6-20   PowerShell Cmdlets to List DHCP Scopes

Creating and Configuring DHCP Scopes

To create and configure a scope, you must define the properties outlined in Table 6-4.

Table 6-4   DHCP Scope Properties

Property	Description
Name and description	Identifies the scope. The name is mandatory.
IP address range	Lists the range of addresses that can be offered for lease. This property is mandatory.
Subnet mask	Used by client computers to determine their location in the organization's network infrastructure. This property is mandatory.
Exclusions	Lists single addresses or blocks of addresses that fall within the IP address range but that will not be offered for lease. This property is optional.
Delay	Amount of time to delay before sending DHCPOFFER. The default setting is 0 milliseconds.
Lease duration	Lists the lease duration. Use shorter durations for scopes that have limited IP addresses, and use longer durations for more static networks. The default setting is 8 days.
Options	You can configure many optional properties on a scope, but typically you configure the following properties: 003: Router (gateway), 006: DNS servers, 015: DNS suffix.
Activation	The scope needs to be activated before it can hand out IP addresses.

For example, imagine that you want to create an IPv4 scope named PearsonScope with an IP range of 192.168.1.100/24 to 192.168.1.200/24 with an exclusion range of 192.168.1.180 to 192.168.200. In addition, it has a DHCP Option 003 with three routers (192.168.1.201, 192.168.1.202, and 192.168.1.203) and a DHCP Option 006 with a DNS server of 192.168.1.210 and a default lease time of 8 days. Figure 6-21 through Figure 6-26 show the graphical configuration steps in the DHCP Manager on a Windows Server 2016 DHCP server.

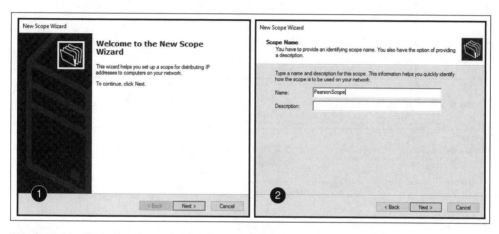

Figure 6-21   Create an Example IPv4 Scope (Welcome Page and Name)

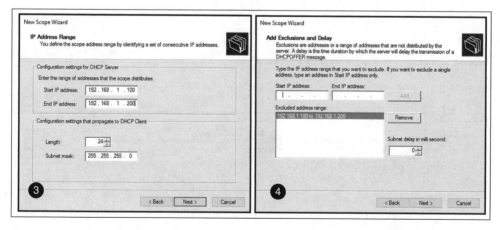

Figure 6-22   Create an Example IPv4 Scope (IP Address Range and Exclusions/Delay)

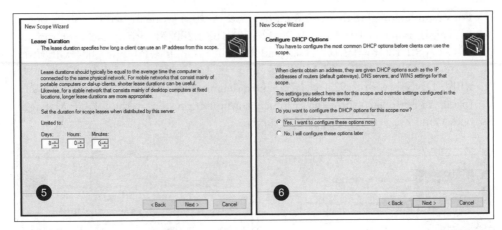

Figure 6-23   Create an Example IPv4 Scope (Lease Duration and DHCP Options)

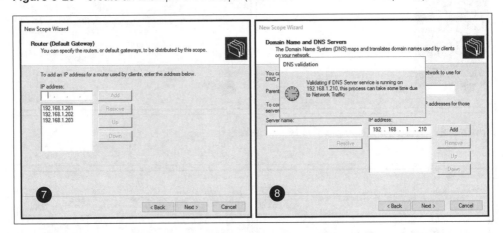

Figure 6-24   Create an Example IPv4 Scope (Router and DNS Server)

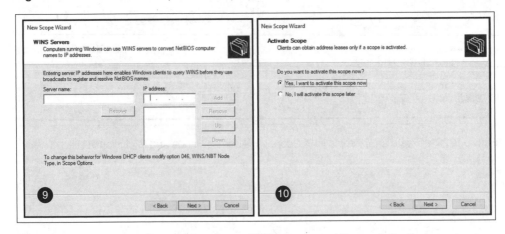

Figure 6-25   Create an Example IPv4 Scope (WINS Server and Scope Activation)

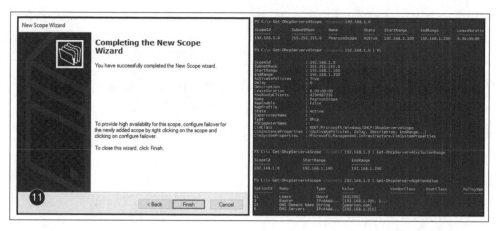

Figure 6-26   Successfully Completing the New Scope Wizard and PowerShell Scope Verification

Creating DHCP Scopes with PowerShell

In Windows Server 2012, Microsoft introduced several new Windows PowerShell cmdlets for configuring and managing DHCP servers. Each cmdlet has parameters that need to be met, depending on actions to be taken. Many of the new cmdlets address scope creation and management (see Table 6-5).

Table 6-5   Windows Server 2016 DHCP Server PowerShell Cmdlets

Cmdlet	Description
Add-DhcpServerv4Scope	Adds an IPv4 scope on the DHCP Server service
Get-DhcpServerv4Scope	Returns the IPv4 scope configuration of the specified scopes
Get-DhcpServerv4ScopeStatistics	Gets the IPv4 scope statistics that correspond to the IPv4 scope identifiers specified for a DHCP Server service
Remove-DhcpServerv4Scope	Deletes the specified IPv4 scopes from the DHCP Server service
Set-DhcpServerv4Scope	Sets the properties of an existing IPv4 scope on the DHCP Server service

TIP   For more information about all Windows Server 2016 DHCP server Power-Shell cmdlets, refer to http://aka.ms/Blsmzw.

If you want a computer or device to obtain a specific address from the scope range, you can reserve that address to be assigned permanently to the device in DHCP. Reservations are useful for tracking IP addresses assigned to devices such as printers. To create a reservation in the DHCP Manager, select the scope in the DHCP console and, from the Action menu, click New Reservation. Figure 6-27 shows an example of a reservation for a printer named Printer1.

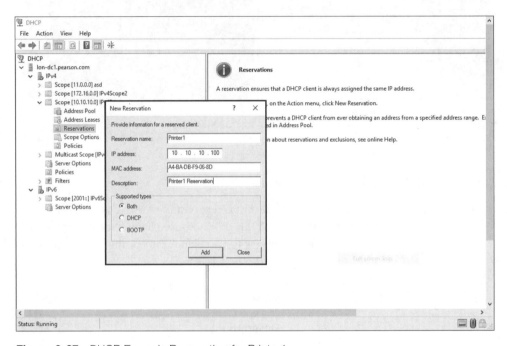

Figure 6-27   DHCP Example Reservation for Printer1

You need to provide the information outlined in Table 6-6 to create the reservation.

Table 6-6   Windows Server 2016 DHCP Server Reservation Properties

Property	Description
Reservation name	A friendly name to reference the reservation
IP address	The IP address from the scope that you want to assign to the device
MAC address	The MAC address of the interface you want to assign the address to
Description	An optional field to provide a comment about the reservation

With the PowerShell cmdlet **Add-DhcpServerv4Reservation**, you can create a DHCP reservation for an IPv4 IP address with a MAC address. You also can add an IPv6 reservation for an IPv6 scope with the PowerShell cmdlet **Add-DhcpServerv6Reservation**.

Figure 6-28 shows all Windows Server 2016 DHCP server PowerShell cmdlets for reservations.

```
PS C:\> get-command *reservation*

CommandType     Name                                    Version     Source
-----------     ----                                    -------     ------
Function        Add-DhcpServerv4Reservation             2.0.0.0     DhcpServer
Function        Add-DhcpServerv6Reservation             2.0.0.0     DhcpServer
Function        Get-DhcpServerv4Reservation             2.0.0.0     DhcpServer
Function        Get-DhcpServerv6Reservation             2.0.0.0     DhcpServer
Function        Remove-DhcpServerv4Reservation          2.0.0.0     DhcpServer
Function        Remove-DhcpServerv6Reservation          2.0.0.0     DhcpServer
Function        Set-DhcpServerv4Reservation             2.0.0.0     DhcpServer
Function        Set-DhcpServerv6Reservation             2.0.0.0     DhcpServer
```

Figure 6-28   Windows Server 2016 DHCP Reservation PowerShell Cmdlets

DHCP Options

Chapter 3, "Configuring and Managing DNS Policies," covered DHCP options in detail. However, you need to understand some additional topics that are more appropriately covered within the context of this chapter.

Common IPv4 DHCP Scope Options

DHCP options are values for common configuration data. They can be applied to the server, scope, class, and reservation levels. Option codes identify DHCP options and come from RFC documentation found on the IETF website. Table 3-2 in Chapter 3 shows the most common DHCP options.

In the following example, you add a DHCP IPv4 option 60 for a DHCP server named DHCP1 with PowerShell:

```
Add-DhcpServerv4OptionDefinition -ComputerName DHCP1 -Name PXEClient
  -Description "PXE Support" -OptionId 060 -Type String
```

With the PowerShell command, you can add a DHCP IPv4 option 43 for a DHCP server named DHCP1 (you have to give it the value for option 43 in hexadecimal):

```
Set-DhcpServerv4OptionValue -ComputerName MyDHCPServer -ScopeId
  "PearsonScope"
-OptionId 043 -Value 0x01,0x04,0x00,0x00,0x00,0x00,0xFF
```

Figure 6-29 shows the PowerShell cmdlets you can use for configuring DHCP options.

```
PS C:\> get-command *DHCP*option*

CommandType     Name                                    Version     Source
-----------     ----                                    -------     ------
Function        Add-DhcpServerv4OptionDefinition        2.0.0.0     DhcpServer
Function        Add-DhcpServerv6OptionDefinition        2.0.0.0     DhcpServer
Function        Get-DhcpServerv4OptionDefinition        2.0.0.0     DhcpServer
Function        Get-DhcpServerv4OptionValue             2.0.0.0     DhcpServer
Function        Get-DhcpServerv6OptionDefinition        2.0.0.0     DhcpServer
Function        Get-DhcpServerv6OptionValue             2.0.0.0     DhcpServer
Function        Remove-DhcpServerv4OptionDefinition     2.0.0.0     DhcpServer
Function        Remove-DhcpServerv4OptionValue          2.0.0.0     DhcpServer
Function        Remove-DhcpServerv6OptionDefinition     2.0.0.0     DhcpServer
Function        Remove-DhcpServerv6OptionValue          2.0.0.0     DhcpServer
Function        Set-DhcpServerv4OptionDefinition        2.0.0.0     DhcpServer
Function        Set-DhcpServerv4OptionValue             2.0.0.0     DhcpServer
Function        Set-DhcpServerv6OptionDefinition        2.0.0.0     DhcpServer
Function        Set-DhcpServerv6OptionValue             2.0.0.0     DhcpServer
```

Figure 6-29   Windows Server 2016 DHCP PowerShell Cmdlets for DHCP Options

PXE Boot Options

PXE-enabled network cards add the DHCP option 60 to their discover packets. Normally, DHCP clients send a DHCP option 67 packet, and then DHCP servers return a DHCP 68 option offer. DHCP uses the same ports used by the Windows Deployment Services PXE server function.

If you deploy DHCP and a PXE server on the same machine, you must set DHCP to make offers that also include the 60 option. A DHCP server then makes the DHCP 60 offer back to the client. You need to set DHCP options 60 (PXE Client), 66 (Boot Server Host Name), and 67 (Bootfile Name). You can set options 66 and 67 in the Scope Options window in the DHCP console, but you must set the 60 option via the command line. The following code sample lists the procedure:

```
netsh
dhcp
server \\<server_machine_name>
add optiondef 60 PXEClient String 0 comment=PXE support
set optionvalue 60 STRING PXEClient
exit
```

After this, a PXE server sends back boot server and boot information to the PXE-enabled network client so that it can accept an operating system installation.

Common IPv6 DHCP Scope Options

Windows Server 2016 DHCP servers support DHCP IPv6, and IPv6 DHCP options can be assigned at the server and scope levels. Table 6-7 lists the IPv6 DHCP scope options.

Table 6-7   Windows Server 2016 IPv6 DHCP Scope Options

Option Code	Name	Description
00021	SIP Server Domain Name List	Specifies the domain names and Session Initiation Protocol (SIP) outbound proxy servers for the client to use.
00022	SIP Server IPv6 Address List	Lists IPv6 addresses indicating SIP outbound proxy servers available to the client. If an organization has more than one server, the server with the highest preference is used.
00023	DNS Recursive Name Server IPv6 Address	Identifies the DNS server used for DNS queries. If an organization has more than one DNS server, the server with the highest preference is used.
00024	Domain Search List	Specifies the domain search list the client should use when resolving hostnames with DNS.
00027	NIS IPv6 Address List	Lists IPv6 addresses indicating NIS servers available to the clients.
00028	NIS + IPv6 Address List	Lists IPv6 addresses indicating NISv2 (NIS +) servers available to the clients.
00029	NIS Domain List	Used by the server to convey the client list of NIS domain name information to the client.
00030	NIS + Domain Name List	Used by the server to convey the client list of NIS + Domain name information to the client.
00031	SNTP Server IPv6 Address List	Provides a list of one or more IPv6 addresses of SNTP servers so that clients can perform time sync with the SNTP server.

Applying DHCP Options

DHCP options are applied in an order of precedence at four different levels:

1. **Server level:** Assigns a server-level option to all DHCP clients of the DHCP server.

2. **Scope level:** Assigns a scope-level option to all clients of a scope. Scope options override server options.

3. **Class level:** Assigns a class-level option to all clients that identify themselves as members of a class. Class options override both scope and server options.

4. **Reserved client level:** Assigns a reservation-level option to one DHCP client. Reserved client options apply to devices that have a DHCP reservation.

DHCP Relay Agent

When attempting to obtain an IP address, clients use broadcasts to initiate communications. Therefore, DHCP servers and clients can communicate only within their IP subnet. As a consequence, many networks have a DHCP server in each subnet. For a DHCP server to respond to a DHCP client request, it must be capable of receiving DHCP requests. You can enable this by configuring a *DHCP relay agent* on each subnet.

A DHCP relay agent is a computer or router that listens for DHCP broadcasts from DHCP clients and then relays them to DHCP servers in different subnets. You configure a DHCP relay agent to point to the IP address of the DHCP server in the remote subnet.

The DHCP relay agent relays any DHCP broadcast packets to unicast packets. These packets are sent to the relay agent's listed DHCP server, which typically is on another IP subnet across a router. The DHCP server sends DHCP offer and acknowledge packets back to the relay agent by using unicast broadcasts. The relay agent then broadcasts these packets on the local subnet, so the client that needs an address can receive it without having to change its core processing.

You also can relay DHCP packets into other subnets by using a router that is compatible with RFC 1542. This means that, upon receiving a DHCP broadcast packet, the router can replay the DHCP broadcast on the other subnets to which it connects. Because this DHCP relay happens within the router, you do not have to create a specific DHCP relay agent on a server running Windows Server. Most modern routers have RFC 1542 capabilities.

For more information regarding RFC 1542, visit https://tools.ietf.org/html/rfc1542.

DHCP Security Options

Because DHCP is not an authentication protocol, you must take precautions to ensure that only valid clients are receiving network information. You also should take precautions to ensure that the names your client computers have registered in your organization's DNS are protected.

Be sure to consider three important points regarding DHCP security options:

- Limit physical access to the network.

- Enable DHCP auditing to track DHCP usage.

- Use DHCP name protection to prevent attacks.

Limited Network Access

DHCP by itself is designed to work before the necessary information is in place for a client computer to authenticate with a domain controller. Administrators need to take precautions to prevent unauthorized computers from obtaining a lease with DHCP.

DHCP Auditing

You should enable audit logging on all DHCP servers. This gives you a historical view of activity and enables you to trace when an unauthorized user obtained an IP address in the network. Be sure to review the audit logs at regular intervals. You can enable DHCP server logging by following these steps:

Step 1.   Open the DHCP Manager.

Step 2.   In the console tree, click the DHCP server you want to configure.

Step 3.   On the **Action** menu, click **Properties**.

Step 4.   On the **General** tab, select **Enable DHCP Audit Logging** and then click **OK**.

Table 6-8 lists some of the most important DHCP server log event codes.

Table 6-8   Windows Server 2016 DHCP Server Log Common Event Codes and DHCP DNS Dynamic Update Event Codes

	Event ID	Description
DHCP Server Log Common Event Codes	00	Log started
	01	Log stopped
	02	Log temporarily paused
	10	New IP address leased
	11	Lease renewed
	12	Lease released
	13	IP address found in use
	14	Lease request could not be satisfied
	15	Lease denied
	20	Bootstrap Protocol (BOOTP) address leased
DHCP DNS Dynamic Update Events Codes	30	DNS dynamic update request
	31	DNS dynamic update failed
	32	DNS dynamic update successful

DHCP Name Protection

A DHCP server can automatically create resource records for DHCP clients in the DNS database.

You should protect the names that DHCP registers in DNS on behalf of other computers or systems from being overwritten by non-Windows operating systems that use the same names. In addition, if DHCP is not configured for conflict detections, you should protect the names from being overwritten by systems that use static addresses that conflict with DHCP-assigned addresses when they use unsecure DNS.

For example, a UNIX-based system named CL1 could potentially overwrite the DNS address that DHCP assigned and registered on behalf of a Windows-based system also named CL1. DHCP Name Protection addresses this issue.

Name squatting describes the conflict that occurs when one client registers a name with DNS, but another client already is using that name. This problem causes the original machine to become inaccessible. It typically occurs with systems that have the same names as Windows operating systems.

DHCP Name Protection addresses this by using a resource record known as a *Dynamic Host Configuration Identifier (DHCID)* to track which machines originally requested which names. The DHCP server provides the DHCID record, which is stored in DNS. When the DHCP server receives a request from a machine with an existing name for an IP address, the DHCP server can refer to the DHCID in DNS to verify that the machine requesting the name is the original machine that used the name. If it is not the same machine, the DNS resource record is not updated. You can implement this for IPv4 and IPv6, and you can configure it at the server scope level. However, the server-level implementation will apply only for newly created scopes.

You can enable DHCP Name Protection for an IPv4 or IPv6 node in this way:

Step 1.   Open the DHCP console.

Step 2.   Right-click the IPv4 or IPv6 node and then open the Property page.

Step 3.   Click **DNS**, click **Advanced**, and click the **Enable Name Protection** check box.

You also can enable DHCP Name Protection for an individual scope in this way:

Step 1.   Expand IPv4 or IPv6, right-click the scope, and open the Property page.

Step 2.   Click **DNS** and **Advanced**, and then click the **Enable Name Protection** check box.

Figure 6-30 shows where to enable DHCP Name Protection in the Windows Server 2016 DHCP Manager.

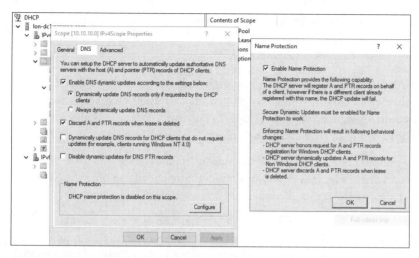

Figure 6-30 DHCP Name Protection

With the following PowerShell command, you can enable DHCP name protection for a scope:

```
Set-DhcpServerv4DnsSetting -ComputerName "dhcpserver.pearson.com"
  -ScopeId 10.10.10.0
-DynamicUpdates "OnClientRequest" -NameProtection $True
```

Just Enough Administration

The new Just Enough Administration (JEA) and Just in Time Administration (JIT) features are new to Windows Server 2016 features and provide a generic RBAC solution that uses PowerShell remotely. *Role-based access control (RBAC)* is a method of regulating access to computer or network resources based on the roles of individual users within an enterprise. In this context, access is the capability of an individual user to perform a specific task, such as viewing, creating, or modifying a file. JEA and JIT enable you to give administration credentials only when needed for a finite time and only for specific tasks. You can implement JEA or JIT for all possible PowerShell cmdlets, as well as for DHCP server PowerShell cmdlets.

For example, suppose you start a remote PowerShell session to your DHCP server with the following PowerShell command, and the *$AdminCred* variable includes DHCP Administrator credentials:

```
Enter-PSSession -Computername dhcp.pearson.com -credential $AdminCred
```

When connected, you have permission to run all DHCP PowerShell cmdlets on dhcp.pearson.com.

When you want to use JEA, start the remote PowerShell session in another way:

```
Enter-PSSession -Computername dhcp.pearson.com -configurationname
  JEA_Demo -credential $NonAdminCred
```

The value *JEA_Demo* for the parameter **-configurationname** is the JEA endpoint, which a highly trusted administrator pre-created through the PowerShell cmdlet **New-PSSessionConfigurationFile**. The JEA endpoint was configured to define which DHCP PowerShell cmdlets you are allowed to use through that endpoint.

Suppose you want to restrict DHCP administrators to allow them just to configure DHCP scope settings. The JEA endpoint defines that you can use only the **Set-DhcpServerv4Scope** PowerShell cmdlet and no other DHCP cmdlets.

When you are connected through a PowerShell remote session with **Enter-PSSession** and are using a JEA/JIT endpoint, your endpoint access is applied to the WinRM Virtual User for this remote session, not the connected user you are logged in as.

Using the following steps, you can restrict permissions to the default directory security group DHCP Administrators so that only members of this group can use the **Set-DhcpServerv4Scope** cmdlet on the DHCP server:

Step 1.   Create a maintenance role capability file in PowerShell ISE and run it:

```
# Fields in the role capability
$MaintenanceRoleCapabilityCreationParams = @{
    Author = 'Pearson Admin'
    CompanyName = 'Pearson'
    VisibleCmdlets = 'Set-DhcpServerv4Scope'
    FunctionDefinitions =
            @{ Name = 'Get-UserInfo'; ScriptBlock = {
  $PSSenderInfo } }
}


# Create the demo module, which will contain the maintenance Role
  Capability File
New-Item -Path "$env:ProgramFiles\WindowsPowerShell\Modules\Demo_
  Module" -ItemType Directory
New-ModuleManifest -Path "$env:ProgramFiles\WindowsPowerShell\
  Modules\Demo_Module\Demo_Module.psd1"
New-Item -Path "$env:ProgramFiles\WindowsPowerShell\Modules\Demo_
  Module\RoleCapabilities" -ItemType Directory


# Create the Role Capability file
New-PSRoleCapabilityFile -Path "$env:ProgramFiles\
  WindowsPowerShell\Modules\Demo_Module\RoleCapabilities\
  Maintenance.psrc" @MaintenanceRoleCapabilityCreationParams
```

Step 2.   Create and register a Demo Session configuration file and run it:

```
# Determine domain
$domain = (Get-CimInstance -ClassName Win32_ComputerSystem).
  Domain


# Replace with your non-admin group name
$NonAdministrator = "$domain\DHCP Administrators"


# Specify the settings for this JEA endpoint
# Note: You will not be able to use a virtual account if you are
  using WMF 5.0 on Windows 7 or Windows Server 2008 R2
$JEAConfigParams = @{
    SessionType = 'RestrictedRemoteServer'
    RunAsVirtualAccount = $true
    RoleDefinitions = @{
        $NonAdministrator = @{ RoleCapabilities = 'Maintenance' }
    }
    TranscriptDirectory = "$env:ProgramData\JEAConfiguration\
  Transcripts"
}


# Set up a folder for the Session Configuration files
if (-not (Test-Path "$env:ProgramData\JEAConfiguration"))
{
    New-Item -Path "$env:ProgramData\JEAConfiguration" -ItemType
  Directory
}


# Specify the name of the JEA endpoint
$sessionName = 'JEA_Demo'


if (Get-PSSessionConfiguration -Name $sessionName -ErrorAction
  SilentlyContinue)
{
    Unregister-PSSessionConfiguration -Name $sessionName
  -ErrorAction Stop
}


New-PSSessionConfigurationFile -Path "$env:ProgramData\
  JEAConfiguration\JEADemo.pssc" @JEAConfigParams


# Register the session configuration
Register-PSSessionConfiguration -Name $sessionName -Path
  "$env:ProgramData\JEAConfiguration\JEADemo.pssc"
```

Step 3.   Test the JEA configuration.

Figure 6-31 illustrates the use of JEA configuration. In this example, the only DHCP server PowerShell cmdlet available for the remotely connected user is the **Set-DhcpServerv4Scope** PowerShell cmdlet.

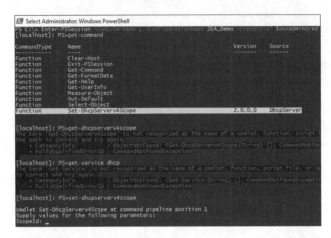

Figure 6-31   Test JEA for DHCP PowerShell Remote Administration

Figure 6-32 shows the information for both the ConnectedUser and the RunAsUser.

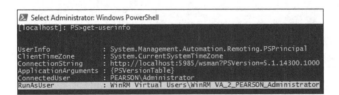

Figure 6-32   Test JEA for DHCP **Get-UserInfo**

The output of **Get-UserInfo** shows the information for both the ConnectedUser and the RunAsUser. The connected user is the account that is connected to the remote session (for example, your account). The connected user does not need to have administrator privileges. The RunAs account is the account that actually performs the privileged actions. By connecting as one user and running as a privileged user, you allow nonprivileged users to perform specific administrative tasks without giving them administrative rights.

TIP   With the PowerShell cmdlet **Get-PSSessionConfiguration**, you can list the JEA endpoints you have set up.

TIP   In the Windows Remote Management operational log in Event Viewer, Event ID 193 records the ConnectedUser's SID and name, as well as the RunAs virtual account's SID. In the PowerShell operational log in Event Viewer, Event ID 4104 records each command invoked if you have enabled Module Logging. You enable PowerShell Module Logging through Group Policy. You can set Turn on Module Logging to Enabled at Computer Configuration\Administrative Templates\ Windows Components\Windows PowerShell.

DHCP High Availability

DHCP is a critical service in modern networks and needs to be available when clients have to get IP configuration information from the central IP configuration delivery service. You have three main possibilities for making DHCP high available: clustering, split scopes, and DHCP failover.

DHCP Clustering

The DHCP Server service can run on Windows Server 2016 in a two-member failover cluster. Both cluster nodes have the DHCP server role installed with identical scopes. Configuration information is stored in shared storage. If one node of the cluster fails, the other member in the cluster detects the failure and starts the DHCP service on the surviving member of the cluster.

Split Scopes

Split scope involves two DHCP servers. In this case, each DHCP server controls a part of the entire range of IP addresses and both servers are active on the same network. For example, if your subnet is 172.16.0.0, you might assign an IP address range of 172.16.0.1 to 172.16.0.150 to DHCP server A (the primary server) and assign the range 172.16.0.151 to 172.16.0.254 to DHCP server B (a secondary DHCP).

DHCP Failover

DHCP manages the distribution of IP addresses in TCP/IP networks of all sizes. When this service fails, clients lose connectivity to the network and all its resources. DHCP failover is a feature in Windows Server 2016 that addresses this issue.

DHCP Failover Overview

DHCP clients renew leases at regular intervals. When a DHCP service fails, clients no longer have IPs. Before Windows Server 2012, DHCP failover was not possible because DHCP servers were independent and unaware of each other. Therefore, configuring two separate DHCP servers to distribute the same pool of addresses could lead to duplicate addresses. Providing redundant DHCP services required that you configure clustering and perform a significant amount of manual configuration and monitoring.

The solution since Windows Server 2012 is the new DHCP failover feature, which is still supported in Windows Server 2016 and enables two DHCP servers to provide IP addresses and optional configurations to the same subnets or scopes. Therefore, you now can configure two DHCP servers to replicate lease information. If one of the servers fails, the other server services the clients for the entire subnet.

TIP   You cannot configure DHCP failover for more than two DHCP servers. In addition, DHCP failover cannot be used with IPv6 scopes and subnets.

Configuring DHCP Failover

When you want to avoid building a failover cluster to implement a high availability (HA) solution for your DHCP server, you need to establish a DHCP failover relationship between the two DHCP servers that you want to configure for the DHCP failover feature. This partnership is stored in Active Directory and needs a unique name. The failover partners exchange this name during configuration. This enables a single Windows Server 2016 DHCP server to have multiple failover relationships with other Windows Server 2012 or Windows Server 2016 DHCP servers, as long as they all have unique names.

To configure the Windows Server 2016 DHCP failover feature, you can choose between two modes. Table 6-9 explains the load sharing and hot standby modes in detail.

Table 6-9   Windows Server 2016 DHCP Failover Modes

Mode	Characteristics
Load sharing	This is the default mode. Both DHCP servers simultaneously supply IP configuration to clients. The server that responds to IP configuration requests depends on how the administrator configures the load distribution ratio. The default ratio is 50:50.

Mode	Characteristics
Hot standby	One DHCP server acts as primary; the other is the secondary. The primary actively assigns IPs for the scope/subnet. The secondary assumes this role only if the primary server becomes unavailable. A DHCP server can simultaneously act as the primary for one scope or subnet and also be the secondary for another. Administrators must configure a percentage of the scope addresses to be assigned to the standby server. These addresses are supplied during the Maximum Client Lead Time (MCLT) interval if the primary is down. The default MCLT value is 5 percent of the scope. The secondary server takes control of the entire IP range after the MCLT interval passes.

You can use two important DHCP failover parameters to configure the behavior of a DHCP server, the required wait time when the partner DHCP server is unavailable, and when to enable automatic transition:

- **MCLT:** The Maximum Client Lead Time parameter determines the amount of time a DHCP server should wait when a partner is unavailable before assuming control of the address range. This value cannot be zero; the default is 1 hour.

- **Auto state switchover interval:** When a server loses the connection with its partner, the server has no way to know what is causing the communication loss. It remains in this state until an administrator changes it to Partner Down state. You can enable automatic transition to Partner Down state through the auto state switchover interval. The default value is 10 minutes.

To configure failover, use the Configuration Failover Wizard, which you launch by right-clicking the IP node or the scope node. The following steps give an example of DHCP failover configuration between two DHCP servers.

Suppose you want to configure a DHCP failover relationship (hot standby mode, with DHCP1 as the primary DHCP server) for a scope between two Windows Server 2016 DHCP servers named DHCP1 and DHCP2 in the domain pearson.com through the following steps. (All DHCP servers must be authorized before DHCP failover feature can be configured.)

Step 1. On DHCP1 in the DHCP Manager, under the IPv4 node, select **Configure Failover**.

Step 2. On the Configure Failover page, select the scope you want to replicate.

Step 3.   On the Specify the Partner Server to Use for Failover page, type the name of your partner server (in this case **DHCP2**) or select **Add Server** to add DHCP2.

Step 4.   On the Create a New Failover Relationship page, leave the Relationship Name value. Here you can configure the Maximum Client Lead Time setting, the DHCP failover mode (load balance or hot standby), Load Balance Percentage, State Switchover Interval, Message Authentication, and Shared Secret. Under Mode, select **Hot Standby**. Leave the default settings at 5% for addresses reserved for the standby server.

Step 5.   Finish the DHCP failover configuration.

After that configuration, the failover scope exists on DHCP1 and DHCP2, with DHCP1 serving as the active (primary) DHCP server and DHCP2 working as the passive (secondary) DHCP server. If DHCP1 stops working, clients obtain their IP addresses and options from DHCP2. Replication traffic between DHCP failover partners is encrypted. The DHCP servers cannot be in different domains, but they can exist in different sites and subnets. DHCP uses TCP port 647 to listen for DHCP failover traffic. The DHCP installation creates the following inbound and outbound firewall rules:

- **Microsoft-Windows-DHCP-Failover-TCP-In**

- **Microsoft-Windows-DHCP-Failover-TCP-Out**

You also can configure DHCP failover through PowerShell cmdlets. Figure 6-33 shows the DHCP failover PowerShell cmdlets.

Figure 6-33   DHCP Failover PowerShell Cmdlets

With the PowerShell cmdlet **Invoke-DhcpServerv4FailoverReplication**, you can invoke scope replication between DHCP failover partners.

When you want to remove a DHCP failover partnership and you want to completely remove its settings, you must go to IPv4 Properties and select the Failover tab. This removes the DHCP failover object completely.

DHCP Policies

With Windows Server 2016 DHCP Policies, you can create policies that deliver specific IP addresses and optional information to clients based on a set of conditions.

This gives you the possibility of having different types of IP devices receive addresses and other options from a subset of IP addresses in the scope range. This strategy can assist you in identifying the device type based on the IP address.

For example, with the DHCP subnet 192.168.1.0/24, you can use policies to dictate that IP-based phones receive addresses from 192.168.1.80 to 192.168.1.100 and have long leases, whereas laptops receive addresses from 192.168.1.101 to 192.168.1.150 with much shorter leases.

Table 6-10 outlines the characteristics of DHCP0.

Table 6-10 Windows Server 2016 DHCP Policies

Characteristics	Description
Policy level	DHCP Policies can be applied at the server or scope levels.
Processing order	DHCP Policies have a unique processing order. Lower-numbered policies are applied before higher-numbered policies.
Conditions	If the DHCP request from the client matches the conditions specified, the settings of the policy are applied. Conditions can be combined with Boolean AND or OR statements. Conditions criteria include vendor class, user class, MAC address, client identifier, FQDN, and relay agent information.
Settings	Settings are the network configurations delivered to the client.
Enabled/Disabled	The policy state is either Enabled or Disabled. Disabled policies are not processed.

DHCP Policy Conditions

Figure 6-34 shows the possible conditions of a DHCP Policy.

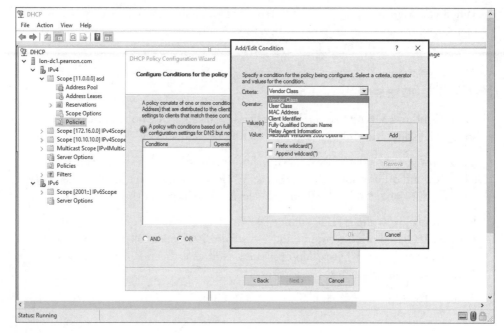

Figure 6-34   DHCP Policy Conditions

DHCP Policies Example

One example of the usefulness of DHCP Policies is registering foreign clients using a guest DNS suffix. Today, thanks to bring your own device (BYOD), devices are not necessarily all domain members. These foreign devices are workgroup or domain-joined devices. You can handle the DNS registrations of such devices via DHCP Policies.

Windows Server 2016 DHCP Policies offer criteria enabling you to group clients based on FQDN. You can use wildcards to group clients based on their DNS suffix or hostnames. Then you can either disable PTR registration for them or register these clients with a different DNS suffix. You can think of the PTR record as the opposite of the A record. Whereas the A record points a domain name to an IP address, the PTR record resolves the IP address to a domain/hostname. PTR records are used for the reverse DNS lookup. Using the IP address, you can get the associated domain/hostname. An A record should exist for every PTR record.

The following configuration explains the implementation of a DHCP Policy at the scope level. Figure 6-35 shows the DHCP Policy Configuration Wizard. The name of the DHCP Policy will be *ForeignDeviceDHCPPolicy*.

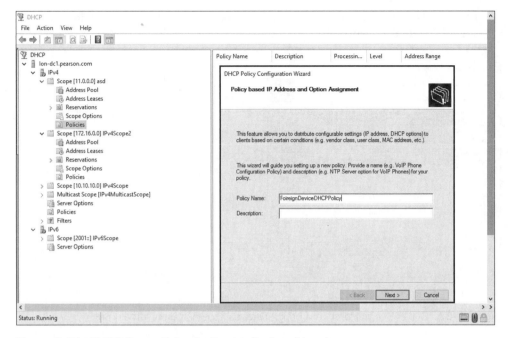

Figure 6-35 DHCP Scope Policy for Foreign Devices (Name)

Figure 6-36 shows possible DHCP Policy criteria for domain-joined foreign devices. For these kinds of devices, you must select the criteria of Fully Qualified Domain Name and also select the operator Is Not Single Label.

Figure 6-36 DHCP Scope Policy for Foreign Devices (FQDN and Is Not Single Label)

Figure 6-37 shows how to define a DHCP Policy condition for foreign devices with a hostname starting with DELL or a suffix of either consuit.ch or also.ch.

Figure 6-37   DHCP Scope Policy for Foreign Devices (Hostname or Domain Suffix)

After you have created the DHCP Policy, you can edit the properties of that policy. Figure 6-38 shows where to find the properties of a DHCP Policy.

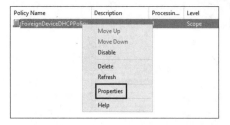

Figure 6-38   DHCP Scope Policy Properties

In the DHCP scope policy properties on the DNS tab, you can select the setting Register DHCP Clients Using the Following DNS Suffix to ensure that all foreign domain or workgroup-joined clients are registered under the guest DNS suffix guestdomain.pearson.com. For successful registration of DNS records, this DNS suffix must be configured on the DNS server. Figure 6-39 shows this setting.

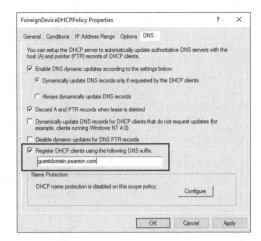

Figure 6-39   DHCP Scope Policy DNS Properties

You also can create, configure, and remove DHCP Policies with PowerShell cmdlets. Figure 6-40 shows the DHCP Policy PowerShell cmdlets.

Figure 6-40   DHCP Policy PowerShell Cmdlets

Exam Preparation Tasks

Review All the Key Topics

Review the most important topics in the chapter, noted with the Key Topics icon in the outer margin of the page. Table 6-11 lists these key topics and the page numbers where each is found.

Table 6-11   Key Topics for Chapter 6

Key Topic Element	Description	Page Number
Text	Verifying running state of DHCP server service	239
Text	DHCP stateful and stateless configuration	240
Section	DHCP Backup	242

Key Topic Element	Description	Page Number
Section	Moving a DHCP Database	243
Section	DHCP Server Migration	243
Tip	DHCP server on Windows Server 2016 Nano Server	245
Step list	DHCP server installation process	245
Section	DHCP Scopes	252
Section	Creating DHCP Scopes with PowerShell	259
Section	Common IPv4 DHCP Scope Options	261
Section	PXE Boot Options	262
Section	DHCP Name Protection	266
Section	Just Enough Administration	267
Section	DHCP Failover	271
Section	DHCP Policies	275

Complete the Tables and Lists from Memory

Print a copy of Appendix B, "Memory Tables" (on the book's website), or at least the section for this chapter, and complete the tables and lists from memory. Appendix C, "Memory Tables Answer Key," also on the website, includes completed tables and lists to check your work.

Definition of Key Terms

Define the following key terms from this chapter and check your answers in the glossary.

DHCP server, DHCP authorization, DHCP failover, DHCP hot standby, DHCP load sharing, DHCP Policy, DHCP reservation, DHCP relay agent

End-of-Chapter Review Questions

1. You have configured a hot standby failover partnership between two Windows Server 2016 DHCP servers named DHCP1 and DHCP2 for the IP scope Scope1. DHCP1 is the active partner. The DHCP service on DHCP1 has crashed after a database corruption. You want to restore Scope1 and ensure that the partnership between both servers is still working after the restore process. Which three commands should you use?

   a. **netsh dhcp server import**

   b. **netsh dhcp server export**

   c. **Backup-DhcpServer**

   d. **Restore-DhcpServer**

   e. **Remove-Item**

   f. **Stop-Service**

2. You must run a PowerShell script to install and configure the DHCP server role on a Windows Server 2016 with the IP address 172.16.1.10. You have to do the following tasks:

   ▪ Install the Windows Server 2016 DHCP server role with management tools

       ▪ Create the necessary security groups

   ▪ Authorize the DHCP server in Active Directory with the following parameters

       ▪ Add the following DHCP IPv4 scope : 172.16.1.150-172.17.1.200/24

       ▪ Configure the following DHCP scope options: Domain: pearson.com, DNS: 172.16.1.10, Gateway: 172.16.1.1

   ▪ Configure lease duration

   You have the following PowerShell script:

```
$DNSDomain="pearson.com"
$DNSServerIP="172.16.1.10"
$DHCPServerIP="172.16.1.10"
$StartRange="172.16.1.150"
$EndRange="172.16.1.200"
$Subnet="255.255.255.0"
$Router="172.16.1.1"

_____A_____ -Name 'DHCP' -_____B_____
_____C_____ /c "netsh dhcp add securitygroups"
Restart-service dhcpserver
_____D_____ -DnsName $Env:COMPUTERNAME
_____E_____ -Name " Scope" -Start $StartRange -End $EndRange
-SubnetMask $Subnet
_____F_____ -DnsDomain $DNSDomain -DnsServer $DNSServerIP
  -Router $Router
```

Match the PowerShell cmdlet in the list that follows (a–m) with the placeholders A–F in the PowerShell script.

a. **IncludeAllSubFeature:** __

b. **IncludeManagementTools:** __

c. **Install-Package:** __

d. **Add-WindowsFeature:** __

e. **Add-DhcpServerinDC:** __

f. **Cmd.exe:** __

g. **Netsh.exe:** __

h. **Add-DhcpServerv4Class:** __

i. **Add-DhcpServerInDC:** __

j. **Add-DhcpServerV4Scope:** __

k. **Add-DhcpServerV4MulticastScope:** __

l. **Set-DhcpServerV4OptionValue:** __

m. **Add-DhcpServerv4OptionDefinition:** __

3. You manage your Windows Server 2016 DHCP servers. You use IPv4 and IPv6 scopes. Which requirement can you not implement through Windows Server 2016 DHCP for IPv6 scopes?

   a. Use the DHCP failover feature in hot standby mode

   b. Deliver the SIP server domain list to DHCP clients

   c. Deliver IP addresses and options

   d. Configure exclusions for scopes

   e. Configure reservations for scopes

4. You have configured a hot standby failover partnership between two Windows Server 2016 DHCP servers named DHCP1 and DHCP2 for the IP scope Scope1, with DHCP1 as the active partner. DHCP1 is not operating, but DHCP2 is not responding to DHCP client requests. Which setting allows DHCP2 to respond to DHCP client requests if DHCP1 is not operating?

   a. Set Maximum Client Lead Time to Zero

   b. Enable State Switchover Interval setting

   c. Enable AutoStateTransition setting

   d. Change Reserve Percentage setting

5. Paul, a DHCP administrator, wants to create a new DHCP IPv4 scope on a Windows Server 2016 DHCP server named DHCP1 using the following PowerShell command:

```
Enter-PSSession -computername DHCP1 -Configurationname DHCPPaul
    -credential $PaulCred.
```

When he tries to use the **Add-DhcpServerv4Scope** PowerShell cmdlet, he gets the following message:

```
"The term 'Add-DhcpServerv4Scope' is not recognized as the name
    of a cmdlet, function, script file, or operable program…."
```

You need to allow Paul to create DHCP IPv4 scopes on DHCP1 through remote PowerShell sessions. Which two steps must you do to allow him the use of the PowerShell cmdlet **Add-DhcpServerv4Scope**?

   a. Add Paul to the DHCP Administrators security group

   b. Add **Add-DhcpServerv4Scope** to the maintenance role capability file

   c. Add **Add-DhcpServerv4Scope** to the session configuration file

   d. Use **Register-PSSessionConfiguration**

   e. Add Paul's computer to TrustedHosts

This chapter covers the following subjects:

- **IPAM fundamentals:** IP Address Management (IPAM) in Windows Server 2016 enables you to deploy, manage, and monitor IP address and name resolution infrastructures; accomplish multiserver management of DNS and DHCP servers; and meet audit and compliance requirements for DDI. Through IPAM, you can automatically discover DHCP and DNS servers. IPAM in Windows Server 2016 has been further enhanced to support critical new capabilities such as DNS management and support for multiple AD forests. IPAM in Windows Server 2016 can now perform most of the DNS management tasks that required the administrator to previously use the DNS Manager. In this chapter, you learn about the benefits of IPAM, the IPAM architecture, deployment requirements, and considerations and improvements in Windows Server 2012 R2 and Windows Server 2016.

- **IPAM provisioning:** The IPAM provisioning process normally is performed through a step-by-step process using the Windows Server 2016 IPAM Provision Wizard. You learn the necessary steps for deploying your first Windows Server 2016 IPAM server, including configuring the discovery of managed DHCP and DNS servers and unblocking these servers to enable central management through IPAM.

- **Creating and managing IP blocks and ranges:** Windows Server 2016 supports IPv4 public and private and IPv6 global and unicast addresses. You learn how to manage DHCP server configuration settings, address spaces, and DHCP scopes through the IPAM management console and PowerShell. This chapter also shows how to import address spaces through CSV files and how to update IPAM address spaces. In addition, you learn how to find, allocate, and reclaim IP addresses and use the IP address tracking feature.

- **Monitoring utilization of IP address spaces:** This chapter covers IPAM utilization monitoring and DHCP and DNS server monitoring through IPAM. It explores IPAM monitoring view and shows how to use the IPAM management console to view and monitor health and configuration events through the Event Catalog.

- **Configuring IPAM database storage using SQL Server:** This chapter covers the database setup and configuration options for IPAM. It explains the possible IPAM database choices, shows how to view and change IPAM database settings through PowerShell cmdlets, and demonstrates the different ways of preparing a Microsoft SQL Server on a separate computer for IPAM with different authentication options. You also learn about the new Windows Server 2016 IPAM feature to purge utilization data from the IPAM database.

- **IPAM and SCVMM:** Here you explore integration between IPAM and SCVMM and how to configure it.

## CHAPTER 7

Implementing Windows Server 2016 IPAM

This chapter covers some core IPAM functionality aspects, including its architecture, benefits, deployment requirements, considerations, and improvements in Windows Server 2012 R2 and Windows Server 2016 IPAM. The chapter prepares you for IPAM provisioning and explains the main purpose and technical features of Windows Server 2016 IPAM. In addition, it delivers an overview on the IPAM modules and main improvements in Windows Server 2016 IPAM, such as support for multiple forests and enhanced DNS server management capabilities.

One of the main topics of the chapter is the IPAM provisioning and deployment process. You get step-by-step instruction on deploying your first IPAM server and preparing and configuring managed servers through Group Policy and PowerShell scripts. You can then centrally manage these servers through IPAM. The chapter also covers DNS management with IPAM and the use of IPAM role-based access control (RBAC) with IPAM built-in security groups and custom IPAM roles.

You learn how to create and manage IP blocks and ranges, as well as how to configure DNS and DHCP server settings through IPAM, address spaces, and DHCP scopes using the IPAM configuration console and PowerShell cmdlets. The chapter demonstrates how to import address space data through CSV files, as well as how to update address spaces and both create and configure IPAM custom fields.

This chapter covers monitoring IPAM utilization and DHCP and DNS servers, as well as viewing and monitoring health and configuration events. You also learn how to use WID and Microsoft SQL Server databases as IPAM database storage and how to manage that with PowerShell cmdlets. You also look into the integration configuration for IPAM and SCVMM.

Key topic selections, memory tables, key term definitions, and exam preparation questions give you get some powerful tools to increase your knowledge about the Windows Server 2016 IPAM configuration for the Microsoft 70-741 exam and your daily work.

"Do I Know This Already?" Quiz

The "Do I Know This Already?" quiz enables you to assess whether you should read this entire chapter or simply jump to the "Exam Preparation Tasks" section for review. If you are in doubt, read the entire chapter. Table 7-1 outlines the major headings in this chapter and the corresponding "Do I Know This Already?" quiz questions. You can find the answers in Appendix A, "Answers to the 'Do I Know This Already?' Quizzes and End-of-Chapter Review Questions."

Table 7-1   "Do I Know This Already?" Foundation Topics Section-to-Question Mapping

Foundation Topics Section	Questions Covered in This Section
IPAM Fundamentals	1, 2
IPAM Provisioning	3, 4
Create and Manage IP Blocks and Ranges	5
Monitor Utilization of IP Address Spaces	6
Configure IPAM Database Storage Using SQL Server	7
IPAM and SCVMM	8

CAUTION   The goal of self-assessment is to gauge your mastery of the topics in this chapter. If you do not know the answer to a question or are only partially sure of the answer, you should mark that question as wrong for purposes of the self-assessment. Giving yourself credit for an answer you correctly guess skews your self-assessment results and might provide you with a false sense of security.

1.   You have a Windows Server 2012 IPAM server named IPAM1 in your domain pearson.com. You also have an existing SQL Server named SQL1. IPAM1 is configured with the WID as storage for IPAM configuration data. You want to migrate your existing IPAM database to SQL1 and you want to use that SQL Server as an external database solution for IPAM1. Which solutions are possible? (Choose two.)

   a. Migrate IPAM database of IPAM1 to SQL1.

   b. Install Microsoft SQL Server on IPAM1.

   c. Upgrade IPAM1 to Windows Server 2012 R2.

   d. Upgrade IPAM1 to Windows Server 2016.

2. You have two forests, named pearson.com and pearsonucertify.com. In pearson.com, you use a Windows Server 2016 IPAM-based IP address configuration solution. In pearsonucertify.com, you have a Windows Server 2012 R2 IPAM-based IP address configuration solution. You have a two-way transitive forest trust between both forests and you want to exchange IPAM configurations through an automatic replication process between IPAM servers in both forests. You want to use the new Windows Server 2016 multiple-forest support feature to replicate IPAM data between both IPAM environments. Which are correct statements for this? (Choose two.)

   a. You can automatically replicate IPAM data between forests.

   b. You can automatically replicate IPAM data between IPAM servers in the same forest.

   c. You cannot exchange IPAM data between IPAM servers.

   d. You cannot exchange IPAM data between IPAM servers in different forests.

   e. You can manage DNS/DHCP servers in different forests through Windows Server 2016 IPAM server.

3. You are in the process of provisioning your first Windows Server 2016 IPAM server through the IPAM configuration console. You add the following servers as managed servers: DHCP1, DHCP2, DHCP3, DNS1, DNS2, and DNS3. After 15 minutes, DHCP2 is still displayed with an IPAM access status of Blocked. You want to force DHCP2 to display an access status of Unblocked. Which configuration should you use?

   a. Perform **gpupdate /force** on DHCP2 again. In the IPAM configuration console, refresh the server access status for DHCP2.

   b. Add DHCP2 to the security filtering list of the IPAM_DHCP Group Policy and perform **gpupdate /force** on DHCP2 again. In the IPAM configuration console, refresh the server access status for DHCP2.

   c. Add DHCP2 to the security filtering list of the IPAM_DC_NPS Group Policy and perform **gpupdate /force** on DHCP2 again. In the IPAM configuration console, refresh the server access status for DHCP2.

   d. In the IPAM configuration console, refresh the server access status for DHCP2.

4. Under which identity is the ipamprovisioning.ps1 PowerShell script running during the deployment of a Windows Server 2016 IPAM server so that this script can correctly prepare managed DHCP servers?

   a. EventLogReader

   b. Administrators

   c. IPAMUG

   d. Domain Administrators

5. You need to import 50 IP addresses from the network 112.20.5.0/24 into your IPAM database through a CSV file named addresses.csv. The CSV file contains data for a field named Division. Which configuration steps should you perform? (Choose two.)

   a. Use **Add-IPAMCustomField** to create the Division field.

   b. Use **Format-Custom** to prepare the Division field.

   c. Use **Add-IPAMCustomValue** to add values to Division.

   d. Use **Import-IPAMAddress** to import from addresses.csv.

   e. Use **Import-IpamSubnet** to import from addresses.csv.

   f. Use **Import-IpamRange** to import from addresses.csv.

   g. Ensure that the RIR field and values are available in addresses.csv.

6. You want to view the DNSSEC signing status of a reverse lookup zone from a DNS server managed through a Windows Server 2016 IPAM server. You want to monitor the signing status in the IPAM configuration console under Monitor and Manage: DNS Zones. You need to verify the reverse lookup zone signing status. Which settings or tools can you use? (Choose two.)

   a. **Get-IPAMDnsZone**

   b. IPAM Configuration Manager Event Catalog

   c. IPAM Configuration Manager DNS and DHCP Servers: DNS Zones

   d. DNS Manager: Reverse Lookup Zones

7. You want to migrate your Windows Server 2016 IPAM database from a local Microsoft SQL Server 2014 to an external Microsoft SQL Server 2016. You have different collations. Which command should you use to start the configuration?

   a. **Move-IpamDatabase**

   b. **Set-IpamDatabase**

   c. **CREATE LOGIN**

   d. **CREATE DATABASE**

8. You want to integrate your IPAM server into System Center Virtual Machine Manager. Which component do you need to add in SCVMM? After that, you must configure an SCVMM IP address pool in IPAM. Which component do you need to add in SCVMM, and which IPAM configuration object should you choose?

Component to add in SCVMM:

   a. Microsoft Windows Server Gateway

   b. Microsoft Windows Server IP Address Management

IPAM configuration object to choose:

   a. VMM logical network

   b. Network site

   c. IP address subnet

   d. IP address range

   e. VM network

Foundation Topics

IPAM Fundamentals

Managing the allocation of IP addresses can be complex. IPAM helps you monitor and administer DHCP and DNS centrally. It provides a central view of where specific IP addresses are allocated. You can configure IPAM to collect statistics from DCs and NPS servers. The resultant data is recorded in the Windows Internal Database or in a Microsoft SQL Server database for Windows Server 2016.

IPAM offers the following benefits:

- IP address space utilization statistics and trend monitoring
- IPv4 and IPv6 address space planning and allocation
- Static IP inventory management, lifetime management, and DHCP and DNS record management
- Service and zone monitoring of DNS servers
- IP address lease and sign-in event tracking
- Remote administration support by using RSAT

IPAM consists of four modules.

- **IPAM Discovery:** You can configure IPAM to use AD DS to discover servers running Windows Server 2008 and newer and servers that are DCs, DHCP, or DNS servers. You also can manually add servers to IPAM.

- **IP Address Space Management:** You can view, monitor, and manage the IP address space. You can dynamically issue addresses or statically assign them. You can also track address utilization and detect overlapping DHCP scopes.

- **Multiserver Management and Monitoring:** You can manage and monitor multiple DHCP servers. Multiserver management enables tasks to run across multiple servers. For example, you can configure and edit DHCP properties and scopes, and you can track the status of DHCP and scope utilization. You can also monitor multiple DNS servers, as well as monitor the health and status of DNS zones across authoritative DNS servers.

- **Operational Auditing and IP Address Tracking:** You can use the auditing tools to track potential configuration problems. You can collect, manage, and view details of configuration changes from managed DHCP servers. You can also collect address lease tracking from DHCP lease logs and sign-in event information from NPS servers and domain controllers.

IPAM Architecture

IPAM consists of the following main components:

- **IPAM server:** The IPAM server performs data collection from the managed servers (DHCP, DNS). Additionally, the IPAM server manages the Windows Internal Database (WID) or a SQL Server database, and it provides RBAC. A single IPAM server can support up to 150 DHCP servers, 500 DNS servers, 6000 DHCP scopes, and 150 DNS zones.

NOTE   The WID is a relational datastore used by Active Directory Rights Management Services (AD RMS), Windows Server Update Services, and the Windows System Resource Manager.

TIP   IPAM on Windows Server 2012 supports WID only. You can use an external SQL database only when you implement IPAM on Windows Server 2016 or Windows Server 2012 R2.

TIP IPAM has IP address utilization trends and reclamation support only with IPv4. IPAM does not check for IP address consistency with routers and switches.

- **IPAM client:** You can collect, manage, and view details of configuration changes from managed DHCP servers. You can also collect address lease tracking from DHCP lease logs and sign-in event information from NPS servers and domain controllers.

When you deploy IPAM, you can select from the following three topologies:

- **Distributed:** You can deploy a Windows Server 2016 IPAM server to each site in the forest. You use the distributed topology when you have multiple sites. Servers in each location can help distribute a workload that might be too large for a single server to handle. You can also use the distributed IPAM topology to separate locations for business units to administer their own IP addressing management.

- **Centralized:** Deploy a single Windows Server 2016 IPAM server for your forest. A single IPAM server provides centralized control and visibility for IP addressing tasks. You can view your entire IP addressing infrastructure from a single console (Server Manager).

- **Hybrid:** Additionally, with a centralized IPAM server, you can deploy an IPAM server to each site. The hybrid topology offers the load sharing and shared administration benefits of the distributed topology, along with the unified management and visibility of the centralized topology. You typically implement the hybrid topology in large organizations when you need to distribute the IPAM load but you still want more central administration.

IPAM Deployment Requirements

Your organization must fulfill the prerequisites for IPAM shown in Figure 7-1 (see the following list for a description).

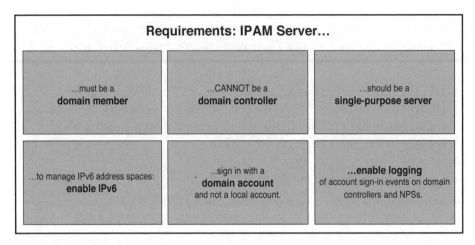

Figure 7-1   IPAM Prerequisites

The IPAM hardware and software requirements follow:

- 2.0-GHz dual-core processor or faster
- Windows Server 2012 operating system or later
- At least 4 GB of RAM
- 80 GB of free hard disk space

If you manage Windows Server 2008 and Windows Server 2008 R2 servers through IPAM, these servers require the following:

- Service Pack 2 (SP2) on Windows Server 2008
- Full version of Microsoft .NET Framework 4.0
- Windows Management Framework 3.0 (KB2506146)
- Windows Management Framework Core (KB968930) with Windows Server 2008 SP2
- Windows Remote Management
- Service Principal Names (SPNs) written to AD DS

IPAM Deployment Considerations

When designing an IPAM deployment, be sure to consider the factors outlined in Figure 7-2.

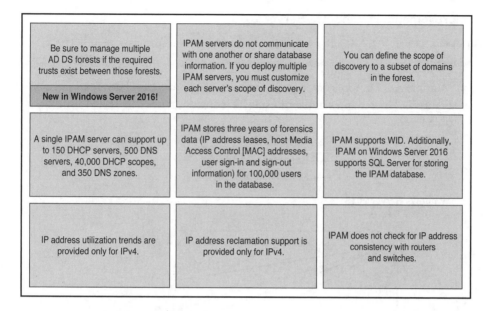

Figure 7-2   IPAM Deployment Considerations

TIP   If you use SQL Server to host the IPAM database, this must be the only SQL instance running on that SQL server.

IPAM Improvements in Windows Server 2012 R2

The following list explains the most important IPAM improvements in Windows Server 2012 R2:

- **RBAC:** You can use RBAC for IPAM to customize access scopes and access policies for IPAM administrators.

- **Virtual address space management:** You can manage physical and virtual networks. Integration between IPAM and SCVMM allows end-to-end address space management. You can view virtual address spaces directly in the IPAM management console.

- **External database support:** You can configure IPAM to use WID. Support for using SQL Server was added in Windows Server 2012 R2.

- **Upgrade and migration support:** You can upgrade the IPAM database from Windows Server 2012 to Windows Server 2012 R2.

- **Enhanced PowerShell support:** IPAM includes more than 50 Windows PowerShell commands.

IPAM Improvements in Windows Server 2016

Windows Server 2016 includes several new features and improvements for IPAM functionality:

- Multiple AD DS forest support (a two-way trust must exist between forests). Figure 7-3 shows an example of using Windows Server 2016 IPAM for multiple forests.

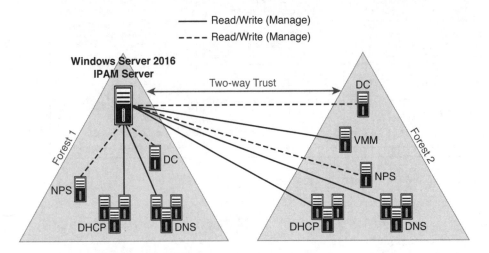

Figure 7-3   IPAM Multiple AD DS Forest Support

- Purge utilization data. You can reduce the size of the IPAM database by purging older IP address utilization data.

- Windows PowerShell support for role-based access control (RBAC).

- Support for IPv4 /32 and IPv6 /128 subnets.

- Enhanced DNS service management. You can manage DNS resource records, conditional forwarders, and zones for AD-integrated and file-backed DNS servers.

- Visualization of DNS resource records that pertain to an IP address.

- Automated inventory of IP addresses based on DNS resource records.

- IP address lifecycle management for DNS and DHCP operations.

TIP   IPAM servers do not communicate with each other or share database information. No IPAM replication feature exists. If you deploy multiple IPAM servers, you must customize each server's discovery scope locally on each IPAM server.

> **TIP**   You can update an existing IPAM installation following an operating system upgrade with the PowerShell cmdlet **Update-IpamServer**. This cmdlet generates a log file in the %System Drive%\System 32\IPAM\Logs folder.

IPAM Provisioning

Implementing IPAM involves several important steps:

Step 1.   Review IPAM functionality and align with implementation goals.

Step 2.   Confirm that the system and environment requirements have been met.

Step 3.   Develop a staged deployment plan.

Step 4.   Deploy IPAM servers.

Step 5.   Deploy IPAM clients.

Step 6.   Assign IPAM administration roles.

Step 7.   Use IPAM for IP infrastructure management.

Assume that the first three steps have been done. Now you have to provision your IPAM server. You can install the IPAM server role by using Server Manager or the PowerShell command **Install-WindowsFeature IPAM -IncludeManagement-Tools**. The following steps illustrate the IPAM installation process through Server Manager:

After successfully installing the IPAM server role through PowerShell, you want to provision the IPAM Server. Figure 7-4 shows where to start the IPAM server provisioning process in Server Manager.

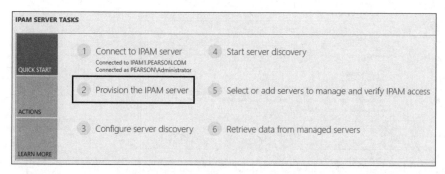

Figure 7-4   IPAM Server Tasks (Provision the IPAM Server)

Read the description on the Before You Begin page and click Next. Figure 7-5 shows the Before You Begin page of the Provision IPAM Wizard.

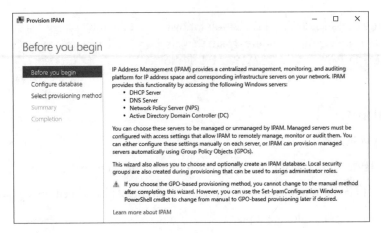

Figure 7-5   IPAM Server Provision IPAM Wizard (Before You Begin)

In the Provision IPAM Wizard on the Configure Database page, select where to store IPAM configuration data. You can choose between Windows Internal Database (WID) and Microsoft SQL Server. In Figure 7-6, Windows Internal Database (WID) is selected.

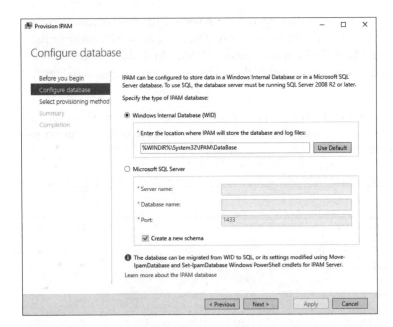

Figure 7-6   IPAM Server Provision IPAM Wizard (Configure Database)

In the Provision IPAM Wizard on the Select Provisioning Method page, you select the provisioning method for managed servers. Select **Group Policy Based** to prepare the managed servers (DHCP, DNS) through GPOs so that the IPAM server can access the DHCP files in either the C:\windows\system32\dhcp folder for managed DHCP servers or the C:\windows\system32\dns folder for DNS servers. You must type a GPO prefix name for GPO-based provisioning. Figure 7-7 shows the Select Provisioning Method page.

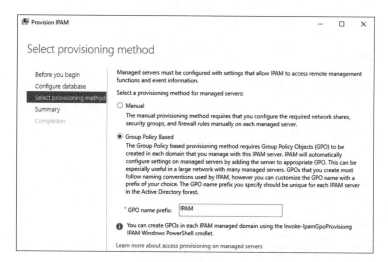

Figure 7-7 IPAM Server Provision IPAM Wizard (Select Provisioning Method)

In the Provision IPAM Wizard on the Summary page, read the summary text and click **Apply**. Figure 7-8 shows the Summary page.

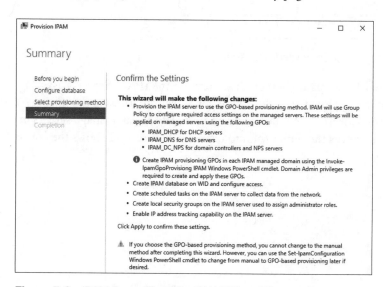

Figure 7-8 IPAM Server Provision IPAM Wizard (Summary)

After you click Apply on the Summary page, the IPAM provisioning process starts. Figure 7-9 shows that the provisioning process has started and Figure 7-10 shows that it has successfully completed.

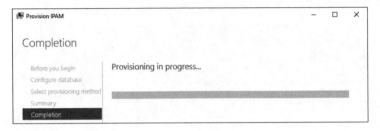

Figure 7-9   IPAM Provisioning in Progress

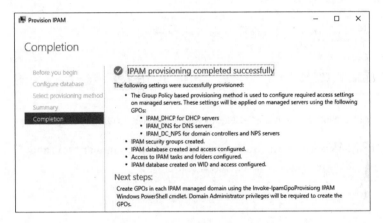

Figure 7-10   IPAM Provisioning Completed Successfully

You then select step 3 (Configure Server Discovery) on the IPAM Server Tasks page in the IPAM management console. There you select the forest and domains to discover (as a new feature of Windows Server 2016, IPAM can manage servers in multiple forests), as well as the server roles to discover. Figure 7-11 shows the completed page.

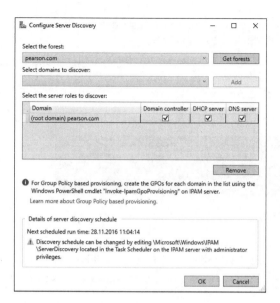

Figure 7-11   IPAM Server Provision (Configure Server Discovery)

After you have selected the Group Policy–based provisioning method, you must determine whether the IPAM GPOs are created on your DC. You can view the three IPAM GPOs in the Group Policy Management Console on the DC. Figure 7-12 shows the three IPAM provisioning GPOs that must exist.

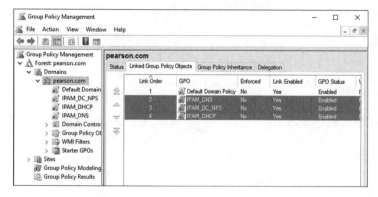

Figure 7-12   IPAM GPOs

If the IPAM GPOs do not exist, you can perform the following PowerShell command on IPAM server to create the three IPAM GPOs: **Invoke-IpamGPOProvisioning** *-Domain pearson.com -GpoPrefix Name IPAM -IpamServerFqdn IPAM1.pearson.com -DelegatedGpoUser Administrator*. Figure 7-13 shows the execution of that PowerShell command.

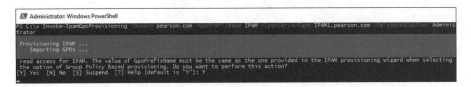

Figure 7-13   Invoke-IpamGPOProvisioning

You then select step 4 (Start Server Discovery) on the IPAM Server Tasks page in the IPAM management console. This step can take 5 to 10 minutes. The server discovery task runs in the background. Figure 7-14 shows where to start the server discovery task.

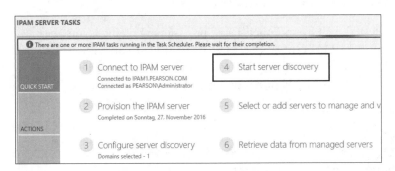

Figure 7-14   IPAM Start Server Discovery Task

TIP   You can view all IPAM tasks in the Task Scheduler of your IPAM server (see Figure 7-15).

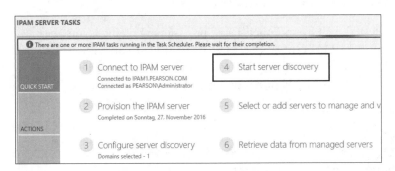

Figure 7-15   IPAM Tasks in Task Scheduler

When the server discovery task is ready, you select step 5 (Select or Add Servers to Manage). There you decide which server types this IPAM server is allowed to manage. Your choices are DC, DNS Server, DHCP Server, and NPS Server. Figures 7-16 and 7-17 illustrate the steps of this configuration choice.

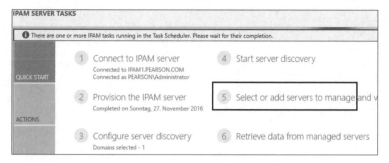

Figure 7-16   IPAM Server Provision (Select or Add Servers to Manage)

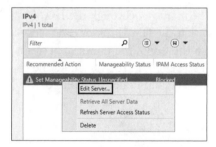

Figure 7-17   IPAM Server Provision (Edit Servers to Manage)

For every DHCP or DNS server in the server inventory list, you must select **Edit Server**. In the Add or Edit Server window, you select the server role you want to manage through IPAM. At Owner, select **Managed** and click **OK**. This step is necessary to add the DHCP or DNS server to the GPO security filtering list, to grant the managed server permission to retrieve the group policy settings. Figure 7-18 illustrates managing the DC, DHCP, and DNS server roles of the managed server named lon-dc1.pearson.com.

Figure 7-18   IPAM Server Provision (Add or Edit Servers to Manage)

You then perform the **gpupdate /force** or **invoke-gpupdate** PowerShell command on all DHCP or DNS servers that should be managed through the IPAM server. This step prepares all managed servers so that the IPAM server can reach the DHCP or DNS data on that servers. Through the GPO, the PowerShell script ipamprovisioning.ps1 has to run on the managed servers. Figure 7-19 shows the **IpamDhcpProvisioning** task in the IPAM_DHCP Group Policy for DHCP servers.

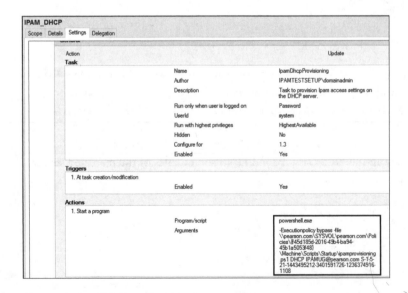

Figure 7-19   IPAM ipamprovisioning.ps1 Script

After applying the GPO and the ipamprovisioning.ps1 PowerShell script on the managed server, you can verify whether the C:\windows\system32\dhcp folder is shared with the share name dhcpaudit so that the IPAM server can access the DHCP server files through that share. Figure 7-20 verifies the existence of the dhcpaudit share.

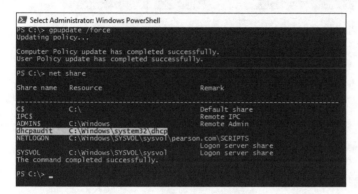

Figure 7-20   IPAM Verifying Managed DHCP Server Settings (dhcpaudit Share)

The ipamprovisioning.ps1 PowerShell script has configured the dhcpaudit share with read share permissions for the IPAMUG security group (IPAM server is a member of that group). See Figure 7-21.

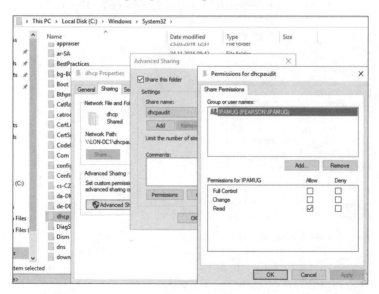

Figure 7-21   IPAM Verifying Managed DHCP Server Settings (dhcpaudit Share Permissions)

The managed servers (in this example, LON-DC1, which has installed the DC, DNS, and DHCP server roles) must be displayed at Server Inventory and IPv4 Managed Servers. Figure 7-22 shows the managed server with IPAM Access Status: Unblocked, which means that IPAM now can manage that server.

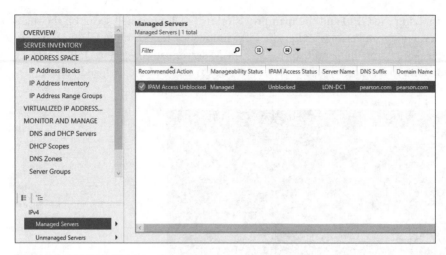

Figure 7-22   IPAM Managed Server Access Status: Unblocked

In the IPAM management console at Event Catalog: DHCP Configuration Events, you can centrally view all DHCP events from all managed DHCP servers (see Figure 7-23). You can do the same under Monitor and Manage > DNS and DHCP Servers > Event Catalog (see Figure 7-24). You can view DHCP scope-specific events at Monitor and Manage > DHCP Scopes > Event Catalog (see Figure 7-25).

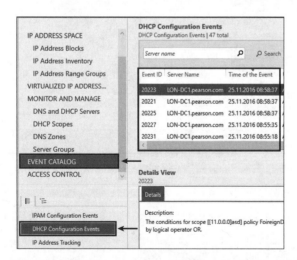

Figure 7-23   IPAM DHCP Configuration Events (All DHCP Servers)

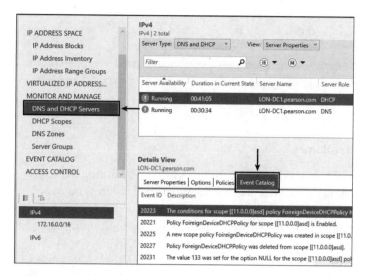

Figure 7-24 IPAM DHCP Configuration Events (One DHCP Server)

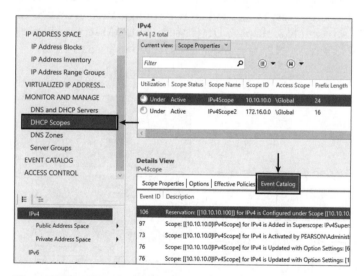

Figure 7-25 IPAM DHCP Configuration Events (DHCP Scope Events)

You also can view IPAM DHCP configuration events by using the PowerShell cmdlet **Get-IpamDhcpConfigurationEvent**.

TIP With the PowerShell cmdlet **Get-IpamIpAddressAuditEvent**, you can get all IP address audit events from an IPAM server over a certain time interval. IPAM enables IP address tracking through correlation of DHCP lease events on managed DHCP servers with user and computer authentication events on managed domain controllers and NPS servers. You can search for correlated events by IP address, client ID, hostname, or username. Use DHCP events between a start date and an end date to correlate data. The data returned includes data for both the start date and the end date. The cmdlet returns only the top 10,000 rows if the query results exceed more than 10,000 rows.

IPAM Network Communication

IPAM communicates with managed servers through RPC or WMI interfaces (see Figure 7-26). IPAM monitors DCs and NPS servers for IP address tracking purposes. In addition to monitoring functions, several DHCP server and scope properties can be configured from the IPAM console. Zone status monitoring and a limited set of configuration functions are also available for DNS servers. Web Services for Management (also known as WS-Management or WS-MAN) is a specification for managing computer systems using web services standards. It is used on IPAM servers to monitor IP address utilization and service status, configure servers and scopes, and audit IP address lease events and DHCP configuration events. SMB is used from the IPAM server only to manage DHCP servers; IPAM servers do not use SMB to manage DNS servers, NPS servers, or DCs. LDAP is used to access Active Directory.

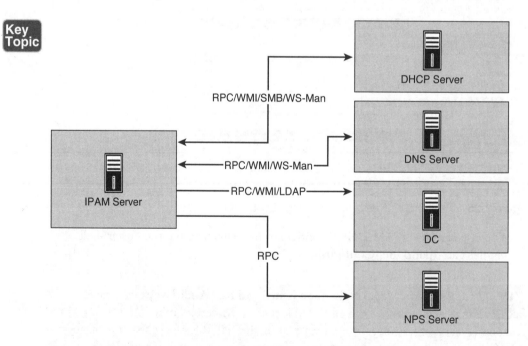

Figure 7-26   IPAM Managed Servers Network Communication

IPAM Administration

With role-based access control (RBAC), you can specify access privileges at different levels. You define who has granular control over operations to create, edit, and delete different types of objects. You must configure the question Where Do I Want to Have Access? in an IPAM access role. For example, you can add the operations Add DNS Records and Configure DNS Server Settings. After that, you have to define the objects for which a user must get access (for example, objects in Asia or the USA), the *IPAM access scope*. The *IPAM Access policy* brings everything together. You combine a role with an access scope to assign permissions to a user or group in an IPAM Access Policy. Figure 7-27 shows the dependencies among IPAM access roles, IPAM access scopes, and IPAM access policies. An IPAM user role must be applied to an IPAM access scope, and both have to be part of the IPAM access policy.

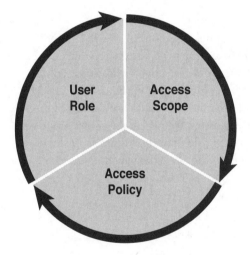

Figure 7-27   IPAM Role-Based Management

You can implement role-based management in IPAM by using the following components:

A *role* is a collection of IPAM operations. You define a user role by selecting the required admin operations. You can associate a role with a user or group in Windows by using an access policy. Nine built-in administrator roles are available, for convenience, but you can also create customized roles to meet your business requirements. You can create and edit roles from the Access Control node in the IPAM management console. Figure 7-28 shows the built-in IPAM administrator roles in Server Manager under Access Control in the IPAM management console.

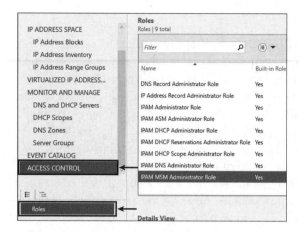

Figure 7-28   IPAM Built-in Administrator Roles

An *access scope* defines the business hierarchy model based on the desired administration levels and controls. An access scope determines the objects to which a user
has access. You can use access scopes to define administrative areas. For example,
you might create access scopes based on geographical location. By default, IPAM
includes an access scope named Global. All other access scopes are subsets of the
Global access scope. Users or groups that you assign to the Global access scope have
access to all objects in IPAM that their assigned role permits. Figure 7-29 shows
where you can configure IPAM access scopes in the IPAM management console.

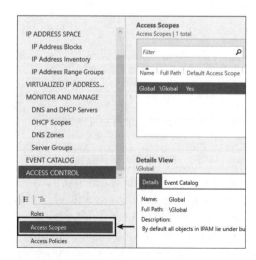

Figure 7-29   IPAM Access Scopes

An *access policy* combines a role with an access scope to assign permissions to a user
or group. For example, you might define an access policy for a user with a role

named IPBlockAdmin and an access scope named Global\Asia. Therefore, this user will have permission to edit and delete IP address blocks that are associated with the Asia access scope. This user will not have permission to edit or delete any other IP address blocks in IPAM. You can create and edit access policies from the Access Control node in the IPAM management console.

IPAM has several built-in role-based security groups that you can use to manage your IPAM infrastructure (see Table 7-2).

Table 7-2   IPAM Security Groups

Security Group	Description
IPAM Users	Members of this group can view all information in server inventory, the IP address space, and the Monitor and Manage view of the IPAM console. They can view IPAM and DHCP operational events under the Event Catalog but cannot view IP address tracking information.
IPAM MSM Administrators	Members of the Multi-Server Management (MSM) Administrators group have IPAM Users privileges and can perform IPAM common management tasks, as well as monitor and manage tasks.
IPAM ASM Administrators	Members of the Address Space Management (ASM) Administrators group have IPAM Users privileges and can perform both common IPAM management tasks and IP address space tasks.
IPAM IP Audit Administrators	Members of the IP Audit Administrators group have IPAM Users privileges. They can perform common IPAM management tasks and view IP address tracking information.
IPAM Administrators	Members of this group have the privileges to view all IPAM data and perform all IPAM tasks.
IPAM DNS Administrator	Members of this group can manage DNS servers and their associated DNS zones and resource records.
DNS Record Administrator	This administrator manages DNS resource records.
IP Address Record Administrator	Members of this group can manage IP addresses, including unallocated addresses. Members also can create and delete IP address instances.
IPAM DHCP Administrator	This administrator completely manages DHCP servers.
IPAM DHCP Reservations Administrator	This administrator manages DHCP reservations.
IPAM DHCP Scope Administrator	This administrator manages DHCP scopes.

Furthermore, the domain security group IPAMUG is created as part of IPAM server deployment. The IPAM server computer account automatically becomes a member of this group; it also has to become a member of the local security group Event Log Readers at the managed server, to grant the IPAM server permission to read DHCP or DNS events from the managed servers (DNS, DHCP) so that these events can be centrally viewed on the IPAM server. Figure 7-30 shows the IPAMUG domain security group, and Figure 7-31 shows the local Event Log Readers security group of a managed server.

Figure 7-30   IPAM IPAMUG Domain Security Group

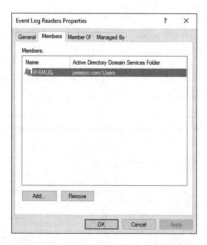

Figure 7-31   IPAM Local Event Log Readers Security Group

In Figure 7-30, the IPAMUG security group contains the computer account of the IPAM server (in this case, IPAM1). The IPAM server was added automatically to that security group during the IPAM server provisioning process. This is important because, after managed DHCP servers get GPO settings, the IPAMUG security group automatically is added to the local security group Event Log Readers on the DHCP servers (this is done through a provisioning PowerShell script that is part of the GPO). The IPAM server then can access DHCP events and display them in the IPAM console in the Server Manager on the IPAM server. Figure 7-31 shows the Event Log Readers security group on a managed DHCP server and the group member IPAMUG.

When you remove the IPAMUG security group from the Event Log Readers security group, you run into problems. The IPAM server loses its permissions to access DHCP events on that DHCP server; in this case, you then miss DHCP events displayed on the IPAM server.

Windows Server 2016 IPAM also has the capability to manage IPAM role-based access control (RBAC) through PowerShell commands. Suppose you want to change the access scope of a DNS zone named usa.pearson.com from Chicago to NewYork:

```
Get-IpamDnsZone -ZoneType Forward -ZoneName usa.pearson.com


ZoneName                 : usa.pearson.com
ZoneType                 : Forward
AccessScopePath          : \Global\Chicago
IsSigned                 : False
DynamicUpdateStatus      : None
ScavengeStaleRecords     : False


$x = Get-IpamDnsZone -ZoneType Forward -ZoneName usa.pearson.com
Set-IpamAccessScope -IpamDnsZone -InputObject $x -AccessScopePath
  \Global\NewYork


Get-IpamDnsZone -ZoneType Forward -ZoneName usa.pearson.com


ZoneName                 : usa.pearson.com
ZoneType                 : Forward
AccessScopePath          : \Global\NewYork
IsSigned                 : False
DynamicUpdateStatus      : None
ScavengeStaleRecords     : False
```

To create an IPAM access policy, complete the following steps:

Step 1.   In the IPAM configuration console, click **Access Control**. In the lower navigation pane, right-click **Access Policies**, and then click **Add Access Policy**.

Step 2.   The Add Access Policy dialog box opens. In User Settings, click **Add**.

Step 3.   The Select User or Group dialog box opens. Click **Locations**.

Step 4.   The Locations dialog box opens. Browse to the location that contains the user account, select the location, and then click **OK**. The Locations dialog box closes.

Step 5.   In the Select User or Group dialog box, in Enter the Object Name to Select, type the user account name for which you want to create an access policy. Click **OK**.

Step 6.   In Add Access Policy, under User Settings, the User Alias now contains the user account to which the policy applies. In Access Settings, click **New**.

Step 7.   In Add Access Policy, change Access Settings to **New Setting**.

Step 8.   Click **Select Role** to expand the list of roles. Select one of the built-in roles or, if you have created new roles, select one of the roles that you created. For example, if you created the PearsonIPAMRole role to apply to the user, click **PearsonIPAMRole**.

Step 9.   Click **Add Setting**.

Step 10.   The role is added to the access policy. To create additional access policies, click **Apply** and then repeat these steps for each policy that you want to create. If you do not want to create additional policies, click **OK**.

Step 11.   In the IPAM client console display pane, verify that the new access policy is created.

Configuring IPAM Options

You can configure IPAM by using GPOs that are deployed during the initial provisioning process. When you provision an IPAM server, it creates three GPOs in any of the domains that you select and links them to the domain root in the GPMC. When you use provisioning through GPOs, you are also asked to provide a prefix for the GPOs so that they can be easily identified in the GPMC. The following GPOs are created:

- **<Prefix>_DHCP:** Applies settings that allow IPAM to monitor, manage, and collect information from managed DHCP servers on the network. This GPO sets up IPAM provisioning scheduled tasks and adds Windows Firewall inbound rules for Remote Event Log Management (RPC-EMAP and RPC), Remote Service Management (RPC-EMAP and RPC), and DHCP Server (RPCSS-In and RP).

- **<Prefix>_DNS:** Applies settings that allow IPAM to monitor and collect information from managed DNS servers on the network. This GPO sets up IPAM provisioning scheduled tasks and adds Windows Firewall inbound rules for RPC (TCP, Incoming), RPC Endpoint Mapper (TCP, Incoming), Remote Event Log Management (RPC-EMAP and RPC), and Remote Service Management (RPC-EMAP and RPC).

- **<Prefix>_DC_NPS:** Applies settings that allow IPAM to collect information from managed domain controllers and NPS servers on the network for IP address tracking purposes. It sets up IPAM provisioning scheduled tasks and adds Windows Firewall inbound rules for Remote Event Log Management (RPC-EMAP and RPC) and Remote Service Management (RPC-EMAP and RPC).

You must use the following command to create the GPOs in the preceding list:

```
Invoke-IpamGpoProvisioning -Domain pearson.com -GpoPrefixName IPAM
  -IpamServerFqdn IPAM1.pearson.com -DelegatedGpoUser Administrator
```

Configure IPAM Managed Servers

You can get, add, configure, or remove IPAM managed servers with PowerShell, as Table 7-3 shows.

Table 7-3   Configuring IPAM Managed Servers with PowerShell

Task	Command
Add managed servers to IPAM server inventory	**Add-IpamServerInventory -Name "dhcp2.pearson.com" -ServerType DHCP**
Get list of managed servers	**Get-IpamServerInventory -AddressFamily IPv4 | Format-List Name, ServerType**
Get all IPv4 DHCP servers in the IPAM server inventory	**Get-IpamServerInventory -AddressFamily IPv4 -ServerType DHCP | Format-List Name, ServerType**
Modify properties of a managed server and make it manageable	**Set-IpamServerInventory -Name "dhcp01" -ManageabilityStatus Managed -PassThru**
Remove a server from IPAM inventory	**Remove-IpamServerInventory -Name "dhcp01"**

> **NOTE**   To learn more about IPAM Server cmdlets in Windows PowerShell, visit https://technet.microsoft.com/en-us/library/jj553807.aspx.

Configuring IPAM Domains

You can get, add, configure, or remove IPAM domains and forests with PowerShell, as Table 7-4 illustrates.

Table 7-4   Configuring IPAM Domains and Forests with PowerShell

Task	Command
Get all discovery domains that are configured in IPAM.	**Get-IpamDiscoveryDomain**
Get a specific discovery domain.	**Get-IpamDiscoveryDomain -Name "pearson.com"**
Configure IPAM to discover DHCP and DNS servers in the domain named usa.pearson.com. Set the **DiscoverDc** parameter to False to direct IPAM, not to discover DCs, instead of DHCP and DNS servers.	**Add-IpamDiscoveryDomain -Name "usa.pearson.com" -DiscoverDc $False -PassThru**
Modify an existing discovery domain. This command modifies an existing discovery domain to prevent server discovery of DCs in the domain.	**Set-IpamDiscoveryDomain -Name "pearson.com" -DiscoverDc $False -PassThru**
Remove a domain from IPAM. This command removes the domain named pearson.com from the IPAM discovery domain configuration and stores the result in the variable named *$X*.	*$X* = **Remove-IpamDiscoveryDomain -Name pearson.com**

Managing DNS Using IPAM

You can use IPAM to perform the following DNS management tasks:

- **View DNS servers and zones:** You can view all managed DNS servers, in addition to the forward lookup zones and reverse lookup zones on those DNS servers. Zone status and health information are available for forward lookup zones but not for reverse lookup zones. Suppose you have created two reverse lookup zones for the subnets 172.16.0.0 and 10.10.0.0 in the DNS Manager. You can see the reverse lookup zones in the DNS Manager, but you cannot view them in the IPAM management console (see Figure 7-32).

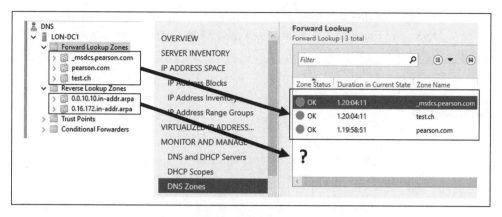

Figure 7-32   No Display of Reverse Lookup Zones in IPAM Management Console

TIP   Instead of using the IPAM management console to view IPv4 reverse lookup zones, you can use the following PowerShell command: **Get-IpamDnsZone -ZoneType "IPv4Reverse" | FL ***.

- **Create new zones:** To create DNS zones, in the navigation pane, click the **DNS and DHCP Servers** node. Right-click the DNS server to which you want to add a zone, and then click **Create DNS Zone** (see Figure 7-33). You can create zones through IPAM in the IPAM management console.

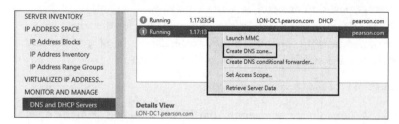

Figure 7-33   IPAM Create DNS Zone

- **Create DNS records:** You can create DNS records for any zone that IPAM manages. Figure 7-34 shows where you can add DNS records in the IPAM management console.

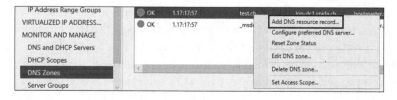

Figure 7-34   IPAM Add DNS Resource Records

- **Manage conditional forwarders:** Figure 7-35 shows how to configure a DNS conditional forwarder through the IPAM management console.

Figure 7-35   IPAM DNS Conditional Forwarder

This example creates a DNS conditional forwarder (stored in a custom Active Directory partition named DNSForwarders.pearson.com) to a DNS server with the IP address 172.16.0.88 that is responsible for the zone pearsonucertify.com. With the following PowerShell command, you can view the settings of conditional forwarders created through IPAM:

```
Get-IpamDnsConditionalForwarder | FL *
```

- **Open the DNS console for any server that IPAM manages:** You can open the Microsoft Management Console (MMC) for DNS by right-clicking a server on the DNS and DHCP Servers page and then selecting Launch MMC.

Create and Manage IP Blocks and Ranges

With Windows Server 2016 IPAM, you can manage, monitor, and add or remove IP blocks and ranges. You can visualize the configuration details of the IP address ranges, check out utilization trends, or view the Event Catalog. You'll find that all this information is quite useful when you are managing a large network with many subnets and IPs. You can search for a particular IP address, create a DHCP lease from a managed DHCP server, add a new DNS entry in a specified zone, or create a custom configuration. You can add address spaces or import/export address spaces from/to CSV files. Finding available IP addresses through IPAM is also easier now. After an IP address is assigned to a host, the range is automatically updated to display the usage status.

Managing IP Addressing

Windows Server 2016 IPAM address space management supports IPv4 public and private addresses and IPv6 global and unicast addresses. On a Windows Server 2016 IPAM server, you can manage the DHCP server settings as in Figure 7-36.

Figure 7-36   IPAM DHCP Server Configuration Settings

Adding Address Spaces to IPAM

You can add DHCP scopes to IPAM through the following steps in the IPAM administration console:

Step 1.   In Server Manager, in the IPAM navigation pane, on the DNS and DHCP Servers tab, right-click the DHCP server role for your managed DHCP server, and then click **Create DHCP Scope**.

Step 2.   Create a new DHCP scope with the following properties:

- Scope name: PearsonScope

- Start IP address: 172.16.32.0.100

- End IP address: 172.16.32.0.200

- Activate scope on creation: No

- Option: 006 DNS Servers

Step 3.   In the IPAM management console on the DNS and DHCP Servers tab, select **Launch MMC**.

Step 4.   In the DHCP console, verify the presence of the scope and the scope options that you created.

Figure 7-37 shows how you can see all possible scope options when you create a DHCP scope through the IPAM management console.

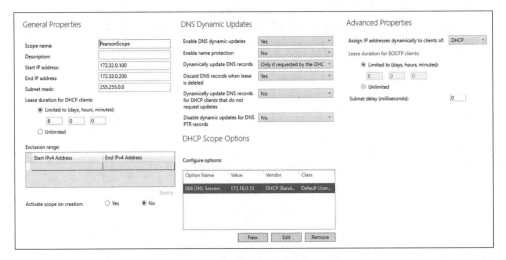

Figure 7-37   IPAM Create DHCP Scope in IPAM Management Console

Figure 7-38 shows how you can verify the successful creation of the DHCP scope through the PowerShell command shown.

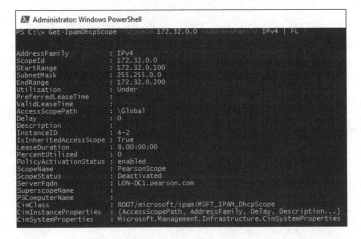

Figure 7-38   IPAM Verify DHCP Scope with PowerShell

Importing and Updating Address Spaces

You can use IPAM to import and update IP address space information from a CSV file.

The required fields are identical to those that are required when adding IP address data in IPAM using the IPAM administrative interface. You must include field names on line 1 of the CSV file, followed by corresponding data; each entry must be on a separate line.

You also can use custom field names, but you must define them in the IPAM administrative interface before importing them. In addition, you can use the following PowerShell cmdlets: **Add-IpamCustomField**, **Get-IpamCustomField**, **Remove-IpamCustomField**, and **Rename-IpamCustomField**.

Consider this example of adding a custom value to a user-defined custom field:

```
Add-IpamCustomValue -Name "Divisions" -Value "Support"
```

You can specify fields in any order, as long as the data values are also in the same order. Data and field names are not case sensitive, and they can be enclosed in quotes and include spaces. You can import the following into IPAM using CSV files:

- IP addresses

- IP address ranges

- IP address blocks

Table 7-5 lists the mandatory fields for importing address spaces into IPAM.

Table 7-5 Mandatory Fields for Importing Address Spaces into IPAM

IP Addresses	IP Address Range	IP Address Block
IP address	Network	Network
Managed by service	Start IP address	Start IP address
Service instance	End IP address	End IP address
Device type	Managed by service	RIR
IP address state	Service instance	
Assignment type	Assignment type	

Consider the following example of a CSV file for importing two IP addresses into the IPAM database, assuming that dhcp1.pearson.com is a valid service instance on the network:

```
IP address,managed by service,service instance,device type,ip address
    state,assignment type
172.32.0.101,ms dhcp,dhcp1.pearson.com,host,in-use,static
172.32.0.102,ms dhcp,dhcp1.pearson.com,host,in-use,static
```

This example shows a CSV file for importing an IP address block of 65.52.0.0/14:

```
Network, start IP address, end IP address, RIR
65.52.0.0/14, 65.52.0.0, 65.52.255.255, ARIN
```

TIP When you want to import a public address space through a CSV file into your IPAM server, the Regional Internet Registry (RIR) field is required.

If a field is missing or contains bad data, an error report is automatically created in the Documents folder of the current user. For example, the following data generates an error if a Managed by Service value of MS DHCP is specified. This value is reserved for DHCP scopes on managed DHCP servers. To avoid this error, use a value of IPAM for Managed by Service. This example includes optional quotes around the field names and data values:

```
"Network", "Start IP address", "End IP address", "Managed by service",
    "Service instance",
"Assignment Type" "192.168.100.0/24", "192.168.100.1",
    "192.168.100.254" "IPAM", "router", "dynamic"
```

Finding, Allocating, and Reclaiming IP Addresses

You can use IPAM to find, allocate, and reclaim an IP address under the following circumstances:

- IP is not reserved in range.

- IP does not exist in IPAM.

- IP is not excluded in range.

- IP does not respond to ping.

- PTR is not found.

Finding and Allocating IP Addresses in IPAM

You can find available IPs within a range by right-clicking IP Address Range in the IPAM configuration console at the Server Manager and then clicking Find and Allocate Available IP Address. When IPAM searches for available addresses, it follows this process:

1. The search begins with the first address in the range that is unassigned in IPAM.

2. If the address range belongs to a managed DHCP scope, the search automatically ignores IP reservation and exclusions.

3. When a ping and DNS query have completed with no response, the address is added to the list.

Reclaiming IP Addresses in IPAM

If you reclaim IPs in IPAM, they are removed from the IPAM database. IP address reclamation does not affect DHCP reservations and DNS records. To reclaim IP addresses, right-click one or more IP Address Ranges in the IPAM configuration console at the Server Manager, and then click Reclaim IP Addresses.

TIP When you also want to remove DHCP reservations and DNS records with the IPAM administrative console, first go to the IP addresses view; select one or more IP addresses, right-click, and then click Delete DHCP Reservation, Delete DNS Host Record, or Delete DNS PTR Record.

IP Address Tracking

Windows Server 2016 IPAM offers the IP address tracking feature to search for IP address records using the parameter IP address, the client ID, the hostname, and the username. Using the PowerShell cmdlet **Get-IpamCapability**, you can list the optional capability **IpAddressTracking**. Figure 7-39 gives the output of that PowerShell cmdlet and shows that IP address tracking is enabled by default.

Figure 7-39   IPAM Optional Capability for IP Address Tracking

You also can use the IP address tracking feature in the IPAM management console at the Event Catalog in the bottom corner of the IPAM management console.

Figure 7-40 shows four different IP address tracking searches for IP address, client ID, hostname, and username (Administrator).

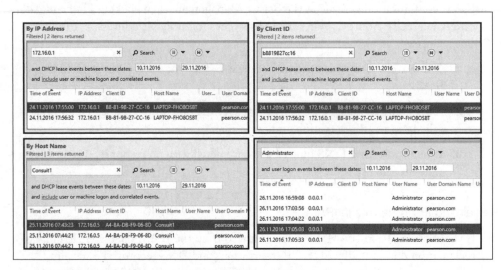

Figure 7-40   IPAM IP Address Tracking in IPAM Management Console

TIP   Searches using wildcards or regular expressions are not supported in the IP address tracking feature.

Monitor Utilization of IP Address Spaces

IPAM maintains utilization data for IP address ranges, address blocks, and range groups. You can configure thresholds for the utilized percentage of the IP address space and then use those thresholds to determine under- or overutilization. You can perform utilization trend building and reporting for IPv4 address ranges, blocks, and range groups.

With Windows Server 2016 IPAM, you can monitor DHCP and DNS servers from any physical location in an enterprise. One of the IPAM benefits is its capability to simultaneously manage multiple DHCP servers or DHCP scopes that are spread across one or more DHCP servers:

- **IPAM Monitoring View:** Use this view to check the status and health of selected sets of Windows Server DNS and DHCP servers from a single IPAM administrative interface. This view displays the basic health of servers and recent configuration events that occurred on these servers. You can also use this monitoring view to organize managed servers into logical server groups.

- **DHCP Server Monitoring:** Use this view to track various server settings, server options, the number of scopes, and the number of active leases that are configured on a server.

- **DNS Server Monitoring:** Use this view to track all zones that are configured on the server, along with details about the zone type. You can also use the view to see the total number of zones that are configured on the server and the overall zone health status, as derived from the zone status of individual forward lookup zones on the server.

In the IPAM management console, you can use the Monitor and Manage: DNS and DHCP Servers, DHCP Scopes, DNS Zone Monitoring, and Server Groups views to view and monitor health and configuration for all DNS and DHCP servers. In the DNS and DHCP Servers section, you can view the DHCP server properties and events (see Figure 7-41) and the DNS server properties and events (see Figure 7-42).

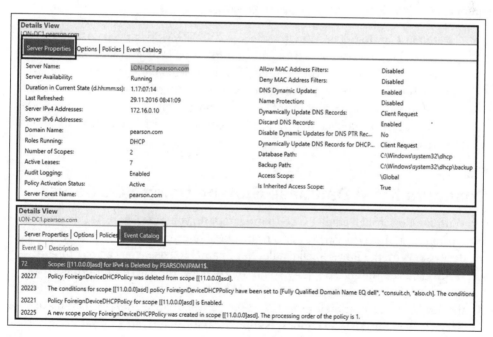

Figure 7-41   IPAM DHCP Server Properties and Events

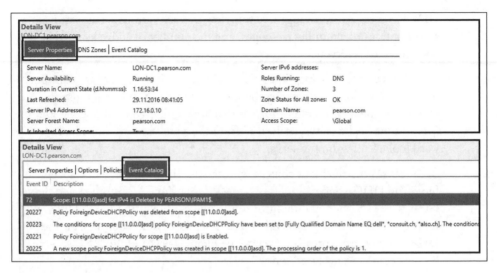

Figure 7-42   IPAM DNS Server Properties and Events

- **Event Catalog:** The Windows Server 2016 IPAM Event Catalog provides a central repository for auditing all configuration changes that occur on managed DHCP servers from a single IPAM management console. The IPAM configuration events console gathers all the configuration events. You can use these configuration Event Catalogs to view, query, and generate reports about consolidated configuration changes, along with details that are specific to each record.

Configure IPAM Database Storage Using SQL Server

With the PowerShell cmdlet **Get-IpamDatabase**, you can view IPAM database settings from the local WID or also from a local or external Microsoft SQL Server database. With the PowerShell cmdlet **Set-IpamDatabase**, you can reconfigure IPAM database settings. Suppose you have to change the Microsoft SQL database server and database name so that the IPAM server gets the information that this is the new database location for this IPAM server: **Set-IpamDatabase -Database-Server "PearsonDB1" -DatabaseName "PearsonIpamData1" -DatabasePort 1433 -DatabaseAuthType Windows**.

Suppose you want to migrate your existing IPAM WID to a Microsoft SQL Server database. You can use the PowerShell cmdlet **Move-IpamDatabase**. You also can use that command to migrate from one Microsoft SQL Server database to another. The cmdlet creates a new IPAM schema and copies all data from the existing IPAM database. When the cmdlet finishes copying the data, it changes the IPAM configuration settings to refer to the new database as the IPAM database. If you migrate from WID, the cmdlet renames the existing data and log files by appending a time stamp to the filenames.

When you have separate computers for the IPAM server and the Microsoft SQL Server, you must create an IPAM SQL database in the following way:

Windows authentication:

```
CREATE LOGIN [pearson\IPAM1$] FROM WINDOWS
CREATE DATABASE IPAM_DB1
GO
USE IPAM_DB1
CREATE USER IPAM FOR LOGIN [pearson\IPAM1$]
ALTER ROLE DB_OWNER ADD MEMBER IPAM
USE MASTER
GRANT VIEW ANY DEFINITION TO [pearson\IPAM1$]
```

SQL authentication:

```
CREATE LOGIN IPAMUSER WITH PASSWORD = 'Pa$$w0rd0'
CREATE DATABASE IPAM_DB1
GO
USE IPAM_DB1
CREATE USER IPAM FOR LOGIN IPAMUSER
ALTER ROLE DB_OWNER ADD MEMBER IPAM
GO
USE MASTER
GRANT VIEW ANY DEFINITION TO IPAMUSER
GO
```

When you have the IPAM server and the Microsoft SQL Server on the same machine, you must create an IPAM SQL database in the following way:

Windows authentication:

```
CREATE LOGIN [NT AUTHORITY\Network Service] FROM WINDOWS
CREATE DATABASE IPAM_DB1
GO
USE IPAM_DB 1
CREATE USER IPAM FOR LOGIN [NT AUTHORITY\Network Service]
ALTER ROLE DB_OWNER ADD MEMBER IPAM
GO
USE MASTER
GRANT VIEW ANY DEFINITION TO [NT AUTHORITY\Network Service]
GO
```

SQL authentication:

```
CREATE LOGIN IPAMUSER WITH PASSWORD = 'Pa$$w0rd0'
CREATE DATABASE IPAM_DB
GO
USE IPAM_DB
CREATE USER IPAM FOR LOGIN IPAMUSER
ALTER ROLE DB_OWNER ADD MEMBER IPAM
GO
USE MASTER
GRANT VIEW ANY DEFINITION TO IPAMUSER
GO
```

Purging Utilization Data from IPAM Database

Windows Server 2016 IPAM introduced the capability to delete utilization data from the IPAM database by performing the following steps:

Step 1.   In the IPAM configuration console, browse to one of the following locations: IP Address Blocks, IP Address Inventory, or IP Address Range Groups.

Step 2.   Click **Tasks**, and then click **Purge Utilization Data**.

Step 3.   Choose the date for which you want to delete database records.

Step 4.   Click **OK**. IPAM deletes all the records you have specified.

Figure 7-43 shows the Purge Utilization Data window.

Figure 7-43   Purge Utilization Data Window

IPAM and SCVMM

Windows Server 2016 introduced the capability to integrate IPAM with System Center Virtual Machine Manager (SCVMM). You can integrate IPAM with Virtual Machine Manager by performing the following steps:

Step 1. On the IPAM server, configure an account that SCVMM uses to communicate with IPAM and grant the account membership to the IPAM ASM Administrator role.

Step 2. In SCVMM console, add and configure the Microsoft Windows Server IP Address Management network service by performing the following steps:

   a. In the Fabric workspace, add a network service named IPAM.

   b. On the Manufacturer and Model page, select **Microsoft and Microsoft Windows Server IP Address Management**.

   c. Configure the service to run in the context of the user account that you created in Step 1.

   d. Specify the fully qualified domain name (FQDN) of the IMAP server.

   e. Verify that the configuration provider is Microsoft IP Address Management Provider.

   For each logical network in SCVMM, the IPAM server has an address space with a name that is based on the name of the logical network. The logical network is contained within the address space, with the name of the logical network displayed under the heading VMM Logical Network. Table 7-6 helps interpret some of the information that you see on the IPAM Server.

Table 7-6 VMM Versus IPAM Terminology

VMM Name	IPAM Name
Logical network	Virtualized IP address space
	Provider IP address space: VMM Logical Network column
Network site	Virtualized IP address space
	Provider IP address space: Network Site column
IP address subnet	IP address subnet (same name in IPAM as in VMM)
IP address pool	IP address range
VM network	Virtualized IP address space
	Customer IP address space: VM Network column

  f. If you use the IPAM server to delete a logical network, then delete the IP address subnets assigned to that logical network. You should not delete the name associated with the VMM Logical Network on the IPAM server. The two servers will then be able to synchronize correctly and the logical network will be deleted. If you delete the name associated with the VMM Logical Network field on the IPAM server, you must go to the VMM server and delete the network sites and the logical network. After the two servers synchronize, the deletion will be complete.

  g. If you cannot control the time synchrony of the IPAM server and the VMM server, you must update permissions on the IPAM server so that the provider software can query the current time setting on the IPAM server. To do this, on the IPAM server, run wmimgmt. msc to open the WMI Control (Local) snap-in. Right-click **WMI Control (Local)**, click **Properties**, and then click the **Security** tab. Navigate to Root\CIMV2, click the **Security** button, select the account, and then, for Remote Enable, check the **Allow** box.

Exam Preparation Tasks

Review All the Key Topics

Review the most important topics in the chapter, noted with the Key Topics icon in the outer margin of the page. Table 7-7 lists these key topics and the page numbers where each is found.

Table 7-7 Key Topics for Chapter 7

Key Topic Element	Description	Page Number
List	Requirements for Windows Server 2008/R2 servers as managed servers	292
List	IPAM improvements in Windows Server 2012 R2	293
List	IPAM improvements in Windows Server 2016	294
Section	IPAM Provisioning	295
Figure 7-26	IPAM Managed Servers Network Communication	306
Section	IPAM Administration	307

Key Topic Element	Description	Page Number
Table 7-4	Configuring IPAM Domains and Forests with PowerShell	314
Section	Managing DNS Using IPAM	314
Section	Managing IP Addressing	317
Section	Importing and Updating Address Spaces	319
Section	Finding, Allocating, and Reclaiming IP Addresses	320
Text	Monitoring DHCP and DNS servers	322
Section	Configure IPAM Database Storage Using SQL Server	324
Step List	IPAM and SCVMM integration	327

Complete the Tables and Lists from Memory

Print a copy of Appendix B, "Memory Tables" (on the book's website), or at least the section for this chapter, and complete the tables and lists from memory. Appendix C, "Memory Tables Answer Key," also on the website, includes completed tables and lists to check your work.

Definition of Key Terms

Define the following key terms from this chapter and check your answers in the glossary.

IPAM, IPAM provisioning, IPAM database, IPAM managed servers, RBAC, IPAM roles, IPAM access scope, IPAM access policy, IPAMUG

End-of-Chapter Review Questions

1. You have Windows Server 2016 DHCP Servers distributed through New York, Chicago, and Denver (domain: pearson.com). You use a Windows Server 2016 IPAM server named IPAM1 as an IP management solution. You have configured the following user roles: NYAdmins, CHAdmins, and DEAdmins. You have configured the following IPAM access scopes:

User Role	Access Scope	Access Policy
NYAdmins	\Global\NY	NYAccessPolicy
CHAdmins	\Global\CH	CHAccessPolicy
DenverAdmins	\Global\DE	DEAccessPolicy

In the past, admins from Chicago configured all DHCP superscopes. Now admins from Denver should manage a DHCP superscope named Downtown created on IPAM1.

Which PowerShell commands should you use for this? (Choose two.)

- **a. Set-IpamScope**
- **b. Set-IpamRange**
- **c. Get-IpamDHCPSuperScope**
- **d. Set-IpamAccessScope**

2. You are responsible for 22 Hyper-V hosts and 12 VMware hosts. The forest pearson.com has only two DHCP servers and two DNS servers. All hosts, virtual machines, and IP address spaces are managed centrally through a SCVMM 2016 server named VMM1. One hundred fifty virtual machines from your customers running on a Windows Server 2016 Hyper-V cluster are also managed through VMM1. Because of the acquisition of another company, you have to integrate the physical and virtual IP address space management IPAM solution of this company into your environment. You create a two-way forest trust between the two forests. The other company has a Windows Server 2016 IPAM server named IPAM2016 with 30 DHCP servers and 25 DNS servers to manage. You want to determine the next steps to use IPAM with SCVMM for physical and virtual IP address space management to centralize the administration. Which implementation should you use?

- **a.** Deploy an IPAM server on pearson.com.
- **b.** Add the pearson.com forest to IPAM2016.
- **c.** Use a third-party IPAM solution.
- **d.** Synchronize IPAM2016 and VMM1.

3. You have two Windows Server 2016 DHCP servers named DHCP1 and DHCP2 that are managed through a Windows Server 2016 IPAM server named IPAM1. You have created an IP scope named ChicagoScope with an IP range from 172.16.0.100/24 to 172.16.0.200/24 on DHCP1. You configure a DHCP Policy named DHCPPolicyChicago on IPAM1. In the Server Policy window on IPAM1, you define DHCP Policy conditions and settings and create the DHCP policy. After that, on IPAM1, you configure DHCP failover between DHCP1 and DHCP2 in hot standby mode. After replication, ChicagoScope is present on DHCP2, but DHCPPolicy Chicago is missing in ChicagoScope on DHCP2.

You must ensure that DHCPPolicyChicago can be automatically replicated successfully between DHCP1 and DHCP2. Which configuration is necessary?

- **a.** Create a scope policy on DHCP2.
- **b.** Create a scope policy on DHCP1.
- **c.** Select Import Policy on DHCP1.
- **d.** Select Import Policy on DHCP2.

4. You centrally manage your DNS and DHCP servers with Windows Server 2016 IPAM server. You want to delegate administration for DNS and DHCP using role-based access control (RBAC). You have created the access roles named IPAMZoneAdmins, IPAMIPAddressAdmins, IPAMScopeAdmins, and IPAMRRAdmins. You need to create the necessary access scopes before using them to create access policies.

Which PowerShell command will not run?

- **a.** $zone = Get-IpamDnsZone -ZoneType Forward -ZoneName pearson.com, Set-IpamAccess Scope -IpamDnsZone -InputObject $zone -AccessScopePath \Global\USA -PassThru
- **b.** $ip = Get-IpamAddress -IPAddress 10.12.1.1, Set-IpamAccessScope -IpamIPNumber -InputObject $ip -AccessScopePath \Global\USA -PassThru
- **c.** $scope = Get-IpamDhcpScope -AddressFamily "Ipv4" -ScopeID 10.0.0.0, Set-IpamAccess Scope -IpamDhcpScope -InputObject $scope -AccessScopePath \Global\USA -PassThru
- **d.** $record = Get-IpamDnsResourceRecord -ZoneName pearson.com -RecordName "PearsonServer" -RecordType A, Set-IpamAccessScope -IpamDnsResourceRecord -InputObject $record -AccessScopePath \Global\USA -PassThru

This chapter covers the following subjects:

- **Managing DHCP server properties using IPAM:** IP Address Management (IPAM) in Windows Server 2016 enables you to centrally configure DHCP server properties for managed DHCP servers. Using the IPAM configuration console, you can display DHCP servers and perform DHCP server-specific tasks such as enabling DHCP audit logging and enabling or disabling DNS dynamic update. This chapter covers the most important DHCP server properties and how to configure them using IPAM.

- **Configuring DHCP scopes and options using IPAM:** Here you learn how to configure predefined DHCP options and values. Configuration examples illustrate DHCP options using IPAM, and you explore the configuration of DHCP scopes using IPAM and some configuration restrictions.

- **Configuring DHCP Policies and failover using IPAM:** You can use IPAM to activate or deactivate DHCP Policies. This chapter covers how to edit, enable, disable, or move the processing order of DHCP Policies for single or multiple DHCP servers.

- **Managing DNS server properties using IPAM:** In Windows Server 2016, you have some enhanced options for managing DNS server and zones using IPAM. You learn how to manage DNS server properties using IPAM or DNS Manager, as well as how to create and edit DNS zones and DNS conditional forwarders.

- **Managing DNS zones and records using IPAM:** This chapter covers enhanced Windows Server 2016 IPAM DNS possibilities. It details how to manage DNS zone settings using IPAM and how to manage subdomains through the IPAM configuration console and DNS Manager.

- **Managing DNS and DHCP servers in multiple Active Directory forests using IPAM:** Windows Server 2016 IPAM offers the new feature to manage DHCP, DNS, or NPS servers distributed through different forests. This chapter covers how to implement an IPAM multiple forest management environment.

- **Using RBAC to delegate DNS and DHCP server administration using IPAM:** This section covers DNS and DHCP delegated administration in IPAM using the RBAC feature. It explains how to use IPAM user roles, access scopes, and access policies to restrict administrative permissions and implement a least privilege–based security design for IPAM administration.

## CHAPTER 8

Managing DNS and DHCP Using Windows Server 2016 IPAM

This chapter covers the configuration of DHCP server properties, options, and values using Windows Server 2016 IPAM tools and PowerShell. It explains all the DHCP server tasks and properties that you can perform through IPAM and compares the possibilities with older Windows Server versions. You also learn about some exclusions and DHCP server properties that cannot be configured through IPAM tools.

You investigate DHCP scope and option configuration using IPAM, as well as how to create and edit DHCP scopes in IPAM. Other important topics include DHCP Policies and the DHCP failover relationship configuration for single or multiple DHCP servers with IPAM. In addition, you learn where to find configuration settings in the IPAM configuration console and how to implement an example DHCP failover relationship scenario.

Windows Server 2016 IPAM offers some enhanced DNS server, zones, and resource record configuration possibilities. This chapter covers DNS server management, shows how to create and edit DNS zones and DNS conditional forwarders using IPAM, and details which PowerShell cmdlets are available for managing DNS zones and records using IPAM. DNS zone settings are explained in detail, along with coverage of subdomain management in the IPAM configuration console.

For larger companies with many forests, the new Windows Server 2016 IPAM capability of managing servers in different forests is an important improvement. This chapter covers this feature as well, including the prerequisites for a multiple-forest IPAM environment and its configuration using IPAM.

Windows Server 2016 IPAM offers RBAC possibilities so that you can restrict administrative privileges based on IPAM user roles, access scopes, and access policies. This chapter gives an example of delegating permissions to DHCP administrators so that only specific administrators can run predefined operations on IPAM.

Key topic selections, memory tables, key term definitions, and exam preparation questions give you some powerful tools to increase your knowledge about managing DNS and DHCP using Windows Server 2016 IPAM for the Microsoft 70-741 exam and your daily work.

"Do I Know This Already?" Quiz

The "Do I Know This Already?" quiz enables you to assess whether you should read this entire chapter or simply jump to the "Exam Preparation Tasks" section for review. If you are in doubt, read the entire chapter. Table 8-1 outlines the major headings in this chapter and the corresponding "Do I Know This Already?" quiz questions. You can find the answers in Appendix A, "Answers to the 'Do I Know This Already?' Quizzes and End-of-Chapter Review Questions."

Table 8-1   "Do I Know This Already?" Foundation Topics Section-to-Question Mapping

Foundation Topics Section	Questions Covered in This Section
Manage DHCP Server Properties Using IPAM	1, 2
Configure DHCP Scopes and Options Using IPAM	3
Configure DHCP Policies and Failover Using IPAM	4
Configure DNS Server Properties Using IPAM	5
Manage DNS Zones and Records Using IPAM	6
Manage DNS and DHCP Servers in Multiple Active Directory Forests Using IPAM	7
Using RBAC to Delegate DNS and DHCP Server Administration Using IPAM	8

CAUTION   The goal of self-assessment is to gauge your mastery of the topics in this chapter. If you do not know the answer to a question or are only partially sure of the answer, you should mark that question as wrong for purposes of the self-assessment. Giving yourself credit for an answer you correctly guess skews your self-assessment results and might provide you with a false sense of security.

1. You are responsible for your Windows Server 2016 IPAM server, IPAM1. IPAM1 is configured to manage DHCP servers in multiple forests; pearson. com and pucert.com are the two forests to manage. On IPAM1, you open the configuration console; then you select DNS and DHCP Servers, Server Type DHCP, and the Server Properties view. The following DHCP servers are listed:

    ■ dhcp1.pearson.com

    ■ dhcp2.pearson.com

- dhcp3.pearson.com

- dhcp4.usa.pearson.com

- dhcp1.pucert.com

- dhcp2.pucert.com

You want to enable the name protection feature for dhcp3.pearson.com and dhcp2.pucert.com through IPAM. Which is a possible way to do that?

- **a.** Select dhcp3.pearson.com and dhcp2.pucert.com together and use Edit DHCP Server Properties in the IPAM configuration console.

- **b.** Use the **Set-DhcpServerv4DnsSetting** PowerShell cmdlet with the **NameProtection** parameter.

- **c.** Select dhcp3.pearson.com and select Edit DHCP Server Properties in the IPAM configuration console. Then select dhcp2.pucert.com and use Edit DHCP Server Properties in the IPAM configuration console.

- **d.** Use the **Get-IpamDhcpServer** PowerShell cmdlet.

2. You have configured DNS Dynamic Update Credentials through your Windows Server 2016 IPAM server named IPAM1 for the three DHCP servers DHCP1, DHCP2, and DHCP3 in the forest pearson.com. Last Friday, a backup of all IPAM configuration data was started. You also have backed up all DHCP servers locally and Active Directory. You have to run a restore process for DHCP1. Which additional configuration should you do?

- **a.** Select all three DHCP servers in the IPAM configuration console and configure new DNS Dynamic Update Credentials.

- **b.** Select DHCP1 in the IPAM configuration console and configure new DNS Dynamic Update Credentials only for DHCP1.

- **c.** Restore ipam.mdf and ipam_log.ldf, select all three DHCP servers in the IPAM configuration console, and configure new DNS Dynamic Update Credentials.

- **d.** Use the **Set-IpamDiscoveryDomain** PowerShell cmdlet to discover the restored Active Directory Credentials from Active Directory.

3. You have two configured DHCP scopes named Scope1 and Scope2, and you want to disable dynamic updates for DNS PTR records for both scopes in IPAM. Which configuration process is a possible solution?

   a. Select both DHCP scopes in the IPAM configuration console and use Edit Scope to disable dynamic updates for DNS PTR records for both scopes.

   b. Use the **Set-IpamDhcpScope** PowerShell cmdlet to disable dynamic updates for DNS PTR records for both scopes.

   c. Select both DHCP scopes in the IPAM configuration console and use Set Access Scope to disable dynamic updates for DNS PTR records for both scopes.

   d. Remove Scope2. Select Scope1 and use Edit Scope to disable dynamic updates for DNS PTR records. Use Duplicate DHCP Scope and name the new scope Scope2.

4. You have a domain named pearson.com with two sites named Chicago and Denver. You also have a Windows Server 2016 IPAM server named IPAM1 that centrally manages all DNS and DHCP servers. Visitor devices must be automatically registered in visitors.pearson.com. The zone is created as an AD-integrated DNS zone with a forest-wide replication scope. You have four DHCP servers: DHCP1 and DHCP2 (Chicago), and DHCP3 and DHCP4 (Denver). You want to configure (with least administrative effort) visitor devices to be automatically registered in visitors.pearson.com with their IP address and hostname. You want to apply the configuration only to the following scopes: Scope2 (DHCP2): 10.10.0.0/24; Scope4 (DHCP4): 172.16.0.0/16. Which configuration is a valid solution for this scenario?

   a. On IPAM1, configure a DHCP Policy for DHCP2 with the Register DHCP Clients Using a Different DNS Suffix setting enabled, and use the DHCP failover feature to replicate the policy to DHCP4.

   b. On DHCP1, create a DHCP Policy with the Register DHCP Clients Using a Different DNS Suffix setting enabled, and use the DHCP failover feature to replicate the policy to DHCP4.

   c. On IPAM1, create a DHCP Policy for DHCP2 with the Register DHCP Clients Using a Different DNS Suffix setting enabled, and import this DHCP Policy into DHCP4.

   d. On IPAM1, select Scope2 and Scope4, and use Configure DHCP Policy. Enable the Register DHCP Clients Using a Different DNS Suffix setting and create the DHCP Policy.

5. You have a Windows Server 2016 IPAM server named IPAM1. You centrally manage 20 of your DNS servers through that IPAM server. You select DNS as the server type and Server Properties as the view. You see the list of your DNS servers. You want to configure Debug Logging on 10 of your DNS servers. The configuration has to be done through the IPAM configuration console. Which configuration is possible?

    a. Select the 10 DNS servers and select Launch MMC. Configure Debug Logging once.

    b. Select the first DNS server and select Launch MMC. Configure Debug Logging. Repeat these two steps for all other DNS servers.

    c. Change to Server Inventory and select the 10 DNS servers. Select Edit Server and configure Debug Logging once.

    d. Change to Server Groups and select the 10 DNS servers. Select Launch MMC and configure Debug Logging once.

6. You use the New Domain setting in the DNS Manager to create a subdomain named USA under the existing zone pearson.com. The subdomain is not displayed in the IPAM configuration console under Forward Lookup. The zone pearson.com is displayed with a green bullet. You also want to display the subdomain in the IPAM configuration console. What configuration do you need so that the subdomain usa.pearson.com is displayed in the IPAM configuration console under Forward Lookup?

    a. Remove the subdomain and use New Delegation in the DNS Manager to create the usa.pearson.com zone.

    b. Remove the subdomain, select the DNS server in the DNS and DHCP Servers list, and use Create DNS Zone to create the usa.pearson.com zone.

    c. Select pearson.com, Reset Zone Status, and then Retrieve Server Data.

    d. Remove the subdomain and create usa.pearson.com with the New Zone Wizard in the DNS Manager.

7. You are responsible for a forest named pearson.com and a Windows Server 2016 IPAM server named IPAM1. Now you want to manage the DHCP and DNS servers of an additional forest named pucert.com through IPAM1. You created DNS conditional forwarding between pearson.com and pucert.com in both directions. You also created a two-way forest trust. You clicked the Get Forests button in the IPAM configuration console and you added the pucert.com forest. Now you perform the **InvokeGpoProvisioning** Power-Shell command on IPAM1 to deploy the necessary GPOs. The command fails. Which configuration do you do next?

   a. Grant computer accounts of managed servers in pucert.com GPOApply permission.

   b. Grant the administrative account of pearson.com the permission to cre-ate IPAM GPOs in pucert.com.

   c. Add IPAM1 to the IPAMUG security group of pucert.com.

   d. Add pucert.com managed servers to the pearson\IPAMUG security group.

8. You want to allow administrators to become members of the security group IPv6Admins to create, modify and delete only AAAA resource records in the DNS zones eu.pucert.com and usa.pucert.com. Which IPAM components do you use? (Choose all that apply.)

   a. Create a new user role.

   b. Use the default user role DNS Record Administrator Role.

   c. Create a new access policy.

   d. Create a new access scope.

   e. Use the default access scope.

   f. Used the default access policy.

   g. Set the access scope.

Foundation Topics

Manage DHCP Server Properties Using IPAM

With Windows Server 2016 IPAM, you can configure DHCP server properties. Through the IPAM configuration console under DNS and DHCP Servers, you can select DHCP as the server type and choose the Server Properties view to display the available DHCP servers. By using the context menu of one or more DHCP servers, you can view DHCP server tasks. Figure 8-1 shows the possible DHCP server tasks in Windows Server 2012 R2 IPAM.

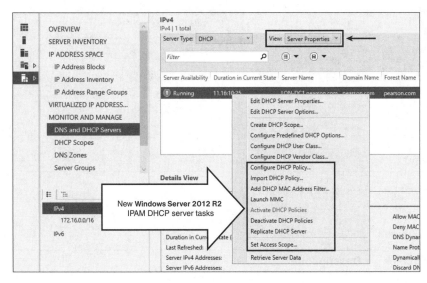

Figure 8-1   IPAM DHCP Server Tasks

DHCP server tasks through Windows Server 2016 IPAM are about the same as with Windows Server 2012 R2.

TIP   You cannot use the Create DHCP Scope configuration option on multiple DHCP servers. To duplicate a DHCP scope, create the scope on at least one DHCP server and then use the Duplicate DHCP Scope configuration option available in the DHCP Scopes view. Figure 8-2 shows the Duplicate DHCP Scope setting.

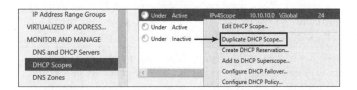

Figure 8-2   IPAM Duplicate DHCP Scope

DHCP Server Properties

To configure DHCP server properties through IPAM, select **Edit DHCP Server Properties** in the IPAM configuration console. Figure 8-3 shows all possible DHCP server properties configuration options, and Table 8-2 describes them further.

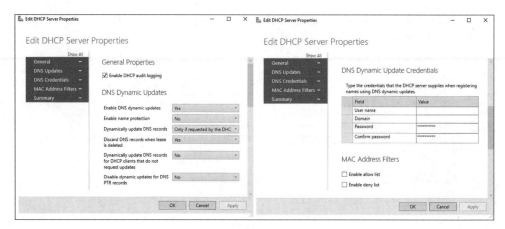

Figure 8-3   IPAM DHCP Server Properties

Table 8-2   IPAM DHCP Server Properties

IPAM DHCP Server Property	Description
Enable DHCP Audit Logging	DHCP audit logging is enabled by default. This tracks the history of client requests, including associated IP address and DNS registrations and administrative configuration changes made to the server. You also can configure DHCP audit logging through PowerShell. The following example enables the DHCP audit log, sets the path for the audit log to D:\dhcpauditlog\directory, and defines a minimum size of 100 MB: **Set-DhcpServerAuditLog -ComputerName "dhcpserver.pearson.com" -Enable $True -Path "D:\ dhcpauditlog\" -MaxMBFileSize 100**.
Enable DNS Dynamic Updates	This enables you to perform dynamic updates on the DNS server.
Enable Name Protection	If this is enabled, DNS name protection is enabled. If this parameter is enabled and an existing DNS record matches the name, the DNS update for the client fails instead of being overwritten.
Dynamically Update DNS Records	This specifies to perform dynamic updates on the DNS server. You also can use the PowerShell cmdlet **Set-DhcpServerv4DnsSetting** to configure how the DHCP server updates the DNS server with the client-related information. The following example sets the DNS update configuration settings to always update DNS with lease entries and deletes the client entry from DNS when the lease expires: **Set-DhcpServerv4DnsSetting -ComputerName "dhcpserver.pearson. com" -DynamicUpdates "Always" -DeleteDnsRRon LeaseExpiry $True**.

IPAM DHCP Server Property	Description
Discard DNS Records When Lease Is Deleted	This discards DNS A and PTR records when the lease is deleted.
Dynamically Update DNS Records for DHCP Clients That Do Not Request Updates	You have to enable this setting only if you have older clients that do not support the dynamic update feature.
Disable Dynamic Updates for DNS PTR Records	When you enable this setting, no PTR resource records are registered on the DNS server.
DNS Dynamic Update Credentials	You must be a member in the Administrators or DHCP Administrators group to configure the DNS Dynamic Update Credentials. You must type in the credentials used to perform DNS dynamic updates on the DNS server. Keep in mind that these credentials are *not backed up* with either synchronous or asynchronous backup. After a DHCP database is restored, new credentials must be configured.
MAC Address Filters	With this setting, you can enable or disable the MAC allow or deny list.

Using the PowerShell command in Figure 8-4, you can list IPAM DHCP server properties.

Figure 8-4   List IPAM DHCP Server Properties with PowerShell

TIP No **Set-IpamDhcpServer** PowerShell cmdlet exists for configuring DHCP server properties through IPAM PowerShell.

TIP You cannot configure the DHCP server general setting Automatically Update Statistics in the IPAM configuration console in Server Manager. You also cannot configure the Database path and the Backup path through the IPAM configuration console. Figure 8-5 shows where to configure these settings in the local DHCP server management console.

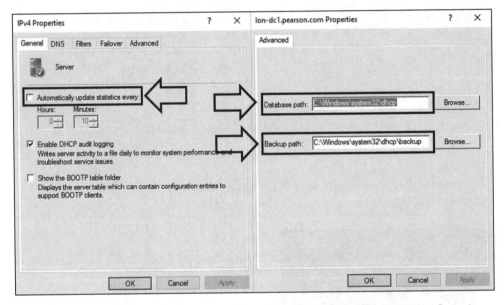

Figure 8-5 Use Local DHCP Management Console Instead of IPAM Configuration Console

DHCP Server Options

Through the IPAM configuration console, under DNS and DHCP Servers, you can select DHCP as the server type and use the Server Properties view to display the available DHCP servers. By using the context menu of one or more DHCP servers, you can select DHCP Server Options. Figure 8-6 shows an example of DHCP server options configured through Windows Server 2016 IPAM.

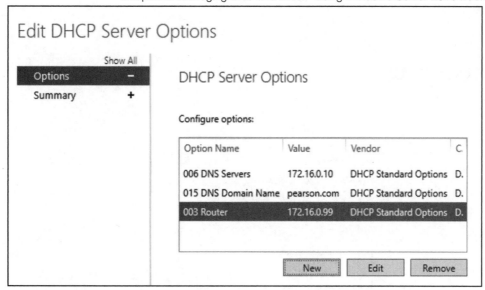

Figure 8-6 IPAM DHCP Server Options

When you select multiple DHCP servers and you want to configure DHCP server options, you can choose among the following configuration actions:

- Add

- Overwrite

- Find and replace

- Delete

Figure 8-7 shows the configuration actions in the DHCP Server Options window.

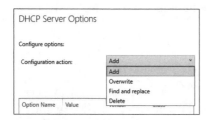

Figure 8-7 IPAM DHCP Server Options Configuration Actions for Multiple DHCP Servers

When you choose Overwrite for multiple DHCP servers and an option does not exist, it will be created. When you choose Add, this does not overwrite an option if it already exists. When you choose the Find and Replace configuration option, you get two additional fields (see Figure 8-8). You must type in the option value you want to replace with another value.

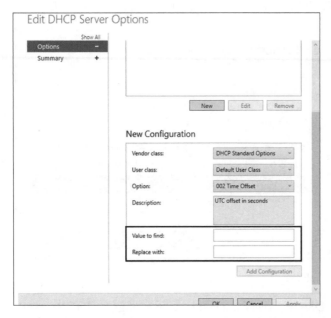

Figure 8-8 IPAM DHCP Server Options Configuration Action Find and Replace

Configure DHCP Scopes and Options Using IPAM

A DHCP server also can deliver DHCP options to clients. The clients must get the DNS servers, the default gateway, or other additional options. DHCP options are values for common configuration data that apply to the server, scopes, reservations, and class options. You can apply DHCP options at the server, scope, class, and reservation levels. An option code identifies the DHCP options, and most option codes come from the RFC documentation found on the Internet Engineering Task Force (IETF) website.

Configuring Predefined DHCP Options and Values

Through the IPAM configuration console under DNS and DHCP Servers, you can select DHCP as the server type and use the Server Properties view to display the available DHCP servers. By right-clicking one or multiple DHCP servers, you can configure predefined DHCP options and values for one or multiple DHCP servers. Figures 8-9 and 8-10 show an example of predefined DHCP options configured through the IPAM configuration console for multiple DHCP servers. In this example, DHCP option 060 will be added and option 043 will be edited so that an Aruba client can get the Aruba master controller IP address through these options.

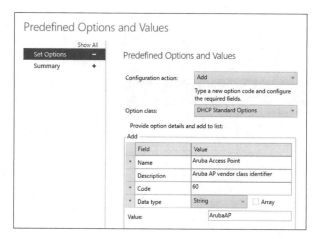

Figure 8-9   Add Predefined IPAM DHCP Server Option 060 to Multiple DHCP Servers

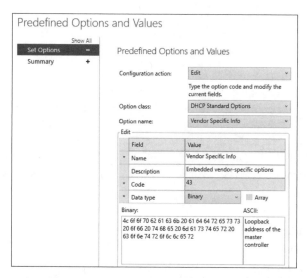

Figure 8-10   Edit Predefined IPAM DHCP Server Option 043 to Multiple DHCP Servers

Configuring DHCP Scopes Using IPAM

In the IPAM configuration console under DHCP Scopes, you can select one or multiple scopes, and you can configure scope settings through IPAM. Figure 8-11 shows which DHCP scope tasks are possible through IPAM; Table 8-3 explains all Windows Server 2016 IPAM server scope tasks.

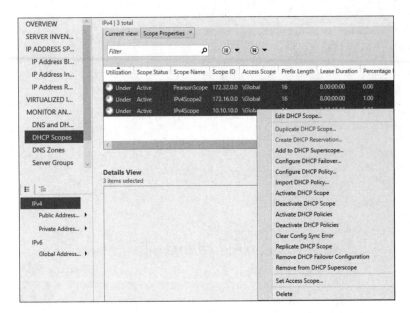

Figure 8-11   IPAM DHCP Server Scope Tasks

Table 8-3   IPAM DHCP Server Scope Tasks

IPAM DHCP Server Scope Task	Description
Edit DHCP Scope	Scope options: ■ Scope Name ■ Description ■ Start IP Address ■ End IP Address ■ Subnet Mask ■ Lease Duration ■ Exclusion Range If multiple scopes are selected, you can configure only the description and lease duration (see Figure 8-12). DNS Dynamic Update options: ■ Enable DNS Dynamic Updates ■ Enable Name Protection ■ Dynamically Update DNS Records ■ Discard DNS A and PTR Records When Lease Is Deleted ■ Dynamically Update DNS Records for DHCP Clients That Do Not Request Updates ■ Disable Dynamic Updates for DNS PTR Records

IPAM DHCP Server Scope Task	Description
Edit DHCP Scope (*continued*)	If multiple scopes are selected, you can enable or disable only DNS dynamic updates (see Figure 8-12). DHCP Scope options: ■ Add, overwrite, delete vendor class and user class options and values ■ All DHCP scope options can be configured simultaneously for multiple scopes (see Figure 8-12). Advanced Properties: ■ Assign IP Addresses Dynamically to DHCP Clients, BOOTP Clients, or Both ■ Lease Duration for BOOTP Clients ■ Subnet Delay All advanced properties can be configured simultaneously for multiple scopes (see Figure 8-12).
Duplicate DHCP Scope	This creates a new scope on a single DHCP server. The new scope is configured with the same DNS dynamic update options, scope options, and advanced properties of the scope that is selected for duplication, but you can change these values before you create the new scope. You must select the DHCP server on which to create the new scope. You are also required to provide a start IP address, end IP address, and subnet mask. DHCP failover relationships are not duplicated.
Create DHCP Reservation	This enables you to add a new DHCP reservation to the selected scope. This option is not available when multiple scopes are selected. You must specify a name, IP address, client ID, and reservation type.
Add to DHCP Superscope	This adds one or more DHCP scopes to a superscope. If multiple scopes are selected, they must belong to the same DHCP server. You can create a new superscope using the selected DHCP scopes or select an existing superscope on the DHCP server.
Configure DHCP Failover	This enables DHCP failover on one or more scopes. If multiple scopes are selected, they must belong to the same DHCP server. You can create a new DHCP failover relationship or choose an existing relationship.
Configure DHCP Policy	This creates a scope-level DHCP policy for one or more scopes. If a policy with the same name exists in the scope, policy creation fails for that scope.
Import DHCP Policy	This imports a server-level or scope-level DHCP Policy from a DHCP server that you specify to the selected scopes or servers.

IPAM DHCP Server Scope Task	Description
Activate DHCP Scope	This activates the selected scopes on managed DHCP servers. All scopes that you select must be inactive to use this option.
Deactivate DHCP Scope	This deactivates the selected scopes on managed DHCP servers. All scopes that you select must be active to use this option.
Activate DHCP Policies	This causes all DHCP Policies on the selected scope to be active. This is the same action as right-clicking a scope-level policy container in the DHCP console and then clicking Activate. All policies that apply to this scope are activated. This setting does not override the server-level policy setting. You cannot activate scope-level policies when policies are inactive at the server level. Policies that are in a disabled state are not enabled by this setting.
Deactivate DHCP Policies	This causes all DHCP Policies that apply to the selected scope to be inactive. This includes server-level policies that apply to clients that receive an IP address lease from the selected scope. This is the same action as right-clicking the scope-level policies container in the DHCP console and then clicking Deactivate. This setting does not change the enabled or disabled status of policies.
Clear Config Sync Error	This removes the error status from the DHCP failover configuration synchronization state of the selected scopes. You should clear the configuration synchronization error if DHCP failover partners were replicated manually with no errors but the Failover Config Sync Status column in the IPAM console continues to display an error.
Replicate DHCP Scope	This performs scope replication for the selected DHCP scopes from the selected DHCP server to its failover partner. If one or more of the selected scopes are not enabled for DHCP failover, an error is reported and this scope is skipped. The selected scopes must all be from the same DHCP server.
Remove DHCP Failover Configuration	This deconfigures DHCP failover on one or more scopes by removing them from the failover relationship. The scope is also removed from the DHCP failover partner server.
Remove from DHCP Superscope	This removes one or more scopes from a DHCP superscope.
Set Access Scope	This configures the selected DHCP scopes to be members of an access scope. The access scope must already be configured. By default, all scopes are members of the Global access scope.
Delete	This deletes the selected scopes on managed DHCP servers.

Figure 8-12 shows which IPAM DHCP server scope tasks can be done simultaneously through Edit DHCP Scope.

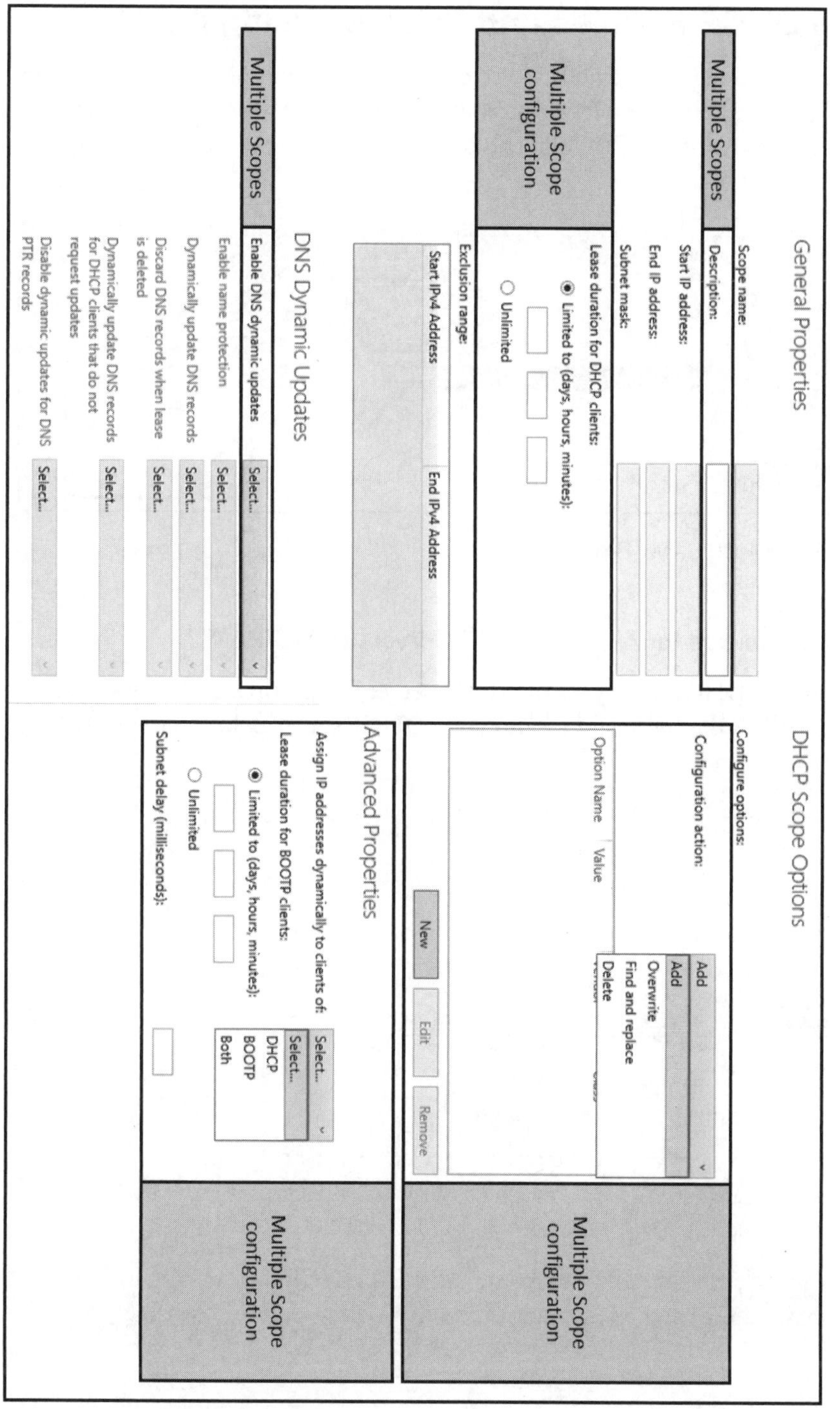

General Properties

Multiple Scopes

Scope name:

Description:

Start IP address:

End IP address:

Subnet mask:

Multiple Scope
configuration

Lease duration for DHCP clients:

◉ Limited to (days, hours, minutes):

○ Unlimited

Exclusion range:

Start IPv4 Address   End IPv4 Address

DNS Dynamic Updates

Multiple Scopes

Enable DNS dynamic updates   Select...

Enable name protection   Select...

Dynamically update DNS records   Select...

Discard DNS records when lease
is deleted   Select...

Dynamically update DNS records
for DHCP clients that do not
request updates   Select...

Disable dynamic updates for DNS
PTR records   Select...

DHCP Scope Options

Configure options:

Configuration action: Add
                               Add
                               Overwrite
                               Find and replace
                               Delete

Option Name   Value

                New   Edit   Remove

Multiple Scope
configuration

Advanced Properties

Assign IP addresses dynamically to clients of: Select...
                                                    Select...
                                                    DHCP
                                                    BOOTP
                                                    Both

Lease duration for BOOTP clients:

◉ Limited to (days, hours, minutes):

○ Unlimited

Subnet delay (milliseconds):

Multiple Scope
configuration

Figure 8-12   Edit DHCP Scope

Configure DHCP Policies and Failover Using IPAM

You can activate or deactivate DHCP Policies for one or multiple DHCP servers in the IPAM configuration console. If you want to edit, enable, disable, delete, or move the processing order of DHCP Policies, you have to change the view to Policies (see Figure 8-13).

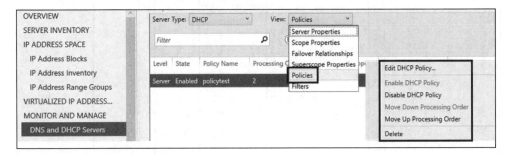

Figure 8-13   IPAM DHCP Server Policies and Tasks

Creating DHCP Policies for Multiple DHCP Servers Using IPAM

You can create a DHCP Policy on the IPAM server for multiple DHCP servers. Figure 8-14 shows the successful creation of a DHCP server policy in the IPAM configuration console.

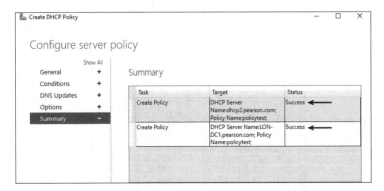

Figure 8-14   Successful DHCP Policy Creation on Multiple DHCP Servers Using IPAM

TIP   You cannot delete DHCP Policies in the IPAM DHCP Server Properties view. Instead, you have to use the Policies view in the IPAM configuration console.

Configuring DHCP Failover Using IPAM

You can use the IPAM configuration console to configure the DHCP failover feature. You first choose the DHCP scope and then select **Configure DHCP Failover Relationship**. In the example in Figure 8-15, a DHCP failover relationship for DHCP scope 10.10.10.0/24 will be implemented for the DHCP servers lon-dc1.pearson.com and dhcp2.pearson.com with enabled message authentication, 1 hour value (default value) for MCLT, default settings for reserved addresses for the standby server (5%), and a default State Switchover interval of 60 minutes. Hot standby mode is chosen so that dhcp2.pearson.com works as a standby server for the active DHCP server lon-dc1.pearson.com. Figure 8-16 shows these settings and where you can change them.

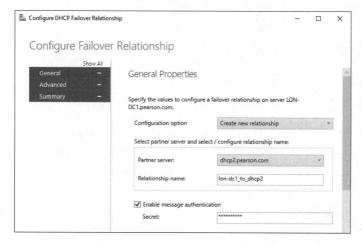

Figure 8-15   Configuring DHCP Failover Relationship Using IPAM (General Properties)

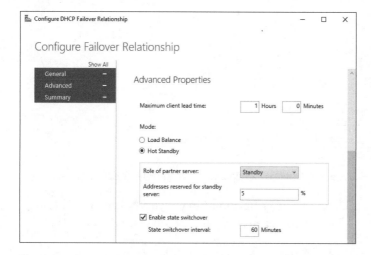

Figure 8-16   Configuring DHCP Failover Relationship Using IPAM (Advanced Properties)

The DHCP Failover Configuration summary displays a success message (see Figure 8-17).

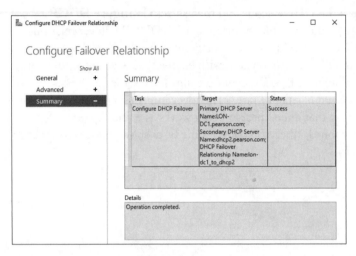

Figure 8-17   Completed DHCP Failover Relationship Configuration Using IPAM (Summary)

In the IPAM configuration console, you can replicate the DHCP scope, or you can remove the DHCP failover configuration. Figure 8-18 shows these two settings.

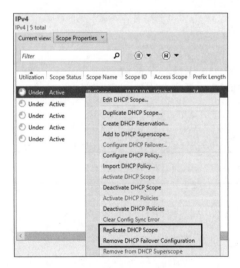

Figure 8-18   IPAM DHCP Failover Relationship Configuration Using IPAM (Replicate, Remove)

You can edit an existing DHCP Failover Relationship under DNS and DHCP Servers and also with the View: Failover Relationships setting (see Figure 8-19).

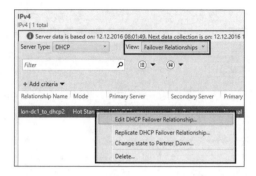

Figure 8-19   Edit IPAM DHCP Failover Relationship

Configure DNS Server Properties Using IPAM

You cannot configure DNS server settings directly in the IPAM configuration console in the Server Manager. Instead, you have to switch to the DNS Manager. There you can configure settings such as Root Hints, Debug Logging, and Event Logging and Monitoring. Since Windows Server 2016, you can configure some DNS server settings through IPAM with IPAM DNS PowerShell cmdlets.

Managing DNS Server Properties Using IPAM

In the IPAM configuration console, you can configure the following DNS server tasks:

- **Launch MMC:** You need to launch the DNS Manager to configure the DNS server settings shown in Figure 8-20.

- **Create DNS Zone:** Through the IPAM configuration console, you can create a new DNS zone (forward lookup zone, IPv4 reverse lookup zone, or IPv6 reverse lookup zone). You can choose a primary, secondary, or stub zone; opt for storage in Active Directory or a zone file; select an AD zone replication scope of domain, forest, legacy, or custom; and choose a dynamic update setting of Allow Only Secure Dynamic Updates, Allow Both Nonsecure and Secure Dynamic Updates, or Do Not Allow Dynamic Updates.

- **Create DNS Conditional Forwarder:** Through the IPAM configuration console, you can create a DNS conditional forwarder.

- **Set Access Scope:** Through the IPAM configuration console, you can set the access scope and disable the Inherit Access Scope from Parent setting.

- **Retrieve Server Data:** Through the IPAM configuration console, you can retrieve server data to refresh DNS server settings on the IPAM server.

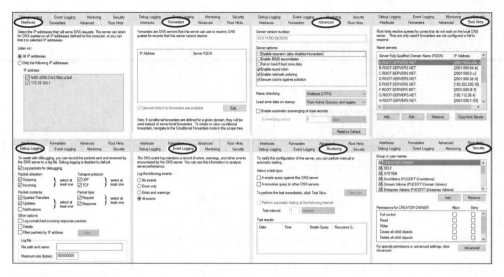

Figure 8-20   DNS Server Properties Through Launching DNS Manager Console

Filtering the View of DNS Server Settings

To filter the view of DNS server settings in IPAM, you need to perform the following steps:

Step 1.   In the Server Manager, click **IPAM**.

Step 2.   In the navigation pane, in Monitor and Manage, click **DNS Zones**. The navigation pane divides into an upper navigation pane and a lower navigation pane.

Step 3.   In the lower navigation pane, click **Forward Lookup**. All IPAM-managed DNS forward lookup zones are displayed in the display pane search results.

Step 4.   Click the zone whose records you want to view and filter.

Step 5.   In the display pane, click **Current View** and then click **DNS Server**.

Step 6.   In the display pane, click **Add Criteria**. Figure 8-21 shows the possible DNS Server criteria you can choose for filtering in this view.

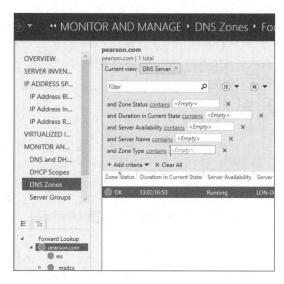

Figure 8-21   IPAM DNS Server Filtering

Manage DNS Zones and Records Using IPAM

When you deploy Windows Server 2016 IPAM, you can perform server discovery to add DHCP and DNS servers to the IPAM server management console. The IPAM server then dynamically collects DNS data every six hours from the DNS servers that it is configured to manage. IPAM stores this DNS data in its IPAM database. IPAM provides you with notification of the day and time the server data was collected and tells you the next day and time data collection from DNS servers will occur.

TIP   Windows Server 2016 IPAM does not support third-party DNS servers and non-domain-joined servers.

Managing DNS Zones and Records with PowerShell

You can use the PowerShell cmdlets in Table 8-4 to manage DNS zones and records.

Table 8-4   IPAM DNS Zones and Records PowerShell Cmdlets

IPAM PowerShell Cmdlet	Description
Get-IpamDnsResourceRecord	Gets IPAM DNS resource records
Get-IpamDnsZone	Gets information about IPAM DNS zones

Managing DNS Zone Settings Through IPAM

You can edit DNS zone settings in the IPAM configuration console. Figure 8-22 shows all configurable settings, and Table 8-5 further describes them.

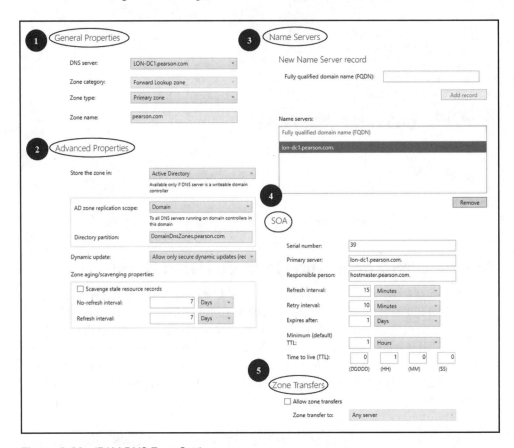

Figure 8-22   IPAM DNS Zone Settings

Table 8-5   IPAM DNS Zone Settings

IPAM DNS Zone Setting	Description
1 DNS Server	The DNS server where the zone exists.
Zone Category	The zone category (forward lookup zone, IPv4 reverse lookup zone, IPv6 reverse lookup zone). This cannot be modified afterward.
Zone Type	The zone type (primary zone, secondary zone).
Zone Name	The zone name (cannot be modified afterward).

	IPAM DNS Zone Setting	Description
2	Store the Zone In	Storage location of the zone data (Active Directory or zone file).
	AD Zone Replication Scope	When Active Directory is selected as the zone storage location in the previous field, you can define the AD zone replication scope here (domain, forest, legacy, custom).
	Directory Partition	The Active Directory partition where the DNS data is stored, when Active Directory is selected as the storage location for DNS data for that zone.
	Dynamic Update	The dynamic update setting. You can choose Allow Only Secure Dynamic Update (most secure setting, usable only together with Active Directory), Allow Both Nonsecure and Secure Dynamic Updates, or Do Not Allow Dynamic Updates.
	Scavenge Stale Resource Records	When to automatically remove old, stale resource records.
	No-Refresh Interval	Default value = 7 days
	Refresh Interval	Default value = 7 days
3	New Name Server Record	Manual addition of a new NS resource record manually.
	Name Servers	List of all NS resource records.
4	Serial Number	The starting serial number (the number version of your zone). If you apply this SOA to a domain that is already created, the serial number increments by one.
	Primary Server	The FQDN of the name server that is the original or primary source of data for this zone.
	Responsible Person	A domain name (FQDN) that specifies the mailbox of the person responsible for this zone.
	Refresh Interval	The time interval (in minutes) before the zone should be refreshed.
	Retry Interval	The time interval (in minutes) before a failed refresh should be retried.
	Expires After	The time interval that specifies the upper limit on the time interval that can elapse before the zone is no longer authoritative.
	Minimum (Default) TTL	The minimum TTL for resource records in that zone.
	Time to Live (TTL)	The TTL for resource records in that zone.

IPAM DNS Zone Setting	Description
5 Allow Zone Transfer	Setting that enables you to transfer zone data to secondary DNS servers.
Zone Transfer To	Setting that enables you to allow a zone transfer to any server, only servers listed on the Name Servers tab, or DNS servers in a defined server list.
Automatically Notify	Setting that enables you to push resource record changes immediately to secondary servers and define the secondary DNS servers that must be notified about changes.

Managing Subdomains Through IPAM

When you want to add a subzone, you can do so through the IPAM configuration console with Create DNS Zone. For example, you would type USA.pearson.com as the name for the subzone USA in the Create DNS Zone window. Another possibility for installing a subzone is to install a first child DC with DNS server for an Active Directory subdomain through the Active Directory Installation Wizard. This automatically generates a subdomain on the DNS server of that domain controller and a DNS delegation on the forest root DNS server. This subdomain (such as a subdomain created manually through the Create DNS Zone in the IPAM configuration console) then displays correctly (see Figure 8-23).

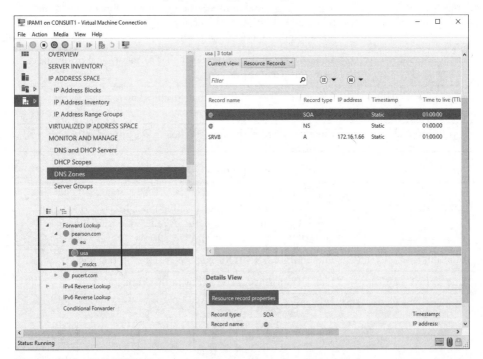

Figure 8-23   IPAM DNS Subzone

When the subzone displays with an empty white bullet under Forward Lookup (see Figure 8-24), it has no data, or the actual zone information was not retrieved from the DNS server. To refresh the information displayed, you must select Reset Zone Status and Retrieve Server Data, as in Figures 8-25 and 8-26.

Figure 8-24   IPAM Subzone with No Data

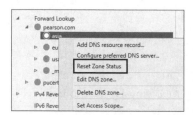

Figure 8-25   IPAM Reset Zone Status

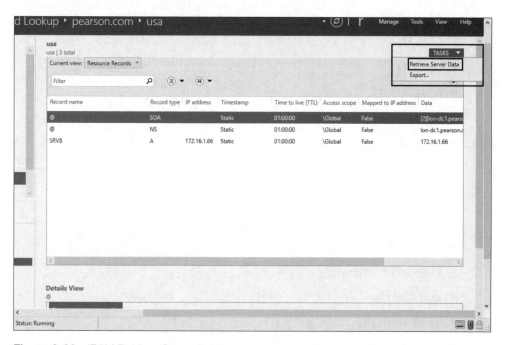

Figure 8-26   IPAM Retrieve Server Data

> **TIP**   When you add a subdomain in the DNS Manager (see Figure 8-27), the subdomain is not listed under Forward Lookup in the IPAM management console.

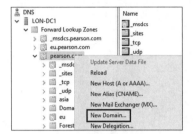

Figure 8-27   Add Subdomain in DNS Manager

Managing DNS Resource Records Using IPAM

A Windows Server 2016 IPAM server can collect the following DNS resource record types:

- AFS database
- ATM address
- CNAME
- DHCID
- DNAME
- Host A or AAAA
- Host information
- ISDN
- MX
- Name servers
- Pointer (PTR)
- Responsible person
- Route location
- Route through
- Service location

- SOA
- SRV
- Text
- Well-known services
- WINS
- WINS-R
- X.25

You can run the following DNS server inventory tasks through Windows Server 2016 IPAM:

- Automatically build an IP address inventory from DNS resource records

- Manually create an IP address inventory from DNS A and AAAA resource records

- View DNS resource records for a specific DNS zone, and filter the records based on type, IP address, resource record data, and other filtering options

- Automatically create a mapping between IP address ranges and DNS reverse lookup zones

- Create IP addresses for the PTR records that are present in the reverse lookup zone and that are included in that IP address range. You can also manually modify this mapping, if needed.

You can add a DNS resource record in the IPAM configuration console by following these steps:

Step 1. In Server Manager, click **IPAM**. The IPAM client console appears.

Step 2. In the navigation pane, in Monitor and Manage, click **DNS Zones**. The navigation pane divides into an upper navigation pane and a lower navigation pane.

Step 3. In the lower navigation pane, click **Forward Lookup**. All IPAM-managed DNS forward lookup zones appear in the display pane search results. Right-click the zone where you want to add a resource record, and then click **Add DNS Resource Record**.

You can delete a DNS resource record in the IPAM configuration console using the following steps:

Step 1.   In Server Manager, click **IPAM**. The IPAM client console appears.

Step 2.   In the navigation pane, in Monitor and Manage, click **DNS Zones**. The navigation pane divides into an upper navigation pane and a lower navigation pane.

Step 3.   Click to expand Forward Lookup and the domain where the zone and resource records that you want to delete are located. Click the zone and, in the display pane, click **Current View**. Click **Resource Records**.

Step 4.   In the display pane, locate and select the resource records you want to delete.

Step 5.   Right-click the selected records and click **Delete DNS Resource Record**.

Filtering the View of DNS Resource Records

To filter the view of DNS resource records in IPAM, complete the following steps:

Step 1.   In Server Manager, click **IPAM**.

Step 2.   In the navigation pane, in Monitor and Manage, click **DNS Zones**. The navigation pane divides into an upper navigation pane and a lower navigation pane.

Step 3.   In the lower navigation pane, click **Forward Lookup**. All IPAM-managed DNS forward lookup zones appear in the display pane search results.

Step 4.   Click the zone whose records you want to view and filter.

Step 5.   In the display pane, click **Current View** and then click **Resource Records**. The resource records for the zone are shown in the display pane.

Step 6.   In the display pane, click **Add Criteria** (in Figure 8-28, the criteria Record Type with a value of A is selected to display all A resource records from the zone pearson.com).

Figure 8-28   IPAM DNS Resource Records Filtering

Saving Views of IPAM DNS Zone Information

You can create saved views of your IPAM-managed DNS zones and resource records based on different criteria definitions. Figure 8-29 shows possible DNS zone criteria, and Figure 8-30 gives an example of saved DNS zone views.

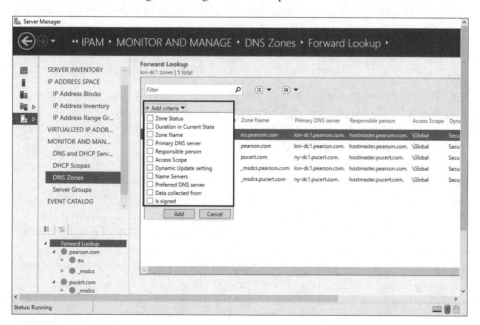

Figure 8-29   IPAM DNS Zone Criteria

Figure 8-30 IPAM Saved DNS Zone Views

Manage DNS and DHCP Servers in Multiple Active Directory Forests Using IPAM

You can now use IPAM to manage your DNS and DHCP servers across multiple AD DS forests. Microsoft will ask about that in the 70-741 exam! IPAM also can automate periodic service monitoring of DHCP and DNS servers across multiple forests in Windows Server 2016.

Prerequisites for Managing Multiple Active Directory Forests with IPAM

When you have to manage DHCP and DNS servers in different AD DS forests, you must fulfill some prerequisites before your IPAM server can collect data from these servers, or you can do central configuration for DHCP and DNS servers distributed across different forests:

- To manage DHCP, DNS, or NPS servers in other forests through Windows Server 2016 IPAM, you must build a two-way trust between the forests.

- Managed servers in other forests have to get Group Policy settings from IPAM GPOs in their forest. The administrative user account performing the GPO provisioning at the Windows Server 2016 IPAM server in forest1 needs permission to create Group Policies in forest2.

Figure 8-31 shows the execution of the **Invoke-GpoProvisioning** PowerShell command in the forest pearson.com on ipam1.pearson.com to create the IPAM GPOs on the forest pucert.com for managed servers in that forest. The first try failed because of the missing access to create GPOs in pucert.com. The administrative account of pearson.com then was added to the Administrators security group of pucert.com to grant access to create the IPAM GPOs in pucert.com. After that change, the forest-to-forest IPAM GPO provisioning process was successful.

Figure 8-31   IPAM GPO Provisioning for Multiple-Forest IPAM Management

Configuring Multiple-Forest IPAM Management

In the following example, DHCP and DNS servers in the two forests pearson.com and pucert.com have to be managed through an IPAM server named ipam1.pearson. com. Figure 8-32 shows that scenario.

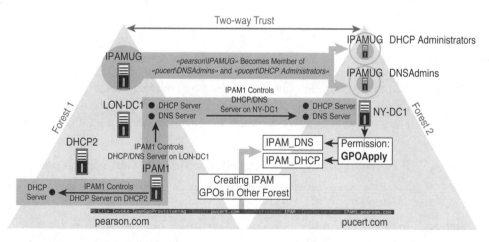

Figure 8-32   IPAM Multiple-Forest Management

The following steps are necessary to implement that IPAM multiple-forest environment scenario:

Step 1.   To start the discovery process for the Active Directory forest pucert.com, open the Server Manager and click **IPAM**. In the IPAM client console, click **Configure Server Discovery**, and then click **Get Forests**. This initiates a background task that discovers trusted forests and domains (in this case, forest pucert.com).

Step 2.   In the Configure Server Discovery dialog box, click **Select the Forest**, then choose pucert.com (the forest with the additional managed servers to integrate into IPAM), and click **OK**. Figure 8-33 shows the complete configured Configure Server Discovery dialog box.

Figure 8-33   IPAM Configure Server Discovery Dialog Box (Get Forests)

Step 3.   Add the Domain Admins security group of pearson.com to the Administrators security group of pucert.com to give the Administrator account of pearson.com permission to create the IPAM provisioning GPOs on the pucert.com forest.

Step 4.   Perform the following PowerShell command on ipam1.pearson.com:

```
Invoke-GpoProvisioing -domain pucert.com -gpoprefix IPAM
   -IpamServerFqdn ipam1.pearson.com
```

Step 5.   In the GPMC tool on the domain controller of pucert.com, verify that the three IPAM GPOs were successfully created (IPAM_DHCP, IPAM_DNS, and IPAM_DC_NPS). Ensure that managed servers have permission to apply GPO settings. Figure 8-34 shows that DHCP/DNS server NY-DC1 has GPOApply permission for the IPAM_DHCP and IPAM_DNS Group Policy.

Figure 8-34   IPAM Security Filtering in Multiple-Forest IPAM Management

Step 6.   Perform **gpupdate /force** on all managed servers in the pucert.com forest.

The IPAM server from pearson.com is a member of the pearson\IPAMUG security group. The pearson\IPAMUG security group is automatically added to the pucert\ DHCPAdmins and pucert\DNS Admins security groups so that ipam1.pearson.com has the permission to manage DNS and DHCP servers in the other forest. Figure 8-35 shows the membership of the two security groups.

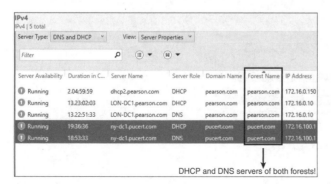

Figure 8-35   IPAMUG Group Membership

After that, you can configure the managed servers in both forests through the IPAM configuration console. Figure 8-36 shows that you now can manage DHCP and DNS servers from both forests.

Server Availability	Duration in C...	Server Name	Server Role	Domain Name	Forest Name	IP Address
Running	2.04:59:59	dhcp2.pearson.com	DHCP	pearson.com	pearson.com	172.16.0.150
Running	13.23:02:03	LON-DC1.pearson.com	DHCP	pearson.com	pearson.com	172.16.0.10
Running	13.22:51:33	LON-DC1.pearson.com	DNS	pearson.com	pearson.com	172.16.0.10
Running	19:36:36	ny-dc1.pucert.com	DHCP	pucert.com	pucert.com	172.16.100.1
Running	18:53:33	ny-dc1.pucert.com	DNS	pucert.com	pucert.com	172.16.100.1

DHCP and DNS servers of both forests!

Figure 8-36   Multiforest Management of DHCP and DNS Servers Through Windows Server 2016 IPAM

Managing DNS Servers and Zones in a Multiple-Forest IPAM Environment

When IPAM is configured to manage DNS servers and zones in multiple forests, you can manage DNS zones centrally through the IPAM configuration console. To manage all forward lookup zones on DNS servers in multiple forests, select **DNS Zones** and **Forward Lookup**. Figure 8-37 shows example DNS zones for the forests pearson.com and pucert.com.

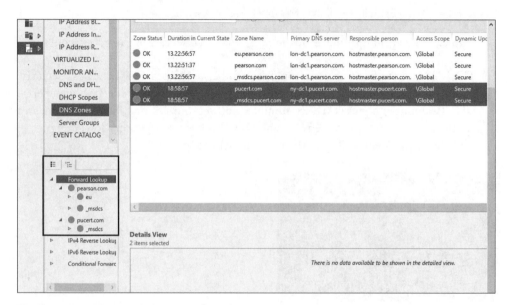

Figure 8-37   IPAM DNS Zones Multiforest Management

TIP   If you try to edit two zones on two different DNS servers in different forests (pearson.com and pucert.com) simultaneously through IPAM, you will get the error message "Selected zones do not have any server in common with same hosting type" (see Figure 8-38).

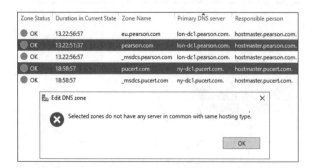

Figure 8-38   Edit Zones of DNS Servers in Multiple Forests Through IPAM

> **TIP**   Creating a new DNS zone on two DNS servers in two different forests through the IPAM configuration console is not possible. Figure 8-39 shows the grayed-out Create DNS Zone setting. However, you can create and edit a DNS conditional forwarder (also stored in Active Directory) on DNS servers in different forests. Figure 8-40 shows where to edit or delete DNS conditional forwarders in the IPAM configuration console.

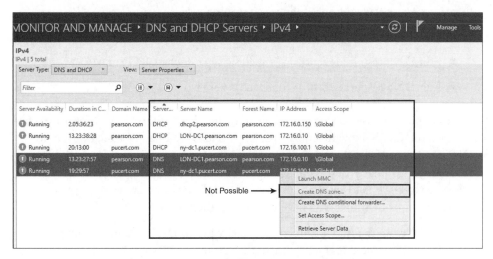

Figure 8-39   Create New DNS Zone on DNS Servers in Multiple Forests Through IPAM

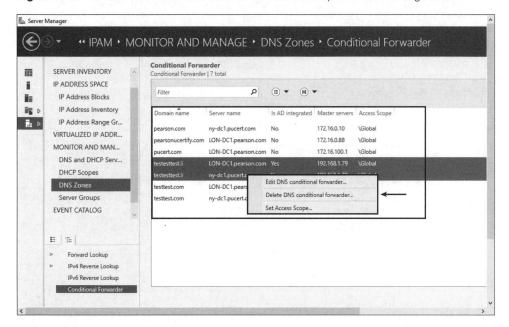

Figure 8-40   Edit or Delete DNS Conditional Forwarders on DNS Servers in Multiple Forests Through IPAM

Using RBAC to Delegate DNS and DHCP Server Administration Using IPAM

Role-based access control (RBAC) in Windows Server 2016 enables you to specify access at various levels (DNS server, DNS zone, and DNS resource records). Using RBAC, you can specify who has granular control over operations to create, edit, and delete different types of DNS resource records. You can configure access control so that users are restricted to the following permissions:

- Edit only specific DNS resource records

- Edit DNS resource records of a specific type, such as PTR or MX

- Edit DNS resource records for specific zones

For example, suppose you want to allow only members of the Active Directory security group DHCPFailoverAdmins to edit a single DHCP failover relationship for a DHCP scope and you do not want to allow other administrative tasks on IPAM for the members of that group. You also do not want to give them permissions to create other new DHCP failover relationships or to replicate or delete existing relationships. To implement that, you have to perform the following steps:

Step 1.   Create the Active Directory security group DHCPFailoverAdmins and add selected user accounts to that group.

Step 2.   Add a new IPAM user role named DHCPFailoverAdmin with the allowed operations in Figure 8-41.

Figure 8-41   IPAM User Role Operations

Step 3.   Create a new IPAM access scope named DHCPFailover (see
Figure 8-42).

Figure 8-42   IPAM Access Scope DHCPFailover

Step 4.   Create a new IPAM access policy with a user alias of Pearson\
DHCPFailoverAdmins and the access scope DHCPFailover (see
Figure 8-43).

Step 5.   Apply the Access Scope to the DHCP scope that is configured with a
DHCP failover relationship (see Figure 8-44) and verify the applied
access scope (Figure 8-45).

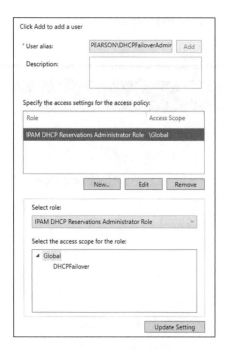

Figure 8-43   IPAM Access Policy

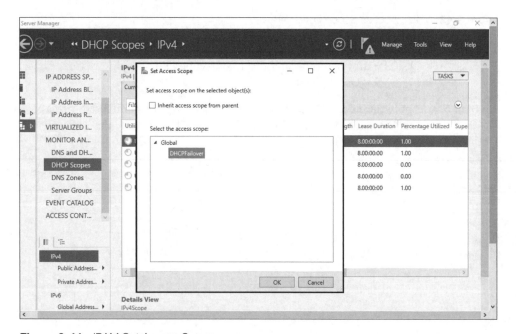

Figure 8-44   IPAM Set Access Scope

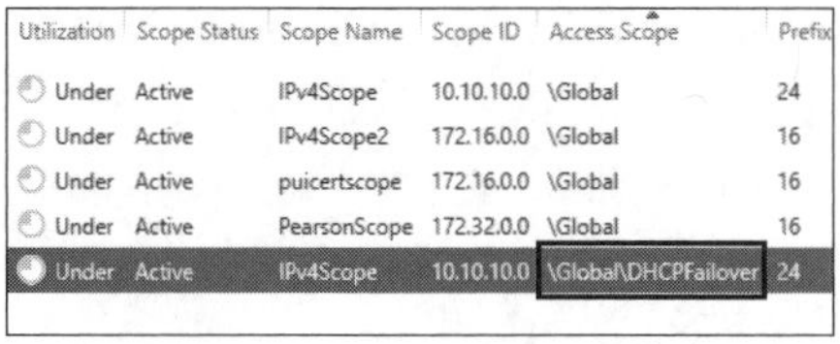

Utilization	Scope Status	Scope Name	Scope ID	Access Scope	Prefix
Under	Active	IPv4Scope	10.10.10.0	\Global	24
Under	Active	IPv4Scope2	172.16.0.0	\Global	16
Under	Active	puicertscope	172.16.0.0	\Global	16
Under	Active	PearsonScope	172.32.0.0	\Global	16
Under	Active	IPv4Scope	10.10.10.0	\Global\DHCPFailover	24

Figure 8-45   IPAM Set Access Scope Verification

After this configuration, if users that are members of the Active Directory security group DHCPFailoverAdmins try to edit a DHCP failover relationship of another scope, they will get the error message in Figure 8-46.

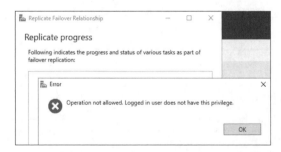

Figure 8-46   No Privilege to Edit DHCP Failover Relationship

If those users try to manually replicate the DHCP scope where the access scope DHCPFailover is applied, they will get the error message in Figure 8-47.

Figure 8-47   No Privilege to Replicate DHCP Failover Relationship

If those users try to remove a DHCP failover configuration, they will get the error message in Figure 8-48.

Figure 8-48   No Privilege to Remove DHCP Failover Relationship

Exam Preparation Tasks

Review All the Key Topics

Review the most important topics in the chapter, noted with the Key Topics icon in the outer margin of the page. Table 8-6 lists these key topics and the page numbers where each is found.

Table 8-6   Key Topics for Chapter 8

Key Topic Element	Description	Page Number
Table 8-2	IPAM DHCP Server Properties	340
List	DHCP Server options configuration actions	343
Section	Configuring Predefined DHCP Options and Values	344
Section	Configuring DHCP Scopes Using IPAM	345
Text	Manage DHCP Policies using IPAM	350
Section	Creating DHCP Policies for Multiple DHCP Servers Using IPAM	350
Section	Configuring DHCP Failover Using IPAM	351

Key Topic Element	Description	Page Number
Section	Managing DNS Server Properties Using IPAM	353
Step List	Filtering the view of DNS server settings	354
Table 8-4	IPAM DNS Zones and Records PowerShell Cmdlets	355
Table 8-5	IPAM DNS Zone Settings	356
Section	Managing Subdomains Through IPAM	358
Step List	Filtering the view of DNS resource records	362
Section	Saving Views of IPAM DNS Zone Information	363
Section	Prerequisites for Managing Multiple Active Directory Forests with IPAM	364
Section	Configuring Multiple-Forest IPAM Management	365
Section	Managing DNS Servers and Zones in a Multiple-Forest IPAM Environment	368
List	Delegate DHCP server administration	370

Complete the Tables and Lists from Memory

Print a copy of Appendix B, "Memory Tables" (on the book's website), or at least the section for this chapter, and complete the tables and lists from memory. Appendix C, "Memory Tables Answer Key," also on the website, includes completed tables and lists to check your work.

Definition of Key Terms

Define the following key terms from this chapter and check your answers in the glossary.

Create DHCP Scope, Edit DHCP Scope, **Get-IpamDhcpServer**, Automatically Update Statistics, DHCP database path, DHCP backup path, DHCP server options, Remove DHCP Failover Configuration, DNS server properties, **Get-IpamDnsResourceRecord, Get-IpamDnsZone,** Get Forests

End-of-Chapter Review Questions

1. You are a member of the DHCP Administrators security group on all your DHCP servers, and you are responsible for your Windows Server 2016 IPAM server, IPAM1. IPAM1 is configured to manage DHCP servers in your domain of pearson.com. The DHCP servers have the following characteristics:

    ■ **DHCP1:** This is the recovered DHCP server.

    ■ **DHCP2:** This DHCP server is running out of local disk space.

    ■ **DHCP3:** This DHCP server has stale update statistics data.

    ■ **DHCP4:** This DHCP server's backup path needs to be changed.

    You want to configure some DHCP server properties through IPAM DHCP server properties in the IPAM configuration console. You must change the following settings:

    ■ Enable DHCP Audit Log

    ■ Change the DNS Dynamic Update Credentials

    ■ Change the Automatically Update Statistics Setting

    ■ Change the DHCP Backup Path

    Which settings can you configure through the IPAM server configuration console?

    a. Change the DNS Dynamic Update Credentials on DHCP1

    b. Change the DNS Dynamic Update Credentials on DHCP2

    c. Change the DHCP Audit Log Path for DHCP2

    d. Configure Automatically Update Statistics for DHCP3

    e. Change the Backup Path for DHCP4

2. You are a member of the DHCP Administrators security group on all your DHCP servers, and you are responsible for your Windows Server 2016 IPAM server, IPAM1. You select multiple DHCP server IPv4 scopes, and you want to know which scope options you can configure in this way. Which scope options can you configure in one step for multiple scopes through the IPAM management console in Server Manager?

   a. Scope name

   b. Description

   c. Start IP address

   d. End IP address

   e. Subnet mask

   f. Lease duration

   g. Exclusion range

3. You want to change the State Switchover Interval setting through your IPAM server, IPAM1. Where in the IPAM configuration console can you configure that?

   a. Monitor and Manage > DNS and DHCP Servers > Edit DHCP Server Properties

   b. Monitor and Manage > DHCP Scopes

   c. Monitor and Manage > DNS and DHCP Servers > View: Failover Relationships > Edit DHCP Failover Relationship

   d. IP Address Space > Server Groups

4. You want to enable automatic scavenging of stale records with a scavenging period of 1 day for five of your DNS servers. You want to do this through your IPAM server IPAM1; you do not want to use PowerShell for it because your administrators do not have PowerShell command knowledge. What is the preferred method?

   a. Server Inventory

   b. Server Groups

   c. Launch MMC

   d. DNS and DHCP Servers

5. You have installed a subdomain named usa.pearson.com, with the first domain controller of that domain as the authoritative DNS server for the subdomain. All your DNS servers have Windows Server 2016 installed and managed through your IPAM server, IPAM1. The subzone is displayed with an empty white bullet in the IPAM console. Which configuration options must you perform to get the subzone correctly displayed with a green bullet? (Choose two.)

   a. Reset Zone Status

   b. Configure Preferred DNS Servers

   c. Retrieve Server Data

   d. Reload

This chapter covers the following subjects:

- **Auditing the changes performed on the DNS and DHCP servers:** Windows Server 2016 IPAM can audit configuration changes performed on managed DNS and DHCP servers. It offers operational auditing and IP address tracking functionality. This chapter covers the key IPAM audit capabilities and features and explains the IPAM scheduled tasks and monitoring views, logical groups, and the use of custom fields in the IPAM configuration console and with PowerShell. You get information about IPAM and DHCP configuration event criteria, how to use IPAM criteria filtering, and how to purge IPAM Event Catalog data. You also get best practices for using the IPAM Event Catalog.

- **Auditing the IPAM address usage trail:** This chapter looks at the use and configuration of the IPAM utilization feature, describes how to use and configure utilization thresholds with the IPAM configuration console and PowerShell, and examines how to use the utilization trends feature. It also delivers best practices for auditing and managing IPAM.

- **Auditing DHCP lease events and user logon events:** Here you learn about the IPAM IP address tracking feature and how to use it to get audit information about DHCP lease and user login events through the IPAM configuration console.

## CHAPTER 9

Windows Server 2016 IPAM Audit Changes and Events

This chapter covers auditing of IPAM-managed DNS and DHCP server configuration changes and auditing of DNS events and DHCP lease events. It examines the monitoring and managing of virtual IP address spaces in IPAM and explains both IPAM operational auditing and IP address tracking.

This chapter also looks at IPAM audit capabilities and features, IPAM scheduled tasks, monitoring views, logical groups, and the use of custom fields in the IPAM configuration console and PowerShell. It examines IPAM and DHCP configuration event criteria and demonstrates filtering to get individual information about DHCP and DNS data. It covers purging IPAM Event Catalog data and explains some best practices for using the IPAM Event Catalog.

In addition, this chapter covers the use and configuration of the IPAM utilization feature, shows how to use and configure utilization thresholds with the IPAM configuration console and PowerShell, and demonstrates how to use the utilization trends feature. It delivers best practices for auditing and managing IPAM.

You also learn about the IPAM IP address tracking feature and how you can use it to audit DHCP lease and user login events.

With key topic selections, memory tables, key term definitions, and exam preparation questions, you gain some powerful tools to increase your knowledge about Windows Server 2016 IPAM audit changes and events for both the Microsoft 70-741 exam and your daily work.

"Do I Know This Already?" Quiz

The "Do I Know This Already?" quiz allows you to assess whether you should read this entire chapter or simply jump to the "Exam Preparation Tasks" section for review. If you are in doubt, read the entire chapter. Table 9-1 outlines the major headings in this chapter and the corresponding "Do I Know This Already?" quiz questions. You can find the answers in Appendix A, "Answers to the 'Do I Know This Already?' Quizzes."

Table 9-1 "Do I Know This Already?" Foundation Topics Section-to-Question Mapping

Foundation Topics Section	Questions Covered in This Section
Audit the Changes Performed on the DNS and DHCP Servers	1
Audit the IPAM Address Usage Trail	2
Audit DHCP Lease Events and User Logon Events	3

CAUTION The goal of self-assessment is to gauge your mastery of the topics in this chapter. If you do not know the answer to a question or are only partially sure of the answer, you should mark that question as wrong for purposes of the self-assessment. Giving yourself credit for an answer you correctly guess skews your self-assessment results and might provide you with a false sense of security.

1. You want to refresh configuration information for your DNS servers, DNS server service status information, and DNS zone status events managed through a Windows Server 2016 IPAM server in the IPAM configuration console. Which scheduled tasks should you run? (Choose three.)

   a. **AddressExpiry**

   b. **AddressUtilization**

   c. **Audit**

   d. **DnsServerConfiguration**

   e. **ServerAvailability**

   f. **ServerConfiguration**

   g. **ServerDiscovery**

   h. **ServiceMonitoring**

2. You are the administrator of your company. You are responsible for your IPAM address usage trail audit functionality. NPS servers are not part of your network environment. Which IP address tracking events cannot be collected on your Windows Server 2016 IPAM server, and which search criteria cannot be used for IPAM IP address tracking?

   Event:

   a. New IP lease

   b. Renew IP lease

   c. Lease expiry

      d. Security event 4768

      e. Security event 672

    Search criteria:

      a. IPAddress

      b. IPScope

      c. ClientID

      d. MACAddress

      e. Hostname

      f. ClassID

      g. Username

3. You are the administrator of your company. You want to track lease and user logon information from 5/20/2016 until 5/23/2016 from a DHCP client named Client1 on your Windows Server 2016 IPAM server. In Server Manager, you open the IPAM management tool. Which two selections must you choose to track this information?

      a. Monitor and Manage

      b. Event Catalog

      c. IP Address Space

      d. IPAM Configuration Events

      e. DHCP Configuration Events

      f. IP Address Tracking

Foundation Topics

Audit the Changes Performed on the DNS and DHCP Servers

Windows Server 2016 IPAM offers operational auditing and IP address tracking functionality.

You can use auditing tools to track configuration problems and relevant events. You can collect, manage, and view configuration change details from DHCP and DNS servers. IPAM facilitates the monitoring and tracking of DHCP service status and utilization of DHCP scopes.

IPAM enables tagging servers with built-in and user-defined custom field values to visualize these servers and group them into logical groups and subgroups.

IPAM can monitor DNS zone health on multiple DNS servers by displaying the aggregated zone status across DNS servers. IPAM can track the status of the service of the DNS and DHCP servers. Details that can be tracked include server name, username, and the date and time a configuration was made. You can collect IP address lease tracking from DHCP lease logs and sign-in events from network policy servers and domain controllers.

Windows Server 2016 IPAM offers the following auditing features:

- Automated inventory of IP addresses based on DNS resource records

- Capability to visualize all DNS resource records that pertain to an IP address

- IP address lifecycle management for DNS and DHCP operations

- New Windows Server 2016 feature: Multiple ADDS forest support (audit events across multiple forests)

IPAM stores three years of forensics data—including IP address leases, host Media Access Control (MAC) addresses, and user sign-in and sign-out information—for 100,000 users in the database.

IPAM provides IP address utilization trends only for IPv4, not for IPv6. IP address reclamation support also is provided only for IPv4. Note that IPAM does *not* check for IP address consistency with routers and switches.

> **TIP**   For IPAM's IP address tracking and auditing feature to work, you must enable logging of account sign-in events on domain controllers and NPSs.

IPAM Scheduled Tasks

Windows Server 2016 IPAM offers eight tasks with the specified periodicity. Table 9-2 shows the IPAM tasks that you can view in the Task Scheduler by navigating to Microsoft > Windows > IPAM (only the DnsServerConfiguration task is a new Windows Server 2016 task).

Table 9-2   IPAM Scheduled Tasks

Task Name	Description	Default Frequency
AddressExpiry	Tracks IP address expiry state and logs notifications.	1 day
AddressUtilization	Collects IP address space usage data from DHCP servers to display current and historical utilization.	2 hours

Task Name	Description	Default Frequency
Audit	Collects DHCP and IPAM server operational events. Also collects events from domain controllers, NPS, and DHCP servers for IP address tracking.	1 day
DnsServerConfiguration (new in Windows Server 2016 IPAM)	Collects configuration information from DNS servers for display in IP address space and server-management functions.	6 hours
ServerAvailability	Collects service status information from DHCP and DNS servers.	15 minutes
ServerConfiguration	Collects configuration information from DHCP servers for display in IP address space and server-management functions.	6 hours
ServerDiscovery	Automatically discovers domain controllers, DHCP servers, and DNS servers in the domains you select.	1 day
ServiceMonitoring	Collects DNS zone status events from DNS servers.	30 minutes

IPAM is not enabled by default and must be installed as a server feature. When the IPAM Server feature is installed, IP address audit functionality is automatically enabled. To disable IP address audit, start the Task Scheduler on the IPAM server, navigate to Microsoft > Windows > IPAM, and disable the Audit task.

IPAM Monitoring Views

IPAM enables automated, periodic service monitoring of DHCP and DNS servers across single or multiple forests. In the IPAM configuration console, monitoring and management of DHCP and DNS servers is organized into the views in Table 9-3.

Table 9-3   IPAM Configuration Console Monitoring Views

View	Description
DNS and DHCP servers	Managed DHCP and DNS servers are arranged by their network interface in /32 subnets for IPv4 and /128 subnets for IPv6. You can select the view to see only DHCP scope properties, only DNS server properties, or both.
DHCP scopes	This view enables scope utilization monitoring. Utilization statistics are automatically collected periodically from a managed DHCP server. You can track important scope properties such as Name, ID, Prefix Length, and Status.
DNS zone monitoring	You enable zone monitoring for forward lookup zones. Zone status is based on events that IPAM collects. The status of each zone is summarized.

View	Description
Server groups	You can organize managed DHCP and DNS servers into logical groups. For example, you might organize servers by business unit or geography. You define groups by selecting the grouping criteria from the built-in fields or user-defined fields.

With the PowerShell cmdlet **Get-IpamCustomField**, you can list all default custom fields. Figure 9-1 shows the default custom field list.

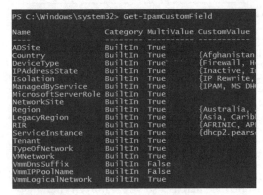

Figure 9-1   IPAM Custom Field List

To audit the status and health of selected sets of Windows Server DNS and DHCP servers from a single IPAM interface, use the IPAM Monitor and Manage view (see Figure 9-2).

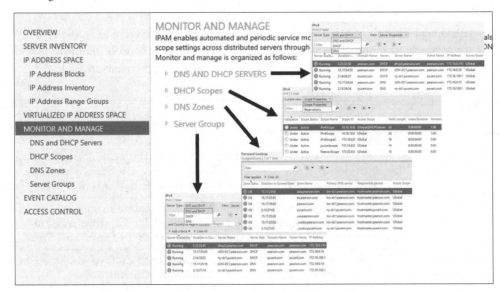

Figure 9-2   IPAM Monitor and Manage View

The IPAM Monitor and Manage view displays the basic health of servers and recent configuration events that occurred on these servers.

For DHCP servers, you can use the DNS and DHCP Servers view to track various server settings, server options, the number of scopes, and the number of active leases that are configured on a server. For DNS servers, you can use this view to track all zones that are configured on the server, along with details about the zone type. You can also use the view to see the total number of zones that are configured on the server and the overall zone health status derived from the zone status of individual forward lookup zones on the server.

You can start the DNS Manager console for any managed DNS server from a central console in the IPAM server, and you can retrieve server data from the selected set of servers.

The DNS Zones monitoring view displays all the forward lookup and reverse lookup zones on all the DNS servers that IPAM is currently managing.

For the forward lookup zones, IPAM also displays all the servers that are hosting the zone, the aggregate health of the zone across all of these servers, and the zone properties.

You can organize your managed servers into logical server groups.

Configuring Logical Groups and Custom Fields with the IPAM Console

IPAM enables you to create custom logical groups to improve the audit experience for IP address ranges. To create custom groups, perform the following steps:

Step 1. In the IPAM navigation pane, under IP Address Space, click **IP Address Range Groups**.

Step 2. On the Server Manager menu, click **Manage** and then click **IPAM Settings**.

Step 3. In the IPAM Settings dialog box, click **Configure Custom Fields**. Figure 9-3 shows the IPAM Settings window.

Figure 9-3   IPAM Settings

Step 4.   In the Configure Custom Fields dialog box, under Add Custom Fields, scroll to the bottom of the list, type **Building** for the Custom Field Name, and then select **Yes** under Multi-Value.

Step 5.   Press Enter or Tab to commit the new custom field name. A blank line opens that you can use for additional custom fields.

Step 6.   Click **Building** and then, under Custom Field Value, type the following values: Headquarters, Operations, Sales, Datacenter. Press Enter after you type each one. Figure 9-4 shows how the Configure Custom Fields window should look.

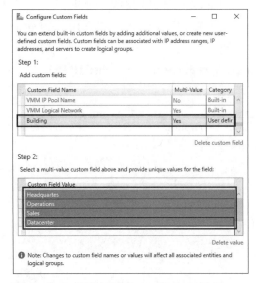

Figure 9-4   IPAM Configure Custom Fields

Step 7.   Repeat the previous step to add another custom field named Floor with the following two custom field values: First, Second. Click **OK** twice, and then click **Close**.

Step 8.   You can apply the custom fields to an IP address range. Click **IP Address Ranges**, right-click the IP address range, and then click **Edit IP Address Range**. Figure 9-5 shows the custom fields Building and Floor applied to an IP address range.

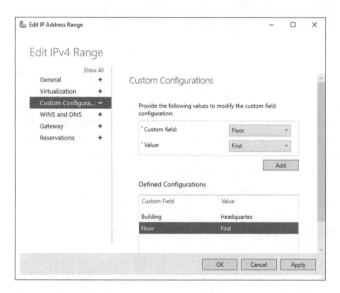

Figure 9-5   IPAM Custom Fields Applied to IP Address Range

Step 9.   Edit the other IP address ranges and apply the custom fields. You can also select multiple IP address ranges and add custom fields to all the ranges in one step. Refresh the IP Address Ranges view, right-click the column header, and then select **Building** and **Floor**. Both fields are now displayed with each IP address range in the list, as Figure 9-6 shows.

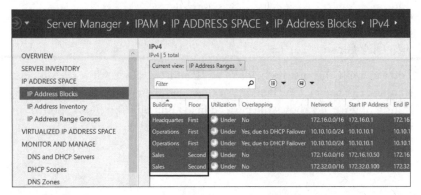

Figure 9-6   IPAM Custom Fields Used in IP Address Range List

Step 10.   Select **IP Address Range Groups** and right-click **IPv4**. Select **Add IP Address Range Group**. Under Provide Name of the Address Range Group, type **Building/Floor**. Under Custom Fields, select **Building** and then select **Floor** so that items are grouped first by building and then by floor. Click **OK**, and then click the arrow next to IPv4. Verify that you can view IP address ranges by building and floor (see Figure 9-7).

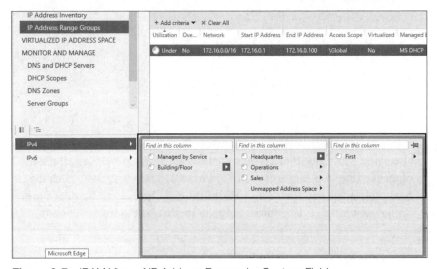

Figure 9-7   IPAM View of IP Address Ranges by Custom Fields

IPAM also enables you to create custom logical groups to improve the audit experience for DNS or DHCP servers. To apply custom fields to one or multiple DHCP or DNS servers, go to Server Inventory (second setting below Overview in the IPAM configuration console in the Server Manager), select the servers, and use the Edit Server task to apply custom fields. Figure 9-8 shows how to apply the custom fields Building and Floor to managed servers.

Figure 9-8   IPAM Applying Custom Fields to Managed Servers

Suppose that you have configured the SCVMM integration and you have created a logical network named BernNet1 on a SCVMM server with the three subnets 172.16.1.0/24, 172.16.2.0/24, and 172.16.3.0/24 (see Figures 9-9 and 9-10). Now you want to apply the custom configuration with the custom field Building and a value of Datacenter to that virtual IP address space. Configure the custom configuration as shown in Figure 9-11.

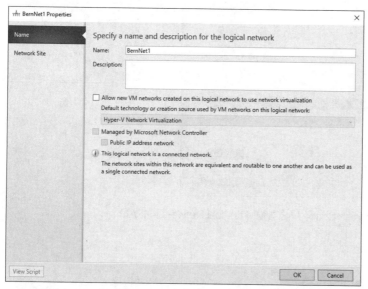

Figure 9-9   SCVMM Logical Network Properties

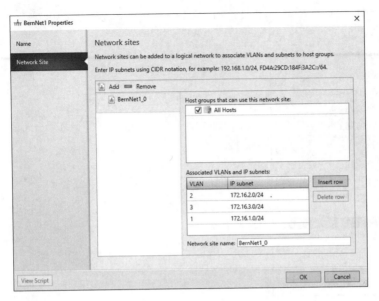

Figure 9-10   SCVMM Logical Network Site Settings

Figure 9-11   Edit IP Address Space of SCVMM Logical Network in IPAM

Configuring Custom Fields with IPAM in PowerShell

You also can configure custom fields with PowerShell. Table 9-4 describes the Power-Shell cmdlets available to manage IPAM custom fields in Windows Server 2016 IPAM.

Table 9-4 IPAM Custom Field PowerShell Cmdlets

Cmdlet	Description and Example
Add-IpamCustomField	Add-IpamCustomField -Name "CustomField01" -MultiValue -PassThru
	This cmdlet adds a free-form or multivalued custom field to IPAM. The example adds a multivalued custom field named CustomField01 to the IPAM server.
Add-IpamCustomFieldAssociation	Add-IpamCustomFieldAssociation -CustomFieldOne "VmmLogicalNetwork" -CustomFieldTwo "NetworkSite" -AssociationValue Storage:Site01", "Storage:Site02", "Public:Site03" -PassThru
	This cmdlet adds a free-form/multivalued custom field to IPAM. The example adds an association between values of two custom fields (VmmLogicalNetwork and NetworkSite).
Get-IpamCustomField	Get-IpamCustomField -Name "Building"
	This cmdlet lists custom fields in IPAM. The example retrieves the custom field named Building.
Get-IpamCustomFieldAssociation	Get-IpamCustomFieldAssociation -CustomFieldOne "ManagedByService" -CustomFieldTwo "ServiceInstance"
	This cmdlet gets associations between two custom fields defined in IPAM. The example gets the associations between two custom fields ManagedByService and ServiceInstance.
Remove-IpamCustomField	Remove-IpamCustomField -Name "Building"
	This cmdlet removes a custom field from IPAM. The example removes the custom field Building from the IPAM server.

Cmdlet	Description and Example
Remove-IpamCustomFieldAssociation	Get-IpamCustomFieldAssociation -CustomFieldOne "ManagedByService" | Remove-IpamCustomField Association
	This cmdlet removes an association between two custom fields that are defined in IPAM. The example gets all associations specified by the custom field and then passes them to the current cmdlet by using the pipeline operator. The cmdlet prompts you for confirmation and then removes all the associations.
Rename-IpamCustomField	Rename-IpamCustomField -Name "Building" -newName "HeadquarterBuilding" -PassThru
	This cmdlet renames a custom field in IPAM. The example renames the user-defined custom field named Building to HeadquarterBuilding.
Rename-IpamCustomValue	Rename-IpamCustomValue -Name "Building" -Value "Headquarters" -NewValue "Operations" -PassThru
	This cmdlet changes a value for a custom field. The example changes the value from Headquarters to Operations for the custom field named Building.
Set-IpamCustomFieldAssociation	Set-IpamCustomFieldAssociation -CustomFieldOne "VmmLogicalNetwork" -CustomFieldTwo "NetworkSite" -AddAssociateValue "Storage:Site03" -RemoveAssociationValue "Public:Site03" -PassThru
	This cmdlet modifies associations of values for custom fields defined in IPAM. This example modifies an existing association between the two custom fields VmmLogicalNetwork and NetworkSite.

Viewing Changes Performed on IPAM-Managed Servers

In the Windows Server 2016 IPAM configuration console under the Event Catalog, you can view changes performed on managed servers. You can choose between IPAM Configuration Events and DHCP Configuration Events. No DNS Configuration Events list exists (see Figure 9-12).

Figure 9-12   Accessing the Event Catalog IPAM Configuration Events and DHCP
Configuration Events

You can filter the IPAM and DHCP Configuration Event list with different criteria.
Table 9-5 shows all possible criteria for both lists.

Table 9-5   IPAM and DHCP Configuration Event Criteria

IPAM Configuration Event Criteria	DHCP Configuration Event Criteria
Event ID	Event ID
Time of the event	Server name
Username	Time of the event
User domain name	Username
User forest name	User domain name
Task category	User forest name
Keywords	Scope name
Operational code	Scope ID (in description)
Network ID of IP address block (in description)	Option number (in description)
IP address subnet ID (in description)	Option name (in description)
Network ID of IP address range (in description)	Reservation name (in description)
IP address (in description)	Relationship name (in description)
IP address space (in description)	Policy name (in description)
Logical group name (in description)	Filter MAC address (in description)
Custom field name (in description)	Superscope name (in description)

Suppose that you want to view all events based on multi-server management tasks through IPAM. Select the criteria Task Category and add the search value Multi-Server Management. Figure 9-13 shows that example configuration.

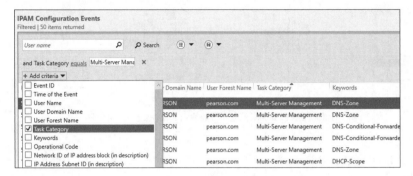

Figure 9-13   IPAM Configuration Events List Criteria Filtering

You can purge Event Catalog data. In the IPAM configuration console (in the top-right corner) at Tasks, select **Purge Event Catalog Data** and select both the data type for which you want to purge catalog data and a time window (see Figure 9-14).

Figure 9-14   Purge IPAM Event Catalog Data

IPAM Configuration Events

The list in Figure 9-15 shows some examples of IPAM configuration events displayed in the Event Catalog.

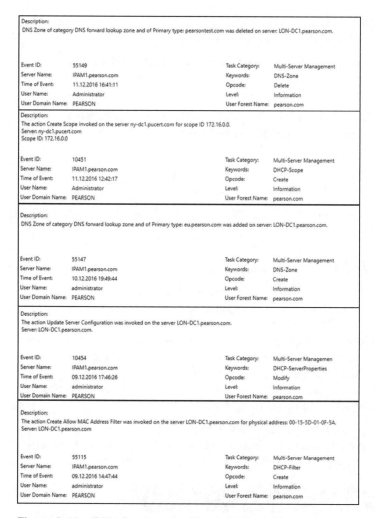

Figure 9-15   IPAM Configuration Events Example List

Best Practices for Using the IPAM Event Catalog

The following list outlines the best practices for using the IPAM Event Catalog, which provides a centralized repository for auditing all configuration changes that occur on managed DHCP servers from a single IPAM management console. The IPAM configuration events console gathers all the configuration events. You can use these configuration event catalogs to view, query, and create reports about configuration changes, along with details that are specific to each record.

- Account logon event auditing should be enabled on DCs and NPS servers. Without this preconfiguration, the IPAM server cannot display account logon events in the IPAM Event Catalog.

- The security event log size should be large enough to allow the periodic audit task to complete data collection before it is rolled over.

- For better performance and disk space management, IPAM Event Catalog data purge should be performed periodically to reduce the amount of data used for IPAM events.

- The audit log file location for both DHCP IPv4 and IPv6 leases must be configured in a common order. The IPAM audit task selects the log files from one network share per server.

- The DHCP audit log file should be large enough for one day, to ensure that no lease events are lost because of size overruns.

- Be sure to select an optimal time period for a query. Typically, a query interval of 3 days to 15 days is optimal.

Audit the IPAM Address Usage Trail

Use the Windows Server 2016 IPAM address space management feature to view, monitor, and manage the IP address space on a network. The address space management feature supports IPv4 public and private addresses, in addition to IPv6 global and unicast addresses. IPAM maintains utilization data for IP address ranges, address blocks, and range groups. You can configure thresholds for the utilized percentage of the IP address space and then use those thresholds to determine under- or overutilization. You also can perform utilization trend building and reporting for IPv4 address ranges, blocks, and range groups.

In the IPAM Overview window, you can change the default utilization thresholds. The default settings are 20 percent for underutilization and 80 percent for overutilization. Figure 9-16 shows where to find these settings and change the values.

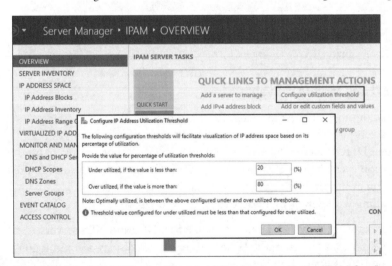

Figure 9-16   IPAM Utilization Threshold Configuring with the IPAM Configuration Console

When you create or edit an IP address range, you can configure the Utilization Calculation settings. The default setting is Automatic, which means that the default utilization threshold values for under- and overutilization are used.

With the PowerShell cmdlet **Set-IpamAddressUtilizationThreshold**, you can set over- or underutilization thresholds so that IPAM can generate an alert when a block, subnet, or range utilization exceeds or drops below the threshold.

This command sets the address overutilization threshold to 70:

```
Set-IpamAddressUtilizationThreshold -OverUtilizationThreshold 70
 -PassThru
```

This command sets the address underutilization threshold to 40:

```
Set-IpamAddressUtilizationThreshold -UnderUtilizationThreshold 40
 -PassThru
```

In the Details view, you can create a graphical display for Utilization Trends for IP Address Ranges, IP Address Subnets, and IP Address Blocks (see Figure 9-17).

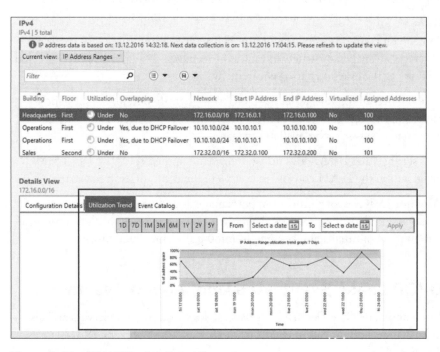

Figure 9-17   IPAM Utilization Trend Example

Best Practices for Monitoring, Auditing, and Managing

Every time a new device or a virtual machine is provisioned, or whenever a tablet leaves the wireless network, the IP address allocation landscape changes. The IPAM database needs to be kept up to date.

The following list outlines the best practices for using Windows Server 2016 IPAM monitoring, auditing, and managing capabilities to get a centralized track and maintain a near-real-time view of all the adds, moves, and changes occurring on the network.

- When editing options across multiple DHCP scopes and servers, leverage advanced constructs in multiedit scenarios to add, overwrite, delete, or find-and-replace to cater to the exact scenario requirement.

- Create and save queries to quickly identify services and zones that are not in a healthy state.

- Use the duplicate scope functionality to create new scopes with similar settings. The typical scenarios in which this can be leveraged are migrating scopes from one server to another and configuring split scopes.

- When you configure vendor and user classes across multiple DHCP servers, leverage advanced constructs in multiedit scenarios to add, overwrite, or delete to cater to the exact scenario requirement.

- Use the overall forward lookup zone view to identify potential issues and to determine servers that might have a problem. Isolate whether the issue is due to a zone event or server availability state.

- For settings that IPAM does not support, launch the DHCP or DNS MMC from within the IPAM console to complete the configuration scenario.

- Monitor DHCP scope utilization percentage and utilization status to identify over- and underutilized scopes. Take the necessary actions to align scope utilization to an optimal state, keeping in mind utilization trend history.

Audit DHCP Lease Events and User Logon Events

IPAM can automatically collect IP address lease logs from DHCP servers and also user and machine authentication events from DCs and NPS servers. IPAM stores this data in its database.

IPAM provides an interface to query this data, intelligently correlates this data in the right context, and provides a view of the IP address activity on the network.

For tracking IP address leases in the network, the IP address tracking feature in the Event Catalog is an efficient tool to audit DHCP lease events and user logon events.

You can search the events database pivoted on an IP address, client ID (MAC address), hostname, or username to retrieve the associated DHCP lease events. IPAM automatically correlates the DHCP lease events with user and machine authentication events, allowing you to quickly get a perspective on which user logged on from which machine at a particular time, or which IP address was allocated to which machine and user. This makes it a useful tool for forensic investigators.

Figure 9-18 shows an example of tracking by IP address.

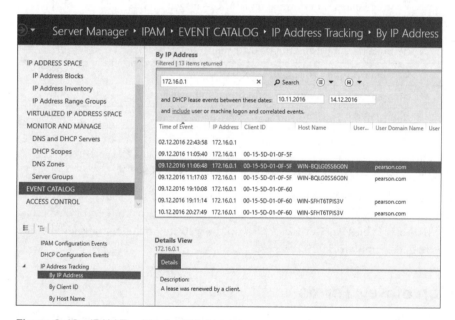

Figure 9-18   IPAM Tracking by IP Address

Exam Preparation Tasks

Review All the Key Topics

Review the most important topics in the chapter, noted with the Key Topics icon in the outer margin of the page. Table 9-6 lists these key topics and the page numbers where each is found.

Table 9-6   Key Topics for Chapter 9

Key Topic Element	Description	Page Number
List	IPAM audit capabilities	384
Table 9-2	IPAM Scheduled Tasks	384
Table 9-3	IPAM Configuration Console Monitoring Views	385
Step List	Configuring logical groups and custom fields with the IPAM console	387
Table 9-4	IPAM Custom Field PowerShell Cmdlets	393
Section	Viewing Changes Performed on IPAM-Managed Servers	394
Section	IPAM Configuration Events	396
List	Best practices for using the IPAM Event Catalog	397
Text	Use and configure IPAM utilization	398
List	Best practices for monitoring, auditing, and managing	400
Section	Audit DHCP Lease Events and User Logon Events	400

Complete the Tables and Lists from Memory

Print a copy of Appendix B, "Memory Tables" (on the book's website), or at least the section for this chapter, and complete the tables and lists from memory. Appendix C, "Memory Tables Answer Key," also on the website, includes completed tables and lists to check your work.

Definition of Key Terms

Define the following key terms from this chapter and check your answers in the glossary.

IP address tracking, custom fields, utilization trends, utilization thresholds, purge Event Catalog data, logical groups, IPAM scheduled tasks

End-of-Chapter Review Questions

1. Windows Server 2016 IPAM can use IPAM tasks that can be viewed in the Task Scheduler. Which of the following tasks is a new Windows Server 2016 task?

   a. **AddressExpiry**

   b. **AddressUtilization**

   c. **Audit**

   d. **DnsServerConfiguration**

   e. **ServerAvailability**

   f. **ServerConfiguration**

   g. **ServerDiscovery**

   h. **ServiceMonitoring**

2. You want to group and display your IP address spaces on your IPAM server based on physical building. Which PowerShell cmdlets should you use to prepare IPAM for this? (Choose two.)

   a. **Add-IpamCustomFieldAssociation**

   b. **Set-IpamCustomFieldAssociation**

   c. **Add-IpamCustomField**

   d. **Add-IpamCustomValue**

3. You want your IPAM server to generate an alert in the case of an overloaded IP address range. The overload must exceed 80 percent to generate an alert. What is the proper action in this scenario?

   a. Change the overutilization threshold settings with **Set-IpamRange**

   b. Change the overutilization threshold setting with **Set-IpamAddressUtilizationThreshold**

   c. Leave the IPAM overutilization threshold default settings

   d. Change the IPAM underutilization threshold settings

This chapter covers the following subjects:

- **Implementing Remote Access and S2S VPN solutions using a RAS gateway:** Windows Server 2016 Remote Access supports site-to-site VPN connections using a Windows Server 2016 server as a gateway between networks. This chapter covers the different kinds of S2S VPN connections and shows how to manage such interfaces with the Routing and Remote Access management tool and PowerShell.

- **Configuring different VPN protocol options:** This chapter explains the tunnel protocols that a Windows Server 2016 VPN server supports, its security system access settings, and how to configure a Windows Server 2016 VPN server's VPN protocol settings through new PowerShell cmdlets.

- **Configuring authentication options:** Here you get the available Windows Server 2016 authentication methods and their differences. This chapter shows where to configure them in the Routing and Remote Access management tool and through PowerShell cmdlets.

- **Configuring VPN Reconnect:** The chapter explains the purpose of the VPN Reconnect feature, the system requirements for using the feature, and how to configure it.

- **Creating and configuring connection profiles:** You investigate the purpose of the CMAK utility, which is used to create and manage VPN and dial-in connection profiles, and see how you can deliver connection profiles to the users.

- **Scenarios for RAS VPN and S2S VPN and appropriate protocols:** The chapter explains the most common RAS VPN and S2S VPN scenarios and appropriate protocols.

- **Installing and configuring DirectAccess:** You get an overview of the features of Windows Server 2016 DirectAccess in this chapter, including the key components of Windows Server 2016 DirectAccess solutions. You look at the core functionality and new features, especially the simplified installation and configuration possibilities.

- **Implementing DirectAccess server requirements:** This chapter covers two kinds of DirectAccess deployments, Basic DirectAccess deployment and Advanced DirectAccess deployment, and looks at the configuration steps to implement them.

- **Implementing DirectAccess client requirements:** DirectAccess clients have to be, at minimum, Windows 7 clients so that they can use DirectAccess. This chapter explains some important DirectAccess client requirements.

- **Troubleshooting DirectAccess:** Windows Server 2016 DirectAccess monitoring capabilities such as DirectAccess Dashboard and Operation and Remote Access Client Status can help you identify DirectAccess problems. Here you get step-by-step instructions on how to perform troubleshooting with DirectAccess problems.

## CHAPTER 10

Windows Server 2016 VPN and DirectAccess Solutions

This chapter covers the implementation of Remote Access and S2S VPN solutions using Windows Server 2016 RAS gateway. It covers the different kinds of S2S VPN connections through Windows Server 2016 demand-dial interfaces and shows how to manage them. It explains the differences between persistent and on-demand S2S VPN connections and also explains the different VPN protocol options and authentication methods.

In addition, this chapter explains the use of the Connection Manager Administration Kit utility and shows how to use it to create and manage VPN and dial-in connection profiles. You learn how you can deliver connection profiles to users and get an overview of the different possibilities for delivering VPN connection profiles. Use and configuration of the app-triggered VPN feature is also included in this chapter.

You learn how to install, configure, and implement Windows Server 2016 DirectAccess solutions in different facets. The chapter explains DirectAccess key infrastructure components and DirectAccess configuration components, and you learn how they interact in a running Windows Server 2016 DirectAccess Server environment. You also learn about the DirectAccess client's requirements and the DirectAccess troubleshooting methodology, and you see how to use PowerShell commands to verify DirectAccess IPv6 IPsec VPN connections.

Key topic selection, memory tables, key term definitions, and exam preparation questions give you powerful tools to increase your knowledge of VPN and DirectAccess solutions for the Microsoft 70-741 exam and your work.

"Do I Know This Already?" Quiz

The "Do I Know This Already?" quiz enables you to assess whether you should read this entire chapter or simply jump to the "Exam Preparation Tasks" section for review. If you are in doubt, read the entire chapter. Table 10-1 outlines the major headings in this chapter and the corresponding "Do I Know This Already?" quiz questions. You can find the answers in Appendix A, "Answers to the 'Do I Know This Already?' Quizzes and End-of-Chapter Review Questions."

Table 10-1   "Do I Know This Already?" Foundation Topics Section-to-Question Mapping

Foundation Topics Section	Questions Covered in This Section
Implementing Remote Access and S2S VPN Solutions Using RAS Gateway	1, 2, 3
Configure Different VPN Protocol Options	4
Configure Authentication Options	5
Configure VPN Reconnect	6
Create and Configure VPN Connection Profiles	7
Scenarios for RAS VPN and S2S VPN and Appropriate Protocols	8
Install and Configure DirectAccess	9
Implement DirectAccess Server Requirements	10
Implement DirectAccess Client Requirements	11
Troubleshooting DirectAccess	12

CAUTION   The goal of self-assessment is to gauge your mastery of the topics in this chapter. If you do not know the answer to a question or are only partially sure of the answer, you should mark that question as wrong for purposes of the self-assessment. Giving yourself credit for an answer you correctly guess skews your self-assessment results and might provide you with a false sense of security.

1. You are responsible for managing your network environment. You have one domain named pearson.com and two sites named New York and Berlin. The two sites are physically connected through the Internet, and you want to use a persistent connection. You must implement an IPsec-encrypted tunnel connection between the two sites. You have a Windows Server 2016 Remote Access server named RAS1 in New York and another Windows Server 2016 Remote Access server named RAS2 in Berlin. Which components do you have to configure on both servers to implement the router-to-router VPN S2S connection? (Choose two.)

    a. Demand-dial interface

    b. VPN connection profile

    c. IPHTTPS interface

    d. Dial-out credentials

    e. KDC Proxy

2. You have configured a site-to-site VPN connection with Windows Server 2016 Remote Access, and you want to have detailed statistics information about your S2S VPN interfaces. Which PowerShell cmdlet can you use for that?

   a. **Get-VpnS2Sinterface**

   b. **Get-VpnS2SinterfaceStatistics**

   c. **Get-VpnDemandDialInterface**

   d. **Get-VpnS2SDemandDialInterface**

3. You must configure a Windows Server 2016 S2S VPN connection between two sites. The connection must be persistent. Where do you configure this? (Choose two.)

   a. On the properties page of the Demand dial interface, on the Options tab

   b. On the answering router by clearing the Idle Timeout and Session Timeout boxes on the network policy's Constraints tab

   c. On the calling router Remote Access server properties page

   d. On the L2TP port settings on the calling router

4. You want to configure a custom IPsec policy for incoming VPN connections and S2S VPN connections to your Windows Server 2016 RRAS VPN server for which the authentication method is not PreSharedKey. Which PowerShell cmdlet can you use?

   a. **Set-VpnAuthProtocol**

   b. **Set-VpnConnectionIPsecConfiguration**

   c. **Set-NetIPsecDospSetting**

   d. **Set-VpnServerIPsecConfiguration**

5. You want to configure your Windows Server 2016 VPN server so that only EAP authentication protocol connections are allowed. Which PowerShell cmdlet can you use to verify which user authentication protocols your VPN server accepts?

   a. **Get-VpnConnection**

   b. **Get-VpnServerConfiguration**

   c. **Get-VpnS2Sinterface**

   d. **Get-VpnAuthProtocol**

6. You want to allow your mobile user to reconnect VPN connections automatically in the case of travel. For example, when a train emerges from a tunnel, the wireless mobile broadband card has to reconnect automatically to the Internet and the VPN tunnel also has to automatically reconnect without user interaction so that the mobile user can continue to access internal resources. Which components are not prerequisites? (Choose two.)

   a. IKEv2

   b. Certificates

   c. PEAP

   d. MS-CHAPv2

   e. PSK

7. You have to plan the deployment of different VPN connection profiles to your clients. Which technologies can you use?

   a. _____

   b. _____

   c. _____

   d. _____

   e. _____

8. Some of your employees want to use their own mobile devices to work with internal web applications. You must decide which connection technology you want to use that provides a user-friendly and easy kind of authentication to these applications when they have to access them through Internet. What are the best technology solutions for this scenario? (Choose two.)

   a. VPN connection with L2TP/IPsec

   b. VPN connections with SSTP

   c. S2S VPN connection

   d. Web Application Proxy

   e. ADFS

9. You want to set up a Windows Server 2016 DirectAccess solution with a single Edge Windows Server 2016 DirectAccess server. Which key components do you not need for that?

   a. Network Location Server

   b. KDC Proxy

   c. Certificate Authority

   d. Network Connectivity Assistant

     e. Group Policy

     f. Active Directory

     g. IPv6 internal network

10. You have configured a Windows Server 2016 DirectAccess Edge server. The Getting Started Wizard on the DirectAccess server was completed successfully. DirectAccess clients cannot automatically establish the IPv6 IPsec DirectAccess tunnel. You have verified all client settings, such as Network Connectivity Assistant (NCA), NRPT settings, and firewall configurations with the IPsec Connection Security Rules on the clients. The DirectAccess tunnel still cannot be established with any of your DirectAccess clients. Figure 10-1 shows the firewall settings on your DirectAccess server.

Figure 10-1   DirectAccess Server Firewall Settings

Which command can you use on the DirectAccess server to solve the problem?

     a. Set-NetFirewallRule

     b. Gpupdate /force

     c. Restart-computer

     d. New-NetFirewallRule

11. You have to plan your DirectAccess client requirements. Which of the following are true statements? (Choose all that apply.)

     a. A DirectAccess client must be domain-joined.

     b. A DirectAccess client does not have to be domain-joined.

     c. A DirectAccess client uses L2TP/IPsec to connect to a DirectAccess server.

     d. A DirectAccess client uses IPsec to connect to a DirectAccess server.

     e. A DirectAccess client gets all client settings through PowerShell,

     f. A DirectAccess client gets all client settings through Group Policy.

     g. DirectAccess clients cannot connect to DirectAccess servers located in different domains.

     h. DirectAccess clients can connect to DirectAccess servers located in different domains.

12. You have deployed a multisite DirectAccess configuration. The Remote Access Management console is unable to show the DirectAccess configuration. Which step troubleshoots this problem?

   a. Use **Set-DAEntryPointDC** to point to another domain controller.

   b. Use the Operation Status tab in the Remote Access management console.

   c. Use **Get-DnsClientNrptRule** to verify NRPT settings.

   d. Manually edit the DirectAccess Server Settings Group Policy.

Foundation Topics

Implementing Remote Access and S2S VPN Solutions Using RAS Gateway

Remote access technologies in Windows Server 2016 enable users to connect securely to data and resources in corporate networks. In Windows Server 2016, four component technologies—virtual private network (VPN), DirectAccess, routing, and Web Application Proxy—are combined into a single, unified server role called Remote Access. You can configure and manage the Remote Access server role in Windows Server 2016 by using the Remote Access Management console.

VPN connections enable offsite users to access a server on a private network by using the infrastructure that a public network provides. A VPN connection can use different encapsulation, authentication, and data encryption technologies. Figure 10-2 shows some of the main differences among them. RAS Gateway is a software-based, multitenant, BGP-capable router. It is designed for cloud service providers and large organizations that host multiple tenant virtual networks using Hyper-V Network Virtualization (HNV). A site-to-site (S2S) VPN connection gives you the capability to connect two networks at different physical locations across the Internet. With Microsoft Azure, you also can use point-to-site (P2S) VPN connections to connect single clients to Microsoft Azure sites.

> **TIP** VPN, DirectAccess, and routing technologies are available in Windows Server 2016, Windows Server 2012 R2, and Windows Server 2012. Web Application Proxy was a new feature in Windows Server 2012 R2 and is still available in Windows Server 2016 to forward request to web applications to an ADFS server or directly to an internal web application server (pass-through).

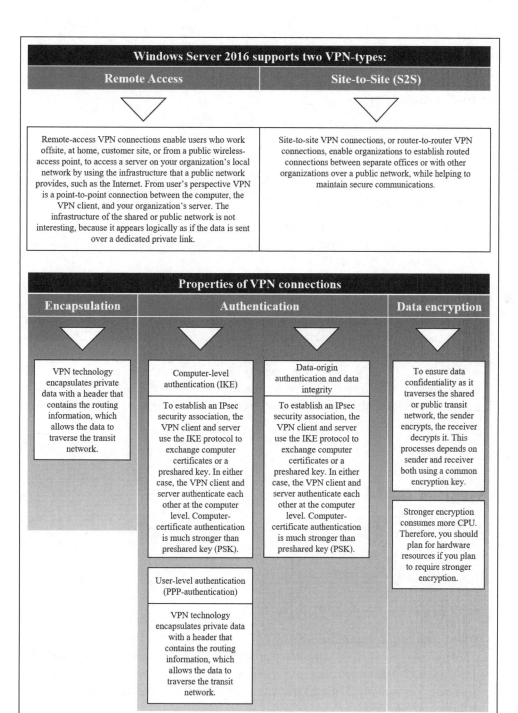

Windows Server 2016 supports two VPN-types:

Remote Access	Site-to-Site (S2S)
Remote-access VPN connections enable users who work offsite, at home, customer site, or from a public wireless-access point, to access a server on your organization's local network by using the infrastructure that a public network provides, such as the Internet. From user's perspective VPN is a point-to-point connection between the computer, the VPN client, and your organization's server. The infrastructure of the shared or public network is not interesting, because it appears logically as if the data is sent over a dedicated private link.	Site-to-site VPN connections, or router-to-router VPN connections, enable organizations to establish routed connections between separate offices or with other organizations over a public network, while helping to maintain secure communications.

Properties of VPN connections

Encapsulation	Authentication		Data encryption
VPN technology encapsulates private data with a header that contains the routing information, which allows the data to traverse the transit network.	Computer-level authentication (IKE)	Data-origin authentication and data integrity	To ensure data confidentiality as it traverses the shared or public transit network, the sender encrypts, the receiver decrypts it. This processes depends on sender and receiver both using a common encryption key.
	To establish an IPsec security association, the VPN client and server use the IKE protocol to exchange computer certificates or a preshared key. In either case, the VPN client and server authenticate each other at the computer level. Computer-certificate authentication is much stronger than preshared key (PSK).	To establish an IPsec security association, the VPN client and server use the IKE protocol to exchange computer certificates or a preshared key. In either case, the VPN client and server authenticate each other at the computer level. Computer-certificate authentication is much stronger than preshared key (PSK).	Stronger encryption consumes more CPU. Therefore, you should plan for hardware resources if you plan to require stronger encryption.
	User-level authentication (PPP-authentication)		
	VPN technology encapsulates private data with a header that contains the routing information, which allows the data to traverse the transit network.		

Figure 10-2   Windows Server 2016 Remote Access and S2S

> **TIP**   Computer-level authentication occurs only for L2TP/IPsec connections.

Site-to-Site (S2S) VPN

With an S2S VPN connection, the following takes place:

- Two portions of a private network are connected.

- The VPN client authenticates itself to the VPN server.

- You must create a demand-dial interface.

- You can create three types of site-to-site VPNs: Point-to-Point Tunneling Protocol (PPTP), Layer 2 Tunneling Protocol (L2TP), and Internet Key Exchange Version 2 (IKEv2).

- A persistent or on-demand connection can be used.

An S2S VPN connection links two portions of a private network. The calling router (VPN client) authenticates itself to the answering router, which is the VPN server. For mutual authentication, the answering router authenticates itself to the calling router. In an S2S VPN connection, packets sent from either router across the VPN connection typically do not originate at the router. You must create a *demand-dial interface* (see Figure 10-3) on the calling router. This interface is a VPN profile that connects to the answering router.

Figure 10-3   Windows Server 2016 Demand-Dial Interface

When creating a demand-dial interface, you must specify the same information you would when creating a VPN profile. Furthermore, you must specify the credentials (see Figure 10-4) used to connect to the answering router. The name of the answering router's demand-dial interface must match the name of the user account that the calling router specifies.

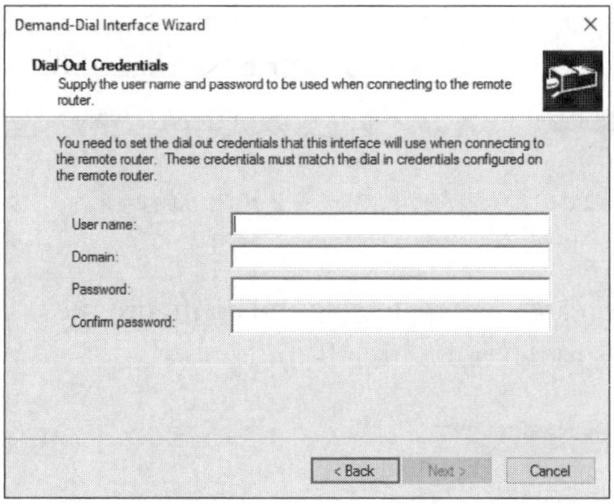

Figure 10-4   Windows Server 2016 Dial-Out Credentials

You can restrict a calling router from initiating unnecessary connections by using demand-dial filtering or dial-out hours (see Figure 10-5). You can use demand-dial filtering to configure the type of traffic that can initiate a connection, or you can specify the traffic that cannot initiate a connection. You also can configure times during which a calling router can or cannot initiate a connection.

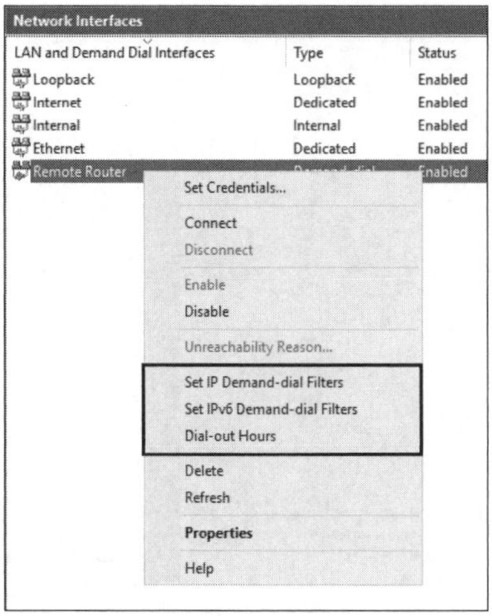

Figure 10-5   Windows Server 2016 Demand Dial-Out Filters and Hours

Since Windows Server 2016, you also can create and configure S2S VPN demand-dial interfaces through PowerShell. Consider some examples:

Example 1: Create an S2S VPN demand-dial interface named PearsonEDGE to the destination 131.107.0.1. The protocol is IKEv2 and the authentication method is preshared key. Traffic to 10.1.0.0/24 and subnet 2001:db8:1::/48 is sent over this interface if no other interface on the server has the same routes with a metric less than 100. When the interface is in a disconnected state, the connection is triggered if no other interface on the server has the same routes with a metric less than 100:

Add-VpnS2SInterface -Name "PearsonEDGE" 131.107.0.1 -Protocol IKEv2
-AuthenticationMethod PSKOnly

-SharedSecret "ABC123" -IPv4Subnet 10.1.0.0/24:100 -IPv6Subnet
2001:db8:1::/48:100

After the demand-dial interface has been created, you can view and configure the settings in the Routing and Remote Access tool (see Figure 10-6).

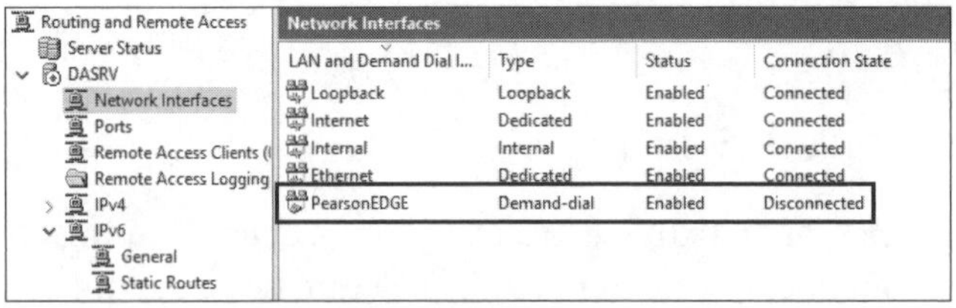

Figure 10-6   Windows Server 2016 Demand-Dial Interface Settings

To get all the details about the S2S VPN demand-dial interface, you should verify the settings through the **Get-VpnS2SInterface** PowerShell cmdlet (see Figure 10-7).

Figure 10-7   Verifying S2S VPN Demand-Dial Interface Settings with PowerShell (Example 1)

Example 2: Create an S2S VPN demand-dial interface that uses the EAP authentication method and multiple subnets (131.0.1.0/24, 121.0.0.0/16) to which this VPN interface can route. The following PowerShell command creates this S2S VPN demand-dial interface:

```
Add-VpnS2SInterface -IPv4Subnet @("131.0.1.0/24:254",
  "121.0.0.0/16:124") -UserName

"administrator@pearson.com" -Destination "10.0.0.1" -IPv6Subnet
  @ ("3ffe::/32:24", "2ffe::/32:24")

-AuthenticationMethod "EAP" -Name "PearsonTestS2SInterface"
  -RetryInterval 120 -EncryptionType

"RequireEncryption" -InternalIPv4 1 -InternalIPv6 1 -NumberofTries 20
  -AdminStatus $True

-IdleDisconnectSeconds 300 -PromoteAlternate $True -Password
  "1111_aaaa" -PassThru
```

To get all the details about this S2S VPN demand-dial interface, you should verify the settings through the **Get-VpnS2SInterface** PowerShell cmdlet (see Figure 10-8).

Figure 10-8 Verifying S2S VPN Demand-Dial Interface Settings with PowerShell (Example 2)

With the following PowerShell commands, you can connect both S2S VPN interfaces:

```
Connect-VpnS2Sinterface -name PearsonEDGE -PassThru
Connect-VpnS2Sinterface -name PearsonTestS2Sinterface -PassThru
```

With the following PowerShell commands, you can disconnect both S2S VPN interfaces:

```
Disconnect-VpnS2Sinterface -name PearsonEDGE -PassThru
Disconnect-VpnS2Sinterface -name PearsonTestS2Sinterface -PassThru
```

When you want detailed statistics information about your S2S VPN interfaces, you can use the PowerShell cmdlet **Get-VpnS2SinterfaceStatistics**. Figure 10-9 shows the statistics information that you can display with this command.

Figure 10-9   Get-VpnS2SinterfaceStatistics

Table 10-2 lists the Windows Server 2016 S2S VPN PowerShell cmdlets used to create, configure, connect, or disconnect S2S interfaces, with detailed settings.

Table 10-2   Windows Server 2016 S2S VPN PowerShell Cmdlets

Cmdlet	Description
Add-VpnS2Sinterface	Creates an S2S interface with the specified parameters.
Clear-VpnS2SInterfaceStatistics	Clears statistics for an S2S interface.
Connect-VpnS2Sinterface	Connects an S2S interface that is currently not connected.
Disconnect-VpnS2Sinterface	Disconnects an S2S interface that is currently connected.
Get-VpnS2SInterface	Retrieves configuration details for an S2S interface.
Remove-VpnS2Sinterface	Removes a specified S2S interface.
Set-VpnS2Sinterface	Updates parameters for an S2S interface. This example modifies the initiator authentication method: **Set-VpnS2SInterface -Name "Edge" -AuthenticationMethod EAP -EapMethod EAP -MSCHAPv2 -PassThru**

Persistent or On-demand S2S VPN Connections

Table 10-3 shows the main differences between an on-demand and persistent VPN connection.

Table 10-3   Windows Server 2016 On-demand and Persistent VPN Connections

On-demand	Persistent
When traffic is being forwarded to the remote location, an S2S VPN connection occurs. After transfer has completed, the connection closes shortly thereafter, contingent on the configuration for your Remote Access policy. You also can configure the calling router (VPN client) to close the connection after a specified idle timeout interval. You can configure this in the properties of the demand-dial interface.	A persistent S2S VPN has a constant connection. Additionally, if the connection inadvertently closes or drops, it is reestablished immediately. To configure the connection as persistent, on the properties page of the Demand-dial interface, on the Options tab, select Persistent connection. You also can configure this on the answering router by clearing the Idle Timeout and Session Timeout boxes on the network policy's Constraints tab.

Configure Different VPN Protocol Options

Table 10-4 lists the VPN tunneling ports and shows which port numbers you have to enable on firewalls for each tunneling network traffic.

Table 10-4   Windows Server 2016 Tunnel Protocols

Tunneling Protocol	Firewall Access	Description
PPTP	TCP port 1723	Provides data confidentiality but not data integrity or data authentication.
L2TP/IPsec	UDP port 500, UDP port 1701, UDP port 4500, IP protocol ID 50	Uses either certificates or preshared keys for authentication. Certificate authentication is recommended.
SSTP	TCP port 443	Uses SSL to provide data confidentiality, data integrity, and authentication.
IKEv2	UDP port 500	Supports the latest IPsec encryption to provide data confidentiality, data integrity, and authentication. IKEv2 is the default VPN tunneling protocol in Windows 10, Windows 7, and Windows 8.

With the PowerShell cmdlet **Get-VpnServerIPsecConfiguration**, you can get IPsec parameters configured on a Windows Server 2016 VPN server (see Figure 10-10).

```
PS C:\> Get-VpnServerIPsecConfiguration | FL

TunnelType                    : IKEV2
GrePorts                      : 128
IdleDisconnect                : 300
Ikev2Ports                    : 128
L2tpPorts                     : 128
MMSALifeTime                  : 28800
SADataSizeForRenegotiation    : 33553408
SALifeTime                    : 3600
SstpPorts                     : 128
EncryptionType                : RequireEncryption
```

Figure 10-10   Get-VpnServerIPsecConfiguration

With the PowerShell cmdlet **Set-VpnServerIPsecConfiguration**, you can configure IPsec properties on Windows Server 2016 Routing and Remote Access (RRAS)
servers for incoming S2S VPN interfaces. You can modify the number of seconds to
idle before disconnecting from the VPN server with the following command:

```
Set-VpnServerIPsecConfiguration -IdleDisconnectSeconds 1000 -PassThru
```

You also can set a custom IPsec policy for incoming VPN connections and S2S
VPN connections for which the authentication method is not PSK with the following command:

```
Set-VpnServerIPsecConfiguration -CustomPolicy
  -EncryptionMethod "AES128" -DhGroup "Group2" -PfsGroup "PFS2"
  -CipherTransformConstants "AES128" -IntegrityCheckMethod "SHA256"
  -AuthenticationTransformConstants "SHA256128" -PassThru
```

With the PowerShell cmdlet **Add-VpnIPAddressRange**, you can add a new IPv4
address range from which IPv4 addresses can be assigned to VPN clients.

This example adds the IP address range 40.1.1.10 (starting IP) through 40.1.1.30
(ending IP) to the IPv4 address pool for assignment to VPN clients:

```
Add-VpnIPAddressRange -IPAddressRange 40.1.1.10, 40.1.1.30 -PassThru
```

With the PowerShell cmdlet **Disconnect-VpnUser**, you can disconnect a
VPN connection originated by a specific user or client. With the PowerShell
cmdlet **Get-RemoteAccessConnectionStatistics**, you can get information
about the TotalConnections, TotalDAConnections, TotalVPNConnections,
Total-UniqueUsers, MaxConcurrentConnections, TotalCumulativeConnections,
TotalBytesIn, TotalBytesOut, and TotalBytesInOut.

With the PowerShell cmdlet **New-VpnServerAddress**, you can create a VPN
server address object.

With the PowerShell cmdlet **New-VpnTrafficSelector**, you can create a VPN
traffic selector object that configures the IKE traffic selector. A traffic selector (also
known as a *proxy ID* in IKEv1) is an agreement between IKE peers to permit traffic
through a tunnel if the traffic matches a specified pair of local and remote addresses.
With this feature, you can define a traffic selector within a specific route-based
VPN, which can result in multiple Phase 2 IPsec security associations (SAs). Only

traffic that conforms to a traffic selector is permitted through an SA. With the following example, two IKEv2 VPN traffic selectors are created and then applied to an S2S VPN interface:

```
$LocalTS  = New-VpnTrafficSelector -IPAddressRange 10.10.0.0,
    10.10.255.255 -PortRange 100, 1000 -Protocol 6 -Type IPv4
$RemoteTS = New-VpnTrafficSelector -IPAddressRange 20.20.0.0,
    20.20.255.255 -PortRange 100, 1000 -Protocol 6 -Type IPv4
Set-VpnS2SInterface -Name EDGE1 -LocalVpnTrafficSelector $LocalTS
    -RemoteVpnTrafficSelector $RemoteTS
```

Configure Authentication Options

In Windows Server 2016, Routing and Remote Access supports the authentication methods described in Table 10-5.

Table 10-5 Windows Server 2016 Authentication Methods

Protocol	Description
PAP	Password Authentication Protocol (PAP) uses plain-text passwords and is the least secure authentication protocol. It typically is negotiated if the Remote Access client and Remote Access server cannot negotiate a more secure form of validation. Windows Server 2016 includes PAP to support older client operating systems that support no other authentication method.
CHAP	The Challenge Handshake Authentication Protocol (CHAP) is a challenge/response authentication protocol that uses the industry-standard MD5 hashing scheme to encrypt the response. Various vendors of network access servers and clients use CHAP. However, because CHAP requires that you use a reversibly encrypted password, you should consider using another authentication protocol, such as MS-CHAPv2.
MS-CHAPv2	MS-CHAPv2 is a one-way, encrypted-password, mutual authentication process that works as follows: 1. The authenticator, which is the Remote Access server or computer that is running Network Policy Server (NPS), sends a challenge to the Remote Access client. The challenge consists of a session identifier and an arbitrary challenge string. 2. The Remote Access client sends a response that contains a one-way encryption of the received challenge string, the peer challenge string, the session identifier, and the user password. 3. The authenticator checks the response from the client and sends back a response that contains an indication of the connection attempt's success or failure, along with an authenticated response based on the sent challenge string, the peer challenge string, the client's encrypted response, and the user password. 4. The Remote Access client verifies the authentication response and, if correct, uses the connection. If the authentication response is not correct, the Remote Access client terminates the connection.

Protocol	Description
EAP	If you use EAP, an arbitrary authentication mechanism authenticates a Remote Access connection. The Remote Access client and the authenticator, which is either the Remote Access server or the Remote Authentication Dial-In User Service (RADIUS) server, negotiate the exact authentication scheme they will use. Routing and Remote Access includes support for EAP-TLS by default. You can plug in other EAP modules to the server that is running Routing and Remote Access to provide other EAP methods.

In the Routing and Remote Access tool, you can configure the authentication methods in the properties of Windows Server 2016 under Security and Authentication Methods (see Figure 10-11).

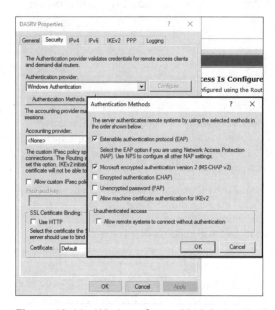

Figure 10-11 Windows Server 2016 Authentication Methods

 Configure VPN Reconnect

Users must be able to access data securely at any time and from anywhere, as well as be able to access it continuously without interruption. For this, you can configure the VPN Reconnect feature. It is available in Windows Server 2016, Windows Server 2012 R2, Windows Server 2012, Windows Server 2008 R2, Windows 10, Windows 8, and Windows 7.

This feature enables users to access organizational data by using a VPN connection, which reconnects automatically if connectivity disconnects.

VPN Reconnect also enables roaming between different networks. VPN Reconnect uses IKEv2, and users who connect via wireless will benefit most from this. Consider a user who travels to work in a train, connects to the Internet with a wireless mobile broadband card, and then establishes a VPN connection to the organization's network. When the train passes through a tunnel, the Internet connection is lost. After the train emerges from the tunnel, the wireless mobile broadband card reconnects automatically to the Internet. With VPN Reconnect, Windows 10 clients automatically reestablish active VPN connections when the network reestablishes Internet connectivity. The reconnection might take several seconds, but users need not reconnect manually or authenticate again to access internal network resources.

System requirements for using the VPN Reconnect feature follow:

- **Server:** Windows Server 2008 R2, Windows Server 2012, or Windows Server 2016

- **Client:** Windows 10, Windows 8, or Windows 7

- **PKI:** A computer certificate from an internal or public CA

You can configure the VPN Reconnect features on the VPN connection when you open the properties of the VPN connection in Protected EAP Properties under Select Authentication Method (see Figure 10-12).

Figure 10-12   Enable Fast Reconnect

Create and Configure VPN Connection Profiles

You can use the *Connection Manager Administration Kit (CMAK)* to customize users' remote connection options by creating predefined connections to remote servers and networks. CMAK is an optional component and is not installed by default. You must install CMAK to create connection profiles that your users can install to access remote networks.

CMAK is part of Windows Server 2016 and can be installed through the **Install-WindowsFeature** *-name CMAK* command. It is also present on a Windows 10 client, and you can install it through Program and Features.

The CMAK Wizard creates an executable file that you can then distribute to your users or include during deployment activities as part of the operating system image. Connection Manager is a client network connection tool that allows a user to connect to a remote network, such as an Internet service provider (ISP) or an organizational network that a VPN server protects.

You can use this tool to customize the remote connection experience for users on your network by creating predefined connections to remote servers and networks.

You can deliver the connection profile, which the CMAK Wizard generates, to users through different methods:

- Including the CMAK profile as part of the image that new computers include. You can install your connection profile as part of the client computer images that install on your organization's new computers.

- Delivering the connection profile on removable media so that the user can install it manually. You can deliver the connection profile installation program on a CD/DVD, universal serial bus (USB) flash drive, or any other removable media that you permit your users to access. Some removable media support autorun capabilities, which allow you to start the installation automatically when the user inserts the media into the client computer.

- Delivering the connection profile with automated software distribution tools. Many organizations use a desktop management and software deployment tool such as Microsoft System Center Configuration Manager, which allows you to package and deploy software that you want your client computers to receive. The installation can be invisible to your users, and you can configure it to report to a management console on whether the installation was successful.

You can use the following technologies to distribute VPN profiles:

- **Configuration Manager:** You can deploy a VPN profile to the following operating systems: Windows 10 Mobile, Windows 10, Windows 8.1, iOS, and Android. Furthermore, to support Windows 10 Mobile, iOS, and Android, the device must be enrolled in Microsoft Intune. The System Center Configuration Manager supports several VPN connections, including Cisco AnyConnect, Pulse Secure, F5 Edge Client, Dell SonicWALL Mobile Connect, Check Point Mobile VPN, Microsoft SSL (SSTP), Microsoft Automatic, IKEv2, PPTP, and L2TP. If you deploy a non-Microsoft VPN profile, you must ensure that the VPN software is installed on the device. Otherwise, the user cannot use the VPN profile to connect to a VPN server.

- **Microsoft Intune:** You can deploy VPN profiles by using Intune, which supports the following VPN profiles natively: Cisco AnyConnect, Pulse Secure, F5 Edge Client, Dell SonicWALL Mobile Connect, and Check Point Mobile VPN. Before you can deploy the VPN profiles, the device must be enrolled in Intune. You can create VPN profiles natively for devices running the Windows, Android, and iOS operating systems by creating a VPN profile in Microsoft Intune. You also can build a VPN policy manually by creating a configuration policy and then specifying the various Open Mobile Alliance Uniform Resource Identifier (OMA-ORI) settings.

- **Group Policy and scripts:** You can use Group Policy preferences to deploy VPN profiles to a user or a computer. You can find the settings for the user or computer configuration at the following locations: **Computer Configuration > Preferences > Control Panel Settings > Network Option** and also **User Configuration > Preferences > Control Panel Settings > Network Option Microsoft** (see Figure 10-13).

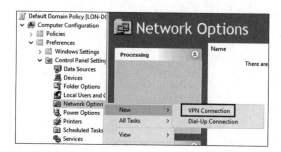

Figure 10-13   Create New VPN Connection through Group Policy

Microsoft has provided a solution for deploying VPN profiles by using a custom Windows PowerShell script and then deploying the Windows PowerShell script using a Group Policy logon script. You also can create and deploy VPN profiles by using the **Add-VPNConnection** PowerShell cmdlet, and then deploy the VPN profile by using a Group Policy logon script. The **Add-VPNConnection** cmdlet is available only on Windows 8 and newer operating systems.

Configuring VPN Connection Profiles with PowerShell

With the **Add-VpnConnection** PowerShell cmdlet, you can add a VPN connection to the Connection Manager phone book. With the **Set-VpnConnection** Power-Shell cmdlet, you can change configurations at existing VPN connections.

When you want to add a VPN connection that uses a custom EAP authentication method, you can use the **New-EapConfiguration** PowerShell cmdlet to create an XML file with the specified EAP configuration. After that, you can use the following command to create a new VPN connection profile using this EAP configuration:

```
Add-VpnConnection -Name "PearsonVPN" -ServerAddress "10.1.11.11"
  -TunnelType L2tp
-EncryptionLevel Required -AuthenticationMethod Eap -SplitTunneling
  -AllUserConnection
-RememberCredential -EapConfigXmlStream $A.EapConfigXmlStream
  -PassThru
```

App-Triggered VPN Feature

An app-triggered VPN enables a VPN profile to connect automatically when a specified app or set of apps starts. This extends a VPN's automatic connection behavior and provides support for app-triggered VPN connections in Windows 10 VPN profiles. Windows 8.1 introduced this functionality as an *on-demand VPN*. You can configure app-triggered VPN connections to start automatically, creating a secure connection when a trusted app needs a network resource. You can create trusted app lists that can include traditional desktop apps or universal apps.

To configure app-triggered VPN, you must do the following:

Step 1.   Find the Package Family Name for universal apps or find the path for desktop apps.

Step 2.   Enable the app to trigger the VPN.

Step 3.   Enable split tunneling for the VPN connection.

You can find the Package Family Name for universal Windows apps when you run the PowerShell cmdlet **Get-AppXPackage** and then search for the value *PackageFamilyName*. Figure 10-14 shows an example.

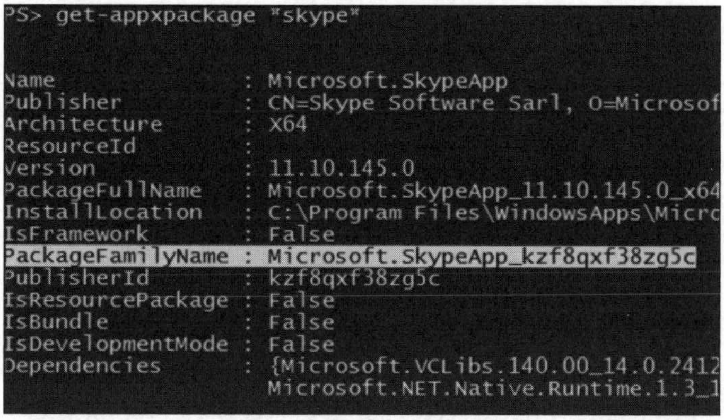

```
PS> get-appxpackage "skype"

Name               : Microsoft.SkypeApp
Publisher          : CN=Skype Software Sarl, O=Microsof
Architecture       : x64
ResourceId         :
Version            : 11.10.145.0
PackageFullName    : Microsoft.SkypeApp_11.10.145.0_x64
InstallLocation    : C:\Program Files\WindowsApps\Micro
IsFramework        : False
PackageFamilyName  : Microsoft.SkypeApp_kzf8qxf38zg5c
PublisherId        : kzf8qxf38zg5c
IsResourcePackage  : False
IsBundle           : False
IsDevelopmentMode  : False
Dependencies       : {Microsoft.VCLibs.140.00_14.0.2412
                     Microsoft.NET.Native.Runtime.1.3_1
```

Figure 10-14 Get the *PackageFamilyName* for an App-Triggered VPN

To enable the app to trigger the VPN, use the PowerShell cmdlet **Add-VpnConnectionTriggerApplication**. The following example enables an app-triggered VPN for Skype:

```
Add-VpnConnectionTriggerApplication -ConnectionName "PearsonVPN"
  -ApplicationID Microsoft.SkypeApp_kzf8qxf38zg5c
```

If you enable split tunneling for a VPN connection, all traffic that is not intended for the internal network is sent out through the local gateway. To use an app-triggered VPN, you must configure the VPN profile for split tunneling. When you create a new VPN profile by using the GUI on Windows 10, split tunneling is disabled. To verify the split tunneling state on a VPN profile, you can run the **Get-VPNConnection** cmdlet. However, because a VPN profile can be global (Allow Other People to Use This Connection) or local (Only Configured for the User), you must run the **Get-VPNConnection** cmdlet twice. Then you will see that the SplitTunneling property is False. To set it to True, which enables split tunneling for the PearsonVPN profile, you must run the following command:

```
Set-VpnConnection -name "PearsonVPN" -AllUserConnection
  -SplitTunneling $true
```

TIP Computers that are members of a domain do not support app-triggered VPNs. They require that you enable split tunneling for the VPN profile.

Scenarios for RAS VPN and S2S VPN and Appropriate Protocols

You can use many different kinds of VPN connections to connect through a VPN tunnel to the corporate network. You can use different tunneling protocols such as PPTP, L2TP, SSTP, and IKEv2. The following sections explain these tunneling protocols and their differences.

Remote Access VPN Connection Scenarios

Remote access VPN connections enable users who work offsite, such as at home, at a customer site, or from a public wireless access point, to access a server on your organization's private network by using the infrastructure that a public network provides, such as the Internet. From the user's perspective, the VPN is a point-to-point connection between the computer, the VPN client, and your organization's server. The exact infrastructure of the shared or public network is irrelevant because it appears logically as if the data is sent over a dedicated private link.

Using remote VPNs in Windows Server 2016 involves four scenarios:

- VPN connections with PPTP

- VPN connections with L2TP/IPsec

- VPN connections with SSTP

- VPN connections with IKEv2

VPN Connections with PPTP

PPTP is a tunnel protocol that uses Microsoft Point-to-Point Encryption (MPPE). Windows Server 2016 VPN server still supports PPTP; it has 128 PPTP ports by default for VPN client connections.

PPTP enables you to encrypt and encapsulate multiprotocol traffic in an IP header that it then sends across an IP network or a public IP network, such as the Internet. For encapsulation, PPTP encapsulates PPP frames in IP datagrams for network transmission. PPTP uses a TCP connection for tunnel management and a modified version of Generic Route Encapsulation (GRE) to encapsulate PPP frames for tunneled data.

Payloads of the encapsulated PPP frames can be encrypted, compressed, or both. Using PPTP, you can encrypt the PPP frame with MPPE by using encryption keys that are generated from the MS-CHAPv2 or EAP-TLS authentication process.

VPN clients must use the MS-CHAPv2 or EAP-TLS authentication protocols to ensure encryption of payloads of PPP frames. PPTP uses the underlying PPP encryption and encapsulates a previously encrypted PPP frame.

For security reasons, PPTP is not recommended for VPN connections because PPTP provides data confidentiality but not data integrity or data authentication.

VPN Connections with L2TP/IPsec

L2TP enables you to encrypt traffic that is sent over any medium that supports point-to-point datagram delivery, such as IP or ATM. L2TP is a combination of PPTP and L2F and represents the best features of both. Unlike PPTP, the Microsoft implementation of L2TP does not use MPPE to encrypt PPP datagrams. L2TP relies on IPsec in transport mode for encryption services. The combination of L2TP and IPsec is L2TP/IPsec. To utilize L2TP/IPsec, both the VPN client and server must support L2TP and IPsec. The Windows 10, Windows 8, and Windows 7 Remote Access clients include client support for L2TP. Windows Server 2016, Windows Server 2012, and Windows Server 2008 operating systems all contain VPN server support for L2TP. L2TP encapsulation consists of two layers, L2TP encapsulation and IPsec encapsulation. L2TP encapsulates and encrypts data as follows:

- **First layer:** The first layer is the L2TP encapsulation. A PPP frame (an IP datagram) is wrapped with an L2TP header and a User Datagram Protocol (UDP) header.

- **Second layer:** The second layer is the IPsec encapsulation. The resulting L2TP message is wrapped with an IPsec ESP header and trailer, an IPsec authentication trailer that provides message integrity and authentication, and a final IP header. The IP header contains the source and destination IP address that corresponds to the VPN client and server. With L2TP, the message is encrypted with AES or 3DES by using encryption keys that the IKE negotiation process generates.

VPN Connections with SSTP

Secure Socket Tunneling Protocol (SSTP) is a tunneling protocol that uses HTTPS protocol over port 443 to pass traffic through firewalls and web proxies that otherwise might block PPTP and L2TP/IPsec traffic.

SSTP provides a mechanism to encapsulate PPP traffic over the SSL channel of the HTTPS protocol. The use of PPP allows support for strong authentication methods such as EAP-TLS. SSL provides transport-level security with enhanced key negotiation, encryption, and integrity checking.

When a client tries to establish an SSTP-based VPN connection, SSTP first establishes a bidirectional HTTPS layer with the SSTP server. SSTP encapsulates PPP frames in IP datagrams for transmission over the network. SSTP uses a TCP connection (443) for tunnel management. SSTP encrypts the message with the SSL channel of the HTTPS protocol.

VPN Connections with IKEv2

Internet Key Exchange Protocol Version 2 (IKEv2) uses the IPsec Tunnel Mode protocol over UDP port 500. IKEv2 supports mobility, making it a good protocol choice for a mobile workforce. IKEv2-based VPNs enable users to move easily between wireless hotspots or between wireless and wired connections. IKEv2 encapsulates datagrams by using IPsec ESP or an Authentication Header (AH) for transmission over the network; it encrypts the message with one of the following protocols by using encryption keys that it generates during the IKEv2 negotiation process: AES 256, AES 192, AES 128, and 3DES encryption algorithms.

IKEv2 is supported only on computers that are running the Windows Server 2016, Windows 10, Windows 8, Windows Server 2012, Windows 7, and Windows Server 2008 R2 operating systems. IKEv2 is the default VPN tunneling protocol in Windows 10, Windows 7, and Windows 8.

On-premises S2S VPN Connection Scenarios

S2S VPN connections, or router-to-router VPN connections, enable your organization to establish routed connections between separate offices or with other organizations over a public network while helping to maintain secure communications.

You can use the same tunneling protocols for S2S VPN connections as for Remote Access scenarios: PPTP, L2TP, SSTP, and IKEv2. Additionally, an S2S VPN connection can be configured in the following two scenarios:

- **S2S VPN connections (on-demand):** When traffic is being forwarded to the remote location, a site-to-site VPN connection occurs. When the transfer completes, the connection closes shortly thereafter, contingent on the configuration for your remote access policy. You also can configure the calling router (VPN client) to close the connection after a specified idle timeout interval. You can configure this in the properties of the demand-dial interface.

- **S2S VPN connections (persistent):** A persistent site-to-site VPN has a constant connection. Additionally, if the connection inadvertently closes or drops, it is reestablished immediately. To configure the connection as persistent, on the properties page of the demand-dial interface, on the Options tab, select Persistent Connection. You also can configure this on the answering router by clearing the Idle Timeout and Session Timeout boxes on the network policy's Constraints tab.

On-premises to Microsoft Azure S2S VPN Connection Scenarios

Virtual networks in Microsoft Azure also enable you to extend your on-premises networks to the cloud. To extend your on-premises network, you can create a VPN between your on-premises computers or networks and an Azure virtual network. Alternatively, you can use ExpressRoute to provide a connection to an Azure virtual network that does not cross the Internet. Using these two methods, you can enable on-premises users to access Azure services as if they were physically located on-premises in your own datacenter. To connect to an Azure virtual network from an on-premises network, you can use these solutions:

- **P2S VPN connection (IPsec-encrypted VPN tunnel from a single on-premises client to an Azure virtual network):** A point-to-site VPN connects a single computer to a virtual network through a VPN tunnel. You must configure a certificate to secure this connection and then install a client configuration package on the client computer. Use point-to-site connections when you have a small number of client computers that you want to connect to an Azure virtual network. Remember that computers with a point-to-site VPN can use that connection from anywhere that they have Internet access. For example, they could connect to the virtual network from a cafe with Wi-Fi.

- **S2S VPN connection (SSTP-based VPN tunnel from your on-premises network to an Azure virtual network):** A site-to-site VPN connects an on-premises TCP/IP network to a virtual network through a VPN tunnel. In the on-premises network, a VPN device routes traffic to the virtual network. You can use either a compatible third-party VPN device or use a server running Windows server with the Routing and Remote Access Service (RRAS) configured. Azure provides scripts that you can use to configure different VPN devices. Use a site-to-site connection when you have many client computers that are all connected to an on-premises network. Unlike point-to-site connections, clients can use site-to-site connections only when they have a direct connection to the on-premises network.

- **ExpressRoute (uses a private connection to Azure datacenters provided by a network provider):** Using ExpressRoute, you increase security, reliability, and bandwidth. The ExpressRoute service can provide a private connection from your datacenter to an Azure virtual network through a connection service provider. This can improve security and achieve higher bandwidth, lower latency, and better reliability. Microsoft works with network service providers to build these connections.

When planning and configuring your VPN connections from your on-premises site to Azure virtual networks, keep the following points in mind:

- Azure supports a maximum of 30 VPN tunnels per VPN gateway. Each point-to-site VPN, site-to-site VPN, or VNet-to-VNet VPN counts as one of those VPN tunnels. A single VPN gateway can support up to 128 connections from client computers.

- Address spaces must not overlap. Carefully plan the address spaces that you want to use in virtual networks and any connected on-premises networks.

- VNet-to-VNet VPNs can connect virtual networks in the same or different Azure subscriptions. Similarly they can connect virtual networks in the same or different Azure regions.

- Redundant tunnels are not supported.

- Cloud services cannot span virtual networks, even when those virtual networks are connected with a VPN.

- All VPN tunnels to a virtual network share the available bandwidth on the Azure VPN gateway. This includes point-to-site VPNs.

- VPN devices must meet certain requirements. These requirements are listed on the Microsoft website, on the page titled "About VPN Devices for Site-to-Site VPN Gateway Connections."

NOTE   You can get an overview and more detailed information about the different Microsoft Azure Gateway solutions at https://docs.microsoft.com/en-us/azure/vpn-gateway/vpn-gateway-about-vpngateways.

Web Application Proxy Scenarios

Web Application Proxy provides reverse proxy functionality for web applications inside your corporate network, to allow users on any device to access them from outside the corporate network through HTTPS. Web Application Proxy preauthenticates access to web applications using AD FS and also functions as an AD FS proxy. You can publish your web applications through a Web Application Proxy to external clients. You can find the Web Application Proxy role on a Windows Server 2016 server under the Remote Access role.

Install and Configure DirectAccess

Windows Server 2012 DirectAccess securely extends network services and resources to remote users while providing seamless access to corporate resources without any user interaction or VPN client. It allows users to move their device among internal, public, and home networks while retaining access to internal servers.

With DirectAccess, users get the experience of being permanently connected to their company intranet from outside any time they have Internet access. Requests for intranet resources (such as email servers, shared folders, or intranet websites) are securely (IPsec IPv6 tunnel) directed to the intranet, without the need for users to connect to a VPN. The connection is established in the background without requiring user interaction.

Windows Server 2016 combines the DirectAccess, VPN (RAS), routing, and Web Application Proxy role features into the Remote Access server role.

> **NOTE**   Be sure to read the "5 New DirectAccess Documents for Windows Server 2016 DirectAccess," at https://blogs.technet.microsoft.com/wsnetdoc/2016/02/17/5-new-directaccess-documents-for-windows-server-2016/.

DirectAccess Infrastructure Components

Windows Server 2008 R2 DirectAccess was difficult, time intensive, and hard to implement. Since Windows Server 2012, the DirectAccess Express Wizard and PowerShell have simplified the DirectAccess implementation process. With Windows Server 2016, DirectAccess has some additional improvements. The following list outlines some of the main prerequisites for a DirectAccess solution:

- At least one Active Directory domain.
- Workgroups not supported.
- DirectAccess clients required to be domain members.
- DirectAccess server required to have minimum one network adapter.
- At least one domain controller and DNS server.
- PKI required to issue certificates. External certificates are not a requirement.
- IPsec policies required to specify protection for network traffic.
- A client running a minimum of Windows 7 (or Windows 8), for DirectAccess.
- Tunneled IP traffic allowed to pass through the perimeter firewall.

DirectAccess Key Components

The following list outlines the most important technologies, services, and components of a Windows Server 2016 DirectAccess solution:

- DirectAccess server
- DirectAccess client
- Active Directory
- DNS server
- NLS
- KDC Proxy
- Certification service
- Certificates
- DNS64
- 6to4/ISATAP/Teredo
- Group Policy
- NCA

DirectAccess Solution Component: DirectAccess Server

A Windows Server 2016 DirectAccess server consists of the following features:

- **DirectAccess Server role:** A DirectAccess server allows remote users to securely access internal resources without connecting to a VPN. The Direct-Access server establishes bidirectional connectivity with an internal network every time a DirectAccess-enabled computer connects to the Internet, even before the user logs on. IT administrators also can manage remote computers outside the office, even when the computers are not connected to the VPN (managed-out support).

- **DirectAccess server setup:** DirectAccess server setup easily can be done through the Getting Started Wizard. This wizard offers easy step-by-step configuration for a DirectAccess server. The wizard runs background PowerShell scripts that execute the most necessary steps (such as creating GPOs). With the setup of the DirectAccess server, you also have configured Direct-Access client settings because the wizard also creates a DirectAccess client Group Policy.

- **DirectAccess and RAS:** In Windows Server 2016 VPN server, Direct-Access and Web Application Proxy are aggregated into one role, named Remote Access.

- **Integrated NLB:** You can easily integrate the Network Load Balancing (NLB) features of the underlying operating system.

- **Multisite deployment:** You can deploy DirectAccess into a multisite network environment. You can use an integrated wizard to configure S2S IKEv2 IPsec tunnels.

- **Single-NIC support:** You can set up a DirectAccess server with a single network card.

- **Kerberos authentication:** With Window Server 2008 and Windows Server 2008 R2, using IPsec certificates was essential for clients to authenticate for the IPsec tunnel to a DirectAccess server. Since Windows Server 2012 Direct-Access, you can use Kerberos authentication for DirectAccess connections from the Internet to corporate networks. Two components that make this possible are KDC Proxy and IP-HTTPS.

- **OTP support:** You can use one-time password authentication (OTP) with highly secure one-time passwords, ensuring that only properly authenticated users are authorized access to the company's critical applications and data.

- **PKI relinquishing:** For Windows Server 2016 DirectAccess, an internal PKI is not mandatory. You can use certificates from public CAs for IPsec tunneling, but DirectAccess can work with self-signed certificates for IP-HTTPS DirectAccess connections and can use Kerberos authentication.

- **Built-in NAT64 and DNS64:** DirectAccess can use NAT64 and DNS64 to allow IPv6 hosts to communicate with IPv4 servers. DNS64 makes it possible to resolve name requests for IPv6 addresses without having IPv6 addresses registered in DNS. The DNS server delivers a synthesized IPv6 address to the requestor.

- **DirectAccess behind NAT:** Windows Server 2016 DirectAccess connections can run through NAT devices.

- **Simplified security policy:** Windows Server 2016 DirectAccess automatically configures the needed Group Policies on the DC with the relevant security settings for DirectAccess clients and DirectAccess servers.

- **Multiple domain support:** Windows Server 2016 DirectAccess supports the deployment of DirectAccess through multiple domains.

- **Force tunneling support:** Windows Server 2016 DirectAccess supports force tunneling, which means that all traffic from the DirectAccess client to any internal resource must go through the DirectAccess IPsec tunnel. Traffic destined for the intranet goes over the IPsec tunnel; traffic to the Internet also has to go over the DirectAccess IPsec tunnel.

- **Manage-out support:** Manage-out support for Windows Server 2016 DirectAccess means that you can manage DirectAccess clients through the DirectAccess tunnel in the outbound direction.

- **Accounting/reporting:** You can use RADIUS Accounting or Windows Internal Database (WID) Accounting.

- **Server Core Support:** Windows Server 2016 DirectAccess can be installed and configured on the Server Core (but not on Windows Server 2016 Nano Server).

- **PowerShell support:** Many PowerShell cmdlets can be used for Windows Server 2016 DirectAccess. For example, to get information about the DirectAccess server configuration, you use **Get-DAServer**.

> **TIP**   NAP was deprecated in Windows Server 2012 R2 and has been removed from Windows Server 2016. You no longer can integrate Windows Server 2016 DirectAccess with NAP to verify security settings of the DirectAccess client.

 DirectAccess Solution Component: DirectAccess Client

A DirectAccess client can be any domain-joined client computer that is running one of the following (Ultimate and Enterprise) editions:

- Windows 7

- Windows 8

- Windows 8.1

- Windows 10

> **TIP**   You cannot use third-party operating systems as DirectAccess clients. With off-premises provisioning, you can join the client computer to a domain without connecting the client computer to your internal premises. This is done with the **djoin** utility.

DirectAccess clients connect into the tunnel by using IPv6 and IPsec. If a native IPv6 network is not available, the client establishes an IPv6-over-IPv4 tunnel by using 6to4 or Teredo. The user does not have to be logged on to the computer. If a firewall or proxy server prevents the client computer using 6to4 or Teredo from connecting to the DirectAccess server, the client computer automatically attempts to connect by using the IP-HTTPS protocol, which uses an SSL connection.

DirectAccess Solution Component: Active Directory

You cannot implement a DirectAccess solution without using Active Directory. At a minimum, the domain must run the Windows Server 2003 domain functional level. Windows Server 2016 DirectAccess provides multiple-domain support, which allows client computers from different domains to access resources that might be located in different trusted domains.

Group Policies (GPO) are an essential part of Active Directory. DirectAccess uses GPOs to deploy DirectAccess server and DirectAccess client settings. The Getting Started Wizard creates a set of GPOs and settings for DirectAccess clients, the DirectAccess server, and selected servers.

DirectAccess enables client authentication requests to be sent over an HTTPS-based Kerberos proxy service (KDC Proxy) that is running on the DirectAccess server. This removes the need to establish a second IPsec tunnel (as in earlier versions) between clients and DCs. However, for a full DirectAccess configuration, two-factor authentication, and force tunneling, you must implement certificates for authentication for every client that will participate in DirectAccess communication. The Kerberos proxy sends Kerberos requests to domain controllers on behalf of the client. PKI is still required for DirectAccess clients running Windows 7.

The DirectAccess clients get the Name Resolution Policy Table (NRPT) settings through the DirectAccess Group Policy. The NRPT is used from DirectAccess clients to find out which DNS server they have to use to resolve the names of resources they access. For internal resources, the clients use the internal DNS servers (delivered through NRPT); for resources on the Internet, they use their locally configured DNS server.

DirectAccess Solution Component: DNS Server

For a successful DirectAccess client connection from outside the company or branch office, you must configure the namespace for the public access. These clients have to resolve the external name to access the DirectAccess server through a DNS server. The suffix for the external connection has to be different from the internal suffix. The suffix for the external connection should not be part of the internal namespace.

For testing purposes, it is also possible to use an IP address for the external name of the DirectAccess server. In a Basic DirectAccess deployment, in which the

DirectAccess server is configured through the Getting Started Wizard and works as an Edge, a self-signed certificate for IP-HTTPS automatically is created. In this case, the name of this certificate becomes the external IP address defined as an external public name (see Figure 10-15) in the Getting Started Wizard. This eliminates the use for external name resolution because the DirectAccess client has to identify the certificate only through IP address, not through FQDN.

Figure 10-15   DirectAccess Server Public Name

Use DNS servers that support dynamic updates. You can use DNS servers that do not support dynamic updates, but you must manually update entries on these servers. DNS servers used for DirectAccess with ISATAP have to be based on Windows Server 2008 with the Q958194 hotfix, Windows Server 2008 with SP2 or later, Windows Server 2008 R2, Windows Server 2012, Windows Server 2012 R2, or Windows Server 2016, or a non-Microsoft DNS server that supports DNS message exchanges over ISATAP.

Internal Name Resolution

An internal DNS server must deliver IP addresses behind hostnames to DirectAccess clients for the following resources:

- IP address of internal dedicated NLS

- DirectAccess server internal interface IP address when DirectAccess Server is NLS

- When using internal CA, the IP address of the internal CA

- IP address of DC, which has to deliver DirectAccess GPO settings

External Name Resolution

External DNS servers must deliver IP addresses behind names for Internet-accessible CRL distribution points for DirectAccess clients. For example, if the URL http://crl.pearson.com/crld/corp-DC1-CA.crl is in the CRL Distribution Points field of the IP-HTTPS certificate of the DirectAccess server, you must ensure that the FQDN crld.pearson.com is resolvable by using Internet DNS servers.

NRPT for Local Name Resolution

If the FQDNs of your CRL distribution points are based on intranet namespace, you must add exemption rules for the FQDNs of the CRL distribution points.

If you are redirecting traffic to an external website through your intranet web proxy servers, the external website is available only from the intranet, and it uses the addresses of your web proxy servers to permit the inbound requests. In this case, you have to add an exemption rule for the external website FQDN and specify that the rule use your intranet web proxy server instead of the IPv6 addresses of intranet DNS servers.

If you have split-brain DNS, you must add exemption rules for the names of resources for which you want DirectAccess clients located on the Internet to access the Internet version instead of the intranet version.

DirectAccess clients attempt to reach the NLS, to find out if they are internal. Clients on the internal network must be able to resolve the name of the NLS, but they must be prevented from resolving the name when they are located on the Internet. To ensure this, NLS FQDN is added as an exemption rule to NRPT.

Split-Brain DNS

When you use the same DNS domain for Internet and intranet name resolution, you must list the FQDNs that are duplicated on the Internet and intranet and decide which resources the DirectAccess client should reach, the intranet or the Internet version. For each name that corresponds to a resource for which you want DirectAccess clients to reach the Internet version, you must add the corresponding FQDN as an exemption rule to the NRPT for your DirectAccess clients.

LLMNR for Local Name Resolution

If a name cannot be resolved with DNS, you must resolve the name on the local subnet. To do this, the DNS Client service in Windows Server 2016, 2012 R2, 2012, and 2008 R2, as well as Windows 10, Windows 8, and Windows 7, can use local name resolution with the Link-Local Multicast Name Resolution (LLMNR) and NetBIOS over TCP/IP protocols.

Local name resolution is needed for peer-to-peer connectivity when the computer is located on private networks, such as single-subnet home networks. When the DNS Client service performs local name resolution for intranet server names and the computer is connected to a shared subnet on the Internet, malicious users can capture LLMNR and NetBIOS over TCP/IP messages to determine intranet server names. You can configure the behavior of local name resolution through the DirectAccess Getting Started Wizard on the Infrastructure Server Setup page.

TIP   You can disable LLMNR in Group Policy at Computer Configuration > Administrative Templates > Network > DNS Client with the setting Turn Off Multicast Name Resolution (see Figure 10-16). You must choose Enabled to disable the LLMNR feature in this policy.

Figure 10-16   Turn Off Multicast Name Resolution

DirectAccess Solution Component: Network Location Server

The Network Location Server (NLS) can be installed on the same server where Windows Server 2016 DirectAccess is installed (this is also possible on a dedicated internal web server). NLS is a web server that allows incoming SSL connections. The Windows Server 2016 web server and the Network Location Server are both automatically installed with the installation of the Windows Server 2016 Direct-Access role.

TIP   Because the FQDN of the network location URL is added as an exemption rule to the NRPT, the intranet web server at that FQDN is not accessible to DirectAccess clients on the Internet.

NLS is used to confirm that the client is in the corporate network and not on the Internet. The client simply has to find the NLS; the NLS then responds to the HTTPS request. As long as the HTTPS request is responded to, the client decides that it is inside the corporate network and does not enable the DirectAccess virtual adapters. The NLS requires an SSL certificate, which must be checked against the Certificate Revocation List (CRL). If the CRL is hosted by the CA and the CRL is unavailable, the certificate for the NLS cannot be verified and the connection check to the NLS fails anyway. The certificate that the web server uses to act as an NLS must have the following requirements:

- In the Subject field, either an IP address of the intranet interface of the web server or the FQDN of the NLS URL

- For the Enhanced Key Usage field, the Server Authentication object identifier (OID)

- For the CRL Distribution Points field, a Certificate Revocation List (CRL) distribution point that is accessible by DirectAccess clients that are connected to the intranet

Figure 10-17 shows the purpose of NLS.

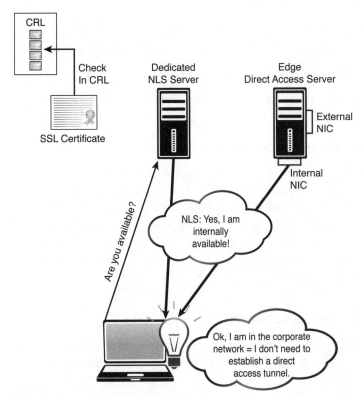

Figure 10-17   NLS Purpose

DirectAccess Solution Component: KDC Proxy

Since Windows Server 2012 DirectAccess, the KDC Proxy service is possible and automatically installed on the DirectAccess Server, to provide a way for Internet clients to use Kerberos authentication. DirectAccess clients create a TLS/SSL secure channel to the KDC Proxy service.

> **TIP**   Force tunnel configuration is not supported with KerbProxy authentication.

To obtain the service ticket for the DirectAccess server, Kerberos messages are sent to the corresponding KDC Proxy service. The service sends the request to a DC in the corporate network, which authenticates the machine based on the Active Directory computer account and returns the response. The KDC Proxy service is not a standalone server role. What value does this change add? You can use the same protocol for external and internal clients: Kerberos.

Some important facts about KDC Proxy follow:

- The KDC Proxy service is installed by default.

- KDC Proxy is a web-based service.

- A TLS/SSL secure channel is used to connect to the KDC Proxy service.

- KDC Proxy is not possible on a standalone server.

- The KDC Proxy SSL certificate needs a revocation check.

DirectAccess Solution Component: Certification Service

A more secure way to install and configure a Windows Server 2016 DirectAccess Server is to use an internal Certificate Authority (CA) based on Active Directory. However, this is not a prerequisite for the deployment of a Windows DirectAccess Server. Some companies find implementing their own public key infrastructure (PKI) an easier and more cost-effective solution. You also can use public CAs for DirectAccess. When you use a dedicated NLS server, it needs an SSL certificate with CRL checking through the CA.

DirectAccess Solution Component: Certificates

The DirectAccess client must have a trusted root certificate for the DirectAccess server authentication certificate. If the client is a domain member, it can be delivered directly through GPO.

In such a case, the client has no problem establishing a DirectAccess connection from outside the company and can use that trusted root certificate to verify the DirectAccess server authentication certificate.

During the installation process of a DirectAccess server, it is possible for the Windows DirectAccess Server setup to create and install the necessary IP-HTTPS and KDC Proxy certificates automatically as self-signed certificates. In this way, no CA has to deploy the certificates. This is the preferred solution for a Basic DirectAccess deployment.

DirectAccess Solution Component: DNS64

DNS64 describes a DNS server that, when asked for a domain's AAAA records and finding only A records, synthesizes the AAAA records from the A records. Two important issues arise with this transition mechanism:

- DNS64 works only when DNS is used to find the remote host address. If IPv4 literals are used, the DNS64 server is never involved.

- Because the DNS64 server needs to return records not specified by the domain owner, DNSSEC validation against the root fails when the DNS server doing the translation is not the domain owner's server.

DirectAccess Solution Component: 6to4

IPv6 packets from DirectAccess clients are encapsulated in an IPv4 header and sent over the 6to4 tunnel adapter to the DirectAccess server. 6to4 is supported when the DirectAccess server is Edge facing with a public IPv4 address assigned to its external NIC.

6to4 uses IP protocol 41 for transport and does not work when the client is behind a NAT. If outbound IP protocol 41 is blocked, the client should fall back to Teredo or IP-HTTPS. In fact, the protocol fallback fails with enough regularity that it is the primary reason to disable 6to4 by default and not to use it for DirectAccess. Figure 10-18 shows a 6to4 adapter in the Device Manager on a DirectAccess server.

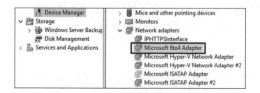

Figure 10-18   Microsoft 6to4 Adapter in Device Manager

DirectAccess Solution Component: ISATAP

DirectAccess works fine without using ISATAP. However, imagine that you want to use managed-out work on the DirectAccess clients through the IPv6 tunnel (which means you want to apply Group Policy to the DirectAccess clients or you have to do some auditing work on them) or you simply want to perform an RDP connection through the DirectAccess tunnel. That requires a help desk computer to have an IPv6 layer of transport available for contacting the IPv6 DirectAccess clients.

When you want to enable ISATAP, you can create a global ISATAP host record on your DNS server. However, this is not a good solution because although ISATAP is desirable, adding IPv6 capabilities to all Windows systems is not desirable for many deployments. This is especially true when Windows naturally favors IPv6 communications over IPv4.

A better option is to configure selective ISATAP. This way, you enable only specific clients to use a custom ISATAP router name. You can achieve this through Group Policy and a dedicated Windows security group for managed-out clients. Figure 10-19 shows an example Group Policy.

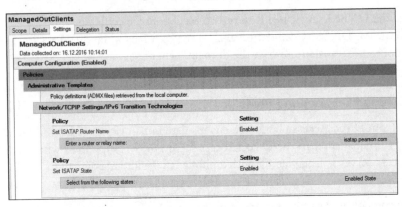

Figure 10-19   ISATAP Group Policy Settings

When you have IPv6 inside your network, you do not need ISATAP.

If you are thinking about installing a DirectAccess server on an Azure VM, keep in mind that Azure does not support using managed-out clients with native IPv6 or ISATAP. Azure does not support IPv6 addressing for Azure VMs, but running an Azure VM with an installed DirectAccess server is technically possible.

DirectAccess Solution Component: Teredo

Teredo is similar to 6to4 in that it enables you to tunnel IPv6 packets over the IPv4 Internet. Teredo functions correctly even when NAT is used for Internet connectivity. Teredo is required because many organizations use private IP addresses, which require NAT to access the Internet. If a NAT device can be configured as a 6to4 router, Teredo is not required.

For use with DirectAccess, using IP-HTTPS is recommending instead of using Teredo and 6to4. You can disable Teredo, 6to4, and ISATAP with the following PowerShell commands:

```
Set-Net6to4Configuration -State disabled
Set-NetTeredoConfiguration -State disabled
Set-NetIsatapConfiguration -State disabled
```

TIP   Teredo is used only when native IPv6, 6to4, or ISATAP transitioning technologies do not provide connectivity.

When you deploy Windows Server 2016 DirectAccess in a cluster with an external load balancer deployment, if remote management is needed, DirectAccess clients cannot use Teredo. Only IP-HTTPS can be used for end-to-end communication.

DirectAccess Solution Component: Group Policy

In Windows Server 2016, the DirectAccess Getting Started Wizard and the Remote Access configuration console transform most configurations into Group Policy settings for the DirectAccess server and the DirectAccess client. The default configuration is that the GPOs are created at the domain level with the default names DirectAccess Client Settings and DirectAccess Server Settings. You can change the GPO names through the GPO Names page (see Figure 10-20) of the Getting Started Wizard. New in Windows Server 2016 is that you also can use existing GPOs.

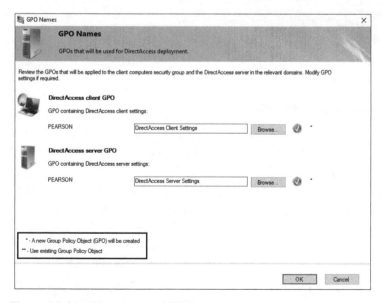

Figure 10-20   DirectAccess GPO Names

DirectAccess Solution Component: WMI Filter

An important part of the Windows Server 2016 DirectAccess configuration is the Group Policy WMI Filter, which can be automatically generated. The default filter defines that only mobile computers get the DirectAccess client Group Policy applied to them.

Normally, these clients are devices that want to use DirectAccess connections from outside the company. You can change this WMI filter from the Group Policy Management Console, perhaps to deploy DirectAccess only to smartphone devices or other mobile devices that want to use DirectAccess connections.

> **CAUTION** When you use virtual machines as test DirectAccess clients and they do not apply the DirectAccess client Group Policy settings, you first must remove the WMI filter. Virtual machines do not have a battery.

Figure 10-21 shows the default WMI filter for the DirectAccess client settings Group Policy.

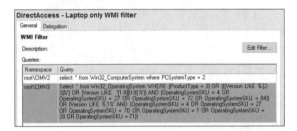

Figure 10-21 DirectAccess Client GPO WMI Filter

DirectAccess Solution Component: NCA

The Network Connection Assistant (NCA) is an integrated part of Windows 8, Windows 8.1, and Windows 10. For Windows 7 SP1, it is an optional feature and must be deployed.

The NCA delivers status information about DirectAccess connections. The NCA service can be seen in the services console (Service name: NcaSvc). If the Direct-Access client is outside the corporate network, the DirectAccess client components are turned on. If the DirectAccess client is inside the corporate network, the Direct-Access client components are turned off. You can verify this status through NCA.

If you are running a version of Windows that is not Enterprise edition (with the exception of Windows 7 Ultimate and Windows 10 Education), DirectAccess will not work.

You can still provision non-Enterprise SKUs such as Windows 10 Professional for DirectAccess. All the DirectAccess settings will be applied without problems, but DirectAccess won't work.

The telltale sign on Windows 8.x and Windows 10 clients is that you won't be able to start the Network Connectivity Assistant (NCA) service (NcaSvc). When you attempt to do so, you will receive the following error message: "Failed to start service Network Connectivity Assistant (NcaSvc)."

When you set up the Basic DirectAccess server deployment, an HTTP Web Probe Host entry (http://DirectAccess-WebProbeHost.pearson.com) is added automatically to the resource list that validates connectivity to the internal network through the DirectAccess IPv6 IPsec tunnel. The NCA tries to reach all resources added into this list. When the NCA can reach the resource, the Network Connectivity Assistant is running and displays a status of Workplace Connection, as connected. Figure 10-22 shows the default NCA setting.

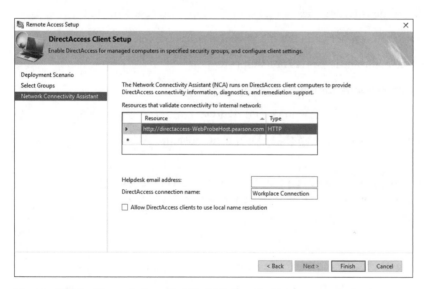

Figure 10-22   Network Connectivity Assistant Settings

Implement DirectAccess Server Requirements

Organizations might choose different DirectAccess server deployment options, depending on their business requirements. Deployment options vary from using the Getting Started Wizard for a simple deployment, to using advanced configuration options for a more complex deployment. This section explains a Basic DirectAccess deployment.

Basic DirectAccess Deployment

Deploying DirectAccess in a Basic DirectAccess deployment scenario means deploying DirectAccess configured with default settings. You use the DirectAccess Getting Started Wizard without configuring infrastructure settings such as CA or Active Directory security groups. To set up a Basic DirectAccess server, you must consider the following:

- Windows Firewall must be enabled on all profiles.

- This option works only with Windows 10, Windows 8.1, and Windows 8.

- A public key infrastructure is not required.

- Domain credentials are required for authentication.

- DirectAccess is automatically deployed to all mobile computers in the current domain.

- Traffic to the Internet does not go over the DirectAccess tunnel.

- The DirectAccess server is the Network Location Server.

- Two-factor authentication is not supported.

- Force tunnel configuration is not supported.

- If you are using ISATAP, you should remove it and use native IPv6.

- Network Access Protection (NAP) is not supported.

> **TIP** If some or all of your client computers are running Windows 7, you must use the Advanced Setup Wizard. The Getting Started Setup Wizard does not support client computers that are running Windows 7.

The basic DirectAccess deployment is divided into three phases:

Phase 1. Configuring the Basic DirectAccess infrastructure

Phase 2. Configuring Basic DirectAccess server

Phase 3. Verifying the Basic DirectAccess deployment

Configuring the Basic DirectAccess Infrastructure (Phase 1)

You must configure the infrastructure required for a Basic DirectAccess deployment using a single DirectAccess server in a mixed IP4/IPv6 environment. For that, you need to ensure that the following tasks are done:

Step 1. Configure the server network settings on the DirectAccess server.

Step 2. Configure routing in the corporate network to make sure traffic is appropriately routed.

Step 3. Configure additional firewalls, if required.

Step 4. Configure DNS settings for the DirectAccess server.

Step 5. Join client computers and the DirectAccess server to the Active Directory domain.

Step 6. Configure GPOs for the deployment, if required.

Step 7. Configure security groups that will contain DirectAccess client computers, as well as any other security groups required in the deployment.

The following sections examine these steps in more detail.

Configuring Server Network Settings

When you deploy the DirectAccess server in an Edge topology with direct connectivity to the internal network and the Internet, the DirectAccess server needs a minimum of two network cards, one with an Internet-facing public static IPv4 or IPv6 address and an internal network card with an internal static IPv4 or IPv6 address.

Suppose you want to use Teredo. You then must use two consecutive public IPv4 addresses. If you are not using Teredo, you can configure a single public static IPv4 address. When you deploy the DirectAccess server behind a NAT device with two network adapters, you need a single internal network-facing static IPv4 or IPv6 address and a single perimeter network-facing static IPv4 or IPv6 address. When you deploy the DirectAccess server behind NAT with one network adapter, you can install the DirectAccess server with only one network adapter with static IPv4 or IPv6 addresses.

TIP If the DirectAccess server has two or more network adapters (one classified in the domain profile and the other in a public/private profile), but you want to use a single NIC topology, then you must ensure that the second NIC, and any additional NICs, are also classified in the domain profile. If the second NIC cannot be configured for the domain profile for any reason, the DirectAccess IPsec policy must be manually scoped to all profiles using the following Windows PowerShell commands:

```
$gposession = Open-NetGPO -PolicyStore <Name of the server GPO>
Set-NetIPsecRule -DisplayName <Name of the IPsec policy>
  -GPOSession $gposession -Profile Any
Save-NetGPO -GPOSession $gposession
```

Configuring Routing

When you use native IPv6, add a route so that the routers on the internal network route IPv6 traffic back through the Remote Access server. You also have to manually configure organization IPv4 and IPv6 routes on the Remote Access servers. Add a published route so that all traffic with an organization (/48) IPv6 prefix is forwarded to the internal network. In addition, for IPv4 traffic, add explicit routes so that IPv4 traffic is forwarded to the internal network.

Configuring Firewalls

When using additional firewalls in your deployment, apply the following Internet-facing firewall exceptions for Remote Access traffic when the Remote Access server is on the IPv4 Internet. (This must be configured on the Remote Access server. All the other exceptions must be configured on the Edge firewall.) *Exception 1:* 6to4 traffic: IP Protocol 41 inbound and outbound. *Exception 2:* IP-HTTPS TCP destination port 443, TCP source port 443 outbound.

For Teredo and 6to4 traffic, these exceptions should be applied for both of the Internet-facing consecutive public IPv4 addresses on the Remote Access server. For IP-HTTPS, the exceptions need to be applied only for the address to which the external name of the server resolves.

TIP When the Remote Access server has a single network adapter and the Network Location Server is on the Remote Access server, then TCP port 62000 is also required.

When using additional firewalls, apply the following Internet-facing firewall exceptions for Remote Access traffic when the Remote Access server is on the IPv6 Internet:

- **Exception 1:** IP Protocol 50
- **Exception 2:** UDP destination port 500 inbound, UDP source port 500 outbound

When using additional firewalls, apply the following internal network firewall exceptions for Remote Access traffic:

- **Exception 1:** ISATAP Protocol 41 inbound and outbound
- **Exception 2:** TCP/UDP for all IPv4/IPv6 traffic

Configuring DNS Server

You must manually configure a DNS entry for the NLS in your deployment. You do so with the following steps:

Step 1.   On the internal network DNS server, run **dnsmgmt.msc** and then press Enter.

Step 2.   In the left pane of the DNS Manager console, expand the forward lookup zone for your domain. Right-click the domain and click **New Host (A or AAAA)**.

Step 3.   From the New Host dialog box, in the Name (Uses Parent Domain Name If Blank) box, enter the DNS name for the Network Location Server website (this is the name the DirectAccess clients use to connect to the Network Location Server). In the IP Address box, enter the IPv4 address of the Network Location Server and then click **Add Host**. In the DNS dialog box, click **OK**.

Step 4.   From the New Host dialog box, in the Name (Uses Parent Domain Name If Blank) box, enter the DNS name for the web probe (the name for the default web probe is directaccess-webprobehost). In the IP Address box, enter the IPv4 address of the web probe and then click **Add Host**. Repeat this process for directaccess-corpconnectivityhost and any manually created connectivity verifiers. In the DNS dialog box, click **OK**.

The following PowerShell commands perform the same steps:

```
Add-DnsServerResourceRecordA -Name <NLS_name> -ZoneName <DNS_zone_
  name> -IPv4Address <NLS_IPv4_address>
Add-DnsServerResourceRecordAAAA -Name <NLS_name> -ZoneName <DNS_zone_
  name> -IPv6Address <NLS_IPv6_address>
```

You also must configure DNS entries for the following:

- **IP-HTTPS server:** DirectAccess clients must be able to resolve the DNS name of the Remote Access server from the Internet.

- **CRL revocation checking:** DirectAccess uses certificate revocation checking for the IP-HTTPS connection between DirectAccess clients and the Direct-Access server, and for the HTTPS-based connection between the Direct-Access client and the NLS. In both cases, DirectAccess clients must be able to resolve and access the CRL distribution point location.

Configuring Active Directory

The Remote Access server and all DirectAccess client computers must be joined to an Active Directory domain. DirectAccess client computers must be a member of domains that belong to the same forest as the DirectAccess server, a forest with a two-way trust with the DirectAccess server forest, or domains that have a two-way domain trust to the DirectAccess server domain. To join the DirectAccess server to a domain, you perform the following steps:

Join the DirectAccess server to the domain:

Step 1.   In Server Manager, click **Local Server**. In the details pane, click the link next to **Computer Name.**

Step 2.   In the System Properties dialog box, click the **Computer Name** tab. On the Computer Name tab, click **Change**.

Step 3.   In Computer Name, type the name of the computer if you are also changing the computer name when joining the server to the domain. Under Member Of, click **Domain**; then type the name of the domain to which you want to join the server (for example, **corp.pearson.com**) and click **OK**.

Step 4.   When you are prompted for a username and password, enter the username and password of a user with rights to join computers to the domain, and then click **OK**.

Step 5.   When you see a dialog box welcoming you to the domain, click **OK**.

Step 6.   When you are prompted to restart the computer, click **OK**.

Step 7.   In the System Properties dialog box, click **Close**.

Step 8.   When you are prompted to restart the computer, click **Restart Now**.

Join clients to the domain:

Step 1.   Run explorer.exe.

Step 2.   Right-click the Computer icon, and then click **Properties**.

Step 3.   On the System page, click **Advanced System Settings**.

Step 4.   In the System Properties dialog box, on the Computer Name tab, click **Change**.

Step 5.   In Computer Name, type the name of the computer if you are also changing the computer name when joining the domain. Under Member Of, click **Domain**; then type the name of the domain you want to join (for example, **corp.pearson.com**) and click **OK**.

Step 6.   When you are prompted for a username and password, enter the username and password of a user with rights to join computers to the domain; then click **OK**.

Step 7.   When you see a dialog box welcoming you to the domain, click **OK**.

Step 8.   When you are prompted to restart the computer, click **OK**.

Step 9.   From the System Properties dialog box, click **Close**. Click **Restart Now** when prompted.

The following PowerShell command also performs the domain join:

```
Add-Computer -DomainName corp.pearson.com, Restart-Computer
```

Configuring GPOs

When you want to deploy DirectAccess, you need two Group Policy objects: one with settings for the DirectAccess server and one with settings for the DirectAccess clients. When you configure DirectAccess, the wizard automatically creates the required GPOs. However, if your organization enforces a naming convention or you do not have the required permissions to create or edit these GPOs, they must be created before configuring DirectAccess.

> **TIP**   Changing the DirectAccess GPOs by using a feature other than the DirectAccess management console or Windows PowerShell cmdlets is not supported.

The DirectAccess client Group Policy settings are explained in the next sections.

DirectAccess Client GPO Settings: Certificates

Figure 10-23 shows the default DirectAccess-IP-HTTPS certificate with the automatically applied name for the default certificate DirectAccess-NLS.pearson.com with a purpose of Server Authentication.

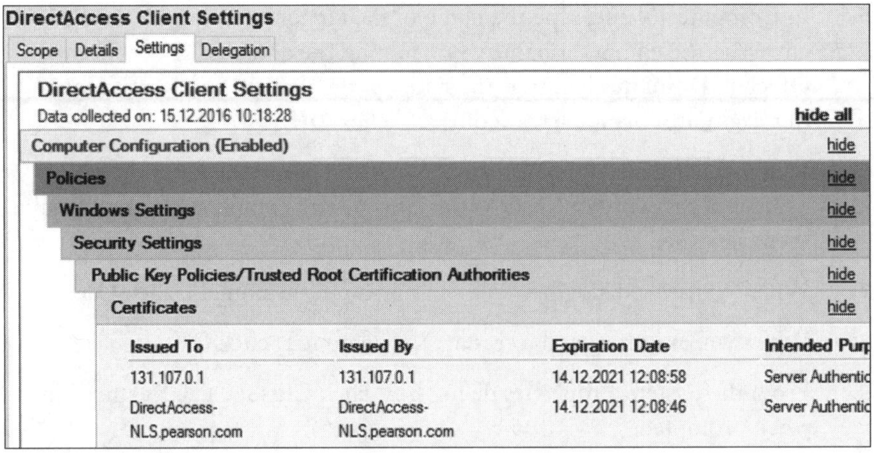

Figure 10-23 DirectAccess Client GPO Certificate Settings

In a production environment, the Issued To field of the certificate contains the FQDN of the Edge DirectAccess server with the public name (for example, edge. external.com). The DirectAccess client must resolve this public name to the IP address of the external interface of the DirectAccess server. In this example, the external IP address is also the name of the certificate and the DirectAccess client does not have to resolve an external public name to find that certificate. The second certificate in the list is the SSL certificate for the NLS server installed on the DirectAccess server itself (self-signed certificate).

DirectAccess Client GPO Settings: Windows Firewall with Advanced Security

Figure 10-24 shows the necessary Windows Firewall settings for the DirectAccess clients. By default, the DirectAccess Setup Wizard allows ICMP traffic for both IPv4 and IPv6 as a firewall exemption so that a ping is possible beside the IPv6 tunnel. The Core Networking–IPHTTPS (TCP-Out) firewall rule allows outbound IPHTTPS tunneling to provide connectivity across HTTP proxies and firewalls.

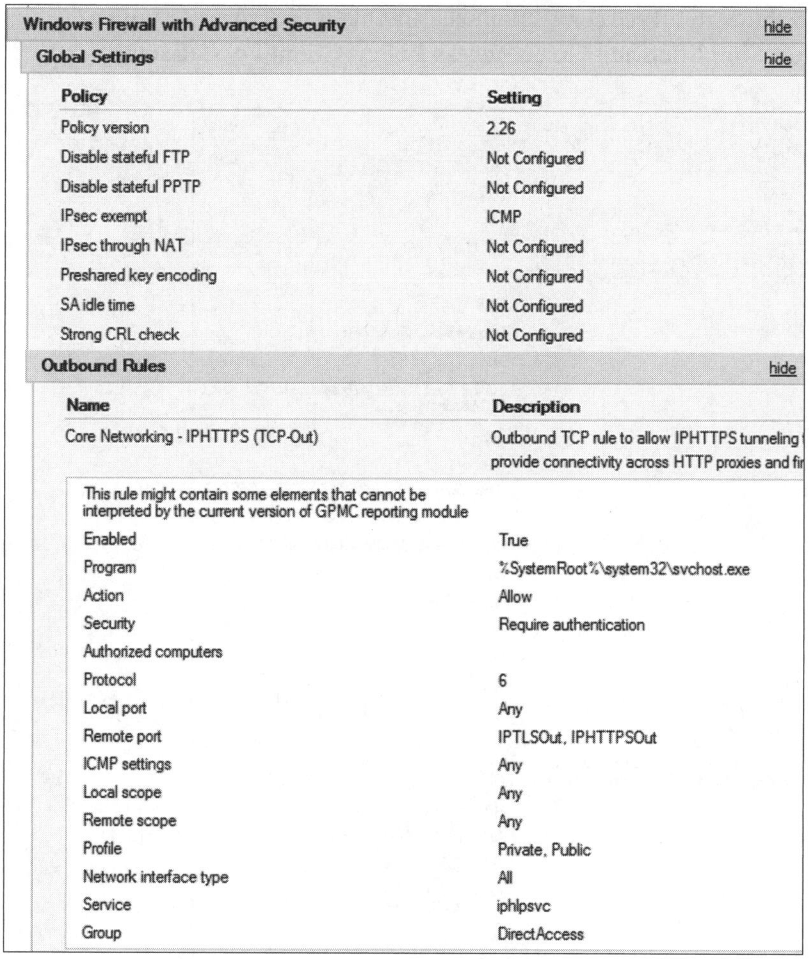

Windows Firewall with Advanced Security	hide

Global Settings	hide

Policy	Setting
Policy version	2.26
Disable stateful FTP	Not Configured
Disable stateful PPTP	Not Configured
IPsec exempt	ICMP
IPsec through NAT	Not Configured
Preshared key encoding	Not Configured
SA idle time	Not Configured
Strong CRL check	Not Configured

Outbound Rules	hide

Name	Description
Core Networking - IPHTTPS (TCP-Out)	Outbound TCP rule to allow IPHTTPS tunneling provide connectivity across HTTP proxies and fir

This rule might contain some elements that cannot be interpreted by the current version of GPMC reporting module

Enabled	True
Program	%SystemRoot%\system32\svchost.exe
Action	Allow
Security	Require authentication
Authorized computers	
Protocol	6
Local port	Any
Remote port	IPTLSOut, IPHTTPSOut
ICMP settings	Any
Local scope	Any
Remote scope	Any
Profile	Private, Public
Network interface type	All
Service	iphlpsvc
Group	DirectAccess

Figure 10-24   DirectAccess Client GPO Windows Firewall with Advanced Security Settings (1)

Figure 10-25 shows the IPsec connection security rules **DirectAccess Policy-ClientToCorpSimplified** and **DirectAccess Policy-ClientToNlaExempt**.

Connection Security Settings	hide
Rules	hide

Name	Description
DirectAccess Policy-ClientToCorpSimplified	

This rule might contain some elements that cannot be interpreted by the current version of GPMC reporting module	
Enabled	True
Authentication mode	Require inbound and outbound
Endpoint 1	Any
Endpoint 2	2002:836b:1:1::/64, fd26:8af3:9a1:7777::/96, 2002:836b:1:3333::1
Endpoint 1 port	Any
Endpoint 2 port	Any
First authentication	{0F6566F4-EE15-4698-9A87-FFC80C6CFCD2}
Second authentication	{AB05D7DE-0235-419C-9AFE-8F0D862E7935}
Data protection	{2A7A63FD-B8AC-4834-A4A6-78BA8BD2158F}
Protocol	Any
Profile	Private, Public
Tunnel endpoint 1	Any
Tunnel endpoint 2	Any
Network interface type	Any

DirectAccess Policy-ClientToNlaExempt	

This rule might contain some elements that cannot be interpreted by the current version of GPMC reporting module	
Enabled	True
Authentication mode	Do not authenticate
Endpoint 1	2002:836b:1:1::/64
Endpoint 2	fd26:8af3:9a1:7777::ac10:7a, 2002:836b:1:1:0:5efe:172.16.0.122
Endpoint 1 port	Any
Endpoint 2 port	443
Protocol	6
Profile	Private, Public
Tunnel endpoint 1	Any
Tunnel endpoint 2	Any
Network interface type	Any

Figure 10-25   DirectAccess Client GPO Windows Firewall with Advanced Security Settings (2)

Figure 10-26 shows the IPsec connection security rule **DirectAccess Policy-ClientToDNS64NAT64PrefixExemption** and the authentication sets. Consider that Kerberos is used as an authentication method. Using Kerberos through the KDC Proxy to authenticate the DirectAccess client through the internal domain controller was a great improvement because as of Windows 8, DirectAccess clients no longer need a client certificate for this. This reduces administrative effort.

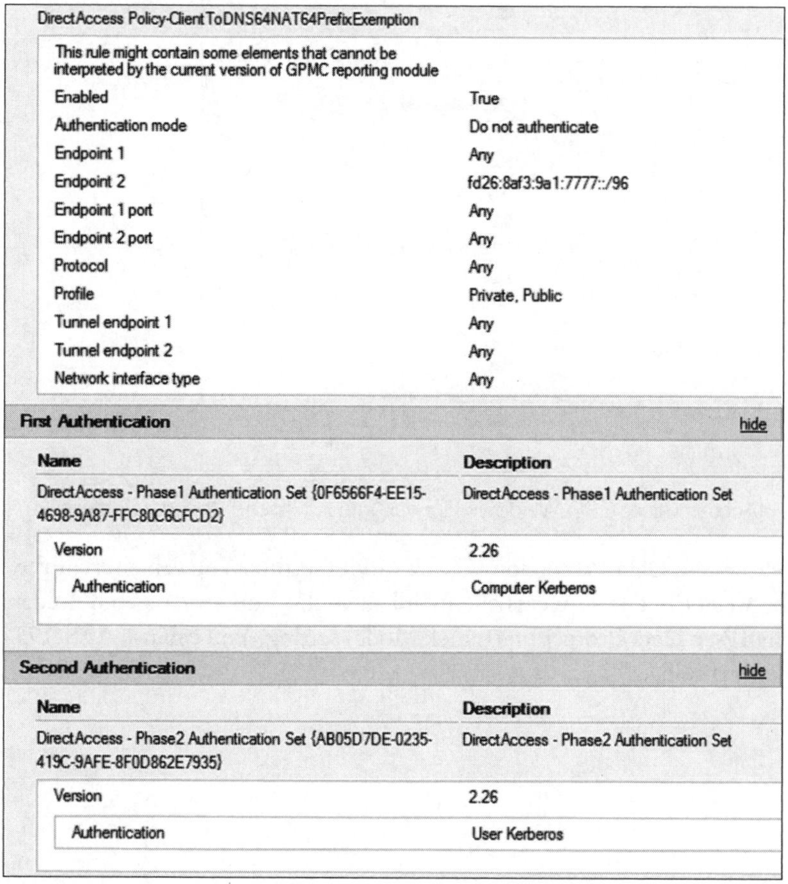

DirectAccess Policy-ClientToDNS64NAT64PrefixExemption

This rule might contain some elements that cannot be interpreted by the current version of GPMC reporting module

Enabled	True
Authentication mode	Do not authenticate
Endpoint 1	Any
Endpoint 2	fd26:8af3:9a1:7777::/96
Endpoint 1 port	Any
Endpoint 2 port	Any
Protocol	Any
Profile	Private, Public
Tunnel endpoint 1	Any
Tunnel endpoint 2	Any
Network interface type	Any

First Authentication   hide

Name	Description
DirectAccess - Phase1 Authentication Set {0F6566F4-EE15-4698-9A87-FFC80C6CFCD2}	DirectAccess - Phase1 Authentication Set
Version	2.26
Authentication	Computer Kerberos

Second Authentication   hide

Name	Description
DirectAccess - Phase2 Authentication Set {AB05D7DE-0235-419C-9AFE-8F0D862E7935}	DirectAccess - Phase2 Authentication Set
Version	2.26
Authentication	User Kerberos

Figure 10-26 DirectAccess Client GPO Windows Firewall with Advanced Security Settings (3)

Figure 10-27 shows the encryption algorithms for DirectAccess. The encryption methods AES-128 and 3DES are configured.

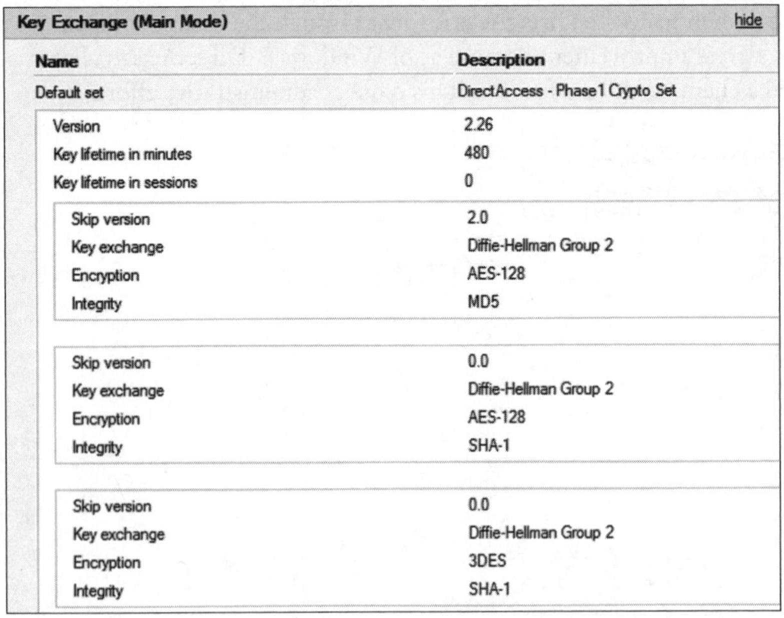

Key Exchange (Main Mode)	hide
Name	**Description**
Default set	DirectAccess - Phase1 Crypto Set
Version	2.26
Key lifetime in minutes	480
Key lifetime in sessions	0
Skip version	2.0
Key exchange	Diffie-Hellman Group 2
Encryption	AES-128
Integrity	MD5
Skip version	0.0
Key exchange	Diffie-Hellman Group 2
Encryption	AES-128
Integrity	SHA-1
Skip version	0.0
Key exchange	Diffie-Hellman Group 2
Encryption	3DES
Integrity	SHA-1

Figure 10-27   DirectAccess Client GPO Windows Firewall with Advanced Security Settings (4)

Figure 10-28 shows the Data Protection (Quick Mode) setting. You can encrypt the data payload between the DirectAccess client and an application server as required by changing the IPsec Data Protection (Quick Mode) setting. You can use AES-192 and AES-128 encryption.

Data Protection (Quick Mode)	hide
Name	**Description**
DirectAccess - Phase2 Crypto Set {2A7A63FD-B8AC-4834-A4A6-78BA8BD2158F}	DirectAccess - Phase2 Crypto Set
Version	2.26
Perfect forward secrecy	Disabled
Skip version	0.0
Protocol	ESP
Encryption	AES-192
ESP integrity	SHA-1
Key lifetime in minutes	60
Key lifetime in kilobytes	100000
Skip version	0.0
Protocol	ESP
Encryption	AES-128
ESP integrity	SHA-1
Key lifetime in minutes	60
Key lifetime in kilobytes	100000

Figure 10-28   DirectAccess Client GPO Windows Firewall with Advanced Security Settings (5)

DirectAccess Client GPO Settings: Name Resolution Policy

Figure 10-29 shows the NRPT settings. Consider the Query Failure setting under Global Settings: Always Fail Back to Link-Local-Multicast Name. When a DNS server is unreachable for name resolution, the DirectAccess client fails back to NLMNR in this case. Under Rule Settings, you see the NRPT entries pearson.com and DirectAccess-NLS.pearson.com, as well as the IPv6 address of the DNS server to resolve the name pearson.com.

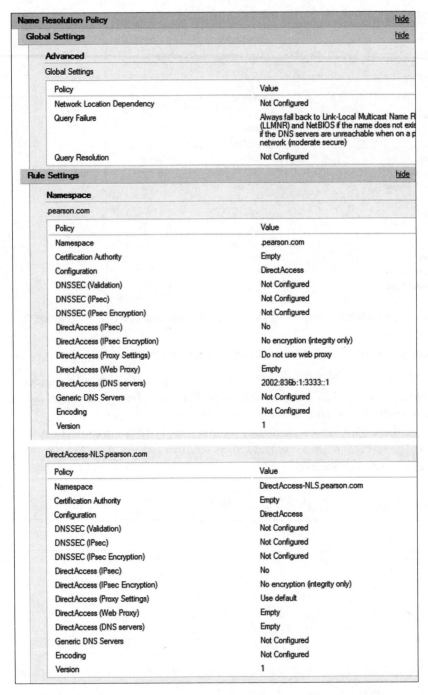

Name Resolution Policy	hide
Global Settings	hide

Advanced

Global Settings

Policy	Value
Network Location Dependency	Not Configured
Query Failure	Always fall back to Link-Local Multicast Name R (LLMNR) and NetBIOS if the name does not exis if the DNS servers are unreachable when on a p network (moderate secure)
Query Resolution	Not Configured

Rule Settings	hide

Namespace

.pearson.com

Policy	Value
Namespace	.pearson.com
Certification Authority	Empty
Configuration	DirectAccess
DNSSEC (Validation)	Not Configured
DNSSEC (IPsec)	Not Configured
DNSSEC (IPsec Encryption)	Not Configured
DirectAccess (IPsec)	No
DirectAccess (IPsec Encryption)	No encryption (integrity only)
DirectAccess (Proxy Settings)	Do not use web proxy
DirectAccess (Web Proxy)	Empty
DirectAccess (DNS servers)	2002:836b:1:3333::1
Generic DNS Servers	Not Configured
Encoding	Not Configured
Version	1

DirectAccess-NLS.pearson.com

Policy	Value
Namespace	DirectAccess-NLS.pearson.com
Certification Authority	Empty
Configuration	DirectAccess
DNSSEC (Validation)	Not Configured
DNSSEC (IPsec)	Not Configured
DNSSEC (IPsec Encryption)	Not Configured
DirectAccess (IPsec)	No
DirectAccess (IPsec Encryption)	No encryption (integrity only)
DirectAccess (Proxy Settings)	Use default
DirectAccess (Web Proxy)	Empty
DirectAccess (DNS servers)	Empty
Generic DNS Servers	Not Configured
Encoding	Not Configured
Version	1

Figure 10-29   DirectAccess Client GPO Name Resolution Policy Settings

DirectAccess Client GPO Settings: Network/DirectAccess Client Experience Settings

Figure 10-30 shows where the DirectAccess client can approve the WebProbeHost record on the DNS server, the friendly name for a successful DirectAccess connection, and the IPsec tunnel endpoints. Figure 10-31 shows how a successful DirectAccess connection is displayed in Windows.

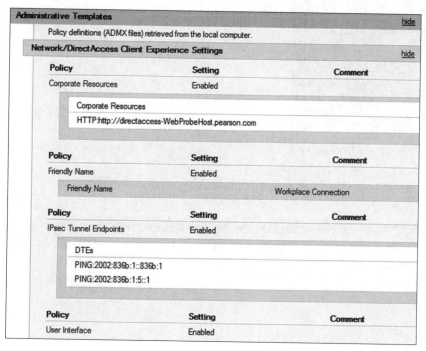

Figure 10-30   DirectAccess Client GPO Network/DirectAccess Client Experience Settings

Figure 10-31   Workplace Connection

DirectAccess Client GPO Settings: Network/Network Connectivity Status Indicator

Figure 10-32 shows the corporate DNS probe host address, probe hostname, site prefix list, website probe URL, and domain location determination URL (URL to the NLS server).

Network/Network Connectivity Status Indicator   hide

Policy	Setting	Comment
Specify corporate DNS probe host address	Enabled	

Corporate DNS Probe Address:	fd26:8af3:9a1:7777::7f00:1
Specify the expected DNS address for the corporate host name to probe.	
Example:	
2001:4898:28:3:38a1:c31:7b3d:bf0	

Policy	Setting	Comment
Specify corporate DNS probe host name	Enabled	

Corporate DNS Probe Hostname:	directaccess-corpConnectivityHost.pearson.c
Specify a corporate host name to resolve to probe for corporate connectivity.	
Example:	
ncsi.corp.microsoft.com	

Policy	Setting	Comment
Specify corporate site prefix list	Enabled	

Corporate Site Prefix List:	2002:836b:1:1::/64,fd26:8af3:9a1:7777::/96 ::836b:1/128,2002:836b:1:5::1/128
Specify the list of corporate IPv6 site prefixes to check for reachability to detect corporate connectivity.	
Syntax:	
The list should be comma-separated with no extra whitespace.	
Example:	
fe80::/9,fe81::/9	

Policy	Setting	Comment
Specify corporate Website probe URL	Enabled	

Corporate Website Probe URL:	http://directaccess-WebProbeHost.pearson.
Specify the URL of the corporate website to use to probe for corporate connectivity.	
Example:	
http://ncsi.corp.microsoft.com/	

Policy	Setting	Comment
Specify domain location determination URL	Enabled	

Corporate Domain Location Determination URL:	https://DirectAccess-NLS.pearson.com:443
Specify the HTTPS URL of the corporate website to use to determine inside or outside domain location.	
Example:	
https://nid.corp.microsoft.com/	

Figure 10-32 DirectAccess Client GPO Network/Network Connectivity Status Indicator Settings

DirectAccess Client GPO Settings: Network/TCPIP Settings/IPv6 Transition Technologies

Figure 10-33 shows the IPHTTPS state and the URL to the KDC Proxy service on the DirectAccess server. Instead of using a public name such as edge.pearson.com, here an IP address is used. In production environments, you must use an FQDN with another suffix, such as the internal domain name.

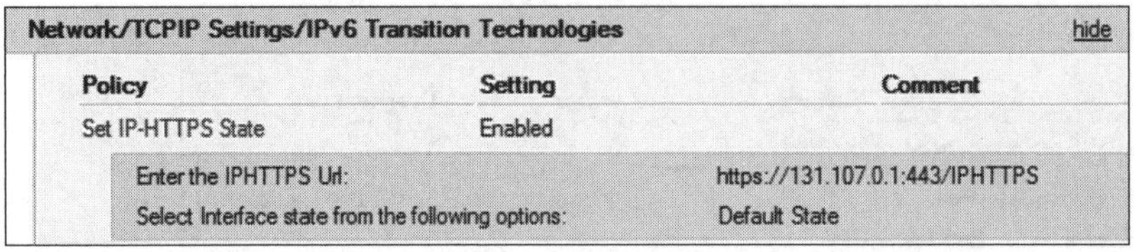

Network/TCPIP Settings/IPv6 Transition Technologies		hide
Policy	**Setting**	**Comment**
Set IP-HTTPS State	Enabled	
Enter the IPHTTPS Url:		https://131.107.0.1:443/IPHTTPS
Select Interface state from the following options:		Default State

Figure 10-33 DirectAccess Client GPO Network/TCPIP and IPv6 Transition Technologies Settings

DirectAccess Client GPO Settings: Security/Kerberos

Figure 10-34 shows that, in a Basic DirectAccess deployment, revocation checking is disabled by default for the self-signed KDC Proxy IP-HTTPS certificate. If security is important for your company, you must use a signed certificate with revocation checking enabled.

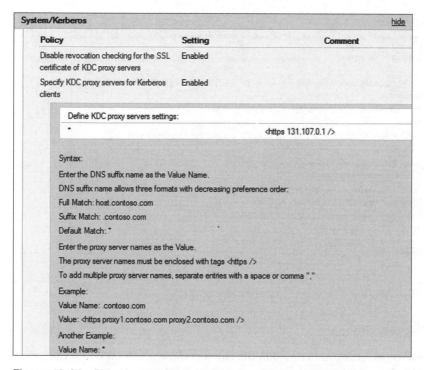

Figure 10-34 DirectAccess Client GPO System/Kerberos Settings

DirectAccess Client GPO Settings: Extra Registry Settings

Figure 10-35 shows the DirectAccess Client GPO Extra Registry settings.

TIP If the GPOs are created manually, they might not be available during Direct-Access configuration. They might not have been replicated to the closest domain controller to the management computer. In this event, the administrator can either wait for replication to complete or force the replication.

Extra Registry Settings	hide

Display names for some settings cannot be found. You might be able to resolve this issue by updating the .ADM files used by Group Policy Management.

Setting	State
SOFTWARE\Policies\Microsoft\Windows\RemoteAccess\Config\GlobalVersion	{47F0EB8D-C285-44CC-AFF6-C11246B51737}
SOFTWARE\Policies\Microsoft\Windows\RemoteAccess\Config\SiteVersion	{47F0EB8D-C285-44CC-AFF6-C11246B51737}
SOFTWARE\Policies\Microsoft\Windows\RemoteAccess\Config\TimeStamp	20161214100902.965000+000
SOFTWARE\Policies\Microsoft\Windows\Tcpip\v6Transition\IPHTTPS\iphttpsinterface\InterfaceRole	0
SOFTWARE\Policies\Microsoft\Windows\Tcpip\v6Transition\IPHTTPS\iphttpsinterface\IPHTTPS_NoRevocationCheck	1
SYSTEM\CurrentControlSet\services\LanmanWorkstation\Parameters\SMB1NATCompatibilityLevel	1

User Configuration (Disabled)	hide

No settings defined.

Figure 10-35   DirectAccess Client GPO Extra Registry Settings

Configuring Security Groups

The DirectAccess settings contained in the client computer Group Policy objects are applied only to computers that are members of the security groups you specify when configuring Remote Access.

To create a security group for DirectAccess clients, follow these steps:

Step 1.   Run dsa.msc. In the left pane of the Active Directory Users and Computers console, expand the domain that will contain the security group, right-click **Users**, point to **New**, and then click **Group**.

Step 2.   On the New Object–Group dialog box, under Group name, enter the name for the security group.

Step 3.   Under Group Scope, click **Global**; under Group Type, click **Security**; and then click **OK**.

Step 4.   Double-click the DirectAccess client computers security group and, on the properties dialog box, click the **Members** tab.

Step 5.   On the Members tab, click **Add**.

Step 6.   In the Select Users, Contacts, Computers, or Service Accounts dialog box, select the client computers that you want to enable for DirectAccess; then click **OK**.

The following PowerShell commands perform the same steps:

```
New-ADGroup -GroupScope global -Name <DirectAccess_clients_group_name>
Add-ADGroupMember -Identity DirectAccess_clients_group_name -Members
   <computer_name>
```

Configuring Basic DirectAccess Server (Phase 2)

You can continue the DirectAccess server configuration with the installation of the RemoteAccess role and the DirectAccess Getting Started Wizard. Here you configure DirectAccess settings and create the necessary DirectAccess Group Policies through PowerShell scripts (in the background).

Installing the Remote Access Role

To deploy DirectAccess, you must install the Remote Access role on a server in your organization that will act as the DirectAccess server. The following steps are necessary to install the Remote Access role:

Step 1. On the Remote Access server, in the Server Manager console, in the Dashboard, click **Add Roles and Features**.

Step 2. Click **Next** three times to get to the server role selection screen.

Step 3. From the Select Server Roles dialog box, select **Remote Access** and then click **Next**.

Step 4. From the Select Features dialog box, click **Next**.

Step 5. Click **Next** and then, from the Select Role Services dialog box, click the **DirectAccess and VPN (RAS)** check box.

Step 6. Click **Add Features**, click **Next**, and then click **Install**.

Step 7. From the Installation Progress dialog box, verify that the installation was successful; then click **Close**.

The following PowerShell commands perform the same steps:

```
Install-WindowsFeature RemoteAccess -IncludeManagementTools
```

Configuring DirectAccess with the Getting Started Wizard

The following steps are necessary to configure DirectAccess with the Getting Started Wizard:

Step 1.   In Server Manager, click **Tools** and then click **Remote Access Management**.

Step 2.   In the Remote Access Management console, select the role service to configure in the left navigation pane, and then click **Run the Getting Started Wizard**.

Step 3.   Click **Deploy DirectAccess Only**. Figure 10-36 shows the Configure Remote Access page of the Getting Started Wizard.

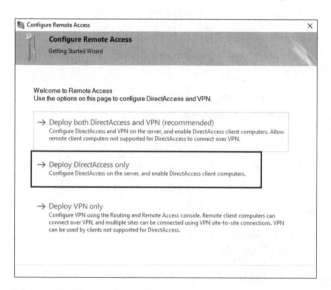

Figure 10-36   Configure Remote Access Page of the Getting Started Wizard

Step 4.   Select the topology of your network configuration and type the public name to which Remote Access clients will connect. Click **Next**. Figure 10-37 shows the Configure DirectAccess and VPN Settings page of the Getting Started Wizard.

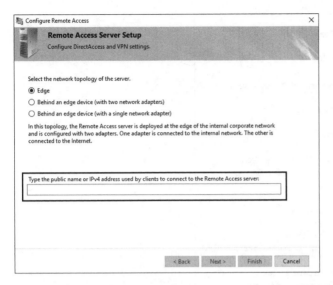

Figure 10-37   Configure DirectAccess and VPN Settings Page of the Getting Started Wizard

Step 5.   Click **Finish**.

Step 6.   Because no PKI is used in this deployment, if certificates are not found, the wizard automatically provisions self-signed certificates for IP-HTTPS and the Network Location Server and also automatically enables Kerberos proxy. In addition, the wizard enables NAT64 and DNS64 for protocol translation in the IPv4-only environment. When the wizard successfully applies the configuration, click **Close**. Figure 10-38 shows all configuration steps the Getting Started Wizard applies.

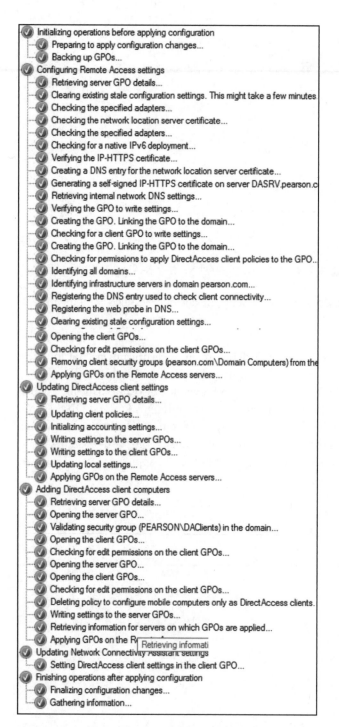

Figure 10-38 DirectAccess Getting Started Wizard GPO Configuration Steps

Step 7.   In the console tree of the Remote Access Management console, select **Operations Status**. Wait until the status of all monitors display as Working. In the Tasks pane, under Monitoring, click **Refresh** periodically to update the display. Figure 10-39 shows a successful Operations Status.

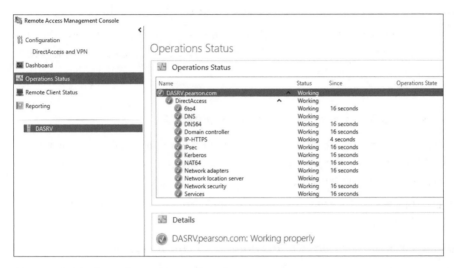

Figure 10-39   DirectAccess Operations Status

TIP   By default, the Getting Started Wizard deploys DirectAccess to all mobile devices in the domain by applying a WMI filter to the client settings GPO. In the wizard on the DirectAccess Client Setup page, the setting Enable DirectAccess for Mobile Computers Only is activated by default. This setting creates the WMI filter, which filters all domain devices with a battery.

CAUTION   If you perform tests with VMs as DirectAccess clients, remember that a VM does not have a battery. When the VM is a member of the selected security group and the Enable DirectAccess for Mobile Computers Only is also selected, the VM cannot apply the DirectAccess client GPO settings. For those testing scenarios, you must disable this setting.

Updating Clients with the DirectAccess Configuration

The following steps are necessary to update the DirectAccess clients with its DirectAccess client configurations:

Step 1.   Open PowerShell as an administrator.

Step 2.   In the PowerShell window, type **gpupdate** and then press Enter.

Step 3.   Wait for the computer policy update to complete successfully.

Step 4.   Type **Get-DnsClientNrptPolicy** and then press Enter.

Step 5.   Type **Get-NCSIPolicyConfiguration** and then press Enter.

Step 6.   Type **Get-DAConnectionStatus** and then press Enter. Because the client can reach the Network Location Server URL, the status displays as ConnectedLocally.

Verifying the Basic DirectAccess Deployment (Phase 3)

To verify that you have correctly configured your Basic DirectAccess deployment and the DirectAccess client has successfully established a DirectAccess IPv6 IPsec tunnel, perform the following steps:

Step 1.   Connect a DA client computer to the corporate network and obtain the Group Policy.

Step 2.   Click the **Network Connections** icon in the notification area.

Step 3.   Click the **DirectAccess Connection**. You will see the status Connected Locally.

Step 4.   Connect the client computer to the external network and attempt to access internal resources. You should be able to access all corporate resources.

Advanced DirectAccess Deployment

DirectAccess can be deployed in many different scenarios. The most used follow:

- Deploy a single DirectAccess server using the Getting Started Wizard.
- Deploy a single DirectAccess server with Advanced Settings.
- Deploy DirectAccess in a cluster.
- Deploy multiple DirectAccess servers in a multisite deployment.
- Deploy DirectAccess with OTP authentication.
- Deploy DirectAccess in a multiforest environment.
- Manage DirectAccess clients remotely (managed-out clients).
- Deploy Windows Server 2016 DirectAccess using Microsoft Azure.

The following list describes the most important prerequisites when deploying a single DirectAccess server using the Getting Started Wizard:

- Windows Firewall must be enabled on all profiles.

- This deployment is supported only for clients running Windows 10, Windows 8.1 Enterprise, Windows 8 Enterprise, and Windows 7 Ultimate.

- A public key infrastructure is not required.

- This option is not supported for deploying two-factor authentication. Domain credentials are required for authentication.

- DirectAccess is automatically deployed to all mobile computers in the current domain.

- Traffic to the Internet does not go through DirectAccess. Force tunnel configuration is not supported.

- DirectAccess server is the Network Location Server.

- Network Access Protection (NAP) is not supported.

- Changing policies by using a feature other than the DirectAccess management console or Windows PowerShell cmdlets is not supported.

The following list describes the most important prerequisites when deploying a single DirectAccess server with Advanced Settings:

- A public key infrastructure must be deployed.

- Windows Firewall must be enabled on all profiles.

- Force tunnel configuration is not supported with KerbProxy authentication.

- Changing policies by using a feature other than the DirectAccess management console or Windows PowerShell cmdlets is not supported.

- Separating NAT64/DNS64 and IPHTTPS server roles on another server is not supported.

The following list describes the most important prerequisites when deploying a DirectAccess server in a cluster:

- Default load balancing is through the Network Load Balancing (NLB) feature in Windows Server.

- External load balancers are supported.

- Unicast mode is the default and recommended mode for NLB.

- Changing policies by using a feature other than the DirectAccess management console or Windows PowerShell cmdlets is not supported.

- When NLB or an external load balancer is used, the IPHTTPS prefix must remain /59.

- Load-balanced nodes must be in the same IPv4 subnet.

- In external load balancer deployments, if remote management is needed, DirectAccess clients cannot use Teredo. Only IPHTTPS can be used for end-to-end communication.

- All known hotfixes for NLB external load balancing must be installed.

The following list describes the most important prerequisites when deploying DirectAccess servers in a multisite deployment:

- Clients running Windows 7 always connect to a specific site. They cannot connect to the closest site based on the location of the client (unlike clients running Windows 10, Windows 8.1, and Windows 8).

- One-time password authentication does not support a PIN change.

- A public key infrastructure must be deployed.

- Changing policies by using a feature other than the DirectAccess management console or Windows PowerShell cmdlets is not supported.

The following list describes the most important prerequisites when deploying a DirectAccess server with OTP authentication:

- Clients running Windows 7 Enterprise and Windows 7 Ultimate must use DCA 2.0 to support one-time password authentication.

- One-time password authentication does not support a PIN change.

- A public key infrastructure must be deployed.

- Changing policies by using a feature other than the DirectAccess management console or Windows PowerShell cmdlets is not supported.

The most important prerequisite when deploying DirectAccess servers in a multi-forest environment is that two-way trust is required.

The following list describes the most important prerequisites when managing DirectAccess clients remotely:

- Windows Firewall must be enabled on all profiles.

- Computers that are running the following operating systems are supported as DirectAccess clients. Note that only Windows operating systems support DirectAccess:

  - Windows Server 2016

  - Windows 10 Enterprise

  - Windows Server 2012 R2

  - Windows 8.1 Enterprise

  - Windows Server 2012

  - Windows 8 Enterprise

  - Windows Server 2008 R2

  - Windows 7 Ultimate

  - Windows 7 Enterprise

- Changing policies by using a feature other than the DirectAccess management console or Windows PowerShell cmdlets is not supported.

The following list describes the most important prerequisites when deploying Windows Server 2016 DirectAccess using Microsoft Azure:

- The minimum Azure VM resources include four cores, single or multiple NICs, a static private and ILPIP address, an Azure network security group (NSG), and inbound HTTPS allow rule (443).

- When you install the DirectAccess server in the Azure VM, you might get the error message "One or more network adapters should be configured with a static IP address. Obtain a static address and assign it to the adapter." You can ignore it because Azure handles all IP address assignment for hosted VMs.

- You cannot enable NLB for DirectAccess.

- You cannot use an external Azure load balancer.

- You cannot use manage-out support because IPv6 or ISATAP is not supported in Azure.

DirectAccess PowerShell Cmdlets

Table 10-6 lists and explains all of these cmdlets.

Table 10-6   Windows Server 2016 DirectAccess PowerShell Cmdlets

Cmdlet	Description
Add-DAAppServer	Adds a new application server security group to the DirectAccess (DA) deployment.
Add-DAClient	Adds one or more client computer security groups (SGs) to the DA deployment, adds one or more DA client GPOs in one or more domains, adds one or more SGs of down-level clients to the DA deployment in a multisite deployment, or adds one or more down-level DA client GPOs in one or more domains in a multisite deployment.
Add-DAClientDnsConfiguration	Adds the specified DNS suffix, DNS server addresses, or proxy server set to the NRPT.
Add-DAEntryPoint	Adds an entry point to a multisite deployment.
Add-DAMgmtServer	Adds the specified management servers to the DA deployment.
Add-DnsClientNrptRule	Adds a rule to the NRPT.
Disable-DAManualEntryPointSelection	Disables a manually selected DirectAccess site and reverts the selection to the default.
Disable-DAMultiSite	Disables a multisite deployment that contains a single entry point.
Disable-DAOtpAuthentication	Disables OTP authentication for DA users.
Enable-DAManualEntryPointSelection	Allows a user to manually choose which DirectAccess entry point to use for connectivity.
Enable-DAMultiSite	Enables and configures a multisite deployment, and adds the first entry point.
Enable-DAOtpAuthentication	Enables and configures OTP authentication for DA users.
Get-DAAppServer	Displays the list of application server security groups that are part of the DA deployment and the properties of the connections made to the application servers in the groups.
Get-DAClient	Displays the list of client security groups that are part of the DA deployment and the client properties.

Cmdlet	Description
Get-DAClientDnsConfiguration	Displays all the NRPT entries and the local name resolution property.
Get-DAClientExperienceConfiguration	Gets the configuration for the DirectAccess client user experience.
Get-DAConnectionStatus	Returns the DirectAccess status of the user.
Get-DAEntryPoint	Displays the settings for an entry point.
Get-DAEntryPointDC	Retrieves a list of entry points and the associated domain controllers (DC).
Get-DAEntryPointTableItem	Gets the list of entry points that have been configured for DirectAccess.
Get-DAMgmtServer	Displays the configured management servers. *Management server* here refers to update servers, domain controllers, and other servers.
Get-DAMultiSite	Retrieves global settings applied to all entry points in a multisite deployment.
Get-DANetworkLocationServer	Displays the detailed NLS configuration.
Get-DAOtpAuthentication	Displays OTP authentication settings for DA.
Get-DAPolicyChange	Gets a list of IP addresses that need to be added and deleted to an IPsec rule based on the differences detected between the IP addresses for the existing rule and the IP addresses derived from the input parameters. The cmdlet then creates a Windows PowerShell script (.ps1) that updates the IPsec rule in the appropriate policy stores.
Get-DAServer	Displays the properties of the DA server.
Get-DnsClientNrptGlobal	Gets the NRPT global settings.
Get-DnsClientNrptPolicy	Gets the NRPT configured on a computer.
Get-DnsClientNrptRule	Retrieves the DNS client NRPT rules.
New-DAEntryPointTableItem	Configures a new entry point for multisite DirectAccess.
Remove-DAAppServer	Removes the specified list of application server SG from the DA deployment, removes the specified application servers from the specified DA application server SG, and removes the application server GPO in the specified domains.

Cmdlet	Description
Remove-DAClient	Removes one or more client computer SGs from the DA deployment, removes one or more DA client GPOs from domains, removes one or more SGs of down-level clients (down-level clients can connect only to the specified site) from the DA deployment in a multisite deployment, and removes one or more down-level DA client GPOs from domains in a multisite deployment.
Remove-DAClientDnsConfiguration	Removes the NRPT entry corresponding to the specified DNS suffix from the NRPT.
Remove-DAEntryPoint	Removes an entry point from a multisite deployment.
Remove-DAEntryPointTableItem	Removes a DirectAccess entry point from the specified configuration store.
Remove-DAMgmtServer	Removes the specified management servers from the DA deployment.
Remove-DnsClientNrptRule	Removes the specified DNS client NRPT rule.
Rename-DAEntryPointTableItem	Renames a DirectAccess entry point.
Reset-DAClientExperienceConfiguration	Restores the specified DirectAccess client configuration to the defaults.
Reset-DAEntryPointTableItem	Resets the specified DirectAccess entry point configuration to the default configuration.
Set-DAAppServerConnection	Configures the properties of the connection to application servers and the IPsec security traffic protection policies for the connection.
Set-DAClient	Configures the properties related to a DA client.
Set-DAClientDnsConfiguration	Configures the DNS server and proxy server addresses of an NRPT entry and configures the local name resolution property.
Set-DAClientExperienceConfiguration	Modifies the configuration of the specified DirectAccess client user experience.
Set-DAEntryPoint	Configures settings for the entry point.
Set-DAEntryPointDC	Modifies DC settings for the entry point.
Set-DAEntryPointTableItem	Modifies the configuration of a DirectAccess entry point stored in a Group Policy Object.
Set-DAMultiSite	Configures global settings for all entry points in a multisite deployment.

Cmdlet	Description
Set-DANetworkLocationServer	Configures the NLS.
Set-DAOtpAuthentication	Configures OTP authentication settings for DA.
Set-DAServer	Sets the properties specific to the DA server.
Set-DnsClientNrptGlobal	Modifies the global NRPT settings
Set-DnsClientNrptRule	Modifies a DNS client NRPT rule for the specified namespace.
Update-DAMgmtServer	Updates the list of Management servers of the DA deployment.

Implement DirectAccess Client Requirements

The requirements for implementing a DirectAccess client are as follows:

- A DirectAccess client can be any domain-joined computer that is running an Enterprise edition of Windows 10, Windows 8.1, Windows 8, or Windows 7.

- The DirectAccess client computer must connect to the DirectAccess server by using IPv6 and IPsec.

- If a native IPv6 network is not available, the client establishes an IPv6-over-IPv4 tunnel by using 6to4 or Teredo. Note that the user does not have to be logged on to the computer for this step to complete.

- If a firewall or proxy server prevents the client computer using 6to4 or Teredo from connecting to the DirectAccess server, the client computer automatically attempts to connect by using the IP-HTTPS protocol, which uses an SSL connection to the DirectAccess server.

- The Getting Started Wizard on the DirectAccess server creates a set of GPOs and settings for DirectAccess clients. The DirectAccess clients get all settings from these GPOs.

- When you deploy multiple endpoints, the DirectAccess client computer automatically selects the closest endpoint if it is running Windows 10, Windows 8.1, or Windows 8. For DirectAccess client computers running Windows 7, you must specify the endpoint manually.

- DirectAccess client computers can connect to DirectAccess servers located in different domains.

- You cannot use 6to4 for DirectAccess if clients are located behind an IPv4 NAT device. When DirectAccess clients are located behind a NAT device, you can use Teredo. Clients that have a private IPv4 address use Teredo to encapsulate IPv6 packets in an IPv4 header and then send them over the IPv4-based Internet. You can configure Teredo for DirectAccess clients and the DirectAccess server by using a GPO.

- IP-HTTPS is used by clients that are unable to connect to the DirectAccess server by using ISATAP, 6to4, or Teredo.

Troubleshooting DirectAccess

You can monitor DirectAccess connectivity by using the Remote Access Management Console. This console contains information on how DirectAccess server components work. By using the Remote Access Management console, you also can monitor DirectAccess client connectivity information. By monitoring DirectAccess connectivity, you can obtain information about DirectAccess role service health that helps you troubleshoot potential connectivity issues. The Remote Access Management Console includes the following monitoring components:

- **Dashboard:** The Remote Access Management Console offers a centralized view (dashboard) for monitoring the most important DirectAccess components. It contains the information on the operation and configuration status and the DirectAccess and VPN client status.

- **Operation Status:** Operation Status provides information about the health of each DirectAccess component: DNS, DNS64, domain controllers, IP-HTTPS, Kerberos authentication, NAT64, network adapters, Network Location Server, and network security and services. If the DirectAccess component is healthy, it shows a green check mark. If any issue arises with the Direct-Access component, it shows a blue question mark. Clicking the component gives you more detailed information about the related issue, the cause of the issue, and how to resolve it.

- **Remote Access Client Status:** Remote Access Client Status displays information about the DirectAccess client computers that connect to the Direct-Access server. The information displaying in this window includes the username, hostname, ISP address, protocol/tunnel, and duration. For each DirectAccess client connection, you can view more detailed information.

- **Remote Access Reporting:** Remote Access Reporting provides the same information as Remote Access Client Status, but as a historical DirectAccess client usage report. You can choose the start date and end date for the report. In addition, Remote Access Reporting displays server load statistics, which is statistical connectivity information for the total DirectAccess sessions, the average sessions per day, the maximum concurrent sessions, and unique DirectAccess clients.

Organizations should develop a troubleshooting methodology for DirectAccess connectivity to quickly eliminate any problem that DirectAccess client computers face. Troubleshooting methodology should contain step-by-step instructions on how to diagnose the problem. You can use the following list to troubleshoot DirectAccess connectivity:

- Whenever DirectAccess client computers are not able to connect to the DirectAccess server, we recommend that you follow the methodology for problem diagnostics. Troubleshooting methodology includes the following steps:

  Step 1. Check whether DirectAccess supports the correct operating system version.

  Step 2. Check whether the DirectAccess client computer is a member of the domain.

  Step 3. Check whether the DirectAccess client computer received computer configuration Group Policy settings for DirectAccess.

  Step 4. Check whether the DirectAccess server computer received computer configuration Group Policy settings for DirectAccess.

  Step 5. Check whether the DirectAccess client computer has a global IPv6 address.

  Step 6. Check whether the DirectAccess client computer can connect to the IPv6 addresses of the DirectAccess server.

  Step 7. Ensure that the DirectAccess client computer is assigned the domain firewall profile.

  Step 8. Check whether the DirectAccess client computer has IPv6 reachability to its intranet DNS servers and whether the DirectAccess client computer can use intranet DNS servers to resolve and to reach intranet FQDNs.

  Step 9. Check whether the DirectAccess client computer can establish both IPsec infrastructure and intranet tunnels with the DirectAccess server.

  Step 10. Use the following command-line tools to perform the checks, per your troubleshooting methodology: **netsh**, **ping**, **nslookup**, **ipconfig**, **certutil**, and **nltest**.

  Step 11. Use the following graphical user interface (GUI) tools for performing the checks, per your troubleshooting methodology: Remote Access Server Management Console, Group Policy Management Console and Group Policy Management Editor, Windows Firewall Advanced Security, Event Viewer, and certificates.

- Verify the DirectAccess Group Policy configuration settings for DirectAccess clients:

  Step 1. Switch to your DirectAccess client.

  Step 2. Restart the DirectAccess client, and then sign in.

  Step 3. Open a command prompt window and type the following commands:

  `gpupdate /force, gpresult /R`

  Step 4. Verify that DirectAccess Client Settings GPO displays in the list of the Applied Policy objects for the Computer Settings.

  Step 5. Close the command prompt window.

- Move the client computer to the Internet virtual network:

  Step 1. Simulate moving a DirectAccess client out of the corporate network and to the Internet and then enabling the Internet network adapter.

  Step 2. Close the Network Connections window.

- Verify connectivity to the DirectAccess server:

  Step 1. On your DirectAccess client, open a command prompt window, type **ipconfig**, and then press Enter.

  Step 2. Notice the IP address that starts with 2002. This is the IP-HTTPS address.

  Step 3. At the command prompt, type the following command and press Enter:

  `Netsh name show effectivepolicy`

  Step 4. Open Settings, select **Network and Internet**, and then click **DirectAccess**.

  Step 5. Verify that Your DirectAccess client is set up correctly for single-site DirectAccess (displayed under Location).

  Step 6. Click the **Collect** button under Troubleshooting info.

Exam Preparation Tasks

Review All the Key Topics

Review the most important topics in the chapter, noted with the Key Topics icon in the outer margin of the page. Table 10-7 lists these key topics and the page numbers where each is found.

Table 10-7   Key Topics for Chapter 10

Key Topic Element	Description	Page Number
Text	Setting up and configuring Site-to-Site VPN connections	410
Table 10-2	Windows Server 2016 S2S VPN PowerShell Cmdlets	416
Table 10-3	Windows Server 2016 On-demand and Persistent VPN Connections	417
Table 10-4	Windows Server 2016 Tunnel Protocols	417
Table 10-5	Windows Server 2016 Authentication Methods	419
Section	Configure VPN Reconnect	420
Text	CMAK	422
Section	Configuring VPN Connection Profiles with PowerShell	424
Section	App-Triggered VPN Feature	424
Text	DirectAccess functionality	431
List	DirectAccess infrastructure components	431
List	DirectAccess key components	432
Section	DirectAccess Solution Component: DirectAccess Client	434
Section	DirectAccess Solution Component: Active Directory	435
Section	DirectAccess Solution Component: DNS Server	435
Section	DirectAccess Solution Component: Network Location Server	438
Section	DirectAccess Solution Component: KDC Proxy	440
Section	DirectAccess Solution Component: Certification Service	440
Section	DirectAccess Solution Component: Certificates	440
Section	DirectAccess Solution Component: DNS64	441
Section	DirectAccess Solution Component: 6to4	441

Key Topic Element	Description	Page Number
Section	DirectAccess Solution Component: ISATAP	442
Section	DirectAccess Solution Component: Teredo	442
Section	DirectAccess Solution Component: Group Policy	443
Section	DirectAccess Solution Component: WMI Filter	444
Section	DirectAccess Solution Component: NCA	444
Section	Basic DirectAccess Deployment	446
Section	Configuring GPOs	451
Section	Configuring Security Groups	464
Step List	Installing and configuring the Remote Access role	465
Step List	Updating clients with the DirectAccess configuration	470
Section	Advanced DirectAccess Deployment	470
Table 10-6	Windows Server 2016 DirectAccess PowerShell Cmdlets	474
List	Requirements for implementing a DirectAccess client	477

Complete the Tables and Lists from Memory

Print a copy of Appendix B, "Memory Tables" (on the book's website), or at least the section for this chapter, and complete the tables and lists from memory. Appendix C, "Memory Tables Answer Key," also on the website, includes completed tables and lists to check your work.

Definition of Key Terms

Define the following key terms from this chapter and check your answers in the glossary.

DirectAccess server, DirectAccess client, Network Connectivity Assistant, Teredo, ISATAP, 6to4, Network Location Server, WebProbe resource record, IPHTTPS, IPsec, KDC Proxy

End-of-Chapter Review Questions

1. On which object can you configure a persistent site-to-site VPN connection?

    a. Connection Request Policy on the answering router

    b. Connection Request Policy on the calling router

    c. Network Policy on the answering router

    d. Network Policy on the calling router

2. You want to set up Windows Server 2016 as a VPN server. You want to open only UDP port 500 on your firewall to allow VPN connections, and you also want to configure the number of seconds to idle before disconnecting with PowerShell. Which VPN tunnel protocol and which PowerShell cmdlet provide the best options for configuring the idle disconnecting?

    a. Set-VpnS2Sinterface

    b. Set-VPNServerIPsecConfiguration

    c. Set-VpnServerConfiguration

    d. PPTP

    e. L2TP

    f. SSTP

    g. IKEv2

3. You want to create a new VPN connection profile and use a preconfigured XML file with specified authentication for that. Which PowerShell cmdlet do you use to define the custom authentication method?

    a. Add-VpnConnection

    b. Set-VpnConnection

    c. New-EapConfiguration

    d. Set-VpnConnectionIPsecConfiguration

4. You have a Microsoft Azure site with one Azure VPN gateway. One hundred active mobile client P2S VPN connections are connected to this gateway. You plan to add another 50 client P2S VPN connections in the next months. To improve the availability, you also want to have redundant tunnels to Microsoft Azure. What are the best solutions in this scenario? (Choose two.)

    a. Add another Azure VPN gateway

    b. Use ExpressRoute instead of P2S tunnels

    c. Use S2S tunnels instead of P2S tunnels

    d. Use a high-performance Azure VPN gateway

This chapter covers the following subjects:

- **Implementing RADIUS:** This chapter explains the overall purpose and scenarios for RADIUS servers, proxies and clients, and use of both the RADIUS protocol and Windows Server 2016 Network Policy Servers (NPS) to implement RADIUS solutions.

- **Implementing RADIUS proxy:** This chapter examines different scenarios for using Windows Server 2016 NPS as a RADIUS proxy.

- **Implementing RADIUS clients:** You learn how to configure a Windows Server 2016 VPN server as a RADIUS client with the NPS console, Routing and Remote Access console, or PowerShell commands (with the learning focus on PowerShell commands).

- **Configuring NPS templates:** This chapter explains the elements and use of NPS templates and demonstrates how you can use them to reduce time and cost efforts when you have to configure multiple NPS servers.

- **Configuring RADIUS Accounting:** You can configure a Windows Server 2016 NPS server for RADIUS Accounting so that the NPS server logs accounting information to log files on the local hard disk or on a Microsoft SQL Server database.

- **Certificates:** This chapter discusses the use of certificates for Windows Server 2016 NPS servers. It tells which authentication methods are dependent on which kind of certificates, explains the differences in certificate-based authentication methods, and shows how to configure certificate templates for EAP/PEAP.

- **Connection request policies:** Connection request policies are condition sets and settings that allow administrators to designate which RADIUS servers do the authentication and authorization of connection requests that a Windows Server 2016 NPS server receives from RADIUS clients.

- **Network Policies for VPN wireless and wired clients:** In this chapter, you learn about creating Windows Server 2016 NPS Network Policies and using network policy categories. You also explore the ordering of Network Policies, network policy key settings, and configuration of NPS for VLANs.

- **Importing and exporting NPS policies:** You can export Windows Server 2016 NPS Network Policies, connection request policies, and shared secrets for RADIUS clients and members of RADIUS server groups for a Windows Server 2016 NPS server.

## CHAPTER 11

Windows Server 2016 Network Policy Server

This chapter covers the overall purpose and scenarios for RADIUS servers, proxies and clients, and the RADIUS protocol and Windows Server 2016 Network Policy Servers (NPS) for implementing RADIUS solutions. It describes how to configure NPS UDP port information, to forward connection requests to another NPS server or RADIUS server, register NPS servers in Active Directory, and configure a Windows Server 2016 VPN server as a RADIUS client.

In addition, the chapter covers different scenarios using Windows Server 2016 NPS as a RADIUS proxy. It shows how to configure a Windows Server 2016 VPN server as a RADIUS client with the NPS console, Routing and Remote Access console, or PowerShell commands (with a learning focus on PowerShell commands). You also learn in this chapter how to configure a Windows Server 2016 DirectAccess server as a RADIUS client and how to plan and configure OTP certificate templates.

Furthermore, you learn about using NPS templates to reduce time and cost efforts when you have to configure multiple NPS servers. To pass the exam, you must know how to configure a Windows Server 2016 NPS server for RADIUS Accounting so that the NPS server logs accounting information to log files on the local hard disk or on a Microsoft SQL Server database. You also have to learn the different NPS Accounting options and differences, how to use certificates for Windows Server 2016 NPS servers, and which authentication methods are dependent on which kinds of certificates.

This chapter explains the differences in certificate-based authentication methods and shows how to configure certificate templates for EAP/PEAP. You learn about connection request policies, condition sets and settings that allow administrators to designate which RADIUS servers do the authentication and authorization of connection requests that a Windows Server 2016 NPS server receives from RADIUS clients.

This chapter also covers the default connection request policies, details how to create new connection requests and Network Policies, and discusses the main connection request policy tasks. (*Important:* At the time of writing this book, no PowerShell cmdlets existed to create or manage connection requests or Network Policies.)

The key topic selections, memory tables, key term definitions, and exam preparation questions give you powerful tools to increase your knowledge about Windows Server 2016 Network Policy Server for the Microsoft exam 70-741 and your work.

"Do I Know This Already?" Quiz

The "Do I Know This Already?" quiz enables you to assess whether you should read this entire chapter or simply jump to the "Exam Preparation Tasks" section for review. If you are in doubt, read the entire chapter. Table 11-1 outlines the major headings in this chapter and the corresponding "Do I Know This Already?" quiz questions. You can find the answers in Appendix A, "Answers to the 'Do I Know This Already?' Quizzes and End-of-Chapter Review Questions."

Table 11-1   "Do I Know This Already?" Foundation Topics Section-to-Question Mapping

Foundation Topics Section	Questions Covered in This Section
Implementing RADIUS	1
Implementing RADIUS Proxy	2
Implementing RADIUS Clients	3
Configure NPS Templates	4
Configure RADIUS Accounting	5
Certificates	6
Connection Request Policies	7
Network Policies for VPN Wireless and Wired Clients	8
Import and Export NPS Policies	9

CAUTION   The goal of self-assessment is to gauge your mastery of the topics in this chapter. If you do not know the answer to a question or are only partially sure of the answer, you should mark that question as wrong for purposes of the self-assessment. Giving yourself credit for an answer you correctly guess skews your self-assessment results and might provide you with a false sense of security.

1. You are responsible for configuring a Windows Server 2016 NPS server named NPS1 in the forest pearson.com. You have another forest named pearsonucertify.com. You want NPS1 to have permissions to read dial-in properties of pearsonucertify.com user accounts. Which configuration step accomplishes this?

    a. Add NPS1 to the RAS and IAS Servers security group of pearsonucertify.com.

    b. Add NPS1 to the RAS and IAS Servers security group of pearson.com.

    c. Register nps2.pearsonucertify.com on pearsonucertify.com and replicate NPS server configuration settings from NPS1 to NPS2.

    d. Use the Azure AD Connect tool to synchronize pearsonucertify.com user accounts to Microsoft Azure and register NPS1 on Azure AD.

2. You are responsible for implementing a Windows Server 2016 NPS server as a RADIUS server and RADIUS proxy. Which configuration setting do you have to configure?

    a. Use the default connection request policy.

    b. Create a new proxy connection request policy and move it to the top in the ordered list.

    c. Create a new proxy connection request policy and move it under the default connection request policy in the ordered list.

    d. Create a new network policy to forward requests to RADIUS server.

3. You must configure a Windows Server 2016 VPN server named VPN1 as a RADIUS client so that connection requests are forwarded to a Windows Server 2016 RADIUS server named R1. The VPN server feature is installed on VPN1. Local NPS is not installed on VPN1. External RADIUS Accounting is enabled on VPN1. Which PowerShell cmdlets can you use to configure this? (Choose two.)

    a. On VPN1, use **Add-RemoteAccessRadius**.

    b. On VPN1, use **Add-WindowsFeature NPAS**.

    c. On R1, use **New-NpsRadiusClient**.

    d. On VPN1, use **New-NpsRadiusClient**.

4. You are responsible for planning the implementation of 200 Windows Server 2016 VPN servers as RADIUS clients and 12 Windows Server 2016 servers as RADIUS servers in different sites of your network environment. Which kinds of settings can you preconfigure through NPS templates? (Choose four.)

    a. Shared secrets

    b. Network policy conditions

    c. SQL Server logging settings

    d. RADIUS clients

    e. IP filters

    f. RADIUS authentication/accounting port numbers

    g. Remote RADIUS servers

5. Your Windows Server 2016 NPS server works as a RADIUS server. It stops processing connection requests and prevents users from accessing network resources. The NPS server is configured to use local NPS log files. Which configuration can prevent such problems? (Choose three.)

    a. Keep NPS log files separate from the system partition.

    b. Use an NPS replica server.

    c. Use a RADIUS server group.

    d. Use SQL logging instead of NPS log files.

6. You want to configure your Windows Server 2016 NPS server to allow VPN clients to connect through the PEAP authentication method. Which components do you have to prepare to make that possible? (Choose four.)

    a. Network policy condition: NAS Port Type: Virtual (VPN)

    b. Network policy condition: Service Type

    c. Network policy constraint: Authentication Methods

    d. Network policy constraints: NAS Port Type

    e. PEAP certificate template and certificate

    f. Encrypted shared secret

    g. Type of network access server

7. You have to create a new connection request policy on your Windows Server 2016 NPS server. Which two configuration options are not viable solutions for this task? (Choose two.)

    a. **New-NpsConnectionRequestPolicy**

    b. New Connection Request Policy Wizard

    c. NPS Getting Started Standard Configuration

    d. NPS templates

8. Which RADIUS attributes do you have to use in a network policy for wireless connectivity on your Windows Server 2016 NPS server to identify VLAN membership as criteria, to define whether a user is allowed or denied authentication? (Choose three.)

    a. **Tunnel-Medium-Type**

    b. **Tunnel-Pvt-Group-ID**

    c. **Tunnel-Server-Auth-ID**

      d. Filter-Id

      e. Login-LAT-Group

      f. Tunnel-Type

9. You want to replicate Network Policies and connection request policies from a Windows Server 2016 NPS server named NPS1 to another Windows Server 2016 NPS server named NPS2. Which PowerShell cmdlets can you use to accomplish this? (Choose two.)

      a. Export-BinaryMiLog

      b. Export-ScheduledTasks

      c. Export-NpsConfiguration

      d. Import-NpsConfiguration

      e. Export-Clixml

      f. Import-Clixml

Foundation Topics

Implementing RADIUS

With the use of a RADIUS server, you can collect and maintain network access user authentication, authorization, and accounting data in a central location.

A Windows Server 2016 RADIUS server manages centralized connection, authentication, and authorization. Organizations that maintain network access, such as ISPs, must manage a variety of network access methods from a single administration point, regardless of the type of network access equipment they use.

The RADIUS standard supports this requirement. RADIUS is a client/server protocol that enables network access equipment, used as RADIUS clients, to submit authentication and accounting requests to a RADIUS server.

You can use Windows Server 2016 NPS as a RADIUS server in these scenarios (see Figure 11-1):

- Using a domain or local SAM user accounts database as a user account database for clients.

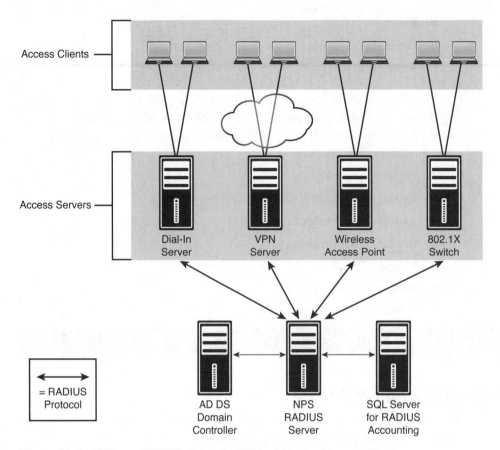

Access Clients

Access Servers

Dial-In
Server

VPN
Server

Wireless
Access Point

802.1X
Switch

= RADIUS
Protocol

AD DS
Domain
Controller

NPS
RADIUS
Server

SQL Server
for RADIUS
Accounting

Figure 11-1 NPS as a RADIUS Server for Different Kinds of Access Clients

- Using Remote Access on multiple dial-up servers, VPN servers, or demand-dial routers. You want to centralize both the configuration of Network Policies and connection logging and accounting.

- Outsourcing dial-up, VPN, or wireless access to a service provider. The access servers can use RADIUS to authenticate and authorize connections that are made by members of your organization.

- Centralizing authentication, authorization, and accounting for a heterogeneous set of access servers.

> **TIP**   What is the RADIUS client? Clients such as wireless portable computers and other computers running client operating systems are *not* the RADIUS clients. RADIUS clients are network access servers such as wireless access points, 802.1X-capable switches, and VPN and dial-up servers because they use the RADIUS protocol to communicate with RADIUS servers such as Windows Server 2016 NPS servers.

TIP   By default, Windows Server 2016 NPS listens for RADIUS traffic on ports
1812, 1813, 1645, and 1646 for both IPv6 and IPv4 for all installed network adapters.
However, many access servers use ports 1645 for authentication requests and 1646
for accounting requests. No matter which port numbers you decide to use, make sure
that NPS and your access server are configured to use the same ones. To configure
NPS UDP port information, you can do the following steps:

Step 1.	Open the NPS console.
Step 2.	Right-click **Network Policy Server**, and then click **Properties**.
Step 3.	Click the **Ports** tab and examine the settings for the ports. If your RADIUS authentication and RADIUS Accounting UDP ports vary from the default values provided (1812 and 1645 for authentication, and 1813 and 1646 for accounting), type your port settings in Authentication and Accounting.
Step 4.	To use multiple port settings for authentication or accounting requests, separate the port numbers with commas.

The Windows Server 2016 Network Policy Server (NPS) is part of the Network
Policy and Access Services server role. Figure 11-2 shows the installed Network
Policy and Access Service (NPAS) role.

Figure 11-2   Verify Installed NPAS Role

You can use a Windows Server 2016 NPS server as a RADIUS server, client, or
proxy to forward connection requests to another NPS server or RADIUS server.

Registering the NPS Server in Active Directory

A Windows Server 2016 NPS server should be registered in Active Directory (see
Figure 11-3). The RADIUS server must have access to the user account information
in Active Directory.

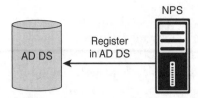

Figure 11-3   Register NPS Server in AD DS

You can register the NPS server using the NPS console (see Figure 11-4), but you also can do so through the command prompt with the command **netsh ras add registeredserver**. In addition, you can add the computer account of the NPS server as a member of the RAS and IAS Servers computer security group to register the NPS server in Active Directory.

Figure 11-4   Register Server in Active Directory

Figure 11-5 shows the default message after successful registration of the NPS server in Active Directory. Membership in the Domain Admins security group (or equivalent) is the minimum required to complete this procedure.

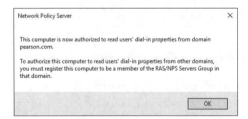

Figure 11-5   Successful Registration of NPS Server in Active Directory

A Windows Server 2016 NPS as a RADIUS server can verify network access authentication credentials. If the user's credentials are approved and RADIUS authorizes the connection attempt, the RADIUS server authorizes the user's access based on configured conditions. It also logs the network access connections in an accounting log.

When the NPS server is a member of a domain, it performs authentication by comparing user credentials that it receives from network access servers with the credentials that are stored for the user account in AD DS. In addition, NPS authorizes connection requests by using Network Policies and by checking user account dial-in properties in AD DS.

When using Windows Server 2016 Network Policy Server as a RADIUS server, you configure network access servers, such as wireless access points and VPN servers, as RADIUS clients.

RADIUS Client Configuration

To configure a Windows Server 2016 VPN server as a RADIUS client, you also must install the NPAS role on the Windows Server 2016 VPN server. In the NPS console, you can configure authentication and accounting request forwarding to the RADIUS server group (if you have only one RADIUS server, you also have to create a RADIUS server group and then add the RADIUS server to this group). Figure 11-6 shows the settings of a connection request policy.

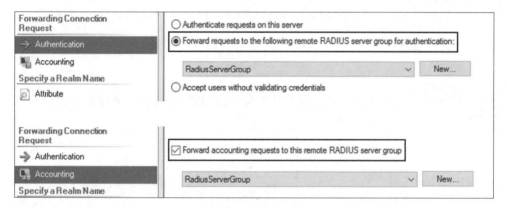

Figure 11-6 Default Windows Server 2016 NPS RADIUS Client Connection Request Policy

You also have to configure Network Policies that the NPS server uses to authorize connection requests, and you can configure RADIUS Accounting so that the NPS server logs accounting information to log files on the local hard disk or in a Microsoft SQL Server database. In the case of configuring an NPS server as a RADIUS client, you have to add a remote RADIUS server group with the Authentication/Accounting and Load Balancing settings (see Figure 11-7).

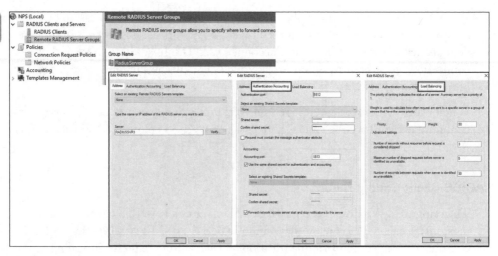

Figure 11-7   Windows Server 2016 NPS RADIUS Client Settings

A Windows Server 2016 NPS server enables the use of a heterogeneous set of wireless, switch, remote access, or VPN equipment. You also can use the Routing and Remote Access Service to configure forwarding to a RADIUS server (see Figure 11-8).

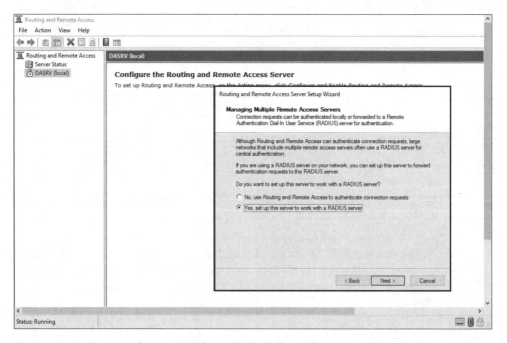

Figure 11-8   Windows Server 2016 Setup RADIUS Client Through Routing and Remote Access Service

When you set up a Windows Server 2016 VPN server as a RADIUS client, you have to know the names of the RADIUS servers you want to connect to.

The Routing and Remote Access Server Setup Wizard asks you for the Primary and Alternate RADIUS servers and the shared secret; it does not ask you about the Remote RADIUS Server Group as in the NPS console.

The wizard automatically adds two Remote RADIUS Server Groups to the list in the NPS console. These are named Microsoft Routing and Remote Access Service Authentication Servers and Microsoft Routing and Remote Access Service Accounting Servers.

A RADIUS server has access to user account information and can verify network access authentication credentials. If the user's credentials are authentic and RADIUS authorizes the connection attempt, the RADIUS server authorizes the user's access based on configured conditions (see Figure 11-9). It then logs the network access connection in an accounting log.

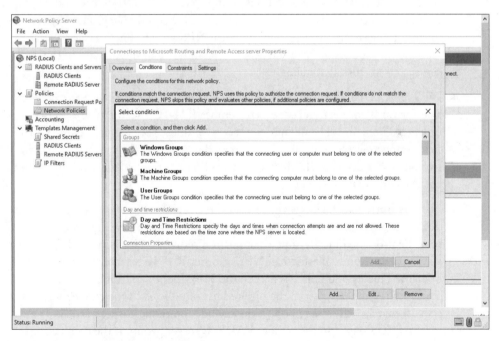

Figure 11-9   Windows Server 2016 NPS Network Policy Conditions

Using RADIUS, you can collect and maintain the network access user authentication, authorization, and accounting data in a central location instead of on each access server.

Implementing RADIUS Proxy

When using an NPS server as a RADIUS proxy, you configure the NPS server to forward to other RADIUS servers. You can create different NPS configurations for the following solutions:

- Wireless access

- Organizational dial-up or VPN remote access

- Outsourced dial-up or wireless access

- Internet access

- Authenticated access to extranet resources for business partners

The following configuration examples demonstrate how you can configure NPS as a RADIUS server and a RADIUS proxy:

- **NPS as a RADIUS server:** NPS is configured as a RADIUS server, the default connection request policy is the only configured policy, and all connection requests are processed by the local NPS server. The NPS server can authenticate and authorize users whose accounts are in the domain of the NPS server and in trusted domains.

- **NPS as RADIUS proxy:** NPS server is configured as a RADIUS proxy that forwards connection requests to remote RADIUS server groups in two untrusted domains. The default connection request policy is deleted, and two new connection request policies are created to forward requests to each of the two untrusted domains. In this example, NPS does not process any connection requests on the local server.

- **NPS as both RADIUS server and RADIUS proxy:** In addition to the default connection request policy, which specifies that connection requests must be processed locally, a new connection request policy is created that forwards connection requests to an NPS or other RADIUS server in an untrusted domain. This second policy is named the Proxy policy. In this example, the Proxy policy appears first in the ordered list of policies. If the connection request matches the Proxy policy, the connection request is forwarded to the RADIUS server in the remote RADIUS server group. If the connection request does not match the Proxy policy but does match the default connection request policy, NPS processes the connection request on the local server.

- **NPS as a RADIUS server with remote accounting servers:** The local NPS server is not configured to perform accounting and the default connection request policy is revised so that RADIUS Accounting messages are forwarded to an NPS server or other RADIUS server in a remote RADIUS server group. Although accounting messages are forwarded, authentication and authorization messages are not forwarded; the local NPS server performs these functions for the local domain and all trusted domains.

- **NPS with Remote RADIUS to Windows User Mapping:** NPS acts as both a RADIUS server and a RADIUS proxy for each individual connection request by forwarding the authentication request to a remote RADIUS server while using a local Windows user account for authorization. This configuration is implemented by configuring the Remote RADIUS to the Windows User Mapping attribute as a condition of the connection request policy.

To configure NPS as a RADIUS server, you can use either standard configuration or advanced configuration in the NPS console or in Server Manager. To configure NPS as a RADIUS proxy, you must use advanced configuration.

Implementing RADIUS Clients

To implement a Windows Server 2016 RADIUS client, you simply have to add the RADIUS client to the list of RADIUS clients on the Windows Server 2016 RADIUS server. You can do this in the NPS console with New RADIUS Client (see Figure 11-10). You must type in a friendly name, IP address, or DNS name of the RADIUS client and a shared secret.

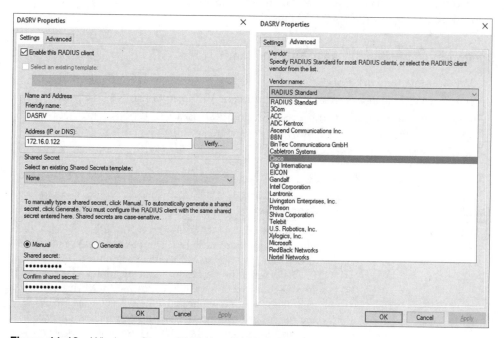

Figure 11-10 Windows Server 2016 New RADIUS Client Settings

When you use a Microsoft VPN Server or a Microsoft DirectAccess server as a RADIUS client, you can use RADIUS Standard as the vendor name. When your RADIUS client is a Cisco device, you have to choose Cisco as the vendor name.

You also can add the RADIUS client to the Windows Server 2016 RADIUS server through the PowerShell cmdlet **New-NpsRadiusClient** (see Figure 11-11).

Figure 11-11   New-NpsRadiusClient Cmdlet

With the PowerShell cmdlet **Get-NpsRadiusClient**, you can display all settings of the RADIUS client you have applied (see Figure 11-12).

Figure 11-12   Get-NpsRadiusClient Cmdlet

With the PowerShell cmdlet **Remove-NpsRadiusClient**, you can remove the RADIUS client from the list of RADIUS clients on a Windows Server 2016 NPS RADIUS server. With the PowerShell cmdlet **Set-NpsRadiusClient**, you can change settings for the RADIUS client.

Configuring a VPN Server as a RADIUS Client

When using Network Policy Server as a RADIUS server, you configure network access devices, such as wireless access points or VPN servers, as RADIUS clients to forward authentication and accounting requests to a RADIUS server. Table 11-2 lists some of the most important PowerShell cmdlets you can use to configure RADIUS servers and clients.

Table 11-2   Windows Server 2016 Remote Access RADIUS PowerShell Cmdlets

Cmdlet	Description
Add-RemoteAccessRadius	Adds a new external RADIUS server for VPN authentication, accounting for DirectAccess (DA) and VPN, or one-time password (OTP) authentication for DA. The RADIUS server properties for authentication and accounting are the same except for the **AccountingOnOffMsg** parameter, which is applicable only to accounting RADIUS, and the **MsgAuthenticator** parameter, which is applicable only to authentication RADIUS. These properties are not relevant for DA OTP authentication.

Cmdlet	Description
Get-RemoteAccessRadius	Displays the list of RADIUS servers, including RADIUS for VPN authentication, RADIUS for DirectAccess and VPN accounting, and RADIUS for OTP authentication for DirectAccess.
Remove-RemoteAccessRadius	Removes an external RADIUS server from being used for VPN authentication, accounting for both DirectAccess and VPN, and OTP authentication for DirectAccess. ■ If a RADIUS server is currently being used for multiple purposes, it can be removed for one or more of those purposes. However, the cmdlet then must be run separately for each purpose. ■ If the last RADIUS server being used for accounting is removed, the accounting type automatically switches to Windows accounting. ■ The user is not allowed to delete the last RADIUS server being used for VPN authentication if RADIUS authentication is configured.
Set-RemoteAccessRadius	Edits the properties associated with an external RADIUS server being used for VPN authentication, accounting for DirectAccess and VPN, and OTP authentication for DirectAccess. ■ You cannot use this cmdlet to change the purpose for which a RADIUS server is currently being used. You can modify only other properties of the server. ■ The RADIUS server properties for authentication and accounting are the same except for the **AccountingOnOffMsg** parameter, which is applicable only to accounting RADIUS, and the **MsgAuthenticator** parameter, which is applicable only to RADIUS authentication. These parameters are not relevant for DirectAccess OTP authentication. ■ If a user tries to edit the properties of a RADIUS server for a particular purpose but specifies a parameter that is not applicable to that purpose, this cmdlet still runs, but the parameter is ignored and a warning message displays; the other parameters specified still are modified.

Cmdlet	Description
Set-RemoteAccessAccounting	Sets the enabled state for the inbox and RADIUS Accounting for both external RADIUS and Windows accounting, and configures the settings when enabled.

- Both inbox accounting and RADIUS Accounting can be active at the same time. RADIUS Accounting includes Windows accounting, external RADIUS Accounting, and accounting on the local Network Policy Server (NPS), but only one type of accounting can be active at any time. The **RadiusServer**, **SharedSecret**, **RadiusPort**, **RadiusScore**, **RadiusTimeout**, and **AccountingOnOffMsg** parameters are applicable only when RADIUS Accounting is enabled and cannot be specified when inbox accounting is enabled.

- If Windows Accounting is enabled for VPN, it will not work for DirectAccess because this is not a supported configuration for DirectAccess. For accounting to work for DirectAccess in this scenario, either NPS needs to be installed locally or an external RADIUS server needs to be configured for accounting.

- If the current configuration is Windows accounting, a user can switch to external RADIUS Accounting by doing one of the following:

Option 1. Running the same cmdlet to enable RADIUS Accounting and specifying an external RADIUS server.

Option 2. Adding an external RADIUS server using the **Add-RemoteAccessRadius** cmdlet. This enables RADIUS Accounting without running this cmdlet.

Option 3. Switching back to Windows accounting by deleting all the configured external RADIUS servers.

TIP You cannot use the **Add-RemoteAccessRadius** PowerShell cmdlet to add an external RADIUS server into the RADIUS Server Group on a Windows Server 2016 VPN server. If VPN is not installed, the authentication type is Windows Authentication on the VPN server. Figure 11-13 shows the output of the **Add-RemoteAccessRadius** PowerShell cmdlet and the wrong authentication setting on the VPN server in the Routing and Remote Access console.

```
PS C:\> Add-RemoteAccessRadius -ServerName 172.16.0.10 Authentication 'Odysee2008' -PassThru
Add-RemoteAccessRadius : You cannot use a RADIUS server for authentication because Windows authentication is
configured on server localhost.
```

Figure 11-13   Add-RemoteAccessRadius (Windows Authentication Error)

TIP You cannot use the **Remove-RemoteAccessRadius** PowerShell cmdlet to remove an external RADIUS server from the RADIUS Server Group on a Windows Server 2016 VPN server if the external RADIUS server you want to remove is the last RADIUS server in the list of RADIUS servers on the VPN server (see Figure 11-14).

Figure 11-14 **Remove-RemoteAccessRadius** Error (Last RADIUS Server in List)

Configuring a DirectAccess Server as a RADIUS Client

Suppose you want to use a Managed Secure Authentication Service with a Mobile Signature Service (MSS) from a third-party company as a two-factor authentication solution to implement secure login authentication for remote devices. You also want to implement that through the use of Windows Server 2016 DirectAccess with OTP and a RADIUS server.

Figure 11-15 shows such an example deployment in which a user requests remote access with Windows Server 2016 DirectAccess. The DirectAccess server (RADIUS client) sends the RADIUS requests to the RADIUS server to authenticate the users. The RADIUS server invokes the MSS over SOAP and provides the answer back to the RADIUS client. The RADIUS server also can be connected to Active Directory, where the end user's details such as phone number and credentials are stored.

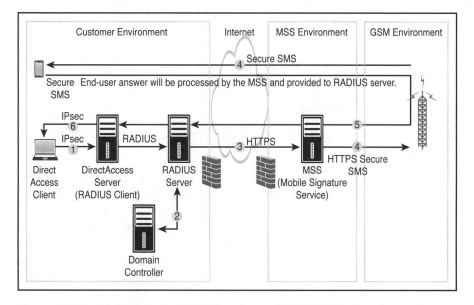

Figure 11-15 Windows Server 2016 DirectAccess MSS RADIUS Client Scenario

The authentication data flow for that scenario involves the following steps:

Step 1.   When a user tries to connect to the Windows Server 2016 DirectAccess server (RADIUS client), the DirectAccess server makes a request to the defined RADIUS server to authenticate the end user with the MobileID.

Step 2.   The RADIUS server (optionally) verifies the user credentials against Active Directory and/or maps to a valid mobile phone user.

Step 3.   The RADIUS server (which enabled the MobileID plug-in) calls the MobileID service.

Step 4.   The third-party MSS platform ensures that the end user's signature request is allowed and forwards the signature request to the end user's mobile phone.

Step 5.   The MSS platform processes the end user answer and provides it to the RADIUS server.

Step 6.   After the RADIUS server verifies the third-party MSS platform response, the answer is forwarded to the RADIUS client. The Windows Server 2016 DirectAccess server processes this answer to grant or reject the DirectAccess connection request.

To configure the Windows Server 2016 DirectAccess server for this scenario, you have to do the following:

Step 1.   Deploy a Single Remote Access server with Advanced Settings.

Step 2.   On the Remote Access server, open Server Manager and click **Remote Access** in the left pane.

Step 3.   Right-click **Remote Access Server** in the Servers pane, and select **Remote Access Management**.

Step 4.   Click **Configuration**.

Step 5.   In the DirectAccess Setup window, under Step 2–Remote Access Server, click **Edit**.

Step 6.   Click **Next** three times, and in the Authentication section, select **Two-Factor Authentication** (Use Computer Certificates is selected automatically) and Use OTP (see Figure 11-16). Verify that the root CA is set to the name of the CA of the organization. Click **Next**.

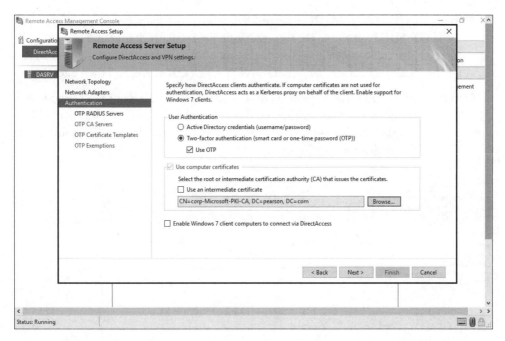

Figure 11-16   Windows Server 2016 DirectAccess OTP RADIUS Client Configuration

Step 7.   In the OTP RADIUS Servers section, double-click the blank **Server Name** field (see Figure 11-17).

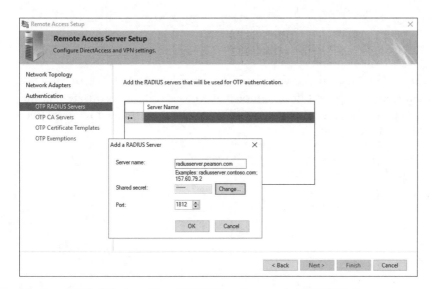

Figure 11-17   Windows Server 2016 DirectAccess Add RADIUS Server

Step 8. In the Add a RADIUS Server dialog box, type the server name of the RADIUS server in the Server Name field. Click **Change** next to the Shared Secret field, and type the same password that you defined at the RADIUS server (see Figure 11-17). Click **OK** twice, and then click **Next**.

Step 9. In the OTP CA Servers section, select the organization's CA server under Detected CA Servers and add this CA to the OTP CA Servers list. This CA then can be used to issue certificates to DirectAccess clients for OTP authentication (see Figure 11-18).

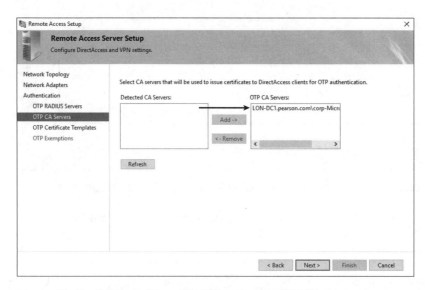

Figure 11-18 Windows Server 2016 DirectAccess OTP CA Servers

Step 10. In the OTP Certificate Templates section, select the OTP certificate template and the certificate template used to enroll the certificate that the DirectAccess server uses to sign OTP certificate enrollment requests (see Figure 11-19).

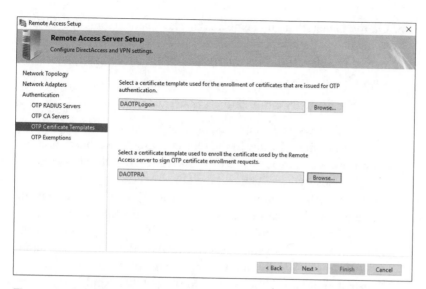

Figure 11-19 Windows Server 2016 DirectAccess OTP Certificate Templates

The certificate templates must have been created previously on the organization's internal CA. The following two lists describe the necessary steps to create both certificate templates.

To create a certificate template used to sign OTP certificate requests:

a. On the internal CA, select the **certtmpl.msc** utility from the command line.

b. In the Certificate Templates Console, in the details pane, right-click the **Computer** template and click **Duplicate Template**.

c. On the Compatibility tab in the Properties of New Template dialog box, in the Certification Authority list, click **Windows Server 2016**; in the Resulting Changes dialog box, click **OK**. In the Certificate Recipient list, click **Windows Server 2016**; in the Resulting Changes dialog box, click **OK**.

d. In the Properties of New Template dialog box, click the **General** tab.

e. On the General tab, in Template Display Name, type **DAOTPRA** as the name. Set the Validity Period to 2 days, and set the Renewal Period to 1 day. If the Certificate Templates warning displays, click **OK**.

f. Click the **Security** tab, and then click **Add**.

g. In the Select Users, Computers, Service Accounts, or Groups dialog box, click **Object Types**. In the Object Types dialog box, select **Computers** and then click **OK**. In the Enter the Object Names to Select box, type the name of the DirectAccess server and click **OK**; in the Allow column, select the **Read**, **Enroll**, and **Autoenroll** check boxes. Click **Authenticated Users**, select the **Read** check box under the Allow column, and clear all other check boxes. Click **Domain Computers** and uncheck **Enroll** under the Allow column. Click **Domain Admins** and **Enterprise Admins**, and click **Full Control** under the Allow column for both. Click **Apply**.

h. Click the Subject Name tab, and then click **Build from This Active Directory Information**. In the Subject Name Format list, select **DNS Name**; make sure that the DNS Name box is checked, and click **Apply**.

i. Click the **Extensions** tab, select **Application Policies**, and then click **Edit**. Remove all existing application policies. Click **Add**; in the Add Application Policy dialog box, click **New**, enter **DA OTP RA** in the Name field, enter **1.3.6.1.4.1.311.81.1.1** in the Object Identifier field, and click **OK**. In the Add Application Policy dialog box, click **OK**. In the Edit Application Policies Extension dialog box, click **OK**. In the Properties of New Template dialog box, click **OK**.

To create and deploy a certificate template for OTP certificates issued by the organization's CA:

a. In the Certificate Templates Console, in the details pane, right-click the **Smartcard Logon** template and click **Duplicate Template**.

b. In the Properties of New Template dialog box, on the Compatibility tab in the Certification Authority list, click **Windows Server 2016**; in the Resulting Changes dialog box, click **OK**. In the Certificate Recipient list, click **Windows Server 2016**; in the Resulting Changes dialog box, click **OK**.

c. In the Properties of New Template dialog box, click the **General** tab.

d. On the General tab, in Template Display Name, type **DAOTPLogon**. In Validity Period, in the drop-down list, click **Hours**. In the Certificate Templates dialog box, click **OK** and make sure that the number of hours is set to 1. In Renewal Period, type **0**.

e. Click the **Security** tab, select **Authenticated Users** in the Allow column, and select the **Read** and **Enroll** check boxes. Click **OK**. Click **Domain Admins and Enterprise Admins**, and click **Full Control** in the Allow column for both. Click **Apply**.

f. Click the **Subject Name** tab, and then click **Build from This Active Directory Information**. In the Subject Name Format list, select **Fully Distinguished Name**; also make sure that the User Principal Name (UPN) box is checked, and click **Apply**.

g. Click the **Server** tab, select the **Do Not Store Certificates and Requests in the CA Database** check box and clear the **Do Not Include Revocation Information in Issued Certificates** check box. In the Properties of New Template dialog box, click **Apply**.

h. Click the **Issuance Requirements** tab, select the **This Number of Authorized Signatures** check box, and set the value to **1**. In the Policy Type Required in Signature list, select **Application Policy**; in the Application Policy list, select **DA OTP RA**. In the Properties of New Template dialog box, click **OK**.

i. Click the **Extensions** tab, and in Application Policies, click **Edit**. Delete Client Authentication, keep SmartCardLogon, and click **OK** twice.

j. Close the Certificate Templates Console.

k. On the Start screen, type **certsrv.msc** and then click **Enter**.

l. In the Certification Authority console tree, expand the name of the CA, click **Certificate Templates**, right-click **Certificate Templates**, point to **New**, and click **Certificate Template to Issue**.

m. In the list of certificate templates, click **DAOTPRA** and **DAOTPLogon**, and click **OK**.

n. In the details pane of the console, you should see the DAOTPRA certificate template with Intended Purpose of DA OTP RA and also the DAOTPLogon certificate template with Intended Purpose of Smart Card Logon.

o. Restart the services.

     p. Close the Certification Authority console.

     q. Open an elevated command prompt. Type **CertUtil.exe -SetReg DBFlags +DBFLAGS_ENABLEVOLATILEREQUESTS**, and click **Enter**.

Step 11. In the OTP Exemptions section, select **Require All Users to Authenticate Using Two-Factor Authentication** if all users must use OTP authentication. Choose **Do Not Require Users in the Specified Security Group to Authenticate Using Two-Factor Authentication** if you want to exclude some users from OTP authentication (see Figure 11-20).

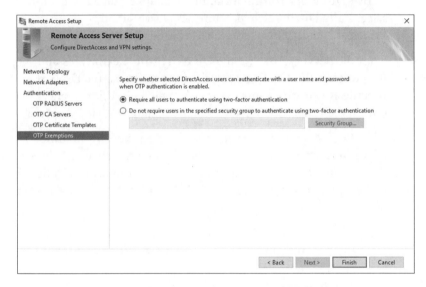

Figure 11-20 Windows Server 2016 DirectAccess OTP Exemptions

Step 12. Create a Probe user with the username DAProbeUser and the password DAProbePass on the RADIUS server.

OTP Certificate Template Planning for Windows Server 2016 DirectAccess Server RADIUS Client

When you want to configure a Windows Server 2016 DirectAccess server as a RADIUS client, each DirectAccess client requires an OTP authentication certificate to gain access to the internal network. You must configure two templates on your internal CA for the OTP certificate. Note the following when configuring the OTP certificate templates:

- All users who need to perform OTP authentication must have read and enroll permissions for this template (see Figure 11-21).

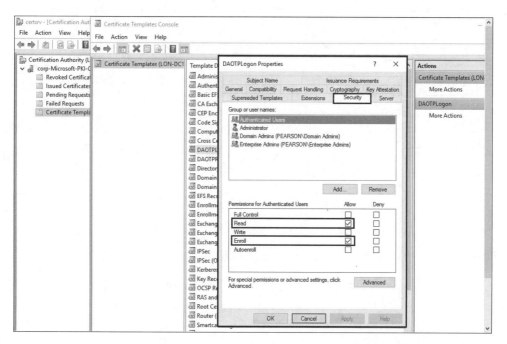

Figure 11-21   Windows Server 2016 DirectAccess OTP Certificate Template (Security)

- The subject name should be built from AD information, to ensure that the subject name matches the OTP username and not the name of the Remote Access server that performs the certificate request. The subject name must be in the fully distinguished name format, and the subject alternative name must be in UPN format. This ensures that the enrolled OTP certificate is valid for smart card Kerberos authentication (see Figure 11-22).

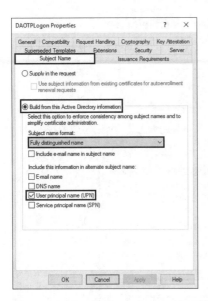

Figure 11-22   Windows Server 2016 DirectAccess OTP Certificate Template (Subject Name)

■ The intended purpose of the certificate must be Smart Card Logon (see Figure 11-23).

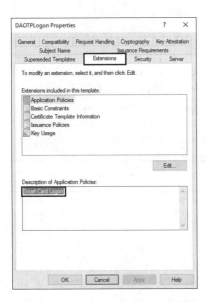

Figure 11-23   Windows Server 2016 DirectAccess OTP Certificate Template (Purpose)

■ Issuance must require one authorized signature. The signature must be configured with the predefined DirectAccess OTP application policy set in the registration authority signing certificate template (see Figure 11-24).

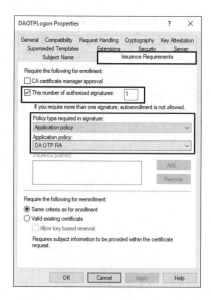

Figure 11-24   Windows Server 2016 DirectAccess OTP Certificate Template (Issuance Requirements)

- The validity period should be set to 1 hour (see Figure 11-25).

- The renewal period should be set to 0 (see Figure 11-25).

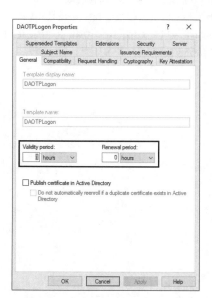

Figure 11-25   Windows Server 2016 DirectAccess OTP Certificate Template (General)

■ Certificates and requests should not be stored in the CA database (see Figure 11-26).

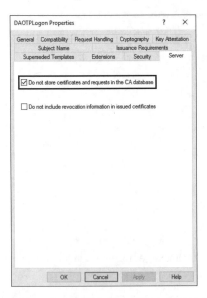

Figure 11-26 Windows Server 2016 DirectAccess OTP Certificate Template (Server)

■ The certificate Enhanced Key Usage parameter must be set correctly, as follows: For the DirectAccess registration signing certificate template, use the key 1.3.6.1.4.1.311.81.1.1 (see Figure 11-27); for the OTP authentication certificate template, use the key 1.3.6.1.4.1.311.20.2.2 (see Figure 11-28).

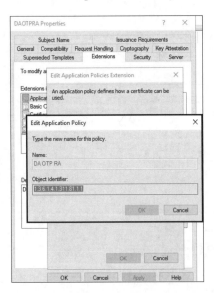

Figure 11-27 Windows Server 2016 DirectAccess Registration Signing Certificate Template (Key)

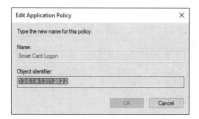

Figure 11-28 Windows Server 2016 DirectAccess OTP Authentication Certificate Template (Key)

Configure NPS Templates

You can use NPS templates to precreate configuration elements such as RADIUS clients or preshared keys (PSK), which you can reuse on a local NPS server or export for other NPS servers. NPS templates are a way for companies with many NPS servers and access clients to reduce time and cost effort. The following settings can be configured with Windows Server 2016 NPS templates:

- Shared Secrets

- RADIUS Clients

- Remote RADIUS Servers

- IP Filters

Figure 11-29 shows where to configure NPS templates.

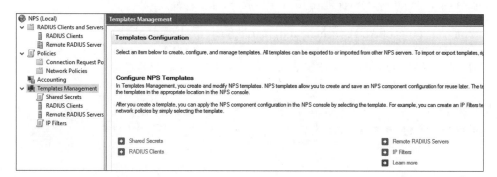

Figure 11-29 Windows Server 2016 NPS Templates

You can rename, delete, duplicate, or view usage with NPS templates. Figure 11-30 shows the possible NPS templates tasks, and Figure 11-31 gives an example of the use of a shared secret NPS template.

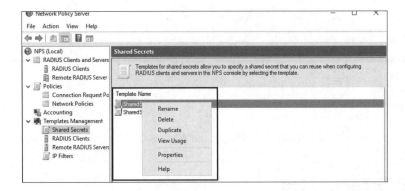

Figure 11-30   Windows Server 2016 NPS Template Tasks

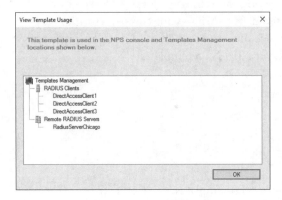

Figure 11-31   Windows Server 2016 NPS View Template Usage

You can apply a RADIUS client and Shared Secret NPS template in the New
RADIUS Client window; you can apply a Remote RADIUS Server NPS template in
the Add RADIUS Server window. See Figures 11-32 and 11-33.

TIP   You also can list your Shared Secret NPS templates with the PowerShell
cmdlet **Get-NpsSharedSecretTemplate**.

Figure 11-32   Apply Windows Server 2016 NPS RADIUS Client and Shared Secret Template

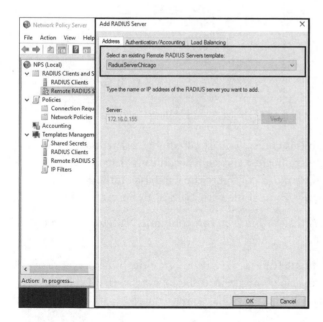

Figure 11-33   Apply Windows Server 2016 NPS Remote RADIUS Server Template

Configure RADIUS Accounting

You can configure a Windows Server 2016 NPS server for RADIUS Accounting so that the NPS server logs accounting information to log files on the local hard disk or on a Microsoft SQL Server database. Figure 11-34 shows the four different NPS accounting options you can configure in the Accounting Configuration Wizard; the following list describes them further:

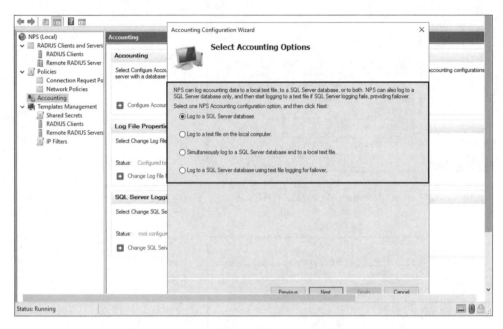

Figure 11-34 Apply Windows Server 2016 NPS RADIUS Accounting Options

- **SQL logging only:** With this choice, you can configure a data link to a SQL Server that allows NPS to connect to and send accounting data to the SQL Server. In addition, the wizard can configure the database on the SQL Server to ensure that the database is compatible with NPS SQL Server logging.

- **Text logging only:** With this setting, you can configure NPS to log accounting data to a text file.

- **Parallel logging:** With this setting, you can configure the SQL Server data link and database. You can also configure text file logging so that NPS logs simultaneously to the text file and the SQL Server database.

- **SQL logging with backup:** With this setting, you can configure the SQL Server data link and database. In addition, you can configure text file logging that NPS uses if SQL Server logging fails.

NPS Log File Properties

Figure 11-35 shows the log file properties and which log information you can choose.

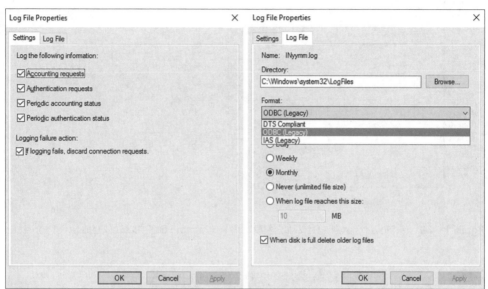

Figure 11-35   Windows Server 2016 NPS Log File Properties

TIP   To prevent NPS log files from filling the hard drive, it is recommended that you keep them on a partition that is separate from the system partition. If RADIUS Accounting fails due to a full hard disk drive or other causes, NPS stops processing connection requests, preventing users from accessing network resources.

NPS SQL Server Logging

When you set up NPS Accounting and you have selected Log to a SQL Server Database on the Accounting Configuration Wizard to use SQL Server as a repository for NPS Radius Accounting information, you have to enter the data link information (SQL Server name, authentication, SQL database name). Figure 11-36 shows the Data Link Properties window.

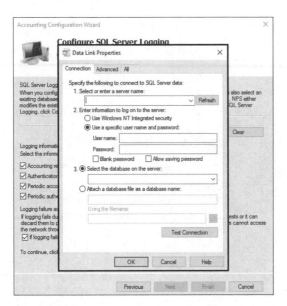

Figure 11-36 Windows Server 2016 NPS RADIUS Accounting SQL Server Data Link Properties

TIP Windows Server 2016 NPS formats accounting data as XML and sends it to the **report_event** stored procedure in the SQL Server database that you designate in NPS. For SQL Server logging to function properly, you must have a stored procedure named **report_event** in the SQL Server database that can receive and parse the XML documents from NPS.

ping user-name

These ping requests include fictional usernames.

When NPS processes these requests, the event and accounting logs become filled with access reject records, making it more difficult to keep track of valid records. When you configure a registry entry for **ping user-name**, NPS matches the registry entry value against the username value in ping requests by other servers.

A **ping user-name** registry entry specifies the fictional username (or a username pattern, with variables, that matches the fictional username) sent by RADIUS proxy servers and network access servers.

When NPS receives ping requests that match the **ping user-name** registry entry value, NPS rejects the authentication requests without processing the requests.

ping user-name is not installed by default. You must add **ping user-name** to the registry. You can add an entry to the registry using a registry editor.

You can add **ping user-name** to the following registry key as a string value: HKEY_LOCAL_ MACHINE\System\CurrentControlSet\Services\IAS\ Parameters. Item: **ping user-name**, value: *REG_SZ*, data: *User name*.

 ## Certificates

To establish an IPsec security association, the VPN client and the VPN server must use the IKE protocol to exchange computer certificates. In either case, the VPN client and server authenticate each other at the computer level. Computer certificate authentication is recommended because it is a much stronger authentication method than using a preshared key. L2TP VPN connections can use certificates for encryption, integrity, and data authentication. If you want to configure a Windows Server 2016 NPS server with PEAP, you need a certificate. You can use certificates from an internal Certificate Authority (CA) or a public CA.

Using Certificates for Windows Server 2016 NPS Servers

When you use the Windows Server 2016 NPS for a VPN server, you use the following authentication methods so that the NPS server hosts the connection request policies and Network Policies for the VPN connections:

- Protected Extensible Authentication Protocol (PEAP)

- Extensible Authentication Protocol (EAP)

- Microsoft Encrypted Authentication (MS-CHAP)

- Microsoft Encrypted Authentication version 2 (MS-CHAPv2)

MS-CHAPv2 and MS-CHAP can work without using certificates, but PEAP must use certificates.

You can configure a Windows Server 2016 NPS for the following two configuration scenarios:

- Dial-up or VPN connections

- 802.1X wireless or wired connections

Figure 11-37 shows the standard NPS configuration scenarios.

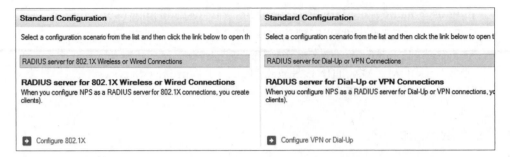

Figure 11-37   Windows Server 2016 NPS Standard Configuration Scenarios

When you use NPS as a RADIUS server for dial-up or VPN connections, your choices are MS-CHAP, MS-CHAPv2, EAP-MSCHAPv2, PEAP, and Smart Card or Other Certificate. For 802.1X wireless or wired connections, your choices are Smart Card or Other Certificates, EAP-MSCHAPv2, and PEAP.

When you select Smart Card or Other Certificates or PEAP, and you have not prepared a valid certificate on the NPS server, you get an error message like the one in Figure 11-38.

Figure 11-38   Windows Server 2016 PEAP Certificate Not Found Error

Table 11-3 shows the certificates that are required to successfully deploy each of the certificate-based authentication methods on a Windows Server 2016 NPS server.

Table 11-3 Windows Server 2016 NPS Certificates for EAP or PEAP

Certificate	Required for EAP-TLS and PEAP-TLS?	Required for PEAP-MS-CHAPv2?	Details
CA certificate in the Trusted Root Certificate Authorities certificate store for the Local Computer and Current User	Yes. CA certificate is enrolled automatically for domain members. For non–domain members, the certificate must be manually imported into the certificate store.	Yes. The certificate is enrolled automatically for domain members. For non–domain members, the certificate must be manually imported into the certificate store.	For PEAP-MS-CHAPv2, this certificate is required for mutual authentication between client and server.
Client computer certificate in the certificate store of the client	Yes. Client computer certificates are required unless user certificates are distributed on smart cards. Client certificates are enrolled automatically for domain members. For non–domain members, the certificate must be manually imported or obtained with the web enrollment tool.	No. User authentication is performed with password-based credentials, not certificates.	If you deploy user certificates on smart cards, client computers do not need client certificates.
Server certificate in the certificate store of the NPS server	Yes. Configure AD CS to autoenroll server certificates to members of the RAS and IAS servers group in AD.	Yes. In addition to using AD CS for server certificates, you can purchase server certificates from other CAs that client computers already trust.	The NPS server sends the server certificate to the client computer; the client computer uses the certificate to authenticate the NPS server.
User certificate on a smart card	No. This certificate is required only if you choose to deploy smart cards instead of autoenrolling client computer certificates.	No. User authentication is performed with password-based credentials, not certificates.	For EAP-TLS and PEAP-TLS, if you do not autoenroll client computer certificates, user certificates on smart cards are required.

Configuring Certificate Templates for EAP and PEAP

With PEAP-MS-CHAPv2, PEAP-TLS, or EAP-TLS as the authentication method, a Windows Server 2016 NPS server must use a server certificate that meets the minimum server certificate requirements. A client accepts the authentication attempt of the server when the server certificate meets the following requirements:

- The subject name contains a value. If you issue a certificate to your server running NPS that has a blank subject name, the certificate is not available to authenticate your NPS server.

- The computer certificate on the server chains to a trusted root Certificate Authority (CA) and does not fail any of the checks that are performed by CryptoAPI and that are specified in the remote access policy or network policy.

- The computer certificate for the NPS server or VPN server is configured with the Server Authentication purpose in Extended Key Usage (EKU) extensions. (The object identifier for Server Authentication is 1.3.6.1.5.5.7.3.1.)

- The server certificate is configured with a required algorithm value of RSA.

- The Subject Alternative Name extension, if used, must contain the DNS name of the server.

When using PEAP and EAP-TLS, NPS servers display a list of all installed certificates in the computer certificate store, with the following exceptions:

- Certificates that do not contain the Server Authentication purpose are not displayed.

- Certificates that do not contain a subject name are not displayed.

- Registry-based and smart card logon certificates are not displayed.

Connection Request Policies

Connection request policies are condition sets and settings that allow administrators to designate which RADIUS servers do the authentication and authorization of connection requests that the NPS server receives from RADIUS clients.

Connection request policies allow you to designate whether the local NPS server processes connection requests locally or whether they are forwarded for processing to another RADIUS server. With connection request policies, you can use NPS servers as a RADIUS server or RADIUS proxy, based on a variety of factors:

- Time of day and day of the week

- Realm name in the connection request

- Connection type you are requesting

- RADIUS client's IP address

Default Connection Request Policy

The default connection request policy uses NPS as a RADIUS server and processes all authentication requests locally. You can delete the default connection request policy if you do not want the NPS server to act as a RADIUS server and process connection requests locally. When you install an NPS server, the default connection request policy is created with the following conditions:

- Authentication is not configured.

  - Accounting is not configured to forward accounting information to a remote RADIUS server group. Attribute manipulation is not configured with rules that change attributes in forwarded connection requests.

  - Forwarding Request is turned off, which means that the local NPS authenticates and authorizes connection requests.

- Advanced attributes are not configured.

- The default connection request policy uses NPS as a RADIUS server.

Figure 11-39 shows the Overview, Conditions, and Settings of the default NPS connection request policy.

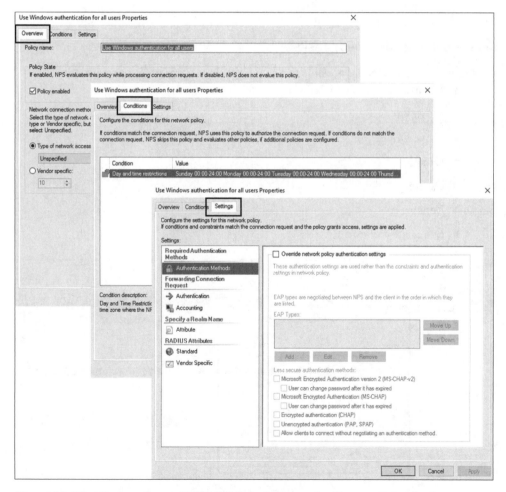

Figure 11-39   Windows Server 2016 NPS Default Connection Request Policy Settings

Creating a New Connection Request Policy

If the NPS server has to work as both a RADIUS server, processing connection requests locally, and a RADIUS proxy, add a new connection request policy using the following steps; then verify that the default connection request policy is the last policy processed by placing it last in the list of policies:

Step 1.   In Server Manager, click **Tools**, and then click **Network Policy Server**.

Step 2.   In the console tree, double-click **Policies**.

Step 3.   Right-click **Connection Request Policies**, and then click **New Connection Request Policy**.

Step 4.   Use the New Connection Request Policy Wizard to configure your connection request policy and, if not previously configured, a remote RADIUS server group.

Connection Request Policy Tasks

Figure 11-40 shows the possible tasks you can do with connection request policies on a Windows Server 2016 NPS server:

- Move Up
- Move Down
- Disable
- Delete
- Rename
- Duplicate Policy

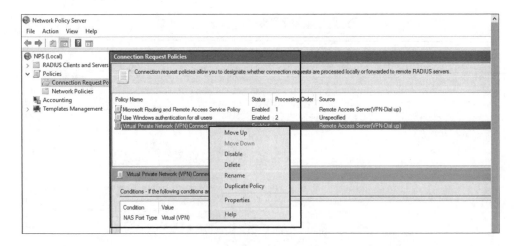

Figure 11-40   Windows Server 2016 NPS Connection Request Policy Tasks

Network Policies for VPN Wireless and Wired Clients

A Windows Server 2016 NPS network policy is a set of conditions, constraints, and settings that enable you to designate who is authorized to connect to the network and the circumstances under which they can or cannot connect.

Figure 11-41 shows where you can create a new Windows Server 2016 NPS network policy.

Figure 11-41 Windows Server 2016 NPS New Network Policy

Each network policy has four categories of properties (see Figure 11-42).

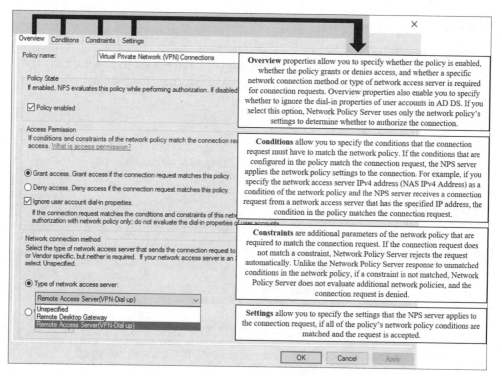

Figure 11-42 Windows Server 2016 NPS Network Policy Categories

Network Policy Ordering

When a Windows Server 2016 NPS performs the authorization of a connection request, it compares the request with each network policy in the ordered list of policies, starting with the first policy and then moving down the list of configured policies.

If NPS finds a policy whose conditions match the connection request, NPS uses the matching policy and the dial-in properties of the user account to perform authorization. If the dial-in properties of the user account are configured to grant access or control access through network policy and the connection request is authorized, NPS applies the settings that are configured in the network policy to the connection.

If NPS does not find a network policy that matches the connection request, the connection request is rejected unless the dial-in properties on the user account are set to grant access.

If the dial-in properties of the user account are set to deny access, NPS rejects the connection request.

Network Policy Key Settings

When you use the New Network Policy Wizard to create a network policy, the value that you specify in Network Connection Method is used to automatically configure the Policy Type condition. Figure 11-43 shows the choices.

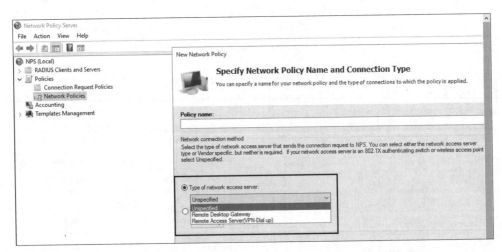

Figure 11-43   Windows Server 2016 Network Policy Network Connection Method

If you select Unspecified, NPC evaluates the network policy that you create for all connection types that are using any kind of network access server. If you specify a network connection method, NPS evaluates the network policy only if the connection request originates from the type of network access server that you specify.

On the Specify Access Permission page, you must select Access Granted if you want the policy to allow users to connect to your network. If you want the policy to prevent users from connecting to your network, select Access Denied. Figure 11-44 shows the Specify Access Permission page.

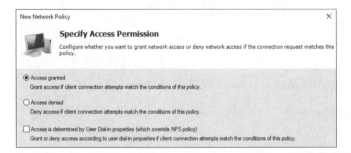

Figure 11-44   Windows Server 2016 Network Policy Specify Access Permission

When you want access permission to be determined by the user's dial-in properties in AD DS, you can select Access Is Determined by User Dial-in Properties.

You can create a network policy for 802.1X wired or wireless with the following steps:

Step 1.   On the NPS server, in Server Manager, click **Tools** and then click **Network Policy Server**.

Step 2.   Click **NPS (Local)**. Select the server.

Step 3.   In Getting Started and Standard Configuration, select **RADIUS Server for 802.1X Wireless or Wired Connections**.

Step 4.   Click **Configure 802.1X Using a Wizard**. The New IEEE 802.1X Secure Wired and Wireless Connections Wizard opens.

Step 5.   Follow the instructions in the wizard to finish creating your new policies.

Network Policy Conditions

Figure 11-45 lists all possible conditions in an NPS network policy.

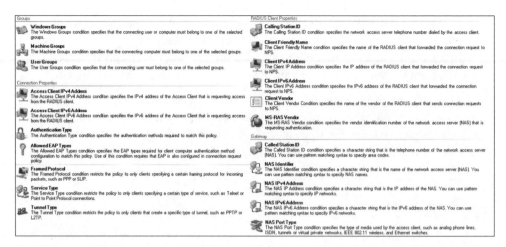

Figure 11-45   Windows Server 2016 Available Network Policy Conditions

Configuring NPS for VLANs

You can provide visitors with wireless access to the Internet without allowing them access to your organization's network.

With VLANs, you can create logical network resources groups that exist in different physical locations or subnets. For example, members of your marketing department and their network resources might be located in several different buildings at your organization, but you can place all of these resources on one VLAN that uses the same IP address range. The VLAN then functions as a single subnet.

You can also use VLANs when you want to segregate a network between different groups of users. After you have determined how you want to define your groups, you can create security groups in Active Directory and then add members to the groups.

You can use the following steps to configure a network policy for VLANs:

Step 1.   On the NPS server, in Server Manager, click **Tools** and then click **Network Policy Server**.

Step 2.   Double-click **Policies**, click **Network Policies**, and then, in the details pane, double-click the policy that you want to configure.

Step 3.   In the policy Properties dialog box, click the **Settings** tab.

Step 4.   In RADIUS Attributes, ensure that Standard is selected.

Step 5.   In the details pane, the Service-Type attribute is configured with a default value of Framed. By default, for policies with access methods of VPN and dial-up, the Framed-Protocol attribute is configured with a value of PPP. To specify additional connection attributes required for VLANs, click **Add**. The Add Standard RADIUS Attribute dialog box opens.

Step 6.   In Add Standard RADIUS Attribute, in Attributes, scroll down and add the following attributes:

- **Tunnel-Medium-Type:** Select a value appropriate to the previous selections you have made for the policy. For example, if the network policy you are configuring is a wireless policy, select **Value: 802 (Includes All 802 Media Plus Ethernet Canonical Format)**.

- **Tunnel-Pvt-Group-ID:** Enter the integer that represents the VLAN number to which group members will be assigned.

- **Tunnel-Type:** Select **Virtual LANs (VLAN)**.

After Step 6, the configuration should look like Figure 11-46.

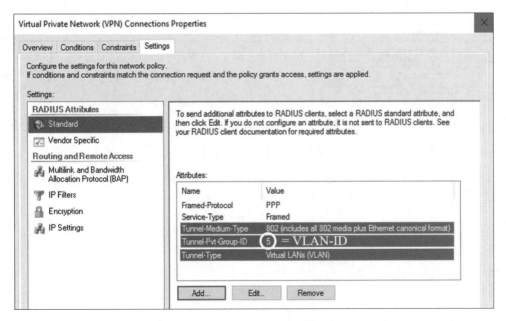

Figure 11-46   Windows Server 2016 Network Policy for VLANs

Step 7.   In Add Standard RADIUS Attribute, click Close.

Import and Export NPS Policies

You can export NPS Network Policies, connection request policies, and shared secrets for RADIUS clients and members of RADIUS server groups for a Windows Server 2016 NPS server through the NPS console (see Figure 11-47).

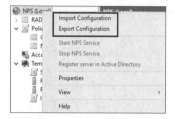

Figure 11-47   Windows Server 2016 Network Policy Import/Export

After selecting **Export Configuration**, you get an information dialog box, which informs you that unencrypted shared secrets are part of the configuration file. The dialog box also tells you that the SQL Server Logging settings are not exported to the file and must be manually configured (see Figure 11-48).

Figure 11-48   Windows Server 2016 Export Shared Secret Dialog Box

After importing the NPS settings, you get another information dialog box about SQL Server Logging settings (see Figure 11-49).

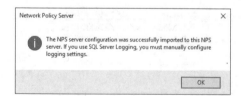

Figure 11-49   Windows Server 2016 NPS Import Configuration Dialog Box

You also can import or export the NPS settings through PowerShell with the cmdlets **Import-NpsConfiguration** and **Export-NpsConfiguration**.

Exam Preparation Tasks

Review All the Key Topics

Review the most important topics in the chapter, noted with the Key Topics icon in the outer margin of the page. Table 11-4 lists these key topics and the page numbers where each is found.

Table 11-4   Key Topics for Chapter 11

Key Topic Element	Description	Page Number
Section	Implementing RADIUS	489
Section	Registering the NPS Server in Active Directory	491
Section	RADIUS Client Configuration	493
Figure 11-7	Windows Server 2016 NPS RADIUS Client Settings	494
Section	Implementing RADIUS Proxy	496
Section	Implementing RADIUS Clients	497
Table 11-2	Windows Server 2016 Remote Access RADIUS PowerShell Cmdlets	498
Step List	Configuring a DirectAccess server as a RADIUS client	502
List	OTP certificate templates	509
Section	Configure NPS Templates	513
List	RADIUS Accounting options	516
Figure 11-35	Windows Server 2016 NPS Log File Properties	517
Section	NPS SQL Server Logging	517
Section	ping user-name	518
Section	Certificates	519
Table 11-3	Windows Server 2016 NPS Certificates for EAP or PEAP	521
Section	Configuring Certificate Templates for EAP and PEAP	521
Section	Connection Request Policies	522
Section	Default Connection Request Policy	522
Step List	Creating a new connection request policy	524
Section	Connection Request Policy Tasks	524

Key Topic Element	Description	Page Number
Section	Network Policies for VPN Wireless and Wired Clients	525
Section	Network Policy Ordering	526
Section	Network Policy Key Settings	526
Step List	Configuring NPS for VLANs	528
Section	Import and Export NPS Policies	530

Complete the Tables and Lists from Memory

Print a copy of Appendix B, "Memory Tables" (on the book's website), or at least the section for this chapter, and complete the tables and lists from memory. Appendix C, "Memory Tables Answer Key," also on the website, includes completed tables and lists to check your work.

Definition of Key Terms

Define the following key terms from this chapter and check your answers in the glossary.

RADIUS client, RADIUS server, RADIUS proxy, RADIUS protocol, NPS server, connection request policy, Network Policy, Network Access Protection, Health Registration Authority, HCAP

End-of-Chapter Review Questions

1. You want to implement some Windows Server 2016 NPS servers as RADIUS servers. You must use EAP authentication. Which scenarios can you configure? (Choose four.)

   a. Use a domain or local SAM user accounts database as the user account database for clients.

   b. Remotely manage mobile devices through Enterprise Mobility solutions.

   c. Use the NPS servers as on-premises MFA authentication servers.

   d. Use Remote Access on multiple dial-up servers, VPN servers, or demand-dial routers. Centralize both the configuration of Network Policies and connection logging and accounting.

    e. Outsource dial-up, VPN, or wireless access to a service provider. The access servers can use RADIUS to authenticate and authorize connections that are made by members of your organization.

    f. Use the Azure MFA authentication server as a RADIUS client for the NPS servers.

    g. Centralize authentication, authorization, and accounting for a heterogeneous set of access servers.

2. You want to set up high-availability solutions to forward VPN authentication requests to different RADIUS servers. You install and configure two Windows Server 2016 NPS servers as RADIUS proxy servers. Your domain name is pearson.com. You want to forward connection requests to untrusted domains. Which components on the RADIUS proxy servers do you have to configure to allow them to work as RADIUS proxies to forward requests to Windows Server 2016 RADIUS servers in the domains pucertify.com, eu.pucertify.com, and usa.pucertify.com? You also want to prevent administrative overhead and incorrect configuration on both RADIUS proxy servers. (Choose four.)

    a. Create three connection request policies.

    b. Create one connection request policy.

    c. Create an attribute manipulation rule.

    d. Add remote RADIUS server groups.

    e. Add three new Network Policies.

    f. Add a RADIUS proxy server group to pearson.com.

    g. Copy NPS proxy configuration between both RADIUS proxy servers with a script.

    h. Configure one RADIUS proxy server group and add the servers into that group.

3. You have to set up 100 servers worldwide. You have to configure 50 VPN servers to forward authentication requests to Windows Server 2016 RADIUS servers in different locations. You also have to configure 50 Windows Server 2016 DirectAccess servers with OTP to forward authentication requests to Windows Server 2016 RADIUS servers. Which PowerShell cmdlet do you have to use on your Windows Server 2016 RADIUS servers to integrate the VPN servers, and how many certificate templates do you need for the DirectAccess OTP RADIUS clients? (Choose two.)

    a. **Add-RemoteAccessRadius**

    b. **New-NpsRadiusClient**

    c. **Add-NpsRadiusClient**

d. **New-VPNServerAddress**

e. 2 certificate templates

f. 1 certificate template

4. You have 200 RADIUS servers in your enterprise. You have configured NPS templates to reduce administrative overhead. Which settings can you configure with NPS templates? (Choose four.)

a. Shared Secrets

b. Connection Request Policies

c. Network Policies

d. Network Access Protection

e. Remote RADIUS Servers

f. RADIUS Clients

g. IP Filters

5. You configure a Windows Server 2016 NPS server as a RADIUS server, and you configure RADIUS Accounting with SQL Server as a repository for accounting data. If no usable stored procedure exists, which SQL query command do you have to run?

a.
```
CREATE
PROCEDURE
[
dbo
].[Report_NPS]
```

b.
```
CREATE
PROCEDURE
[
dbo
].[Report_Event]
```

c.
```
CREATE
PROCEDURE
[
dbo
].[Report_XML]
```

d.

```
CREATE

PROCEDURE
[
dbo
].[Report_RADIUS]
```

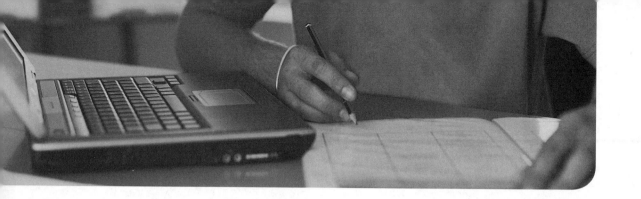

This chapter covers the following subjects:

- **Configuring IPv4 addresses and options:** This chapter covers configuring Windows Server 2016 IPv4 addresses and network interface settings manually through the GUI and PowerShell commands, as well as through DHCP. The chapter also explores which PowerShell cmdlets you can use to troubleshoot IPv4 network configuration settings.

- **Determining and configuring appropriate IPv6 addresses:** Here you investigate the configuration of local Windows Server 2016 IPv6 settings through the GUI and PowerShell cmdlets. The chapter covers general and advanced IPv6 network interface settings and discusses the differences between IPv4 and IPv6 address assignment. You see some examples of IPv6 configurations with PowerShell, learn the most important facts about IPv6 addresses, and see how to configure IPv6 through DHCPv6 and IPv6 prefix policies.

- **Configuring IPv4 or IPv6 subnetting:** This chapter details the most important facts about IPv4 and IPv6 subnetting.

- **Implementing IPv6 stateless addressing:** Here you investigate stateless IPv6 addressing and how to configure it with PowerShell cmdlets.

- **Configuring interoperability between IPv4 and IPv6 by using ISATAP, 6to4, and Teredo scenarios:** Information covered includes IPv6 over IPv4 tunneling and different scenarios for configuring and using 6to4, Teredo, and ISATAP.

- **Configuring Border Gateway Protocol (BGP):** In addition to explaining the use of BGP for software-defined networking (SDN) and important BGP features, you learn how to use BGP for Windows Server 2016 RAS Gateways with multitenant capability and how to use PowerShell cmdlets to configure BGP.

- **Configuring IPv4 and IPv6 routing:** You explore the most important PowerShell cmdlets to configure IPv4 and IPv6 routing.

## CHAPTER 12

Implementing Windows Server 2016 IPv4 and IPv6 Addressing

This chapter covers configuring Windows Server 2016 IPv4 addresses and network interface settings manually through the GUI and PowerShell commands (as well as through DHCP, although the primary focus is on the PowerShell commands). The chapter also explores which PowerShell cmdlets you use to troubleshoot IPv4 network configuration settings.

You also look into the differences between IPv4 and IPv6 address assignment, learn the most important facts about IPv6 addresses, and see how to configure IPv6 through DHCPv6 and IPv6 prefix policies.

In addition you learn the most important facts about IPv4 and IPv6 subnetting, stateful and stateless IPv6 addressing, IPv6 over IPv4 tunneling, 6to4, Teredo, and ISATAP, and you learn how to use them in different scenarios. You also look at the base Windows Server 2016 configuration for 6to4, Teredo, and ISATAP.

The chapter looks at BGP for software-defined networking (SDN) and important BGP features as well. You see how to use BGP for Windows Server 2016 RAS Gateways with multitenant capability and you check out many PowerShell cmdlets that you can use to configure BGP.

The key topic selections, memory tables, key term definitions, and exam preparation questions give you some powerful tools to increase your knowledge about Windows Server 2016 IPv4 and IPv6 addressing for the Microsoft 70-741 exam and your daily work.

"Do I Know This Already?" Quiz

The "Do I Know This Already?" quiz enables you to assess whether you should read this entire chapter or simply jump to the "Exam Preparation Tasks" section for review. If you are in doubt, read the entire chapter. Table 12-1 outlines the major headings in this chapter and the corresponding "Do I Know This

Already?" quiz questions. You can find the answers in Appendix A, "Answers to the 'Do I Know This Already?' Quizzes and End-of-Chapter Review Questions."

Table 12-1 "Do I Know This Already?" Foundation Topics Section-to-Question Mapping

Foundation Topics Section	Questions Covered in This Section
Configure IPv4 Addresses and Options	1
Determine and Configure Appropriate IPv6 Addresses	2
Configure IPv4 or IPv6 Subnetting	3
Implement IPv6 Stateless Addressing	4
Configure Interoperability Between IPv4 and IPv6 by Using ISATAP, 6to4, and Teredo Scenarios	5
Configure Border Gateway Protocol (BGP)	6
Configure IPv4 and IPv6 Routing	7

CAUTION The goal of self-assessment is to gauge your mastery of the topics in this chapter. If you do not know the answer to a question or are only partially sure of the answer, you should mark that question as wrong for purposes of the self-assessment. Giving yourself credit for an answer you correctly guess skews your self-assessment results and might provide you with a false sense of security.

1. You want to configure an additional DNS server on your network interface. Which PowerShell cmdlet should you use?

   a. **Set-NetIPAddress**

   b. **New-NetIPAddress**

   c. **Set-DnsClientServerAddress**

   d. **Set-DnsClient**

2. You have implemented four new 100-Gbps network adapters on your Windows Server 2016 Hyper-V host. You want to improve throughput and reduce network latency using these network adapters for SET and SDN. Which PowerShell cmdlet can you use to enable this on your network adapters?

   a. **Enable-NetAdapterRdma**

   b. **Enable-NetAdapterPacketDirect**

   c. **Enable-NetAdapterSriov**

   d. **Enable-NetAdapterVmq**

3. You have two Hyper-V VMs named VM1 and VM2. The IPv4 configuration follows:

   - VM1: 192.168.66.5/19

   - VM2: 192.168.34.12/19

   No router is configured between these two VMs, and both VMs are using a network switch named Switch1 (private). You use Windows Server 2016 Network Controller and the Datacenter Firewall.

   Which configuration change must you implement to allow both VMs to reach each other through the network?

   a. **Set-NetIPAddress 192.168.36.7/19** on VM1

   b. Change Switch1 to public

   c. **Set-NetIPAddress 192.168.98.3/19** on VM1

   d. Configure the Datacenter Firewall to allow network traffic between VM1 and VM2

4. You need to add a new IPv6 subnet to the routing table of your ISATAP router, to allow the stateless configuration of IPv6 hosts in that subnet automatically. Which parameter of the **New-NetRoute** PowerShell cmdlet should you use?

   a. **Advertising**

   b. **Forward**

   c. **Publish**

5. You need to implement a transition mechanism to implement a mix of IPv4 and IPv6 network solutions. Network traffic must traverse NAT. Which transition mechanism is not a valid solution for this scenario?

   a. Teredo

   b. 6to4

   c. ISATAP

6. You need to configure a RAS Gateway and you must enable BGP for each tenant. Which PowerShell command can you use to accomplish this?

   a. **Enable-RemoteAccessRoutingDomain**

   b. **Set-RemoteAccessConfiguration**

   c. **Enable-NetworkSwitchFeature**

   d. **Enable-BgpRouteFlapDampening**

7. You have configured an Azure P2S VPN connection and successfully connected to Azure from your P2S client. You want to know which IP address is used as a gateway to the Azure VNet. Which PowerShell cmdlet can you use to determine this information?

   a. **Get-NetIPAddress**

   b. **Get-NetRoute**

   c. **Get-NetIPInterface**

   d. **Get-BgpCustomRoute**

Foundation Topics

Configure IPv4 Addresses and Options

You can configure IPv4 addresses manually or automatically. To configure an IPv4 address manually, enter the IPv4 address by using the Windows Server 2016 GUI or by using PowerShell. An IPv4 address is configured automatically when a server runs DHCP and assigns an IPv4 address to the computers. Static IP addresses are usually configured on servers, routers, switches, or other network devices that need to maintain persistent IP configuration that does not change over time. Figure 12-1 shows the general and advanced TCP/IP settings of a network card.

To configure a static IP address for a server in an IPv4 configuration, you need to determine the following settings:

- IPv4 address

- Subnet mask

- Default gateway

- DNS servers

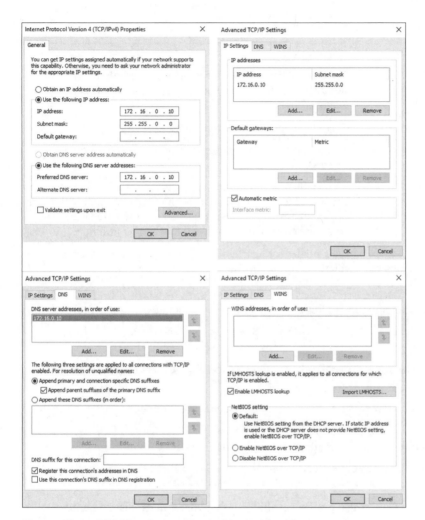

Figure 12-1 TCP/IPv4 Properties of a Network Interface

Windows Server 2016 includes PowerShell cmdlets that you can use to manage network configuration. Table 12-2 describes some of the Windows PowerShell cmdlets that are available for configuring IPv4.

Table 12-2   IPv4 IP Address PowerShell Cmdlets

Cmdlet	Description
New-NetIPAddress	Use this cmdlet to create a new IP address and bind it to a network adapter. You cannot use this command to change an IP address.
Set-NetIPAddress	This cmdlet changes the configuration of an IP address.
Set-NetIPInterface	You can use this cmdlet to enable or disable DHCP for an interface.
New-NetRoute	This cmdlet creates routing table entries, including the default gateway (0.0.0.0). You cannot use this cmdlet to modify the next hop of an existing route; instead, you must remove an existing route and create a new route with the correct next hop.
Set-DNSClientServerAddress	This cmdlet configures the DNS server that is used for an interface.

The following command applies a new IPv4 address to a network interface:

```
New-NetIPAddress -InterfaceAlias "Ethernet" -IPAddress 172.16.0.10
  -PrefixLength 24 -DefaultGateway 172.16.0.1
```

With the following command, you configure two DNS servers on the network interface:

```
Set-DNSSclientServerAddress -InterfaceAlias "Ethernet"
  -ServerAddresses 172.16.0.10, 172.16.0.11
```

You can configure a static IP address by using the **netsh** command-line tool:

```
Netsh interface ipv4 set address name="Local Area Connection"
  source=static addr=172.16.0.10 mask=255.255.255.0 gateway=172.16.0.1
```

Windows Server 2016 also has PowerShell cmdlets that you can use to enable DHCP for an interface. Table 12-3 describes some of the available PowerShell cmdlets for configuring DHCP on an interface.

Table 12-3   Configuring DHCP on a Network Interface with PowerShell Cmdlets

Cmdlet	Description
Get-NetIPInterface	Obtains a list of interfaces and their configuration. This does not include IPv4 configuration of the interface.
Set-NetIPInterface	Enables or disables DHCP for an interface.
Get-NetAdapter	Obtains a list of network adapters in a computer.
Restart-NetAdapter	Disables and re-enables a network adapter. This forces a DHCP client to obtain a new DHCP lease.

With the following command, you enable DHCP for a network adapter:

```
Set-NetIPInterface -InterfaceAlias "Ethernet" -Dhcp Enabled
Restart-NetAdapter -Name "Ethernet"
```

Table 12-4 shows PowerShell cmdlets for troubleshooting IPv4 network configurations.

Table 12-4   PowerShell Cmdlets to Troubleshoot IPv4 Network Configurations

Cmdlet	Description
Get-NetAdapter	Obtains a list of network adapters in a computer.
Get-NetIPv4Protocol	Gets information about the IPv4 protocol configuration. Note that **Get-NetIPv6Protocol** gets information about the IPv6 protocol configuration.
Restart-NetAdapter	Disables and re-enables a network adapter.
Get-NetIPInterface	Obtains a list of interfaces and their configuration.
Get-NetIPAddress	Obtains a list of IP addresses that are configured for interfaces.
Get-NetRoute	Obtains the list of routes in the local routing table.
Get-NetConnectionProfile	Obtains the type of network (public, private, domain) to which a network adapter is connected.
Get-DnsClient	Retrieves configuration details specific to the different network interfaces on a specified computer.
Get-DNSClientCache	Obtains the list of resolved DNS names that are stored in the DNS client cache.
Get-DnsClientGlobalSetting	Retrieves global DNS client settings, such as the suffix search list.
Get-DNSClientServerAddress	Obtains the list of DNS servers that are used for each interface.
Register-DnsClient	Registers all the IP addresses on the computer on the configured DNS server.
Set-DnsClient	Sets the interface-specific DNS client configurations on the computer.
Set-DnsClientGlobalSetting	Configures the global DNS client settings, such as the suffix search list.
Set-DnsClientServerAddress	Configures the computer's network adapter with the IP addresses of the DNS server.

Cmdlet	Description
Set-NetIPAddress	Sets information about the IP address configuration.
Set-NetIPv4Protocol	Sets information about the IPv4 protocol configuration. Note that **Set-NetIPv6Protocol** returns information about the IPv6 protocol configuration.
Set-NetIPInterface	Modifies the IP interface properties.
Test-Connection	Runs connectivity tests that are similar to those used by **ping**.
Test-NetConnection	Displays the results of a DNS lookup, the IP interfaces, an option to test a TCP connection, IPsec rules, and confirmation of connection establishment.
Resolve-Dnsname	Performs a DNS name query resolution for the specified name.

Determine and Configure Appropriate IPv6 Addresses

Address assignment on IPv6 networks is slightly different than with IPv4 networks. IPv6 addresses can be assigned manually with one or more IPv6 addresses on the interface, through stateful address autoconfiguration using a DHCPv6 server, as stateless based on receipt of router advertisement messages, or with both stateful and stateless address autoconfiguration. The main difference between address assignment in IPv6 and in IPv4, however, is that the IPv6 protocol was designed to be configured automatically. Specifically, an IPv6 network interface typically has at least two addresses:

- An automatically generated link-local address, used for traffic on the local link

- An additional unicast address (either a global address or a unique local address), used for traffic that needs to be routed beyond the local link

Configuring Local IPv6 Settings (GUI)

Figure 12-2 shows the default TCP/IPv6 properties of a network interface on a Windows Server 2016 server.

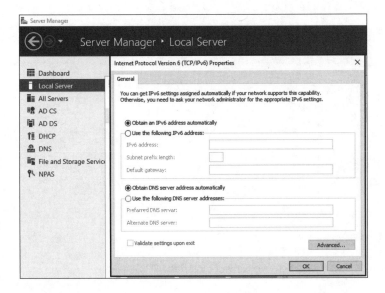

Figure 12-2   Default TCP/IPv6 Properties of a Network Interface

General Tab

When configuring IPv6 settings on a network interface, you have multiple options;
default settings are stateful or stateless address autoconfiguration. On the General tab
of the Internet Protocol Version 6 (TCP/IPv6) Properties dialog box, you can configure to obtain an IPv6 address automatically or specify an IPv6 address manually
(including the subnet prefix length, which should be set to 64 as the default value—
specify the default gateway IPv6 unicast address). You also can choose between
obtaining the DNS server IPv6 address automatically from a DHCPv6 server or
manually specifying the preferred and alternate DNS server IPv6 addresses.

Advanced TCP/IP Settings

From the General tab, you can click Advanced to access the Advanced TCP/IP
Settings dialog box (see Figure 12-3). This is similar to the Advanced TCP/IPv4
Settings dialog box, except that it has no WINS tab (IPv6 does not use NetBIOS or
WINS) and no Options tab (filtering is defined only for IPv4 traffic). For IPv6, the
dialog box has IP Settings and DNS settings.

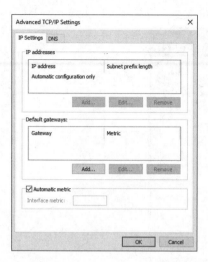

Figure 12-3   Advanced TCP/IPv6 Properties of a Network Interface (IP Settings)

Here you can configure the following:

- **Multiple IPv6 addresses:** For each IPv6 address, you must specify an IPv6 address and a subnet prefix length. The Add button is available only if Use the Following IPv6 Address is selected on the General tab.

- **Multiple default gateways:** For each gateway, you must specify the IPv6 address of the gateway and whether you want the metric for the default route associated with this default gateway to be manually specified.

- **Route metrics:** You can use a specific metric for the routes or default gateways or use a metric determined by the speed of the connection or adapter.

DNS Tab

From the DNS tab, shown in Figure 12-4, you can configure the settings described in the list that follows.

- **DNS Server Addresses, in Order of Use:** Specifies the IPv6 addresses of DNS servers to query for resolving DNS domain names. DNS servers are queried in the order in which they are listed here.

- **Append Primary and Connection-Specific DNS Suffixes:** Specifies that resolution for unqualified names is limited to the domain suffixes of the primary suffix and all connection-specific suffixes. The connection-specific DNS suffixes are configured in the DNS suffix for this connection.

- **Append These DNS Suffixes (in Order):** Lists the DNS suffixes to search in the order listed.

- **DNS Suffix for This Connection:** Provides a space for you to specify a DNS suffix for this connection, unless configured by stateful address autoconfiguration (DHCPv6).

- **Register This Connection's Addresses in DNS:** Specifies that the computer attempts dynamic registration of the IP addresses (through DNS) of this connection with the full computer name of this computer.

- **Use This Connection's DNS Suffix in DNS Registration:** If the checkbox is selected, this registration is in addition to the DNS registration of the full computer name.

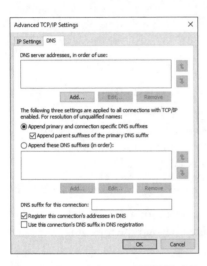

Figure 12-4   Advanced TCP/IPv6 Properties of a Network Interface (DNS)

IPv4 and IPv6 Assignment Differences

On IPv4 networks, you can assign addresses to an interface in three ways:

- Manually, by using static addresses

- Dynamically, by using DHCP server

- Automatically, by using APIPA

Administrators of small networks often configure IPv4 addresses manually; midsize and large organizations typically use DHCP. Automatic address configuration by using APIPA is usually done only on very small networks, such as a home or office LAN that connects to the Internet using a personal router.

IPv6 address assignment is slightly different. For example, IPv6 addresses can be assigned to an interface in four ways:

- Manually, by configuring one or more IPv6 addresses on the interface

- Stateful, by using address autoconfiguration through a DHCPv6 server

- Stateless, by using autoconfiguration based on the receipt of router advertisement messages

- Stateful and stateless (both), by address autoconfiguration

TIP   The operating system always automatically configures IPv6 link-local addresses on an interface, regardless of whether stateful or stateless address autoconfiguration is deployed. The address block FE80::/10 is reserved for link-local unicast addressing. To conform to standard /64 addressing on subnets, the actual link-local addresses are assigned with the prefix FE80::/64.

The big address assignment difference between IPv6 and IPv4 is that IPv6 was made to be configured automatically. You typically do not need to assign addresses manually or deploy a DHCPv6 server; instead, you can use stateless address autoconfiguration. Network adapters on IPv6 hosts are mostly multihomed with multiple addresses assigned. An IPv6 interface typically has at least two addresses:

- An automatically generated link-local address, used for traffic on the local link

- An additional unicast address (either a global address or a unique local address), used for traffic that needs to be routed beyond the local link

Configuring Local IPv6 Network Settings with PowerShell

In Windows Server 2016, you can configure IPv6 addresses, default gateways, and DNS servers with Windows PowerShell cmdlets, such as those described in Table 12-5.

Table 12-5   PowerShell Cmdlets to Configure IPv6 Settings

Cmdlet	Description
Set-NetIPAddress	Modifies IP address configuration properties of an existing IP address
Set-NetIPInterface	Modifies IP interface properties
Set-NetIPv6Protocol	Modifies information about the IPv6 protocol configuration
Set-NetNeighbor	Modifies a neighbor cache entry
Set-NetRouteWindows	Modifies one or more entries in the routing table
Set-DnsClientServerAddress	Modifies DNS server addresses associated with an interface

Use the **Get-NetAdapter** PowerShell cmdlet to display a list of names and indexes of the network interface on computers running Windows Server 2016 (see Figure 12-5).

```
PS C:\> get-netadapter | ? interfacealias -eq 'Ethernet' | FL

MacAddress                  : 00-15-5D-01-0F-54
Status                      : Up
LinkSpeed                   : 1 Gbps
MediaType                   : 802.3
PhysicalMediaType           : Unspecified
AdminStatus                 : Up
MediaConnectionState        : Connected
DriverInformation           : Driver Date 2006-06-21 Version 10.0.14300.1000 NDIS 6.60
DriverFileName              : netvsc.sys
NdisVersion                 : 6.60
ifOperStatus                : Up
ifAlias                     : Ethernet
InterfaceAlias              : Ethernet
ifIndex                     : 2
ifDesc                      : Microsoft Hyper-V Network Adapter
ifName                      : ethernet_32769
DriverVersion               : 10.0.14300.1000
LinkLayerAddress            : 00-15-5D-01-0F-54
Caption                     :
Description                 :
ElementName                 :
InstanceID                  : {2AA4A15A-65D1-4829-9919-BF190A3148A7}
CommunicationStatus         :
DetailedStatus              :
HealthState                 :
InstallDate                 :
Name                        : Ethernet
OperatingStatus             :
OperationalStatus           :
PrimaryStatus               :
StatusDescriptions          :
AvailableRequestedStates    :
EnabledDefault              : 2
EnabledState                : 5
OtherEnabledState           :
RequestedState              : 12
TimeOfLastStateChange       :
TransitioningToState        : 12
```

Figure 12-5   Get-NetAdapter

You also can use the **Get-NetIPAddress** PowerShell cmdlet to display address information for all local IPv6 interfaces (see Figure 12-6).

```
PS C:\> Get-NetIPAddress | ? addressfamily -eq IPv6

IPAddress          : fe80::d956:ac88:c6fc:d3f0%2
InterfaceIndex     : 2
InterfaceAlias     : Ethernet
AddressFamily      : IPv6
Type               : Unicast
PrefixLength       : 64
PrefixOrigin       : WellKnown
SuffixOrigin       : Link
AddressState       : Preferred
ValidLifetime      : Infinite ([TimeSpan]::MaxValue)
PreferredLifetime  : Infinite ([TimeSpan]::MaxValue)
SkipAsSource       : False
PolicyStore        : ActiveStore

IPAddress          : fe80::5efe:172.16.0.10%3
InterfaceIndex     : 3
InterfaceAlias     : isatap.{2AA4A15A-65D1-4829-9919-BF190A3148A7}
AddressFamily      : IPv6
Type               : Unicast
PrefixLength       : 128
PrefixOrigin       : WellKnown
SuffixOrigin       : Link
AddressState       : Preferred
ValidLifetime      : Infinite ([TimeSpan]::MaxValue)
PreferredLifetime  : Infinite ([TimeSpan]::MaxValue)
SkipAsSource       : False
PolicyStore        : ActiveStore

IPAddress          : ::1
InterfaceIndex     : 1
InterfaceAlias     : Loopback Pseudo-Interface 1
AddressFamily      : IPv6
Type               : Unicast
PrefixLength       : 128
PrefixOrigin       : WellKnown
SuffixOrigin       : WellKnown
AddressState       : Preferred
ValidLifetime      : Infinite ([TimeSpan]::MaxValue)
PreferredLifetime  : Infinite ([TimeSpan]::MaxValue)
SkipAsSource       : False
PolicyStore        : ActiveStore
```

Figure 12-6   Get-NetIPAddress

You can use the **New-NetIPAddress** PowerShell cmdlet to apply a new global unicast IPv6 address with prefix length 64 and a gateway to the Ethernet interface (see Figure 12-7).

```
PS C:\> New-NetIPAddress -InterfaceAlias "Ethernet" -IPAddress 2001:DB6:3FA8::D1:9C4A ' -PrefixLength 64 -DefaultGateway 2001:DB6:3FA8::1C0

IPAddress           : 2001:db6:3fa8::d1:9c4a
InterfaceIndex      : 2
InterfaceAlias      : Ethernet
AddressFamily       : IPv6
Type                : Unicast
PrefixLength        : 64
PrefixOrigin        : Manual
SuffixOrigin        : Manual
AddressState        : Tentative
ValidLifetime       : Infinite ([TimeSpan]::MaxValue)
PreferredLifetime   : Infinite ([TimeSpan]::MaxValue)
SkipAsSource        : False
PolicyStore         : ActiveStore

IPAddress           : 2001:db6:3fa8::d1:9c4a
InterfaceIndex      : 2
InterfaceAlias      : Ethernet
AddressFamily       : IPv6
Type                : Unicast
PrefixLength        : 64
PrefixOrigin        : Manual
SuffixOrigin        : Manual
AddressState        : Invalid
ValidLifetime       : Infinite ([TimeSpan]::MaxValue)
PreferredLifetime   : Infinite ([TimeSpan]::MaxValue)
SkipAsSource        : False
PolicyStore         : PersistentStore
```

Figure 12-7   New-NetIPAddress

After that, the interface is multihomed because it now has one link-local IPv6 address and one global IPv6 address.

You can use the **Netsh.exe** utility to do the same configuration. For example, you can use the **netsh** command to configure the IPv6 unicast address 2001:db1:230a:1290::5 on the interface named Ethernet. You also can add a default route (::/0) that uses the same interface to add a default gateway. In addition, you can add DNS servers with the **Netsh** utility. Figure 12-8 shows an example of this configuration.

```
PS C:\> netsh interface ipv6 add address Ethernet 2001:db1:230a:1290::5
PS C:\> netsh interface ipv6 add route ::/0 Ethernet fe80::2ba:ff:fe1a:113c
Ok.
PS C:\> netsh interface ipv6 add dnsserver Ethernet 2001:db1:39:3abd::3
```

Figure 12-8   Configuring IPV6 Network Interface Settings with the **netsh.exe** Utility

About IPv6 Addresses

Each IPv6 address is 128 bits long. The prefix is the part of the address that contains the bits with fixed values or the subnet prefix's bits. The prefix is equivalent to the network ID for IPv4 addresses. IPv6 subnets, prefixes, routes, and address ranges are represented in the same way as CIDR notations. An IPv6 prefix is represented in address/prefix length notation. For example, 2001:DB8::/48 (a route prefix) and 2001:DB8:0:2D4C::/64 (a subnet prefix) are IPv6 address prefixes. IPv6 uses prefixes instead of a subnet mask.

When a unicast IPv6 address is assigned to a host, the prefix is 64 bits. The remaining 64 bits are allocated to the interface identifier, which uniquely identifies the host on that network. The interface identifier can be generated randomly, assigned by DHCPv6, or based on the MAC address of the network. By default, the host bits are generated randomly unless assigned by DHCPv6.

Table 12-6 shows IPv6 equivalents to some common IPv4 addresses. Table 12-7 describes the three types of IPv6 addresses, which can be categorized based on type and scope.

Table 12-6   IPv6 Equivalents to IPv4 Addresses

Type of Address	IPv4 Address	IPv6 Address
Unspecified address	0.0.0.0	::
Loopback address	127.0.0.1	::1
Autoconfigured addresses	169.254.0.0/16	FE80::/64
Broadcast address	255.255.255.255	Uses multicast instead
Multicast addresses	224.0.0.0/24	FF00::/8

Table 12-7   Types of IPv6 Addresses

Unicast	Multicast	Anycast
A unicast address identifies a single interface within the scope of the type of unicast address. With the appropriate unicast routing topology, packets addressed to a unicast address are delivered to a single interface. Effectively, a packet is delivered from a single interface to another single interface. To accommodate load-balancing systems, RFC 3513 allows multiple interfaces to use the same address, as long as they appear as a single interface to the IPv6 implementation on the host.	A multicast address identifies multiple interfaces. With the appropriate multicast routing topology, packets addressed to a multicast address are delivered to all interfaces that are identified by the address. A multicast address is used for one-to-many communication, with delivery to multiple interfaces or all the interfaces in the set.	An anycast address identifies multiple interfaces. With the appropriate routing topology, packets addressed to an anycast address are delivered to a single interface that is also the nearest interface identified by the address. The nearest interface is defined as being closest in terms of routing distance. An anycast address is used for one to one-of-many communication, with delivery to a single interface in the set. An example of this is a proxy server in which you have multiple servers located across your network, but you want to forward packets to only the closest one.

Configuring IPv6 with DHCPv6

On a Windows Server 2016 DHCP server, the DHCP console displays two nodes, one for creating and configuring IPv4 scopes and the other for creating and configuring IPv6 scopes. Using the following steps, you can create a new IPv6 scope named HQ IPv6 with an available range from fd00::0:0:0:1 until fd00::ffff:ffff:ffff:ffff:

Step 1.   On your DHCPv6 server, from the taskbar, open Server Manager and start the DHCP Console.

Step 2.   In the DHCP Console, expand and right-click **IPv6**, and then click **New Scope**.

Figures 12-9 through 12-13 demonstrate the necessary configuration steps.

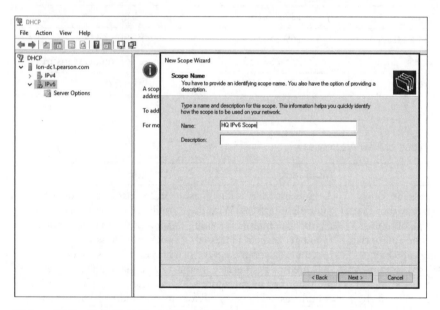

Figure 12-9   New IPv6 Scope Wizard (Scope Name)

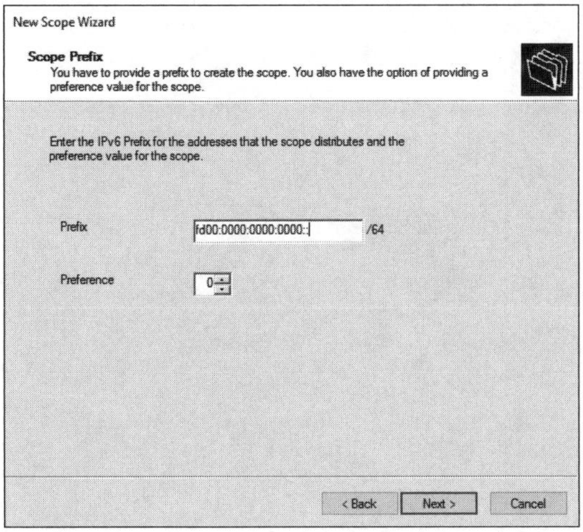

Figure 12-10   New IPv6 Scope Wizard (Scope Prefix)

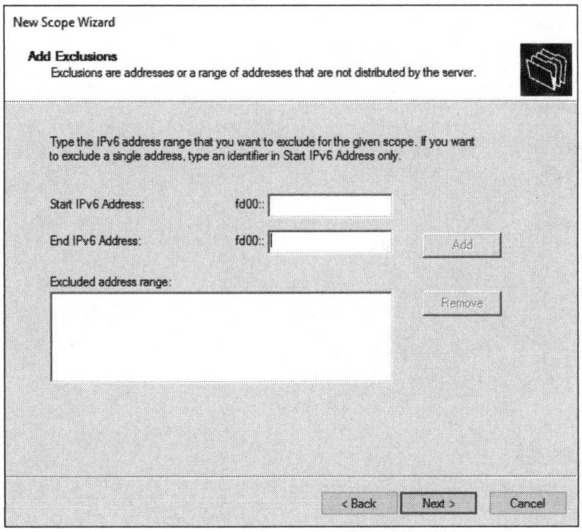

Figure 12-11   New IPv6 Scope Wizard (Add Exclusions)

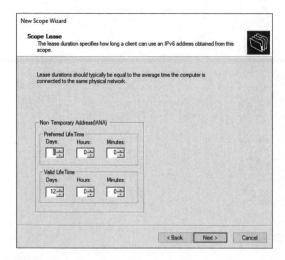

Figure 12-12   New IPv6 Scope Wizard (Scope Lease)

Figure 12-13   New IPv6 Scope Wizard (Activate Scope Now)

TIP   IPv6 host (AAAA) resource records that IPv6 nodes require are registered in DNS dynamically.

When a name can be resolved to both an IPv4 address and an IPv6 address, both addresses are returned to the client. The client then chooses which address to use, based on prefix polices. In these prefix policies, each prefix has a precedence level assigned to it. A higher precedence is preferred over a lower precedence. Table 12-8 displays typical prefix policies for Windows Server 2016.

Table 12-8   Prefix Policies for Windows Server 2016

Prefix	Precedence	Label	Description
::1/128	50	0	IPv6 loopback
::/0	40	1	Default gateway
::FFFF:0:0/96	10	4	IPv4-compatible address
2002::/16	7	2	6to4
2001::/32	5	5	Teredo
FC00::/7	3	13	Unique local
::/96	1	3	IPv4-compatible address (deprecated)
FEC0::/10	1	11	Site local (deprecated)
3FFE::/16	1	12	6Bone (deprecated)

TIP   You can view the prefix policies by using the **Get-NetPrefixPolicy** PowerShell cmdlet (see Figure 12-14).

Figure 12-14   Get-NetPrefixPolicy

In Windows Server 2016, you can see a new networking feature named Packet Direct. Soon you will see affordable 100-Gbps switches hitting the market. Packet Direct will improve throughput and reduce latency for networks up to this speed. Packet Direct is integrated with SDN and SET (Switched Embedded Teaming). You can configure Packet Direct through the PowerShell cmdlets listed in Table 12-9.

Table 12-9   Packet Direct PowerShell Cmdlets

Cmdlet	Description
Enable-NetAdapterPacketDirect	Enables the Packet Direct feature on the network adapter
Disable-NetAdapterPacketDirect	Disables the Packet Direct feature on the network adapter
Get-NetAdapterPacketDirect	Displays the Packet Direct settings of the network adapter
Set-NetAdapterPacketDirect	Configures Packet Direct on the network adapter

Configure IPv4 and IPv6 Subnetting

In most organizations, you need to perform subnetting to divide your network into smaller subnets and allocate those subnets for specific purposes or locations. To do this, you need to understand how to select the correct number of bits to include in the subnet masks. In some cases, you also need to combine multiple networks into a single larger network through supernetting.

When you subdivide a network into subnets, you must create a unique ID for each subnet. These unique IDs are derived from the main network ID when you allocate some of the bits in the host ID to the network ID. This enables you to create more networks.

Using subnets, you can accomplish the following:

- Use a single large network across multiple physical locations

- Reduce network congestion by segmenting traffic and reducing broadcasts on each segment

- Increase security by dividing the network and using firewalls to control communication

- Overcome limitations of current technologies, such as exceeding the maximum number of hosts that each segment can have

When determining subnet addresses, you should keep the following in mind:

- Choose the number of subnet bits based on the number of subnets required.

- Use 2^n to determine the number of subnets available from n bits.

For five locations, the following three subnet bits are required:

- 5 locations = 5 subnets required

- 2^n = 4 subnets (not enough)

- 2^3 = 8 subnets

Before you define a subnet mask, estimate how many subnets and hosts for each subnet you require. This enables you to use the appropriate number of bits for the subnet mask. You can calculate the number of subnet bits that you need in the network. Use the formula 2^n, where n is the number of bits. The result is the number of subnets your network requires. Table 12-10 indicates the number of subnets you can create by using a specific number of bits.

Table 12-10 2^n, n, and Subnets

Number of Bits (n)	Number of Subnets (2^n)
1	2
2	4
3	8
4	16
5	32
6	64

To quickly determine the subnet addresses, you can use the lowest value bit in the subnet mask. For example, if you choose to subnet the network 192.168.0.0 by using 3 bits, the subnet mask then is 255.255.224.0. The decimal 224 is 11100000 in binary, and the lowest bit has a value of 32, so that is the increment between each subnet address.

Table 12-11 shows the subnet addresses for this example; the 3 bits that you have chosen to use to subnet the network appear in bold.

Table 12-11 IPv4 Subnet Mask Example

Binary Network Number	Decimal Network Number
192.168.**000**00000.00000000	192.168.0.0
192.168.**001**00000.00000000	192.168.32.0
192.168.**010**00000.00000000	192.168.64.0
192.168.**011**00000.00000000	192.168.96.0
192.168.**100**00000.00000000	192.168.128.0
192.168.**101**00000.00000000	192.168.160.0
192.168.**110**00000.00000000	192.168.192.0
192.168.**111**00000.00000000	192.168.224.0

You can use a subnet calculator to determine the appropriate subnets for your network instead of calculating them manually. Subnet calculators are widely available on the Internet.

Implement IPv6 Stateless Addressing

With stateless autoconfiguration, IPv6 address configuration is based on the receipt of router advertisement messages only. Stateless autoconfiguration includes a router prefix but does not include additional configuration options such as DNS servers.

When you use an ISATAP router to provide stateless IPv6 to deliver an IPv6 IP address automatically to a host, forwarding *and* advertising must be enabled on the ISATAP interface. To verify that both are enabled, you can use the following PowerShell command:

```
Get-NetIPInterface -InterfaceIndex Ethernet -PolicyStore ActiveStore |
  Format-List.
```

You should enable the **Publish** parameter for the IPv6 network in which the host resides:

```
New-NetRoute -InterfaceIndex 22 -Destination Prefix 2001:db8:0:2::/64
  -Publish Yes.
```

This command adds the IPv6 network 2001:db8:0:2::/64 to the routing table and enables IPv6 stateless configuration for that network for DHCPv6 clients.

Configure Interoperability Between IPv4 and IPv6 by Using ISATAP, 6to4, and Teredo Scenarios

Instead of replacing IPv4, most companies add IPv6 to an existing IPv4 network. Since Windows Server 2008 and Vista, Windows supports the simultaneous use of IPv4 and IPv6. Transitioning from IPv4 to IPv6 requires coexistence between the two protocols. Too many applications and services rely on IPv4 for it to be removed quickly; however, several technologies aid in the transition by allowing communication between IPv4-only and IPv6-only hosts. ISATAP, 6to4, and Teredo allow IPv6 communication over IPv4 networks, to help provide connectivity between IPv4 and IPv6 networks.

IPv6 over IPv4 Tunneling

IPv6 over IPv4 tunneling is the process by which IPv6 packets are encapsulated with an IPv4 header so that IPv6 packets can be sent over an IPv4-only infrastructure. Within the IPv4 header, the IPv4 Protocol field of the IPv4 header is set to 41 to indicate an encapsulated IPv6 packet. The Source and Destination fields of the IPv4 header are set to the IPv4 addresses of the tunnel endpoints.

You can configure tunnel endpoints manually as part of the tunnel interface or have them derived automatically. Stateless configuration occurs when the subnet router assigns the IPv6 address automatically and the DHCPv6 server assigns only other IPv6 configuration settings.

You can manually configure IPv6 over IPv4 tunneling or use automated technologies such as ISATAP, 6to4, or Teredo that implement IPv6 over IPv4 tunneling.

Differences Among ISATAP, 6to4, and Teredo

Table 12-12 shows the differences in the transition mechanisms of 6to4, Teredo, and ISATAP. Each mechanism has its individual singularities. Which transition mechanism should you choose for which kind of transition requirement? Which transition mechanism should you choose if you have to transport your network traffic through a NAT device? Which mechanism cannot be used with NAT? The next section answers these and other questions.

Table 12-12   Comparing Transition Mechanisms

Transition Mechanism	Description
6to4	6to4 is a mechanism by which a router with a public IPv4 address can be an IPv6 gateway/provider for a whole set of LANs. The IPv6 prefix starts with 2002:, followed by the 32 bits of the public IPv4 address. This gives a /48 prefix that can be used to provide 65536 LANs with a /64 each. The problem is that, to reach the normal IPv6 Internet, the 6to4 router needs to use public 6to4 relays, which are not always reliable. The inbound and outbound traffic use different relays most of the time because the reliability of 6to4 networks leaves a lot to be desired. These days, using 6to4 is strongly discouraged.
Teredo	Teredo is a built-in mechanism that gives a single system behind an IPv4 NAT access to IPv6. Similar to 6to4, it uses public relays. Teredo combines this with a setup protocol using Teredo servers (by default, those hosted by Microsoft) to detect and break through the IPv4 NAT. It is not very reliable, but Teredo is used only when explicitly connecting to an IPv6 address, not when connecting to a hostname and looking up the addresses in DNS.
ISATAP	ISATAP is a managed technology for providing IPv6 on an IPv4 network. It emulates IPv6 connectivity on the IPv4 infrastructure. IPv6 router discovery usually uses multicast. This is not possible on an infrastructure based on IPv6-over-IPv4 tunnels, so ISATAP solves that in a different way. An ISATAP router is provided on the network and its IPv4 address is made known to the ISATAP hosts (usually using the hostname isatap in DNS). The ISATAP hosts then can use that address to set up their IPv6 connectivity.

Configuring 6to4

When configuring 6to4 settings on a computer running Windows Server 2016, you can use **ipconfig /all** to display the status of the 6to4 tunnel adapter.

If the computer is configured with a private IP address, the operating system assumes that the computer is located behind a NAT device. Therefore, the media state of the 6to4 tunnel adapter has a status of Disconnected because the 6to4 technology cannot work with NAT devices.

> **TIP**   6to4 cannot work with NAT.

If the computer is configured with a public IP address, the operating system enables the 6to4 tunnel adapter so that the computer can be configured to connect to IPv6 by using the 6to4 technology.

You can enable 6to4 router functionality in Windows Server 2016 in the following ways:

- **Enable Internet Connection Sharing (ICS):** When you enable ICS, Windows Server 2016 is configured automatically as a 6to4 router.

> **TIP**   You can enable ICS on a Windows Server 2016 server with the following PowerShell commands: **Set-Service** *SharedAccess -StartupType Automatic* and **Start-Service** *SharedAccess*.

- **Use Windows PowerShell:** You can use the PowerShell commands listed in Table 12-13.

Table 12-13   6to4 PowerShell Cmdlets

Cmdlet	Description
Get-Net6to4Configuration	Retrieves the 6to4 configuration of a computer or a GPO.
Set-Net6to4Configuration	Sets the 6to4 configuration for both client computers and servers. With **Set-Net6to4Configuration -State Disabled**, you can disable 6to4. The default value for the *State* parameter is *Default*, which means that 6to4 is enabled if the host has link-local-only IPv6 connectivity and a public IPv4 address. If no global IPv6 address or IPv4 address is present, the host does not have a 6to4 interface. If no global IPv6 address is present but a global IPv4 address is present, the host has a 6to4 interface. You can modify the relay name on the persistent store with **Set-Net6to4Configuration -RelayName "pearson6to4relay.com"**.

Cmdlet	Description
Reset-Net6to4Configuration	Resets the GPO settings for a 6to4 configuration. The **Reset-Net6to4Configuration** cmdlet resets the GPO settings for a 6to4 configuration to the Not Configured state. Group Policy settings have three possible states: Not Configured, Enabled, and Disabled.

You also can use the **netsh** command to perform 6to4 configuration tasks. You can disable 6to4 with the following command: **netsh interface ipv6 6to4 set state disabled**.

Configuring Teredo

Teredo enables you to tunnel IPv6 packets over the IPv4 Internet; however, Teredo functions correctly even when NAT is used for Internet connectivity.

> **TIP**   Teredo does work with NAT.

Teredo is required because many organizations use private IP addresses, which require NAT to access the Internet. If a NAT device can be configured as a 6to4 router, Teredo is not required. Teredo is used only when native IPv6, 6to4, or ISATAP transitioning technologies do not provide connectivity.

IPv6 communication between two Teredo clients over the IPv4 Internet requires a Teredo server hosted on the IPv4 Internet.

> **TIP**   Teredo needs a Teredo server. Several public Teredo servers are available for use on the Internet. Windows Server 2016 uses a Microsoft-provided Teredo server at teredo.ipv6.microsoft.com.

The Teredo server facilitates communication between the two Teredo clients by acting as a known central point for initiating communication.

Typically, hosts behind a NAT device are allowed to initiate outbound communication but are not allowed to accept inbound communication. To work around this problem, both Teredo clients initiate communication with the Teredo server. After connection is initiated with the Teredo server, and after the NAT device has allowed outbound communication, any further communication occurs directly between the two Teredo clients.

You can configure a Windows Server 2016 server as the following:

- Teredo client

- Tereo relay

- Teredo server

To configure Teredo, use the Windows PowerShell cmdlet **Set-NetTeredo-Configuration**. The default configuration for Teredo is as a client. When a computer is configured as a Teredo client, Teredo is disabled when the computer is attached to a domain network. To enable Teredo on the domain network, you must configure the computer as an enterprise client.

Using the **Netsh** command, you can configure Teredo servers other than the default servers at teredo.ipv6.microsoft.com.

Configuring ISATAP

ISATAP is an address-assignment technology that you can use to provide unicast IPv6 connectivity between IPv6 and IPv4 hosts over an IPv4 intranet. IPv6 packets are tunneled in IPv4 packets for transmission over the network. Communication can occur directly between two ISATAP hosts on an IPv4 network, or communication can go through an ISATAP router if one network has only IPv6-only hosts.

An ISATAP address that is based on a private IPv4 address is formatted like this:

[64-bit unicast prefix]:0:5EFE:w.x.y.z

An ISATAP address that is based on a public IPv4 address is formatted in this way:

[64-bit unicast prefix]:200:5EFE:w.x.y.z

For example, FD00::5EFE:192.168.137.133 is an example of a private IPv4 address, and 2001:db8::200:5EFE:131.107.137.133 is an example of a public IPv4 address.

What is an ISATAP router? If no IPv6-only hosts exist, the ISATAP router advertises the IPv6 prefix that ISATAP clients use. The ISATAP interface on client computers is configured to use this prefix. When applications use the ISATAP interface to deliver data, the IPv6 packet is encapsulated in an IPv4 packet for delivery to the IPv4 address of the destination ISATAP host. If there are IPv6-only hosts, the ISATAP router also unpacks IPv6 packets. ISATAP hosts send packets to the IPv4 address of the ISATAP router. The ISATAP router then unpacks the IPv6 packets and sends them on to the IPv6-only network.

> **TIP**   All ISATAP nodes are connected to a single IPv6 subnet. All ISATAP nodes are part of the same AD DS site, which might not be desirable. For this reason, you should use ISATAP only for limited testing. For intranet-wide deployment, you should instead deploy native IPv6 support.

ISATAP hosts do not require manual configuration. They can create ISATAP addresses by using standard address autoconfiguration mechanisms. Although the ISATAP component is enabled by default in Windows 10 and Windows Server 2016 operating systems, it assigns ISATAP-based addresses only if it can resolve the name ISATAP on your network.

> **TIP**   By default, DNS servers on Windows Server 2008 or later have a global query block list that prevents ISATAP resolution even when the host record is created and properly configured. You need to remove ISATAP from the global query block list in DNS if you are using an ISATAP host record to configure ISATAP clients. You can do that with the PowerShell cmdlet **Set-DnsServerGlobalQueryBlockList** or the following command: **dnscmd /config /globalqueryblocklist**.

You have three possibilities to configure hosts with an ISATAP router:

- Use the PowerShell cmdlet **Set-NetIsatapConfiguration Router x.x.x.x**.
- Use **netsh interface IPv6 ISATAP Set Router x.x.x.x**.
- Configure the **ISATAP Router Name** GPO setting (see Figure 12-15).

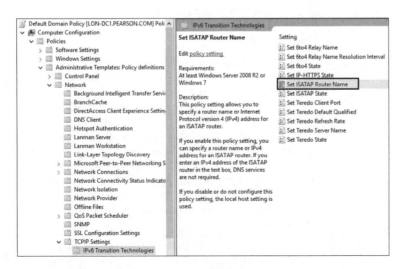

Figure 12-15   ISATAP Router Name GPO Setting

TIP The ISATAP interface for an ISATAP router must have forwarding and advertising enabled. Use the following **Set-NetIPInterface** cmdlet to enable router advertisements on the ISATAP interface: **Set-NetIPInterface -Advertising Enabled**.

Configure Border Gateway Protocol (BGP)

To plan your Windows Server 2016 SDN configuration, you need to ensure that your network environment meets the requirements. One of the physical network requirements for SDN is the Boarder Gateway Protocol (BGP).

With Windows Server 2016, you can use a RAS Gateway (Windows Server Gateway in System Center), which is a software-based, multitenant, BGP-capable router.

A Windows Server 2016 RAS Gateway is designed for providers and large organizations that host multiple tenant virtual networks using Hyper-V Network Virtualization. RAS Gateway provides dynamic routing with BGP. This reduces the need for manual route configuration on routers because BGP is a dynamic routing protocol and automatically learns routes between sites that are connected using S2S VPN connections.

BGP Features

Table 12-14 lists the BGP features available on a Windows Server 2016 RAS Gateway.

Table 12-14 BGP Features on a Windows Server 2016 RAS Gateway

Feature	Description
BGP routing as a role service of Remote Access	Using Windows Server 2016 as a BGP router, you can now install the Routing role service of the Remote Access server role without installing the Remote Access Service (RAS) role service when you want to use Remote Access as a BGP LAN router. This reduces the BGP router memory footprint and installs only the components required for dynamic BGP routing. The Routing role service is useful when only a BGP router VM is required and you don't require use of DirectAccess or a VPN. In addition, using Remote Access as a LAN router with BGP provides you with the dynamic routing advantages of BGP on your internal network.
BGP statistics (message counters, route counters)	A Windows Server 2016 BGP router supports displaying the message and route statistics, if required, by using the **Get-BgpStatistics** Windows PowerShell command.

Feature	Description
Equal Cost Multi Path Routing (ECMP) support	A Windows Server 2016 BGP router supports ECMP and can have more than one equal-cost route plumbed into the BGP routing table and stack. The BGP router selection of the route for transmitting data packets is random when ECMP is enabled.
HoldTime configuration	A Windows Server 2016 BGP router supports configuration of the HoldTimer value according to your network requirements. This timer can be dynamically changed to accommodate interoperability with third-party devices or to maintain a specific maximum time for BGP peering session timeout.
Internal BGP and External BGP support	A Windows Server 2016 BGP router supports both iBGP and eBGP peering. To configure either, you must ensure that the appropriate ASNs are assigned to the local and remote BGP Routers. All four BGP deployment topologies employ the use of eBGP peering, and the fourth topology uses iBGP peering as well.
Interoperability with third-party solutions	A Windows Server 2016 BGP router is based on the latest BGP version 4 specification and has been tested for interoperability with most of the major third-party BGP routing devices.
IPv4 and IPv6 transport peering support	A Windows Server 2016 BGP router supports both IPv4 and IPv6 peering. However, you must configure the BGP identifier as the IPv4 address of the BGP router. For all BGP router deployment topologies, either of the two peering types (IPV4 or IPv6) can be used.
IPv4 and IPv6 unicast route learning and advertisement capability (Multiprotocol Network Layer Reachability Information [NLRI])	Regardless of the transport you use, a Windows Server 2016 BGP router can exchange IPv4 and IPv6 routes if other BGP routers announce the appropriate capability while establishing the session. To configure IPv6 routing, the parameter **IPv6Routing** must be enabled, and a local global IPv6 address must be configured at the router level.
Mixed mode and passive mode peering	With a Windows Server 2016 BGP router, you can configure BGP peering sessions in either mixed mode (the BGP router acts as both initiator and responder) or passive mode (the BGP router does not initiate peering but does respond to incoming requests). Mixed mode is the default and is recommended for BGP peering. This is true unless you want to use passive mode for debugging or diagnostic purposes. For all BGP router deployment topologies, mixed-mode peering is required to enable automatic restarts in case of failure events.

Feature	Description
Route attribute rewrite capability	You can add, modify, or remove the following attributes from the BGP router ingress and egress route advertisements by using the BGP routing policies *Next-Hop*, *MED*, *Local-Pref*, and *Community*.
Route filtering	A Windows Server 2016 BGP router supports filtering ingress or egress route advertisements based on multiple route attributes such as *Prefix*, *ASN-Range*, *Community*, and *Next-Hop*.
Route reflector (RR) and RR client	A Windows Server 2016 BGP router can act as a route reflector and an RR client. This is useful in complex topologies where RR can simplify the network by forming RR clusters.
Route refresh support	A Windows Server 2016 BGP router supports route refresh and advertises this capability on peering by default. It is capable of sending a fresh set of route updates when requested by a peer via route refresh message, as well as sending a route refresh to update its routing table in case of routing policy changes for a peer. This enables changing or updating the BGP routing policies in Windows Server 2016 without needing to restart peering.
Static route configuration support	You can configure static routes or interfaces on the BGP router by using the **Add-BgpCustom Route** Windows PowerShell command. The static routes that you configure can be the prefixes or the name of the interfaces from which the routes must be chosen. However, only the routes with resolvable next hops are plumbed into the BGP routing tables and advertised to peers.
Transit routing support	The BGP router supports transit routing for iBGP-to-iBGP connections, iBGP-to-eBGP connections, and eBGP-to-eBGP connections.

Feature	Description
Route flap dampening	Windows Server 2016 supports route flap dampening to BGP routing. When a route is constantly being advertised and withdrawn, making the routing table unstable, you can configure the BGP router to assign a dampening weight to the route and monitor it for flaps, suppressing or unsuppressing it, as required. This helps maintain a stable routing table and involves less processing by the BGP router.
	You can enable BGP route flap dampening with the following PowerShell command:
	Enable-BgpRouteFlap Dampening -RoutingDomain "Pearson"
	With **Clear-BgpRouteFlapDampening**, you can clear the route flap dampening information for the specified set of BGP routes:
	Clear-BgpRouteFlap Dampening -Prefix 172.168.10.0/24, 10.10.1.128/25 -Force
	With **Set-BgpRouteFlap Dampening**, you can configure the RFD settings:
	Set-BgpRouteFlapDampening -HalfLifeTimeOK 600 -ReuseThreshold 500 -SuppressThreshold 2000 -MaxSuppressValue 2400
Route aggregation	Route aggregation to the Windows Server 2016 BGP router enables you to configure aggregate routes and replace the more granular route advertisements with summary or aggregate routes to peers. This results in fewer route advertisement messages transmitted on the network.

TIP When you install a RAS gateway, you must specify whether BGP is enabled for each tenant by using the **Enable-RemoteAccessRoutingDomain** PowerShell cmdlet with the **-Type** parameter value of **All**. To install Remote Access as a BGP-enabled LAN router without multitenant capabilities, you can use the command **Install-RemoteAccess -VpnType RoutingOnly**. The following example code illustrates how to install RAS in multitenancy mode with all RAS features (P2S VPN, S2S VPN, and BGP routing) enabled for two tenants, Pearson and Pucertify. Before using the following commands, you must create the tenant compartments on the Hyper-V Host with the **Add-VmNetworkAdapterRoutingDomainMapping** PowerShell cmdlet. For example, to add a tenant that has the specified routing domain to the virtual network adapter named InternalNIC that belongs to the

multitenant VM Gateway01, the following command also adds the virtual subnet
that has the ID 6000 to the virtual network adapter:

```
Add-VMNetworkAdapterRoutingDomainMapping -VMName "Gateway01"
  -VMNetworkAdapterName
"InternalNIC" -RoutingDomainID "{5a07361e-6a54-49fc-9210-bfbf14a5c56f}"
  RoutingDomainName "Pearson"
-IsolationID 6000 -IsolationName "Pearson GatewayVsid"):
$Pearson_RoutingDomain = "PearsonTenant"
$PUcertify_RoutingDomain = "PucertifyTenant"
Enable-RemoteAccessRoutingDomain -Name $Pearson_RoutingDomain
  -Type All -PassThru
Enable-RemoteAccessRoutingDomain -Name $PUcertify_RoutingDomain
  -Type All -PassThru
```

If you cannot use the **Install-RemoteAccess** PowerShell cmdlet, first you must install the RemoteAccess PowerShell module with **Install-WindowsFeature RSAT-
RemoteAccess-PowerShell**.

BGP allows routers to route inbound traffic to the MUX by using ECMP. For
outbound network traffic, it uses the route provided by the host, listens for route
updates for VIPs from SLB MUX, and removes SLB MUXs from the SLB rotation if the keepalive fails. You must create a BGP peer on the router that your SDN
infrastructure uses to receive routes for the VIP logical networks advertised by the
SLB MUXs and HNV gateways. Typically, you configure BGP peering in a managed switch or router as part of the network infrastructure.

Network Controller is a new Windows Server 2016 server role. It provides two
application programming interfaces (APIs): the Southbound API and the Northbound API. The Southbound API enables Network Controller to communicate
with the network; the Northbound API gives you the capability to communicate
with Network Controller. By using Network Controller, you can deploy, configure,
and manage Hyper-V hosts and VMs that are members of a RAS Gateway pool so
you can provide RAS Gateway services to your tenants. You can use Network Controller to automatically deploy VMs running RAS Gateway to support BGP routing
so that you can manage the routing of network traffic between your tenants' VM
networks and their remote sites.

BGP PowerShell Cmdlets

You can use the PowerShell cmdlets in Table 12-15 to configure BGP.

Table 12-15   PowerShell Cmdlets to Configure BGP on Windows Server 2016

Cmdlet	Description
Add-BgpCustomRoute	Adds custom routes to the BGP routing table
Add-BgpPeer	Adds a BGP peer to the current router
Add-BgpRouteAggregate	Adds a new aggregate route for specific BGP routes
Add-BgpRouter	Adds a BGP router
Add-BgpRoutingPolicy	Adds a BGP routing policy to the policy store
Add-BgpRoutingPolicyForPeer	Adds BGP routing policies to BGP peers
Clear-GbpRouteFlapDampening	Clears the route dampening information for the specified set of BGP routes
Disable-BgpRouteFlapDampening	Disables route dampening for the flapping BGP routes
Enable-BgpRouteFlapDampening	Enables route dampening for the flapping BGP routes
Get-BgpCustomRoute	Gets custom route information from the BGP router
Get-BgpPeer	Gets configuration information for BGP peers
Get-BgpRouteAggregate	Gets all the aggregate BGP routes configured by the administrator
Get-BgpRouteFlapDampening	Gets the configuration of a BGP route dampening engine
Get-BgpRouteInformation	Gets route information for network prefixes from the BGP router
Get-BgpRouter	Gets configuration information for BGP routers
Get-BgpRoutingPolicy	Gets configuration information of BGP routing policies
Get-BgpStatistics	Retrieves BGP peering-related message and route advertisement statistics
Remove-BgpCustomRoute	Removes custom routes from the BGP router
Remote-BgpRouteAggregate	Removes BGP peers from a router
RemoveBgpRouter	Removes the set of specified aggregate BGP routes
Remove-BgpRoutingPolicy	Removes the BGP router for tenants
Remove-BgpRoutingPolicyForPeer	Removes routing policies from the policy store
Set-BgpPeer	Updates the configuration of the specified BGP peer
Set-BgpRouteAggregate	Updates the properties of the specified aggregate BGP route
Set-BgpRouteFlapDampening	Configures the BGP route dampening engine

Cmdlet	Description
Set-BgpRouter	Updates the configuration of the local BGP router for the specified tenant ID
Set-BgpRoutingPolicy	Modifies a routing policy configuration
Set-BgpRoutingPolicyForPeer	Modifies BGP routing policies for BGP peers
Start-BgpPeer	Starts routing sessions for BGP peers
Stop-BgpPeer	Stops routing sessions for BGP peers

Next we look at some examples for configuring BGP with PowerShell cmdlets.

You can add an interface named Ethernet to the local BGP router with the following PowerShell command:

```
Add-BgpCustomRoute -Interface "Ethernet" -PassThru
```

You can add routing information from the network prefix 172.23.90.0/29 to the local BGP router with the following PowerShell command:

```
Add-BgpCustomRoute -Network "172.23.90.0/29" -PassThru
```

You can add routing information from the interface Int1 and the network prefix 172.23.90.0 to the BGP router for the routing domain in a multitenant environment named Rd1 with the following PowerShell command:

```
Add-BgpCustomRoute -Interface "Int1" -Network "172.23.90/29"
-RoutingDomain "Rd1" -PassThru
```

You must create a BGP peer on the router that your SDN infrastructure uses to receive routes for the VIP logical networks advertised by the SLB MUXs and HNV gateways. Adding a BGP peer to the BGP router automatically starts establishing a BGP peering session with that neighbor using the following PowerShell command:

```
Add-BgpPeer -Name "RedTenantSite1" -LocalIPAddress 192.168.1.10
-PeerIPAddress 14.1.1.10 -PeerASN 64512 -PassThru
```

If you add a new BGP peer to the BGP router, the BGP router listens for incoming connections from neighbors. *PeeringMode* is set to *Manual*. Unless this peering is started manually, the incoming connections requests are dropped:

```
Add-BgpPeer -Name "RedTenantSite1" -LocalIPAddress 192.168.1.10
-PeerIPAddress 14.1.1.10 -PeerASN 64512  -OperationMode Server
  -PeeringMode Manual -PassThru
```

To reduce the number of BGP peers, you can use route reflectors. Adding a new route reflector client BGP peer to the BGP router automatically starts a BGP peering session. You can use the following PowerShell command for that:

```
Add-BgpPeer -Name RRC1 -LocalIPAddress 14.1.1.1 -PeerIPAddress
  192.168.1.20 -PeerASN 64510 -PassThru -RouteReflectorClient $true
```

A BGP route is hidden when the AS path of an aggregate route is more than half of the maximum BGP packet size (4096 bytes). AS paths have the **OverflowASPathSize** flag set for that. If you want to leak a BGP route whose AS path length can overflow, adding the AS path statically in the default route configuration is recommended. You can do this by adding a static custom route aggregation with the following Power-Shell command:

```
Add-BgpRouteAggregate -RoutingDomain "Pearson" -Prefix "172.12.0.0/16"
  -AttributePolicy "X_StaticAggAttrib" -PreserveASPath enable
```

You can add a local BGP router with the following PowerShell command:

```
Add-BgpRouter -BgpIdentifier 10.1.1.10-LocalASN 64522 -PassThru.
```

To set up a BGP router, use the following PowerShell commands:

```
Add-BgpRouter -BgpIdentifier "<Local Gateway's Enterprise IP Address>"
  -LocalASN 63311
Add-BgpPeer -Name CloudPeer -LocalIPAddress "<Local Gateway's
  Enterprise IP Address>" -PeerIPAddress -PeerASN 63322 -PassThru
Start-BgpPeer -Name CloudPeer
Get-BgpPeer -Name CloudPeer
Get-BgpRouteInformation
```

Configure IPv4 and IPv6 Routing

When a host transmits a packet to a remote network, IPv4 consults the internal routing table to determine the appropriate router for the packet to reach the destination subnet. If the routing table does not contain any routing information about the destination subnet, IPv4 forwards the packet to the default gateway. The host assumes that the default gateway contains the required routing information. The default gateway is used in most cases.

With the PowerShell cmdlet **New-NetRoute**, you can create routing table entries, including the default gateway (0.0.0.0). You cannot use this cmdlet to modify the next hop of an existing route; instead, you must remove an existing route and create a new route with the correct next hop.

With the **Get-NetRoute** PowerShell cmdlet, you can display the routing table. Figure 12-16 shows an example of a local routing table.

```
PS C:\> get-netroute

ifIndex DestinationPrefix                    NextHop                    RouteMetric PolicyStore
------- -----------------                    -------                    ----------- -----------
2       255.255.255.255/32                   0.0.0.0                            256 ActiveStore
1       255.255.255.255/32                   0.0.0.0                            256 ActiveStore
2       224.0.0.0/4                          0.0.0.0                            256 ActiveStore
1       224.0.0.0/4                          0.0.0.0                            256 ActiveStore
2       172.16.255.255/32                    0.0.0.0                            256 ActiveStore
2       172.16.0.10/32                       0.0.0.0                            256 ActiveStore
2       172.16.0.0/16                        0.0.0.0                            256 ActiveStore
1       127.255.255.255/32                   0.0.0.0                            256 ActiveStore
1       127.0.0.1/32                         0.0.0.0                            256 ActiveStore
1       127.0.0.0/8                          0.0.0.0                            256 ActiveStore
2       ff00::/8                             ::                                 256 ActiveStore
1       ff00::/8                             ::                                 256 ActiveStore
2       fe80::d956:ac88:c6fc:d3f0/128        ::                                 256 ActiveStore
3       fe80::5efe:172.16.0.10/128           ::                                 256 ActiveStore
2       fe80::/64                            ::                                 256 ActiveStore
2       2001:db6:3fa8::d1:9c4a/128           ::                                 256 ActiveStore
2       2001:db6:3fa8::/64                   ::                                 256 ActiveStore
2       2001:db1:230a:1290::5/128            ::                                 256 ActiveStore
2       2001:db1:230a:1290::/64              ::                                 256 ActiveStore
1       ::1/128                              ::                                 256 ActiveStore
2       ::/0                                 fe80::2ba:ff:fe1a:113c             256 ActiveStore
2       ::/0                                 2001:db6:3fa8::1c0                 256 ActiveStore
```

Figure 12-16   Get-NetRoute

With the **Remove-NetRoute** PowerShell cmdlet, you can remove routing table entries.

To identify the routing path through your network, you can use the PowerShell cmdlet **Test-NetConnection -TraceRoute**.

Exam Preparation Tasks

Review All the Key Topics

Review the most important topics in the chapter, noted with the Key Topics icon in the outer margin of the page. Table 12-16 lists these key topics and the page numbers where each is found.

Table 12-16   Key Topics for Chapter 12

Key Topic Element	Description	Page Number
Table 12-2	IPv4 IP Address PowerShell Cmdlets	542
Table 12-3	Configuring DHCP on a Network Interface with PowerShell Cmdlets	542
Table 12-4	PowerShell Cmdlets to Troubleshoot IPv4 Network Configurations	543
Section	Configuring Local IPv6 Settings (GUI)	544
Section	IPv4 and IPv6 Assignment Differences	547
Table 12-5	PowerShell Cmdlets to Configure IPv6 Settings	548
Table 12-6	IPv6 Equivalents to IPv4 Addresses	551
Table 12-7	Types of IPv6 Addresses	551

Key Topic Element	Description	Page Number
Step List	Configuring IPv6 with DHCPv6	552
Table 12-8	Prefix Policies for Windows Server 2016	555
Table 12-12	Comparing Transition Mechanisms	559
Section	Configuring 6to4	559
Section	Configuring Teredo	561
Section	Configuring ISATAP	562
List	Possibilities for configuring hosts with an ISATAP router	563
Text	Using BGP for software-defined networking	564
Table 12-14	BGP Features on Windows Server 2016 RAS Gateway	564
Table 12-15	PowerShell Cmdlets to Configure BGP on Windows Server 2016	569
Section	Configure IPv4 and IPv6 Routing	571

Complete the Tables and Lists from Memory

Print a copy of Appendix B, "Memory Tables" (on the book's website), or at least the section for this chapter, and complete the tables and lists from memory. Appendix C, "Memory Tables Answer Key," also on the website, includes completed tables and lists to check your work.

Definition of Key Terms

Define the following key terms from this chapter and check your answers in the glossary.

Stateful IPv6 configuration, stateless IPv6 configuration, IPv6 WINS tab, IPv6 Options tab, IPv6 link-local addresses, IPv6 prefix, AAAA resource records, IPv6 prefix policy, 6to4, Teredo, ISATAP, GlobalQueryBlockList, ISATAP router, software-defined networking (SDN), BGP, ECMP, BGP route reflector, BGP route flap dampening, RAS Gateway, Network Controller

End-of-Chapter Review Questions

1. You have configured a Windows Server 2016 DirectAccess server for some of your Windows mobile clients. One of these clients is located outside the company, and one of your traveling employees has to access local company resources through a DirectAccess tunnel from the Los Angeles airport terminal. He reports that he cannot access internal file servers from the domain usa.pearson.com. You are the administrator and you use the DirectAccess managed-out feature to connect remotely to the DirectAccess client to find out the cause of that problem. Hostnames from pearson.com and eu.pearson.com will be correctly resolved. You see that all internal resources from usa.pearson.com cannot be resolved from that DirectAccess client. The following internal DNS servers are responsible:

   - DNS1 (10.10.0.10): pearson.com

   - DNS2 (192.168.1.5): eu.pearson.com

   - DNS3 (172.16.0.10): usa.pearson.com

   Which PowerShell cmdlet can you use to resolve internal resources from the DNSSEC-protected domain usa.pearson.com?

   a. **Get-DnsClientNRPTPolicy**

   b. **Resolve-DnsName**

   c. **Add-DnsClientNrptRule**

   d. **Get-DnsClientCache**

   e. **Get-NetRoute**

2. You need to debug how an application is actually reaching a network resource through hostname and IPv6 and also determine what IPv6 address and interface your host is using so that he can reach that resource. Which PowerShell cmdlets can you use? (Choose two.)

   a. **Get-NetTCPSetting**

   b. **Resolve-DnsName**

   c. **Find-NetRoute**

   d. **Get-NetRoute**

3. You have a client with an IP address of 192.168.194.5/19. What is the client's subnet?

    a. 192.168.160.0

    b. 192.168.64.0

    c. 192.168.32.0

    d. 192.168.192.0

4. You use **ipconfig /all** on your client and see only the Teredo and ISATAP interfaces. You also want to see the 6to4 interface. What is a possible reason for no 6to4 interface to be displayed?

    a. The client has no link-local IPv6 address configured.

    b. The client has the ISATAP interface enabled.

    c. The client has no global IPv6 address configured.

    d. The client has the Teredo interface enabled.

5. You want to use the **Enable-RemoteAccessRoutingDomain** PowerShell cmdlet to enable BGP for tenants. You cannot use this cmdlet or all other PowerShell cmdlets, such as **Install-Remote Access** or **Add-VmNetworkAdapterRoutingDomainMapping**. Which feature must you install so that you can configure a RAS Gateway as a BGP-enabled LAN router with this PowerShell cmdlet?

    a. **RSAT-RemoteAccess-Mgmt**

    b. **RSAT-RemoteAccess-PowerShell**

    c. **RemoteAccess**

    d. **Routing**

    e. **MSMQ-Routing**

This chapter covers the following subjects:

- **Installing and configuring DFS namespaces:** This chapter explores the different network file usage scenarios for branch offices and delves into the differences in DFSN, DFSR, and the Storage Replica feature. It explains the two types of DFS namespace scenarios and their differences and use.

- **Configuring DFS replication scheduling:** You look at DFSR and its capabilities, learn how to configure it with the DFS Management tool, and get step-by-step instruction in setting up a DFSR scenario for automatic file replication with DFSR.

- **Configuring Remote Differential Compression (RDC) settings:** This chapter discusses Remote Differential Compression (RDC), a client/server protocol that you can use to efficiently update files over a limited-bandwidth network.

- **Configuring fault tolerance:** When DFS is used together with Active Directory and domain-based namespaces, with multiple DFS servers and domain controllers, you can implement DFS fault tolerance functionality. This subject covers some aspects of this topic.

- **Recovering DFSR databases:** This chapter explains some DFS recovery aspects, such as the ConflictAndDeleted and Preexisting folders.

- **Optimizing DFS Replication:** New Windows Server 2016 offers DFS optimizing capabilities such as DFS database cloning. This chapter also explains the advantages of integrating the Data Deduplication feature and DFSR.

- **Installing and configuring BranchCache:** You learn some basic concepts and components of BranchCache, including protocols, main benefits, and overall functionality of the BranchCache feature.

- **Implementing distributed and hosted cache modes:** Here you learn how to configure BranchCache client and server settings, to implement distributed or hosted cache mode.

- **Implementing BranchCache for web, file, and application servers:** This chapter explains the components you have to use on web servers, file servers, and application servers, if you want to cache content from them.

- **Troubleshooting BranchCache:** You learn how to use command-line tools and PowerShell cmdlets to monitor and troubleshoot BranchCache configurations.

## CHAPTER 13

Implementing Windows Server 2016 DFS and Branch Office Solutions

This chapter focuses on two topics: Distributed File System (DFS) and BranchCache.

Here you learn about installing and configuring Windows Server 2016 DFS servers and DFS namespaces (DFSN), and using the DFS Replication (DFSR) feature. You learn about DFS usage scenarios for branch offices and examine the differences in DFSN, DFSR, and Storage Replica (a new feature in Windows Server 2016).

This chapter explains the DFS namespace types and their differences. You get information about administrative permissions required to create and manage Windows Server 2016 DFS. You work through step-by-step instructions to set up a DFS domain-based namespace scenario.

You learn about DFSR and its capabilities and how to configure it with the DFS Management tool. You also work through step-by-step instructions for setting up a DFSR scenario for automatic file replication with DFSR. Other topics include DFSR scheduling; configuration of DFS Replication groups; and PowerShell cmdlets for creating DFS health reports, forcing DFSR synchronization, and getting detailed DFSR configuration settings.

In addition, you learn about Remote Differential Compression (RDC), how to enable or disable RDC, and when to use the cross-file RDC feature.

The chapter explains the new Windows Server 2016 feature of DFS database cloning and gives the advantages of using the built-in Data Deduplication feature for DFSR.

Furthermore, this chapter explains some basic concepts and components of BranchCache, including its protocols, benefits, and main functionality. It also covers the BranchCache modes and their differences, as well as BranchCache requirements. You learn about BranchCache client and server settings and how to configure them, and you look at BranchCache troubleshooting and monitoring capabilities.

Key topic selections, memory tables, key term definitions, and exam preparation questions give you some powerful tools to increase your knowledge about implementing Windows Server 2016 DFS and branch office solutions for the Microsoft 70-741 exam and your daily work.

"Do I Know This Already?" Quiz

The "Do I Know This Already?" quiz enables you to assess whether you should read this entire chapter or simply jump to the "Exam Preparation Tasks" section for review. If you are in doubt, read the entire chapter. Table 13-1 outlines the major headings in this chapter and the corresponding "Do I Know This Already?" quiz questions. You can find the answers in Appendix A, "Answers to the 'Do I Know This Already?' Quizzes and End-of-Chapter Review Questions."

Table 13-1   "Do I Know This Already?" Foundation Topics Section-to-Question Mapping

Foundation Topics Section	Questions Covered in This Section
Install and Configure DFS Namespaces	1
Configure DFS Replication and DFSR Scheduling	2
Configure Remote Differential Compression (RDC) Settings	3
Configure Fault Tolerance	4
Recover DFS Databases	5
Optimize DFS Replication	6
Install and Configure BranchCache	7
Implement Distributed and Hosted Cache Modes	8
Implement BranchCache for Web, File, and Application Servers	9
Troubleshoot BranchCache	10

CAUTION   The goal of self-assessment is to gauge your mastery of the topics in this chapter. If you do not know the answer to a question or are only partially sure of the answer, you should mark that question as wrong for purposes of the self-assessment. Giving yourself credit for an answer you correctly guess skews your self-assessment results and might provide you with a false sense of security.

1. You have configured a DFS domain-based namespace. Your environment consists of three sites named Headquarter, BranchOffice1, and BranchOffice2. The following DFS namespace servers are present:

    - Headquarter: DFS1, DFS2
    - BranchOffice1: DFS3, DFS4
    - BranchOffice2: DFS5, DFS6

    You want to exclude folder targets for the Marketing folder on DFS3 and the Accounting folder on DFS4 that are outside the client's site. The clients have to fail back to the in-site server if this server becomes available again. Which are possible configurations? (Choose three.)

    a. On the folder properties, change the Effective Referrals Ordering setting.

    b. On the folder target properties, disable Enable Referrals for This Folder Target.

    c. Use the **Set-DfsnFolder -EnableInSiteReferrals $false** PowerShell command.

    d. Use the **Set-DfsnFolder -EnableInSiteReferrals $true** PowerShell command.

    e. Use the **Set-DfsnFolder -EnableTargetFailback $true** PowerShell command.

    f. Use the **Set-DfsnFolder -EnableTargetFailback $false** PowerShell command.

2. You have to implement DFS Replication for a folder named data on DFS1 so that the folder content automatically is replicated between the two DFS servers DFS1.pearson.com and DFS2.pucertify.pearson.com. Place the configuration steps in the correct order:

a. Create a new replication group.

b. Install DFS namespaces and the DFS Replication role on DFS1 and DFS2.

c. Remove DFS2 from pucertify.pearson.com and add DFS2 to pearson.com.

d. Add DFS1 and DFS2 as replication group members.

e. Configure replication scheduling.

f. Select the full mesh replication topology.

g. Define DFS1 as a primary member.

h. Define the local path on other members.

i. Define the folder to replicate.

j. Push initial replication by restarting the DFSR service on DFS1 and DFS2.

k. Wait for AD replication.

Step 1. _____

Step 2. _____

Step 3. _____

Step 4. _____

Step 5. _____

Step 6. _____

Step 7. _____

Step 8. _____

Step 9. _____

Step 10. _____

Step 11. _____

3. You have configured DFS Replication between the two DFS servers DFS1 (site1) and DFS2 (site2). You have a new high-performance WAN connection between site1 and site2. You cannot increase CPU resources on DFS1. You want to optimize CPU utilization on DFS1 when DFSR has to replicate data to DFS2. Which of the following is the correct setting to implement for this scenario?

   a. **Set-DfsrConnection -DisableCrossFileRDC $true**

   b. **Set-DfsrConnection -DisableCrossFileRDC $false**

   c. **Set-DfsrConnection -DisableRDC $false**

   d. **Set-DfsrConnection -DisableRDC $true**

4. You have four domain controllers: DC1, DC2, DC3, and DC4. All are running Windows Server 2016. All servers are members of the domain pearson. com. Your topology consists of three sites: Headquarters, BranchOffice1, and BranchOffice2. In sites Headquarters and BranchOffice1, you have two Windows Server 2016 DFS servers configured with domain-based namespaces. In site BranchOffice2, you use DFS standalone namespaces on two separate DFS servers. You want to implement a more fault-tolerant solution for the DFS standalone namespaces. Which is the best solution?

   a. Configure NLB with round robin for BranchOffice2 servers.

   b. Replace the standalone namespace with a domain-based namespace.

   c. Add another DFS server to BranchOffice2.

   d. Move the standalone namespace servers from BranchOffice2 to Headquarters.

5. You want to restore copies of preexisting files and folders in the replicated folder C:\Data to the location C:\DataTest. You want to overwrite existing files that have the same names in the specified location. Which PowerShell cmdlet and parameter do you have to use? (Choose two.)

   a. **CopyFiles**

   b. **Restore-DfsrPreservedFiles**

   c. **RestoreAllVersions**

   d. **AllowClobber**

   e. **Get-DfsrPreservedFiles**

6. You want to optimize network bandwidth usage for initial DFS Replication. Which new Windows Server 2016 feature can you use?

    a. Data Deduplication

    b. Remote Differential Compression

    c. DFS database cloning

    d. Storage Replica

7. You must configure BranchCache for use with a Windows Server 2016 file server named FS1 residing at the Headquarters site. You also have two other servers named SRV1 and SRV2 at Headquarters. The BranchOffice site has no servers. All servers and clients are members of the domain pearson.com. You want to configure BranchCache for 20 Windows 10 clients at the BranchOffice site. On which machines do you need to install the Branch-Cache feature?

    a. FS1

    b. SVR1

    c. SVR2

    d. Windows 10 clients

8. You have configured SVR1.pearson.com as a BranchCache host in your BranchOffice site. When you use the **Get-BCStatus** PowerShell cmdlet on the BranchCache clients, you notice that they are configured to find the BranchCache host through SCP. The clients cannot identify SVR1 as their BranchCache host. Which command do you have to run on SRV1?

    a. **Clear-BCCache**

    b. **Disable-BCServerOnBattery**

    c. **Enable-BCLocal**

    d. **Export-BCSecretKey**

    e. **Enable-BCHostedServer**

    f. **Set-BCMinSMBLatency**

    g. **Set-BCAuthentication**

9. Which command do you have use if you want to use the BranchCache feature for your application server?

    a. **Install-WindowsFeature BranchCache, BITS**

    b. **Install-WindowsFeature BranchCache**

   c. **Install-WindowsFeature BranchCache, FS-BranchCache**

   d. **Install-WindowsFeature BranchCache, FS-Data-Deduplication**

10. You have configured Windows Server 2016 BranchCache in hosted cache
   mode with two BranchCache hosts in your BranchOffice. You need to verify
   the Peer Discovery Firewall rules state on BranchCache clients. Which commands can you use for that? (Choose two.)

   a. **Get-NetFirewallProfile**

   b. **Netsh branchcache show status**

   c. **Netsh branchcache show status all**

   d. **Get-BCStatus**

Foundation Topics

Install and Configure DFS Namespaces

You can use DFS namespaces to create virtual views of your shared folders. You
can create either a domain-based or standalone namespace. Each type has different
characteristics. A domain-based namespace can be used when high availability of the
namespace is required.

Scenarios for Implementing DFS

You can implement DFS for the following network file usage scenarios in branch
offices:

- File sharing

- Data collection

- Data distribution

Branch Office File Sharing

Large organizations that have many branch offices often need to share files or col-
laborate between these locations. DFS can help replicate files between branch
offices or from a branch office to a hub site. Having files in multiple branch offices
also benefits users who travel from one branch office to another. The changes users
make to their files in a branch office are replicated to other branch offices.

TIP   DFS replicates a file only after it is closed. Therefore, DFS is not recommended for replicating database files or any files that are held open for long periods of time. Windows Server 2016 has a new feature called Storage Replica. In some scenarios, if many users have to work together on many documents in parallel, Storage Replica seems to be a better replication solution than DFSR because it uses SMB to replicate the data. Storage Replica replicates smaller units (blocks) and no files, and no file blocking occurs with Storage Replica. Table 13-2 outlines the Storage Replica features.

Table 13-2   Storage Replica Features

Feature	Details
Type	Host based
Synchronous	Yes
Asynchronous	Yes
Storage hardware agnostic	Yes
Replication unit	Volume (Partition)
Windows Server Stretch Cluster creation	Yes
Server-to-server replication	Yes
Cluster-to-cluster replication	Yes
Transport	SMB3
Network	TCP/IP or RDMA
Network constraint support	Yes
RDMA	iWARP, InfiniBand, RoCEv2
Replication network port firewall requirements	TCP 445 or 5445
Multipath/multichannel	Yes (SMB3)
Kerberos support	Yes (SMB3)
Overwrite encryption and signing	Yes (SMB3)
Per-volume failovers allowed	Yes
Thin-provisioned storage support	Yes
Management UI in-box	PowerShell, Failover Cluster Manager

Branch Office Data Collection

DFS technologies can collect files from a branch office and replicate them to a hub site, thus allowing the files to be used for several purposes. Critical data can be replicated to a hub site by using DFS and then backed up at the hub site using standard backup procedures. This increases data recoverability at the branch office if a server fails because files are available and backed up in two separate locations. Additionally, companies can reduce branch office costs by eliminating backup hardware and on-site IT personnel expertise. Replicated data can also be used to make branch office file shares fault tolerant. If the branch office server fails, clients in the branch office can access the replicated data at the hub site.

Branch Office Data Distribution

You can use DFS to publish and replicate documents, software, and other large object (LOB) data throughout your organization. DFS can also increase data availability and distribute client load across various file servers.

You can use DFS namespaces to create a virtual representation of shared folder structures. Two types of DFS namespaces exist:

- Domain-based
- Standalone

Domain-based Namespaces

A domain-based namespace can be used in these cases:

- HA (high availability) for namespace is required. This is accomplished by replicating the namespace to multiple namespace servers.

- You must hide the name of the namespace servers from users. Domain-based namespace servers also make it easier to replace a namespace server or migrate the namespace to a different server. Users can then access the \\domainname\ namespace format instead of the \\servername\share format. Windows Server provides support for access-based enumeration and increases the number of folder targets from 5,000 to 50,000. With *access-based enumeration (ABE)*, you can hide folders that someone does not have permission to view.

To use the DFS features, the following requirements must be met:

- The forest must be at the forest functional level of Windows Server 2008 or newer.

- The domain must be at the domain functional level of Windows Server 2008 or newer.

- The namespace servers must be running Windows Server 2008 or newer.

Figure 13-1 shows an example scenario for a domain-based DFS namespace deployment.

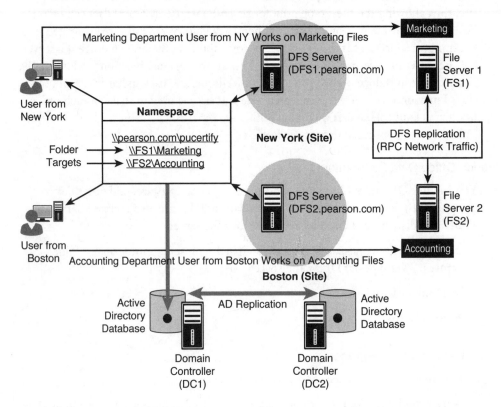

Figure 13-1 Domain-based DFS Namespace Scenario

When implementing DFS, you must have a general understanding of the overall topology of your DFS implementation. DFS topology functions as follows:

1. **The user accesses a folder in the DFS namespace.** When a user attempts to access a folder in a namespace (Accounting), the client computer contacts the server that is hosting the namespace root (DFS1 or DFS2). The host server can be a standalone server that is hosting a standalone namespace, or it can be a domain-based configuration (see Figure 13-1) that is stored in Active Directory and then replicated to other DCs providing high availability. The namespace server sends back to the client computer a referral containing a list of servers that host the shared folders (called folder targets) and are associated with the folder being accessed. DFS is a site-aware technology, so to ensure the most reliable access, client computers can be configured to access the namespaces that arrive within their site first.

2. The client accesses the first server in the referral. A referral is a list of targets that a client computer receives from a DC or namespace server when the user accesses a root or folder with namespace targets. The client computer caches the referral information and then contacts the first server in the referral. This referral typically is a server in the client's own site, unless no server is located within the client's site; in that case, the administrator can configure the target priority.

In Figure 13-1, the pucertify folder that is published within the namespace actually contains two folder targets distributed on two file servers in different sites. One share is named Marketing and is located on a file server named FS1 in New York; the other share is located on file server FS2 in Boston. Shared folders can be kept synchronized by DFSR. The Marketing folder is synchronized to FS2, and the Accounting folder is synchronized to FS1. Even though multiple servers host the source folders, this is transparent to users, who access only a single folder in the namespace. If one of the target folders becomes unavailable, users are redirected to the remaining targets within the namespace.

Table 13-3 shows the permissions required to create and manage a DFS namespace.

Table 13-3 DFS Namespace Administrative Permissions

Task	Groups That Can Perform the Tasks by Default
Create a domain-based namespace	Domain Admins
Add a namespace server to a domain-based namespace	Domain Admins
Manage a domain-based namespace	Local administrators on namespace server
Create a standalone namespace	Local administrator on namespace server
Manage a standalone namespace	Local administrator on namespace server
Create a replication group or enable DFSR on a folder	Domain Admins

Standalone Namespaces

A standalone namespace is used in these cases:

- An organization has no AD DS implementation.

- A company does not meet the requirements for a domain-based namespace, and requirements specify more than 5,000 DFS folders. Standalone DFS namespaces support up to 50,000 folders with targets.

- A company still hosts a DFS namespace in a failover cluster.

Deploying DFS Namespaces

Many implementations consist of content that is published within the DFS namespace. To configure a namespace for publishing content to users with Windows Server 2016, perform the following procedures:

Step 1. **Create a namespace.** Use the New Namespace Wizard to create the namespace within the DFS Management console. When a new namespace is created, you must provide the name of the server that you want to use as the namespace server, as well as specify the namespace name and type (either domain based or standalone). You can also specify whether the namespace is enabled for Windows Server 2008 mode.

Step 2. **Create a folder in the namespace.** Add a folder in the namespace that will be used to contain the content. There you can add folder targets or perform separate tasks to add, edit, or remove folder targets.

Step 3. **Add folder targets.** Now you have to create the folder targets. The folder target is a shared folder's UNC path on a specific server. Browse for shared folders on remote servers and create them as needed. You also can add multiple folder targets to increase the folder's availability. If you add multiple folder targets, consider using DFSR to ensure that the content is the same between the targets.

Step 4. **Set the ordering method for targets in referrals.** A referral is an ordered list of targets that a client computer receives from the namespace server when a user accesses a namespace root or folder. When a client receives the referral, the client attempts to access the first target in the list. If the target is not available, the next target is attempted. By default, targets in the client's site are always listed first in the referral. You can configure the method for ordering targets outside the client's site on the Referrals tab of the Namespace Properties dialog box. You have the choice of configuring the lowest cost and random order, or configuring the ordering method to exclude targets outside the client's site.

With the following steps, you set up a DFS domain-based namespace named pucertify with two Windows Server 2016 servers named dfs1.pearson.com and dfs2.pearson.com:

Step 1. Install the DFS-Namespaces and DFS-Replication roles and the necessary tools on DFS1 and DFS2 with PowerShell (see Figure 13-2).

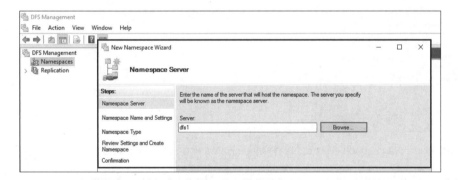

```
PS C:\> get-windowsfeature *DFS*

Display Name                                    Name                      Install State
------------                                    ----                      -------------
[ ] Active Directory Federation Services        ADFS-Federation           Available
    [ ] DFS Namespaces                          FS-DFS-Namespace          Available
    [ ] DFS Replication                         FS-DFS-Replication        Available
    [ ] DFS Management Tools                    RSAT-DFS-Mgmt-Con         Available

PS C:\> invoke-command -ComputerName DFS1, DFS2 -ScriptBlock {Install-windowsFeature FS-DFS-Namespace, FS-DFS-Replication, RSAT-DFS-Mgmt-Con}

Success Restart Needed Exit Code   Feature Result                             PSComputerName
------- -------------- ---------   --------------                             --------------
True    No             Success     {DFS Namespaces, DFS Replication, DFS Mana... DFS2
True    No             Success     {File and iSCSI Services, DFS Namespaces, ... DFS1
```

Figure 13-2 Installing DFS-Namespaces and DFS-Replication Roles with PowerShell

If you do not also install the File Server role on both servers, you cannot use the DFS PowerShell cmdlets. You install the File Server role on DFS1 and DFS2 with the following PowerShell command: **Install-windowsfeature FS-FileServer**.

Step 2. With the **New-DfsnRoot** PowerShell cmdlet, you can create the DFS domain-based namespace. You can also do this with the DFS Management tool. Open the DFS Management tool and select **Namespaces** and **New Namespace**. Enter the name of the server that will host the namespace (in this case, **DFS1**). Figure 13-3 shows the Namespace Server page of the New Namespace Wizard.

Figure 13-3 New Namespace Wizard (Namespace Server)

Step 3. On the Namespace Name and Settings page, type the name of the namespace (in this case, **pucertify**). Figure 13-4 shows the Namespace Name and Settings page. Figure 13-5 shows the Edit Settings page, where you can configure the shared folder permissions.

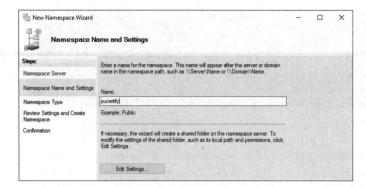

Figure 13-4   New Namespace Wizard (Namespace Name and Settings)

Figure 13-5   New Namespace Wizard (Namespace Name and Settings, Edit Settings)

Step 4.   On the Namespace Type page, select **Domain-based Namespace** and **Enable Windows Server 2008 Mode**. Figure 13-6 shows the Namespace Type page.

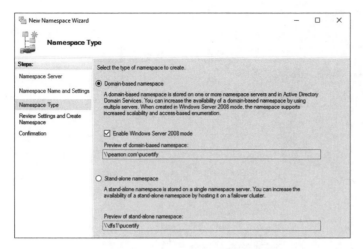

Figure 13-6   New Namespace Wizard (Namespace Type)

Step 5.   On the Review Settings and Create Namespace page, select **Create**. Figure 13-7 shows the Review Settings and Create Namespace page, and Figure 13-8 shows the Confirmation page.

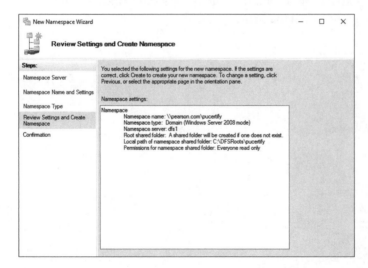

Figure 13-7   New Namespace Wizard (Review Settings and Create Namespace)

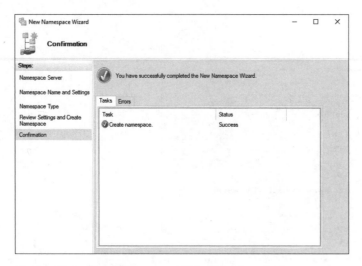

Figure 13-8   New Namespace Wizard (Confirmation)

Step 6.   Now you can add new folders. In this example, you add two folders
named Marketing and Accounting with the folder targets \\FS1\
marketing and \\FS1\Accounting. Figure 13-9 shows the New Folder
window and how to add the Marketing folder.

Figure 13-9   Windows Server 2016 DFS Management Tool (New Folder)

Figure 13-10 shows the possible DFS namespace tasks in the DFS Management
tool, and Table 13-4 describes these in more detail.

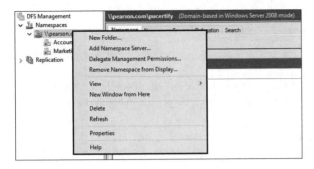

Figure 13-10   Windows Server 2016 DFS Management Tool Namespace Tasks

Table 13-4   Windows Server 2016 DFS Namespace Tasks

Task	Description
New Folder	Adds a new folder to the existing namespace
Add Namespace Server	Adds namespace servers
Delegate Management Permissions	Adds DFS administrators for that namespace
Remove Namespace from Display	Hides the namespace display from the DFS Management tool

Figure 13-11 shows the possible namespace folder tasks in the DFS Management tool, and Table 13-5 describes them in more detail.

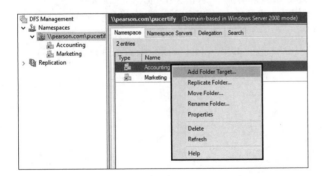

Figure 13-11   Windows Server 2016 DFS Management Tool Namespace Folder Tasks

Table 13-5   Windows Server 2016 DFS Namespace Folder Tasks

Task	Description
Add Folder Target	Adds folder targets to the folder.
Replicate Folder	Replicates between two or more folder targets. If you have only one folder target for a folder configured, you get the dialog box shown in Figure 13-12.
Move Folder	Moves a folder to another server.
Rename Folder	Renames a folder.
Properties	Figures 13-13 and 13-14 show the available folder properties. Normally, every folder inherits the settings from the root. Here, however you also can configure other settings for Exclude Targets Outside of the Client's Site or Clients Fail Back to Preferred Targets. A referral is an ordered list of targets that a client computer receives from a DC or namespace server when the user accesses a namespace root or folder with targets. After the client receives the referral, the client attempts to access the first target in the list. If the target is not available, the client attempts to access the next target. Targets on the client's site are always listed first in a referral. Targets outside the client's site are listed according to the ordering method. You also can use the following PowerShell command to exclude folder targets outside the client's site: **Set-DfsnFolder** -*EnableInsiteReferrals*. To use PowerShell to set the ordering method for a target in namespace root referrals, use the **Set-DfsnRoot** PowerShell cmdlet with the parameters **EnableSiteCosting** (specifies the lowest-cost ordering method) or **EnableInsiteReferrals** (specifies excluding targets outside the client's site). On the Advanced tab of the DFS folder properties (see Figure 13-15), you can configure which users can see the folder.

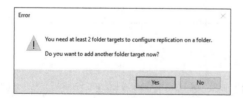

Figure 13-12   Replicate Folder Error

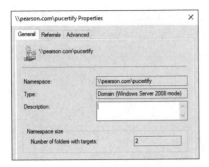

Figure 13-13 DFS Folder Properties (General)

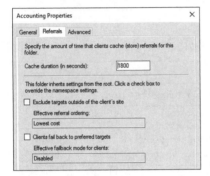

Figure 13-14 DFS Folder Properties (Referrals)

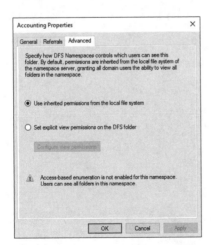

Figure 13-15 DFS Folder Properties (Advanced)

Figure 13-16 shows the Folder Target tasks in the DFS Management tool, and Table 13-6 describes them further.

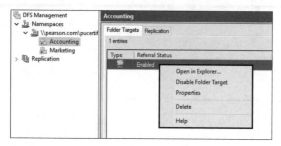

Figure 13-16 DFS Folder Target Tasks

Table 13-6 Windows Server 2016 DFS Folder Target Tasks

Task	Description
Open in Explorer	Displays the Folder Target in Windows Explorer.
Disable Folder Target	Disables the Folder Target
Properties	See Figures 13-17 and 13-18 for the Folder Target General and Advanced properties.

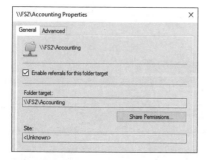

Figure 13-17 DFS Folder Target Properties (General)

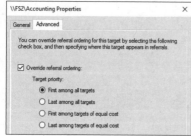

Figure 13-18 DFS Folder Target Properties (Advanced)

Configuring DFS with PowerShell

Table 13-7 lists all possible DFS Namespace PowerShell cmdlets.

Table 13-7 Windows Server 2016 DFS Namespace PowerShell Cmdlets

Cmdlet	Description
Get-DfsnAccess	Gets permissions for a DFS namespace folder
Get-DfsnFolder	Gets settings for a DFS namespace folder
Get-DfsFolderTarget	Gets settings for targets of a DFS namespace folder
Get-DfsRoot	Gets settings for DFS namespaces
Get-DfsnRootTarget	Gets settings for root targets of a DFS namespace
Get-DfsServerConfiguration	Gets DFS namespace settings for a DFSN root server
Grant-DfsnAccess	Grants permissions to users and groups to access a DFS namespace folder
Move-DfsnFolder	Moves or renames a DFS namespace folder
New-DfsnFolder	Creates a folder in a DFS namespace
New-DfsnFolderTarget	Adds a target to a DFS namespace folder
New-DfsnRoot	Creates a DFS namespace
New-DfsnRootTarget	Adds a root target to a DFS namespace
Remove-DfsnAccess	Removes users and groups from the ACL for a folder in a DFS namespace
Remove-DfsnFolder	Removes a DFS namespace folder
Remove-DfsnFolderTarget	Removes a target for a DFS namespace folder
Remove-DfsnRoot	Removes a DFS namespace
Remove-DfsnRootTarget	Removes a target for a DFS namespace root
Revoke-DfsnAccess	Revokes permissions for users to access and enumerate the contents of a DFS namespace folder
Set-DfsnFolder	Changes settings for a DFS namespace folder
Set-DfsnFolderTarget	Changes settings for a target of a DFS namespace folder
Set-DfsnRoot	Changes settings for a DFS namespace
Set-DfsnRootTarget	Changes settings for a root target of a DFS namespace
Set-DfsServerConfiguration	Changes settings for a DFS namespace root server

With the PowerShell cmdlet **Get-DfsnServerConfiguration**, you can list all configurations of your Windows Server 2016 DFS namespace server. Figure 13-19 shows example output of this command.

```
PS C:\> Get-DfsnServerConfiguration | FL

cmdlet Get-DfsnServerConfiguration at command pipeline position 1
Supply values for the following parameters:
ComputerName: DFS1


ComputerName                 : DFS1
LdapTimeoutSec               : 30
SyncIntervalSec              : 3600
UseFqdn                      :
EnableInsiteReferrals        :
EnableSiteCostedReferrals    :
LdapTimeout                  : 30
NamespaceServer              : DFS1
PreferLogonDC                :
SyncInterval                 : 3600
UseFullyQualifiedDomainNames :
```

Figure 13-19   Get-DfsnServerConfiguration Example Output

You can use the PowerShell cmdlet **Remove-DfsnFolder** to remove a DFS folder, as Figure 13-20 shows.

```
PS C:\> Remove-DfsnFolder -Path \\pearson\pucertify\Marketing

Confirm
Performing operation "Delete DFS Namespace folder" on Target "\\pearson\pucertify\Marketing"
[Y] Yes  [N] No  [S] Suspend  [?] Help (default is "Y"): Y
```

Figure 13-20   Remove-DfsnFolder

When you remove the same folder through the DFS Management tool, you will get the message that this will not delete shared folders (folder targets) referenced by the folder (see Figure 13-21).

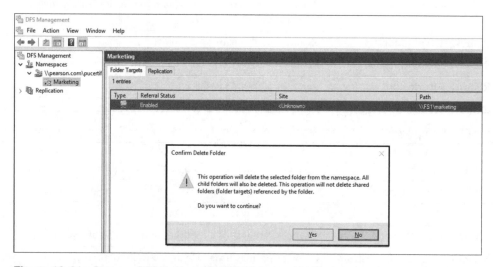

Figure 13-21   Remove DFS Folder with DFS Management Tool

You can modify settings for the DFS root with the PowerShell cmdlet **Set-DfsnRoot**. You can use this cmdlet to enable or disable the following settings:

- Site costing

- In-site referrals

- Access-based enumeration

- Root scalability

- Target failback

With the following command, you can enable root scalability, which allows the DFS namespace server to poll domain controllers for updates:

```
Set-DfsnRoot -Path "\\Pearson\PUcertify" -EnableRootScalability $True
 -TimeToLiveSec 900
```

The command also sets the referral TTL interval to 900 seconds. If the **EnableRootScalability** value is *$True*, DFS namespace servers connect to the nearest DC for periodic namespace updates. If this value is *$False*, the servers connect to the DC, which is a PDC emulator.

Configure DFS Replication and DFSR Scheduling

DFSR provides a way to keep folders synchronized between servers across well-connected and limited-bandwidth connections. DFSR has the following characteristics:

- DFSR uses RDC, a client/server protocol that can be used to efficiently update files over a limited-bandwidth network. RDC detects data insertions, removals, and rearrangements in files, enabling DFSR to replicate only the changed file blocks when files are updated.

- DFSR uses a hidden staging folder to stage a file before sending or receiving it. Staging folders act as caches for new and changed files to be replicated from sending members to receiving members. The sending member begins staging a file when it receives a request from the receiving member. The process involves reading the file from the replicated folder and building a compressed representation of the file in the staging folder. After it has been constructed, the staged file is sent to the receiving member; if remote differential compression is used, only a fraction of the staging file might be replicated. The receiving member downloads the data and builds the file in its staging folder. When the file download completes on the receiving member, DFSR decompresses the file and installs it into the replicated folder. Each replicated folder has its own staging folder, which, by default, is located in the local path of the replicated folder in the DfsrPrivate\Staging folder.

- DFSR detects volume changes by monitoring the file system update sequence number (USN) journal and replicates changes only after the file is closed.

- DFSR uses a version vector exchange protocol to determine which files must be synchronized. The protocol sends less than 1 KB per file across the network to synchronize the metadata associated with changed files on the sending and receiving members.

- DFSR uses a conflict resolution heuristic of "last writer wins" for files that are in conflict (that is, a file that is updated at multiple servers simultaneously) and "earliest creator wins" for name conflicts. Files and folders that lose the conflict resolution are moved to a folder known as the Conflict and Deleted folder. You can also configure the service to move deleted files to the Conflict and Deleted folder for retrieval, in case the file or folder is deleted. Each replicated folder has its own hidden Conflict and Deleted folder, which is located in the local path of the replicated folder in the DfsrPrivate\ConflictandDeleted folder.

Configuring Windows Server 2016 DFSR with the GUI

The following steps describe how to set up a DFSR scenario with two DFS servers named DFS1 and DFS2 as replication partners, to replicate a folder named data on DFS1 between them:

Step 1. Install the **DFS-Namespaces** and **DFS-Replication** roles and the necessary tools on DFS1 and DFS2 with PowerShell (see Figure 13-22).

Figure 13-22   Installing DFS-Namespaces and DFS-Replication Role with PowerShell

If you do not install the File Server role on both servers, you cannot use the DFS PowerShell cmdlets. You should also install the File Server role on DFS1 and DFS2 with the following PowerShell command: **Install-windowsfeature FS-FileServer**.

Step 2. In the DFS Management tool, at Replication, select **New Replication Group**. To configure DFSR replication between two or more servers, select **Multipurpose Replication Group** (see Figure 13-23).

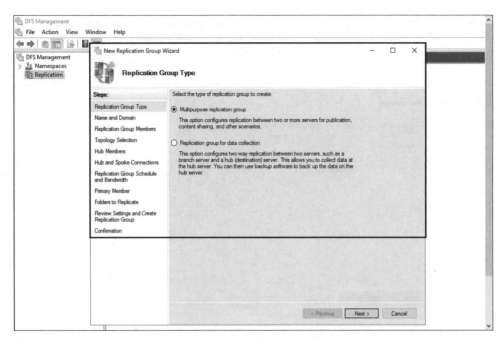

Figure 13-23   Replication Group Type

Step 3.   From the Name and Domain page of the New Replication Group Wizard, type a name (in this case, **ReplicaGroup1**). The replication group object is saved in Active Directory; you cannot replicate when the DFSR partner servers are in different domains (see Figure 13-24).

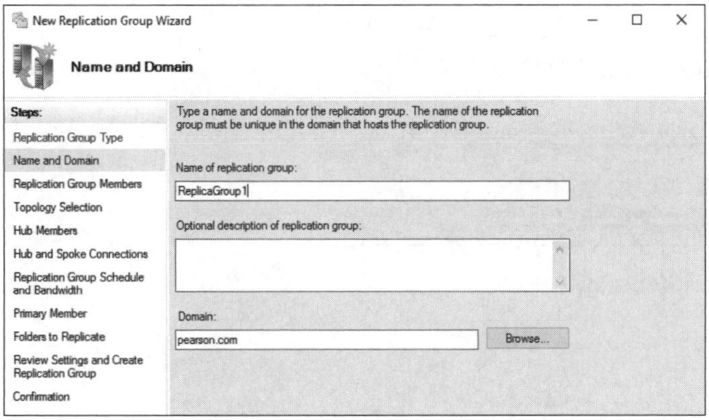

Figure 13-24   DFS Replication: Name and Domain

Step 4. From the Replication Group Members page of the New Replication Group Wizard, add the two DFS servers DFS1 and DFS2. Figure 13-25 shows how the page should look.

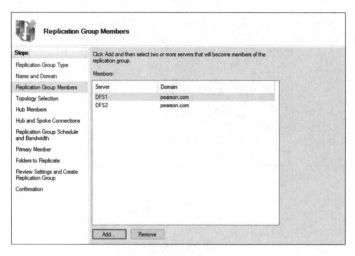

Figure 13-25 DFS Replication: Replication Group Members

Step 5. From the Topology Selection page of the New Replication Group Wizard, select **Full Mesh** (see Figure 13-26).

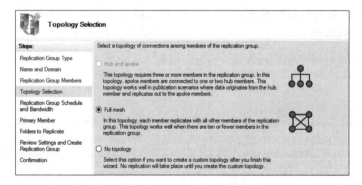

Figure 13-26 DFS Replication: Topology Selection

Step 6. From the Replication Group Schedule and Bandwidth page of the New Replication Group Wizard, select **Replicate Continuously Using the Specified Bandwidth** with the default setting (see Figure 13-27).

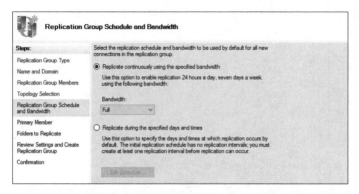

Figure 13-27 DFS Replication: Replication Group Schedule and Bandwidth

Step 7. From the Primary Member page of the New Replication Group Wizard, select **DFS1** as primary member because the DATA folder, which has to be replicated, is located there (see Figure 13-28).

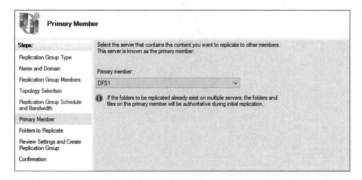

Figure 13-28 DFS Replication: Primary Member

Step 8. From the Folders to Replicate page of the New Replication Group Wizard, click **Add** and type **C:\Data** into the field Local Path of Folder to Replicate (see Figure 13-29).

Figure 13-29 DFS Replication: Primary Member Add Folders to Replicate

Afterward, the Folders to Replicate page looks like Figure 13-30.

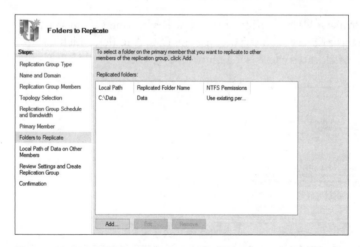

Figure 13-30 DFS Replication: Add Replicated Folders

Step 9. From the Local Path of Data on Other Members page of the New Replication Group Wizard, the member details must look like those in Figure 13-31.

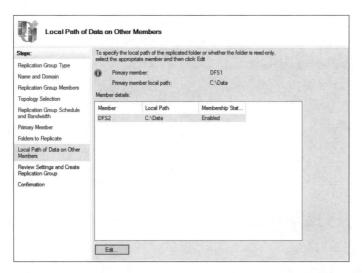

Figure 13-31   DFS Replication: Local Path of Data on Other Members

Step 10.   Verify the review settings in the Review Settings and Create Replication Group page (see Figure 13-32) and the Confirmation page (see Figure 13-33).

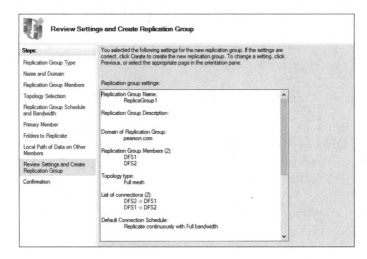

Figure 13-32   DFS Replication: Review Settings and Create Replication Group

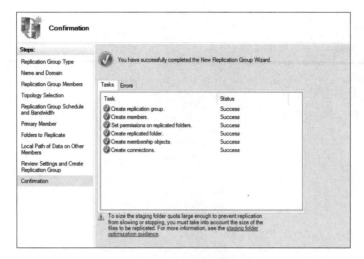

Figure 13-33   DFS Replication: Confirmation

   Step 11.   After successfully completing the New Replication Wizard, you get the
            Replication Delay message shown in Figure 13-34. The replication group
            object in Active Directory must be replicated to other DCs.

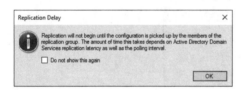

Figure 13-34   DFS Replication: Replication Delay Message

   Step 12.   After this configuration, you can restart the DFS Replication service
            on DFS1 and DFS2 to push the start of the initial replication with the
            PowerShell command: **Invoke-command -computername DFS1,
            DFS2 -ScriptBlock {Restart-Service DFSR}.**

You can configure DFSR scheduling in the DFS Management tool on the connection's properties (see Figure 13-35).

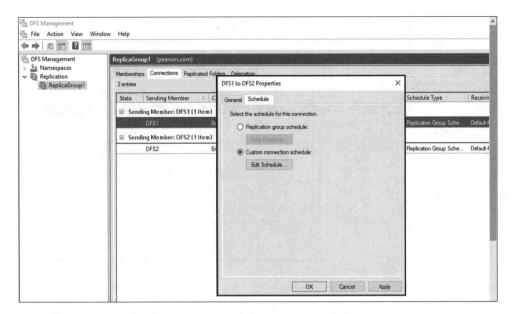

Figure 13-35   Windows Server 2016 DFSR Group Schedule

You cannot edit the default DFSR group schedule. You can configure only the custom group schedule, based on Universal Coordinated Time (UTC) or the local time of the receiving member. Figure 13-36 shows the Edit Schedule window of a custom group schedule.

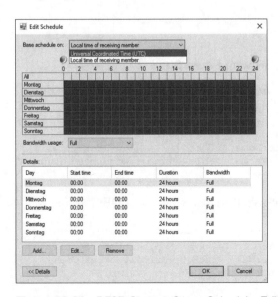

Figure 13-36   DFSR Custom Group Schedule: Edit Schedule

If you want to delete a DFS Replication group, you must explicitly confirm that (see Figure 13-37).

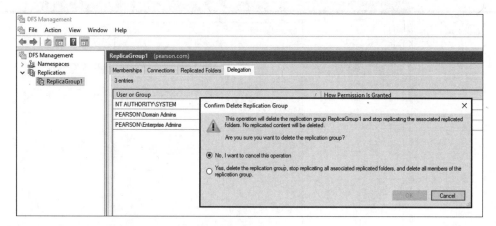

Figure 13-37   Confirm Delete Replication Group

You also can configure DFSR group scheduling with PowerShell commands. Figure 13-38 shows the available cmdlets.

Figure 13-38   Windows Server 2016 DFSR Group Schedule PowerShell Cmdlets

Configuring Windows Server 2016 DFSR with PowerShell

You can configure the same scenario with PowerShell commands. You create the DFS Replication group with the following command:

```
New-DfsReplicationGroup -GroupName "ReplicaGroup1" |
  New-DfsReplicatedFolder -FolderName "PUcertify" | Add-DfsrMember
  -ComputerName "DFS1","DFS2" | Format-Table dnsname,groupname -auto
  -wrap
```

With the **Set-DfsrMembership** PowerShell cmdlet, you can set DFS1 as the primary member:

```
Set-DfsrMembership -GroupName "ReplicaGroup1" -FolderName "PUcertify"
  -ContentPath "C:\Data" -ComputerName "DFS1" -PrimaryMember $True
  -Force | Format-Table *name,*path,primary* -auto -wrap
```

Figure 13-39 shows an example of the successful creation of a DFSR group with PowerShell.

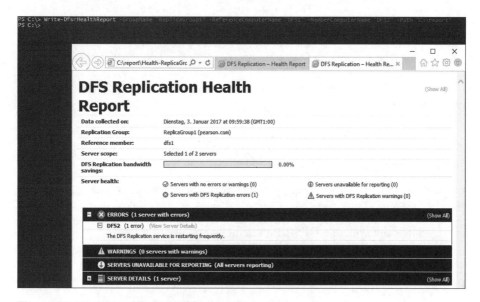

```
PS C:\> New-DfsReplicationGroup -GroupName "ReplicaGroup2" | New-DfsReplicatedFolder -FolderName "PUCentify2" | Add-Dfsr
Member -ComputerName "DFS1","DFS2"

GroupName                    : ReplicaGroup2
ComputerName                 : DFS1
DomainName                   : pearson.com
Identifier                   : 5c3797d2-1e6c-41c6-8bce-782ee1c6b6d4
Description                  :
DnsName                      : DFS1.pearson.com
Site                         : Default-First-Site-Name
NumberOfConnections          : 0
NumberOfInboundConnections   : 0
NumberOfOutboundConnections  : 0
NumberOfInterSiteConnections : 0
NumberOfIntraSiteConnections : 0
IsClusterNode                : False
State                        : Normal

GroupName                    : ReplicaGroup2
ComputerName                 : DFS2
DomainName                   : pearson.com
Identifier                   : 3db85c29-0e86-45aa-a0b7-9590e8a4cece
Description                  :
DnsName                      : DFS2.pearson.com
Site                         : Default-First-Site-Name
NumberOfConnections          : 0
NumberOfInboundConnections   : 0
NumberOfOutboundConnections  : 0
NumberOfInterSiteConnections : 0
NumberOfIntraSiteConnections : 0
IsClusterNode                : False
State                        : Normal
```

Figure 13-39   New-DfsReplicationGroup Example

With the PowerShell cmdlet **Write-DfsrHealthReport,** you can generate a DFSR health report to verify replication and get information about replication bandwidth savings through the use of RDC or errors. Figure 13-40 shows an example of this command and example output of an error in the report when the problem lies in the DFS Replication service on DFS2.

```
PS C:\> Write-DfsrHealthReport -GroupName "ReplicaGroup1" -ReferenceComputerName "DFS1" -MemberComputerName "DFS2" -Path "C:\report"
PS C:\>
```

C:\report\Health-ReplicaGro [🔍 ▾ ⬡]   DFS Replication – Health Report   DFS Replication – Health Re... ×   ⌂ ☆ ⚙ ⊕

DFS Replication Health Report   (Show All)

Data collected on:	Dienstag, 3. Januar 2017 at 09:59:38 (GMT1:00)
Replication Group:	ReplicaGroup1 (pearson.com)
Reference member:	dfs1
Server scope:	Selected 1 of 2 servers
DFS Replication bandwidth savings:	[ ] 0.00%

Server health: ⊘ Servers with no errors or warnings (0)   ⊕ Servers unavailable for reporting (0)
                  ✖ Servers with DFS Replication errors (1)   ⚠ Servers with DFS Replication warnings (0)

■ ✖ **ERRORS (1 server with errors)**   (Show All)
  ⊟ **DFS2 (1 error)** (View Server Details)
     The DFS Replication service is restarting frequently.

⚠ **WARNINGS (0 servers with warnings)**

⊕ **SERVERS UNAVAILABLE FOR REPORTING (All servers reporting)**

■ ▦ **SERVER DETAILS (1 server)**   (Show All)

Figure 13-40   Write-DfsrHealthReport Example

With the PowerShell cmdlet **Sync-DfsReplicationGroup,** you can force the synchronization of DFS Replication. Take a look at this example:

```
Sync-DfsReplicationGroup -GroupName "ReplicaGroup1" -SourceComputer
  Name DFS1 -DestinationComputerName DFS2 -DurationInMinutes 1
```

With the **Get-DfsrServiceConfiguration** PowerShell cmdlet, you can display some important DFSR settings, such as whether to use RPC dynamic port mapping or the DebugLogPath, which defines the place of the DFSR log files. Figure 13-41 shows an example for the **Get-DfsrServiceConfiguration** PowerShell cmdlet and also an example of a DFSR debug log file; LON-DC1.pearson.com is used as the domain controller.

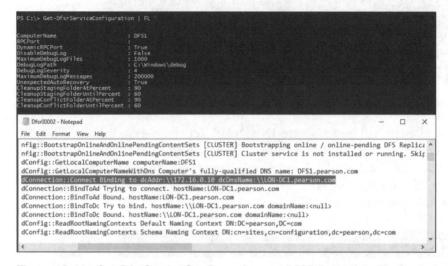

Figure 13-41   Get-DfsrServiceConfiguration and DFSR Debug Log File Content

With the **Get-DfsrBacklog** PowerShell cmdlet, you can list pending file updates between two DFS Replication partners.

The following example retrieves the first 100 unreplicated changes between the local computer and the upstream computer, DFS2, for the replication group Repli-Group1 and the replicated folder named Data:

```
Get-DfsrBacklog -SourceComputerName "DFS2" -GroupName "RepliGroup1"
    -FolderName "Data"
```

Table 13-8 lists the available DFSR PowerShell cmdlets.

Table 13-8 Windows Server 2016 DFSR PowerShell Cmdlets

Cmdlet	Description
Get-DfsrBacklog	Retrieves the list of pending file updates between two DFS Replication partners. Updates can be new, modified, or deleted files and folders. The maximum number of files that this command displays is 100. The **Verbose** parameter displays a count of all backlogged updates. Any files or folders listed in the DFS Replication backlog have not yet replicated from the source computer to the destination computer. This does not necessarily indicate a problem. A backlog indicates latency, and a backlog could be expected in your environment, depending on configuration, rate of change, network, and other factors.
Get-DfsrCloneState	Gets the status of a database cloning operation.
Get-DfsrConnection	Gets a connection between DFS Replication partners.
Get-DfsrConnectionSchedule	Gets a connection schedule between DFS Replication partners.
Get-DfsReplicatedFolder	Gets a replicated folder from a replication group.
Get-DfsReplicationGroup	Retrieves a replication group.
Get-DfsrGroupSchedule	Retrieves a replication group schedule.
Get-DfsrMember	Gets member computers in a replication group.
Get-DfsrMembership	Gets membership settings for members of replication groups.
Get-DfsrServiceConfiguration	Gets settings for the DFS Replication service on group members.
Get-DfsrState	Gets the DFS Replication state for a member.
Reset-DfsrCloneState	Cancels a cloning operation.
Start-DfsrPropagationTest	Creates a propagation test file in a replicated folder.
Suspend-DfsReplicationGroup	Suspends replication between computers, regardless of schedule.
Sync-DfsReplicationGroup	Synchronizes replication between computers, regardless of schedule.
UpdateDfsrConfigurationFromAD	Initiates an update of the DFS Replication service.

Cmdlet	Description
Write-DfsrHealthReport	Generates a DFS Replication health report. This cmdlet generates a DFS Replication health, or diagnostic, report for two or more servers. A health report contains administrative information about replication state, efficiency, and any potential replication issues. The cmdlet creates the reports as an HTML file, with an associated XML file.
Write-DfsrPropagationReport	Generates reports for propagation test files in a replication group.

Configure Remote Differential Compression (RDC) Settings

DFSR uses Remote Differential Compression (RDC), a client/server protocol that can be used to efficiently update files over a limited-bandwidth network.

You can enable and disable RDC in the DFS Management tool under the properties of the DFSR connection. Figure 13-42 shows where to enable and disable RDC.

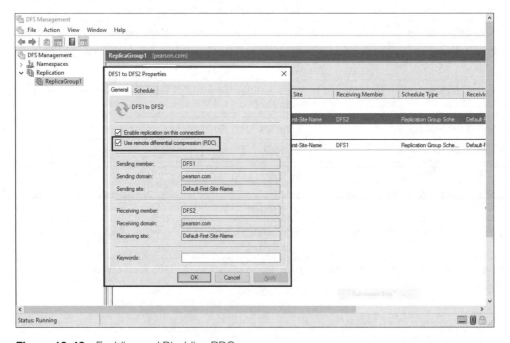

Figure 13-42   Enabling and Disabling RDC

RDC detects insertions, removals, and rearrangements in files, enabling DFSR to replicate only the changed file blocks when files are updated.

By default, RDC is used only for files that are 64 KB or larger.

DFSR also supports cross-file RDC, which allows DFSR to use remote differential compression even when a file with the same name does not exist at the client. Cross-file RDC can determine files that are similar to the file that needs to be replicated; it uses blocks of similar files that are identical to the replicating file, to minimize the amount of data that needs to be replicated.

Cross-file RDC uses up to five existing previously replicated files on a volume to seed a new replicating file. Applying cross-file RDC over very low-bandwidth network connections with files that are very similar results in very large bandwidth savings and potentially large time savings.

When you use cross-file RDC on very high-bandwidth network connections, cross-file RDC can add too much local processing time and negatively affect performance. In extremely large datasets (millions of files on a volume with a great deal of similarity), cross-file RDC can also negatively affect CPU and disk utilization. Consider disabling cross-file RDC when you replicate over LANs and very high-performance WANs.

You can enable and disable cross-file RDC with the following PowerShell cmdlet:

```
Set-DfsrConnection -DisableCrossFileRDC $true
```

 ## Configure Fault Tolerance

DFS is integrated with Active Directory to create fault-tolerant DFS roots. If you have multiple servers in your domain, any or all participating servers can host and provide fault tolerance for a given DFS root. Active Directory is used to ensure that DCs share a common DFS topology, thus providing redundancy and fault tolerance. For example, when you have three domain controllers in a domain, named DC1, DC2, and DC3, the domain-based DFS namespace will be replicated to all three DCs; this provides the fault tolerance for the domain-based DFS namespace. Up to 32 DCs can host the same root.

You also can use standalone DFS servers, which does not take advantage of Active Directory and does not provide root-level fault tolerance. A DC can host a single DFS root, and you can have an unlimited number of DFS roots in each domain.

If you need to load-balance only static (read-only) data, you can do so with a standalone DFS namespace by creating identical standalone namespaces (and identical targets) on separate DFS servers and then using DNS round robin to distribute the workload among servers. Remember, however, that DNS-based load balancing does not take the DFS server's availability into account. DNS queries are resolved to each DFS server in a round-robin manner, regardless of whether an individual DFS server is actually available.

TIP   At the Windows Server 2016, 2012 R2, 2012, 2008 R2, and 2008 domain functional levels, DFS Replication is also used to replicate SYSVOL folder contents (GPOs) between DCs. If you created a new domain at the Windows Server 2008 domain functional level or higher, DFS Replication is automatically used to replicate SYSVOL. If you created the domain at a lower functional level, you need to migrate from FRS to DFS Replication for SYSVOL.

Suppose that you have a domain named pearson.com with two sites, Chicago and Berlin. You have two DFS servers: dfs1.pearson.com at the Chicago site and dfs2.pearson.com at the Berlin site.

To make the DFS namespace server fault tolerant in its own sites, you need to add one more DFS namespace server in every site. Then you create a new connection to DFS3 and DFS4 (see Figure 13-43).

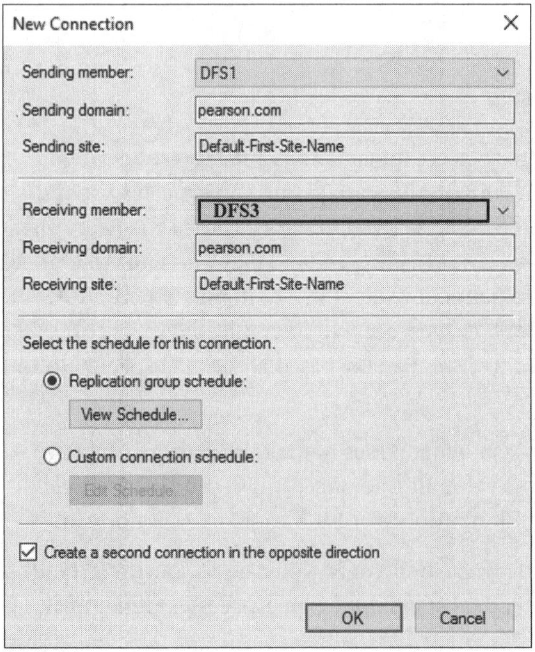

Figure 13-43   Windows Server 2016 DFS New Connection

Recover DFS Databases

When DFSR detects database corruption, it rebuilds the database and then resumes replication normally, with no files arbitrarily losing conflicts.

When replicating with a read-only partner, DFSR resumes replication without waiting indefinitely for an administrator to set the primary flag manually. The database corruption recovery feature rebuilds the database by using local file and USN information and marks each file with a normal replicated state.

You cannot recover files from the ConflictAndDeleted and Preexisting folders except from backup.

Use the Windows PowerShell cmdlets **Get-DfsrPreservedFiles** and **Restore-DfsrPreservedFiles** to allow the recovery of files from these folders. You can restore these files and folders into their previous location or a new location. You can choose to move or copy the files, and you can keep all versions of a file or only the latest version.

Optimize DFS Replication

DFS includes database-management tasks that use database cloning to help you perform initial database replication. Furthermore, DFS includes tasks that can recover the DFS database in case of data corruption. A new Windows Server 2016 feature is the capability to clone the DFS database for initial replication, to dramatically improve performance during initial synchronization. You also can use the Data Deduplication feature to reduce bandwidth consumed when replicating file data.

DFS Database Cloning

The initial replication can take a long time and consume a large amount of network bandwidth when replicating a large set of files. Windows Server 2016 provides a feature that clones the database for the initial replication. To create a clone of the database, use the **Export-DfsrClone** PowerShell cmdlet to export the DFSR database and volume configuration XML file settings for a given local computer volume. On a large dataset, exports can take a long time to complete. You can use the **Get- DfsrCloneState** PowerShell cmdlet to determine the status of the export operation.

After you clone the data and copy the exported database and XML file to the new DFS member server, use the **Import-DfsrClone** PowerShell cmdlet to inject the database onto a volume and validate the files on the file system. This provides dramatic performance improvements during the initial synchronization. The following cmdlet exports a database and creates a clone of the database in a folder named PUCertify:

```
Export-DfsrClone -Volume C: -Path "C:\PUCertify"
```

After copying the cloned database to the C:\PUCertify folder on the new DFS member server, you can use the following PowerShell cmdlet to import the cloned database:

```
Import-DfsrClone -Volume C: -Path "C:\PUCertify"
```

With the PowerShell cmdlet **Get-DfsrCloneState**, you can get the status of a DFS database cloning operation. The DFS Replication service can return the cloning states described in Table 13-9.

Table 13-9 Windows Server 2016 DFSR Database Cloning States

Clone State	Description
Ready	The DFS Replication service is ready to perform cloning. This is the status both before cloning starts and after cloning completes.
Started DB Export	The DFS Replication service has begun the export process and is validating prerequisites.
Started DB Import	The DFS Replication service has begun the import process and is validating prerequisites.
Processing DB Export	The DFS Replication service is exporting the database.
Processing DB Import	The DFS Replication service is importing the database.
Resetting	The DFS Replication service is canceling and rolling back the import or export.
Shut down	The DFS Replication database was shut down due to a requested backup or restore operation.
Shutting down	The DFS Replication database is shutting down because of a requested backup or restore operation, or because a requested service shut down.

Data Deduplication and DFSR

Data Deduplication is a server built-in feature (File and Storage services role) as of Windows Server 2012 on Microsoft server operating systems. It helps provide a more robust and efficient DFS environment when combined with DFSR. Data Deduplication offers the advantages in Table 13-10.

Table 13-10 Data Deduplication Advantages

Advantage	Description
Optimization of storage capacity	Data Deduplication enables a server to store more data in less physical disk space. You can configure Data Deduplication only per volume, not per folder.
Bandwidth consummation reduction	In combination with DFSR, Data Deduplication can greatly reduce the bandwidth consumed when replicating file data, as long as replication partners are also running Windows Server 2016.
Scale and performance	Data Deduplication is highly scalable in Windows Server 2016. It can run on multiple volumes without affecting other services and applications running on the server. Data Deduplication can be throttled to accommodate other heavy workloads on the server so that no performance degradation occurs for important server tasks.
Reliability data integrity	Windows Server 2016 uses checksum consistency and validation to ensure that the integrity of data affected by Data Deduplication remains intact. Data Deduplication also maintains redundant copies of the most frequently used data on a volume to protect against data corruption.
Simplified management	Windows Server 2016 and Windows PowerShell 5.0 contain integrated support for Data Deduplication. Management through Windows Server 2016 is accomplished with known tools. You can install Windows Server 2016 with the PowerShell command **Install-WindowsFeature FS-Data-Deduplication**, and you can configure it in Server Manager or with the PowerShell cmdlets in Figure 13-44.

Figure 13-44 Data Deduplication PowerShell Cmdlets

TIP Data Deduplication is available and fully supported in the new Nano Server deployment option for Windows Server 2016.

Install and Configure BranchCache

BranchCache reduces the network use on WAN connections between branch offices and headquarters by locally caching frequently used files on computers in the branch office. When the client requests data, BranchCache retrieves it from a server. Because BranchCache is a passive cache, it does not increase WAN use. BranchCache caches only the read requests and does not interfere when a user saves a file. BranchCache in Windows Server 2016 has many benefits. It allows more than one hosted cache server per location, uses Extensible Storage Engine (ESE) database technology from Exchange Server, and requires only a single GPO for BranchCache deployment.

BranchCache Protocols

BranchCache reduces the network use on WAN connections between branch offices and headquarters by locally caching frequently used files on computers in the branch office. BranchCache improves the performance of applications that use one of the following protocols:

- **HTTP or HTTPS:** These protocols are used by web browsers and other applications.

- **SMB, including signed SMB traffic protocol:** This protocol is used for accessing shared folders.

- **BITS:** BITS is a Windows component that distributes content from a server to clients by using only idle network bandwidth. Microsoft System Center Configuration Manager also uses BITS.

Main Benefits of BranchCache

The primary benefits of BranchCache are as follows:

- Reduces the network use on WAN connections between headquarters and branch offices

- Locally caches frequently used files on computers in the branch office

- Improves the performance of applications that use HTTP or HTTPS, SMB, or BITS

BranchCache Clients

BranchCache is supported on client operating systems Windows 7 and newer, and server operating systems Windows Server 2008 R2 and newer.

BranchCache Functionality in Windows Server 2016

Windows Server 2016 BranchCache offers some improvements. The following list shows which functionality has changed:

- BranchCache allows for more than one hosted cache server per location.

- The underlying database uses the ESE database technology from Exchange Server. This enables a hosted cache server to store up to terabytes of data.

- You do not need a GPO for each location. To deploy BranchCache, you need only a single GPO that contains the settings. This also enables clients to switch between hosted cache mode and distributed mode when they are traveling and moving client computers between locations, without needing to use site-specific GPOs.

BranchCache Modes

You can configure BranchCache in two different modes (see Figure 13-45):

- **Hosted cache mode (HCM):** This mode operates by deploying a computer that is running Windows Server 2008 R2 or newer versions as a hosted cache server in the branch office. Client computers locate the host computer so that they can retrieve content from the hosted cache when it is available. If the content is not available in the hosted cache, the content is retrieved from the content server over a WAN link. The content is then provided to the hosted cache, which serves successive client requests.

- **Distributed cache mode (DCM):** For smaller remote offices, you can configure BranchCache in distributed cache mode without requiring a server. In this mode, local client computers running Windows 7 or newer maintain a copy of the content and make it available to other authorized clients that request the same data. This eliminates the need to have a server in the branch office. However, unlike hosted cache mode, this configuration works per subnet only. In addition, clients that hibernate or disconnect from the network cannot provide content to other requesting clients.

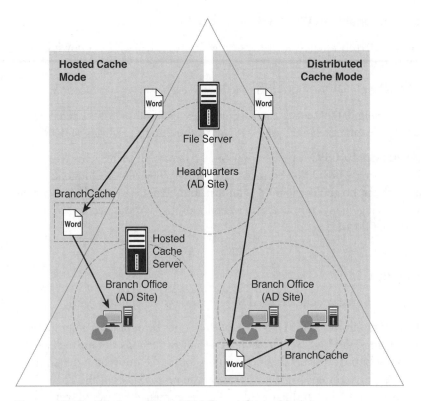

Figure 13-45   Windows Server 2016 BranchCache Modes

TIP   When using BranchCache, you can use both modes, but you can configure only one mode per branch office.

BranchCache Requirements

The BranchCache feature has the following requirements:

- Install the BranchCache feature (and, optionally, the BranchCache for Network Files role service).

- Configure client computers using either GPO or the **netsh** command.

- DCM: Configure the client firewall to enable incoming traffic (HTTP, WS-Discovery).

- HCM: Configure the firewall to enable incoming HTTP traffic from the hosted cache server.

Implement Distributed and Hosted Cache Modes

You can implement Windows Server BranchCache for different scenarios. You can use BranchCache distributed mode, in which the BranchCache is located on the clients, or you can use hosted cache mode, in which the BranchCache is centralized on a hosted BranchCache server in a branch location. The following section explains how to configure the settings for these two modes.

Configuring BranchCache Client Settings

You do not have to install the BranchCache feature on client computers because BranchCache is already included if the client is running Windows 7 or newer as a service. However, BranchCache is disabled by default on client computers. To enable and configure BranchCache, you must perform the following steps:

To enable BranchCache settings by using GPO, perform the following steps for a domain-based GPO:

Step 1.   On the DC, open the Group Policy Management console.

Step 2.   Create a GPO that will be linked to the OU in which client computers are located.

Step 3.   In the GPO, browse to Computer Configuration > Policies > Administrative Templates: Policy Definitions (ADMX Files) Retrieved from the Local Computer > Network and then click **BranchCache**.

Step 4.   Enable the Turn on BranchCache setting in the GPO.

Figure 13-46 shows where to find the Turn on BranchCache setting in the Branch-Cache client GPO.

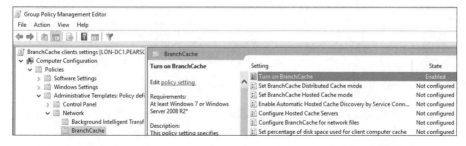

Figure 13-46   Turn on BranchCache Setting in the BranchCache Client GPO

To enable BranchCache mode through GPO, perform the following steps:

Step 1.   On the DC, open the Group Policy Management console.

Step 2.   Open the GPO where the BranchCache client settings are located.

Step 3.   In the GPO, browse to Computer Configuration > Policies > Administrative Templates: Policy Definitions (ADMX Files) Retrieved from the Local Computer > Network and click **BranchCache**.

Step 4.   Select either **Distributed Cache Mode** or **Hosted Cache Mode**. You can also enable both distributed cache mode and automatic hosted cache discovery through Service Connection Point policy settings. The client computers operate in distributed cache mode unless they find a hosted cache server in the branch office. If they find a hosted cache server in the branch office, they work in hosted cache mode.

Figure 13-47 shows how to configure the BranchCache mode with the Enable Automated Hosted Cache Discovery by Service Connection Point setting, which can be used to automatically identify the hosted cache server through Active Directory. This is possible only if the hosted cache server was registered in Active Directory with the PowerShell cmdlet **Enable-BCHostedServer -RegisterSCP**. If this is enabled in addition to Turn on BranchCache, clients attempt to discover hosted cache servers in the local branch office. You also can use the **Enable-BCHostedClient** PowerShell cmdlet to configure BranchCache in hosted cache mode.

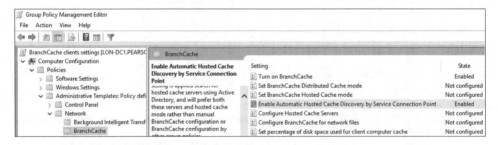

Figure 13-47   Enable Automated Hosted Cache Discovery by Service Connection Point

You also can use the **Enable-BCHostedClient** PowerShell cmdlet to configure BranchCache in hosted cache mode. The following commands enable hosted cache mode by using SVR1.pearson.com as the hosted cache server for HTTPS and clients running Windows 10:

```
Enable-BCHostedClient -ServerNames SVR1.pearson.com -UseVersion
   Windows10
```

The following cmdlet enables hosted cache mode and registers Service Connection Points in AD DS:

```
Enable-BCHostedServer -RegisterSCP
```

The following cmdlet enables distributed cache mode on the server:

```
Enable-BCDistributed
```

You also can use the **netsh** command to configure BranchCache settings:

```
netsh branchcache set service mode=distributed
netsh branchcache set service mode=hostedclient
  location=SVR1.pearson.com
```

In addition, you must configure the client firewall. In distributed cache mode, BranchCache clients use the HTTP protocol for data transfer between client computers and the WS-Discovery protocol for cached content discovery. You should configure the client firewall to enable the following incoming rules:

- BranchCache–Content Retrieval (Use HTTP).

- BranchCache–Peer Discovery (Use WS–Discovery). In hosted cache mode, BranchCache clients use the HTTP protocol.

In hosted cache mode, you should configure the client firewall to enable the incoming rule, BranchCache–Content Retrieval (Use HTTP).

After you configure BranchCache, clients can access the cached data in Branch-Cache-enabled content servers, which are available locally in the branch office. You can modify BranchCache settings and perform additional configuration tasks:

- Set the cache size

- Set the location of the hosted cache server

- Clear the cache

- Create and replicate a shared key for use in a server cluster

Configuring BranchCache Server Settings

When you want to use BranchCache for a file server, you have to install the Branch-Cache service and the BranchCache for Network Files role service on the file server (see Figure 13-48).

Figure 13-48   Install BranchCache on File Server

You also have to enable BranchCache on the Offline Settings for a file share. Figure 13-49 shows the setting.

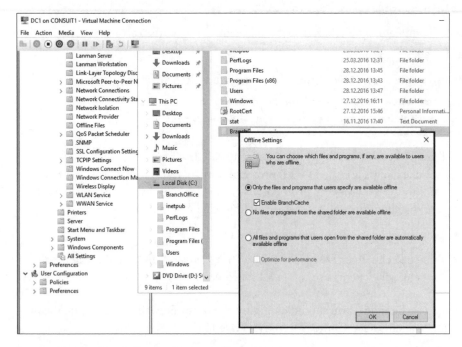

Figure 13-49   Enable BranchCache on Shared Folder

To configure the BranchCache host server, you also have to install the BranchCache service and the BranchCache for Network Files role service. When BranchCache clients automatically have to find the host through its Service Connection Point (SCP) in Active Directory, you must register the host with the PowerShell cmdlet **Enable-BCHostedServer -RegisterSCP**.

With the PowerShell cmdlet **Get-BCStatus**, you can verify the correct Branch-Cache configuration on the file server, BranchCache host, or BranchCache client.

Figure 13-50 shows the output of **Get-BCStatus** on a configured file server.

Figure 13-50   Get-BCStatus on File Server

Implement BranchCache for Web, File, and Application Servers

BranchCache-enabled content servers include web servers, application servers, and file servers.

You can configure your organization's internal web servers as BranchCache-enabled content servers by installing the BranchCache feature on a computer running IIS in the main office.

File servers located in the organization main office can be enabled as BranchCache content servers by installing the File Services server role and the BranchCache for Network Files role service.

Application servers can be enabled as BranchCache-enabled content servers by installing and enabling BITS. Furthermore, BranchCache should be installed and enabled on the application server.

WSUS and Configuration Manager branch distribution points also can use Branch-Cache to share content across WAN links.

Troubleshoot BranchCache

After the initial configuration, verify that BranchCache is configured correctly and functioning correctly.

You can use the **netsh branchcache show status all** command to display the BranchCache service status. Figure 13-51 shows example output of that command.

```
PS C:\> netsh branchcache show status all

BranchCache Service Status:
-----------------------------------------------------------------------
Service Mode        = Local Caching
Current Status      = Running
Service Start Type  = Automatic
This machine is not configured as a hosted cache client.

Local Cache Status:
-----------------------------------------------------------------------
Maximum Cache Size       = 5% of hard disk
Active Current Cache Size = 0 Bytes
Local Cache Location      = C:\Windows\ServiceProfiles\NetworkService\AppData\Local\PeerDistRepub (Default)

Publication Cache Status:
-----------------------------------------------------------------------
Maximum Cache Size       = 1% of hard disk
Active Current Cache Size = 0 Bytes
Publication Cache Location = C:\Windows\ServiceProfiles\NetworkService\AppData\Local\PeerDistPub (Default)

Networking Status:
-----------------------------------------------------------------------
Content Retrieval URL Reservation          = Configured      (Required)
Hosted Cache URL Reservation               = Configured      (Not Required)
Hosted Cache HTTP URL Reservation          = Configured      (Not Required)
SSL Certificate Bound To Hosted Cache Port = Not Configured  (Not Required)
Content Retrieval Firewall Rules           = Enabled         (Not Required)
Peer Discovery Firewall Rules              = Enabled         (Not Required)
Hosted Cache Server Firewall Rules         = Enabled         (Not Required)
Hosted Cache Client Firewall Rules         = Enabled         (Not Required)

Warning: The Windows Firewall is Currently Disabled.
```

Figure 13-51   netsh branchcache show status all

You can also use the Windows PowerShell cmdlet **Get-BCStatus** to provide BranchCache status and configuration information. The client and hosted cache servers display additional information, such as the location of the local cache, the size of the local cache, and the status of the firewall rules for HTTP and WS-Discovery protocols that BranchCache uses.

In addition, you can use the following tools to monitor BranchCache:

- **Event Viewer:** Use the Event Viewer to monitor BranchCache events that are recorded in both the application log and the operational log. In the Event Viewer console, the application log is located in Windows Logs > Application, and the operational log is located in Application and Service Logs > Microsoft > Windows > BranchCache.

- **Performance Monitor:** In the Performance Monitor, you can add many BranchCache counters, as in Figure 13-52.

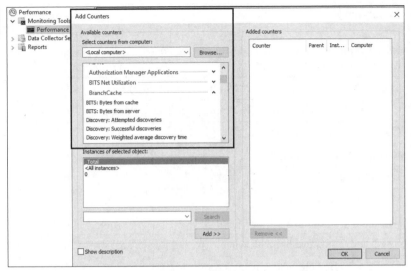

Figure 13-52   Monitor BranchCache Counters with Performance Monitor

Exam Preparation Tasks

Review All the Key Topics

Review the most important topics in the chapter, noted with the Key Topics icon in the outer margin of the page. Table 13-11 lists these key topics and the page numbers where each is found.

Table 13-11   Key Topics for Chapter 13

Key Topic Element	Description	Page Number
Tip and Table 13-2	Features of Storage Replica and advantages against DFSR	584
Section	Domain-based Namespaces	585
Table 13-3	DFS Namespace Administrative Permissions	587
Section	Standalone Namespaces	587
Step List	Deploying DFS namespaces	588
Figure 13-18	DFS Folder Target Properties (Advanced)	596
Section	Configuring DFS with PowerShell	597

Key Topic Element	Description	Page Number
Step List	Set up Windows Server 2016 DFSR with the DFS Management tool	600
Section	Configuring Windows Server 2016 DFSR with PowerShell	608
Section	Configure Remote Differential Compression (RDC) Settings	612
Section	Configure Fault Tolerance	613
Section	Recover DFS Databases	615
Section	DFS Database Cloning	615
Section	Data Deduplication and DFSR	616
Figure 13-44	Data Deduplication PowerShell Cmdlets	617
Section	Install and Configure BranchCache	617
Section	Configuring BranchCache Client Settings	621
Section	Configuring BranchCache Server Settings	623
Section	Troubleshoot BranchCache	625
Figure 13-52	Monitor BranchCache Counters with Performance Monitor	627

Complete the Tables and Lists from Memory

Print a copy of Appendix B, "Memory Tables" (on the book's website), or at least the section for this chapter, and complete the tables and lists from memory. Appendix C, "Memory Tables Answer Key," also on the website, includes completed tables and lists to check your work.

Definition of Key Terms

Define the following key terms from this chapter and check your answers in the glossary.

DFS, DFSR, DFSN, Storage Replica, DFS domain-based namespace, DFS standalone namespace, RDC, cross-file RDC, SYSVOL, DFS database cloning, BranchCache

End-of-Chapter Review Questions

1. You have configured a DFS solution with four Windows Server 2016 file servers, named DFS1, DFS2, DFS3, and DFS4, distributed across two sites in your domain pearson.com. Now you want to change the settings for a DFS namespace folder with the PowerShell cmdlet **Set-DfsnFolder** on DFS1. You notice that this and all other DFS PowerShell cmdlets are not usable on DFS2. Which component do you have to install on DFS2?

   a. Install the FS-FileServer feature.

   b. Install the FS-DFS-Namespace feature.

   c. Install the FS-SMB1 feature.

   d. Install the FS-NFS feature.

2. You must verify a connection-based DFS Replication schedule that inherits its schedule settings from a replication group with the members DFS2 and DFS1. You also want to get information about a custom connection-based replication schedule from DFS1 to DFS2 that blocks replication between 9 a.m. and 5 p.m. Monday through Friday and allows full bandwidth replication for all remaining time blocks. Which PowerShell command or commands can you use?

   a. **Get-DfsrGroupSchedule**

   b. **Get-DfsrConnectionSchedule**

   c. **Get-DfsReplicationGroup**

   d. **Get-DfsrMember**

3. You have a high-bandwidth network connection between the sites Chicago and Denver, and your users do not frequently reopen files after modification or added content on a member of a DFS Replication group. Which PowerShell cmdlet can boost performance?

   a. **Set-DfsrMembership -MinimumFileStageSizing**

   b. **Set-DfsrMembership -ConflictandDeletedQuotaInMB**

   c. **Set-DfsrMembership -DisableMembership**

   d. **Set-DfsrMembership -RemoveDeletedFiles**

This chapter covers the following subjects:

- Implementing NIC Teaming or the Switch Embedded Teaming (SET) solution and identifying when to use each

- Receive Side Scaling

- Quality of service with Data Center Bridging

- SMB Direct on RDMA-enabled network adapters

- SMB Multichannel

- Receive Side Scaling on a VMQ-capable network adapter

- Virtual Machine Multi-Queue

- Single-root I/O Virtualization on a supported network adapter

- Software-defined networking

- Requirements and scenarios for implementing Hyper-V Network Virtualization (HNV) using Network Virtualization Generic Route Encapsulation (NVGRE) encapsulation or Virtual Extensible LAN (VXLAN) encapsulation

- Scenarios for implementing Software Load Balancer (SLB) for north–south and east–west load balancing

- Implementation scenarios for various types of Windows Server Gateways, including L3, GRE, and S2S, and their use

- Requirements and scenarios for distributed firewall policies and Network Security Groups

Implementing Windows Server 2016 High-Performance Network Solutions

This chapter covers Switch Embedded Teaming (SET) and how you can enable it through PowerShell on a VMSwitch. It shows how to create a Hyper-V SET-enabled virtual switch, illustrates SET compatibilities and incompatibilities, and explains the differences in the load-balancing algorithm options. You learn about the advantages of RSS and how to enable or disable RSS with PowerShell cmdlets.

In addition, you look at QoS and DCB, SMB Direct and RDMA, SMB Multi-channel configuration, the use of Dynamic VMQs, and RSS. You also investigate VMMQ and SR-IOV on supported network adapters and see how you can use PowerShell commands to configure SR-IOV.

This chapter also discusses SDN and determines scenarios for implementing Software Load Balancer (SLB) for north–south and east–west load balancing. You learn about the advantages and capabilities of software-defined networking and check out the SDN components and requirements. You also work through a step-by-step example of an SDN configuration.

Furthermore, you learn about the different versions of HNV, check out NVGRE and VXLAN, see how SLB works, and understand SLB core functionality. You also learn about the use of northbound and southbound APIs.

This chapter also compares the different gateway types and RAS Gateway scenarios and explains the use of RAS Gateway pools. It looks at the Datacenter Firewall and its benefits for CSPs and tenants. It also gives an example of Datacenter Firewall ACL configuration.

Key topic selections, memory tables, key term definitions, and exam preparation questions give you powerful tools to increase your knowledge about implementing Windows Server 2016 high-performance network solutions for the Microsoft 70-741 exam and your work.

"Do I Know This Already?" Quiz

The "Do I Know This Already?" quiz enables you to assess whether you should read this entire chapter or simply jump to the "Exam Preparation Tasks" section for review. If you are in doubt, read the entire chapter. Table 14-1 outlines the major headings in this chapter and the corresponding "Do I Know This Already?" quiz questions. You can find the answers in Appendix A, "Answers to the 'Do I Know This Already?' Quizzes and End-of-Chapter Review Questions."

Table 14-1   "Do I Know This Already?" Foundation Topics Section-to-Question Mapping

Foundation Topics Section	Questions Covered in This Section
Implement NIC Teaming or the Switch Embedded Teaming (SET) Solution and Identify When to Use Each	1
Receive Side Scaling	2
Quality of Service with Data Center Bridging	3
SMB Direct on RDMA-Enabled Network Adapters	4
SMB Multichannel	5
Receive Side Scaling on a VMQ-Capable Network Adapter	6
Single-Root I/O Virtualization on a Supported Network Adapter	7
Software-Defined Networking	8
Requirements and Scenarios for Implementing Hyper-V Network Virtualization (HNV) Using Network Virtualization Generic Route Encapsulation (NVGRE) Encapsulation or Virtual Extensible LAN (VXLAN) Encapsulation	9
Scenarios for Implementation of Software Load Balancer (SLB) for North–South and East–West Load Balancing	10
Implementation Scenarios for Various Types of Windows Server Gateways, Including L3, GRE, and S2S, and Their Use	11
Requirements and Scenarios for Distributed Firewall Policies and Network Security Groups	12

CAUTION   The goal of self-assessment is to gauge your mastery of the topics in this chapter. If you do not know the answer to a question or are only partially sure of the answer, you should mark that question as wrong for purposes of the self-assessment. Giving yourself credit for an answer you correctly guess skews your self-assessment results and might provide you with a false sense of security.

1. You plan to implement an LBFO solution. Your solution has to fulfill the following requirements:

   - Support for Hyper-V Network Virtualization SDN version 2 (HNVv2)
   - Requires identical NICs in a team
   - Up to 32 NICs in a team
   - Provides teaming in a VM

   Which requirements are not covered with SET? (Choose two.)

   a. Support for Hyper-V Network Virtualization SDN version 2 (HNVv2)

   b. Requires identical NICs in a team

   c. Up to 32 NICs in a team

   d. Provides teaming in a VM

2. You want to efficiently expand your Windows Server 2016 Hyper-V VMs to multiple virtual CPUs. You want to distribute network receiving processing across these processors. You also want additional security to protect the system from malicious remote hosts that might attempt to force the system into an unbalanced state. Which command should you use?

   a. **Enable-NetAdapterIPSecOffload**

   b. **Set-NetAdapterRss**

   c. **Set-VMNetworkAdapter**

   d. **Set-ReceiveConnector**

3. You use Data Center Bridging and previously you managed DCB settings from a switch. You have a Windows Server 2016 server. Now you plan to manage DCB settings at the system level.

   Which preconfiguration tasks do you need to perform on your Windows Server 2016 server so that you can manage DCB settings for a NIC device locally, and which PowerShell cmdlets can you use always, regardless of whether DCB is installed?

   Preconfiguration tasks:

   a. **Install-WindowsFeature "data-center-bridging"**

   b. **Set-NetQoSdcbxSetting -Willing 0**

   c. **import-module netqos**

   d. **import-module dcbqos**

   e. **import-module netadapter**

PowerShell commands, regardless of whether DCB is installed:

    f. Get-NetAdapterQos

    g. Set-NetQosPolicy

    h. Disable-NetAdapterQos

    i. Enable-NetAdapterQos

    j. Get-NetQosFlowControl

    k. Set-NetQosTrafficClass

4. You set up a Windows Server 2016 hyperconverged solution using Storage Spaces Direct. You have set up the Hyper-V virtual switch with SET and RDMA. You must verify the capability of a device to access host memory directly without CPU intervention. You verify this capability with the following PowerShell command: **Get-SmbClientNetworkInterface**. You get the following output:

Interface Index	RSS Capable	RDMA Capable	Speed	Friendly Name
5	False	False	0 bps	NIC1
16	False	False	0 bps	NIC2
15	False	False	10 bps	NIC3
17	True	True	20 bps	NIC4
14	True	True	20 bps	NIC5
12	False	False	100 bps	NIC6
4	False	False	100 bps	NIC7

You want to enable NIC6 and NIC7 to allow more throughput and lower latency and to get less CPU impact for these network cards. Which Power-Shell command should you use?

    a. Set-NetAdapter

    b. Enable NetAdapterVmq

    c. Enable-NetAdapterRDMA

    d. New-VMSwitch

5. You have set up a Windows Server 2016 Hyper-V failover cluster with four nodes. You want to use multiple RSS- and RDMA-capable network cards on the same subnet with SMB Multichannel configured. Which kind of IP addresses should you use for the SMB Multichannel automatic configuration?

    a. IPv6 site local unicast

    b. IPv6 link local

    c. IPv6 unique local unicast

    d. IPv6 global unicast

6. You want to distribute network traffic among multiple VMs on a single Windows Server 2016 Hyper-V host with a vSwitch. You have 8 physical 10 GB network cards and 32 logical processors. You want to increase the scalability of the VMs' networking. Which configuration settings should you verify or configure? (Choose six.)

    a. Verify that Hyperthreading is enabled

    b. TeamingMode: Switch Independent

    c. TeamingMode: Switch Dependent

    d. LoadBalancingAlgorithm: Dynamic

    e. LoadBalancingAlgorithm: TransportPorts

    f. Enable VMQ on network adapters

    g. Set Base and Max CPUs with **Set-NetAdapterVmq**

    h. Set BaseProcessorGroup with **Set-NetAdapterVmq**

    i. Enable vRSS with **Enable-NetAdapterRSS**

    j. Enable vRSS with **Set-NetAdapter**

7. You have the following Windows Server 2016 Hyper-V hosts and VMs environment:

VM Name	Guest Operating System	Hyper-V Host Operating System
VM1	Windows Server 2012	Windows Server 2008 R2
VM2	Windows 7	Windows Server 2012
VM3	Windows 8	Windows Server 2016
VM4	Windows Server 2012	Windows Server 2016

For which VMs can you enable SR-IOV and with which PowerShell commands can you do that?

VMs:

    a. VM1

    b. VM2

    c. VM3

    d. VM4

PowerShell commands:

e. Set-VMHost

f. New-VMSwitch

g. Set-VMNetworkAdapter

h. Set-VMProcessor

8. You have to determine software-defined networking deployment scenarios and network requirements for deploying SDN. To do so, you need to know about the main SDN components and their capabilities. You must apply the relevant SDN capabilities and components to the corresponding network requirements (you can apply some SDN components more than once).

SDN components:

a. Network Controller (NC)

b. Southbound API (S-API)

c. Northbound API (N-API)

Network Requirement	SDN Component
Automating the configuration of the network infrastructure	
Network Controller communicates with the network	
Administrator communicates with the Network Controller	
Windows PowerShell, REST API, management application	

9. You host a multitenant deployment for the two companies Pearson Corporation and Pearson UCertify Corporation. You use Windows Server 2016 Virtual Machine Manager to manage the Pearson and Pearson UCertify networks. Pearson has a SQL Server with the IP address of 10.1.1.11 and a web server of 10.1.1.12. Pearson UCertify has a SQL Server with the IP address of 10.1.1.11 and a web server of 10.1.1.12. These are the network virtualization policy configurations on SCVMM:

VSID	CA	PA
7001	172.16.1.11	192.168.1.10/24
7001	172.16.1.12	192.168.2.20/24
8001	172.16.1.11	192.168.1.10/24
8001	172.16.1.12	192.168.2.20/24

You have created all necessary PA logical networks through the Network Controller. You have configured two Hyper-V hosts named Host1 and Host2 in the following manner:

Host1:

- Pearson: VSID=8001, 172.16.1.11 → 192.168.1.10/24; 172.16.1.12 → 192.168.2.20/24

- Pearson UCertify: VSID=8001, 172.16.1.11 → 192.168.1.10/24; 172.16.1.12 → 192.168.2.20/24

Host2:

- Pearson: VSID=7001, 172.16.1.11 → 192.168.1.10/24; 172.16.1.12 → 192.168.2.20/24

- Pearson UCertify: VSID=8001, 172.16.1.11 → 192.168.1.10/24; 172.16.1.12 → 192.168.2.20/24

Now VMs from Pearson and Pearson UCertify interact as if they were on their original intranets. They cannot interact with each other. With the virtualization mappings and transformation, you successfully have decoupled the virtual network architecture from the physical network infrastructure.

You can use VXLAN or NVGRE as the encapsulation type for this configuration. You must identify whether the technical statements about Windows Server 2016 HNV2 and VXLAN are correct before you decide which encapsulation type is the best for you. (Choose True or False)

Technical Statement About Windows Server 2016 HNV	Choice
Is using the Azure Virtual Filtering Platform (VFP) switch	
Cannot be used with any other third-party switch extension	
Broadcasts and subnet multicasts implemented using unicast replication	
Is using Hyper-V switch extensions in the SDN stack	
Can use cross-subnet multicast routing	
For a VM establishing a connection to another VM in the same VSID, the Host Agent is responsible for MAC address resolution	
For a VM establishing a connection to another VM in another VSID, nondefault routes are supported	

Technical Statement About Windows Server 2016 VXLAN	Choice
Forwarding table of the external switch does not grow with the increase in the VMs behind the physical port on the server	
1 PA per NIC team member	

10. You have deployed some Windows Server 2016 VMs in a customer virtual network named Cust1Net. You use Windows Server 2016 System Center Virtual Machine Manager and SDN to manage SLB to distribute tenant customer network traffic among virtual network resources. Two Windows Server 2016 web servers named SRV01 and SRV02 are members of a customer virtual network named Cust1Net that is configured for SLB access.

Select the correct terms:

The Network Controller processes SLB commands that come in through the northbound API from the Windows Server 2016 System Center Virtual Machine Manager.

The Network Controller communicates through the southbound API to the SLB Host Agent.

Choices: *Northbound API, Southbound API*

SRV01 and SRV02 communicate through east–west TCP/UDP traffic.

Choices: *East–West; South–North*

11. You want to use the Windows Server 2016 SDN feature with SCVMM 2016 to deploy a RAS Gateway using SCVMM 2016. You want to securely connect your remote tenant network and your datacenter using IPsec through a RAS Gateway to enable S2S connectivity between them. You want the simplest possible solution.

Which preparations do you need to complete before you can begin to create the GRE VIP logical network? (Choose two.)

    a. Deploy the Network Controller

    b. Create an IP pool for GRE VIP addresses

    c. Deploy the Software Load Balancer

    d. Import the gateway service template

12. You have implemented a Windows Server 2016 SDN solution. You want to use the Network Controller to centrally manage your network security. Which new security features does Network Controller offer?

    a. Antimalware solution

    b. Distributed firewall policies

    c. Network traffic encryption

    d. Network Security Groups

Foundation Topics

Implement NIC Teaming or the Switch Embedded Teaming (SET) Solution, and Identify When to Use Each

NIC Teaming enables you to combine up to 32 network adapters and use them as a single network interface. With Switch Embedded Teaming (SET), you can team up to eight physical network adapters into one or more software-based virtual NICs. This section covers NIC Teaming and SET and illustrates their differences.

What Is Switch Embedded Teaming (SET)?

With Windows Server 2016, you can use Switch Embedded Teaming (SET) within a Hyper-V virtual switch to team up to eight physical NICs into one or more software-based virtual NICs. These virtual network adapters deliver fast performance and fault tolerance in the event of a network adapter failure.

You must install SET member network adapters in the same physical Hyper-V host so they are placed in a SET team.

You can also use Remote Direct Memory Access (RDMA)–capable network adapters within a SET team, which enables you to use both RDMA and SET teams while utilizing fewer network adapters in your servers. This also means that you do not have to team at the host level. The big benefit here is that RDMA can be managed at the virtual switch.

With Windows Server 2016, NIC Teaming is integrated into the Hyper-V virtual switch. The teaming is switch independent and configuration of static ports or Link Aggregation Control Protocol (LACP) is not needed. You can manage the Hyper-V SET using Windows PowerShell or SCVMM; you cannot manage it using the older NIC Teaming GUI.

You also can create converged networking with just two RDMA-capable NICs.

The new Hyper-V SETs are much easier to create. You do not need to first create the NIC team in Server Manager and then bind it to a Hyper-V virtual switch. With the new SET feature, NIC Teaming configuration is a one-step process. The following shows the Windows PowerShell code to create a new SET:

```
New-VMSwitch -name SETSW -NetAdapterName "NIC1", "NIC2"
  -EnableEmbeddedTeaming $true
```

With Windows Server 2012, four NICs (host) are required to provide RDMA networking for the host and NIC Teaming for the VMs. Windows Server 2016 introduces new support for vNICs in the Windows Server 2016 host, and both the host vNICs and the VM vNICs provide support for RDMA. This Hyper-V virtual switch must have SET enabled.

> **TIP**   SET is supported in the Hyper-V virtual switch only in Windows Server 2016. You cannot deploy SET in Windows Server 2012 R2.

The new Hyper-V switch support for RDMA allows both the host and the VMs to share the RDMA support in the physical NICs, enabling you to reduce and converge the required host infrastructure. Microsoft states that the Hyper-V virtual switch support for RDMA provides near-native RDMA performance to the vNICs. Figure 14-1 compares the Windows Server 2012 R2 and Windows Server 2016 SET and RDMA structure.

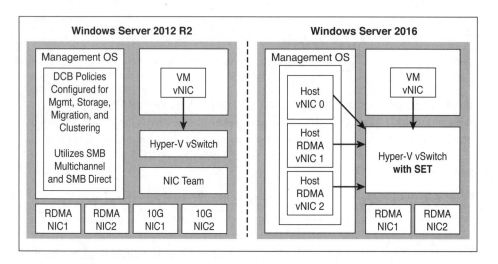

Figure 14-1   Hyper-V Virtual Switch with SET and RDMA

You can create a Hyper-V SET-enabled virtual switch with two NICs using Windows PowerShell:

```
New-VMSwitch RDMASwitch -NetAdapterName "NIC1", "NIC2"
  -EnableEmbeddedTeaming $true
Add-VMNetworkAdapter -SwitchName MyRDMAswitch -Name SMBRDMA1
Add-VMNetworkAdapter -SwitchName RDMAswitch -Name SMBRDMA2
Enable-NetAdapterRDMA  "vEthernet (SMBRDMA_1)", "vEthernet
  (SMBRDMA_2)"
```

SET Compatibility

Table 14-2 outlines the technologies that SET is compatible and incompatible with in Windows Server 2016.

Table 14-2 SET Compatibility

Compatible with SET	Incompatible with SET
Data Center Bridging (DCB)	802.1X authentication
Hyper-V Network Virtualization	IPsec Task Offload (IPsecTO)
Receive side checksum offloads	QoS in host or native OS
Remote Direct Memory Access (RDMA)	Receive Side Coalescing (RSC)
SDN quality of service (QoS)	Receive Side Scaling (RSS)
Transmit side checksum offloads	Single-root I/O virtualization (SR-IOV)
Virtual Machine Queues (VMQ)	TCP Chimney Offload
Virtual Receive Side Scaling (RSS)	Virtual Machine QoS (VM-QoS)

> **TIP**   You cannot configure a team name for a SET team as you can with NIC Teaming. When you deploy SET, all network adapters are active and none are in standby mode. Another difference between NIC Teaming and SET is that NIC Teaming provides the choice of three different teaming modes, whereas SET supports only Switch Independent mode. When you use SET in conjunction with Packet Direct, the teaming mode Switch Independent and the load balancing mode Hyper-V Port are required. You can use SET for live migration.

The **Set-VMSwitchTeam** cmdlet has a **LoadBalancingAlgorithm** option that takes one of two possible values: **HyperVPort** or **Dynamic**. To set or change the load distribution algorithm for a switch-embedded team, use this option. In the following example, the VMSwitch named TeamedvSwitch uses the Dynamic load-balancing algorithm:

```
Set-VMSwitch -Name TeamedvSwitch -VMSwitchLoadBalancingAlgorithm
  Dynamic
```

Table 14-3 shows the differences between the **HyperVPort** and **Dynamic Load-BalancingAlgorithm** values for a VM switch team.

Table 14-3   HyperVPort Versus Dynamic

HyperVPort	Dynamic
Every vmSwitch port is affinitized to a team member.	Every vmSwitch port is affinitized to a team member.
Every packet is sent on the team member to which the port is affinitized.	All ARP/NS packets are sent on the team member to which the port is affinitized.
No secure MAC replacement is done.	Packets sent on the team member that is the affinitized have no source MAC address replacement done.
	Packets sent on the team member other than the affinitized team member have source MAC address replacement done.

Receive Side Scaling

Windows Server 2016 supports virtual RSS on the VM network path. This offers better network traffic loads for VMs. A VM can take advantage of virtual RSS improvements only if the processor on the Hyper-V host supports RSS and you have configured the virtual machine to use multiple processor cores.

You must run the following PowerShell command to enable RSS for all network adapters in your VM: **Enable-NetAdapterRss -name "*"**. After that, you can see in the Device Manager of the VM on the network adapter's advanced properties that RSS is enabled (see Figure 14-2).

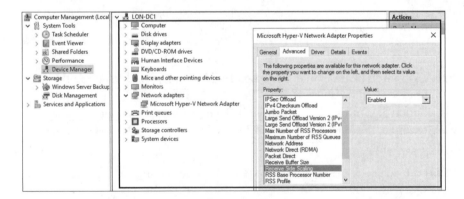

Figure 14-2   Enable Receive Side Scaling (RSS)

You also can use the following command to enable RSS: **netsh interface tcp set global rss=enabled**. With **netsh interface show global**, you can check the status of RSS; you can do the same with the PowerShell cmdlet **Get-NetAdapterRss** (see Figure 14-3).

```
PS C:\> get-netadapterRss

Name                                          : Ethernet
InterfaceDescription                          : Microsoft Hyper-V Network Adapter
Enabled                                       : True
NumberOfReceiveQueues                         : 0
Profile                                       : NUMAStatic
BaseProcessor: [Group:Number]                 : 0:0
MaxProcessor: [Group:Number]                  : 0:0
MaxProcessors                                 : 1
RssProcessorArray: [Group:Number/NUMA Distance] : 0:0/0
IndirectionTable: [Group:Number]              :
```

Figure 14-3   Get-NetAdapterRss

Quality of Service with Data Center Bridging

QoS is a collection of technologies that enable you to meet the service requirements of a workload or an application by measuring network bandwidth; detecting changing network conditions, such as congestion or the availability of bandwidth; and then prioritizing or throttling network traffic. This means you can prioritize traffic with precedences and higher-priority processes first. You can use QoS for voice or video streaming network traffic.

Data Center Bridging (DCB) is a suite of IEEE standards that enable converged fabrics in your data center, where storage, data networking, cluster interprocess communication, and management traffic all share the same Ethernet network infrastructure. DCB provides hardware-based bandwidth allocation to a specific type of traffic and enhances Ethernet transport reliability with the use of priority-based flow control.

SMB Direct on RDMA-Enabled Network Adapters

SMB Direct supports network adapters that have RDMA capability, can perform at full speed with very low data latency, and use very little CPU processing time.

TIP   SMB Direct is enabled by default on Windows Server 2016.

Considerations for SMB Direct

When deploying SMB Direct, be sure to consider the following points:

- SMB Direct is supported on Windows Server 2016, Windows Server 2012 R2, and Windows Server 2012.

- You can use SMB Direct in a failover cluster; however, you need to make sure that the cluster networks used for client access are adequate for SMB Direct. Failover clustering supports using multiple networks for client access, along with network adapters that are RSS and RDMA capable.

- You can use SMB Direct on the Hyper-V management operating system to support using Hyper-V over SMB and to provide storage to a virtual machine that uses the Hyper-V storage stack. However, RDMA-capable network adapters are not directly exposed to a Hyper-V client. If you connect an RDMA-capable network adapter to a virtual switch, the virtual network adapters from the switch will not be RDMA capable.

- If you disable SMB Multichannel, SMB Direct is also disabled. Because SMB Multichannel detects network adapter capabilities and determines whether a network adapter is RDMA capable, the client cannot use SMB Direct if SMB Multichannel is disabled.

RDMA

RDMA over Ethernet is a technology that can transfer data more efficiently between two computers. RDMA-capable NICs can transfer data at full speed with low latency while using very little CPU power. Windows Server 2016 and Windows Server 2012 use RDMA to provide the SMB Direct functionality. Currently, three different types of NICs support RDMA:

- InfiniBand

- Internet Wide Area RDMA Protocol (iWARP)

- RDMA over Converged Ethernet (RoCE)

You can enable and disable RDMA on a network adapter with the PowerShell commands **Disable-NetAdapapterRmda** and **Enable-NetAdapterRdma**.

Figure 14-4 shows all available RDMA PowerShell cmdlets.

Figure 14-4   RDMA PowerShell Cmdlets

TIP   In Windows Server 2012, RDMA NICs do not work in a virtual switch and you cannot team RDMA NICs. You can use RDMA NICs only for storage with Windows Server 2012.

Packet Direct

Windows Server 2016 supports Packet Direct, which you can use to create a low-latency data path. You can enable it in the Hyper-V virtual switch with a single network adapter.

Packet Direct (PD) extends the current NDIS model. It works by allowing PD clients to explicitly manage networking traffic from a NIC. PD gives PD clients control of the high-performance send and receive functionality of the NIC through the Packet Direct client interface (PDCI).

Figure 14-5 shows the new Windows Server 2016 Packet Direct PowerShell cmdlet.

Figure 14-5 Packet Direct PowerShell Cmdlets

SMB Multichannel

SMB Multichannel enables you to aggregate network bandwidth and network fault tolerance if multiple paths are available between the SMB client and SMB server. SMB Multichannel enables server applications to take advantage of all available network bandwidth to a branch office and makes them resilient if a WAN link fails, as long as multiple paths are available over the network to the branch office.

You can integrate SMB Multichannel and SMB Direct. This allows CSV traffic to stream across multiple networks in the cluster and fully utilize network adapters that support RDMA.

Using SMB Multichannel for Failover Clustering is much easier now. A Windows Server 2016 failover cluster automatically recognizes and configures multiple NICs on the same subnet. Both RSS-capable and RDMA-capable NICs can be used. Simplified SMB Multichannel offers the following benefits:

- Clustering automatically recognizes all NICs on nodes that are using the same switch or subnet.

- SMB Multichannel is enabled automatically.

- Networks with IPv6 link local IP addresses are recognized on cluster-only (private) networks.

- A single IP address resource is configured on each CAP network name, by default.

- Cluster validation no longer produces warnings when multiple NICs are found on the same subnet.

Figure 14-6 shows how you can verify the SMB Multichannel settings with PowerShell.

Figure 14-6   Get-SMBServerConfiguration

Receive Side Scaling on a VMQ-Capable Network Adapter

Dynamic VMQ is similar to RSS. On a host, RSS processes incoming network traffic so that a single CPU core does not slow it down. RSS does this by spreading the calculations across multiple CPU cores.

For a Hyper-V host that has several virtual machines with significant incoming traffic, dynamic VMQ is similar to RSS.

Dynamic VMQ dynamically distributes incoming network traffic processing to physical host CPU cores based on processor usage and network load. During periods of heavy network loads, dynamic VMQ automatically employs more processors. Figure 14-7 shows the behavior of the network traffic flow with and without using VMQ.

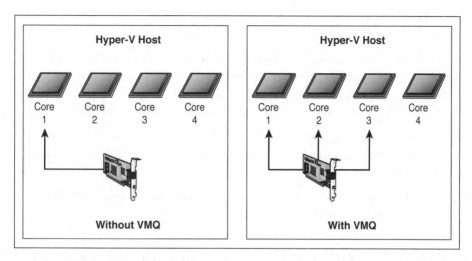

Figure 14-7   With and Without VMQ

Dynamic VMQ is enabled by default in Windows Server 2016. You can enable or disable it by using the **Enable-NetAdapterVmq** and **Disable-NetAdapterVmq** Windows PowerShell cmdlets, respectively. Figure 14-8 shows the available PowerShell cmdlets for VMQ.

Figure 14-8   VMQ PowerShell Cmdlets

Dynamic VMQ hashes the destination MAC address, puts the traffic for a particular virtual machine in a specific queue, and distributes the interrupts to the CPU cores. Dynamic VMQ handles this by offloading these functions to the network adapters. In dynamic VMQ, a rare circumstance can occur when processing that is happening on a CPU core generates a large amount of inbound traffic. This triggers dynamic VMQ to use another, less-busy CPU core; because the traffic load has not changed, it jumps back to the original CPU core or another one. This process then continues, which is why it is known as the ping-pong effect. Although dynamic VMQ is more automatic, RSS can better avoid the ping-pong effect in this situation.

Virtual Machine Multi-Queue

VMMQ is a new feature of Windows Server 2016 Hyper-V that is based on the investments in RSS and VMQ in previous versions. Previously, a single VM could be allocated a single VMQ (which is an I/O queue on the NIC and helps speed up performance), and this queue was affinitized to a single processor core.

Today network adapters have huge numbers of queues, often more than the VMs running on the box. vRSS enables multiple cores in the VM to process traffic, but the traffic still originates from the single queue. With VMMQ, multiple queues are allocated to a single VM, with each queue affinitized to a core in the VM.

Even the default queue in Hyper-V (which VMs use without their own queue) utilizes multiple queues now. The NIC distributes traffic between queues, avoiding overhead on the CPU.

Remember that, even with VMMQ, the VM must have multiple cores (vCPUs) to enable each queue allocated to be bound to a specific core.

 # Single-Root I/O Virtualization on a Supported Network Adapter

SR-IOV enables multiple VMs to share the same PCI Express physical hardware resources. Only network adapters specific to Hyper-V support this feature.

Receive Side Coalescing (RSC) is an offload technology that helps you reduce how much CPU time is used in network processing. RSC provides multiple benefits:

- RSC reduces the number of CPU cycles used for network storage and live migration.

- I/O-heavy database applications and database replication are processed faster with RSC.

- Performance is enhanced on file servers that are deployed with the Windows Server File Services server role. If your file server is also configured as a BranchCache-enabled content server, RSC improves BranchCache performance.

You can use Windows PowerShell to manage RSC. You can use the cmdlets **Get-NetAdapterRsc** and **GetNetAdapterStatistics** to see the network adapter's RSC configuration. Use the cmdlet **EnableNetAdapterRsc** to enable RSC.

> **TIP**   If you want to use RSC in a virtualized environment, the network adapter must support SR-IOV.

Software-Defined Networking

Software-defined networking (SDN) centralizes the configuration and management of the physical and virtual network devices (switches, routers, and gateways) so that you can provide an automated means of responding to application and workload requirements.

In Windows Server 2016, virtualization features, including Hyper-V Network Virtualization (HNV), Hyper-V Virtual Switch, and RAS Gateway, are integrated features of SDN.

With SDN, you can do the following:

- Virtualize the network, breaking a direct connection between applications and virtual servers and physical networks

- Define traffic flow policies across physical and virtual networks

- Manage a virtualized network infrastructure

Microsoft implemented SDN in Windows Server 2012, Windows Server 2012 R2, and Windows Server 2016 Hyper-V by providing the components listed in Table 14-4.

Table 14-4 SDN Components

SDN Component	Description
Hyper-V Network Virtualization (HNV)	Abstracts your applications and workloads from the underlying physical network by using virtual networks.
Hyper-V virtual switch	Connects VMs to virtual or physical networks. The Hyper-V virtual switch also provides security, isolation, and service-level policy enforcement.
Network Controller (a new Windows Server 2016 feature)	Provides centralized management, configuration, monitoring, and troubleshooting of the virtual and physical network infrastructure.
RRAS Multitenant Gateway	Extends network boundaries to Microsoft Azure or another provider to deliver on-demand hybrid infrastructure.
NIC Teaming	Configures multiple NICs as a team for bandwidth aggregation and traffic failover, to guard against loss of connectivity following a network component failure.

TIP   You can integrate Microsoft System Center with SDN to extend your SDN capabilities.

Benefits of SDN

SDN enables you to take advantage of a cloud-based infrastructure to overcome the limitations in your on-premises infrastructure, regardless of whether those limitations are short term or persistent. This enables you to do the following:

- You can move traffic from your on-premises infrastructure to your private or public cloud infrastructure.

- You can use software components to abstract hardware components of your network.

- A cloud-based infrastructure has far broader limits that let you scale up when needed.

SDN Requirements

Table 14-5 outlines what you need to plan before you implement SDN.

Table 14-5   SDN Requirements

Physical Network	Physical Computer Hosts
You must be able to access all your physical networking components, including these: - VLANs - Routers - BGP devices - DCB with enhanced transmission selection (if using RDMA) - DCB with priority-based flow control (if using RDMA that is based in RDMA over Converged Ethernet [RoCE])	These computers run the Hyper-V role and host the SDN infrastructure and tenant virtual machines. These hosts must have the following characteristics: - Have Windows Server 2016 installed - Have the Hyper-V role enabled - Have an external Hyper-V virtual switch created with at least one physical NIC - Be reachable with a management IP assigned to the Management Host virtual NIC (vNIC)

SDN Configuration

Now you can deploy a software-defined network using SCVMM or scripts. This section helps you evaluate the SDN features available with Windows Server 2016. In particular, it focuses on using Virtual Machine Manager (VMM) 2016 to deploy SDN on a single physical host. It covers several SDN capabilities in Windows Server 2016, including the Network Controller and SLB.

TIP   You can download SDN scripts at http://aka.ms/Iu57tt.

To deploy SDN on a single physical host, you need the following:

- A physical machine with 16 cores
- Windows Server 2016 Data Center with the 9D Update
- SQL Server 2014
- Windows Assessment and Deployment Kit
- SCVMM 2016
- SCVMM Templates for SDN Deployment

In phase 1, you have to prepare the physical host. After that, you can deploy the SDN in phase 2. Both actions are explained in detail in the next sections.

Phase 1: Preparing the Physical Host

The physical host will be used as the Hyper-V host. All you need to do is install Windows 2016 and enable Hyper-V. After you have enabled the Hyper-V role, you create three virtual switches on the host from the Hyper-V Manager UI or with PowerShell:

```
New-VMSwitch -SwitchName "SDN" -SwitchType Internal
New-VMSwitch -SwitchName "Public" -SwitchType Internal
New-VMSwitch -SwitchName "Private" -SwitchType Internal
```

Next, you need to create the virtual hard disks for the SDN infrastructure VMs and you must create seven virtual machines for testing purposes:

Step 1. Based on Windows Server 2016 DC with 9D Update, create virtual hard disks (VHDs) for the SDN infrastructure VMs.

Step 2. Create seven VMs with the following names: SCVMM, RRAS, Remote, HOST01, HOST02, HOST03, and HOST04, based on the Windows Server 2016 DC with 9D VHD. Table 14-6 lists the minimum processor and memory settings for the virtual machines you need.

Table 14-6 VM List

VM Name	Processor	Memory
SCVMM	4	2 GB
RRAS	2	2 GB
HOST01	2	2 GB
HOST02	2	2 GB

VM Name	Processor	Memory
HOST03	2	2 GB
HOST04	2	2 GB
Remote	2	2 GB

Step 3.   Review the topology view from the physical host (see Figure 14-9).

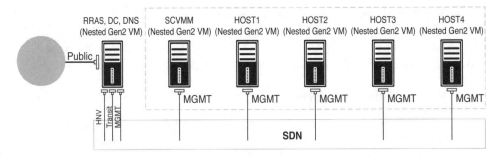

Figure 14-9   Topology View from the Physical Host

Step 4.   Connect these seven VMs to the virtual switches as follows:

- **Remote:** Public, Private

- **RRAS:** Three vNICs connect to SDN, one NIC connects to Public

- **SCVMM, HOST01, HOST02, HOST03, and HOST04:** SDN

Step 5.   Name the vNICs of SCVMM with following names: MGMT, HNV, Transit, Public.

Step 6.   Apply VLAN IDs for the SCVMM vNICs: 7 for MGMT, 10 for Transit, and 11 for HNV.

Step 7.   Enable trunk mode on NIC of HOST01 to HOST04 to allow VLAN 7, 10, and 11. You can use the following PowerShell command: **Set-VMNetworkAdapterVlan** *-Trunk*.

Step 8.   Manually set up static IPs to these seven VMs on their vNICs (see Table 14-7).

Table 14-7 VM IP Addresses

VM Name	NIC1	NIC2	NIC3	NIC4
Remote	Public:	Private:		
	IP: 50.50.50.1/8	IP: 60.60.60.1/8		
	GW: 50.50.50.1	GW: 60.60.60.1		
	DNS: 50.50.50.2	DNS: 60.60.60.1		
SCVMM	SDN (MGMT):			
	IP: 10.184.108.50/8			
	GW: 10.184.108.1			
	DNS: 10.184.108.1			
HOST01	SDN (MGMT):			
	IP: 10.184.108.11/8			
	GW: 10.184.108.1			
	DNS: 10.184.108.1			
HOST02	SDN (MGMT):			
	IP: 10.184.108.12/8			
	GW: 10.184.108.1			
	DNS: 10.184.108.1			
HOST03	SDN (MGMT):			
	IP: 10.184.108.13/8			
	GW: 10.184.108.1			
	DNS: 10.184.108.1			
HOST04	SDN (MGMT):			
	IP: 10.184.108.14/8			
	GW: 10.184.108.1			
	DNS: 10.184.108.1			
RRAS	SDN (MGMT):	SDN (HNV):	SDN (Transit):	Public:
	IP: 10.184.108.1/8	IP: 10.10.56.1/8	IP: 10.10.10.1/8	IP: 50.50.50.2/8
	GW: 10.184.108.1	GW: 10.10.56.1	GW: 10.10.10.1	GW: 50.50.50.1
	DNS: 10.184.108.1	DNS: 10.184.108.1	DNS: 10.184.108.1	

Step 9. Enable nested virtualization on HOST01 through HOST04 with PowerShell:

```
Set-VMProcessor -VMName HOST01-ExposeVirtualizationExtension
   $true

Get-VMNetworkAdapter -VMName HOST01 |
   Set-VMNetworkAdapter-MacAddressSpoofing
```

Step 10. Prepare the VMs based on the information in Table 14-8.

Table 14-8 VM and VM Configuration Steps

VM	VM Configuration Steps
RRAS VM	■ Rename the computer to RRAS.
	■ Install the ADDS role and configure the RRAS server as the DC. Create a root domain named SDN.LAB.
	■ Install the DNS Server role and configure the DNS.
	■ Install the Remote Access role.
	■ Create an Active Directory security group for Network Controller management named SDNMGMT. You need to create an Active Directory security group for Network Controller management. The group should be a domain local group. Members of this group will be able to create, delete, and update the deployed Network Controller configuration. You need to create at least one user account that is a member of this group and have access to its credentials.
	■ Create an Active Directory security group for Network Controller clients named SDNCLIENT. You need to create an AD security group for Network Controller clients. The group should be a domain local group. When the Network Controller is deployed, any members of this group will have permissions to communicate with the Network Controller via a REST-based interface. You need to create at least one user account that is a member of this group. After the Network Controller is deployed, VMM can be configured to use this user's account credentials to establish communication with the Network Controller.
HOST01 - HOST04	■ Rename the computer as HOST01 - HOST04.
	■ Join VMs to the SDN.LAB domain.
	■ Enable the Hyper-V role on the VM. Do not use Hyper-V to create a vSwitch based on the vNIC.

VM	VM Configuration Steps
SCVMM	<ul><li>Rename the computer as SCVMM.</li><li>Join the VM to the domain.</li><li>Install .NET Framework V3.5.</li><li>Install the Windows Assessment and Deployment Kit.</li><li>Install SQL Server 2014.</li><li>Install SCVMM.</li></ul>
Remote	<ul><li>Rename the VM as Remote.</li><li>Install the Remote Access role.</li><li>Install IIS and change the default page of the default website to something meaningful, such as the HTML page with content that can show the page is on the remote host.</li></ul>

Phase 2: Deploying the SDN

Figure 14-10 shows an overview of the SDN topology for the scenario. Consider the Network Controller (NC) component on HOST3.

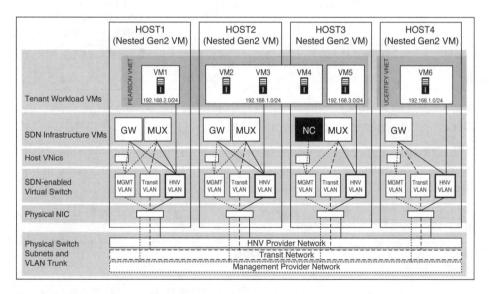

Figure 14-10 SDN Topology

Planning the Network Topology

Table 14-9 outlines the network configuration with detailed IPv4 address data for the gateways and reservations for each VM for the planned SDN topology.

Table 14-9   SDN Network Topology Example

Network Name	Subnet	Mask	VLAN ID on Trunk	Gateway	Reservations (Examples)
Management	10.184.108.0	24	7	10.184.108.1	10.184.108.1 (Router)
					10.184.108.4 (NC)
					10.184.108.11 (HOST1)
					10.184.108.12 (HOST2)
					10.184.108.13 (HOST3)
					10.184.108.14 (HOST4)
HNV Provider	10.10.56.0	23	11	10.10.56.1	10.10.56.1 (Router)
					10.10.56.2 (SLB/MUX1)
Transit	10.10.10.0	24	10	10.10.10.1	10.10.10.1 (Router)
Public VIP	41.40.40.0	27	—	41.40.40.1	41.40.40.40.1 (Router) 41.40.40.2 (SLB/MUX) 41.40.40.4 (S2S VPN VIP)
Private VIP	20.20.20.0	27	—	20.20.20.1	20.20.20.1 (Default GW)
GRE VIP	31.30.30.0	24	—	31.30.30.1	31.30.30.1 (Default GW)

Deploying the Network Controller and SDN

Table 14-10 describes the necessary steps for deploying the Windows Server 2016 Network Controller component and setting up the SDN topology displayed in Figure 14-10.

Table 14-10   Tasks for Deploying Network Controller and SDN

Task Number	Task	Description
1	Prepare an SSL self-signed certificate	You need an SSL certificate to establish secure communication (https) between SCVMM and the Network Controller.
2	Export the certificate	After requesting the certificate, use the Certificates snap-in to export it and its private key into a .pfx file.

Task Number	Task	Description
3	Import the service template and copy VHDs	Download all SDN Network Controller templates from GitHub and copy the VHDs to the VMM Library.
4	Set up Network Settings in SCVMM	On SCVMM, uncheck Create Logical Networks Automatically.
5	Add Hyper-V hosts to SCVMM	Add the Hyper-V hosts to SCVMM.
6	Create the Management logical network	Create the Management logical network and Management logical switch for Management network connectivity for the VMM host, Network Controller hosts, and tenant virtual machine hosts.
7	Create the IP address pool in the Management logical network	You must create an IP address pool in SCVMM for the Management logical network.
8	Create a Management logical switch	The Management logical switch provides the Management network connectivity to the Network Controller VMs.
9	Apply a logical switch on Hyper-V hosts	You must apply a Management switch on HOST1, HOST2, HOST3, and HOST4. You also need to create a vNIC. Both are done in SCVMM.
10	Import a service template into the VMM library	Import the Network Controller Standalone Generation 2 VM.xml service template into the SCVMM library. Here you apply the SSL certificate that you prepared earlier.
11	Configure and deploy the service	After preparing the service template, you can deploy the service. Deployment times vary, depending on your hardware, but are typically between 30 and 60 minutes.
12	Add the Network Service Wizard	After deploying the service, you can add the new network service. Here you select Microsoft Network Controller as the model.
13	Create the HNV Provider network for tenant VM connectivity	The HNV Provider network is used to validate that the Network Controller has been deployed successfully and that tenant VMs within the same virtual network can ping each other.
14	Create the HNV Provider logical network IP address pool	You need to create a static IP address pool that is associated with this logical network.
15	Create a tenant virtual network and VMs	Create your own tenant virtual network and connect two VMs to it using SCVMM.

The following sections look at these tasks in more detail.

Task 1: Preparing an SSL Self-signed Certificate

Use the following PowerShell command to create a self-signed certificate for SDN deployment:

```
New-SelfSignedCertificate -KeyUsageProperty All -provider "Microsoft
  Strong Cryptographic Provider" -FriendlyName "SingleNodeDC" -DnsName
  @("SingleNodeDC. pearson.com")
```

Task 2: Exporting the Certificate

Now use the Certificates snap-in to export the certificate and its private key into a .pfx file. When exporting, choose Personal Information Exchange–PKCS #12 (.PFX) and accept the default of Include All Certificates in the Certification Path If Possible (see Figure 14-11). The Certificate Export Wizard requires you to protect the private key using either security or a password. Be sure to assign a password; you will need it later during Network Controller deployment.

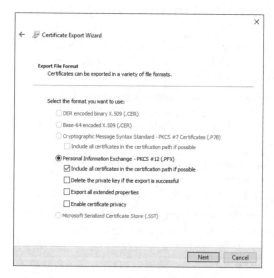

Figure 14-11   Exporting the Certificate

Later, you should place this SingleNodeNC.PFX certificate file directly into the ServerCertificate.cr folder for use during deployment. Details of the ServerCertificate.cr folder are included in the following sections.

Task 3: Importing the Service Template and Copying VHDs

Copy all SDN templates from GitHub (see Figure 14-12) to the folder C:\
Programdata\Virtual Machine Manager Library Files\. Also copy the Windows
Server 2016 + 8D sysprep VHD to the folder C:\Programdata\Virtual Machine
Manager Library Files\VHDS.

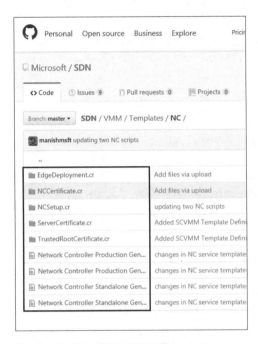

Figure 14-12   SDN GitHub Templates

Task 4: Setting Up Network Settings in SCVMM

Open the SCVMM Console and go to **Settings** > **Network Settings**. Uncheck
Create Logical Networks Automatically.

Task 5: Adding Hyper-V Hosts to SCVMM

Perform these steps to add Hyper-V hosts to SCVMM:

Step 1.   Open the VMM Console, click **Fabric**, and then click **Servers, All
Hosts**.

Step 2.   Right-click **All Hosts** and select **Add Hyper-V Hosts and Clusters**.

Step 3.   Select **Windows Server Computer in a Trusted Active Directory
Domain**.

Step 4.   On the Credentials page, choose to use an existing Run As Account, click **Browse**, and then click **Create Run As Account** to create a Run_As account named pearson\Administrator.

Step 5.   Type **HOST** in Computer Names and click **Next** to search the hosts.

Step 6.   You will see HOST01 to HOST04 displayed on the Target Resources page. Click **Select All**, and then click **Next** twice.

Step 7.   On the Summary page, confirm the settings and click **Finish**. All four hosts are added to the **All Host** group.

Task 6: Creating the Management Logical Network

Perform the following steps to create the Management logical network and switch. The Management logical network models the Management network connectivity for the VMM host, Network Controller hosts, and tenant virtual machine hosts. It is recommended that you create this Management network specifically to provide connectivity to Network Controller–managed infrastructure virtual machines.

Step 1.   Open the Fabric workspace in the VMM Console, expand Networking, and select **Logical Networks**.

Step 2.   Right-click the **Logical Network** node and select **Create Logical Network**.

Step 3.   Specify **MGMT** as the name and optional description for this network. Click **Next**.

Step 4.   On the Settings page, be sure to select **One Connected Network**; all Management networks need to have routing and connectivity between all hosts in that network. Check the box **Create a VM Network with the Same Name** to automatically create a VM network for your Management network. Click **Next**.

Step 5.   In the Network Site panel, click **Add** to add a new network site. Select the host group for the hosts that the Network Controller will manage. Insert your Management network IP subnet information. This network should already exist and be configured in your physical switch. Click **Next** when you are ready to proceed.

Step 6.   Review the summary information and click **Finish** to complete.

For an HA Network Controller deployment, you need a REST IP address that can be assigned to the Network Controller service. This REST IP address will be reserved from the Management logical network IP address space. Now create an IP address pool for the Management logical network and reserve an IP address for the Network Controller service.

Task 7: Creating the IP Address Pool in the Management Logical Network

Perform the following steps to create the IP address pool for the logical network in SCVMM:

Step 1.   Right-click the Management logical network in VMM and select **Create IP Pool** from the drop-down menu.

Step 2.   Provide a name and optional description for the IP pool, and ensure that the Management network is selected for the logical network. Click **Next**.

Step 3.   From the Network Site panel, select the subnet that the IP address pool will service. Click **Next**.

Step 4.   From the IP Address Range panel, type the starting and ending IP addresses. *Important:* Don't use the first three IP addresses of your available subnet. For example, if your available subnet is from .1 to .254, start your range at .4 or greater.

Step 5.   In IP Addresses to Be Reserved for Other Uses, type one of the IP addresses from the specified range. This is the IP address that you will later use as the REST IP of the Network Controller Service. Click **Next**.

Step 6.   Next, configure the default gateway address.

Step 7.   DNS information is not required.

Step 8.   WINS server information is generally not required. Click **Next**.

Step 9.   Review the summary information and click **Finish**.

Task 8: Creating a Management Logical Switch

The Management logical switch needs to be deployed on the Network Controller host(s). It provides the Management network connectivity to the Network Controller VMs.

Perform the following steps to deploy the Management logical switch on the Network Controller:

Step 1.   Click **Create Logical Switch** on the ribbon in the VMM Console.

Step 2.   Review the Getting Started information and click **Next**.

Step 3.   Provide MGMT-LSWITCH as the name and optional description. For the Uplink mode, be sure to select **No Uplink Team**. Click **Next**.

Step 4.   For Minimum Bandwidth mode, choose the default option. Click **Next**.

Step 5.   Uncheck all the switch extensions in Extensions. This is a crucial step because selecting any of the switch extensions at this stage could block Network Controller onboarding later.

Step 6.   You can add a virtual port profile and choose a port classification for host management on this page, if you want, but these are not required. Click **Next**.

Step 7.   Create a new uplink port profile directly from the Logical Switch Wizard. Click **Add** and select **New Uplink Port Profile**.

Step 8.   Provide a name and optional description for your uplink port profile.

   a. Use the defaults for the Load Balancing Algorithm and Teaming Mode settings.

   b. Make sure you select all the network sites that are part of the Management logical network you created. Leave the Load Balancing Algorithm setting as Host Default, and leave the Teaming Mode setting as Switch Independent.

   c. Select the uplink port profile you created and click **New Virtual Network Adapter**. This adds a host virtual network adapter (vNIC) to your logical switch and uplink port profile so that when you add the logical switch to your hosts, the vNICs get added automatically. Provide a name for the vNIC.

   d. Select **This Network Adapter Will Be Used for Host Management**, and then select **Inherit Connection Settings from the Host Adapter**. This enables you to take the vNIC adapter settings from the adapter that already exists on the host.

   e. If you created a port classification and virtual port profile earlier, you can select it now. Click **Next** and then **Finish**.

Task 9: Applying a Logical Switch on Hyper-V Hosts

Perform the following steps to apply the previously created logical switch to a vNIC:

Step 1.   Click **VMs and Services**.

Step 2.   Right-click the host under the **All Hosts** group.

Step 3.   Click **Virtual Switches** on the left; then click **New Virtual Switch** and choose the logical switch you just created.

Step 4.   Click **New Virtual Network Adapter** to also create a vNIC.

Task 10: Importing the Service Template into the VMM Library

Perform the following steps to import the Network Controller Standalone Generation 2 VM template:

Step 1.   In VMM, navigate to Library.

Step 2.   In the top of the left pane, in the Templates section, select **Service Templates**.

Step 3.   In the ribbon at the top, click **Import Template**.

Step 4.   Browse to your service template folder, select the **Network Controller Standalone Generation 2 VM.xml** file, and follow the prompts to import it.

Step 5.   The service template uses the virtual machine configuration parameters listed in Table 14-11. Update the parameters for your environment as you import the service template.

Table 14-11 lists the resource types of the SDN service template and describes the functionality of each resource type.

Table 14-11   SDN Service Template Parameter

Resource Type	Resource Name and Description
WinServer.vhd	Select the base image that you prepared earlier and imported into the SCVMM library folder.
NCSetup.cr	Map to the NCSetup.cr library resource in your SCVMM library.
ServerCertificate.cr	Select the Server Certificate.cr library resource that you downloaded earlier and imported into the SCVMM library. Also put the SingleNodeDC.pfx SSL certificate that you prepared earlier inside this folder. Make sure that you have only one certificate in the ServerCertificate.cr folder.
TrustedRootCertificate.cr	The folder should be left empty. Map to the TrustedRootCertificate.cr folder in your SCVMM library.
NCCertificate.cr	Map to the NCCertificate.cr library resource in your SCVMM library.

Task 11: Configuring and Deploying the Service

You deploy a Network Controller service instance with the following steps:

Step 1. Select the Network Controller service template and click **Configure Deployment**. You must type the service name **NCService** and select a destination for the service instance. The destination must map to a host group that contains Windows Server RTM hosts and that the Network Controller will manage.

Step 2. On the left side of the Configure Deployment window are several settings that you must configure. Table 14-12 summarizes each field's values.

Table 14-12 SDN Service Template Configuration

Setting	Requirement	Value
ClientSecurityGroup	Required	Pearson\SDNCLIENTS
DiagnosticLogShare	Optional	
DiagnosticLogShareUsername	Optional	
DiagnosticLogSharePassword	Optional	
LocalAdmin	Required	Select a Run As account that will be used as the local administrator on the Network Controller VMs.
Management	Required	MGMT
MgmtDomainAccount	Required	Select a Run As account that will be used to prepare the Network Controller. This user must be a member of the Management security group, which has privileges to manage the Network Controller.
MgmtDomainAccountName	Required	Example: Pearson\Administrator. The domain username is added to the Local Administrators group of the Network Controller VMs during deployment.
MgmtDomainAccountPassword	Required	The password for the Management Run As account maps to the MgmtDomain account.
MgmtDomainFQDN	Required	Pearson.com
MgmtSecurityGroup	Required	Pearson\MGMT
ServerCertfiicatePassword	Required	This is the password needed to import the SSL certificate into the machine.

It is normal for the VM instances to initially be red. Click **Refresh Preview** to have the deployment service automatically find suitable hosts for the VMs to be created. Input the Network Controller name as SingleNodeNC. After you configure these settings, click **Deploy Service** to begin the service deployment job. Deployment times need to be between 30 and 60 minutes.

Task 12: Adding the Network Service Wizard

Perform the following steps to add the Windows Server 2016 Network Controller as a network service to SCVMM.

Step 1.   Navigate to the Fabric Node in the VMM console.

Step 2.   Right-click **Network Service** under Networking and click **Add Network Service**.

Step 3.   Select the Add Network Service Wizard and click **Next**.

Step 4.   Input **NCService** as your Network Controller network service name. Then click **Next**.

Step 5.   Select **Microsoft** for the manufacturer and select **Microsoft Network Controller** for the model. Click **Next**.

Step 6.   From the Credentials tab, provide the RunAs account that you want to use to configure the Network Service. This should be the same account that you included in the Network Controller clients group. Click **Next**.

```
SERVERURL=https://SingleNodeNC.pearson.com;servicename=NCService
```

In this example, the service account included in the Network Controller clients group is named NCService.

Step 7.   On the Review Certificates page, a connection is made to the Network Controller virtual machine to retrieve the certificate. Verify that the certificate shown is the one you expect. Make sure that you select the **These Certificates Have Been Reviewed and Can Be Imported to the Trusted Certificate Storebox** check box. Click **Next**.

Step 8.   On the next screen, click **Scan Provider** to connect to your service and list the properties and their status. This is also a good test of whether the service was created correctly and whether you're using the right string to connect to it. Examine the results and ensure that the property *Network-Controller = true* is set. When it completes successfully, click **Next**.

Step 9.   Configure the host group in VMM that your Network Controller will manage. Click **Next**.

Step 10.   Click **Finish** to complete the Add Network Service Wizard. When the service has been added to VMM, you should see it appear in the Network Services list in the VMM Console.

Task 13: Creating the HNV Provider Network for Tenant VM Connectivity

The Network Controller is connected to the Management network, which is used to deploy and manage the Network Controller through SCVMM.

You need to create the HNV Provider network that the Network Controller manages in your SDN fabric. This network is used to confirm that the Network Controller has been deployed successfully.

Perform the following steps to create the HNV Provider network that the Network Controller manages so that tenant virtual machines within the same virtual network can ping each other:

Step 1.   Start the Create Logical Network Wizard.

Step 2.   Type **HNV** as the name and optional description for this network. Click **Next**.

Step 3.   On the Settings page, verify that One Connected Network is selected; all HNV Provider networks need to have routing and connectivity between all hosts in that network. Make sure that you check **Allow New VM Networks Created on This Logical Network to Use Network Virtualization**. You will also see a new setting of Managed by the Network Controller. Ensure that you check this box and then click **Next**.

Step 4.   From the Network Site panel, add the network site information for your HNV Provider network. This should include the host group, subnet, and VLAN information for your HNV Provider network. Remember, this network should already exist in your physical network devices, and all your SDN fabric hosts should have physical connectivity to it.

Task 14: Creating the HNV Provider Logical Network IP Address Pool

VMM requires the HNV Provider logical network to have an IP address pool, even if DHCP is available on this network. You need to create a static IP address pool that is associated with this logical network. To create an IP address pool in the HNV Provider logical network, perform the following steps:

Step 1.   Right-click the HNV Provider logical network in VMM and select **Create IP Pool**.

Step 2.   Provide a name and optional description for the IP pool and ensure that the HNV Provider logical network is selected for the logical network. Click **Next**.

Step 3. From the Network Site panel, select the subnet that this IP address pool will service. If you have more than one subnet as part of your HNV Provider network, you need to create a static IP address pool for each subnet. If you have only one site (for example, as with the sample topology), click **Next**.

Step 4. From the IP Address Range panel, configure the starting and ending IP addresses. Click **Next**. *Important:* Don't use the first three IP addresses of your available subnet. For example, if your available subnet is from .1 to .254, start your range at .4 or greater.

Step 5. Configure the default gateway address. Click **Insert** next to the Default Gateways box, type the address, and use the default metric. Click **Next**.

Step 6. DNS information is not required.

Step 7. WINS server information is not required. Click **Next**.

Step 8. Click **Finish**.

Step 9. As part of Network Controller on-boarding, the switch that you deployed on the hosts for the Management logical network connectivity was converted to an SDN switch. This switch can now be used to deploy a Network Controller–managed network, including the HNV Provider logical network. Ensure that you select the network site that corresponds to the HNV Provider logical network in the uplink port profile settings for the Management logical switch.

Make sure HNV_0 and MGMT_0 are both checked.

Task 15: Creating a Tenant Virtual Network and VMs

Now you must create your tenant virtual network and connect two VMs by using underlying SDN components and the System Center Virtual Machine Manager (SCVMM). VM1 and VM2 are on different Hyper-V hosts and in different subnets, but they are connected through a VM Network (VNET). Figure 14-13 shows the configuration; the following list outlines the steps to set up VM1 and VM2 so that both have a network connection through the VM network named pearson.

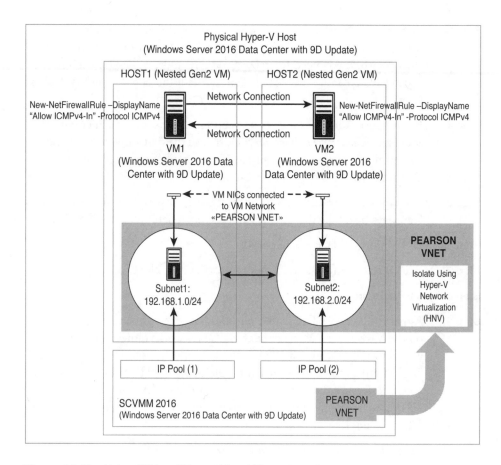

Figure 14-13   Using SDN and Tenant Virtual Network to Connect VMs with SCVMM

Step 1.   Open the SCVMM console. Leave the default login settings as is with the server name as localhost:81001. Select **Connect**.

Step 2.   Open the VM Networks and IP Pools pane. Click **VMs and Services** on the bottom-left side of the console. Click **VM Networks** in the VMs and Services pane. Click **VM Networks** in the menu.

Step 3.   Open the Create VM Network Wizard. Click **Create VM Network** in the menu.

Step 4.   Configure the VM network name and description. Input **pearson** as the name for the virtual network you are creating. Optionally, provide a description for the virtual network. Make sure you set Logical Network to **HNV**. Click **Next**.

Step 5.   Select **Isolation**. Leave the default radio button selection Isolate Using Hyper-V Network Virtualization. Leave the default IP address protocol for both the VM and the logical network as IPv4. Click **Next**.

Step 6.   Create the VM subnets. Click the **Add** button. Enter **Subnet1** as the name for the first VM subnet. Enter the subnet (IP prefix) **192.168.1.0/24** for the first VM subnet. Make sure you use 192.168.1.0/24 as your first subnet. Click **Add** again. Enter a name for the second VM subnet (for example, Subnet2). Enter a subnet for the second VM subnet (for example, 192.168.2.0/24). Click **Next**.

Step 7.   Skip the Connectivity section. We are not providing external connectivity for this virtual network through a VPN tunnel, direct routing, or NAT in this exercise. Click **Next**.

Step 8.   Create the VM network. Click the **View Script** button to see the SCVMM PowerShell script used to create this network. Click **Finish**.

Step 9.   Create an IP pool. Right-click the Virtual Network you just created and select **Create IP Pool**.

Step 10. Specify the IP address pool name and VM subnet. Note that you will be creating a separate IP pool for each VM subnet. Type **IPPool1** as the pool name and, optionally, provide a description. Ensure the VM Network listed is the VM Network you just created. Select the first Subnet1 you created. Click **Next**.

Step 11. Specify an IP address range. Click **Next**. Leave the Starting and Ending IP Addresses as the default. You do not have to reserve an IP address for VIPs or other uses.

Step 12. Specify a gateway. Click **Next**. The lowest IP address in the subnet is the default gateway—this is determined automatically if the field is left blank.

Step 13. Skip Specify a DNS Server. Click **Next**.

Step 14. Skip Specify a WINS Server. Click **Next**.

Step 15. Create the first VM subnet's IP pool. Click **Finish** to confirm the settings.

Step 16. Create the second VM subnet's IP pool. Input **IPPool2** as the second pool name. Repeat steps 9–15 for your second VM subnet, named **Subnet2**.

Step 17. Create a VM. Click **All Hosts** in the VMs and Services pane on the left side of the screen, and click the **VMs** icon in the menu. Click **Create Virtual Machine**.

Step 18.   Now you select the source for the new VM. Use the default option Use an Existing Virtual Machine and click **Browse**. Navigate down to the sysprep Windows Server 2016 VHD you copied to the SCVMM template library. At the VHDX TYPE section, click it, then click **OK**, and click **Next**.

Step 19.   Specify Virtual Machine Identity. Input **VM1** as the name for the VM. Generation 2 must be selected. Leave Turn on Shielding Support in the Virtual Machine After Deploying It unchecked. Click **Next**.

Step 20.   Configure the hardware. Under Compatibility, click **Hyper-V** profile. At General in the left menu pane, select **Processor** and ensure that Number of Processors is set to **2**. Maintain the default settings of 2 processors and 2048 MB of memory. At Network Adapters, select **Network Adapter 1**. On the right side of the window, under Connectivity, select **Connected to a VM Network**. Browse to the pearson VM Network you previously created. Select a VM subnet attached to the Subnet1 subnet you previously created. Click **Next**.

Step 21.   Place the VM on a host. Click **Next** to skip Select Destination. Choose the first recommended host on which to deploy this VM. Particularly if you are completing this step for the second time (after reaching step 26 of this exercise), feel free to select a different Hyper-V host (assuming that it is recommended with three or more stars), to spread out the VM deployments. Click **Next**.

Step 22.   Skip Configure Settings. Click **Next**.

Step 23.   Skip the Add Properties section. Select **Start the Virtual Machine After Deploying It**. Click **Next**.

Step 24.   Confirm the settings and deploy the VM. Select **Start the Virtual Machine After Deploying It** and click **Create**. Creating the VM takes some time.

Step 25.   To create another VM, repeat Steps 17–24 with a VM name of VM2 and Subnet2.

Step 26.   Open a console session to the VMs. Check the VM's state. If the status is Stopped, right-click the VM and click **Power On**. Check the VM's status again. When the status of each of your VMs has changed to Running, select **VMs and Services** in the bottom-left side of the VMM console. Click **All Hosts** in the VMs and Services pane. Click **VMs** in the menu. Right-click any one of the VMs you just deployed and select **Connect or View**. Connect via Console. Log in with the password you set up for the VMs.

Step 27.   Validate virtual network connectivity in each of your created VMs. Upon logging in, you may see a Networks pane on the right side. Click **No** (although it does not matter what you pick). Right-click the Windows icon in the Start menu and click a command prompt (Admin). Type **ipconfig** and press Enter. Record the IP address of the VM. Open a console session in another VM and open its command prompt. Ping the first VM from the second VM. You should receive replies.

Step 28.   Configure the firewall policy on both VM1 and VM2 to allow them to ping each other. Run the following PowerShell command: **New-NetFirewallRule -DisplayName "Allow ICMPv4-In" -Protocol ICMPv4.**

Step 29.   Log in to VM1; then open the CMD utility to ping the IP address of VM2 to see whether it works.

You have now attached two VMs on different subnets to a VM network (VNET). The VMs can even route between each other.

Requirements and Scenarios for Implementing Hyper-V Network Virtualization (HNV) Using Network Virtualization Generic Route Encapsulation (NVGRE) or Virtual Extensible LAN (VXLAN) Encapsulation

The following sections examine the requirements and scenarios in more detail.

HNVv1 and HNVv2

Two HNV implementations are available in Windows Server 2016: HNVv1 and HNVv2. Table 14-13 describes the differences.

Table 14-13   HNVv1 Versus HNVv2

HNVv1	HNVv2
HNVv1 is compatible with Windows Server 2012 R2 and System Center 2012 R2 Virtual Machine Manager (VMM). Configuration for HNVv1 relies on WMI management and Windows PowerShell cmdlets (facilitated through the System Center VMM) to define isolation settings and customer address (CA)—virtual network—to physical address (PA) mappings and routing. No additional features have been added to HNVv1 in Windows Server 2016, and no new features are planned.	A significant number of new features are included in HNVv2, which is implemented using the Azure Virtual Filtering Platform (VFP) forwarding extension in the Hyper-V Switch. HNVv2 is fully integrated with Microsoft Azure Stack, which includes the new Network Controller in the SDN stack. Virtual network policy is defined through the Network Controller using a RESTful northbound (NB) API and is plumbed to a Host Agent via multiple southbound interfaces (SBI), including OVSDB.

Suppose that the Pearson Corporation has two networks, ChicagoNet and DenverNet. Both networks have different routing domain IDs; therefore, they cannot interact or communicate with each other. These networks are isolated from each other through the use of the RDID. The RDID and VSID must be unique (see Figure 14-14).

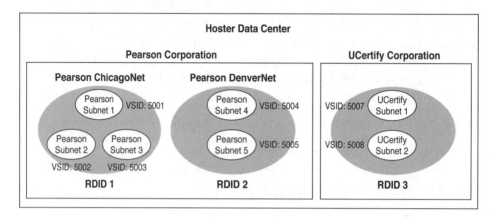

Figure 14-14   Customer Networks and Virtual Subnets

With Layer 3 routing, virtual machines in VSID 5001 can route packets to VMs in VSID 5002 or VSID 5003 by the HNV distributed router, which is present in each Hyper-V host's vSwitch. HNV updates the VSID of the incoming packet to the VSID of the destination VM. This happens only if both VSIDs are in the same RDID. Therefore, virtual network adapters with RDID1 cannot send packets to virtual network adapters with RDID2 without traversing a gateway.

TIP   With Windows Server 2016, broadcast and subnet multicasts are implemented using unicast replication. Cross-subnet multicast routing and IGMP are not supported.

TIP   Hyper-V switch extensions cannot work with HNVv2 in an SDN stack. HNVv2 is implemented using the Azure Virtual Filtering Platform (VFP) switch extension, which cannot be used in conjunction with any other third-party switch extensions.

Network Virtualization Generic Routing Encapsulation (NVGRE)

This network virtualization mechanism uses NVGRE as part of the tunnel header. In NVGRE, the VM's packet is encapsulated inside another packet. The header of this new packet has the appropriate source and destination PA IP addresses, in addition to the virtual subnet ID, which is stored in the Key field of the GRE header (see Figure 14-15).

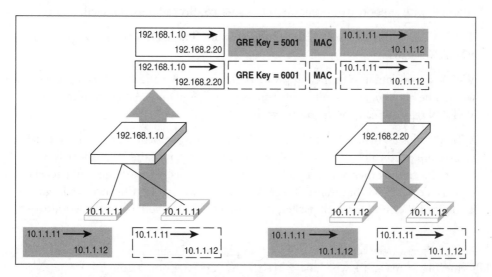

Figure 14-15   Network Virtualization—NVGRE Encapsulation

The virtual subnet ID allows hosts to identify the customer VM for any given packet, even though the PAs (provider addresses) and the CAs (customer addresses) on the packets may overlap.

Sharing the PA has a big impact on network scalability and can substantially reduce the number of IP and MAC addresses that the network infrastructure needs to learn. For instance, if every end host has an average of 30 VMs, this reduces the number of IP and MAC addresses that the networking infrastructure needs to learn by a factor of 30. The embedded virtual subnet IDs in the packets also enable easy correlation of packets to the actual customers.

The PA sharing scheme for Windows Server 2012 R2 is one PA per VSID per host. For Windows Server 2016, the scheme is one PA per NIC team member.

With Windows Server 2016 and later, HNV fully supports NVGRE and VXLAN out of the box; it does *not* require upgrading or purchasing new network hardware such as NICs (network adapters), switches, or routers. This is because these packets on the wire are regular IP packets in the PA space, which is compatible with today's network infrastructure. However, to get the best performance, use supported NICs with the latest drivers that support task offloads.

Virtual eXtensible Local Area Network (VXLAN)

The Virtual eXtensible Local Area Network (VXLAN) protocol has been widely adopted, with support from vendors such as Cisco, Brocade, Arista, Dell, and HP.

The VXLAN protocol uses UDP as the transport. The UDP destination port for VXLAN is 4789.

VXLAN is essentially a tunneling protocol that wraps Layer 2 on a Layer 3 network. The network is split into different segments, and only VMs within the same VXLAN segment can communicate with each other.

VXLAN adds 50 bytes of additional overhead for the protocol. For that reason, it gives more overhead and all packets need to wrapped out of the VXLAN before being sent to the other VM. This also creates an issue when sending small packets such as Telnet/SSH that transmit a packet for each keystroke; this incurs a large amount of overhead for each packet, even though it not a very common workload.

> **TIP**   In Windows Server 2016, HNVv2 is implemented using the Azure Virtual Filtering Platform (VFP), which is an NDIS filtering extension within the Hyper-V switch. VFP supports inner MAC forwarding for NVGRE and VXLAN encapsulation types, as well as outer MAC VLAN-based forwarding.

Scenarios for Implementing Software Load Balancer (SLB) for North–South and East–West Load Balancing

SLB maps virtual IP addresses (VIPs) to dynamic IP addresses (DIPs) that are part of a cloud service set of resources in the datacenter. When public traffic arrives from the Internet, the SLB MUX examines the traffic, which contains the VIP as a destination, and maps and rewrites the traffic so that it arrives at an individual DIP. For inbound network traffic, this transaction is performed in a two-step process that is split between the MUX virtual machines (VMs) and the Hyper-V host where the destination DIP is located. The two steps are load-balancing and NAT.

SLB Core Functionality

The following list explains the core functionality of SLB and under what circumstances it can be used:

- Use layer 4 load-balancing services for north–south and east–west TCP/UDP traffic.

- Use SLB on a Hyper-V network virtualization-based network.

- Use SLB with a VLAN-based network for DIP VMs connected to an SDN-enabled Hyper-V virtual switch.

- One SLB instance can handle multiple tenants.

- SLB and DIP support a scalable and low-latency return path, as implemented by Direct Server Return (DSR).

- SLB functions when you are also using Switch Embedded Teaming (SET) or single-root input/output virtualization (SR-IOV).

- SLB includes Internet Protocol version 4 (IPv4) support.

- For site-to-site gateway scenarios, SLB provides NAT functionality to enable all site-to-site connections to use a single public IP.

- You can install SLB, including the Host Agent and the MUX, on Windows Server 2016, Full, Core, and Nano installations.

SLB Scale and Performance

The following list describes performance-relevant aspects of SLB solutions:

- SLB is ready for cloud scale, including scale-out and scale-up capability for MUXes and Host Agents.

- One active SLB Manager Network Controller module can support eight MUX instances.

SLB High Availability

The following list addresses high-availability issues you have to consider when planning SLB solutions:

- You should deploy SLB to more than two nodes in an active/active configuration.

- MUXes can be added and removed from the MUX pool without impacting the SLB service. This maintains SLB availability when individual MUXes are being patched.

- Individual MUX instances have an uptime of 99 percent.

- Health monitoring data is available to management entities.

SLB Alignment

The following list points out some integration issues concerning SLB scenarios:

- You can deploy and configure SLB with SCVMM.

- SLB provides a multitenant unified edge by seamlessly integrating with Microsoft appliances such as the RAS Multitenant Gateway, Datacenter Firewall, and Route Reflector.

A northbound interface is an interface that allows a particular component of a network to communicate with a higher-level component. Conversely, a southbound interface allows a particular network component to communicate with a lower-level component.

Northbound API

The Network Controller northbound API enables you to gather network information from the Network Controller that enables you to monitor and configure the network. With the Network Controller northbound API, you can configure, monitor, troubleshoot, and deploy new devices on the network by using the following:

- Windows PowerShell

- REST API

- A management application with a graphical user interface—for example, System Center Virtual Machine Manager or System Center Operations Manager

Datacenter Firewall in Windows Server 2016 helps you install and configure firewall policies to protect your virtual networks from unwanted network traffic. You manage the Datacenter Firewall policies by using Network Controller northbound APIs.

You can use SLB in SDN to distribute network traffic across available network resources. Windows Server SLB provides Layer 4 load balancing for both north–south and east–west TCP/UDP traffic.

Southbound API

The Windows Server 2016 Network Controller uses the southbound API to communicate with network devices, services, and components. With the southbound API, Network Controller can do the following:

- Discover network devices

- Detect service configurations

- Gather all the information you need about the network

- Send information to the infrastructure (for example, configuration changes you have made)

Chapter 14: Implementing Windows Server 2016 High-Performance Network Solutions   677

Implementation Scenarios for Various Types of Windows Server Gateways, Including L3, GRE, and S2S, and Their Use

To understand the topology for various types of gateways, you need to understand the corresponding scenarios that these gateways are used in. Three types of gateways are available via Windows Server 2016 SDN solutions for connectivity with a non-SDN infrastructure (see Table 14-14).

Table 14-14 Gateway Types

IPsec Gateway	GRE Gateway	L3 Forwarding Gateway
IPsec gateways are used to connect virtual networks with other virtualized or physical networks (on-premises) over the public Internet. The Enterprise gateway and the HNV gateway establish the secure IPsec connection over public Internet IP addresses to exchange data between the two networks.	GRE gateways are used to connect virtual networks with other physical networks over dedicated connectivity. The physical network gateway (GRE terminating device) and the HNV gateway establish the connection identified by the unique GRE key to exchange data between the two networks.	L3 gateways are used to connect virtual networks with other physical networks over a VLAN-isolated network. The physical network gateway (a Layer 3 router) and the HNV gateway establish the connection over this network, isolated by unique VLAN ID to exchange data between the two networks.

RAS Gateway is a software-based, multitenant, BGP-capable router. It is designed for cloud service providers and large organizations that host multiple tenant virtual networks using Hyper-V Network Virtualization (HNV). RAS Gateway provides the following features:

- **Site-to-site VPN:** Enables you to connect two networks at different physical locations across the Internet with a site-to-site VPN connection

- **Point-to-site VPN:** Gives organization employees or administrators the capability to connect to your organization's network from remote locations

- **GRE tunneling:** Enables connectivity between tenant virtual networks and external networks

- **Dynamic routing with BGP:** Reduces the need for manual route configuration on routers because it is a dynamic routing protocol and automatically learns routes between sites that are connected with site-to-site VPN connections

You can implement RAS Gateway in the scenarios outlined in Table 14-15.

Table 14-15 RAS Gateway Scenarios

RAS Gateway Scenario	Description
Multitenant-aware VPN gateway	The RAS Gateway works as a VPN gateway that is aware of the virtual networks deployed on the Hyper-V hosts. Deploying RAS Gateway with this configuration means that you can connect to the RAS Gateway by using a site-to-site VPN from a remote location, or you can configure individual users with VPN access to the RAS Gateway. The RAS Gateway operates like any other VPN gateway: It allows remote users to connect directly to the virtual networks on the Hyper-V servers. The main difference is that the RAS Gateway is multitenant aware, so you can have multiple virtual networks with overlapping address spaces located on the same virtual infrastructure. This configuration is useful for organizations that have multiple locations or multiple business groups that share the same address spaces and must be able to route traffic to the virtual networks. Hosting providers also can use this configuration to give remote clients direct network access between their on-premises network and the hosted networks.
Multitenant-aware network address translation (NAT) gateway for Internet access	In this scenario, the RAS Gateway provides access to the Internet for virtual machines on virtual networks. The RAS Gateway is configured as a NAT device, which translates addresses that can connect to the Internet to addresses used on the virtual networks. In this configuration, RAS Gateway is also multitenant aware, so all virtual networks behind the RAS Gateway can connect to the Internet, even if they use overlapping address spaces.
Forwarding gateway for internal physical network access	In this configuration, RAS Gateway provides access to internal network resources that are located on physical networks. For example, an organization might have some servers that are still deployed on physical hosts. When configured as a forwarding gateway, RAS Gateway enables computers on the virtual networks to connect to those physical hosts.

Using a Network Controller, you can deploy and manage hosts and VMs that are members of a RAS Gateway pool so that you can provide RAS Gateway services to your tenants. You can use the Network Controller to automatically deploy VMs running RAS Gateway to support the following features:

- Capability to add and remove gateway virtual machines from the RAS Gateway pool and specify the level of backup required

- S2S VPN gateway connectivity between remote tenant networks and your datacenter using IPsec

- S2S VPN gateway connectivity between remote tenant networks and your datacenter using GRE

- P2S VPN gateway connectivity so that tenant administrators can access resources on your datacenter from anywhere

- Layer 3 forwarding capability

- BGP routing so that you can manage the routing of network traffic between your tenants' VM networks and their remote sites

Requirements and Scenarios for Distributed Firewall Policies and Network Security Groups

Windows Server 2016 offers the new Datacenter Firewall capability. The Datacenter Firewall is a network layer, 5-tuple (protocol, source and destination port numbers, and source and destination IP addresses), stateful, multitenant firewall. When it is deployed and offered as a service by the service provider, tenant administrators can install and configure firewall policies to help protect their virtual networks from unwanted traffic originating from Internet and intranet networks.

> **TIP**   Both the cloud service provider admin and the tenant admin can manage Datacenter Firewall policies by using the Network Controller.

Benefits of the Datacenter Firewall for CSPs

The following list describes the main benefits of the new Windows Server 2016 Datacenter Firewall feature:

- It is a software-based firewall solution that is highly scalable and manageable, and it can easily be offered to tenants.

- It offers the capability to easily move tenant virtual machines to different computer hosts without disrupting tenant firewall configuration, for these reasons:

    - It is deployed as a vSwitch port Host Agent firewall.

    - Tenant virtual machines get the policies assigned to their vSwitch Host Agent firewall.

    - Firewall rules are configured in each vSwitch port, independent of the host that runs the virtual machine.

- It provides protection to tenant virtual machines, regardless of the tenant guest operating system.

Benefits of the Datacenter Firewall for Tenants

Tenants can use Datacenter Firewall rules to protect against unwanted network traffic:

- Define firewall rules that can help protect Internet-facing workloads on their virtual networks

- Define firewall rules that can help protect traffic between virtual machines on the same L2 virtual subnet and also between virtual machines on different L2 virtual subnets

- Define firewall rules that can help protect and isolate network traffic between tenant on-premises networks and their virtual networks at the service provider

Configure Datacenter Firewall Access Control Lists (ACL)

The Datacenter Firewall enables you to configure and manage Access Control rules to allow or deny firewalls for your workload VMs for both east–west and north–south network traffic in your datacenter. The firewall rules are plumbed in the vSwitch port of workload VMs, so they are distributed across your workload in the datacenter. Using the northbound API, you can define the firewall rules for both incoming and outgoing traffic from the workload VM. You can also configure each firewall rule to log the traffic that the rule either allowed or denied. The Datacenter Firewall enables you to apply firewall policies at the VM interface level or at the subnet level.

Through the Windows Server 2016 Datacenter Firewall, you can apply specific ACLs to network interfaces. If ACLs are also set on the virtual subnet to which the network interface is connected, both ACLs are applied, but the network interface ACLs are prioritized above the virtual subnet ACLs.

If you want to override the default ACL on the virtual subnet with a specific ACL for an individual network interface, follow these steps:

Step 1. Get or create the NIC to which you will add the ACL:

```
$nic = get-networkcontrollernetworkinterface -ConnectionUri $uri
  -ResourceId "MyVM_Ethernet1"
```

Step 2. Get or create the ACL you will add to the NIC:

```
$acl = get-networkcontrolleraccesscontrollist -ConnectionUri $uri
  -resourceid "AllowAllACL"
```

Step 3. Add the ACL to the *AccessControlList* property of the NIC:

```
$nic.properties.ipconfigurations[0].properties.AccessControlList
  = $acl
```

Exam Preparation Tasks

Review All the Key Topics

Review the most important topics in the chapter, noted with the Key Topics icon in the outer margin of the page. Table 14-16 lists these key topics and the page numbers where each is found.

Table 14-16   Key Topics for Chapter 14

Key Topic Element	Description	Page Number
Section	What Is Switch Embedded Teaming (SET)?	639
Table 14-2	SET Compatibility	641
Section	Receive Side Scaling	642
Section	Quality of Service with Data Center Bridging	643
Section	SMB Direct on RDMA-Enabled Network Adapters	643
Section	RDMA	644
Section	Packet Direct	645
Section	SMB Multichannel	645
Section	Receive Side Scaling on a VMQ-Capable Network Adapter	646
Section	Virtual Machine Multi-Queue	647
Section	Single-Root I/O Virtualization on a Supported Network Adapter	648
Section	Software-Defined Networking	649
List	Benefits of SDN	650
Table 14-5	SDN Requirements	650
Section	SDN Configuration	650
Table 14-13	HNVv1 Versus HNVv2	671
Section	Network Virtualization Generic Routing Encapsulation (NVGRE)	672
Section	Scenarios for Implementing Software Load Balancer (SLB) for North–South and East–West Load Balancing	674
Table 14-14	Gateway Types	677
Table 14-15	RAS Gateway Scenarios	678
List	RAS Gateway pools	678
Text	Datacenter firewall and distributed firewall policies	679

Complete the Tables and Lists from Memory

Print a copy of Appendix B, "Memory Tables" (on the book's website), or at least the section for this chapter, and complete the tables and lists from memory. Appendix C, "Memory Tables Answer Key," also on the website, includes completed tables and lists to check your work.

Definition of Key Terms

Define the following key terms from this chapter and check your answers in the glossary.

SET, RSS, RDMA, DCB, HVN, RSC, SMB Direct, Packet Direct, SMB Multichannel

End-of-Chapter Review Questions

1. You want to create a Hyper-V SET-enabled virtual switch with two network adapters, and you want to enable RDMA. You want to use PowerShell cmdlets and parameters to configure that. Fill in the relevant PowerShell cmdlet or parameter required to complete this configuration.

    _____ Switch1 -NetAdapterName "NIC1", "NIC2"

    - _____ $true

    Add-VMNetworkAdapter -SwitchName Switch1 -Name SMBRDMA1

    Add-VMNetworkAdapter -SwitchName Switch1 -Name SMBRDMA2

    _____ "vEthernet (SMBRDMA_1)", "vEthernet (SMBRDMA_2)"

    Choices:

PowerShell Cmdlets	PowerShell Parameters
New-VMSwitch	EnableIov
Enable-NetAdapterRDMA	EnablePacketDirect
Enable-NetworkSwitchFeature	EnableEmbeddedTeaming
Enable-NetworkSwitchVlan	MinimumBandwithMode

2. You have configured some of your Windows Server 2016 VMs to use multiple processor cores. You cannot distribute the received network traffic among these multiple processors because the processor of the Hyper-V does not support this feature. However, you can reduce the number of processor cycles that are used, leading to better scalability. Which PowerShell cmdlets can you use?

    a. **Enable-NetAdapterRss**

    b. **Enable-NetAdapterRsc**

    c. **Enable-NetAdapterBinding**

    d. **Enable-NetAdapterQos**

3. You have disabled SMB Multichannel with the PowerShell command **Set-SmbServer Configuration -EnableMultiChannel $false**. You want to use high throughput, low latency, and low CPU utilization capabilities offered by your RDMA-capable network adapters. Which feature can you not use as long as SMB Multichannel is disabled?

    a. RDMA

    b. SMB Direct

    c. SET

    d. Receive Side Scaling

4. Which benefits does the SMB Multichannel feature offer? (Choose all that apply.)

    a. Clustering automatically recognizes all NICS on nodes using the same switch or subnet.

    b. SMB Multichannel is enabled automatically.

    c. Networks with IPv6 link local IPv6 addresses are recognized on cluster-only networks.

    d. Single IP address resource is configured on each CAP network name, by default.

    e. Cluster validation produces less warning when multiple NICs are on the same subnet.

5. You have to extend your Windows Server 2016 SDN configuration, and you want to add a virtual gateway for a tenant. What components do you have to verify before you can add a virtual gateway JSON object and add it to the Windows Server 2016 Network Controller? (Choose three.)

    a. GatewayPool

    b. VirtualNetwork

    c. Logical network

    d. VirtualSubnet

    e. Network Proxy

    f. Private Cloud plug-in

## CHAPTER 15

Final Preparation

The first 14 chapters of this book cover the technologies, protocols, design concepts, and considerations required to be prepared to pass the Microsoft Certified Solutions Associate (MCSA) Networking with Windows Server 2016 70-741 exam. Although these chapters supply detailed information, most people need more preparation than just reading the covered material. This chapter details a set of tools and a study plan to help you complete your exam preparation.

This short chapter has two main sections. The first section lists the exam preparation tools that you might find useful at this point in the study process. The second section provides a suggested study plan now that you have covered all the necessary material in the book.

> **NOTE** Appendix B, "Memory Tables," and Appendix C, "Memory Tables Answer Key," are available as soft-copy appendixes on the website for this book. You can access it by going to www.pearsonITcertification.com/register, registering your book, and entering this book's ISBN, 9780789757043.

Tools for Final Preparation

This section lists some information about the available tools and how to access them.

Pearson Test Prep Practice Test Software and Questions on the Website

Register this book to get access to the Pearson IT Certification test engine (software that displays and grades a set of exam-realistic multiple-choice questions). Using the Pearson Test Prep practice test software, you can either study by going through the questions in study mode or take a simulated (timed) 70-741 exam.

The Pearson Test Prep practice test software comes with two full practice exams, available either online or as an offline Windows application. To access the practice exams that were developed with this book, see the instructions in the card inserted in the sleeve at the back of the book. This card includes a unique access code that enables you to activate your exams using the Pearson Test Prep software.

Accessing the Pearson Test Prep Software Online

The online version of this software works on any device that has a browser and connectivity to the Internet, including desktop machines, tablets, and smartphones. To start using your practice exams online, simply follow these steps:

Step 1.   Go to http://www.PearsonTestPrep.com.

Step 2.   Select **Pearson IT Certification** as your product group.

Step 3.   Enter your email and password for your account. If you don't have an account on PearsonITCertification.com or CiscoPress.com, you need to establish one by going to PearsonITCertification.com/join.

Step 4.   On the My Products tab, click the **Activate New Product** button.

Step 5.   Enter the access code printed on the insert card in the back of your book to activate your product.

Step 6.   The product now is listed in your My Products page. Click the **Exams** button to launch the exam settings screen and start your exam.

Accessing the Pearson Test Prep Software Offline

If you want to study offline, you can download and install the Windows version of the Pearson Test Prep software. The book's companion website has a download link for this software, or you can just enter this link in your browser:

http://www.pearsonitcertification.com/content/downloads/pcpt/engine.zip

To access the book's companion website and the software, simply follow these steps:

Step 1.   Register your book by going to PearsonITCertification.com/register and entering the ISBN, 9780789757043.

Step 2.   Respond to the challenge questions.

Step 3.   Go to your account page and select the **Registered Products** tab.

Step 4.   Click the **Access Bonus Content** link under the product listing.

Step 5.   Click the **Install Pearson Test Prep Desktop Version** link on the Practice Exams section of the page to download the software.

Step 6. When the software finishes downloading, unzip all the files on your computer.

Step 7. Double-click the application file to start the installation, and follow the on-screen instructions to complete the registration.

Step 8. When the installation is complete, launch the application and click the **Activate Exam** button on the My Products tab.

Step 9. Click the **Activate a Product** button in the Activate Product Wizard.

Step 10. Enter the unique access code found on the card in the sleeve at the back of your book and click the **Activate** button.

Step 11. Click **Next**, and then click **Finish** to download the exam data to your application.

Step 12. You can now start using the practice exams. Select the product and click the **Open Exam** button to open the exam settings screen.

Note that the offline and online versions sync, so exams and grade results recorded on one version are available to you on the other as well.

Customizing Your Exams

At the exam settings screen, you can choose to take exams in one of three modes:

- Study Mode
- Practice Exam Mode
- Flash Card Mode

Study Mode enables you to fully customize your exam and review answers as you are taking it. This is the mode you want to use first, to assess your knowledge and identify information gaps. Practice Exam Mode locks certain customization options, to present a realistic exam experience. Use this mode when you are testing your exam readiness. Flash Card Mode strips out the answers and presents you with only the question stem. This mode is great for late-stage preparation when you really want to challenge yourself without the benefit of seeing multiple-choice options. Flash Card Mode does not provide the detailed score reports that the other two modes do, so do not use it if you are trying to identify your knowledge gaps.

In addition to choosing your mode, you can select the source of your questions. You can opt to take exams that cover all the chapters, or you can narrow your view to just a single chapter or the chapters that make up specific parts in the book. By default, exams cover material in all chapters. If you want to narrow your focus to individual chapters, simply deselect all the chapters and then, in the Objectives area, select only the ones you want.

You can also select your desired exam banks. Each exam bank comes with a full exam of questions that cover topics in every chapter. In addition, the two exams printed in the book are available, along with two additional exams of unique questions. You can have the test engine serve up exams from all four banks or from just one bank by selecting your desired banks in the exam bank area.

You can make several other customizations to your exam at the exam settings screen, including the time of the exam, the number of questions served up, whether to randomize questions and answers, whether to show the number of correct answers for multiple answer questions, and whether to serve up only specific types of questions. You can also create custom test banks by selecting only questions that you have marked or questions on which you have added notes.

Updating Your Exams

If you are using the online version of the Pearson Test Prep software, you should always have access to the latest version of the software and the exam data. If you are using the Windows desktop version, every time you launch the software, it checks for updates to your exam data and automatically downloads any changes that were made since the last time you used the software. This requires a connection to the Internet at the time you launch the software.

For multiple reasons, exam data might not fully download when you activate your exam. If you find that figures or exhibits are missing, you might need to manually update your exams.

To update an exam that you have already activated and downloaded, simply select the **Tools** tab and click the **Update Products** button. This is an issue only with the desktop Windows application.

If you want to check for updates to the Pearson Test Prep exam engine software, Windows desktop version, simply select the **Tools** tab and click the **Update Application** button. This ensures that you are running the latest version of the software engine.

Premium Edition

In addition to the free practice exam on the website, you can purchase additional exams with expanded functionality directly from Pearson IT Certification. The Premium Edition of this book contains an additional two full practice exams and an eBook (in both PDF and ePub format). The Premium Edition title also points you to the specific part of the eBook that relates to each question.

Because you have purchased the print version of this title, you can purchase the Premium Edition at a deep discount. Look for a coupon code in the book sleeve that contains a one-time-use code and instructions for where you can purchase the Premium Edition.

To view the Premium Edition product page, go to www.informit.com/title/9780789757043.

Memory Tables

As with most Cert Guides from Pearson, this book purposely organizes information into tables and lists for easier study and review. Rereading these tables before the exam can be useful. However, it is easy to skim over the tables without paying attention to every detail, especially when you remember having seen the table's contents when you read the chapter.

This book's Appendixes B and C give you another review tool for tables. Appendix B lists partially completed versions of many of the tables from the book. You can open Appendix B (a PDF is available on the book website after you register), print it, and then attempt to complete the tables. This strategy exercises the memory connectors in your brain and makes you think about the information as you fill out the tables, forcing a little more contemplation about the facts.

Appendix C, also a PDF located on the book website, lists the completed tables so you can check yourself. You can also just refer to the tables printed in this book.

End-of-Chapter Review Tools

Chapters 1–14 have several useful features in the "Exam Preparation Tasks" section at the end of the chapter. You might have already worked through these in each chapter. Looking over the questions and exercises again can be useful as you make your final preparations for the exam.

Suggested Plan for Final Review/Study

This section lists a suggested study plan to implement when you finish reading Chapter 14. You can follow the entire plan or just take suggestions from it.

The plan involves four steps:

Step 1. **Review key topics and "Do I Know This Already?" (DIKTA) quiz questions.** You can use the table that lists the key topics in each chapter or just flip through the pages looking for key topics. Reviewing the DIKTA questions from the beginning of the chapter can also be helpful for review.

Step 2. **Complete the memory tables.** Open Appendix B from the book's website and either print the entire appendix or print only the tables by major part. Then complete the tables.

Step 3. **Review the "End-of-Chapter Review Questions" sections.** Complete the questions at the end of each chapter to identify areas where you need more study.

Step 4. **Use the Pearson Test Prep practice test software.** The Pearson Test Prep practice test software helps you study by using a bank of unique exam-realistic questions that are available only with this book.

Summary

The tools and suggestions in this chapter were designed with one goal in mind: to help you develop the skills required to pass the MCSA 70-741 exam. From the beginning, this book was put together not just to give you the facts, but also to help you learn how to *apply* the facts. Regardless of your experience level leading up to the exam, we hope that the structure of this book and its broad range of preparation tools help you pass with ease.

Answers to the "Do I Know This Already?" Quizzes and End-of-Chapter Review Questions

Chapter 1

Do I Know This Already? Quiz

1. B, D. Domain controller SRV records are typically registered automatically if you install a new domain controller. DCs register the following SRV records automatically: _ldap, _kerberos, _gc, and _kpasswd. If you have to set up Skype for Business or other services, you might have to add SRV records manually. SRV records can be created manually and automatically. TXT and MX records normally have to be added manually into the zone. (*Exception:* You can write PowerShell scripts to automatically add resource records such as TXT or MX. Records normally are registered automatically through the dynamic update process, but they also can be added manually in the DNS manager console.)

2. B. Round robin is enabled by default on a Windows Server 2016 DNS server. With this setting, you can distribute web requests and network traffic through web servers. If you enable DNSSEC, you get more security. With the Enable Cache Against Pollution setting enabled in the DNS server properties, your DNS server ignores DNS resource records that come from servers that are not authoritative for them, to provide more security. If you enable BIND secondaries, you can use UNIX BIND DNS servers together with Microsoft DNS servers.

3. C. DNS data such as resource records in an Active Directory–integrated DNS zone are stored in the DomainDNSZones or ForestDNSZones Active Directory partition as AD objects and are replicated through the RPC network protocol. By default, this kind of network traffic runs encrypted. If you store resource records in a primary zone and you want to replicate them to a secondary DNS server, the terminology changes from *zone replication* to *zone transfer*. In this scenario, you have to allow zone transfer first, and the zone transfer network traffic between primary and secondary DNS servers is unencrypted. If you use an Active Directory–integrated DNS zone and you want to replicate that zone to a secondary

DNS server, you also first have to enable zone transfer. In this case, zone transfer also produces unencrypted network traffic.

4. C. Here you want to replicate DNS data through Active Directory replication only to a specific DNS server, not to all servers in the domain or all servers in the forest, which are the two base possibilities through DomainDNSZones and ForestDNSZones. You must create a custom application directory partition and define the replication partners individually. In the zone properties of the test.com zone, you must change the replication scope to the name of the custom application directory partition.

5. A, B. You want to back up only the DNS data from the zone; you do not want to back up the complete Active Directory, including DNS zone data. Therefore, a system state backup is not the right choice; you would back up too much. With the **Export-Csv** PowerShell cmdlet, you cannot back up the DNS zone. With the **dnscmd.exe** tool, you can back up (export) zone data into a bak-file. With the PowerShell command **Export-DnsServerZone**, you also can back up DNS data from the zone.

6. C. In the registry database of a DNS server, normally the ISATAP entry is part of the Global Query Block List. Although you can add an ISATAP host resource record manually to the zone, this still is blocked and clients cannot use it until you remove the ISATAP entry from the registry.

7. B. If conditional forwarders are defined for a given domain, they are used instead of server-level forwarders.

8. B. You can ignore the note because a DNS delegation still was created with the setup of DNS3. You do not have to create a DNS delegation again. Canceling the wizard and trying to set up DNS4 as an additional domain controller for usa.pearson.com with PowerShell are not necessary because that requires too much administrative effort. The **Install-ADDSDomainController** PowerShell cmdlet has a parameter named **CreateDNSDelegation**.

   In this case, you can set that parameter to a value of *$false*. Restarting DNS2 and repeating all steps in the Active Directory Installation Wizard is not a solution because it is not a network connectivity problem from DNS4 to DNS3. When you install an additional domain controller such as DNS4, you must have network connectivity to the forest root domain controller. Verifying network connectivity to the forest root domain controllers is not a mistake, but repeating all steps in the Active Directory Installation Wizard is not required and takes too much effort.

9. B. By default, the Windows Server 2016 DNS server opens a pool of 5000 UDP sockets: 2500 for IPv4 and 2500 for IPv6. The default socket pool size value is 2500.

10. A, C. Cache locking is configured as a percent value. For example, if the cache locking value is set to 50, the DNS server will not overwrite a cached entry for half the duration of the TTL. By default, the cache locking percent value is 100. This means that cached entries are not overwritten for the entire duration of the TTL. A low cache locking value increases the chance of a successful cache poisoning attack. Network traffic might be directed to a malicious site. After you have configured the new value for cache locking, you have to restart the DNS service. Clearing the DNS server cache is not necessary.

11. B. When you enable debug logging, you get information about the DNS request types and DNS query packet content. Debug logging is disabled by default on a Window Server 2016 DNS server. As in earlier versions, a Windows Server 2016 DNS server maintains a DNS server log. You can view the DNS server events in the Event Viewer in the Applications and Service Logs folder. It records common events such as Start/Stop DNS Service, Change DNS Configuration Settings, background loading, and zone signing events. You do not have to enable analytic event logging to get the requested information. DNS server analytic events enable you to track activity on the DNS server. An analytic event gets logged every time the server sends or receives DNS information. You can view Windows Server 2016 DNS analytic and debug logs in the Event Viewer. DNS monitoring does not deliver DNS request types and query packet contents.

12. B. Paul must become a member of the security group DNSAdmins because he needs administrative permissions to manage only the DNS server. If you add him to the Domain Admins security group, he gets too-broad permissions. If you add him to the Administrators security group, he gets local administrator permissions. If you add him to the DNSUpdateProxy security group, he cannot manage the DNS server.

End-of-Chapter Review Questions

1. A, C, E. You can protect your Windows Server 2016 DNS server against DNS amplification attacks with the new Response Rate Limiting (RRL) feature. This feature is disabled by default on a Windows Server 2016 DNS server.

With the PowerShell cmdlet **Set-DnsServerResponse RateLimiting**, you can enable RRL on a Windows Server 2016 DNS server. DNS servers usually use the global query block list to block name resolution to an ISATAP router, and the name ISATAP cannot be resolved to the IP address of the ISATAP router. For test purposes, you might want to remove the ISATAP entry from the DNS global query block list so that the DNS server can use the added hostname resource record named ISATAP to deliver the IP address of the ISATAP router to DNS clients.

You can add or remove entries in the DNS global query block list with the PowerShell cmdlet **Set-DnsServerGlobalQueryBlocklist** or using the **dnscmd.exe** tool or registry editing tools.

With Windows Server 2016, you can use DNS server zone transfer policies to specify whether to deny or ignore a zone transfer, based on criteria such as subnet or domain names.

With the PowerShell cmdlet **Set-DnsServerZone TransferPolicy**, you can update a zone transfer policy on a DNS server, to redefine the conditions of that zone transfer policy.

With the PowerShell cmdlet **Set-DnsServerRecursion Scope**, you can modify recursion scopes.

With the PowerShell cmdlet **Set-DnsServerCache**, you can modify the cache settings for a DNS server, such as the maximum cache size or the cache locking percent value. With the PowerShell cmdlet **Set-DnsGlobalNamesZone**, you can change the configuration settings for a GlobalNames zone.

2. B, D. With the PowerShell cmdlets **Set-DnsServerResponseRateLimiting** or **Set-DnsServerRRL**, you first have to enable the new Windows Server 2016 Response Rate Limiting (RRL) feature to protect against DDoS attacks. To exclude App1 from RRL and to ensure that RRL has no negative impact on App1 name resolution, add App1 to the RRL exception list using **Add-DnsServerResponseRateLimitExceptionList**.

    With the PowerShell cmdlet **Set-DnsServerDnsSec ZoneSetting**, you can configure DNSSEC settings for a zone on a DNS server.

    With the PowerShell cmdlet **Set-DnsServerEDns**, you can configure Extended DNS (EDNS) configuration settings, such as the EDNS information caching timeout. EDNS integrates some DNS protocol extensions concerning DNS data transport of UDP network packets.

    With the PowerShell cmdlet **Add-DnsServer SigningKey**, you can add a key signing key (KSK) or zone signing key (ZSK) to a signed zone.

3. B. On a Windows Server 2016 DNS server, you can enable both analytical and audit logging with the **tracelog.exe** tool. This can be done through the following command: **tracelog.exe -start Dns -guid #{EB79061A-A566-4698-9119-3ED2807060E7} -level 5 -matchanykw 0xFFFFFFFF -f C:\analytic_audit.etl**.

    With the **Set-DnsServerDiagnostics** PowerShell cmdlet, you can set DNS server debugging and logging parameters, and you can enable debug logging instead of analytical logging.

With the PowerShell cmdlet **Set-DnsServerSetting**, you can easily import the DNS server settings from one DNS server to the other. You can get the DNS server settings from DNS1 with the following command: **Get-DnsServerSetting -computername DNS1 -all | Export-Clixml C:\DNS1settings.xml, $a = Import-Clixml C:\ DNS1settings.xml**. After that, you can import the DNS server settings from DNS1 to DNS2 with the command **Set-DnsServerSetting -computername DNS2 $a**.

The **Wusa.exe** tool is the Windows Update Standalone Installer that can be used to install update packages.

4. A. On a Windows Server 2016 Nano Server, you can configure some basic local settings through the Nano Server Recovery Console.

   You must enable the DHCP client on the Nano Server using the F4 key so that the Nano Server can obtain IP address configuration from the DHCP server. You do not have to reconfigure the NAP server on NAP1 because Windows Server 2016 DHCP server no longer supports DHCP NAP. You do not have to remove and re-create the DHCP reservation on the DHCP server because the other reservations for N01, N02, and N03 have worked fine. If you used the wrong MAC address for the reservation of N04 and you change the reservation for N04 to the correct MAC address, the Nano Server N04 still won't get an IP address if the DHCP client is not enabled on its network interface.

   You do not have to disable a firewall rule on the Nano Server N04 to get an IP address from the DHCP server.

5. B. Under the Advanced tab of the DNS server setting, you have the option Disable Recursion. Normally, this setting is not enabled on a DNS server. If you enable it, this DNS server cannot forward to any other DNS server independently if forwarding is configured through forwarders or conditional forwarders. Recursion (forwarding) is completely disabled in this case. That is the cause of the problem.

   With the Store This Conditional Forwarder in Active Directory setting, you can save the forwarder in the Active Directory database, and the forwarder will be replicated automatically through AD replication to other DNS servers.

   If recursion still is disabled, this will not solve the problem on this DNS server. The Use Root Hints If No Forwarders Are Available setting is a forwarder setting, not a conditional forwarder setting. In this question, a conditional forwarder was configured instead of a forwarder. Netmask ordering typically is enabled on a DNS server. This has nothing to do with the forwarding possibility on a DNS server, so it is not the correct answer.

6. B. You get maximum performance with a Windows Server 2016 Nano Server. Using a Server Core is also an option, to get faster performance than with GUI-based Windows Server 2016; however, Nano Server is smaller than a Server Core, so it is the smallest kind of DNS server you can use with Windows Server 2016.

You can deploy a new Windows Server 2016 Nano Server with DNS server through the **New-NanoServer Image** PowerShell cmdlet. A Nano Server offers up to 93 percent smaller VHD size, 92 percent fewer critical patches, and 80 percent fewer reboots. With the **Install-WindowsFeature** PowerShell cmdlet, you also can install the DNS server role; however, this question asks for a completely new DNS server, which means you also have to build the virtual hard disk for the DNS server. The **Add-WindowsFeature** PowerShell cmdlet does the same thing as the **Install-WindowsFeature** cmdlet. The **New-Container** PowerShell cmdlet creates a container from an existing container image. You cannot install a DNS server into a docker-based container.

7. C. When you want to create a DNS delegation, you can do that during the promotion process for a new domain controller of a new child domain. When you install the first domain controller of a new child domain in the Active Directory Installation Configuration Wizard in the DNS Options page, the option Create DNS Delegation is automatically selected and grayed out. The DNS delegation on a forest root DNS server automatically is created and a forwarder from the child DNS server to the forest root DNS server also is created.

You do not have to use the PowerShell cmdlet **Add-DnsServerForwarder** to add a forwarder on the child domain DNS server; additionally, you cannot create a DNS delegation manually with this command, so it is not the correct answer.

With the PowerShell cmdlet **Install-ADDSForest**, you can build a new forest with the installation of the forest root domain controller. You cannot create child domains with that PowerShell cmdlet.

Using the PowerShell cmdlet **Install-ADDSDomainController**, you cannot install a new first child domain controller with a delegated DNS server; instead, you can add more domain controllers to existing domains.

8. C. In the Recovery Console of a Windows Server 2016 Nano Server, you cannot define or configure the DNS server; Nano Server must use its network interface. Instead, you can do this with the PowerShell cmdlet **Set-DnsClientServerAddress**. You can define the computer name, gateway address, and IPv6 address of the Nano Server in the Nano Server Recovery Console.

Chapter 2

Do I Know This Already? Quiz

1. A, E. A stub zone hosts only the SOA record, NS record, and A record of authoritative DNS servers of a zone. In a stub zone, you have listed master DNS servers from a zone, and you can find the IP addresses of those master servers. You need this information to know about these DNS servers so that you can configure forwarding to them. Client resource records and records from other servers, such as mail servers and file servers, are not transferred to a stub zone.

2. A. With a file-based DNS zone, you cannot use the secure dynamic update feature. This is not correct. All other answers are correct.

3. D. You simply can copy the zone file from the DNS server of the product-ive domain to the DNS server of the future domain and import that file. You can select the zone file in DNS manager only if you copy it to the %systemroot%\system32\dns folder of that DNS server. When you create a forest trust between the two forests, you still cannot replicate Active Directory data between the forests. No option exists for replicating this through dif-ferent forests. When you create a stub zone on the DNS server of the future domain, you lose all DNS records except SOA, NS, and A records of DNS servers. All resource records of all other servers and clients are not transferred to a stub zone. When you convert the stub zone to a primary zone, you do not have all the DNS data of pearson.com as in the productive domain. When you transfer the DNS data of pearson.com to a secondary DNS server, this server is not authoritative for the zone; instead, the zone in the future domain then is read only and DNS data is not saved in Active Directory.

4. B. You can secure the zone transfer from BIND1 to SEC1 through IPsec. You cannot use the Transaction Signature (TSIG) network protocol and TSIS resource records for that because Microsoft DNS servers do not support TSIG; instead, they use GSS-TSIG. It is not possible to configure Windows Servers running Microsoft DNS service to perform zone transfers from servers running BIND DNS configured as the master with TSIG protection. You also cannot use the HMAC-MD5 algorithm because Windows Server 2016 does not support this.

5. C. You should create an AD-integrated stub zone on DNS servers in usa.pearson.com because all DNS server records (NS records) in usa.pearsonucertify.com will be transferred from the DNS servers (master) in usa.pearsonucertify.com to the stub zone DNS server in usa.pearson.com.

You must select the stub zone type for the usa.pearson.com zone because the NS and A records of the DNS servers in usa.pearsonucertify.com are interesting only for you to know, not for clients or other servers. When you know the IP addresses of the new DNS servers in the zone usa.pearsonucertify.com through the stub zone, you can implement conditional forwarding on the DNS servers of usa.pearson.com to the new DNS servers of usa.pearsonucertify.com. When you create a conditional forwarder on a DNS server in usa.pearson.com, you can do that only if you know about the IP address of the DNS servers you want to forward.

You must get that IP address automatically through the use of a stub zone. You also can use a file-based stub zone, but this is not the best solution; you get more security and automatic replication of the stub zone to the other AD-integrated DNS server in the same domain only if you integrate the stub zone into Active Directory. Creating a secondary zone also will deliver NS and A records of the DNS server from usa.pearsonucertify.com, but it will do so for all other resource records as well (clients and other servers); this is not necessary because you have to know only about DNS servers.

6. A, B. You can use the **dnscmd** command-line utility and the **Set-DnsServerGlobalNameZone** PowerShell cmdlet to enable GlobalNames support.

7. D. Since Windows Server 2016, a DNS server supports the standards NSEC3 and RSA/SHA-2.

8. A. With Windows Server 2016, you have enhanced zone-level statistics possibilities. You can use **ZoneQueryStatistics** to get information about DNSKEY records on your DNS server. You cannot use **ZoneUpdateStatistics** because that gives you information about dynamic update behaviors. You cannot use **ZoneTransferStatistics** because that gives you information about zone transfer between master and secondary DNS servers. You cannot use **RRLStatistics** because that gives you information about Response Rate Limiting (RRL) behaviors, which is a new feature of Windows Server 2016.

9. C. DNS records added dynamically are time stamped. Static records that you enter manually have a time stamp value of 0; therefore, they will not be affected by aging and will not be scavenged out of the database. Instead, you must remove them manually. An exception to the exception arises if you use the new Windows Server 2016 PowerShell cmdlets, such as **Add-DnsServerResourceRecordPtr** or **Add-DNSServerResourceRecordA**. These cmdlets have a parameter named **AgeRecord**. Using this parameter, the DNS server can use a time stamp for the record that these cmdlets add.

10. C. You can use TLSA records. With Windows Server 2016 and DNSSEC, a
new protocol called DANE (DNS-Based Authentication of Named Entities)
enables you to securely specify exactly which TLS/SSL certificate an application or service should use to connect to your site. You can use TLSA records
in four ways:

1) to specify the CA that will provide RLS certificates for the domain, 2) to
specify the exact TLS certificate that should be used, 3) to specify the trust
anchor to be used for validating the TLS certificate for the domain, and 4)
to specify the exact TLS certificate that should be used for the domain, but
without needing the TLS certificate to be signed by a valid CA (for self-signed
certificates).

You cannot use TSIG, RRSIG, or DNSKEY resource records to verify the
CA, certificate, or trust anchor.

11. D. You can stop the analytical event tracing on the DNS server with the
tracelog -stop DNS command. You cannot stop analytical event tracing on
the DNS server with the **Set-DnsServer Diagnostics -EnableLogging-
ForServerStartStopEvent $true** PowerShell command because that
gives you log start and stop events of the DNS server. You also cannot use
Set-DnsServer Diagnostics -DebugLogging 0x10000 to stop analytical
event tracing on the DNS server because that enables DNS logging for sent
packages. You cannot use the PowerShell cmdlet **Stop-PefTraceSession**
because that stops a specified trace session of the Message Analyzer utility.

End-of-Chapter Review Questions

1. B. Since Windows Server 2016, you can use and add TLSA resource records
or other unknown resource records. TLSA resources are needed for DANE
configuration. You can use the DANE protocol to secure your SSL/TLS certificates via DNSSEC.

You can easily generate TLSA resource records through the TLSA online
generator: https://www.huque.com/bin/gen_tlsa.

If you change the DNS zone to an AD-integrated zone with forest replication on a Windows Server 2012 R2 DNS server, this server does not support
TLSA resource records. If you add another Windows Server 2016 DNS server
as the secondary, you still cannot use TLSA resource records because a secondary zone is read-only and you cannot add any records manually there. If
you enable BIND secondaries to use UNIX DNS servers as secondaries, you
still have no DNS server where you can add TLSA resource records.

2. B. With the PowerShell command **Start-DnsServerZoneTransfer**, you can immediately start the DNS zone transfer process between the DNS server, DNS1, and the secondary DNS server, DNS2. This is the fastest solution. Converting the zone eu.pearson.com to an AD-integrated zone is not necessary because it is still saved in Active Directory on DNS1. You can change the zone on DNS2 from a secondary zone to an AD-integrated zone, but then you have AD replication of the DNS zone data and no zone transfer, which this question requires. For security reasons, using two DNS servers is recommended with an AD-integrated zone. With the **Repadmin /replicate DNS2 DNS1 DC=eu,DC=pearson,DC=com** command, you force the AD replication of the domain partition eu.pearson.com. If you add DNS2 to the notify list on DNS1, this reduces the zone transfer time for the zone transfer from DNS1 to DNS2 in the case of changes or new resource records on the zone, but it does not immediately force the zone transfer.

3. D. With the **Add-DnsServerResourceRecord** PowerShell cmdlet, you cannot change the TTL value of an existing resource record. With that PowerShell cmdlet, you can add a new resource record and define a new TTL for that record. For example: **Add-DnsServer ResourceRecord -ZoneName "Contoso.com" -A -Name "SRV1" -Allow UpdateAny -IPv4Address "10.10.1.12 -TimeToLive 04:00:00 -AgeRecord**.

4. A, D. Download and install the Windows Driver Kit (WDK) to get the **tracelog.exe** command-line utility. You can see **tracelog.exe** included when you install the WDK, Visual Studio, and the Windows SDK for desktop apps. With **tracelog.exe**, you can enable or disable DNS analytical logging. Debug logging is another option on the DNS server, but this is not the analytical logging feature. With the **Test-DnsServer** PowerShell cmdlet, you can run some tests on the DNS server, but this is not the DNS analytical feature. With **nslookup** and the **-d2** parameter, you can test zone transfers, security options, and MX record resolution. With the **-d2** parameter, you can get detailed debugging information through the analytical DNS logging feature.

Chapter 3

Do I Know This Already? Quiz

1. B. DHCP Policies are a possible cause because you can configure DHCP scope options through a DHCP Policy based on different criteria. It seems that a DHCP Policy is responsible for delivering other options to some clients. The DHCP failover feature is not the possible cause here because you have only a single DHCP server. DNS Policy also is no cause of this because you

cannot deliver DHCP options through DNA Policies. With DNSSEC, you sign zones; this has nothing to do with which DHCP options a DHCP client gets.

2. C. You can use the Name Protection feature of the DHCP server to protect against name squatting attacks. Such conflicts happen if one client registers a name with DNS but another client is already using that name. With DHCP server policies (new Windows Server 2012 feature), you can create policies that deliver specific IP address and option information to clients based on a set of conditions. This enables you to have different types of IP devices receive addresses and other options from a subset of IP addresses in the scope range; it does not protect against such name squatting conflicts. With DNS server policies (new Windows Server 2016 feature), you can manipulate how a DNS server handles queries based on different factors.

As an example, you might create a DNS Policy to respond to queries asking for the IP address of a web server to respond with a different IP address based on the closest datacenter to the client. This differs from netmask reordering because the client does not have the same local subnet address of the web server, but the web server is closer than others from the client's perspective. DNSSEC enables a DNS zone and all records in the zone to be signed cryptographically so that client computers can validate the DNS response.

DNS is often subject to various attacks, such as spoofing and cache tampering. DNSSEC helps protect against these threats.

3. A. You configure the DNS server's IP address for the network interface of a DNS client through the **Set-DnsClientServerAddress** PowerShell cmdlet.

4. B. With the **Sync-DnsServerZone** PowerShell cmdlet, you synchronize DNS zone data and root hint data for a zone to the persistent storage. With the **Start-DnsServerZoneTransfer** PowerShell cmdlet, you start a zone transfer for a secondary DNS zone from master servers.

With the **Add-DnsServerZoneTransferPolicy** PowerShell cmdlet, you add a zone transfer policy to a DNS server.

With the **Set-DnsServerZoneTransferPolicy** PowerShell cmdlet, you update a zone transfer policy on a DNS server.

5. A, D, E, F. You should verify the DHCP Policies as a possible cause that clients from the Paris subnet are getting the wrong DNS server for name resolution through DHCP options configured through DHCP Policy. You also should verify the DNS server zone scope settings on the DNS server because name resolution could be restricted through a DNS Policy based on subnet criteria. You also have to verify the DNS server client subnet settings on a

DNS server because the subnet Paris might have been accidentally added to a DNS server policy zone scope.

In addition, you should verify the DNS server recursion policy settings because selective recursion might be enabled, preventing clients from the subnet Paris from being forwarded to other DNS servers responsible for pearsonucertify.com. You do not have to verify DNS server options. You also do not have to verify DNS server zone transfer policies because you use them to manage which zones can be transferred between DNS servers.

6. B. You use the **Get-NetRoute** PowerShell cmdlet to list the routing table of the client. There you can see the IP address of the client-side tunnel endpoint of the Point-to-Site tunnel to Azure. You cannot use the PowerShell cmdlet **Get-AzureVNetGateway** because it shows you the configuration settings of the VPN gateway on Azure. You also first must install the Azure PowerShell module to make that command possible on the client. You cannot use the **Get-NetIPInterface** PowerShell cmdlet because it shows you only the interface settings, not the routing table. You cannot use the PowerShell cmdlet **Get-VpnConnection** because it also does not display the routing table.

7. D. DirectAccess clients on the Internet use the preconfigured NRPT settings to evaluate the DNS servers for name resolution to access internal resources. The DHCP server at the airport delivers an IP address, gateway, and DNS server so that public name resolution can happen.

The Name Resolution Policy Table (NRPT) delivers the DNS servers for the company name resolution. The entries in the NRPT are delivered through DirectAccess GPOs, which are created as part of the setup for the Direct-Access server. The DHCP server of the company normally is not responsible for delivering any IP settings for a DirectAccess client on the Internet.

8. B, C, D. You can use the **Set-DnsServerRecursionScope** PowerShell cmdlet to deactivate recursion for all clients through the existing default recursion scope. You must use the **Add-DnsServerRecursionScope** PowerShell cmdlet to add a scope for internal clients to allow recursion.

You can use the **Add-DnsServerQueryResolutionPolicy** PowerShell cmdlet to create the DNS server policy to configure selective recursion with different settings for external and internal clients.

You would not use the PowerShell cmdlet **Add-DnsServer ResourceRecord** here because it is necessary if you create DNS Policy zones and want to add records to those zones.

You would not use the **Add-DnsServerClientSubnet** PowerShell cmdlet because you do not want to configure recursion policy for a special subnet.

End-of-Chapter Review Questions

1. C. You should use **Add-DnsServerQuery ResolutionPolicy -Name MalwarePolicy -Action IGNORE -ClientSubnet 'EQ, CHSubnet1' -Disable $false** because this new DNS server policy blocks all name resolution traffic from subnet CHSubnet1. The existing policy CHPolicy allows name resolution, but the blocking policy is more powerful than this.

    The parameter action has the value **IGNORE**, which means to not respond.

    You should not use **Add-DnsServerQuery ResolutionPolicy -Name MalwarePolicy -Action DENY -ClientSubnet 'EQ, CHSubnet1' -Disable $false** because the parameter **Action** with a value of *DENY* means that it delivers a response with **SERV-FAIL**.

    You should not use **Add-DnsServerQuery ResolutionPolicy -Name MalwarePolicy -Action DENY -ClientSubnet 'EQ,NYSubnet2' -Disable $false** because the parameter **Action** with a value of **DENY** means that it delivers a response with **SERV-FAIL**.

    You should not use **Set-DnsServerQuery ResolutionPolicy -Name NYPolicy -Action IGNORE -ClientSubnet 'EQ, NYSubnet2' -Disable $true** because the subnet 192.168.6.0/24 is not a member of the zone scope NYScope. If the subnet is not part of the zone scope and DNS server policy, you cannot block name resolution traffic by disabling NYPolicy.

2. A. You should use the command **Add-DnsServerClientSubnet -Name "AllowedNET" -IPv4Subnet 172.16.0.0/16 -PassThru**. If you do not define the subnet behind the subnet name AllowedNET before you add the DNS server query resolution policy, it cannot identify the subnet.

    With the PowerShell cmdlet **Remove-DnsServerClientSubnet**, you remove an existing subnet. With the PowerShell cmdlet **Add-DnsServerResourceRecord**, you add a DNS resource record to a DNS server zone scope.

    With the PowerShell cmdlet **Add-DnsServerZoneScope**, you add a DNS server zone scope.

3. B. You should use the PowerShell command **Add-DnsServerZoneTransfer Policy -Name "IntTransfer" -Action IGNORE -ServerInterfaceIP "ne,10.0.0.50" -PassThru -ZoneName "pearson.com"** because this denies zone transfer traffic to DNS3.

    You do not have to use **Add-DnsServerZoneTransferPolicy -Name "IntTransfer" -Action ALLOW -ServerInterfaceIP "ne,10.0.0.49" -PassThru -ZoneName "pearson.com"** or **Add-DnsServer**

ZoneTransferPolicy -Name "IntTransfer" -Action ALLOW -ServerInterfaceIP "ne,10.0.0.51" -PassThru -ZoneName "pearson.com" because you do not have to allow DNS2 and DNS3 again.

With the PowerShell command **Add-DnsServerZoneTransferPolicy -Name "IntTransfer" -Action IGNORE -ServerInterfaceIP "ne,10.0.0.10" -PassThru -ZoneName "pearson.com"**, you deny any zone transfer traffic to DNS1; this is wrong because DNS1 is the master DNS, not the secondary DNS server.

Chapter 4

Do I Know This Already? Quiz

1. **B.** In versions before Windows Server 2016, it was possible to enable or disable DNSSEC validation on the Advanced tab of the DNS server. In Windows Server 2016 DNS server, this setting is no longer possible. Instead, you can use PowerShell to enable or disable DNSSEC validation. You can do this with the following PowerShell command: **(Get-DnsServer).DNS Setting. EnableDnsSec**. With the PowerShell cmdlet **Get-DnsServerDnsSecZoneSetting**, you can verify DNSSEC zone settings. With the **dnscmd.exe** command, you also can enable DNSSEC validation on a Windows Server 2016 DNS server, but you must use 1 instead of 2 for the **EnableDNSSEC** parameter.

2. **B.** If the key master DC1 is offline and cannot be recovered, it is still possible to move the role to another server. This is known as seizing. When you want to seize the key master role, DC2 must have access to the zone's existing private key data. This is the case if the keys are stored in AD (only for AD-integrated zones) or another shared location, such as a certificate or hardware security module (HSM).

    If the zone's private key data is not available, the role can still be seized, but new keys must be generated and the zone must be re-signed with them. Any distributed trust anchors for the zone must then be redistributed. Because you have no hardware solution (HSM module) in this scenario, you cannot get the key data from there. The zone is a file-based zone. When an AD-integrated zone is signed with DNSSEC, the private keys are also replicated to all DNS servers running DCs, with one exception: Private keys are not replicated to an RODC. Replication is not done to DC3, then, because it is an RODC. This is the reason you cannot get key data from Active Directory; you can get key data only from a certificate in this case.

3.   A. You cannot use the DNSSEC Zone Signing Wizard to create DS records with that wizard. Only DNSKEY records can be automatically created through the wizard.

After you create them, you can view them in the DNS Manager in the Trust-Points folder. You can use the DS record set (DSSET), a file in the C:\ windows\system32\dns folder, to import DS records. You can import DS records from that file with the following PowerShell command for a zone named pearson.com: **Import-DnsServerResourceRecordDS -ZoneName pearson.com -DSSetFile "c:\windows\system32\dns\dsset-pearson.com**. You also manually can add DS records with the DNS Manager or directly through PowerShell.

4.   B. If trust anchors are not removed when a zone is unsigned, DNS servers will continue to attempt validation of DNS responses for the zone. However, this validation will fail and, therefore, DNS resolution for the zone will fail. When you unsign the zone, all RRSIG records automatically are removed from the zone if you use the DNSSEC Zone Signing Wizard for that. The NRPT settings do not have to be reconfigured because the DNSSEC clients still have to be enabled for DNSSEC to use it with other DNSSEC-enabled DNS servers or zones. The RRset is a set of DNSSEC records and is removed automatically through the unsigning process.

5.   B. You can force the rollover with the PowerShell cmdlet **Step-DnsServerSigningKey Rollover**. For example, you can get the keys for the signed zone sec.pearson.com with the following PowerShell cmdlet: **Get-DnsServerSigningKey -ZoneName "sec.pearson.com"**. After that, you can force the KSK rollover that is waiting for a parent DS update on sec.pearson.com with the following PowerShell command: **Step-DnsServerSigning KeyRollover -KeyID <ID> -ZoneName "sec.pearson.com" -force**.

With the PowerShell cmdlet **Invoke-DnsServerSigning KeyRollover**, you can initiate a rollover of input keys for the specified DNS zone.

With the PowerShell cmdlet **Enable-DnsServerSigning KeyRollover**, you can enable rollover on the input key.

With the **Grant-HgsKeyProtectorAccess** PowerShell cmdlet, you can grant access to a Host Guardian Service (HGS) for a key protector. The HGS is used to protect Hyper-V shielded virtual machines. This has nothing to do with the question and, therefore, is a wrong answer.

6.   A, D. You use the prepublishing rollover method for the ZSK that makes the new DNSKEY record available before signing. You propagate the key to all client caches, remove the old signatures, and create new ones with the new key. This does not double the size of your zone. It replaces signatures as they expire. You can roll over each zone and ZSK separately. You use the double signing method for KSK because you simultaneously sign the zone with both (old and new) keys. Both signatures are held in the zone until the old public key expires. When the time passes, the old key is removed. This reduces risk and is preferred for the KSK rollover.

7. A, C. On client1, you must update the GPO settings from the Default Domain Policy, which delivers the NRPT settings and makes client1 a DNSSEC-enabled client. After that, you can verify the **DNSSECValidationRequired** value with the **Get-DnsClientNrptPolicy** PowerShell cmdlet. You get the following output:

```
Namespace                             : .sec.pearson.com
QueryPolicy                           :
SecureNameQueryFallback               :
DirectAccessIPSecCARestriction        :
DirectAccess ProxyName                :
DirectAccessDnsServers                :
DirectAccessEnabled                   :
DirectAccessProxyType                 : NoProxy
DirectAccessQueryIPSecEncryption      :
DirectAccessQueryIPSecRequired        : False
NameServers                           :
DNSSECIPSecCARestriction              :
DNSSECQueryIPSecEncryption            :
DnSecQueryIPSecRequired               : False
DNSSECValidationRequired              : True
NameEncoding                          : Utf&WithoutMapping
```

You cannot use the **Resolve-Dnsname** PowerShell cmdlet to verify the **DNSSECValidationRequired** setting. With that you can query a signed zone with DNSSEC validation required, and if a trust anchor is present on DNS1, the query is successful even if validation is required.

8. B. Only one DS trust anchor has to be installed for the parent zone. Delegations establish a chain of authentication for child zones. If all zones in the chain are signed with DNSSEC, resolving DNS servers can have a single DS trust anchor installed, provided that appropriate DS records are available in the parent zone. This way, it is not necessary to install a trust anchor for every zone that a caching DNS server can validate. Build a chain of trust where it is sufficient for the DNS server to have only one DS trust anchor installed for the parent zone.

9. B, C. With **dnscmd** */retrieveroottrustanchor*, you can install the root trust
    anchor. With the PowerShell command **Add-DnsServerTrustAnchor
    -Root**, you also can do so. With the PowerShell command **Import-
    DnsServerTrustAnchor**, you can import a trust anchor through the specified
    DS set file but not the root trust anchor. With **Add-DnsServerTrustAnchor
    -KeyProtocol DNSSEC -CryptoAlgorithm RsaSha256**, you can install
    trust anchors but not the root trust anchor; you also have to know the
    Base64Data value, which is the key data.

10. D, E. NSEC3 records hash the names of existing hosts. A zone that uses
    NSEC3 also has a NSEC3PARAM record. This is necessary for the proper
    functioning of NSEC3.

End-of-Chapter Review Questions

1. B. You cannot change the replication scope or zone type of a signed zone as
    long it is a signed zone. First, you must unsign the zone. Then you can change
    the replication scope of the zone from application directory partition to forest-
    wide replication. After that, you must re-sign the zone. When you create a
    new zone, you can choose to get the DNSSEC parameters for the zone from
    another zone through a file, but then the zone has another name and this is
    not wanted.

2. A. You must use the Key Master tab of the DNSSEC properties of the zone,
    and there you must select Use the Following DNS Server as the Key Master.
    You also must choose DC3 as the new key master. You must do that at DC3.

    In this question, you are sure about the proper functionality of AD replication
    between DC3 in Azure and the on-premises domain controllers because AD
    replication was successfully tested. This also means that DC3 can resolve all
    necessary resource records of the other domain controllers. Thus, it should be
    possible to get all the names of the other domain controllers in the drop-down
    list on the Key Master page.

    You cannot use the **Reset-DnsServerZoneKey MasterRole -SeizeRole**
    PowerShell command because, with the **SeizeRole** parameter, you do not
    perform an online role transfer, in which you can reach the original key mas-
    ter, DC1; instead, you seize the role to DC3, which means that keys must be
    generated, the zone must be re-signed, and trust anchors must be redistrib-
    uted. This is not necessary if the key master is online and reachable, as in this
    scenario.

    You also cannot use the **Reset-DnsServerZone KeyMasterRole -Force**
    PowerShell command because the **Force** parameter does not give you any
    confirmation about the transfer process.

3.   F, I. DLV records are not necessary in a pure Windows environment. They are used together with BIND. BIND also is not necessary in this environment because you have only Windows servers. All other DNSSEC deployment steps are usable.

4.   B. An RODC at a branch site cannot transfer DNS data or keys from Active Directory to a domain controller in a headquarters (HQ) site because such keys should not exist in an unsecure branch site. Instead, the RODC creates a secondary zone to transfer the DNS data from a primary DNS server. By default, the RODC uses the nearest writeable DC as the primary. In this case, this can be only DC1 or DC2 because no other domain controllers exist in this environment. The RODC cannot transfer the zone if that was not manually enabled on the primary DNS server.

You can enable zone transfer in the DNS Manager console or through PowerShell with the cmdlet **Set-DnsServerPrimaryZone**. After enabling zone transfer for the RODC, the zone can exist as secondary zone on the RODC. To allow UDP DNS replies larger than 512 bytes through the firewall, DNSSEC must work throughout the network.

In this scenario, however, the zone transfer was not allowed, and this is the more probable cause of the problem. Installing an additional RODC at the branch site is no solution because the RODC zone transfer must be enabled and you have doubled your AD replication traffic from the HQ site to the branch site. Installing an additional writeable domain controller at the branch site is a solution for getting a DNS server with a signed AD-integrated zone at the branch site, but you chose an RODC for the branch site for a reason: It is a physically unsecure site, so you do not want a writeable domain controller there.

5.   A. A zone signed on a Windows Server 2008 R2 cannot be unsigned through the PowerShell cmdlet **Invoke-DnsServerZoneUnsign**. To unsign a zone on a legacy DNS server, you must use legacy procedures on the legacy server.

Chapter 5

Do I Know This Already? Quiz

1.   A, B. DANE enables you to specify which CA is allowed to issue certificates for a resource and can authenticate TLS client or server entities without the use of a CA. DANE increases DNS response performance from Windows Server 2016 DNS servers because of the DNSSEC validation. DANE does not simplify certificate validation in a mixed IPv4/IPv6 environment because

one domain name normally has one associated TLSA record; in this case, one TLSA record cannot match two different certificates.

2. D. Self-Signed Certificate Constraint is not a DANE operation mode. Instead, DANE can work in four different operation modes: 0, 1, 2, and 3. Mode 0 stands for CA specification: DANE accepts TLS certificates from only a specific CA. Mode 1 is for the Specific TLS certificate; only the exact TLS certificate can be used for the domain. This certificate must be issued by a valid CA. Mode 2 is for trust anchor assertion, which specifies the trust anchor to be used for validating the TLS certificates for the domain. Mode 3 is for domain-issued certificates, which specifies the exact TLS certificate that should be used for the domain; the TLS certificate does *not* need to be signed by a valid CA. This allows for the use of self-signed certificates.

3. A, C. You can use TLSA records to associate a TLS server certificate with the domain name where the record is found, thus forming a TLSA certificate association. TLSA records can be used to validate self-signed certificates and X.509 certificates from certification authorities (Symantec, Comodo, StartSSL, CACert, and so on). Normally, you use TLSA records together with DNSSEC and RRSIG records to protect the TLSA record.

4. B. You must use **DomainIssuedCertificates** because only with that value can you use TLSA records for self-signed certificates.

5. D. You should use the **_443._tcp.usa.nutex.com. IN TLSA 3 1 1** TLSA record because it uses the TLSA Usage Field parameter **3 - DANE-EE: Domain Issued Certificate**. This value disables the trust hierarchy inspection. The client has to trust only the referenced certificate in the TLSA record. The Matching-Type field has a value of 1, which means that the SHA-256 hash is used. You should not use **_443._tcp.usa.nutex.com. IN TLSA 0 1 1** because this TLSA record uses the TLSA Usage Field parameter **0 - PKIX-TA: Certificate Authority Constraint**. With this value, the client is invited to accept only defined certificate authorities. The certificate also must pass the trust hierarchy inspection. You should not use **_443._tcp.usa.nutex.com. IN TLSA 1 1 1** because this TLSA record uses the TLSA Usage Field parameter **1 - PKIX-EE: Service Certificate Constraint**. With this value, the client is invited to accept only defined certificates. You should not use **_443._tcp.usa.nutex.com. IN TLSA 2 1 2** because this TLSA record uses the TLSA Usage Field parameter **2 - DANE-TA: Trust Anchor Assertion**. With this value, the client must use a validated trust anchor.

6. D. You should use unknown record support because, with the newly added support for unknown record types (RFC 3597), you can add previously

unsupported record types such as TLSA into Windows DNS server zones in binary format.

In this example, a TLSA record is added. TLSA records are required for DANE. Other examples for such unknown record types are SMIMEA, OPENPGPKEY, TA, and TALINK.

You should not use DANE because DANE is a validation mechanism to validate certificates and certificate authorities. DANE servers can verify whether a certificate really comes from the relevant CA.

You should not use DNS Policies because this feature (also a new Windows Server 2016 feature) controls how a DNS Server handles queries based on different parameters. For example, you might create a DNS Policy to respond to a query asking for the IP address of a web server with a different IP address, based on the closest datacenter to the client.

You should not use Response Rate Limiting because this feature (also a new Windows Server 2016 feature) tries to extenuate DNS amplification attacks. It does not allow you to add unknown records such as TLSA records.

You should not use IPv6 root hints because this feature (also a new Windows Server 2016 feature) allows a Windows Server 2016 DNS server to use IPv6 root servers for name resolution.

7. This is the correct order of steps:

   1. e. Export the X.509 binary certificate data to the .CER file.

   2. i. Open the TLSA record generator.

   3. a. Fill in the Usage, Selector, and Matching Type fields.

   4. c. Paste the X.509 binary data of the certificate into the TLSA record generator.

   5. d. Fill in the port number with 443.

   6. f. Fill in the transport protocol with TCP.

   7. h. Fill in the domain name with pearson.com.

   8. j. Select Generate.

   9. k. Use the key value from the generated TLSA record as the **Certificate-AssociationData** parameter value on your **Add-DnsServerResourceRecord** command.

   10. l. Add the TLSA record with **Add-DnsServerResourceRecord**.

Appendix A: Answers to the "Do I Know This Already?" Quizzes and   713
End-of-Chapter Review Questions

The following steps are incorrect:

b. Use the thumbprint of your certificate as the **CertificateAssociationData** parameter value on your **Add-DnsServerResourceRecord** command. (You cannot use the thumbprint of a certificate as the **CertificateAssociationData** parameter value for your **Add-DnsServer ResourceRecord** command. You need the value generated through the TLSA record generator.)

g. Fill in the domain name with srv01.pearson.com. (You must use the name of the zone for the domain name parameter.)

8.   A. Before you deploy the planned certificate chain, make sure that the TLSA records that match the planned certificate chain are published in addition to the records that match the current chain. After deploying the planned certificate chain, you can remove the TLSA records that match the previous chain. When your TLSA records are CNAME records pointing to a location where your organization's issuing authority maintains suitable TLSA records for you, you can deploy new certificates from that authority without updating the server's TLSA records. The burden of key rollover falls on that authority before it issues any certificates via a new certificate or key. Editing existing TLSA records to match a new certificate chain is not supported or recommended.

End-of-Chapter Review Questions

1.   C. You must use the PEM format X.509 certificate data. You can generate that using the TLSA record generator online tool. You cannot use the public key, thumbprint, or serial number of the certificate to do so.

2.   B. In Figure 5-13, you can see that the zone pearson.com is not signed with DNSSEC. You can add TLSA records to an unsigned zone (as shown in the figure), but then the TLSA record is not protected through a RRSIG record. You must sign the zone pearson.com with DNSSEC. After that, the TLSA record is protected through the RRSIG record. Requesting a new server certificate is not necessary because you have to then repeat the creation of the TLSA record. Removing Everyone from the ACL of the TLSA record removes access to the TLSA record for all; then no one can use the TLSA record for certificate validation. Activating DNSSEC client settings through GPO in the NRPT is necessary when you want to use DNSSEC internally for domain clients, but this will not secure the TLSA record on the DNS server.

3.   B, C. Optimally, developers of application clients that depend on DANE-SRV want to reduce the wait time for end users trying to make a connection to a service. To make this possible, a DNS library might perform the SRV queries and TLSA queries in parallel. Performing TLSA queries in parallel with SRV record queries is not harmful from a security perspective and can yield some operational benefits. You also must use at least one TLSA record that authenticates the server's certificate (RFC 7673).

4. The correct answer follows:

Certificate	Certificate Usage Option
Certificate 0	PKIX-EE
Certificate 1	PKIX-TA
Certificate 2	DANE-TA
Certificate 3	DANE-EE

PKIX-EE is another term for Certificate Usage Option 0. PKIX-EE is another term for Certificate Usage Option 1. DANE-TA is another term for Certificate Usage Option 2. DANE-EE is another term for Certificate Usage Option 3.

Chapter 6

Do I Know This Already? Quiz

1. A. With the PowerShell cmdlet **Export-DhcpServer**, you can export the complete DHCP Server configuration, including scope configuration, to an XML file. This exports or backs up only the configuration settings, not the DHCP data. This is exactly what the question asks for. You can transfer the settings from one DHCP server to another, but not the DHCP data. With the PowerShell cmdlet **Import-DhcpServer**, you can import the previously exported DHCP configuration data into your new Windows Server 2016 DHCP server. With the **Backup-DhcpServer** PowerShell cmdlet, you perform a complete backup of all DHCP data (DHCP leases, reservation leases, and so on). With the **Restore-DhcpServer** PowerShell cmdlet, you can restore DHCP data.

2. C, D. On a Windows Server 2016 Nano Server, running a DHCP Server service is not possible. Therefore, you have to replace the Nano Server with a Windows Server 2016 Datacenter server with GUI or Server Core, install the DHCP server role, and authorize that server in ADDS. Then you can add DHCP2 as a DHCP failover replication partner. You cannot authorize DHCP2 in ADDS because you cannot install a DHCP server role on it. You can add DHCP2 to the domain pearson.com; however, it is still not a DHCP server and cannot work as a DHCP failover replication partner for DHCP1.

3. C. You cannot create a multicast scope with the default New Scope Wizard in the DHCP Manager or through the PowerShell cmdlet **Add-DhcpServerv4Scope**. You must use the New Multicast Scope Wizard in the DHCP Manager or the PowerShell cmdlet **Add-DhcpServerv4 MulticastScope** to create a multicast scope starting with 224.

4. B. You cannot add DHCP option 60 (pre-boot execution [PXE] client) with the **Add-DhcpServerv4OptionDefinition** PowerShell cmdlet. For that, you have to use the **netsh** command. You must configure 60, 66, and 67 because the WDS server also hosts the DHCP server on the same machine.

5. C. You need to install a DHCP relay agent as a solution so that DHCP client requests from Chicago and Subnet2 can be forwarded to DHCP1 as unicast traffic. The relay agent must be in that network, where the DHCP clients come from. Adding a second DHCP server in Subnet1 does not solve the problem because then you have two DHCP servers in the same subnet, which produces new problems. Installing a second DHCP server in Subnet2 and then using the DHCP failover feature seems to be a good idea because then DHCP clients from Subnet2 can get IP addresses from a DHCP server in their own network, but in this scenario, you cannot install an additional DHCP server in Chicago. You have no reason to install a DHCP relay agent in Paris because the Paris DHCP clients have no problems getting IP addresses from the DHCP server in Paris.

6. B. When the DHCP server is configured to perform DNS dynamic updates on behalf of DHCP clients, you can use the DHCP audit logs to monitor that. Event ID 31 is the event type about failed DNS dynamic update events. You cannot view that on a DNS server or the DHCP client. Events with event ID 30 are successful DNS dynamic update events.

7. B. When you have to use default settings, you cannot use the DHCP failover load sharing mode because the default setting for a split is 50:50. In this case, you must configure two DHCP servers manually with 70 percent of the scope on one DHCP server and 30 percent of the scope on the other DHCP server.

8. B. When you want to have less administrative effort and make the DHCP Server service highly available, you can do so through the DHCP failover feature in hot standby mode. Building a failover cluster requires much more administrative effort. A DHCP failover with load sharing mode works for a split-scope configuration and the Hyper-V replica feature makes Hyper-V VMs high available, but for that you need another Hyper-V host.

9. B. When you use DHCP Policies to direct foreign DHCP clients to a guest DNS suffix, you must use the FQDN and the operator Is Not Single Label because, in this question, you have foreign clients that are domain-joined

clients at also.ch domain. Through Group Policies, you cannot register foreign DHCP clients using a guest DNS suffix. You use the DHCP Policy operator Is Single Label when the DHCP clients are workgroup clients and they have no suffix. You use the DHCP Policy condition MAC address to deliver the DHCP options of that DHCP Policy to specific clients with specific MAC addresses. In this case, you do not know about the MAC addresses of the foreign clients, so you cannot preconfigure these MAC addresses on the DHCP Policy as a condition. With a DNS zone scope policy, you can configure different name resolution answers based on different criteria for DNS clients. With a DNS recursion policy, you can configure DNS forwarding.

End-of-Chapter Review Questions

1. C, D, E. You should use the PowerShell cmdlet **Backup-DhcpServer** because it also backs up the failover relationship data, which you can use to restore to the previous relationship state. You should also use the PowerShell cmdlet **Restore-DhcpServer** because, if you have used the previous PowerShell cmdlet or you backed up manually through the DHCP manager, you can restore the failover relationship data with that.

    You can view the restored failover relationship data through IPv4 Properties on the Failover tab. First the replication state appears as Recover Wait. You must wait so that it can sync up with its partner server before resuming normal operations on the network.

    You also should use the PowerShell cmdlet **Remove-Item** because you need to first remove all files from the C:\Windows\System32\DHCP folder. This removes the corrupted database from the location DHCP1 is trying to read it from. After removing the files, you can start the DHCP service.

    You should not use **netsh dhcp server import** because the failover relationship data is not part of the backup with that command.

    You should not use **netsh dhcp server export** because that command does not include the failover relationship data in the backup, and you cannot use the backed-up files to restore it.

    You should not use **Stop-Service** because it stops the DHCP service. It remains stopped after a database corruption.

2. The correct script is

    ```
    $DNSDomain="pearson.com"
    $DNSServerIP="172.16.1.10"
    $DHCPServerIP="172.16.1.10"
    $StartRange="172.16.1.150"
    ```

```
$EndRange="172.16.1.200"
$Subnet="255.255.255.0"
$Router="172.16.1.1"

Install-WindowsFeature -Name 'DHCP' -IncludeManagementTools
cmd.exe /c "netsh dhcp add securitygroups"
Restart-service dhcpserver
Add-DhcpServerInDC -DnsName $Env:COMPUTERNAME
Add-DhcpServerV4Scope -Name "DHCP Scope" -Start $StartRange -End
  $EndRange -SubnetMask $Subnet
Set-DhcpServerV4OptionValue -DnsDomain $DNSDomain -DnsServer
  $DNSServerIP -Router $Router
```

The correct answer is

 a. **IncludeAllSubFeature: B**

 b. IncludeManagementTools: __

 c. Install-Package: __

 d. **Add-WindowsFeature: A**

 e. **Add-DhcpServerinDC: D**

 f. **Cmd.exe: C**

 g. Netsh.exe: __

 h. Add-DhcpServerv4Class: __

 i. Add-DhcpServerInDC: __

 j. **Add-DhcpServerV4Scope: E**

 k. Add-DhcpServerV4MulticastScope: __

 l. **Set-DhcpServerV4OptionValue: F**

 m. Add-DhcpServerv4OptionDefinition: __

3. A. You cannot use the DHCP failover feature for IPv6 scopes. This is possible only for IPv4 scopes. You can deliver IPv6 options; one of them is 00021, the SIP server domain list option. You can deliver IP addresses and options with IPv6 scopes. You also can configure exclusions and reservations for IPv6 scopes.

4. C. You should use the EnableAutoStateTransition setting because the DHCP server DHCP2 is in the PartnerDown state; it is assuming that its failover partner, DHCP1, is not operating. In a hot standby failover configuration, in which DHCP2 is the passive partner, normally this server responds to all client requests that it receives if DHCP goes down. If the Automatic State

Transition setting is enabled, the automatic state transition process moves from the CommunicationsInterrupted state to the PartnerDown state when the state switchover interval expires.

With the PowerShell command **Set-Dhcpserverv4Failover -AutoStateTransition $true**, you can enable the automatic state transition here. If it is disabled, DHCP2 does not go into the PartnerDown state after the switchover interval expires.

You should not set Maximum Client Lead Time (MCLT) to 0 because this defines the maximum amount of time one server can extend a lease for a DHCP client beyond the time known by the partner server. The MCLT defines the temporary lease period given by a failover partner server and also determines the amount of time a server in a failover relationship waits in the PartnerDown state before assuming control over the entire IP address range.

You cannot set the Maximum Client Lead Time to 0; the default setting is 1 hour.

You should not use Enable State Switchover Interval because this is the interval after which a DHCP server automatically transitions its failover partner to a Partner Down state after loss of communication. This works only if automatic state transition is enabled. In this scenario, automatic state transition is disabled, so this interval does not work.

You should not use Change Reserve Percentage setting because, in a failover relationship configured in hot standby mode, administrators can specify a percentage of the address range of the scope as reserved for the hot standby server. The default value is 5 percent.

5. B, D. You should add **Add-DhcpServerv4Scope** to the maintenance role capability file as an additional visible cmdlet value. The maintenance role capability file defines all PowerShell cmdlets that are allowed to use the given Just Enough Administration (JEA) endpoint. You then must reregister the session configuration. When you add Paul to the DHCP Administrators security group, he has full DHCP administrator permissions. You cannot add a Power-Shell cmdlet directly to the session configuration file; instead, the role definition is done in that file; the given PowerShell cmdlets will be applied under the virtual account. Adding Paul's computer to the TrustedHosts list gives the client permission for remote PowerShell sessions, but this still is allowed because Paul had no problem connecting from his client to the DHCP server DHCP1.

Chapter 7

Do I Know This Already? Quiz

1. C, D. Since Windows Server 2012 R2, IPAM can use another SQL Server computer as an external location for its IPAM database. This is also possible with Windows Server 2016. When you migrate the IPAM database of IPAM1 to SQL1, you cannot use the SQL database on the other server for IPAM: IPAM1 is still running Windows Server 2012 and this server version does not support an external IPAM SQL database. When you install Microsoft SQL Server on IPAM1, you can use that database locally for IPAM and you can migrate from the WID database to SQL; however, this question asks about an external database solution.

2. C, E. You cannot exchange or replicate IPAM data between IPAM servers; no mechanism supports that. You also cannot replicate IPAM data between forests. A new feature of Windows Server 2016 IPAM enables you to manage DNS and DHCP servers distributed through multiple forests using Windows Server 2016 IPAM. To do so, you must have a two-way trust between the forests.

3. B. You must verify that the DHCP servers are in the security filtering list of the IPAM_DHCP Group Policy and have read permission. This is a prerequisite so that these managed servers can get the Group Policy settings from the IPAM_DHCP Group Policy. You can also manually add the computer account of the DHCP server into the security filtering list to force this. You then can restart the DHCP server or perform a Group Policy update. To display the DHCP server in the IPAM configuration console under Server Inventory with an IPAM access status of Unblocked, you must refresh the server access status to force the display.

   Simply performing **gpupdate /force** again on DHCP2 will not work if DHCP2 has no read permission for the DHCP_IPAM Group Policy.

   Adding DHCP2 to the IPAM_DC_NPS Group Policy does not help because this Group Policy is for DCs and NPS servers; they must be added to the security filtering list with read permissions, not the managed DHCP server.

   When you refresh the server access status, DHCP2 still has no read permission to the IPAM_DHCP Group Policy.

4. C. During the default Windows Server 2016 IPAM provisioning process, the IPAM_DHCP Group Policy is created. This policy runs the **ipamprovisioning.ps1** PowerShell script on the managed servers. This happens through the identity IPAMUG, which is a domain security group

that has the IPAM server as a member. The IPAMUG security group automatically becomes a member of the local EventLogReaders security group of the managed servers so that the IPAM server can get access to DHCP events. The local Administrators security group and the Domain Administrators security group are not the correct identities the PowerShell script runs by default.

5. A, D. You can add a custom IPAM field through the PowerShell cmdlet **Add-IPAMCustom Field** before the CSV file import occurs. A field named Division does not exist by default in the IPAM database. To make the CSV data import possible, you must create that field. You can use the **Import-IPAMAddress** PowerShell cmdlet to import the IP addresses from the CSV file. You cannot use the **Format-Custom** PowerShell cmdlet to create or prepare a custom IPAM field. You do not have to use the **Add-IPAMCustomValue** PowerShell cmdlet because the values for the Division field come from the CSV file.

   You have a CSV file with IP addresses, so you do not want to import a subnet or a range; you also do not have to use **Import-IpamSubnet** or **Import-IpamRange**. You do not have to ensure that the RIR field exists because here you want to import IP addresses from the file, not an IP address block. When you have public IP address blocks in a CSV file and you want to import them, you must use the RIR field and value.

6. A, D. You cannot view or monitor information about DNS reverse lookup zones in the IPAM management console. Instead, you use the PowerShell cmdlet **Get-IPAMDnsZone** for that. Alternatively, you can do that through the DNS Manager on the DNS server to verify the signing status of the reverse lookup zone. You cannot get reverse lookup zone information through the Event Catalog or the DNS and DHCP Server area of the IPAM configuration console.

7. C. When you want to use separated computers for the IPAM server and the SQL Server hosting the IPAM database, you must first create the IPAM SQL database. This starts with the SQL command **CREATE LOGIN**. Then you can use the SQL command **CREATE DATABASE** to create the new IPAM database. After that, you can use the PowerShell cmdlet **Move-IpamDatabase** to move the IPAM database.

8. B, D. You have to add the network service named Microsoft Windows Server IP Address Management in SCVMM to configure the integration between IPAM and SCVMM. An IP address range in IPAM is the same as an IP address pool in SCVMM.

End-of-Chapter Review Questions

1. C, D. You should use **Get-IpamDhcpSuperScope** because that PowerShell cmdlet enables you to identify the IPAM DHCP Superscope. **$a = Get-IpamDhcpSuperScope Downtown**.

   After that, you can use a variable to change the access scope with the following command: **Set-IpamAccessScope -IpamDhcpSuperscope $a -AccessScopePath \Global\DE**.

   You also should use **Set-IpamAccessScope** because that PowerShell cmdlet enables you to change the access scope for the SuperScope from \Global\CH to \Global\DE. You can do that with the new Windows Server 2016 parameter **IpamDhcpSuperscope** of **Set-IpamAccess Scope**: **Set-IpamAccessScope -IpamDhcpSuperscope Downtown -AccessScopePath \Global\DE**.

   You should not use **Set-IpamScope** because it modifies settings of an existing DHCP scope managed through IPAM, but you cannot modify settings of a superscope or change the access scope with that PowerShell cmdlet.

   You should not use **Set-IpamRange** because that PowerShell cmdlet modifies an existing IP range on IPAM. For example: **Get-IpamRange -StartIPAddress 10.12.1.1 -EndIPAddress 10.12.1.254 | Set-IpamRange -NewManagedBy Service VMM -NewServiceInstance "vmm1.pearson.com" -PassThru**.

2. D. You should synchronize IPAM2016 and VMM1 because the IPAM server IPAM2016 from the other company is a Windows Server 2016 server. You can use it for IPAM–VMM integration to centralize physical and virtual IP address space management. The IPAM server must be at least a Windows Server 2012 R2 for that.

   You must create a VMM user account on the IPAM server and assign the IPAM ASM Administrator role on the global access scope to that account. On the VMM server, you must add the IPAM as a new network service. There you have to select Microsoft Windows Server IP Address Management and define the VMM user account as a Run As account.

   After that, you can add logical networks through VMM or through IPAM, and they will be replicated with all settings through each other. You should not deploy an IPAM server on pearson.com because you still have a centralized solution for IP address space management: the SCVMM server. Additionally, you can use IPAMX from the integrated company's forest in the future, to manage both forests (multiple-forest support is new to Windows Server 2016 IPAM).

You should not add the pearson.com forest to IPAM2016 because it has only two DHCP and DNS servers. All virtual machines' IP addresses on pearson.com are managed through the SCVMM server.

You should not use a third-party IPAM solution because this involves too much administrative effort and produces too many migration costs. In the pearson.com forest, you have a field-tested environment. In the forest of the other company, you also have an existing IP address space-management solution with the existing Windows Server 2016 IPAM server IPAM2016. Migrating to a third-party solution would not be a fast or cheap solution.

3. **B.** You should create a scope policy on DHCP1 because you cannot replicate a DHCP Policy created on the server level. The DHCP Policy created on DHCP1 will be applied to all scopes on DHCP1, but it cannot be replicated through the DHCP failover replication process. This was not possible in Windows Server 2012 and is still not possible in Windows Server 2016.

   If you create the DHCP Policy on the scope level, the DHCP Policy settings apply only to clients for that scope; this DHCP Policy, however, will be replicated to the DHCP failover partner.

   You should not create a scope policy on DHCP2 because here the original scope is on DHCP1. You must create the scope-level DHCP Policy on DHCP1, not on DHCP2.

   You should not select Import Policy on DHCP1 because you still have to create the DHCP Policy in DHCP1; it does not need be imported again. If you have created it in the IPAM console, the DHCP Policy is present and automatically applied to all scopes on DHCP1.

   You should not select Import Policy on DHCP2 because if you import the DHCP Policy on DHCP2, it is still a policy on the server level. It will be applied to the scope on DHCP2, but it still cannot be automatically replicated through DHCP failover replication because it is not a scope-level DHCP Policy.

4. **B.** You should use **$ip = Get-IpamAddress -IPAddress 10.12.1.1, Set-IpamAccessScope -IpamIP Number -InputObject $ip -AccessScopePath \Global\USA -PassThru** because the **Set-IpamAccessScope** PowerShell cmdlet has no **IpamIPNumber** parameter. You can set an access scope for an IP scope and assign the role through the access policy to that IP scope, but any newly configured IP address falls automatically under the \Global access scope.

You cannot apply an access scope to a single IP address. You should not use **$zone = Get-IpamDnsZone -ZoneType Forward -ZoneName pearson.com, Set-IpamAccessScope -IpamDnsZone -InputObject $zone -AccessScope Path \Global\USA -PassThru** because the **Set-IpamAccessScope** PowerShell cmdlet has the parameter **IpamDnsZone** and you can apply an access scope to a DNS zone. This works, so it is the wrong answer.

You should not use **$scope = Get-IpamDhcpScope -AddressFamily "Ipv4"-ScopeID 10.0.0.0, Set-IpamAccess Scope -IpamDhcpScope -InputObject $scope -AccessScopePath \Global\USA -PassThru** because the **Set-IpamAccessScope** PowerShell cmdlet has the parameter **IpamDhcpScope** and you can apply an access scope to an IPAM DHCP scope. This works, so it is the wrong answer.

You should not use **$record = Get-IpamDnsResource Record -ZoneName pearson.com -RecordName "PearsonServer" -RecordType A; Set-IpamAccessScope -IpamDns ResourceRecord -InputObject $record -AccessScopePath \Global\Europe -PassThru** because the **Set-IpamAccessScope** PowerShell cmdlet has the parameter **IpamDnsResourceRecord** and you can apply an access scope to a DNS record. This works, so it is the wrong answer.

Chapter 8

Do I Know This Already? Quiz

1. C. You cannot configure the DHCP name protection feature simultaneously through a multiselection in the IPAM configuration console. From the DNS Dynamic Updates settings, only the setting Enable DNS Dynamic Updates is configurable through the Edit DHCP Server Properties window in the IPAM configuration console. This has nothing to do with the fact that both DHCP servers are in different forests. You can use the **Set-DhcpServerv4Setting** PowerShell cmdlet to configure the DHCP name protection feature on DHCP servers, but then it is not configured through IPAM. When you want to configure this setting through IPAM, you have to configure it twice. You cannot use the PowerShell cmdlet **Get-IpamDhcp Server** to change settings. With that cmdlet, you can display the status of a DHCP name protection setting for one or multiple DHCP servers.

2. B. DNS Dynamic Update Credentials are never part of a backup (synchronous or asynchronous), so after the DHCP database restore, new credentials must be configured for DHCP1. You do not have to configure new credentials for all DHCP servers because only DHCP1 was restored. When you restore

ipam.mdf and ipam_log.ldf, you restore the IPAM WID database files. With that, you restore all IPAM configuration settings, but DHCP1 still has lost its configured credentials because these were not part of the DHCP database backup.

When you use the **Set-IpamDiscoveryDomain** PowerShell cmdlet, you can prevent the server discovery for domain controllers or other managed servers such as DNS or DHCP servers. You cannot use this cmdlet to discover restored credentials.

With the **DiscoverDns**, **DiscoverDhcp**, and **DiscoverDc** parameters of this cmdlet, you can allow or prevent server discovery. No parameter for NPS servers exists.

3. D. You cannot select both scopes and also disable dynamic updates for DNS PTR records for both scopes in the IPAM configuration console in one step. If multiple scopes are selected, you can only enable or disable DNS dynamic updates; you cannot configure Enable Name Protection, Dynamically Update DNS Records, Discard DNS A and PTR Records When Lease Is Deleted, Dynamically Update DNS Records for DHCP Clients That Do Not Request Updates, and Disable Dynamic Updates for DNS PTR Records.

    A PowerShell cmdlet named **Set-IpamDhcp Scope** does not exist, so you cannot use it.

    You cannot use the Set Access Scope setting to configure DHCP scopes. Access scopes are used to configure administrative permissions based on RBAC.

    The only possibility with these answer choices is to use the Duplicate DHCP Scope feature in the IPAM configuration console.

4. C. When you use the DHCP failover feature to replicate the DHCP Policy to DHCP4, Scope2 is replicated to DHCP4 and you have only the DHCP Policy on Scope2 configured, not on both scopes. When you choose DHCP1 to create the DHCP Policy, this is the wrong DHCP server because Scope2 does not exist on DHCP1. You can use the Import DHCP Policy feature to apply the DHCP Policy created on DHCP2 on Scope2 to Scope4 on DHCP4. You cannot use Configure DHCP Policy and select both scopes because you cannot enable the Register DHCP Clients Using a Different DNS Suffix setting in this way. You can enable only the DNS dynamic update setting.

5. B. Debug Logging settings cannot be configured centrally directly through the Windows Server 2016 IPAM configuration console; you must launch the DNS Manager tool. When you select multiple DNS servers, you cannot select Launch MMC; this is not possible. You can select a single DNS server in IPAM and then select Launch MMC, but then you have to repeat this for the

other nine DNS servers to configure Debug Logging through IPAM. When you go to the Server Inventory list and you select Edit Server, you cannot configure Debug Logging of that DNS server. When you go to the Server Groups list, you also can select only a single DNS server to get the Launch MMC setting for each server.

6. B. When you remove the subdomain, select the DNS server in the DNS and DHCP Servers list, and use the Create DNS Zone setting to create usa.pearson.com, the subdomain appears under Forward Lookup.

When you remove the subdomain and use New Delegation in the DNS Manager, this creates a DNS delegation, not a subdomain or zone.

When you use Reset Zone Status and Retrieve Server Data to update the IPAM information in the IPAM configuration console, this is a good idea for getting actual information, but the subdomain still does not display.

You can use the New Zone Wizard in the DNS Manager to create the subdomain and subzone usa.pearson.com, and it displays in IPAM with a white bullet and a Zone Status of No Data. When the first resource record is added to the zone (excluding SOA and NS), it automatically changes to a green bullet or you can force the display with Reset Zone Status and Retrieve Server Data.

7. B. The PowerShell command **Invoke-GpoProvisioning** must create the GPOs on a domain controller in the pucert.com forest. This can be done only with permissions in that forest. You have to grant the administrative account of pearson.com, which is performing the PowerShell command, minimum permission to create GPOs at pucert.com so that the GPOs can be created.

You do not have to grant the computer accounts of the managed servers the GPOApply permission in this step. For example, it is correct that a DHCP server in pucert.com must have the GPOApply permission on IPAM_DHCP GPO and that a DNS server in pucert.com must have the GPOApply permission on IPAM_DNS GPO, but this is not the configuration step to solve the error message for the **InvokeGpoProvisioning** command. You do not have to add IPAM1 to the IPAMUG security group because this is done automatically. Managed servers do not have to be a member of the IPAMUG security group.

8. A, C, D, G. You must create a new user role and then, in Operations and DNS Resource Record Management Operations, select AAAA Record Operations. Then you need to create a new access scope. After that, you create a new access policy and add the IPv6Admins security group and the new user role with the AAAA resource record operation permission. The last step is to select both DNS zones and then select Set Access Scope to apply the new access scope. You cannot edit the default access roles. The only default access scope is the Global scope, which you cannot edit. No default access policy exists.

End-of-Chapter Review Questions

1. B. You can change the DNS Dynamic Update Credentials on DHCP2 because you are member of the DHCP Administrators security group on all DHCP servers. This can be done on DHCP2 and all other DHCP servers in the list except on DHCP1 because this is an evenly recovered DHCP server and the DNS Dynamic Update credentials are not part of a DHCP backup.

    When you recover the DHCP database, you first have to configure new credentials before you can change them. You can enable DHCP audit logging in the IPAM DHCP server properties, but you cannot configure the audit log path there. For that, you can use the **Set-DhcpServer AuditLog** PowerShell cmdlet.

    The Automatically Update Statistics setting cannot be configured through the IPAM DHCP server properties.

    The Backup Path also cannot be configured through the IPAM DHCP server properties.

2. B, F. When you select multiple IPv4 DHCP scopes in the IPAM management console, you can change only the description and the lease duration settings in one step for multiple scopes.

3. A. The State Switchover Interval setting is part of a DHCP failover relationship configuration. If automatic state transition is enabled, a DHCP server in a CommunicationInterrupted state automatically transitions to the Partner-Down state after a defined period of time. This period of time is defined by the State switchover interval; you can configure it under the Edit DHCP Failover Relationship setting.

4. C. In the IPAM configuration console, you can configure the following DNS server tasks: Launch MMC, Create DNS Zone, Create DNS Conditional Forwarder, Set Access Scope, and Retrieve Server Data. For every DNS server, you have to select Launch MMC to configure the automatic scavenging of stale records setting.

5. A, C. When the subzone is displayed with an empty white bullet under Forward Lookup, either it has no data or the actual zone information was not retrieved from the DNS server. To refresh the information displayed, you must select Reset Zone Status and Retrieve Server Data.

Chapter 9

Do I Know This Already? Quiz

1. D, E, H. With the IPAM scheduled task DnsServerConfiguration (new in Windows Server 2016), you can collect configuration information from DNS servers for display in the IP address space and server management functions. With the IPAM scheduled task ServerAvailability, you can collect service status information from DHCP and also DNS servers. With the IPAM scheduled task ServiceMonitoring, you can collect DNS zone status events from DNS servers.

2. **Event: E; Search criteria:** B, D, F. Security event 672 is a correct answer because this security event (672–An authentication service [AS] ticket was successfully issued and validated) comes from an NPS server. Because you have no NPS server in your environment, you cannot get these events. If you do not want to include events such as these, you can choose and exclude user or machine logon and correlated events. IPScope, MACAddress, and ClassID are correct answers because they are not possible IPAM IP address tracking events.

3. B, F. You should choose Event Catalog and IP Address Tracking because there you can configure IP address tracking by IP address, client ID, hostname, and username.

End-of-Chapter Review Questions

1. D. The **DnsServerConfiguration** task is new in Windows Server 2016. With this task, the IPAM server collects configuration information from DNS servers for display in the IP address space and for server-management functions.

2. C, D. IPAM enables you to create custom logical groups to improve the audit experience for DNS or DHCP servers. To apply custom fields to one or multiple DHCP or DNS servers, go to Server Inventory, select the servers, and use the Edit Server task to apply custom fields. For example, if you want to use PowerShell, you first must add a custom field named Building with **Add-IpamCustomField** and then add values with **Add-IpamCustomValue**.

3. C. The default IPAM underutilization threshold setting is 20 percent, and the IPAM overutilization setting is 80 percent. You can leave the overutilization threshold default settings.

Chapter 10

Do I Know This Already? Quiz

1. A, D. When you have to set up a router-to-router S2S (site-to-site) VPN connection between two Windows Server 2016 RAS servers in different sites and you want to use an IPsec-encrypted tunnel and persistent connection, you must create a demand-dial interface on both Windows Server 2016 Remote Access servers. During the interface configuration, you must define the dial-out credentials. You do not have to create a VPN connection profile because, in this scenario, no client has to connect into a VPN tunnel. You also cannot use the IPHTTPS interface for this because IPHTTPS is used for Direct-Access VPN connections, not for S2S router-to-router VPN connections.

2. B. You can get detailed statistics information about your S2S VPN interface through the PowerShell cmdlet **Get-VPNS2SinterfaceStatistics**. You cannot use the **Get-VpnS2S Interface**, **Get-VpnDemandDialInterface,** or **Get-VpnS2SdemandDialInterface** cmdlets.

3. A, B. You need a demand-dial interface for such an S2S VPN connection. You can choose the setting **Persistent** on the **Options** tab of the Properties page of the demand-dial interface; you also can configure it by clearing the Idle Timeout and Session Timeout settings on the NPS server the Remote Access server is using in the network policy and on the **Constraint** tab. On the calling router Remote Access server properties page, you cannot configure a persistent demand-dial VPN S2S connection. On the L2TP port settings on the calling router, you cannot configure this.

4. D. You can set custom IPsec policies for incoming VPN and S2S connections with the PowerShell cmdlet **Set-VpnServerIPsecConfiguration**. The following example command sets a custom IPsec policy like the one asked:

   Set-VpnServerIPsecConfiguration -CustomPolicy-EncryptionMethod "AES128"-DhGroup "Group2" -PfsGroup "PFS2" -CipherTransformConstants "AES128"-IntegrityCheckMethod "SHA256" -AuthenticationTransformConstants "SHA256128" -PassThru

   The PowerShell cmdlet **Set-VpnAuthProtocol** configures the authentication method for incoming S2S VPN interfaces on RRAS servers. This is not the correct answer because you have to configure a custom IPsec policy, not base authentication protocol settings. The following example uses this cmdlet to change the authentication method for incoming connections to Certificate:

   Set-VpnAuthProtocol -UserAuthProtocolAccepted Certificate

The PowerShell cmdlet **Set-Vpn ConnectionIPsec Configuration** sets the IPsec parameters of a VPN connection. The following example first uses the **Add-VpnConnection** PowerShell cmdlet to add a VPN connection, and the second command uses **Set-VpnConnectionIPsec Configuration** to specify values for the **CipherTransformsConstants**, **EncryptionMethod**, **IntegrityCheckMethod**, and **DHGroup** parameters:

Add-VpnConnection -Name "Contoso" -ServerAddress 176.16.1.2 -TunnelType Ikev2, Set-VpnConnectionIPsec Configuration -ConnectionName "Pearson"-AuthenticationTransform Constants None -CipherTransformConstants AES256-EncryptionMethod AES256 -IntegrityCheck Method

The PowerShell cmdlet **Set-NetIPsecDospSetting** modifies existing IPsec DoS protection settings. The following example modifies the internal interface of an IPsec DoS protection setting by using the rule name:

Set-NetIPsecDospSetting -Name PearsonNet-CorpNet -PublicInterface Aliases PearsonNet2

5. D. You can use the PowerShell cmdlet **Get-VpnAuthProtocol** to verify which user authentication protocols your VPN server accepts. The following example receives authentication parameters configured for your Windows Server 2016 VPN server:

    Get-VpnAuthProtocol | FL UserAuthProtocolAccepted

    You can configure this with **Set-VpnAuthProtocol -UserAuth ProtocolAccepted EAP**.

    The PowerShell cmdlet **Get-VpnConnection** retrieves specified VPN connection profile information.

    The PowerShell cmdlet **Get-VpnServerConfiguration** delivers VPN server properties.

    The PowerShell cmdlet **Get-VpnS2Sinterface** delivers configuration details about S2S interfaces.

6. D, E. Since Windows 7 and Windows Server 2008 R2 server, you can use the VPN Reconnect feature. You also need IKEv2, certificates, and PEAP. MS-CHAPv2 and PSK are not prerequisites for the VPN Reconnect feature. Windows Server 2016 VPN servers still support the VPN Reconnect feature.

7. **Explanation:** You can use the following possibilities to distribute VPN connection profiles: *CMAK*, *Microsoft Intune*, *System Center Configuration Manager*, *Group Policies*, and *scripts*.

8. D, E. You can use a Web Application Proxy together with ADFS (Active Directory Federation Services) to allow these users to access the web applications through HTTPS. The Web Application Proxy server can forward the authentication requests to the ADFS server; the ADFS server then delivers an access ticket to the client so that the user can access the web applications. When you use VPN connections (L2TP/IPsec or SSTP), you have a tunnel to the local network of the company, not just to the web applications. SSTP also works with HTTPS, but in this question, the users want to access only their web applications and no other internal resources, so Web Application Proxy is the best solution. An S2S VPN connection is used to connect sites through a VPN tunnel, not single clients with the local network.

9. C, G. You do not need a Certificate Authority and an IPv6 internal network for that. Only the DirectAccess IPsec-encrypted tunnel has to be an IPv6 network, at minimum. When you set up a single Edge Windows Server 2016 DirectAccess server, you can use the Getting Started Wizard; self-signed certificates then are created and installed automatically on the DirectAccess server for IP-HTTPS and the NLS server.

You do not need a Certificate Authority because the certificates do not have to come from this; however, for security reasons, it is more secure to implement a CA for the KDC Proxy and NLS certificate. The Network Location Server (NLS) is used so that DirectAccess clients can approve whether they are internal or external.

The KDC Proxy is used to authenticate DirectAccess clients through Kerberos.

The Network Connectivity Assistant (NCA) is a service on the DirectAccess client that is used to test the connectivity through the IPv6 IPsec tunnel and to allow monitoring.

Group Policies are created to configure DirectAccess server and client settings.

You cannot use DirectAccess without using Active Directory.

10. C. The Getting Started Wizard on the DirectAccess server was successfully completed. This means that the necessary Group Policy objects are successfully created and also the DirectAccess server settings Group Policy. The problem is that the public firewall on the public accessible interface of the DirectAccess server is not enabled and not configured through the Direct-Access server settings Group Policy. The IPsec connection security rule on this interface must be configured through this Group Policy.

When you run **gpupdate /force,** the GPO settings are applied, but because the public firewall profile is disabled, the firewall settings cannot be applied through the Group Policy.

When you restart the DirectAccess server, all firewall profiles are enabled and the public firewall settings also are applied through Group Policy.

You do not have to configure or create firewall rules because this all can be done through the DirectAccess server settings Group Policy.

11. A, D, F, H. DirectAccess clients can be any domain-joined computer that is running an Enterprise edition of the Windows 10, Windows 8.1, Windows 8.0, or Windows 7 operating systems. They also can connect to the Direct-Access server by using IPv6 and IPsec. The Getting Started Wizard on the DirectAccess server creates a set of GPOs and settings for DirectAccess clients. DirectAccess clients get all settings from GPOs. DirectAccess client computers can connect to DirectAccess servers located in different domains.

12. A. You should use the **Set-DAEntryPointDC** PowerShell cmdlet to point to another domain controller. When you have deployed a multisite DirectAccess configuration, you can verify the name of the domain controller closest to the entry point with the PowerShell cmdlet **Get-DAEntrypointDC**.

If the domain controller is not running, use the **Set-DAEntryPointDC** PowerShell cmdlet to point to another domain controller. After that, use **gpresult** to ensure that DirectAccess is getting the DirectAccess Server Group Policy Objects settings.

Using the **Operation Status** tab in the Remote Access Management Console is a good idea to identify problems with DirectAccess components, but in this case, you get no information displayed in the console because the DirectAccess server cannot read information from Active Directory.

When you use the **Get-DnsClientNrptRule** PowerShell cmdlet to verify NRPT settings, you do that on the DirectAccess client. This has nothing to do with the problem that the DirectAccess server cannot display the DirectAccess configuration and gets no information from Active Directory.

You should not manually edit DirectAccess Group Policy settings directly in the GPO; this always must be done through the Remote Access Management console.

End-of-Chapter Review Questions

1. C. A persistent S2S VPN connection has a constant connection. If the connection closes, it is reestablished immediately. You can configure the connection as persistent on the Properties page of the demand-dial interface on the Options tab. Alternatively, you can configure this at the Network Policy of the answering router by clearing the Idle Timeout and Session Timeout settings.

2. C, G. When you want to open only UDP port 500 for the VPN connection, you must choose IKEv2 as the tunnel protocol. Because IKEv2 will use the IPsec protocol, you can configure the idle disconnecting setting with the **Set-VPNServerConfiguration** PowerShell cmdlet.

3. C. When you want to add a VPN connection that uses a custom EAP authentication method, you can use the **New-EapConfiguration** PowerShell cmdlet to create an XML file with the specified EAP configuration. After that, you can use **Add-VpnConnection** to create a new VPN connection profile using this EAP configuration.

4. A, B. One Azure VPN gateway supports up to 128 P2S VPN connections. Only ExpressRoute offers redundant tunneling; Azure P2S and Azure S2S do not offer that. Here you have mobile clients that travel and are not always inside your on-premises site. When using an S2S tunnel solution, clients have a VPN tunnel connection to Azure only if they are at the on-premises site. When you upgrade to a high-performance Azure VPN gateway, you can increase the S2S tunnels to 30, but the P2S limit is still 128.

Chapter 11

Do I Know This Already? Quiz

1. A. You must register NPS1 in the domain or forest where the user accounts reside. In this case, this is the pearsonucertify.com domain. You also need to create a trust relationship between the two forests so that you can add the computer account of NPS1 from the pearson.com domain to the security group of pearsonucertify.com.

   You do not have to add NPS1 to the security group in pearson.com because the user accounts are not in this domain.

   You cannot replicate NPS settings between NPS servers; no such replication function exists. You can use the NPS configuration import/export feature to manually transfer NPS settings from one NPS server to another; you can write a PowerShell script to do that automatically and schedule it to run from time to time.

   NPS1 needs read permissions on the user accounts of pearsonucertify.com.

   You cannot register NPS servers in Azure AD.

2. C. You must create a new connection request policy to forward connection requests to a RADIUS server. This policy is the Proxy policy and has to stay at the top of the ordered list. If the request matches this policy, requests are forwarded to a RADIUS server. If the request does not match this proxy policy, the next policy applies, which is the default connection request policy (local authentication). When you simply use the default connection request policy, local authentication applies, so the NPS server can work only as a RADIUS server.

3. A, C. A RADIUS server cannot be added for authentication when VPN is not installed. In this case, the VPN feature is installed on VPN1. A RADIUS server cannot be added for authentication when the authentication type is Windows or when local NPS is installed. In this case, a local NPS is not installed on VPN1.

   A RADIUS server cannot be added for the purpose of accounting when external RADIUS Accounting is not enabled. In this case, external RADIUS Accounting is enabled on VPN1. This means that you can use the **Add-RemoteAccessRadius** PowerShell cmdlet to add the RADIUS server to VPN1. You also can tell the RADIUS server R1 that VPN1 is the RADIUS client with the **New-NpsRadiusClient** PowerShell cmdlet.

4. A, D, E, G. You can configure only the following kinds of settings through NPS templates on a Windows Server 2016 NPS server: shared secrets, RADIUS clients, IP filters, and remote RADIUS servers.

5. A, C, D. You have to separate NPS log files from the system partition; otherwise, too many log files could bring down the operating system.

   You can use a RADIUS server group to specify load-balancing settings either to determine the order in which the proxy uses the servers or to distribute the flow of RADIUS messages across all servers in the group to keep from overloading one or more servers with too many connection requests. Remote RADIUS server groups are unrelated to and separate from Windows groups.

   You can use SQL logging instead of NPS log files, and you can use another server as the SQL Server. You can use Database Availability Groups (DAG) on SQL Server to make the database highly available there. In this case, the system disk cannot be filled with NPS log file information to bring down the NPS server.

6. A, C, E, G. To allow VPN clients to connect through the PEAP authentication method, you need the network policy condition NAS Port Type: Virtual (VPN). You also have to configure the Authentication Method Microsoft Protected EAP (PEAP). For PEAP to work, you need to prepare a PEAP certificate template on the CA and request a PEAP certificate for the NPS server so

that you can apply that certificate in the network policy on the PEAP authentication method. You must define the type of network access server as Remote Access Server (VPN–Dial-up).

7.   A, D. No PowerShell cmdlet exists for creating, modifying, or removing Windows Server 2016 NPS connection request policies. You cannot create connection request policies through NPS templates.

8.   A, B, F. You must use the **Tunnel-Medium-Type**, **Tunnel-Pvt-Group-ID**, and **Tunnel-Type** attributes as RADIUS attributes.

9.   C, D. You can use the **Export-NpsConfiguration** PowerShell cmdlet to export NPS server settings, Network Policies, and connection request policies into an XML file. You can use the **Import-NpsConfiguration** PowerShell cmdlet to import them on the other server. SQL Server logging settings cannot be exported or imported through those commands.

End-of-Chapter Review Questions

1.   A, D, E, G. You can use the Windows Server 2016 NPS RADIUS servers using a domain or local SAM user accounts database as the user account database for clients; you also can use them as Remote Access servers for multiple dial-up servers, VPN servers, or demand-dial routers, and you can centralize both the configuration of Network Policies and connection logging and accounting.

You can outsource dial-up, VPN, or wireless access to a service provider. The access servers can use the Windows Server 2016 RADIUS servers to authenticate and authorize connections that are made by members of your organization.

You also can centralize authentication, authorization, and accounting for a heterogeneous set of access servers.

You cannot remotely manage mobile devices through Enterprise Mobility with Windows Server 2016 NPS.

You cannot use the NPS servers as on-premises MFA authentication servers.

You also cannot use the Azure MFA authentication server as a RADIUS client because the Azure MFA authentication server can act as a RADIUS server, not as a RADIUS client. An Azure Multi-Factor Authentication Server also can be configured as a RADIUS proxy between RD gateway and NPS servers.

2.   A, C, D, G. You have to create three connection request policies on the RADIUS proxy servers because when you want the NPS proxy to forward

messages to multiple groups (in this case, you have three groups of RADIUS servers, one for every domain), you have to configure one connection request policy per group.

You also must create attribute manipulation rules because you have more than one location to which you want to forward connection requests. However, you must create a connection request policy for each location and then configure the policy with the remote RADIUS server group to which you want to forward messages, as well as with the attribute manipulation rules that tell NPS which messages to forward. These rules are defined through conditions—in this case, the User-Name condition. This is the username that the RADIUS client provides and is included by the NAS in the RADIUS Access-Request message. The value of this attribute is a character string that typically contains a realm name and a user account name.

On the RADIUS proxy servers, you have to add remote RADIUS server groups to tell RADIUS servers the proxy to which they have to forward the requests. The proxy does not need to be registered in Active Directory because it does not need access to the dial-in properties of user accounts.

You can replicate the RADIUS proxy configuration between both servers by using a script that copies the settings. Windows Server 2016 has no RADIUS proxy server group.

3. B, E. When you want to tell the RADIUS server which VPN servers are working as RADIUS clients, you have to use the **New-NPSRadiusClient** PowerShell cmdlet on the RADIUS server to add the VPN servers as RADIUS clients. When you want to configure a Windows Server 2016 DirectAccess server with OTP and you want to use it as a RADIUS client, then you have to configure two certificate templates, one as an OTP certificate template and the second to enroll the certificate used by the DirectAccess server to sign OTP certificate enrollment requests.

4. A, E, F, G. You can configure the Shared Secrets (with autogenerating feature), Remote RADIUS Servers, RADIUS Clients, and IP Filters settings in Windows Server 2016 NPS templates. Network Access Protection (NAP) is deprecated on Windows Server 2016 NPS.

5. B. Windows Server 2016 NPS formats accounting data as XML that it sends to the **report_event** stored procedure in the SQL Server database that you designate in NPS. For SQL Server logging to function properly, you must have a stored procedure named **report_event** in the SQL Server database that can receive and parse the XML documents from NPS. For that reason, you must name the SQL stored procedure **report_event**.

Chapter 12

Do I Know This Already? Quiz

1. C. With the PowerShell cmdlet **Set-DnsClientServerAddress**, you can configure which DNS server(s) a client's network interface must use. With the **Set-NetIPAddress** PowerShell cmdlet, you can modify configurations of an IP address, such as the assigned IP address and prefix length (subnet mask), but not DNS servers. With the **New-NetIPAddress** PowerShell cmdlet, you can add a new IP address to a network interface with the **DefaultGateway** parameter, but no **DNS server** parameter is available.

2. B. Since Windows Server 2016, you can configure the Packet Direct feature on network adapters. You can enable network adapters for using Packet Direct with the PowerShell cmdlet **Enable-NetAdapterPacketDirect**.

    With the PowerShell cmdlet **Enable-NetAdapterRdma**, you can enable RDMA on the network adapters. This also improves throughput and reduces network latency, but Packet Direct is usable only with network adapters that have a minimum of 100 Gbps capability.

    You can enable SR-IOV on a network adapter with the **Enable-NetAdapterSriov** PowerShell cmdlet, but SR-IOV enables network traffic to bypass the software switch layer of the Hyper-V virtualization stack. As a result, the I/O overhead in the software emulation layer is diminished and can achieve network performance that is nearly the same as in nonvirtualized environments.

    You can enable SRIOV with the PowerShell cmdlet **Enable-NetAdapterVmq**, but VMQ is a scaling networking technology for the Hyper-V switch.

3. A. When you use the **Set-NetIPAddress** PowerShell cmdlet to reconfigure the IP address configuration of VM1 so that VM1 is in the same subnet as VM2, both can reach each other. VM1 and VM2 are distributed through two subnets, and when no router is configured to forward IP packets between them, they cannot reach each other. When you change the Hyper-V switch Switch1 to a public switch, this changes nothing for VM1 and VM2; they are still in different subnets. When you change the VM1 IP address to 192.168.93.3/19, you move VM1 to the subnet 192.168.96.0. Configuring the Datacenter Firewall to allow traffic between VM1 and VM2 is not the solution because they are still in different subnets.

4. C. When you add a new route to the routing table of the ISATAP router so that this router can automatically deploy IPv6 addresses to IPv6 hosts through stateless IPv6 configuration, you must use the **Publish** parameter of the **New-NetRoute** PowerShell cmdlet.

For example, with the following command, you add a route for interface 22 (which goes to IPv6 subnet where the IPv6 host resides) and the IPv6 network 2001:db8:0:2::/64: **New-NetRoute -InterfaceIndex 22 -Destination Prefix 2001:db8:0:2::/64 -Publish Yes**. The **Advertising** and **Forward** parameters must be used on the network interface, not in the routing table entry.

5. B. You cannot use 6to4 with NAT. Teredo and ISATAP can break through NAT.

6. A. The PowerShell command **Enable-RemoteAccessRoutingDomain -Type All** enables all tenants for BGP. The PowerShell cmdlet **Set-RemoteAccessConfiguration** modifies the configuration of a remote access role; you cannot configure or enable BGP with that.

    With the PowerShell cmdlet **Enable-NetworkSwitchFeature**, you also cannot enable BGP.

    With the PowerShell cmdlet **Enable-BgpRouteFlapDampening**, you enable route flap dampening, not BGP. When a BGP route is being advertised and withdrawn, making the routing table unstable, you can configure the BGP router to assign a dampening weight to the route, monitor it for flaps, and, accordingly, suppress or unsuppress it as required. This helps maintain a stable routing table and involves less processing by the BGP router.

7. B. When you connect from a client through an Azure P2S VPN connection to an Azure VNet, you can view the gateway address with the **Get-NetRoute** PowerShell cmdlet on the client. The tunnel endpoint of the P2S-tunnel is displayed under **NextHop**.

    With the PowerShell cmdlet **Get-NetIPAddress**, you cannot see routing entries; instead, you can verify local IP address settings.

    With the PowerShell cmdlet **Get-NetIPInterface**, you cannot see routing entries.

    With the PowerShell cmdlet **Get-BgpCustomRoutes**, you can verify BGP custom routes. This is possible only when BGP is enabled.

End-of-Chapter Review Questions

1. C. You can solve the name resolution problem with the following PowerShell cmdlet: **Add-DnsClientNrptRule -Namespace "usa.pearson.com" -DnsSecEnable -NameServers "172.16.0.10"**. It seems that the DNS server DNS3 is not defined in the NRPT table on that client or is not added as a DNSSEC-enabled DNS server.

When you use the PowerShell cmdlet **Get-DnsClientNRPTPolicy**, you can view the NRPT settings, but you cannot solve the problem with that.

With the **Resolve-DnsName** PowerShell command, you can test the name resolution for an individual hostname, but this is not the solution.

With the **Get-DnsClientCache** PowerShell cmdlet, you can view the hostname cache of the client. This is a good idea because when the IP address changes, old information sometimes is still located in the hostname cache. However, this is not the solution in this case.

With the **Get-NetRoute** PowerShell cmdlet, you can view the routing table of that client. You can verify the correct routing settings for the DirectAccess tunnel, but in this case, the client cannot access internal resources in only usa.pearson.com. This means that the client can access resources in the other domains, so the DirectAccess tunnel is established and routing is correct.

2. B, C. You can use **Resolve-DnsName** to resolve the AAAA record to an IPv6 address of the network resource you want to reach. Example: **$r = Resolve-DnsName -name www.pearson. com -type AAAA**. After that, you can display the IPv6 address property of the **$r** variable to find the IPv6 address and the net route with the following PowerShell command: **Find-NetRoute -RemoteIPAddress $r.ipv6address**.

   With the **Get-NetTCPSetting** PowerShell cmdlet, you can view TCP settings, but you cannot find out what IPv6 address and interface your host is using to a specific network resource.

   With the **Get-NetRoute PowerShell** cmdlet, you can view the routing table and search for the specific routing entry. This works faster using **Find-NetRoute**, particularly when you have many routing table entries.

3. D. The client is part of the subnet 192.168.192.0. When you use 19 bits for the subnet mask, which means a subnet mask of 255.255.224.0, you can calculate the following possible subnets: 192.168.0.0, 192.168.32.0, 192.168.64.0, 192.168.96.0, 192.168.128.0, 192.168.160.0, 192.168.192.0, and 192.168.224.0.

4. C. To get a 6to4 interface displayed with **ipconfig /all**, a global IPv6 address must be configured on that client.

5. B. To use such PowerShell cmdlets, you must install the **RSAT-RemoteAccess-PowerShell** feature. The **RSAT-RemoteAccess-Mgmt** feature installs the graphical Remote Access console, but you cannot configure a RAS Gateway as a BGP-enabled LAN router. The RemoteAccess and Routing roles must be installed, but to use this PowerShell cmdlet, you also need to install the **RSAT-RemoteAccess-PowerShell** feature.

Chapter 13

Do I Know This Already? Quiz

1. A, C, E. To use Windows PowerShell to exclude folder targets outside the client's site, use the **Set-DfsnFolder -EnableInsiteReferrals** cmdlet and set the value to **$false**; the DFS namespace server provides in-site referrals first and then provides referrals to other sites.

   To enable failback to the original server in the client's site, use the **Set-DfsnFolder -EnableTargetFailback $true** PowerShell command.

   You also can change the Effective Referrals Ordering setting in the DFS Management tool on the folder properties to enable In-Site Referrals. You have to do that for the Marketing folder on DFS3 and the Accounting folder on DFS4. When you configure the folder target properties and you disable the Enable Referrals for This Folder Target setting, then you have disabled the target completely and no client can access the folder target.

2. The correct configuration order is the following. (First, you must ensure that both DFS servers are in the same domain. DFS Replication between DFS servers in different domains is not possible.)

   Step 1. **c.** Remove DFS2 from pucertify.pearson.com and add DFS2 to pearson.com.

   Step 2. **b.** Install DFS namespaces and the DFS Replication role on DFS1 and DFS2.

   Step 3. **a.** Create a new replication group.

   Step 4. **d.** Add DFS1 and DFS2 as replication group members.

   Step 5. **f.** Select the full mesh replication topology.

   Step 6. **e.** Configure replication scheduling.

   Step 7. **g.** Define DFS1 as a primary member.

   Step 8. **i.** Define the folder to replicate.

   Step 9. **h.** Define the local path on other members.

   Step 10. **k.** Wait for AD replication.

   Step 11. **j.** Push initial replication by restarting the DFSR service on DFS1 and DFS2.

3. A. When you use cross-file RDC on very high-bandwidth network connections, cross-file RDC might add too much local processing time and negatively affect performance. In extremely large datasets (millions of files on a volume with a great deal of similarity), cross-file RDC can also negatively affect CPU and disk utilization. Consider disabling cross-file RDC when you replicate over LANs and very high-performance WANs. With the Power-Shell command **Set-DfsrConnection -DisableCrossFileRDC $true**, you can disable cross-file RDC for a DFSR connection. **Set-DfsrConnection -DisableCrossFileRDC $false** is the default setting.

4. B. You can implement more fault tolerance by configuring Network Load Balancing (NLB) with round robin for the standalone namespace servers. They do not use Active Directory to store namespace information. Because of that, you must distribute the workload among the servers with NLB.

   The best solution for fault tolerance is to migrate the standalone namespace to a domain-based namespace. This is possible because these servers are domain members; when the namespace is saved in Active Directory, it is replicated through AD replication among the domain controllers.

   Adding another DFS server to BranchOffice2 is a good idea because, when one or two of the other DFS servers stop, this additional server can still offer the standalone namespace.

   However, the namespace is still not saved in Active Directory. Moving the standalone namespace servers to Headquarters is not a good idea because then clients from BranchOffice2 cannot find a near DFS server in their site and they instead have to go to the Headquarters site; this reduces performance for the clients.

5. B, D. With the PowerShell cmdlet **Restore-DfsrPreservedFiles**, you can restore preserved files and folders. DFSR preserves conflicted, deleted, and preexisting files and folders. For all three types, DFS Replication moves the files to either <replicated folder>\DfsrPrivate\Conflict And Deleted or <replicated folder>\DfsrPrivate\Preexisting. DFSR records these files in a manifest, either ConflictAndDeletedManifest.xml or PreExisting Manifest.xml, as appropriate. Specify the ConflictAndDeletedManifest.xml manifest to restore conflicted and deleted files and folders. Specify the PreExisting-Manifest.xml manifest to restore preexisting files and folders. You can use the **Get-DfsrPreservedFiles** cmdlet to view preserved files and folders. The **AllowClobber** parameter overwrites existing files that have the same names in the specified location.

6. C. The initial DFS Replication can take a long time and consume a large amount of network bandwidth when replicating a large set of files. Windows

Server 2016 provides a feature that clones the database for the initial replication. To create a clone of the database, use the **Export-DfsrClone** PowerShell cmdlet to export the DFSR database and volume configuration XML file settings for a given local computer volume. On a large dataset, exports might take a long time to complete. You can use the **Get-DfsrCloneState** PowerShell cmdlet to determine the status of the export operation.

7. A. You need to use Distributed BranchCache mode because the BranchOffice site has no servers. You do not have to install the BranchCache feature on the clients because Windows 7 is part of the operating system as a service, but you have to enable the BranchCache service on the clients. You can do so through GPO, PowerShell, or the **netsh** utility locally. You must install the BranchCache feature (and also the BranchCache for Network Files feature) on the file server. You do not have to install BranchCache on SVR1 or SVR2 because they are not part of the BranchOffice site.

8. E. With the PowerShell cmdlet **Enable-BCHostedServer -RegisterSCP**, you must register the BranchCache host in Active Directory. With the PowerShell cmdlet **Clear-BCCache**, you delete all data in all data cache files and all hash cache files.

    The PowerShell cmdlet **Disable-BCServerOnBattery** configures a client to ignore content discovery requests in distributed cache mode when operating on battery power.

    The PowerShell cmdlet **Enable-BCLocal** enables the BranchCache service in local caching mode. In local caching mode, a client stores data in the BranchCache cache and attempts to read data from the local BranchCache cache, but it does not contact peers or attempt to contact a hosted cache server.

    The **Export-BCSecretKey** PowerShell cmdlet exports a secret key to a file.

    The **Set-BCMinSMBLatency** PowerShell cmdlet sets the minimum latency that must exist between client and server before transparent caching functions are used. Use this cmdlet to specify when client computers in branch offices start caching content from content servers based on the network latency, or delay, that occurs when the clients download content over a wide-area network (WAN) link.

    The **Set-BCAuthentication** PowerShell cmdlet specifies the authentication mode for client computers. This can be set on a hosted cache server to enable clients to prove domain membership before uploading data.

9. A. On an application server, you must install and enable BITS and the BranchCache feature.

10. C, D. With the PowerShell command **Get-NetFirewallProfile**, you cannot view the firewall rules; instead, you can see the firewall profile settings.

With **netsh branchcache show status**, you can verify whether the Branch-Cache service is running, check the BranchCache mode, and see whether the firewall is enabled or disabled; however, you cannot view the firewall rules.

With **netsh branchcache show status all**, you can verify the networking status and the Peer Discovery Firewall rules state.

With the PowerShell cmdlet **Get-BCStatus**, you also can verify the Peer Discovery Firewall rules state.

End-of-Chapter Review Questions

1. A. To make it possible on DFS2 to use DFS PowerShell cmdlets, you have to install the File Server role.

2. B. When you want to get information about a specific connection schedule between specific DFS members of a DFS Replication group, you must use the **Get-DfsrConnectionSchedule** PowerShell cmdlet. With the PowerShell cmdlet **Get-DfsrGroupSchedule**, you get only the group schedule settings. With the PowerShell cmdlet **Get-DfsReplicationGroup**, you get the settings of a DFS Replication group, not the connection schedules. With the Power-Shell cmdlet **Get-DfsrMember**, you get the list of members in a replication group.

3. A. DFSR creates a staging folder for each replicated folder. This staging folder contains the marshalled files sent between servers and allows replication without risk of interruption from subsequent handles to the file. By default, files larger than 256 KB stage during replication, unless RDC is enabled and using its default minimum file size; in that case, files larger than 64 KB are staged. When replicating on low-latency, high-bandwidth networks such as LANS and high-end WANs, it might be faster to allow certain files to replicate without first staging. If users do not frequently reopen files after modification or addition to a content set (such as during batch processing that dumps files onto a DFSR server for replication out to hundreds of nodes without any later modification), skipping the RDC and the staging process can lead to significant performance boosts.

You configure this using **Set-DfsrMembership** and the **MinimumFile StagingSize** parameter.

With the **ConflictandDeletedQuotaInMB** parameter, you specify the maximum size, in megabytes, for the ConflictsAndDeleted folder.

With the **DisableMembership** parameter, you disable the membership for a replication folder in a replication group. If you disable membership, DFS Replication stops replicating content on this computer but does not delete the replicated folder or its private replication data. This does not boost replication performance.

With the **RemoveDeletedFiles** parameter, you delete files and folders immediately following inbound replication. If this parameter has a value of **$False**, the DFS Replication member moves deleted files and folders to the ConflictAndDeleted folder when the deletion replicates inbound.

Chapter 14

Do I Know This Already? Quiz

1. C, D. You should use up to 32 NICs in a team because standalone NIC Teaming supports up to 32 NICs in a team. SET supports only eight NICs in a team. You should use "Provides teaming in a VM" because only standalone NIC Teaming can be used to provide NIC Teaming in a VM. NIC Teaming in a VM applies only to vmNICs connected to external switches; vmNICs connected to internal or private switches show as disconnected when they are in a team.

   NIC Teaming in Windows Server 2016 also can be deployed in a VM. SET does not support teaming in a VM. You should not use "Support for Hyper-V Network Virtualization SDN version (HNVv2)" because SET fully supports all the capabilities of HNVv2, including both NV-GRE and VXLAN operation.

   You should not use "Requires identical NICs in a team" because SET requires all NICs in a team to be identical (same manufacturer, model, firmware, and driver).

2. B. You should use the PowerShell command **Set-NetAdapterRss -Name * -Enabled $true** because it enables Receive Side Scaling (RSS) on the VMs.

   You should not use **Enable-NetAdapterIPSecOffload** because that PowerShell cmdlet enables IPSec task offloading, to reduce the workload from the main computer's CPU to a dedicated processor on the network adapter. This has to do with only IPSec network traffic; you cannot distribute the network receiving processing across virtual processors with that.

You cannot use **Set-VMNetworkAdapter** because that PowerShell cmdlet configures many virtual network adapter settings, such as DHCPGuard, RouterGuard, IPSec Task Offloading, and Port Mirroring, but you cannot use it to enable RSS.

You cannot use **Set-ReceiveConnector** because this PowerShell cmdlet is a command from Exchange Server and is usable only with on-premises Exchange servers, not on Exchange Online; you cannot configure the distribution of network receiving processing across virtual processors with it.

3.   Preconfiguration tasks: A, B; PowerShell commands: F, H, I. You should use **Install-WindowsFeature "data-center-bridging"** because if you want to manage DCB locally on a Windows Server 2016 server, you must install the feature for it. If you want to manage DCB only from a switch and you propagate the settings to an end device such as a network card on the server, you do not have to install the DCB feature on the server.

You should use **Set-NetQoSdcbxSetting -Willing 0** because you cannot configure DCB settings such as traffic classes, PFC, and application priority locally at the server if the Willing bit is not set to false on a network card. First, you must set the Willing bit to false with this command. After that, you can enable DCB on the network adapter, or you can configure your DCB settings locally. If the DC Willing bit is true, the network card can accept configurations from a remote device such as another switch through DCB.

You should use **Get-NetAdapterQos** because you can use this PowerShell cmdlet even if you have not installed the DCB feature on the server to display DCB settings on network adapters.

You should use **Disable-NetAdapterQos** because this PowerShell cmdlet can be used without installing the DCB feature on the server to display DCB settings on network adapters.

You should use **Enable-NetAdapterQos** because this PowerShell cmdlet can be used without installing the DCB feature on the server to display DCB settings on network adapters.

You should not use **import-module netqos**, **import-module dcbqos**, or **import-module netadapter** because you do not have to import the modules. Since PowerShell 3.0, if you use a PowerShell cmdlet from a specific module, the module is imported automatically.

You should not use **Set-NetQosPolicy** because you must install DCB to configure existing QoS policies.

You should not use **Get-NetQosFlow Control** because you must install DCB to view QoS flow control settings.

You should not use **Set-NetQosTrafficClass** because you must install DCB to view QoS traffic class settings.

4. C. You should use **Enable-NetAdapterRDMA** because NIC6 and NIC7 are not enabled for RDMA. If you want more throughput, lower latency, and less CPU impact for these network cards, you can use RDMA. If you want to use RDMA and SET for a hyperconverged solution using Storage Spaces Direct, you must identify the network adapters with the **Get-NetAdapter** PowerShell cmdlet. Then you need to create the virtual switch connected to both of the physical network adapters and enable SET with **New-VMSwitch -Name SETSwitch -NetAdapterName "<adapter1>", "<adapter2>" -EnableEmbeddedTeaming $true**. After that, you add the host vNICs to the virtual switch with the **Add-VMNetwork** Adapter PowerShell cmdlet and you configure the host vNIC to use a VLAN with the **Set-VMNetworkAdapter Vlan** PowerShell cmdlet. Then you can enable RDMA on the host vNIC adapters with the **Enable-NetAdapterRDMA** PowerShell cmdlet.

You should not use **Set-NetAdapter** because you cannot enable RDMA or SET with this PowerShell cmdlet.

You should not use **Enable NetAdapterVmq** because this PowerShell cmdlet enables Virtual Machine Queue on the network adapter. VMQ uses hardware packet filtering to deliver packet data from an external virtual machine network directly to virtual machines, which reduces the overhead of routing packets and copying them from the management operating system to the virtual machine. With VMQ, you cannot access host memory directly without the intervention of the CPU. For that, you have the RDMA capability.

You should not use **New-VMSwitch** because, with the **New-VMSwitch** PowerShell cmdlet, you can create a SET switch.

With the parameter **EnableEmbeddedTeaming $true**, you can enable SET for this switch; however, you do not get less CPU impact, which is the requirement in this exam question.

5. B. You should use IPv6 link local addresses because IPv6 link local IP addresses start with FE80. When private (cluster-only) networks with multiple NICs are detected, the cluster automatically recognizes IPv6 link local (FE80) IP addresses for each NIC on each subnet. This saves administrators time because they no longer have to manually configure IPv6 link local (fE80) IP address resources. Simplified SMB Multichannel and multi-NIC networks are new features of Windows Server 2016. Now you can use multiple NICs

on the same failover cluster network subnet and SMB Multichannel is enabled automatically.

You should not use IPv6 site local unicast addresses because this is an obsolete IPv6 alternative. These addresses were similar to the private IP address ranges in IPv4. An organization could choose any IP address in the FEC0::/10 range. Since September 2004, these IPv6 addresses have been obsolete; new implementations must use global unicast IPv6 addresses instead; you cannot use these IPv6 addresses for a simplified SMB Multichannel Windows Server 2016 failover cluster configuration.

You should not use IPv6 unique local unicast addresses because they are used for tunnel configurations to avoid address collisions; you cannot use these IPv6 addresses for a simplified SMB Multichannel Windows Server 2016 failover cluster configuration.

You should not use IPv6 global unicast addresses because they are public accessible IPv6 addresses. The cluster network of a Windows Server 2016 failover cluster is a private network and does not have to be directly available for the public world.

You cannot use these IPv6 addresses for a simplified SMB Multichannel Windows Server 2016 failover cluster configuration in which multiple NICs can be automatically integrated into the same cluster subnet.

6. A, B, D, F, G, I. You should verify that Hyperthreading is enabled because you cannot use vRSS and VMQ without Hyperthreading enabled. With the PowerShell command **Get-WmiObject -Class win32_processor | FT -Property NumberOfCores, NumberOfLogical Processors -auto**, you can verify that Hyperthreading is enabled.

If you see values at **NumberofCores** and **NumberofLogicalProcessors**, Hyperthreading is enabled.

You should use Teaming Mode: Switch Independent because you have to use Switch Independent Teaming Mode as a prerequisite for a VMQ configuration; the difference between dependent teaming mode and independent teaming mode is that the bandwidth of multiple-teamed network adapters shuttles the network to different switches. In independent teaming mode, you can configure your team in active/active or active/standby. If you use active/passive, you use one adapter offline to function as a failover adapter in the event of an adapter failure.

You should use LoadBalancing Algorithm: Dynamic because the virtual adapters are registered separately across physical adapters and received traffic can be balanced; however, sending is balanced using the address hash method.

This gives you an impressive balancing configuration. Dynamic mode also uses flowlets, a technique that breaks an existing TCP stream and moves it to another physical adapter. For example, imagine that you have 2x10 GB cards in a team that uses dynamic load balancing. VM1 produces a massive outbound file transfer that gets balanced to the first adapter. VM2 starts a small outbound transfer that is balanced to the second adapter. VM3 begins its own large transfer and is balanced back to the first adapter. Transfer on the second adapter finishes quickly, leaving two large transfers to share the same 10 GB adapter. Using the Hyper-V port or any address hash load-balancing method, you can do nothing about this except cancel a transfer and restart it, hoping to balance it to the second adapter. With the new method, one of the streams can be dynamically moved to the other adapter, hence the word *Dynamic*. Flowlets require the split to be made at particular junctions in the stream. It is possible for Dynamic to work even when a neat flowlet opportunity does not present itself.

You should use Enable VMQ on Network Adapters because you can use the PowerShell cmdlet **Enable-NetAdapterVmq** to enable every NIC for the VMQ feature. With **Get-NetAdapterVmq**, you can verify that VMQ is enabled on the interfaces.

You should use Set Base and Max CPUs with **Set-NetAdapterVmq** because this defines how CPUs can be used for VMQ on every interface. With the **BaseProcessorNumber** parameter of the PowerShell cmdlet **Set-NetAdapterVmq**, you specify the starting processor for the NIC to use for processing. With the **MaxProcessors** parameter of the PowerShell cmdlet **Set-NetAdapterVmq**, you can define the maximum number of CPUs that can be used from the interface.

You should use Enable vRSS with Enable-NetAdapterRSS because you have to enable vRSS on every VMQ network adapter if you want to use the RSS feature and distribute the workload across multiple CPUs. You also can do that with **netsh interface tcp set global rss=enabled** and in the Device Manager network adapter properties advanced settings.

You should not use TeamingMode: Switch Dependent because, to use VMQ, you must use a Teaming Mode of Switch Dependent; that provides the largest set of VMQ queues.

You should not use LoadBalancingAlgorithm: Transport Ports because this uses the source and destination TCP ports and the IP addresses to create a hash; then it assigns the packets that have that hash value to one of the available network adapters.

You should not use **Set BaseProcessorGroup** with **Set-NetAdapterVmq** because if you are using multiple NICs, you should not overlap the logical processor usage, if possible. For example, the first NIC might use cores 1 through 4 (ProcessorGroup0), the next might use cores 5 through 8 (ProcessorGroup1), and so on. For that, you can group the CPUs into ProcessorGroups, as in this PowerShell example: **Set-NetAdapterVmq -Name NIC1 -BaseProcessor-Group -0 -BaseProcessorNumber 1 -MaxProcessor Number -Max Processors 4, Set-NetAdapterVmq -Name NIC1 -BaseProcessorGroup -1 -BaseProcessorNumber 5 -MaxProcessorNumber 8 -MaxProcessors 4**.

You should not use Enable vRSS with Set-NetAdapter because with the PowerShell cmdlet **Set-NetAdapter**, you cannot enable RSS. For that, you have to use the PowerShell cmdlets **Enable-NetAdapterRss** or **Set-NetAdapterRss**.

7. VMs: C, D; PowerShell commands: F, G. You should use VM3 and VM4 because SR-IOV is supported on the guest machine only as of Windows 8 and Windows Server 2012. The host also has to be at least Windows Server 2012.

    You should use the **New-VMSwitch** PowerShell cmdlet because first you have to create an external virtual switch. You can do that with the following PowerShell command: **New-VMSwitch SR-IOV -netadaptername "SR-IOV" -EnableIoV $true**.

    With **Get-VMSwitch**, you can verify the properties of the created external VMSwitch. There you can verify settings such as **IovVirtualFunctionCount**, **IoVirtualFunctioninUse**, and **IoVQueuePairCount**: The **IovVirtualFunctionCount** parameter is the number of VFs that are currently available for use by guest operating systems. Each software-based NIC can be backed by a VF. Each VM can have up to eight software-based NICs. The **IovVirtualFunctionsInUse** parameter is the current number of VFs in use by guest operating systems. The **IoVQueuePairCount** parameter is the number of pairs that are available as hardware resources on the physical NIC. This varies among hardware vendors. In most cases, there will be as many pairs available as there are VFs. Depending on the vendor, additional functionality might be included in the VFs; for instance, a hardware vendor might support RSS in a guest operating system that is backed by a VF and requires more than one queued pair for this.

    You should use **Set-VMNetworkAdapter** because this PowerShell cmdlet allows you to enable SR-IOV on the virtual network adapter of the VM. *Example:* **Set-VM Network Adapter IOV8222 -IoVWeight 50 -PassThrough**.

You should not use VM1 because the Hyper-V host operating system is not at least Windows Server 2012. You should not use VM2 because the guest operating system is not at least Windows 8.

You should not use **Set-VM Host** because you cannot access any settings about SR-IOV with this PowerShell cmdlet on the host.

You should not use **Set-VMProcessor** because you cannot access any settings about SR-IOV with this PowerShell cmdlet.

8.

Network Requirement	SDN Component
Automating the configuration of the network infrastructure	A
Network Controller communicates with the network	B
Administrator communicates with the Network Controller	C
Windows PowerShell, REST API, management application	A

The correct answer is (from top to bottom): NC, S-API, N-API, NC. You should use the Network Controller for automating the configuration of the network infrastructure because, through SDN, you can use policies and JSON files to automatically set up and configure network components such as virtual networks, gateways, and firewall settings.

For example, you can use policies to configure firewall rules and strengthen the stance of your infrastructure because you can prevent hosts in the same DMZ tier from communicating with one another, thus limiting the reach of an attack. When your segment security is defined by perimeter firewalls, you can't reach this level of control in a scalable and manageable way.

You can use the Network Controller to manage the following physical and virtual network infrastructure components centrally: Hyper-V VMs and virtual switches, physical network switches, physical network routers, firewall software, VPN gateways, and load balancers.

You should use the Southbound API for "Network Controller communicates with the network" because, in SDN, the southbound interface is the OpenFlow (or alternative) protocol specification. Its main function is to enable communication between the SDN controller and the network nodes (both physical and virtual switches and routers) so that the router can discover network topology, define network flows, and implement requests relayed to it via northbound APIs.

The northbound interface describes the area of protocol-supported communication between the controller and applications or higher-layer control programs. You should use the northbound API for "Administrator communicates with Network Controller" because a northbound API interface is an interface that allows a particular component of a network to communicate with a higher-level component. Conversely, a southbound interface allows a particular network component to communicate with a lower-level component.

Northbound flow can be thought of as going upward, while southbound flow can be thought of as going downward. In architectural diagrams, northbound interfaces are drawn at the top of the applicable component and southbound interfaces are drawn at the bottom of the component.

You should use the Network Controller for Windows PowerShell, the REST API, and management applications to centrally manage your network environment through the network controller and to automate the configuration processes.

9.

Technical Statement About Windows Server 2016 HNV	Choice
Is using the Azure Virtual Filtering Platform (VFP) switch	True
Cannot be used with any other third-party switch extension	True
Broadcasts and subnet multicasts implemented using unicast replication	True
Is using Hyper-V switch extensions in the SDN stack	False
Can use cross-subnet multicast routing	True
For a VM establishing a connection to another VM in the same VSID, the Host Agent is responsible for MAC address resolution	True
For a VM establishing a connection to another VM in another VSID, nondefault routes are supported	False

Technical Statement About Windows Server 2016 VXLAN	Choice
Forwarding table of the external switch does not grow with the increase in the VMs behind the physical port on the server	True
1 PA per NIC team member	True

Correct answers (from top to bottom): True, True, True, False, True, True, False, True, True.

You should answer True for the statement "Is using the Azure Virtual Filtering Platform (VFP) switch" because HNVv2 uses the Azure Virtual Filtering Platform (VFP) forwarding extension in the Hyper-V Switch. HNVv2 also is fully integrated into Microsoft Azure Stack, which includes the Network Controller in the SDN stack. VFP is a programmable switch that exposes an easy-to-program abstracted interface to network agents that act on behalf of network controllers such as the VNET controller and the SLB controller. By leveraging host components and doing much of the packet processing on each host running in the datacenter, the Azure SDN data plane scales nodes from 1 GB to 40 GB.

You should answer True for the statement "Cannot be used with any other third-party switch extension" because HNVv2 is implemented using the Azure VFP switch extension, which cannot be used with any third-party switch extension. Hyper-V switch extensions do not work with HNVv2 in the new SDN stack.

You should answer True for the statement "Broadcasts and subnet multicasts implemented using unicast replication" because, with Windows Server 2016 broadcast and subnet, multicasts are implemented using unicast replication. When a VM broadcasts a packet, HNV uses unicast replication to make a copy of the original packet and replace the destination IP and MAC addresses with the addresses of each VM in the same VSID; therefore, it converts the broadcast network traffic into unicast network traffic.

You should answer False for the statement "Is using Hyper-V switch extensions in the SDN stack" because Hyper-V switch extensions do not work with HNVv2 in the new SDN stack. HNVv2 is implemented using the Azure Virtual Filtering Platform (VFP) switch extension. You should answer True for "Can use cross-subnet multicast routing" because, in this scenario, the separated addresses (CAs and PAs), the policy settings of the Hyper-V hosts, and the address translation between the CA and the PA for inbound and outbound VM traffic isolate these sets of servers using either the NVGRE key or the VXLAN VNID. Furthermore, the virtualization mappings and transformation decouple the virtual network architecture from the physical network infrastructure. Although servers in the Pearson network and servers in the Pearson UCertify network reside in their own CA IP subnets (10.1.1/24), their physical deployment happens on two hosts in different PA subnets, 192.168.1/24 and 192.168.2/24, respectively. The implication is that cross-subnet virtual machine provisioning and live migration become possible with HNV.

You should answer True for the statement "For a VM establishing a connection to another VM in the same VSID, the Host Agent is responsible for MAC address resolution" because HNVv2 implements correct L2 switching and L3 routing semantics to work just as a physical switch or router would work. When a VM connected to an HNV virtual network attempts to establish a connection with another VM in the same VSID, it first needs to learn the CA MAC address of the remote VM. If the source VM's ARP table has an ARP entry for the destination VM's IP address, the MAC address from this entry is used. If an entry does not exist, the source VM sends an ARP broadcast with a request for the MAC address that corresponds to the destination VM's IP address to be returned. The Hyper-V switch intercepts this request and sends it to the Host Agent. The Host Agent looks in its local database for a corresponding MAC address for the requested destination VM's IP address.

You should answer False for the statement "For a VM establishing a connection to another VM in another VSID, nondefault routes are supported" because if a VM connected to an HNV virtual network wants to create a connection with a VM in a different VSID, a packet needs to be routed accordingly. HNV assumes a star network topology. Only one IP address in the CA space is used as the next-hop to reach all IP prefixes. This enforces a limitation to a single default route, so nondefault routes are not supported.

You should answer True for the statement "Forwarding table of the external switch does not grow with the increase in the VMs behind the physical port on the server" because VXLAN is a Layer 2 technology that enables you to create an L2 network on top of a Layer 3 network, providing further network isolation. VXLAN provides a virtual L2 network that stretches over multiple physical L2 networks. Therefore, provisioning resources in a cloud environment is not restricted to a single physical Layer 2 network. Physical servers can be a part of a VXLAN network as long as they are connected by IPv4 or IPv6 networks.

You should answer True for the statement "1 PA per NIC team member" because the PA sharing scheme for Windows Server 2012 R2 is 1 PA per VSID per host. For Windows Server 2016, it is one PA per NIC team member.

10. You should choose the statement "The Network Controller processes SLB commands that come in through the northbound API from the Windows Server 2016 System Center Virtual Machine Manager" because, in SDN, the northbound API enables you to configure, monitor, troubleshoot, and deploy new devices (by REST endpoint or a management application as VMM). The northbound API is the interface that enables SCVMM to communicate with the Network Controller.

You should choose the statement "The Network Controller communicates through the southbound API to the SLB Host Agent" because the southbound API allows the Network Controller to communicate with the network. The SLB Host Agent listens for SLB policy updates from the Network Controller. In addition, the Host Agent programs rules for SLB into the SDN-enabled Hyper-V virtual switches that are configured on the local computer. Between the Network Controller and the SLB Host Agent, the SLB MUX component processes inbound network traffic and maps VIPs (virtual IPs) to DIPs (data-center IPs); then it forwards the traffic to the correct DIP. Each MUX also uses BGP to publish VIP routes to edge routers.

You should choose the statement "SRV01 and SRV02 communicate through east–west TCP/UDP traffic" because east–west communication is virtual network internal communication. North–south SLB communication comes from outside the virtual network from WAN.

11. **A, C.** You should deploy the Network Controller because then you have the basic computer and network infrastructure in place to proceed with the RAS Gateway deployment. The Network Controller communicates with network devices, services, and components by using the southbound API. With the southbound API, the Network Controller can discover network devices, detect service configurations, and gather all the needed information about the network. The Network Controller also offers RAS Gateway management. In SCVMM, the RAS Gateway is known as the Windows Server Gateway. Some Network Controller features for RAS follow:

- You can add and remove gateway VMs from the cluster and specify the level of backup required.

- Site-to-site virtual private network (VPN) gateway connectivity between remote tenant networks and your datacenter is accomplished using IPSec.

- Site-to-site VPN gateway connectivity between remote tenant networks and your datacenter is accomplished using Generic Routing Encapsulation (GRE).

- Point-to-site VPN gateway connectivity is supported so that your tenants' administrators can access their resources on your datacenter from anywhere.

- Layer 3 forwarding capability exists.

You should deploy the Software Load Balancer as well. This step is not required when deploying a RAS Gateway, but if you need simplicity and preview validation, this is recommended. You should not create an IP pool for GRE VIP addresses because you can create an IP pool after you have created the GRE VIP logical network. This is not a prerequisite for the RAS Gateway configuration in SCVMM 2016; it is the next step after creating the GRE VIP logical network.

You should not import a gateway service template because, after downloading the gateway service template from the Microsoft SDN GitHub repository, you need to copy the contents to a folder on your VMM server to which the VMM server has access. The download contains two templates, one for Generation 1 VMs and one for Generation 2 VMs. After that, you import the service template. All these steps must be done in SCVMM 2016 after you deploy the network controller and the SLB.

12. B, D. You should use distributed firewall policies because the new Windows Server 2016 SDN Network Controller Datacenter Firewall is a new service. This is a stateful multitenant firewall that tenant administrators can use to install and configure firewall policies to protect virtual networks.

You should use Network Security Groups because, with Windows Server 2016 Network Controller and SDN, the Network Security Groups can be used like Azure Network Security Groups in Azure. Through Network Security Groups, administrators can control access by permitting or denying communication between the workloads within a virtual network, from systems on a customer's networks via cross-premises connectivity, and direct Internet communication. You can apply NSGs on the subnet or NIC levels. You can define rules about which source or destination port protocols are allowed or denied.

You should use an antimalware solution because the Windows Server 2016 Network Controller does not offer this. Instead, it offers the Datacenter Firewall, which administrators can use to install and configure firewall policies to protect virtual machine and networks.

You should use network traffic encryption because you cannot encrypt datacenter or virtual network traffic with the Windows Server 2016 Network Controller and the Datacenter Firewall.

End-of-Chapter Review Questions

1. You should use the following solution:

New-VMSwitch Switch1 -NetAdapterName "NIC1", "NIC2"
-EnableEmbeddedTeaming \$true; Add-VMNetworkAdapter
-SwitchName MyRDMAswitch -Name SMBRDMA1;
Add-VMNetworkAdapter -SwitchName RDMAswitch -Name
SMBRDMA2; Enable-NetAdapterRDMA "vEthernet (SMBRDMA_1)",
"vEthernet (SMBRDMA_2)".

2. B. In this case, you cannot use the **Enable-NetAdapterRss** PowerShell cmdlet to enable Receive Side Scaling because the Hyper-V host processor does not support this feature. To reduce the number of processor cycles that are used, you can enable Receive Side Coalescing with the **Enable-NetAdapterRsc** cmdlet. This solution improves scalability by reducing the overhead for processing a large amount of network I/O traffic by offloading some of the work to the network adapters.

3. B. When you disable SMB Multichannel, SMB Direct is also disabled. With SMB Multichannel, SMB detects whether a network adapter has the RDMA capability and then creates multiple RDMA connections for that single session (two per interface). Without SMB Multichannel, SMB uses regular TCP/IP with the RDMA-capable network adapters (all network adapters provide a TCP/IP stack along with the new RDMA stack). When you disable SMB Multichannel, you still can use SET, RDMA, and RSS.

4. A, B, C, D, E. All answers are correct.

5. A, B, D. When you want to add a virtual gateway for a tenant, you have to verify the existence of the GatewayPool, the VirtualNetwork, and the VirtualSubnet because you have to select the VirtualSubnet to be used for routing between the Gateway and the VirtualNetwork. When you want to connect container endpoints to a tenant virtual network through the SDN stack, you have to install the private cloud plug-in into the container host (tenant) VM. The Network Proxy is used to allocate multiple IP addresses for container host VMs.

Glossary of Key Terms

6to4   6to4 is a transition mechanism in which a router with a public IPv4 address can be an IPv6 gateway or provider for a whole set of LANs.

AAAA resource records   An AAAA resource record is a record that stores a single IPv6 address. It is called 4 A's because IPv6 128-bit addresses are four times as large as IPv4's 32-bit addresses.

AD-integrated zone   An AD-integrated zone saves zone data in the Active Directory database. Advantages include more security and automatic replication of the zone data between DNS servers (which are also domain controllers).

Application Directory partition   An Application Directory partition can be used as a custom partition to save DNS data and to replicate this data only to specific domain controllers. An administrator can individually define the name of the partition, the replication scope, and the enlisted domain controllers.

Automatically Update Statistics   You cannot configure this DHCP server general setting in the IPAM configuration console; you must use the DHCP server management tool or DHCP PowerShell cmdlets.

AXFR   AXFR is the transfer of the complete zone. It happens only during initial configuration of a secondary DNS server.

BGP   Border Gateway Protocol allows the routers to route inbound traffic to the MUX by using equal-cost multipath routing (ECMP). It uses the route provided by the host, listens for route updates for VIPs from SLB MUX, and removes SLB MUXs from the SLB rotation if the keepalive fails.

BGP route flap dampening   BGP route dampening is a way to suppress flapping routes so that they are "suppressed" instead of advertised. An unstable network can cause BGP routes to flap, which can force other BGP routers in the network to constantly reconverge. This wastes valuable CPU cycles and can cause severe problems in the network. As a best practice, most ISPs use route dampening regularly.

BGP route reflector   A BGP route reflector allows all iBGP speakers within your autonomous network to learn about the available routes without introducing loops. BGP route reflectors simplify iBGP configuration. When you configure a route reflector, you must tell the router whether the other iBGP router is a client or nonclient. A client is an iBGP router to which the route reflector will reflect routes; the non-client is just a regular iBGP neighbor.

BranchCache   BranchCache is implemented on network file servers to enable client computers in branch office locations to maintain cached copies of network files locally or on a BranchCache host server in their location. Clients in the branch office use the cached copies of the network files instead of copying them again from the head office file server. BranchCache is designed to reduce file traffic over WAN links and is especially effective for file shares with frequently accessed but infrequently changed files.

Cache Locking   Cache Locking is a DNS server feature that enables you to control whether information in the DNS cache can be overwritten. It can be configured only through the command line.

CAConstraint   CAConstraint is an operation mode of TLSA records. With CAConstraint, you can protect a CA certificate.

chain of trust   A DS resource record allows trust for a KSK, a KSK allows trust for all the zone keys (the DNSKEY RRset), and ZSKs allow trust for other resource records of the zone.

connection request policy   Connection request policies are sets of conditions and settings that enable administrators to designate which RADIUS servers perform the authentication and authorization of connection requests that the server running NPS receives from RADIUS clients. Connection request policies can be configured to designate which RADIUS servers are used for RADIUS accounting. Connection request policy conditions are one or more RADIUS attributes that are compared to the attributes of the incoming RADIUS Access-Request message.

Create DHCP Scope   You cannot use the Create DHCP Scope configuration option on multiple DHCP servers in IPAM. To duplicate a DHCP scope, create the scope on at least one DHCP server and then use the Duplicate DHCP Scope configuration option available in the DHCP Scopes view.

cross-file RDC   Cross-file remote differential compression can determine files that are similar to the file that needs to be replicated. It uses blocks of similar files that are identical to the replicating file to minimize the amount of data that needs to be replicated.

custom fields   IPAM enables you to create custom logical groups to improve the audit experience for IP address ranges. To create custom groups, you create and configure custom fields as criteria for grouping.

DANE   DNS-based Authentication of Named Entities (DANE) offers the option to use the DNSSEC infrastructure to store and sign keys and certificates used by

TLS. DANE is envisioned as the preferred basis for binding public keys to DNS names because the entities that vouch for the binding of public key data to DNS names are the same entities responsible for managing those DNS names.

DANE criteria   DANE can work with two points of criteria: 1) The certificate contains the desired domain name. 2) The certificate is issued under a trusted Certificate Authority.

DANE operation modes   DANE defines four operation modes: CAConstraint, ServiceCertificateConstraint, TrustAnchorAssertation, and DomainIssuedCertificate.

DANE statements   DANE offers three major types of statements: 1) CA Constraints: The client should accept certificates issued under only a specific CA. 2) Service Certificate Constraints: The client should accept only a specific certificate. 3) Trust Anchor Assertion: The client should use a domain-provided trust anchor to validate certificates for that domain.

DCB   Data Center Bridging (DCB) is a suite of standards that enable converged fabrics. Storage, data networking, cluster interprocess communication, and management traffic all share the same Ethernet network infrastructure.

DFS   Distributed File System (DFS) provides highly available access to files, load sharing, and WAN-friendly replication.

DFS database cloning   Windows Server 2016 provides a feature that clones the database for the initial replication to improve that replication.

DFS domain-based namespace   A domain-based namespace can be used when high availability of the namespace is required. This is accomplished by replicating the namespace to multiple namespace servers.

DFS standalone namespace   A standalone namespace is used when a company has not implemented Active Directory or does not meet the requirements for a domain-based namespace, and when requirements specify more than 5,000 DFS folders. Standalone DFS namespaces support up to 50,000 folders with targets. They work well for a company that is hosting a DFS namespace in a failover cluster.

DFSN   You can use DFS namespaces (DFSN) to create a virtual representation of shared folder structures. You can create either a domain-based namespace or a standalone namespace.

DFSR   DFS Replication (DFSR) provides a way to keep folders synchronized between servers across well-connected and limited-bandwidth connections.

DHCP authorization   A DHCP server must be authorized in Active Directory before it can be used. It must be verified as an authorized DHCP server before it can service clients with IP address configurations.

DHCP Backup Path   You cannot configure this DHCP server general setting in IPAM; you must use the DHCP server management tool or DHCP PowerShell cmdlets.

DHCP Database Path   You cannot configure this DHCP server general setting in IPAM; you must use the DHCP server management tool or DHCP PowerShell cmdlets.

DHCP failover   The DHCP failover feature can be used as a high availability or load-balancing solution (since Windows Server 2012). With DHCP failover, two DHCP servers share DHCP scope and lease information, enabling one server to provide DHCP leases to clients if the other server is unavailable.

DHCP hot standby   The DHCP failover feature can work in two modes: hot standby and load sharing. DHCP failover can be configured to provide redundancy in hot standby mode.

DHCP load sharing   The DHCP failover feature can work in two modes: hot standby and load sharing mode. Load sharing mode is the default mode. Two DHCP servers simultaneously serve IP addresses and options to clients on a given subnet. DHCP client requests are load-balanced and shared between the two DHCP servers. The default load-balancing ratio between the two servers is 50:50, but this can be customized to any ratio from 0 to 100 percent.

DHCP Name Protection   DHCP Name Protection is a DHCP server setting that protects against name squatting attacks.

DHCP options   Through DHCP options, DHCP servers can be configured to provide optional data that fully configures TCP/IP on a client.

DHCP Policy   The DHCP Policy feature enables you to group DHCP clients by specific attributes based on fields contained in the DHCP client request packet. The feature enables targeted administration and greater control of the configuration parameters delivered to network devices with DHCP.

DHCP Relay Agent   A DHCP Relay Agent is used between networks if a router does not support the RFC 1541 standard, which means that the router cannot deliver DHCPDISCOVER messages. A DHCP Relay Agent forwards DHCP clients to the DHCP server in the network behind the router.

DHCP reservation   A DHCP reservation is used to tell the DHCP server that it has to always deliver the same IP address to the client.

DHCP server   A DHCP server can lease and renew IP addresses for DHCP clients for a specific amount of time. It also can perform DNS name registration for DHCP clients, and it provides IPv4 and IPv6 protocol support.

DHCP server options   You can configure DHCP server options for multiple DHCP servers in IPAM.

DirectAccess client   Computers that are running the following operating systems are supported as DirectAccess clients: Windows 7 Enterprise/Ultimate, Windows 8/8.1 Enterprise, Windows 10 Enterprise, Windows Server 2008 R2, Windows 2012, Windows 2012 R2, and Windows 2016. Non-Microsoft clients are not allowed to be used with DirectAccess.

DirectAccess server   The DirectAccess server is also known as Unified Remote Access. It is a VPN-like technology that enables DirectAccess clients (only Windows) to establish an IPv6 tunnel to the corporate network through the Internet without user interaction. When the user has Internet connectivity, the DirectAccess tunnel automatically is established to the public IP address and name of the DirectAccess server.

DNS analytical logging   DNS analytical logs are not enabled by default. They typically affect only DNS server performance at very high DNS query rates.

DNS Policies   DNS Policies control how a DNS server handles queries based on different parameters. DNS Policies can be used for application high availability, traffic management, split-brain DNS, filtering, forensics, and time of day–based redirection.

DNS Server policies   DNS Server policies is a new Windows Server 2016 DNS feature (configurable only through PowerShell) that controls how a DNS server handles queries based on different parameters and criteria.

DNS server properties   Most DNS server properties cannot be configured through the IPAM configuration console; instead, you must use the DNS manager tool.

DNS server transfer policies   DNS server transfer policies are a new possibility with Windows Server 2016. With these policies, you can specify whether to deny or ignore zone transfers based on different criteria.

DNS socket pool   The DNS socket pool feature of a Windows Server 2016 DNS server uses port randomization when issuing DNS queries. This provides enhanced security against cache poisoning attacks.

DNSKEY   A DNSKEY record publishes the public key for the zone. These keys require periodic replacement through key rollovers. Windows Server 2016 supports automated key rollovers. Every zone has multiple DNSKEYs that are then broken down into the ZSK and KSK.

DNSSEC   DNSSEC is a suite of extensions that adds security to the DNS protocol by enabling DNS responses to be validated. Specifically, DNSSEC provides origin authority, data integrity, and authenticated denial of existence. With DNSSEC, the DNS protocol is much less susceptible to certain types of attacks, particularly DNS spoofing attacks.

DNSSEC priming   A validating DNS server that uses a DS trust anchor must query the authoritative DNS server to obtain the full DNSKEY resource record set.

DomainDNSZones   DomainDNSZones is a default Active Directory partition used to replicate zone data to all domain controllers in a domain.

DomainIssuedCertificate   DomainIssuedCertificate is an operation mode for DANE and TLSA records that enables you to protect a CA signed or self-signed certificate.

DS record   The registrar where you registered your domain must support DNSSEC. Specifically, it needs to be able to accept and sign Delegation Signer (DS) records that contain the necessary information about the keys used to sign your DNS zone. The registrar also needs to be able to provide these DS records to the parent domain.

ECMP   ECMP (equal-cost multipath routing) is a routing strategy in which next-hop packet forwarding to a single destination can occur over multiple best paths that tie for top place in routing metric calculations. Multipath routing can be used in conjunction with most routing protocols because it is a per-hop decision limited to a single router. It can substantially increase bandwidth by load-balancing traffic over multiple paths.

Edit DHCP Scope   With multiple DHCP servers selected in IPAM, you can configure only the description, lease duration, and capability to enable or disable DNS dynamic updates. Under DHCP Scope and Advanced options, all settings can be configured parallel on multiple DHCP servers through the IPAM configuration console.

ForestDNSZones   A ForestDNSZone is a default Active Directory partition. The msdcs zone saves its zone data by default in the ForestDNSZone partition. Any zone data saved in that partition is replicated to all domain controllers in the forest.

forwarder   A DNS server that forwards DNS queries to other DNS servers is a DNS forwarder.

Get Forests   A new Windows Server 2016 IPAM setting in the Configure Server Discovery dialog box to manage other forests through IPAM.

Get-IpamDhcpServer   PowerShell cmdlet that lists all IPAM DHCP server properties.

Get-IpamDnsResourceRecord   PowerShell cmdlet that gets information about DNS zones from IPAM. (Only two IPAM PowerShell cmdlets can get DNS data from IPAM.)

Get-IpamDnsZone   PowerShell cmdlet to get DNS resource records from IPAM. (Only two IPAM PowerShell cmdlets can get DNS data from IPAM.)

GlobalNames zone   You use a GlobalNames zone if you plan to retire WINS or if you need single-label name resolution.

GlobalQueryBlockList   You need to remove ISATAP from the GlobalQueryBlockList in DNS.

HCAP   Host Credential Authorization Protocol (HCAP) is removed in Windows Server 2016.

Health Registration Authority   The Health Registration Authority (HRA) is removed in Windows Server 2016.

HVN   Hyper-V Network virtualization decouples virtual networks from the physical network infrastructure and removes the constraints of VLAN and hierarchical IP address assignment from virtual machine provisioning.

IP address tracking   Windows Server 2016 IPAM offers operational auditing and IP address tracking functionality. You can use auditing tools to track configuration problems and relevant events. You can collect, manage, and view configuration changes details from DHCP and DNS servers. IPAM facilitates the monitoring and tracking of DHCP service status and utilization of DHCP scopes.

IPAM   Since Windows Server 2012, IP Address Management (IPAM) is implemented as a server role and can be used to plan, track, or centrally manage DNS and DHCP servers.

IPAM access policy   You can create an IPAM access policy for a user and assign the relevant role for the access scope to then apply access to the user. (You cannot deny permission for users with an access policy. If users already have permission granted to perform a procedure because they are members of one or more IPAM administrator groups, they will continue to have that permission even if they have only limited rights granted by role-based access polices.)

IPAM access scope   The one default IPAM access scope is named \Global. All user-defined access scopes are children of that scope.

IPAM database   When you install a Windows Server 2016 IPAM server, you can choose either Windows Internal database (WID) or Microsoft SQL Server database (locally or external) as the storage solution for IPAM data.

IPAM managed servers   IPAM managed servers are DNS or DHCP servers. They can centrally be managed through IPAM. From DCs and NPS servers, an IPAM server only can read data.

IPAM provisioning   Provisioning is the process of enabling required permissions, file shares, and access settings on managed servers so that the IPAM server can communicate with them.

IPAM roles   Nine default built-in IPAM roles enable you to apply access to specific users or groups through IPAM access policies.

IPAM scheduled tasks   Windows Server 2016 IPAM has eight default scheduled tasks: AddressExpiry, AddressUtilization, Audit, DnsServerConfiguration, ServerAvailability, ServerConfiguration, ServerDiscovery, ServiceMonitoring. The scheduled task DnsServerConfiguration is new in Windows Server 2016 IPAM.

IPAMUG   The domain security group IPAMUG automatically is created through the IPAM provisioning process to grant the IPAM server access to managed server resources.

IP-HTTPS   IP-HTTPS enables DirectAccess clients to connect to the DirectAccess server over the IPv4 based Internet. IP-HTTPS is used by clients that are unable to connect to the DirectAccess server by using ISATAP, 6to4, or Teredo. You can configure IP-HTTPS for DirectAccess clients and the DirectAccess server using Group Policy.

IPsec   A DirectAccess client uses Authenticated IP (AuthIP) and IPsec to negotiate and authenticate an encrypted IPsec tunnel to the DirectAccess server.

IPv6 link-local addresses   IPv6 link-local addresses are always configured automatically on an interface by the operating system, regardless of whether stateful or stateless address autoconfiguration is deployed. The address block FE80::/10 is reserved for link-local unicast addressing.

IPv6 Options tab   No IPv6 Options tab exists on the IPv6 advanced network interface settings as in IPv4 because filtering is defined only for IPv4 traffic.

IPv6 prefix   IPv6 prefixes are used instead of a subnet mask.

IPv6 prefix policy   When a name can be resolved to both an IPv4 address and an IPv6 address, both addresses are returned to the client. The client then chooses which address to use, based on IPv6 prefix polices.

IPv6 root hints   Windows Server 2016 now also supports IPv6 addresses for the Internet Root Servers. This is IPv6 root hints.

IPv6 WINS tab   WINS provides a centralized database for registering dynamic mappings of a network's NetBIOS names. IPv6 does not support WINS, so it has no IPv6 WINS tab on the advanced network interface settings as in IPv4.

ISATAP   ISATAP is an address assignment technology that you can use to provide unicast IPv6 connectivity between IPv6 and IPv4 hosts over an IPv4 intranet. IPv6 packets are tunneled in IPv4 packets for transmission over the network. Communication can occur directly between two ISATAP hosts on an IPv4 network, or communication can go through an ISATAP router if one network has only IPv6-only hosts. If no IPv6-only hosts exist, the ISATAP router advertises the IPv6 prefix that ISATAP clients use. The ISATAP interface on client computers is configured to use this prefix. When applications use the ISATAP interface to deliver data, the IPv6 packet is encapsulated in an IPv4 packet for delivery to the IPv4 address of the destination ISATAP host.

ISATAP router   The ISATAP router connects IPv6 hosts through an ISATAP tunnel to IPv4 hosts.

IXFR   IXFR is the incremental zone transfer of zone data. Only changes on a primary DNS server are transferred to the secondary DNS server.

KDC proxy   The Getting Started Wizard configures the DirectAccess server to act as a Kerberos proxy to perform IPsec authentication without requiring certificates. Client authentication requests are sent to a Kerberos proxy service running on the DA server. The KDC proxy sends Kerberos requests to DCs on behalf of the client. This configuration is applicable only for clients running the following operating systems: Windows 10, Windows 8.1, Windows 8 client operating system, Windows Server 2016, Windows Server 2012 R2, or Windows Server 2012. If Windows 7 clients need to be supported for DirectAccess, you must deploy a PKI to issue computer certificates for backward compatibility.

KSK   The KSK is the key signing key. For DNSSEC, this key validates the DNSKEY record. The KSK signs the public ZSK key.

KSK rollover process   Rolling the KSK means generating a new cryptographic public and private key pair and distributing the new public component to parties that operate validating resolvers. These include ISPs, administrators, and other DNS resolver operators.

logical groups   IPAM enables you to create custom logical groups to improve the audit experience for IP address ranges.

msdcs zone   The msdcs zone is automatically created during the installation of a DNS server. It is reserved for registering records for Microsoft domain controllers. Any domain controller in a forest can identify any other domain controller in that forest through the entries in that zone.

Nano Server   Nano Server is a new Windows Server 2016 installation option. A Nano Server is much smaller and faster than a GUI-based or core server.

Nano Server Recovery Console   With the Nano Server Recovery Console, an administrator can handle the base local configuration components of a Nano Server, such as the computer name, IPv4 address, IPv6 address, gateway address, and firewall rules.

Network Access Protection   Network Access Protection (NAP) is removed in Windows Server 2016.

Network Connectivity Assistant   The Network Connectivity Assistant (NCA) is a service that is present on a DirectAccess client. It is installed by default since Windows 8 and can be installed optionally on Windows 7. This service verifies a DirectAccess IPv6 IPsec tunnel and allows monitoring through PowerShell cmdlets. If the NCA is not running, you cannot use PowerShell cmdlets to monitor Direct-Access connections.

Network Controller   Windows Server 2016 introduced Network Controller, which provides a centralized point of automation to manage and configure your datacenter's virtual and physical networks.

Network Location Server   A DirectAccess client uses the network location server (NLS) to determine its location. If the client computer can securely connect to the NLS by using HTTPS, then the client computer assumes that it is on the intranet and the DirectAccess policies are not enforced. If the network location server is not contactable, the client assumes that it is on the Internet. The NLS installs on the DirectAccess server with the web server role.

Network Policy   A Windows Server 2016 NPS offers two types of Network Policies: connection request policies and Network Policies. Health policies for NAP servers are no longer available on a Windows Server 2016 NPS server. Network Policies are sets of conditions, constraints, and settings that allow you to designate who is authorized to connect to the network and under which circumstances they can or cannot connect.

New-NanoServerImage   With the PowerShell cmdlet **New-NanoServerImage**, you can build a new Nano Server vhd or vhdx based on a Server Core or Nano Server image.

NPS   The Network Policy Server (NPS) enables you to create and enforce organization-wide network access policies for client health, connection request authentication, and connection request authorization. You can configure NPS as a RADIUS server, client, or proxy.

NRPT   The Name Resolution Policy Table (NRPT) in Windows Server 2016 enables you to enforce name resolution policies on security-aware DNS clients.

Packet Direct   Packet Direct (PD) extends the current NDIS model with an accelerated network I/O path that is optimized for packet-per-second (pps) counts an order of a magnitude higher than with the traditional NDIS I/O model.

primary zone   A primary zone is the only zone type that can be edited or updated. This is because the data in the zone is the original source of the data for all domains in the zone. Updates made to the primary zone are made by the DNS server that is authoritative for the specific primary zone. Users can also back up data from a primary zone to a secondary zone.

Purge Event Catalog Data   Purging events from the IPAM database does not clear events from the Event Viewer on managed DHCP servers. However, subsequent Event Catalog data retrieval only adds newly generated events in IPAM. Data that was purged is not reintroduced.

query resolution policies   With the new Windows Server 2016 DNS query resolution policies, you can define how queries are handled through criteria such as client subnet, transport protocol, server IP address, FQDN, query type, and time of day.

RADIUS client   A RADIUS client is a client that forwards authentication requests for network connections to a RADIUS server. Examples of RADIUS clients are VPN servers, wireless access points, 802.1X-capable switches, and dial-up servers.

RADIUS protocol   RADIUS messages are sent as UDP messages. UDP port 1812 is used for RADIUS authentication messages and UDP port 1813 is used for RADIUS accounting messages. Some network access servers might use UDP port 1645 for RADIUS authentication messages and UDP port 1646 for RADIUS accounting messages. By default, NPS supports receiving RADIUS messages destined to both sets of UDP ports.

RADIUS proxy   A RADIUS proxy forwards and routes connection requests and accounting messages between RADIUS clients/proxies and RADIUS servers/proxies. A RADIUS proxy uses information within the RADIUS message, such as username or Called-Station-ID, to route the RADIUS message to the appropriate RADIUS server.

RADIUS server   A RADIUS server is a device that receives and processes connection requests or accounting messages sent by RADIUS clients or RADIUS proxies. In the case of connection requests, the RADIUS server processes the list of RADIUS attributes in the connection request. Based on a set of rules and the information in the user account database, the RADIUS server either authenticates and authorizes the connection and sends back an Access-Accept message or sends back an Access-Reject message. The Access-Accept message can contain connection restrictions that are implemented by the access server for the duration of the connection. To configure a Windows Server 2016 RADIUS server, you must install a Network Policy Server (NPS).

RAS Gateway   When you implement network virtualization by using the Hyper-V virtual switch, the switch operates as a router between different Hyper-V hosts in the same infrastructure. The network virtualization policies define how packets will be routed from one host to another. However, a virtual switch cannot route to networks outside the Hyper-V server infrastructure when using network virtualization. If you were not using network virtualization, you would just connect the VM to an external switch, and the VM could connect to the same networks as the host machine. But in a network virtualization scenario, you might have multiple VMs running on a Hyper-V host that share the same IP addresses. You might also want to move the VMs to any host in the network without disrupting network connectivity. You must be able to connect the virtualized networks to the Internet by using a mechanism that is multitenant aware so that traffic to external networks is correctly routed to the internal addresses that the VMs use. Windows Server 2016 provides the RAS Gateway to address these issues.

RBAC   Role-based access control (RBAC) enables you to specify access privileges at various levels, including the DNS server, DNS zone, and DNS resource record levels. By using RBAC in IPAM, you can specify who has granular control over operations to create, edit, and delete different types of DNS resource records.

RDC   Remote differential compression (RDC) detects data insertions, removals, and rearrangements in files, enabling DFSR to replicate only the changed file blocks when files are updated.

RDMA   RDMA supports zero-copy networking by enabling the network adapter to transfer data directly to or from application memory. This eliminates the need to copy data between application memory and the data buffers in the operating system.

recursion policies   With the new Windows Server 2016 DNS recursion policies, you can configure selective recursion name resolution, to configure different recursion settings for different clients on one DNS server.

recursion scope   Recursion scopes are a new Windows Server 2016 feature used to fine-tune recursion settings. A recursion scope contains a list of forwarders and specifies whether recursion is enabled.

Remove DHCP Failover Configuration   With this setting in IPAM, the scope is removed from the DHCP failover partner.

reserve forwarders   On a Nano Server, you can install a package named Microsoft-OneCore-ReverseForwarder. Reverse forwarders enable a subset of Desktop Win32 binaries to run on Nano Server without recompilation.

Response Rate Limiting   The Windows Server 2016 DNS server feature Response Rate Limiting (RRL) works to prevent DNS amplification attacks.

root zone trust anchor   The ICANN publishes the root zone trust anchor and root operators to serve the signed root zone with actual keys.

RSC   Receive Side Coalescing (RSC) distributes network receive processing across multiple CPUs.

RSS   Receive Side Scaling (RSS) uses the NIC queues to distribute incoming traffic across multiple logical processors.

scavenging   Scavenging is a DNS server mechanism to clean up and remove stale resource records based on time stamps.

secondary zone   A secondary zone is a read-only copy of a primary zone. To configure a secondary zone, you must know the IP address of the master DNS server. A stub zone is also a secondary zone.

SEP flag   A SEP flag indicates whether a key is a zone signing key (ZSK) or a key signing key (KSK).

server-level zone transfer policy   With the new Windows Server 2016 DNS server-level zone transfer policies, you can control zone transfer in a more granular form by using DNS zone transfer policies on the server level.

ServiceCertificateConstraint   ServiceCertificateConstraint is an operation mode for DANE and TLSA records. With ServiceCertificateConstraint, you can protect a signed server certificate.

SET   Use Switch Embedded Teaming (SET) within a Hyper-V virtual switch to team up to eight physical Ethernet network adapters into one or more software-based virtual network adapters.

SMB Direct   SMB Direct supports the use of network adapters that have RDMA capability and can function at full speed with very low latency while using very little CPU. For workloads such as Hyper-V or Microsoft SQL Server, this enables a remote file server to resemble local storage.

SMB Multichannel   SMB Multichannel aggregates network bandwidth and network fault tolerance if multiple paths are available between the SMB client and SMB server.

software-defined networking   Software-defined networking (SDN) bypasses the limitations imposed by physical network devices and allows organizations to dynamically manage their networks. SDN uses an abstraction layer in software to manage your network dynamically. When you implement SDN, you can virtualize your network, define policies to manage network traffic, and manage your virtualized network infrastructure.

split DNS   In a split DNS infrastructure, you create two zones for the same domain: one for use by the internal network and the other for use by the external network (typically, users on the Internet). Split DNS directs internal hosts to an internal domain name server for name resolution; external hosts are directed to an external domain name server for name resolution.

stateful IPv6 configuration   Stateful IPv6 configuration occurs when the DHCPv6 server assigns the IPv6 address to the client, along with additional DHCP data.

stateless IPv6 configuration   Stateless IPv6 configuration occurs when the router assigns the IPv6 address automatically, and the DHCPv6 server assigns other IPv6 configuration settings.

Storage Replica   Storage Replica is a new feature that supports storage-agnostic, block-level, synchronous replication between servers or clusters for disaster recovery, as well as to stretch a failover cluster between sites. Synchronous replication mirrors data in physical sites with crash-consistent volumes to ensure that no data loss occurs at the file system level.

stub zone   A stub zone is a special type of secondary zone in which only NS and A records of DNS servers are present (no records of clients or other servers).

SYSVOL   The SYSVOL folder on a domain controller with GPOs can be replicated through DFSR. As a new Windows Server 2016 feature, SMB signing and mutual authentication in Windows 10 and Windows Server 2016 is now required for SYSVOL and NETLOGON shares.

Teredo   Teredo is a built-in transition mechanism that gives a single system behind an IPv4 NAT access to IPv6.

TLSA   TLSA DNS resource records associate a TLS server certificate or public key with the domain name where the record is found. This record is used together with DANE.

TLSA record   The TLSA DNS resource record (RR) associates a TLS server certificate or public key with the domain name where the record is found, thus forming a TLSA certificate association.

transfer policies   With the new Windows Server 2016 DNS transfer policies, you can configure selective DNS server transfer settings for primary/secondary DNS server scenarios.

trust anchors   A recursive or forwarding DNS server recognizes that the zone supports DNSSEC if it has a DNSKEY, also called a trust anchor, for that zone. DNSKEY and DS resource records are also called trust anchors. Trust anchors must be distributed to all nonauthoritative DNS servers that will perform DNSSEC validation of DNS responses for a signed zone.

trust anchor state   The status of a trust anchor can be Valid/Active, Add Pending, Missing, Revoked, DS Pending, or DS Invalid.

trust point   Trust anchors are organized and displayed in the DNS Manager console tree under Trust Points.

TrustAnchorAssertion   TrustAnchorAssertion is an operation mode for DANE and TLSA records in which you can protect a certificate that must be used as a trust anchor.

unknown record support   As of Windows Server 2016, previously unknown resource record types (such as TLSA records) are supported. Now you can add the unsupported record types into the Windows DNS server zones in the binary on-wire format.

utilization thresholds   With the PowerShell cmdlet **Set-IpamAddressUtilizationThreshold**, you can set over- or underutilization thresholds so that IPAM generates an alert when a block, subnet, or range utilization exceeds or drops below the threshold.

utilization trends   IPAM provides IP address utilization trends for IPv4 but not IPv6.

WebProbe resource record   To verify connectivity to the internal network, DirectAccess creates a default web probe that DirectAccess client computers use.

zone-level statistics   Zone-level statistics give DNS server-level statistics to track usage or monitor DNS server performance. You can get statistics about queries, zone transfers, packets, and DNSSEC.

zone transfer   Zone transfer is the process of transferring zone data from a primary DNS server to one or more secondary DNS server(s). On a Windows Server 2016 DNS primary DNS server, zone transfer is disabled by default. Network traffic of zone transfer is not encrypted by default.

zone transfer policy   Zone transfer policies are a new Windows Server 2016 DNS feature to control whether a DNS server allows a zone transfer.

ZSK   ZSK is the zone signing key pair. Each zone in DNSSEC has a ZSK, which is the private portion of the key that digitally signs records in the zone.

Index

Numbers

C